The Culture of National Security

●

New Directions in World Politics
John Gerard Ruggie, General Editor

Sponsored by the Committee on International Peace & Security
of the Social Science Research Council

New Directions in World Politics

John Gerard Ruggie, General Editor

The Culture of National Security:
Norms and Identity in World Politics

•

Edited by

Peter J. Katzenstein

Columbia University Press
New York

Columbia University Press
New York   Chichester, West Sussex
Copyright © 1996 Columbia University Press
All rights reserved

Library of Congress Cataloging-in-Publication Data
The culture of national security : norms and identity in world politics / edited by Peter J.
Katzenstein ; [sponsored by the Committee on International Peace & Security of the Social
Science Research Council]
p.   cm.
Includes bibliographical references and index.
ISBN 0-231-10468-5 (cl)
1. National security. 2. Nationalism. 3. Social institutions.
I. Katzenstein, Peter J. II. Social Science Research Council (U.S.) Committee on International
Peace & Security.
UA10.5.C85   1996
355'.03—dc20   96-14340
                                          CIP

Casebound editions of Columbia University Press books are printed on permanent and durable
acid-free paper.

Printed in the United States of America
c 10 9 8 7 6 5 4 3 2 1

For the graduate students at Cornell

Contents

About the Contributors

Peter J. Katzenstein is Walter S. Carpenter, Jr. Professor of International Studies at Cornell University.

Ronald L. Jepperson is in the Department of Sociology at the University of Washington.

Alexander Wendt is in the Department of Political Science at Yale University.

Dana P. Eyre is in the Department of National Security Affairs at the Naval Postgraduate School.

Mark C. Suchman is in the Department of Sociology at the University of Wisconsin.

Richard Price is in the Department of Political Science at the University of Minnesota.

Nina Tannenwald is in the Department of Political Science at the University of Colorado, Boulder.

Martha Finnemore is in the Department of Political Science at George Washington University.

Elizabeth Kier is in the Department of Political Science at the University of California, Berkeley.

Alistair Iain Johnston is in the Department of Government at Harvard University.

Robert G. Herman is Social Science Analyst, Bureau for Europe and the New Independent States, U.S. Agency for International Development, Washington, D.C.

Thomas U. Berger is in the Department of Political Science at Johns Hopkins University.

Thomas Reisse-Kappen is a member of the Faculty of Public Adminstration at Universitat Konstanz, Germany.

Michael J. Barnett is in the Department of Political Science at the University of Wisconsin.

Paul Kowert is in the Department of International Relations at Florida International University.

Jeffrey Legro is in the Department of Political Science at the University of Minnesota (on leave) and until 1997 a John M. Olin Fellow, Center for International Affairs, Harvard University.

Preface

The revolutionary changes that have marked world politics in recent years offer scholars an extraordinary opportunity for reflection and critical self-appraisal.[1] This is true, in particular, for scholars of international relations. One observer has likened the embarrassment that the end of the Cold War caused us as scholars of international relations and national security to the effects the sinking of the *Titanic* had on the profession of naval engineers. Although our analytical coordinates for gauging global politics have proven to be inadequate for an analysis of a world in rapid change, there has been remarkably little rethinking of our categories of analysis. Instead, in the first half of the 1990s North American scholarship on the theory of international relations was preoccupied with the issue of whether variants of realism or liberalism offered a superior way for explaining the world. Considering the dramatic international developments occurring during these years, many of the academic debates looked arcane to the interested bystander. For it is hard to deny that existing theories of international relations have woefully fallen short in explaining an important revolution in world politics.

What the writer Peter Schneider said of the German Left is also appo-

---

1. See, for example, the symposium on prediction in the social sciences introduced by Michael Hechter in the *American Journal of Sociology* 100,6 (May 1995): 1520–1527.

site for the field of national security studies: it slept right through a revolution. While the balance between demand and supply effected significant changes among security specialists working in think-tanks and, more slowly, even inside government, remarkably little changed in the academy. In a recent review of the scholarship published between 1989 and 1994 in *International Security*, one of the premier journals in the field, Hugh Gusterson concludes that "old stories have been bent to new times rather than questioned or cast away."[2] He identifies only one article between 1989–94, published by a historian, which asks the obvious question—why and how virtually all of the established theories could have been so wrong.

Scholars have made some adjustments in their research. Various forms of realist theorizing, for example, have rediscovered nationalism and ethnicity and are doing so with a breath-taking lack of analytical discomfort. Ever since Kenneth Waltz published his seminal *Theory of International Politics*, this book had been invoked as a text that provided the field of national security studies with a firm base. However, Waltz was very clear that the internal characteristics of states were irrelevant to his theory. The analysis of nationalism and ethnicity thus is a sharp turn for those who previously had written on national security informed by this variant of realist theorizing. It is especially surprising that realists, with their natural focus on states, have not inquired more systematically into the effects of changes in state identity, for example from warfare state to welfare state in Western Europe, that have altered traditional conceptions and instruments of national security.

A second adjustment has been to look for new areas to apply realist theory. A spirited debate about the conditions of peace in Europe has led to an examination of those conditions in other regions of the world. Realist theory, for example, rediscovered in Asia the balance of power and the instabilities of multipolarity which so unexpectedly were missing in Europe in recent years. It was, however, odd that realist analysis continued to neglect domestic politics and transnational relations, the very factors that had much to do with the unexpected end of the Cold War. A style of analysis that had proven to be inadequate in Europe was not refurbished but, implausibly, simply reapplied to Asia.

These adjustments in the core paradigm informing national security

---

2. Hugh Gusterson, "Reading International Security after the Cold War," paper prepared for the second workshop on Culture and the Production of Security/Insecurity, Kent State University, April 28–30, 1995, p. 6.

studies have left unimpressed a growing number of graduate students and younger scholars unpersuaded because, in part, their political and intellectual sensibilities are more firmly grounded in circumstances that differ from those experienced by their elders. The younger generation lived through the waning of the Cold War, not its exacerbation. It was exposed to new intellectual currents in the humanities and cultural studies. And as had been true before, this was an impatient cohort, eager to push ahead.

This volume represents and speaks to these intellectual currents. It reports the results of a project conducted under the auspices of the Committee on International Peace and Security of the Social Science Research Council and funded by the Council through a grant from the MacArthur Foundation. The project was deliberately designed to expose the participants to different intellectual climates at different universities. Workshops held at Cornell University, the University of Minnesota, and Stanford University, attended by the project participants as well as graduate students and faculty members from the respective host institutions, elicited different reactions, depending on the local intellectual culture and the list of participants. The tenor of the discussions at the Cornell meeting, with a heavy representation of realists, was "why this effort?" At Minnesota, a stronghold of cultural and post-modern approaches, the reaction was "show us how!" And at Stanford, in the presence of sociologists and theorists of rational choice, both reactions were articulated at the same meeting. To say that the debates at these meetings were spirited would be misleading. The intellectual level of discussion was extraordinarily high and so was the emotional pitch of the participants. Differences in arguments mattered both substantively and personally.

"Identity" theory, in particular, is deeply contested because it raises for scholars of national security directly and unavoidably pressing moral issues. Even though all of the contributors to this volume show in their scholarship that they regard evidence to be of critical importance in adjudicating competing analytical and political claims, realists and rationalists, at times, tar their sociologically minded critics with the brush of being the vanguard of a new wave of intellectual fascism. The critics, less powerful and more polite, view these scholars at times as the vanguard of political and intellectual conservatism. Does truth speak to power? Does power exploit knowledge? For more than an hour the Stanford meeting erupted into an emotionally charged discussion of these issues, illustrating vividly, painfully and usefully for everyone around the table the magnitude of the intellectual, political, and moral stakes that are involved for all scholars, whether they choose to adhere to or depart from the conventional view of national security.

This project expresses an explicit commitment to engage realism on its own terms. Scholars tend to shy away from conversations that pose fundamental disagreements, preferring instead to live in the comfortable cocoon of the like-minded. Talking across deep intellectual divides is always difficult, often uncomfortable and occasionally hurtful. It is also a useful reminder of the pervasiveness of power in the world of scholarship, of the primacy of institutionally backed validity claims among competing analytical possibilities. Even when such confrontations do not lead to intellectual conversions, they help in sharpening key arguments and circumscribing general claims. Without the willingness of some distinguished scholars of national security to generously commit themselves and their time, this confrontation of perspectives could not have occurred.

In the view of these scholars this was, from the beginning, a fundamentally flawed enterprise. The critics argued that the issues raised in this book have been addressed by the extant literature in a promising way which is leading cumulatively to a theory of national security framed by neo-realist and realist writings. In their reading this volume offers no more than an intellectually incoherent mixture of postmodern interpretivism, nonfalsifiable claims, ex post facto description, and insignificant embellishments of what mainstream realism analyzes elegantly and with precision. I report these objections here and let the reader be the judge.

Science is a social process that develops, refines, and rejects ideas. It is not a football game in which players protect turf—intellectual and otherwise. Hence the inclusion in this volume of the self-critical chapter 12. Some colleagues supportive of this project have urged me quietly to drop this chapter. And, unsurprisingly, the vociferous critics of this book's approach uniformly have applauded it as the most compelling piece in the entire collection. Both reactions are besides the point. The chapter points to some of the most noticeable weaknesses of this book and suggests some avenues for future improvement. This self-critical stance, not the waving of new flags or the dogged defense of received dogma, I take to be the task of an empirically oriented social science.

This project could not have been carried out without the generous support of the Committee on International Peace and Security of the Social Science Research Council. I would like to thank my fellow committee members for their vote of confidence in funding the project and for their useful counsel in its initial stages. I am also deeply indebted to the staffs at the Social Science Research Council and at Cornell University, the University of Minnesota and Stanford University for carrying the administrative burden involved in organizing the three workshops. And I would like to thank the many graduate students and faculty members at these three universities who were active participants and whose comments, criticisms and suggestions were indispensable for shaping my thinking on a broad range of issues. Without their intellectual energy and commitment all of us would have learned much less in the process, and the ultimate product would have been worse.

My special thanks go to the staff of Columbia University Press: to Kate Wittenberg for her strong interest in this project from the very outset; to two readers who gave detailed and searching suggestions that helped the authors to sharpen their arguments; to Jan McInroy for her extraordinarily careful work as copyeditor; to Alan Greenberg for putting together the index in record time; and to Leslie Bialler for much more than his humor and wit along the way.

Most importantly I would like to thank the project participants for their intellectual engagement and enthusiasm; for their ability to cooperate in friendship; for their willingness to disagree in civility; for their hard work; and for their toleration of an "old fogey" in their midst.

I dedicate this volume to all the graduate students at Cornell with whom I have worked over the years. I have learned an enormous amount from you. And without you I could not have conceived of this project. Contradicting current wisdom about the relation between research and teaching, it was our individual discussions and seminars as well as your research papers and dissertations that made me read in unfamiliar fields and thus lure me in new directions in both research and teaching.

Peter J. Katzenstein
May 1996

The Culture of National Security
•

1 • Introduction: Alternative Perspectives on National Security

Peter J. Katzenstein

> *It is always risky to pronounce a verdict of death on ideas, even after an extended period of apparent lifelessness, but I predict that we have seen the last of the "sociologists" in political science. . . . What has happened is that others too have penetrated the characteristically sloppy logic and flabby prose to discover the deeper problems of circularity and vacuousness inherent in the approach.*
> —Brian Barry
> *Sociologists, Economists, and Democracy*

This is a book written by scholars of international relations rummaging in the "graveyard" of sociological studies. Since research and teaching is an eminently social process, it is perhaps understandable that changing political circumstances and intellectual fashions reopen controversies that appeared to some to have been already settled. This process can lead, in the best of circumstances, to what we might call intellectual progress: the diminishing of sloppy logic, flabby prose, circularity in reasoning, and vacuousness of insight.

Put briefly, this book makes problematic the state interests that predominant explanations of national security often take for granted. For example, in the absence of geostrategic or economic stakes, why do the interests of some powerful states in the 1990s, but not in the 1930s or the 1890s, make them intervene militarily to protect the lives and welfare of

For their careful readings and critical comments of previous drafts I would like to thank the members of the project; the participants at the Social Science Research Council/MacArthur Workshops at the University of Minnesota and Stanford University in 1994; and Emanuel Adler, Thomas Christensen, James Goldgeier, Peter Haas, Gunther Hellmann, Ronald Jepperson, Mary F. Katzenstein, Robert Keohane, Jonathan Kirshner, Atul Kohli, Charles Kupchan, John Odell, Judith Reppy, Shibley Telhami, Stephen Walt, Alexander Wendt, and two anonymous readers for Columbia University Press.
1. Although, properly speaking, I am referring to state security, I am adhering to the conventional usage in the field of national security studies.

citizens other than their own? Why did the Soviet Union consider it to be in its interest to withdraw from Eastern Europe in the late stages of the Cold War, while it had rejected such suggestions many times before? Answers to such questions are nonobvious and important. State interests do not exist to be "discovered" by self-interested, rational actors. Interests are constructed through a process of social interaction. "Defining," not "defending," the national interest is what this book seeks to understand.[2]

In the context of a bipolar, ideological struggle, the Cold War made relatively unproblematic some of the cultural factors affecting national security. Theories that abstracted from these factors offered important insights. Now, with the end of the Cold War, the mix of factors affecting national security is changing. Issues dealing with norms, identities, and culture are becoming more salient. An institutional perspective permits us to investigate more closely the context, both domestic and international, in which states and other actors exercise power.

This book offers a sociological perspective on the politics of national security. It argues that security interests are defined by actors who respond to cultural factors. This does not mean that power, conventionally understood as material capabilities, is unimportant for an analysis of national security. States and other political actors undoubtedly seek material power to defend their security. But what other kinds of power and security do states seek and for which purposes? Do the meanings that states and other political actors attach to power and security help us explain their behavior? Answers to such questions, this book argues, raise issues of both theory and evidence.

Our point of departure is influenced greatly by the inability of all theories of international relations, both mainstream and critical, to help us explain fully what John Mueller aptly calls a quiet cataclysm:[3] the dramatic changes in world politics since the mid-1980s, which have profoundly affected the environment for the national security of states.[4] The Soviet Union has ceased to exist, and its successor states, organized in the

2. See Martha Finnemore, *National Interests in International Society* (Ithaca: Cornell University Press, 1996); Stephen D. Krasner, *Defending the National Interest: Raw Materials Investments and U.S. Foreign Policy* (Princeton: Princeton University Press, 1978).

3. John Mueller, *Quiet Cataclysm: Reflections on the Recent Transformation of World Politics* (New York: Harper Collins, 1995).

4. This project thus resembles others that seek to reevaluate or refine international relations theory in light of recent events. See Richard Ned Lebow and Thomas Risse-Kappen, eds., *International Relations Theory and the End of the Cold War* (New York: Columbia University Press, 1995); Robert O. Keohane and Helen Milner, eds., *Internationalization and Domestic Politics* (New York: Cambridge University Press, 1996); Miles Kahler, ed., *Liberalization and Foreign Policy* (forthcoming); and Thomas Risse-Kappen, ed., *Bringing Transnational Relations Back In: Non-State Actors, Domestic Structures, and International Institutions* (Cambridge: Cambridge University Press, 1995).

Commonwealth of Independent States, are in the process of creating a new regional international system while at the same time attempting to effect transitions from authoritarian socialism to democratic capitalism. The international positions of the United States and Japan have changed greatly as international competitiveness and financial power shifted away from the United States in the 1980s and away from Japan in the 1990s. China is undergoing a fundamental transformation in its economic structure and in its links to the international system. And the European Union (EU) appears to have been perhaps an overambitious attempt to accelerate the pace of European integration in the face of German unification. In South Africa, the Middle East, Central America, and Western Europe, long-standing violent conflicts that only a few years ago appeared to be simply unsolvable are now finding negotiated settlements. And in Europe, Central Asia, the Islamic world, and Africa, new conflicts are breaking out.

The main analytical perspectives on international relations, neorealism and neoliberalism, share with all their critics their inability to foreshadow, let alone foresee, these momentous international changes.[5] Furthermore, with the end of the Cold War, international relations specialists, whatever their theoretical orientation, are uncertain about how to interpret the consequences of change.[6] Disagreement is widespread on what are the most important questions, let alone what might constitute plausible answers to these questions. Are we living in a unipolar, a bipolar, or a multipolar world? Is the world increasingly divided into zones of peace among prosperous states at the center and zones of war between poor states on the periphery? Is the risk of war rapidly increasing in Asia while it remains negligible in Western Europe or is the reverse closer to the mark? Is the main

5. Sean M. Lynn-Jones, ed., *The Cold War and After: Prospects for Peace* (Cambridge: MIT Press, 1991); Michael J. Hogan, ed., *The End of the Cold War: Its Meaning and Implications* (New York: Cambridge University Press, 1992); John Lewis Gaddis, *The United States and the End of the Cold War: Implications, Reconsiderations, Provocations* (New York: Oxford University Press, 1992).
6. Ken Jowitt, *New World Disorder: The Leninist Extinction* (Berkeley: University of California Press, 1992); Max Singer and Aaron Wildavsky, *The Real World Order: Zones of Peace, Zones of Turmoil* (Chatham, N.J.: Chatham House, 1993); Robert O. Keohane, Joseph S. Nye, and Stanley Hoffmann, eds., *After the Cold War: International Institutions and State Strategies in Europe, 1989–1991* (Cambridge: Harvard University Press, 1993); Bruce Russett, *Grasping the Democratic Peace: Principles for a Post–Cold War World* (Princeton: Princeton University Press, 1993); Meredith Woo-Cumings and Michael Lorriaux, eds., *Past As Prelude: History in the Making of a New World Order* (Boulder: Westview, 1993); Mike Bowker and Robin Brown, eds., *From Cold War to Collapse: Theory and World Politics in the 1980s* (Cambridge: Cambridge University Press, 1993); Hans Henrik Holm and Georg Sørensen, eds., *Whose World Order? Uneven Globalization and the End of the Cold War* (Boulder: Westview, 1995).

cause of war on the periphery the excessive strength or the deplorable weakness of states? Is ideological conflict between states in the international system diminishing or increasing?

Without thinking specifically about the Cold War and national security, some sociologists wrote in the 1970s and 1980s about large-scale processes of change in and possible transformation of the global system. They privileged factors that appear to be relevant to our understanding of some of the changes that we are now observing. Immanuel Wallerstein, for example, argued that the dynamism inherent in the world capitalist economy would seek increasing integration of the socialist bloc.[7] And John Meyer articulated a model of global sociopolitical organization that embeds states.[8] This has opened up productive lines of research that undermine the plausibility of making a sharp distinction between international anarchy and world government as the only analytical alternatives for thinking about international relations. Taken together, Wallerstein's and Meyer's analyses recognize the importance of combining an analysis of power and wealth with issues of state sovereignty and cultural elements in the international society of states.

The uncertainties that mark international relations scholarship make this the right time to cast about for analytical perspectives that differ on key points from established theories, thus inviting us to take a fresh look at the world we live in. This volume concentrates on two underattended determinants of national security policy: the cultural-institutional context of policy on the one hand and the constructed identity of states, governments, and other political actors on the other. We explore these determinants from the theoretical perspective of sociological institutionalism,[10] with its focus on the character of the state's environment and on the contested nature of political identities. The primary purpose of this book is to

7. Immanuel Wallerstein, "Socialist States: Mercantilist Strategies and Revolutionary Objectives," in Immanuel Wallerstein, *The Politics of the World Economy*, pp. 86–96 (Cambridge: Cambridge University Press, 1984); Immanuel Wallerstein, "Marx, Marxism-Leninism, and Socialist Experiences in the Modern World System," in Immanuel Wallerstein, *Geopolitics and Geoculture: Essays on the Changing World System*, pp. 84–97 (Cambridge: Cambridge University Press, 1991).
8. John W. Meyer, "The World Polity and the Authority of the Nation-State," in Albert Bergesen, ed., *Studies of the Modern World System*, pp. 109–37 (New York: Academic Press, 1980).
9. This is a major difference between the inspiration motivating this book and Frank W. Wayman and Paul F. Diehl, eds., *Reconstructing Realpolitik* (Ann Arbor: University of Michigan Press, 1994).
10. Recent volumes that articulate a similar perspective include Sven Steinmo, Kathleen Thelen, and Frank Longstreth, eds., *Structuring Politics: Historical Institutionalism in Comparative Analysis* (New York: Cambridge University Press, 1992); and Walter W. Powell and Paul J. DiMaggio, eds., *The New Institutionalism in Organizational Analysis* (Chicago: University of Chicago Press, 1991).

establish these causal factors, and the theoretical orientations from which they derive, as relevant for the analysis of national security.

The empirical essays in this volume illustrate how social factors shape different aspects of national security policy, at times in ways that contradict the expectations derived from other theoretical orientations. This book does not offer a theory of national security.[11] To insist on such a theory now would be premature for an approach that is in the early stages of developing a theoretically coherent, empirically oriented research program. And it would be immodest in the midst of a wide-ranging discussion of economic and sociological approaches in the social sciences. Instead, this book seeks to redress the extreme imbalance between structural and rationalist styles of analysis and sociological perspectives on questions of national security.

The authors in this volume adhere to the sociological use of such concepts as norms, identity, and culture as summary labels to characterize the social factors that they are analyzing.[12] These factors result from social processes, purposeful political action, and differences in power capabilities.

The authors use the concept of *norm* to describe collective expectations for the proper behavior of actors with a given identity. In some situations norms operate like rules that define the identity of an actor, thus having "constitutive effects" that specify what actions will cause relevant others to recognize a particular identity. In other situations norms operate as standards that specify the proper enactment of an already defined identity. In such instances norms have "regulative" effects that specify standards of proper behavior. Norms thus either define (or constitute) identities or prescribe (or regulate) behavior, or they do both.

For example, Dana Eyre and Mark Suchman in essay 3 argue that advanced weapon systems are one measure signifying that a state is modern. Governments thus spend their precious funds to buy such weapon systems even if they have only a marginal effect on national security. Anal-

---

11. I argue below that this is no particular liability for the approach chosen for the book; no such theory exists in the field of national security studies.

12. One of the main difficulties in making the sociological approach of this book attractive for scholars of national security lies in the intuitive equation of the concept of norm with morality. The book focuses primarily on the analysis of regulatory norms (defining standards of appropriate behavior) and constitutive norms (defining actor identities). It touches less directly on evaluative norms (stressing questions of morality) or practical norms (focusing on commonly accepted notions of "best solutions"). See also various essays in *Millennium: Journal of International Studies* 22, no. 3 (Winter 1993).

ogously, large battleships at the beginning of the twentieth century and a secure second-strike capability at century's end confer world- or super-power status on states. Similarly, in essay 5, Martha Finnemore argues that global models of statehood have important effects on policies of military intervention. Relatedly, Richard Price and Nina Tannenwald show in essay 4 that a taboo delegitimizing the use of chemical and nuclear weapons has, to different degrees, constrained the self-help behavior of states.

The essays refer to *identity* as a shorthand label for varying construc-tions of nation- and statehood. The process of construction typically is explicitly political and pits conflicting actors against each other. In invok-ing the concept of identity the authors depict varying national ideologies of collective distinctiveness and purpose. And they refer as well to varia-tions across countries in the statehood that is enacted domestically and projected internationally.

For example, Thomas Berger traces in essay 9 the transformation of Germany's and Japan's collective purpose from war to commerce. Thomas Risse-Kappen, in essay 10, argues that the collective identity of democra-tic states has been central to the creation of a transatlantic security com-munity, marked by what Karl Deutsch called "dependable expectations of peaceful change."[13] And Michael Barnett shows in essay 11 that changing and contested notions of Arab national identity help to define security threats and shape the dynamics of alliance formation.

Finally, the authors in this volume invoke the term *culture* as a broad label that denotes collective models of nation-state authority or identity, carried by custom or law. Culture refers to both a set of evaluative stan-dards (such as norms and values) and a set of cognitive standards (such as rules and models) that define what social actors exist in a system, how they operate, and how they relate to one another.[14] Richard Price and Nina Tannenwald (in essay 4) and Dana Eyre and Mark Suchman (in essay 3), respectively, exemplify these two usages of the term. Furthermore, Eliza-beth Kier (essay 6), Alastair Johnston (essay 7), and Thomas Berger (essay 9) invoke specific cultural arguments about France, China, Germany and

---

13. Karl W. Deutsch et al., *Political Community and the North Atlantic Area* (Princeton: Princeton University Press, 1957), p. 5.
14. This distinction between the cognitive and evaluative effects of norms is also made by scholars working from within a cognitive paradigm. See, for example, Alexander L. George, "Domestic Con-straints on Regime Change in U.S. Foreign Policy: The Need for Policy Legitimacy," in Ole R. Hol-sti, Randolph M. Siverson, and Alexander L. George, eds., *Change in the International System*, p. 235 (Boulder: Westview, 1980).

Japan, and, at times, about some of the political and military organizations within these countries.

The definitions of these concepts share an emphasis on what is collective rather than subjective. Sociological approaches to the analysis of national security sometimes seem nebulous in their specification of the factors that affect the behavior of states or other political actors. We can easily conjure up the image of a column of 50,000 tanks stretching from Cleveland to Seattle that tells us something about the size of the Soviet military at the end of the Cold War. It is harder to fathom what force caused Governor Michael Dukakis, the Democratic candidate for president in 1988, to dress up in military fatigues and ride around on a tank—looking foolish in the process—to demonstrate his toughness on the issue of national defense. Collectively shared expectations of the American public about the military toughness of presidential candidates are what made the governor behave the way he did. Collective expectations can have strong causal effects. Such expectations deserve close scrutiny, this book argues, for a better understanding of national security policy.

This essay points to some analytical gaps left by the predominant perspectives. The next essay proposes an approach for filling those gaps. The empirical essays that follow seek to show that perspectives that neglect social factors foreclose important avenues for empirical research and theoretical insight that are relevant for explaining specific aspects of national security.

Why Traditional National Security Issues?

The end of the Cold War has put new national security issues beside the long-standing fear of a nuclear war between the two superpowers and their preparations for large-scale conventional wars: ethnic conflicts leading to civil wars that expose civilian populations to large-scale state violence; an increasing relevance of economic competitiveness and, relatedly, of the "spin-on" of civilian high technology for possible military use; increasing numbers of migrants and refugees testing the political capacities of states; threats of environmental degradation affecting national well-being; and perceived increases in the relevance of issues of cultural identity in international politics, including human rights and religion.

The 1970s and 1980s had already witnessed some evidence of this trend. It divided American realist academics and political practitioners on the one hand and reformers staffing the Brandt, Palme, and Brundtland Commissions and European peace researchers on the other.[15] In the case of Japan, whose power was increasing sharply in the 1980s, opinion also was divided.[16] Did Japan's strategy of "comprehensive security" represent merely a politically convenient ruse to counter American pressure for greater defense expenditures? Or was it a genuine political innovation that reflected the political experiences of Japan since 1945?

In a prescient article published in the early 1980s Richard Ullman made a general case for broadening the concept of security.[17] Ullman viewed national security as more than a goal with different trade-off values in different situations. He insisted that national security is threatened by the consequences of events that quickly degrade the quality of life of state and nonstate actors alike, thus narrowing significantly the future range of political choice.[18] But at the height of the second Cold War in the early 1980s, security specialists did not consider seriously the arguments of European peace researchers. Japanese national security policy was not an important topic. And the political climate in the early 1980s was not favorable to Ullman's argument.

With the end of the Cold War and the breakup of the Soviet Union, the political and intellectual climate has changed.[19] In distinguishing between traditional, narrow definitions and recent, broad conceptions of security studies, Stephen Walt, Edward Kolodziej, and Barry Buzan, among others,

15. Raimo Värynen, "Towards a Comprehensive Definition of Security: Pitfalls and Problems" (paper presented at the thirty-first annual convention of the International Studies Association, Washington, D.C., April 10–14, 1990), pp. 1–2; John P. Lovell, "From Defense Policy to National Security Policy: The Tortuous Adjustment for American Military Professionals," *Air University Review* 32, no. 4 (May–June 1981): 42–54; J. A. Tapia-Valdes, "A Typology of National Security Policies," *Yale Journal of World Public Order* 9, no. 1 (Fall 1982): 10–39; Bruce Andrews, "Surplus Security and National Security: State Policy As Domestic Social Action" (paper presented at the annual convention of the International Studies Association, Washington, D.C., February 22–26, 1978).

16. "Comprehensive Security: Japanese and U.S. Perspectives: A Conference Report of the Northeast Asia–United States Forum on International Policy" (Stanford University, November 1981); J. W. M. Chapman, R. Drifte, and I. T. M. Gow, *Japan's Quest for Comprehensive Security: Defence, Diplomacy, Dependence* (New York: St. Martin's, 1982); Peter J. Katzenstein and Nobuo Okawara, *Japan's National Security: Structures, Norms, and Policy Responses in a Changing World* (Ithaca: Cornell University East Asia Program, 1993).

17. Richard Ullman, "Redefining Security," *International Security* 8, no. 1 (Summer 1983): 129–53.
18. Ibid., pp. 130–35.
19. Two surveys of the field of security studies from 1987 and 1992 illustrate this point very clearly. See Joseph S. Nye Jr. and Sean M. Lynn-Jones, "International Security Studies: A Report of a Conference on the State of the Field," *International Security* 12, no. 4 (Spring 1988): 5–27; and Lynn Eden, " 'New Approaches to the Study of Conflict and Peace in a Changing World': Report on a Conference Held January 16–17, 1992, Center for International Security and Arms Control, Stanford University" Stanford University, Center for International Security and Arms Control, 1992.

have articulated very different views about how to define the concept of security, as well as about the scope of analytical approaches and empirical domains appropriate to security studies.[20] The narrow definition of security tends to focus on material capabilities and the use and control of military force by states.[21] This contrasts with the distinctions among military, political, economic, social, and environmental security threats that affect not only states but also groups and individuals, as well as other nonstate actors.[22]

Since different analytical perspectives suggest different definitions of national security, such disagreements are probably unavoidable.[23] Those

20. Stephen M. Walt, "The Renaissance of Security Studies," *International Studies Quarterly* 35, no. 2 (June 1991): 211–39; Edward A. Kolodziej, "Renaissance in Security Studies? Caveat Lector!" *International Studies Quarterly* 36, no. 4 (December 1992): 421–38; Edward A. Kolodziej, "What Is Security and Security Studies? Lessons from the Cold War," *Arms Control* 13, no. 1 (April 1992): 1–31; Barry Buzan, *People, States, and Fear: The National Security Problem in International Relations* (London: Wheatsheaf Books, 1983); Barry Buzan, "The Case for a Comprehensive Definition of Security and the Institutional Consequences of Accepting It," *Working Papers* 4/1990 (Copenhagen: Centre for Peace and Conflict Research, 1990); Barry Buzan, "New Patterns of Global Security in the Twenty-first Century," *International Affairs* 67, no. 3 (1991): 431–51; Lester R. Brown, *Redefining National Security*, Worldwatch Papers no. 14 (Washington, D.C.: Worldwide Institute, 1977); Joseph J. Romm, *Defining National Security: The Nonmilitary Aspects* (New York: Council on Foreign Relations Press, 1993); Simon Dalby, "Security, Modernity, Ecology: The Dilemmas of Post–Cold War Security Discourse," *Alternatives* 17, no. 1 (Winter 1992): 95–134; Theodore C. Sorenson, "Rethinking National Security," *Foreign Affairs* 69, no. 3 (Summer 1990): 1–18; Martin Shaw, "There Is No Such Thing as Society: Beyond Individualism and Statism in International Security Studies," *Review of International Studies* 19 (1993): 159–75; Ole Waever et al., *Identity, Migration, and the New Security Agenda in Europe* (New York: St. Martin's, 1993); Wilhelm Agrell, "The Problems of Defining and Dealing with the Civilian Aspects of Security" (unpublished paper, Research Policy Institute, University of Lund, Sweden, December 1986); Deborah A. Stone, *Policy Paradox and Political Reason* (Glenview, Ill.: Scott, Foresman, 1988), pp. 69–86; Ronnie D. Lipschutz, "Reconstructing Security: Discursive Practices, Material Changes, and Policy Consequences" (paper prepared for delivery at the 1992 annual meeting of the American Political Science Association, Chicago, September 3–6, 1992); Michael T. Klare and Daniel C. Thomas, eds., *World Security: Challenges for a New Century* (New York: St. Martin's, 1994); Graham Allison and Gregory F. Treverton, eds., *Rethinking America's Security: Beyond Cold War to New World Order* (New York: W. W. Norton, 1992); Peter Digeser, "The Concept of Security" (paper prepared for delivery at the 1994 annual meeting of the American Political Science Association, New York, September 1–4, 1994); James Sperling and Emil Kirchner, "Introduction: The Changing Definition of Security," in Emil Kirchner, Christoph Bluth, and James Sperling, eds., *The Future of European Security*, pp. 1–22 (Brookfield, Vt.: Dartmouth Pub., 1995).
21. Walt, "The Renaissance of Security Studies," p. 212.
22. Kolodziej, "Renaissance in Security Studies?" pp. 422–23; Buzan, "New Patterns of Global Security," pp. 432–33.
23. Proponents on either side of the debate agree that much would be lost, and little gained, if broader security studies were compressed into the well-developed, narrower focus of strategic studies; Walt, "Renaissance of Security Studies," p. 213; Buzan, "The Case for a Comprehensive Definition," pp. 12–13.

interested in the state and in traditional issues of national security tend to favor established realist and liberal approaches developed during the last decades. A new generation of scholars built on these approaches in reinvigorating the field of security studies as an intellectually challenging field of academic scholarship during the 1980s. In contrast, those interested in unconventional, broader definitions of national security—such as economic competitiveness, human rights, or human welfare—as affecting not only states but also nonstate actors tend to favor alternative analytical perspectives.[24]

What scholars and policy makers consider to be national security issues is not fixed but varies over time. At the beginning of the twentieth century, for example, pronatalist policies were widely believed to strengthen national power and security. In the interwar period the focus on eugenics illustrated a partial shift from the quantity to the quality of population as an important measure of national power and security. And after 1945 there was a dramatic discontinuity as national elites no longer viewed population control policies as sources of national security but as sources of national well-being. To take a second example, in the case of plutonium, the very recent past has witnessed an analogous process of issue transformation. Once considered to be only a security issue, plutonium has now become an environmental issue as well.[25] The domain of national security issues thus is variable. In the nineteenth century, the concept covered economic and social dimensions of political life that, for a variety of reasons, were no longer considered relevant when national security acquired a narrower military definition in the first half of the twentieth century, especially during the Cold War. The intellectual move to broaden the concept thus returns the field of national security studies to its own past.

This book is self-conscious in bringing together two fields of study usually kept apart. Its theoretical stance highlights the social determinants of national security policy, but it adopts a traditional, narrow definition of security studies. It does so despite the fact that the argument for a broadening of the field has substantial intellectual merit and is reflected in the

---

24. Why these are the lines of division is not entirely clear. It is possible that nonstate actors and issues that touch less directly on the balance of material capabilities lend themselves perhaps more easily to the sociological perspectives that this book proffers.

25. I would like to thank John Meyer for drawing my attention to this analytical point and these examples.

changing agenda of United States foreign policy as well as in the curricula of many schools of foreign affairs.[26]

Why, then, does this book focus on traditional issues of national security? The main reason is a healthy respect for the sociology of knowledge. Intellectual challenges are often disregarded because they do not meet reigning paradigms on their preferred ground. It might have been easier to point to the limitations of existing theories of national security by investigating some of the "new" security issues. But in all likelihood that exercise would have been pointless. Such a challenge would be dismissed as skirting the hard task of addressing the tough political issues in traditional security studies. This book deals with what most scholars of national security would consider to be hard cases. It chooses political topics and empirical domains that favor well-established perspectives in the field of national security. If the style of analysis and the illustrative case material can establish plausibility here, it should be relatively easy to apply this book's analytical perspective to broader conceptions of security that are not restricted to military issues or to the state.

Existing Analytical Perspectives

Like other subfields in international relations, security studies is influenced by the major theoretical debates in international relations. Structural neorealism and neoliberal institutionalism as the two dominant paradigms agree on the central importance of international anarchy for the analysis of international politics. Even though neoliberalism to date has had little direct influence on national security studies, indirectly, through this shared assumption, it has helped consolidate the orienting Hobbesian framework that motivates most studies of national security.[27]

In addition, neorealism and neoliberalism share other areas of agree-

---

26. Andrew Rosenthal, "U.S. to Unveil Drug Plan with Wide Military Role," *New York Times*, March 9, 1990, p. A5; Elaine Sciolino, "Bush Wants Intelligence Agencies to Reconsider Focus on Military," *New York Times*, December 22, 1991, p. 6; Ken Brown, "Cold War Over, Foreign Affairs Schools Refocus," *New York Times*, November 17, 1993, p. B7.

27. Robert O. Keohane, *International Institutions and State Power: Essays in International Relations Theory* (Boulder: Westview, 1989), p. 6, for example, writes that the "causal impact of international institutions on state policy is not as strong as that of states on international institutions." But in contrast to realist thought, this version of liberalism focuses on deception rather than violence as the most important consequence of international anarchy.

ment on basic theoretical issues.[28] Neorealist and neoliberal perspectives focus on how structures affect the instrumental rationality of actors. Neorealists emphasize that the competitive pressure of an anarchic international system is a constant in history; it determines important types of state behavior such as balancing. In an interdependent world, neoliberals insist, international institutions provide an alternative structural context in which states can define their interests and coordinate conflicting policies. But the assumption of unified state actors and a focus on an anarchical, systemic context of states are common to both.

Kenneth Waltz's formulation of a neorealist theory has had a profound influence on the field of security studies.[29] Waltz's theory is explicitly structural. It argues that the international state system molds states and defines the possibilities for cooperation and conflict. According to Waltz, the international state system has three distinctive characteristics. It is decentralized; the most important actors—states—are unitary and functionally undifferentiated; and differences in the distribution of the capabilities of the most important states distinguish bipolar from multipolar state systems. Waltz is careful to specify only a restricted domain in security affairs as relevant for neorealist theory. But within that domain developments in international politics are driven by the balancing of differences in capabilities in the international system.[30]

Robert Keohane has been very influential in shaping the analytical per-

---

28. Robert Powell, "Anarchy in International Relations Theory: The Neorealist-Neoliberal Debate," *International Organization* 48, no. 2 (Spring 1994): 313–44; Emerson M. S. Niou and Peter C. Ordeshook, " 'Less Filling, Tastes Great': The Realist-Neoliberal Debate," *World Politics* 46, no. 2 (January 1994): 209–34; Michael Zürn, "We Can Do Much Better! Aber muss es auf amerikanisch sein? Zum Vergleich der Disziplin 'Internationale Beziehungen' in den USA und in Deutschland," *Zeitschrift für Internationale Beziehungen* 1, no. 1 (June 1994): 98–109. Grouping different theoretical formulations under these two broad headings is a simplification. Each theory has a major and a minor variant. Neorealists have sought to systematize the insights of traditional realists. And neoliberals distinguish themselves from traditional liberals. Although not unimportant, these differences pale compared with the combined impact that the two main variants, neorealism and neoliberalism, have had on international relations scholarship since the early 1980s. Hence I discuss them here. The first part of the concluding essay examines briefly some attempts of reformulating realist and liberal perspectives to address the issues that this book raises. For some important differences between realism and liberalism, see also Keohane, *International Institutions and State Power*, pp. 1–20, and the discussion in Barry Buzan, Charles Jones, and Richard Little, *The Logic of Anarchy: Neorealism to Structural Realism* (New York: Columbia University Press, 1993), pp. 1–17.

29. Kenneth N. Waltz, *Theory of International Politics* (Reading, Mass.: Addison-Wesley, 1979).

30. This book's approach differs from Waltz's along all three dimensions. First, the international society of states is distinguished by both organizational decentralization and elements of a shared culture. Second, states are not unitary and functionally differentiated. Third, the distribution of capabilities and the number of poles may be less important than some of the effects of the society of

spective of neoliberal institutionalism on questions of political economy and international relations.[31] According to Keohane, international politics after hegemony does not necessarily collapse into the unmitigated power politics that realists infer from conditions of international anarchy. Instead the international order that hegemons have created through institutions can continue to ameliorate the problem of international anarchy. These institutions facilitate monitoring, enhance political transparency, reduce uncertainty, and increase policy-relevant information. The institutional infrastructure of a post-hegemonic system thus can facilitate the coordination of conflicting policies by lowering the transaction costs associated with cooperation. Neoliberals insist that conflict inheres in the international system. But that condition is not immutable. Under some political conditions, international conflict can be ameliorated through collective management.[32]

Structural neorealism and neoliberal institutionalism share a similar, underlying analytical framework, susceptible to the same weakness. Kenneth Waltz privileges systemic effects on national policy and sidesteps the motivations that inform policy. He argues that "neorealism contends that international politics can be understood only if the effects of structure are added to the unit level explanations of traditional realism. . . . The range of expected outcomes is inferred from the assumed motivation of the units and the structure of the system in which they act."[33] Since causes operate at different levels and interact with one another, explanations operating at either level alone are bound to be misleading.[34] Robert Keohane concurs when he writes that "institutional theory takes states' conceptions of their interests as exogenous: unexplained within the terms of

---

states. An additional important difference lies in the fact that the recurrent balancing behavior of states that interests Waltz is of little concern to any of the authors writing in this volume. Some of them are interested in the direction of the balance, others in a variety of aspects of national security policy. A set of essays in two special issues of *Security Studies* (5, nos. 2 and 3 [Winter 1995/96 and Spring 1996]) takes stock of realist and neorealist theory.

31. Robert O. Keohane, *After Hegemony: Cooperation and Discord in the World Political Economy* (Princeton: Princeton University Press, 1984).

32. Robert Axelrod, *The Evolution of Cooperation* (New York: Basic Books, 1984); Kenneth A. Oye, ed., *Cooperation Under Anarchy* (Princeton: Princeton University Press, 1986); Oran Young, *International Governance: Protecting the Environment in a Stateless Society* (Ithaca: Cornell University Press, 1994).

33. Kenneth N. Waltz, "The Origins of War in Neorealist Theory," in Robert I. Rotberg and Theodore K. Rabb, eds., *The Origins and Prevention of Major Wars*, pp. 41–42 (Cambridge: Cambridge University Press, 1989).

34. Ibid., p. 42.

the theory. . . . Nor does realism predict interests. This weakness of systemic theory, of both types, denies us a clear test of their relative predictive power."[35] The consequences of this shortcoming for both neorealism and neoliberalism are in Keohane's view far-reaching. "Without a theory of interests, which requires analysis of domestic politics, no theory of international relations can be fully adequate. . . . Our weak current theories do not take us very far in understanding the behavior of the United States and European powers at the end of the Cold War. . . . More research will have to be undertaken at the level of the state, rather than the international system."[36]

Both neorealism and neoliberalism thus express a widely accepted, though problematic, social science paradigm suggesting a three-step analysis.[37] First, there is the specification of a set of constraints. Then comes the stipulation of a set of actors who are assumed to have certain kinds of interests. Finally, the behavior of the actors is observed, and that behavior is related to the constraining conditions in which these actors, with their assumed interests, find themselves. This perspective highlights the instrumental rationality of actors and focuses on decisions and choice.

Variants of realist and liberal perspectives do acknowledge the importance of social facts. However, in adopting economic styles of analysis, they often misunderstand concepts such as prestige and reputation, which they view as "force effects rather than as social attributions."[38]

Robert Gilpin is one of the most important and insightful realists. He has developed a compelling argument about war and change. While he appreciates the importance of sociological insights for understanding the context of rational behavior, his book argues in an economic mode.[39] Yet a core assumption of Gilpin's basic model embodies an unanalyzed concept of identity, the distinction between revisionist and status quo pow-

35. Robert O. Keohane, "Institutional Theory and the Realist Challenge After the Cold War," in David A. Baldwin, ed., *Neorealism and Neoliberalism: The Contemporary Debate*, p. 285 (New York: Columbia University Press, 1993).
36. Ibid., pp. 294–95.
37. James G. March, "Decision-Making Perspective: Decisions in Organizations and Theories of Choice," in Andrew H. Van De Ven and William F. Joyce, eds., *Perspectives on Organization Design and Behavior*, pp. 205–44 (New York: Wiley, 1981).
38. Francis A. Beer and Robert Hariman, "Realism and Rhetoric in International Relations," in Francis A. Beer and Robert Hariman, eds., *Post-Realism: The Rhetorical Turn in International Relations* (East Lansing, Mich.: Michigan State University Press, in press), p. 21 of manuscript.
39. Robert Gilpin, *War and Change in World Politics* (New York: Cambridge University Press, 1981), pp. xii–xiii.

ers.[40] And Gilpin's analysis of the international system explicitly incorporates recognition by others, or prestige. For Gilpin this is a functional equivalent to the concept of authority in domestic politics and has functional and moral grounding.[41] Gilpin asserts, but does not demonstrate, that "ultimately" prestige rests on military or economic power. But he writes that "prestige, rather than power, is the everyday currency in international relations."[42]

Analogously, Robert Keohane is a leading neoliberal scholar favoring an economic mode of analysis. He writes that "much of my own work has deliberately adopted Realist assumptions of egoism, as well as rationality, in order to demonstrate that there are possibilities for cooperation even on Realist premises."[43] In thinking about egoism and empathy, Keohane poses the central question of "how people and organizations define self-interest."[44] The answer lies in the issue of identity, in variations in the degree of expansiveness and restrictiveness, with which people and organizations relate to one another. To what extent does the "self" incorporate relevant aspects of the "other" in its calculations of gains and losses? The answer to this question takes Keohane away from considerations of more or less myopic calculations of interest to "deeper" questions of values. Keohane concludes that "since the notion of self-interest is so elastic, we have to examine what this premise means, rather than simply taking it for granted."[45] Such relational thinking falls squarely in the sociological rather than the economic mode of analysis.[46]

---

40. Ibid., pp. 10–11. Randall Schweller's interesting paper on neorealism illustrates the same point; see Randall L. Schweller, "Neorealism's Status-Quo Bias," *Security Studies* 5, no. 3 (Spring 1996) (in press). "Predatory states motivated by expansion and absolute gains, not security and the avoidance of relative-gains losses, are the prime movers of neorealist theory" (ibid., p. 36 of manuscript).

41. Gilpin, *War and Change*, pp. 14, 28, 30.

42. Ibid., pp. 30–31.

43. Robert O. Keohane, "Empathy and International Relations," in Jane J. Mansbridge, ed., *Beyond Self-Interest*, p. 227 (Chicago: University of Chicago Press, 1990).

44. Ibid., p. 228.

45. Ibid., p. 236.

46. Keohane writes further: "A complete analysis of regimes would have to show how international regimes could change as a result not of shifts in the allegedly objective interests of states, or in the power distributions and institutional conditions facing governments, but of changes in how people think about their interests, including the possibility that they may be interested in the welfare of others, both from empathy and from principle" (ibid.). In the early 1980s Keohane suggested that a different, sociological line of argument about regimes would be possible, whereby norms would be "internalized" by actors as part of their utility functions; see Robert O. Keohane, "The Demand for International Regimes," in Stephen D. Krasner, ed., *International Regimes*, p. 154 n. 27 (Ithaca: Cornell University Press, 1983). But his subsequent work has continued to draw almost exclusively

Similarly, a theory of historical change popular among realists and rationalists mimics a sociological institutional perspective. Stephen Krasner, for example, gives an account of sovereignty that relies heavily on the concept of punctuated equilibrium and historical path-dependence.[47] In this view, the social determinants that this volume analyzes are acknowledged to exist, but they are banished to a remote past or to a distant future. The big bangs in history contrast sharply with the slight tremors of the present. The social determinants that are thus admitted to exist during epochal shifts, this book claims, exist throughout history, be it heroic or mundane.[48]

Finally, in a bold neorealist analysis of European politics after the Cold War, John Mearsheimer invokes the importance of social factors. Mearsheimer makes a case for a carefully managed process of nuclear proliferation to help stabilize an emerging war-prone, multipolar European system no longer held in check by the Soviet threat from the East and, possibly, the American night-watchman state from the West. Nuclear powers can reduce the dangers of proliferation by helping to "socialize emerging nuclear societies to understand the nature of the forces they are acquiring. Proliferation managed in this manner can help bolster peace."[49] Similarly, Kenneth Waltz has conceded in one of his more recent writings that "systems populated by units of different sorts in some ways perform differently, even though they share the same organizing principle. More needs to be said about the status and role of units in neorealist theory."[50]

This book relaxes the two core assumptions that mark, to different degrees, both neorealism and neoliberalism. First, what happens if, in contrast to neorealism, we conceive of the environment of states not just in

on economic imagery and has followed a rationalist path. See also Robert O. Keohane, "International Relations Theory: Contributions of a Feminist Standpoint," in Rebecca Grant and Kathleen Newland, eds., *Gender and International Relations*, pp. 41–50 (Bloomington: Indiana University Press, 1991). This paper clearly recognizes feminism's sociological orientation toward the articulation of an "institutional vision of international relations" (p. 44) and calls for an "alliance between two complementary critiques of neorealism," neoliberal institutionalism and feminism (p. 47).

47. Stephen D. Krasner, "Sovereignty: An Institutional Perspective," *Comparative Political Studies* 21 (1988): 64–94.

48. I am indebted to John Meyer for drawing my attention to this point.

49. John Mearsheimer, "Back to the Future: Instability After the Cold War," *International Security* 15, no. 1 (Summer 1990): 38.

50. Kenneth N. Waltz, "Realist Thought and Neorealist Theory," *Journal of International Affairs* 44, no. 1 (1990): 37. See also Henry Nau, "Identity and International Politics: An Alternative to Neorealism" (unpublished paper, George Washington University, April 1994).

terms of the physical capabilities of states? Neoliberalism has already effected this move with its focus on institutions. But its efficiency-oriented view of the role of institutions in political life is open to reinterpretation if we also relax a second assumption.[51] What happens if, contrasting with neoliberalism, we do not focus our attention solely on the effects that institutional constraints have on interests? This perspective neglects the crucial fact that institutions can constitute, to varying degrees, the identities of actors and thus shape their interests. Relaxing core assumptions of the two central perspectives in international relations theory, this book argues, is useful for two reasons. It may help us discern new aspects of national security. Alternatively, it may help in accounting for anomalies in existing analyses of national security.

Cultural-Institutional Context and Political Identity

The end of the Cold War and the issues of international politics that are emerging as central make this a propitious time for rethinking established analytical approaches to national security. This book focuses on the effects that culture and identity have on national security. The prevailing theories deliberately slight these effects. For realists, culture and identity are, at best, derivative of the distribution of capabilities and have no independent explanatory power. For rationalists, actors deploy culture and identity strategically, like any other resource, simply to further their own self-interests.

Neorealism, for example, insists that shifts in the balance of relative capabilities are the main determinants of international politics. Yet it is difficult to link the end of the Cold War and the disintegration of the Soviet Union causally to dramatic changes in power capabilities.[52] It is undoubtedly true that the relative economic and military decline of the Soviet Union convinced the Soviet military of the need for fundamental reform.

---

51. One should note here that neoliberalism and institutional economics have been notably unsuccessful in measuring transaction costs, an opaque concept at best that is central to an understanding of how institutions work.

52. John Mueller, "The Impact of Ideas on Grand Strategy," in Richard N. Rosecrance and Arthur A. Stein, eds., *The Domestic Bases of Grand Strategy*, pp. 48–62 (Ithaca: Cornell University Press, 1993); Richard Ned Lebow, "The Long Peace, the End of the Cold War, and the Failure of Realism," *International Organization* 48, no. 2 (Spring 1994): 249–77; see also Robert Herman's essay in this volume.

Realist insights thus are relevant to an interpretation of political developments since the 1980s.[53] But they are no more than partial.

For example, the process of German unification within multilateral
frameworks illustrates well the shortcomings of realist analysis.[54] The Bush
administration did not seek to exploit the weakness of the Soviet Union
through an aggressive foreign policy. It remained instead committed to the
institutional innovation of multilateralism that it had brought to Europe at
the end of World War II.[55] The Soviet Union was willing to accept multilateral institutions to solve its national security problems. Germany
eschewed neutralism in favor of continued membership in the Western
Alliance and a deepening of the process of European integration. After a
brief moment of uncertainty in December 1989 and January 1990, France,
in contrast to Britain, decided in favor of European integration as the most
appropriate way of dealing with the consequences of German unity. Soon
after the disintegration of the Soviet Union, NATO's Cooperation Council,
reinforced subsequently by the Partnership for Peace, became a forum for
the discussion of security issues between the West and all Central and Eastern European states as well as all successor states of the Soviet Union except
Georgia. None of these choices was automatic. None is irreversible. But the
logic of balancing in a world of relative capabilities did not dictate political
action in the halls of government in 1989–1990. Realism does not offer a
compelling explanation of the end of the Cold War.

While neoliberalism helps us understand the importance of institutions
at the end of the Cold War, it is of less use in making intelligible the central features of international politics after the Cold War. During the Cold
War, it may have been reasonable to take for granted state identities, at least
on the central issues of national security along the central front that divided
East from West.[56] Definitions of identity that distinguish between self and

53. William C. Wohlforth, "Realism and the End of the Cold War," *International Security* 19, no. 3
(Winter 1994/95): 91–129.
54. Rey Koslowski and Friedrich V. Kratochwil, "Understanding Change in International Politics:
The Soviet Empire's Demise and the International System," *International Organization* 48, no. 2
(Spring 1994): 244–46; Thomas Risse-Kappen, "Ideas Do Not Float Freely: Transnational Coalitions, Domestic Structures, and the End of the Cold War," *International Organization* 48, no. 2
(Spring 1994): 185–214.
55. John Gerard Ruggie, "Multilateralism: The Anatomy of an Institution," in John Gerard Ruggie,
ed., *Multilateralism Matters: The Theory and Praxis of an Institutional Form*, pp. 3–47 (New York:
Columbia University Press, 1993).
56. This is a simplifying assumption, not an empirical claim. State identities are always politically
reproduced and contested. Furthermore, context makes a difference. The Cold War may have had a
large effect on state identities in Europe. But this does not mean that it necessarily did so, for example, in the Third World.

other imply definitions of threat and interest that have strong effects on national security policies. Furthermore, such definitions of identity are rarely captured adequately with the language of symbolic resources sought by self-interested actors. For most of the major states, identity has become a subject of considerable political controversy. How these controversies are resolved—for example, in the United States, in the member states of the European Union, in Russia and the members of the Commonwealth of Independent States, in China and in many parts of the Third World—will be of great consequence for international security in the years ahead. In sum, recent changes in world politics remind us that other approaches, here a perspective emphasizing social factors, are useful in sharpening our thinking on issues that neorealism and neoliberalism slight.

Social Determinant 1: Cultural-Institutional Context

In sharp contrast to the realist view of the international system as a Hobbesian state of nature, neoliberalism offers a theory of the cultural-institutional context of state action. It defines regimes as particular combinations of principles, norms, rules, and procedures.[57] Power shapes international regimes. Often these regimes emerge when a hegemonic state, such as the United States after 1945, attempts to mold the international order to suit its interests and purposes. But international regimes do not simply mirror power relationships. With the passing of time they acquire their own dynamic. Regimes reduce transaction costs and thus enhance the potential for coordinating conflicting state policies. Regimes present states with political constraints and opportunities that can substantially affect how governments calculate their interests.

While the analysis of economic regimes has become a focus of scholarly attention, American scholars have made relatively few attempts to apply this analytical perspective to issues of national security. In the original volume on international regimes, Robert Jervis, for example, was very tentative in his assessment of whether security regimes have existed since 1945.[58] And in a subsequent essay he reached cautious conclusions about the possibility of relatively high levels of cooperation between states confronting a security dilemma in international politics.[59] Other scholars have given

57. Krasner, *International Regimes*; Volker Rittberger, ed., *International Regimes in East-West Politics* (New York: Pinter, 1990); Volker Rittberger, ed., *Regime Theory and International Relations* (Oxford: Oxford University Press, Clarendon Press, 1993).
58. Robert Jervis, "Security Regimes," in Krasner, *International Regimes*, pp. 173–94.
59. Robert Jervis, "From Balance to Concert: A Study of International Security Cooperation," in Oye, *Cooperation Under Anarchy*, pp. 58–79. Although these are two widely cited papers, it should

greater weight to cultural-institutional factors in their analyses of security regimes and the security cooperation between the United States and the Soviet Union.[60] In the most recent synthetic and authoritative restatement of this line of research, Volker Rittberger has gone furthest in incorporating a prescriptive element as a defining characteristic of a regime.[61]

In an important article, Friedrich Kratochwil and John Gerard Ruggie have noted that these lines of argument subscribe to a view that is too behavioralist.[62] The dominant, neoliberal application of regime theory captures only what in a statistical sense is "normal" about norms. But norms reflect also the premises of action.[63] While above a certain threshold behavioral violations invalidate norms, occasional violations do not. Critics of neoliberal institutionalism have made this their central point. These critics insist that social change engenders a process of self-reflection and political actions that are shaped by collectively held norms.[64]

---

be noted that Jervis was not writing from an unambiguous, neoliberal perspective. His analysis neglects cultural-institutional factors and rests largely on changes in the payoffs of different policies as well as on institutional features that increase transparency and warning time.

60. Harald Müller, "The Internalization of Principles, Norms, and Rules by Governments: The Case of Security Regimes," in Rittberger, *Regime Theory and International Relations*, pp. 361–88; Joseph S. Nye, Jr., "Nuclear Learning and U.S.-Soviet Security Regimes," *International Organization* 41, no. 3 (Summer 1987): 371–402. Alexander George, *U.S.-Soviet Security Cooperation: Achievements, Failures, Lessons* (New York: Oxford University Press, 1988).

61. Volker Rittberger, "Research on International Regimes in Germany: The Adaptive Internalization of an American Social Science Concept," in Rittberger, *Regime Theory and International Relations*, pp. 10–11.

62. Friedrich Kratochwil and John Gerard Ruggie, "International Organization: A State of the Art on an Art of the State," *International Organization* 40, no. 4 (Autumn 1986): 753–75. Other critics have questioned the lack of precision in definition, the analytical usefulness, and the empirical application of the regime concept; see Stephen Haggard and Beth A. Simmons, "Theories of International Regimes," *International Organization* 41, no. 3 (Summer 1987): 491–517; Martin J. Rochester, "The Rise and Fall of International Organization as a Field of Study," *International Organization* 40, no. 4 (Autumn 1986): 777–813.

63. This leads to an important set of analytical distinctions that could be further clarified, relying on Goldstein and Keohane's taxonomy of three types of beliefs; see Judith Goldstein and Robert O. Keohane, "Ideas and Foreign Policy: An Analytical Framework," in Judith Goldstein and Robert O. Keohane, eds., *Ideas and Foreign Policy: Beliefs, Institutions, and Political Change*, pp. 8–11 (Ithaca: Cornell University Press, 1993). "World views" and "principled beliefs" are publicly held and have behavioral implications; they are "intersubjective." "Causal beliefs" can be held privately and do not necessarily make claims on behavior; they are "cognitive."

64. Hayward R. Alker, Jr., "The Presumption of Anarchy in World Politics" (unpublished manuscript, Cambridge, Mass., 1986); Richard K. Ashley, "The Poverty of Neorealism," *International Organization* 38, no. 2 (Spring 1984): 225–86; Richard K. Ashley, "Untying the Sovereign State: A Double Reading of the Anarchy Problematique," *Millennium: Journal of International Studies* 7, no. 2 (1988): 227–62; Richard K. Ashley, "Living on Border Lines: Man, Poststructuralism, and War" (unpublished manuscript, Tempe, Ariz., 1988); Friedrich V. Kratochwil, *Rules, Norms, and Decisions* (New York: Cambridge University Press, 1988).

Although their criticism has not been answered to date, these observers have failed to produce the empirical research necessary to shake the rationalist and behavioral assumptions of neoliberal theory.[65] But this is beginning to change.[66] For example, in the area of arms control Emanuel Adler has relied on a sociological perspective to show how the arms control community in the United States institutionalized its influence in government and how it subsequently diffused and institutionalized its views in international agreements.[67] And several scholars have investigated with interesting results the effects of the culture of military organizations.[68]

Self-reflection does not occur in isolation; it is communicated to others. In the process of communication norms can emerge in a variety of ways: spontaneously evolving, as social practice; consciously promoted, as political strategies to further specific interests; deliberately negotiated, as a mechanism for conflict management; or as a combination, mixing these three types. State interests and strategies thus are shaped by a never-ending political process that generates publicly understood standards for action.[69]

---

65. Keohane, *International Institution and State Power*, pp. 158–79; Goldstein and Keohane, "Ideas and Foreign Policy," pp. 5–6, 26–27.

66. As the research in this volume and many of the volume's references illustrate, the charge of a lack of empirical research has by now lost much of its bite. Cornell graduate students alone are finishing a series of dissertations and books that provide a wealth of empirical research challenging exclusive reliance on rationalist and behavioralist styles of analysis. See Robert Herman, "Ideas, Identity, and the Redefinition of Interests: The Political and Intellectual Origins of the Soviet Foreign Policy Revolution" (Ph.D. diss., Cornell University, 1995); Elizabeth L. Kier, *Imagining War: French and British Military Doctrine Between the Wars* (Princeton: Princeton University Press, 1995); Audie J. Klotz, *Protesting Prejudice: Apartheid and the Politics of Norms in International Relations* (Ithaca: Cornell University Press, 1995); Gil Merom, "Blood and Conscience: Recasting the Boundaries of National Security" (Ph.D. diss., Cornell University, 1994); Richard Price, *A Genealogy of the Chemical Weapons Taboo* (forthcoming); Richard Price, "A Genealogy of the Chemical Weapons Taboo," *International Organization* 49, no. 1 (Winter 1995): 73–104; Christian Reus-Smit, "The Moral Purpose of the State: Social Identity, Legitimate Action, and the Construction of International Institutions" (Ph.D. diss., Cornell University, 1995); Nina Tannenwald, "Dogs That Don't Bark: The United States, the Role of Norms, and the Non-Use of Nuclear Weapons Since 1945" (Ph.D. diss., Cornell University, 1995); Michael Marks, "The Formation of European Policy in Post-Franco Spain: Ideas, Interests, and the International Transmission of Knowledge" (Ph.D. diss., Cornell University, 1993); and Dan Thomas, "Between Reason and Power: International Norms and Political Change in Eastern Europe and the Soviet Union, 1975–1989" (Ph.D. diss., Cornell University, 1995).

67. Emanuel Adler, "Arms Control, Disarmament, and National Security: A Thirty-Year Retrospective and a New Set of Anticipations," *Daedalus* 120, no. 1 (Winter 1991): 1–20; Emanuel Adler, "The Emergence of Cooperation: National Epistemic Communities and the International Evolution of the Idea of Nuclear Arms Control," *International Organization* 46, no. 1 (Winter 1992): 101–46.

68. Jeffrey W. Legro, *Cooperation Under Fire: Anglo-German Restraint During World War II* (Ithaca: Cornell University Press, 1995); Kier, *Imagining War*; Scott D. Sagan, *The Limits of Safety: Organizations, Accidents, and Nuclear Weapons* (Princeton: Princeton University Press, 1993).

69. Harald Müller, "Internationale Beziehungen als kommunikatives Handeln," *Zeitschrift für Internationale Beziehungen* 1, no. 1 (June 1994): 15–44; James Johnson, "Habermas on Strategic and

The behavioral compliance of actors with norms thus is only one part of the story, and that part must be linked to another aspect, the justifications proffered.[70] This line of reasoning is a departure from neoliberal theory, but it would be a great mistake to overemphasize this difference. The most widely accepted definition of what constitutes a regime refers specifically to implicit norms.[71] This definition thus grants scholars a wide measure of latitude in the type of evidence that they collect and in the methods of analysis that they rely on. Since a large amount of the scholarship on international regimes relies on qualitative case histories, the shift in analysis is not very great, so long as analysis adheres to the conventions of an empirically oriented social science.

Social Determinant 2: Collective Identity

International regimes are social institutions that mitigate conflict in a decentralized international society of states. But a rationalist theory of regimes factors out of its analysis the actor identities that often are consequential for the definition of actor interests. Cultural-institutional contexts do not merely constrain actors by changing the incentives that shape their behavior. They do not simply regulate behavior. They also help to constitute the very actors whose conduct they seek to regulate.

International and domestic environments shape state identities.[72] With the end of the Cold War, issues of collective identity have become centrally important, probably more so than the reduction in political uncertainties that inhibit agreements. For example, the shape and speed of the European integration process and the question of how that Europe will relate to the outside world is of critical political importance and has given rise to xenophobia and a new wave of nationalism. Analogous political developments are occurring in Eastern Europe, in the member states of the Commonwealth of Independent States, in many Third World countries, and in the United States. And in Asia the intensification of efforts to create new

Communicative Action," *Political Theory* 19, no. 2 (May 1991): 181–201; Oran Young, *International Cooperation: Building Regimes for National Resources and the Environment* (Ithaca: Cornell University Press, 1989); Young, *International Governance.*

70. David Welch, *Justice and the Genesis of War* (Cambridge: Cambridge University Press, 1993).

71. Krasner, *International Regimes*, p. 2. Issues of definition and conceptualization are considered at length in several essays in Rittberger, *Regime Theory and International Relations.*

72. Alexander Wendt, "The Agent-Structure Problem in International Relations Theory," *International Organization* 41, no. 3 (Summer 1987): 335–70; Alexander Wendt, "Anarchy Is What States Make of It: The Social Construction of Power Politics," *International Organization* 46, no. 2 (Spring 1992): 391–425; Alexander Wendt, "Collective Identity Formation and the International State," *American Political Science Review* 88, no. 2 (Summer 1994): 384–96; Iver B. Neumann, "Identity and Security," *Journal of Peace Research* 29, no. 2 (1992): 221–26.

forms of multilateralism designed to facilitate policy coordination is closely linked to contested definitions of Asian identity.

With few exceptions, neorealism also remains silent on the issue of identity—for two reasons. First, it stresses the ecological dynamics that self-selection and functional imperatives have for states. Second, neorealism seeks to distance itself from traditional realism, which did pay attention, implausibly, to human nature[73] and, plausibly, to issues of national identity. Since neorealists view states as undifferentiated and unitary actors, they sidestep consideration of issues concerning the character of the state and the construction of state identities.[74]

The international and domestic societies in which states are embedded shape their identities in powerful ways. The state is a social actor. It is embedded in social rules and conventions that constitute its identity and the reasons for the interests that motivate actors.[75] On this point the contrast between a sociological perspective on the one hand and neoliberalism and neorealism on the other is substantial. History is more than a progressive search for efficient institutions that regulate property rights. And history cannot be reduced to a perpetual recurrence of sameness, conflict, and balancing. History is a process of change that leaves an imprint on state identity. In a broad historical perspective the eventual success of the national state in Western Europe should not blind us to the wide array of institutional experimentation, both domestic and international, that preceded it.[76] Influenced by a long history of universal empires, regional kingdoms, and subcontinental empires, Asian states also differ greatly from the conventional image of unified, rational states.[77] The historical evidence compels us to relinquish the notion of states with unproblematic identities.

---

73. J. Ann Tickner, *Gender in International Relations: Feminist Perspectives on Achieving Global Security* (New York: Columbia University Press, 1992), p. 30.

74. Relatedly, state theory applied to the analysis of domestic politics or the domestic sources of foreign policy has typically focused on the variability in the autonomy and the capacity of states, not on their identity. See Bruce Andrews, "Social Rules and the State as a Social Actor," *World Politics* 27, no. 4 (July 1975): 521–40; Peter J. Katzenstein, "International Relations and Domestic Structures: Foreign Economic Policies of Advanced Industrial States," *International Organization* 30, no. 1 (Winter 1976): 1–45; Stephen D. Krasner, "Approaches to the State: Alternative Conceptions and Historical Dynamics," *Comparative Politics* 16, no. 2 (January 1984): 223–46; Peter B. Evans, Dietrich Rueschemeyer, and Theda Skocpol, eds., *Bringing the State Back In* (Cambridge: Cambridge University Press, 1985); Peter B. Evans, *Embedded Autonomy: States and Industrial Transformation* (Princeton: Princeton University Press, 1995).

75. Andrews, "Social Rules and the State as a Social Actor," p. 536.

76. Charles Tilly, *Coercion, Capital, and European States, A.D. 990–1990* (Oxford: Blackwell, 1990).

77. Suzanne H. Rudolph, "Presidential Address: State Formation in Asia—Prolegomena to a Comparative Study," *Journal of Asian Studies* 46, no. 4 (November 1987): 731–46.

The identities of states emerge from their interactions with different social environments, both domestic and international. Despite differences in theoretical formulation, the analysis of nationalism offers an important example. Ernest Gellner stresses the importance of the instrumental logic of nationalism; Benedict Anderson emphasizes that national identities are socially constructed; and Ernst Haas combines both perspectives in his discussion of nationalism as an instrumental social construction.[78] All insist that the national identities of states are crucial for understanding politics and that they cannot be stipulated deductively. They must be investigated empirically in concrete historical settings.

The international society of states also shapes varying state identities by virtue of recognizing their legitimacy and admitting them to international organizations whose membership is often restricted only to states.[79] Governments crave the diplomatic recognition by members of the international society of states because it bestows upon them the legitimacy they may need to secure their existence. In Africa and elsewhere, for example, sovereignty constitutes and legitimates states that are extremely weak in terms of material power.[80] Statehood thus depends partly on position in the international society of states.

The analysis of transnational relations and of world systems offers analytical perspectives that also elucidate the relations between states and their social environments.[81] Often the social environments that affect state

78. Ernest Gellner, *Nations and Nationalism* (Ithaca: Cornell University Press, 1983); Benedict Anderson, *Imagined Communities* (London: Verso, 1983); Ernst B. Haas, "Nationalism: An Instrumental Social Construction," *Millennium: Journal of International Studies* 22, no. 3 (Winter 1993): 505–45.

79. John Gerard Ruggie, "Continuity and Transformation in the World Polity: Toward a Neorealist Synthesis," *World Politics* 35, no. 2 (January 1983): 261–85; John Gerard Ruggie, "International Structure and International Transformation: Space, Time, and Method," in Ernst-Otto Czempiel and James N. Rosenau, eds., *Global Changes and Theoretical Challenges: Approaches to World Politics for the 1990s*, pp. 21–36 (Lexington, Mass.: D. C. Heath, Lexington Books, 1989); Raymond Duvall and Alexander Wendt, "Institutions and International Order," in Czempiel and Rosenau, *Global Changes and Theoretical Challenges*, pp. 51–74.

80. Robert H. Jackson and Carl G. Rosberg, "Why Africa's Weak States Persist: The Empirical and the Juridical in Statehood," *World Politics* 35, no. 1 (October 1982): 1–24; Robert H. Jackson, *Quasi-States: Sovereignty, International Relations, and the Third World* (Cambridge: Cambridge University Press, 1990); Meyer, "The World Polity"; George M. Thomas and John W. Meyer, "Regime Changes and State Power in an Intensifying World State-System," in Bergesen, *Studies of the Modern World System*, pp. 139–58.

81. Robert O. Keohane and Joseph S. Nye, eds., *Transnational Relations and World Politics* (Cambridge: Harvard University Press, 1972); Immanuel Wallerstein, *The Modern World System: Capitalist Agriculture and the Origins of the European World-Economy in the Sixteenth Century* (New York: Academic Press, 1974); Immanuel Wallerstein, *The Modern World System II: Mercantilism and the Consolidation of the European World-Economy, 1600–1750* (New York: Academic Press, 1980).

identity link international and domestic environments in a way that defies the reification of distinct domestic and international spheres of politics. After 1945, for example, the institutionalization of the welfare state created a system of "embedded liberalism" based on the compromise between advocates of domestic welfare capitalism and proponents of a liberal international order.[82] In her research on European guestworkers Yasemin Soysal has demonstrated one of the consequences of embedded liberalism for changing notions of citizenship in Western Europe.[83] In contrast to past practice, European nation-states have become responsible for the welfare of all persons, not just citizens, living within their borders. Traditionally defined on the basis of nationality, individual rights in Western Europe are now codified into notions of universal personhood rather than nationality. This is a novel and important change in the matrix of factors affecting the international relations of Europe.

This book analyzes the effect of political identities. It views states as social actors. It analyzes political identities in specific historical contexts. And it traces the effects that changing identities have on political interests and thus on national security policies.

Neorealist and neoliberal theories adhere to relatively sparse views of the international system. Neorealism assumes that the international system has virtually no normative content. The international system constrains national security policies directly without affecting conceptions of state interest. Neoliberalism takes as given actor identities and views ideas and beliefs as intervening variables between assumed interests and behavioral outcomes.[84] In this view states operate in environments that create constraints and opportunities.

These analytical perspectives overlook the degree to which social environments and actors penetrate one another. The domestic and international environments of states have effects; they are the arenas in which actors contest norms and through political and social processes construct and reconstruct identities. The cultural-institutional context and the degree to which identities are constructed both vary. In some situations neorealist and neoliberal assumptions may be warranted. But these perspectives often overlook important political effects that condition international politics and thus affect issues of national security.

---

82. Ruggie, "Continuity and Transformation in the World Polity"; Peter J. Katzenstein, *Small States in World Markets: Industrial Policy in Europe* (Ithaca: Cornell University Press, 1985).
83. Yasemin Nuhoglu Soysal, *Limits of Citizenship: Migrants and Postnational Membership in Europe* (Chicago: University of Chicago Press, 1994).
84. Goldstein and Keohane, "Ideas and Foreign Policy," p. 5.

This book makes two analytical moves simultaneously. It stipulates a more social view of the environment in which states and other political actors operate. And it insists that political identities are to significant degrees constructed within that environment. It thus departs from materialist notions and the rationalist view of identities as exogenously given. That is, this book seeks to incorporate into the analysis of national security both the cultural-institutional context of the political environment and the political construction of identity. The empirical studies illustrate how both factors help to shape the definition of interests and thus have demonstrable effects on national security policies.

Why Bother?

Neorealism offers an orienting framework of analysis that gives the field of national security studies much of its intellectual coherence and commonality of outlook. Furthermore, neorealism holds forth the promise of a tight, deductive theory as the ultimate prize of theorizing about national security. Kenneth Waltz himself, however, has been very circumspect in his theoretical claims. He argues that his theory, formulated at the level of the international system, seeks to explain only the recurrence of the balancing behavior of states in history.

Neorealism is too general and underspecified to tell us anything about the direction of balancing, let alone about the content of the national security policies of states. Therefore, particular studies of national security, typically, adapt some features of Waltz's theory and, in addition, import more or less loosely clustered groups of variables from other fields (such as organization theory, comparative politics, or political psychology) and graft them onto the orienting framework that neorealism provides. The theoretical contribution of these studies lies in the formulation and testing of, at best, loosely linked hypotheses. The politically substantive and most interesting scholarship in the field is historical in nature and offers little hope of moving to a deductive style of "theory" anytime soon.

This book puts at center stage analytical concepts that the existing literature on national security acknowledges only obliquely. Some studies seek to explain aspects of national security with reference to social facts. But they tend to do so in a manner that subordinates the causal force of social facts to a materialist or rationalist view of the world. In this view, for example, identities and norms either are derivative of material capabilities or are deployed by autonomous actors for instrumental reasons. Based on the assumption that rationality is a natural rather than a constructed concept, these books view ideologies largely in the service of rational calculations.

The "myths of empires," for example, that Jack Snyder analyzes in accounting for the conditions under which great powers overexpand result from different patterns of domestic politics. While Snyder acknowledges that international factors also play a role, he argues that specific domestic coalitions develop aggressive strategic perspectives that serve particular political interests. Elites manipulate mass publics through propaganda. In this view imperial ideologies are rationalizations for parochial interests, products that entrepreneurs sell in political markets. As Snyder writes, his theory of domestic politics roots its analysis "securely in a rational-choice framework. . . . It is more accurate to say that statesmen and societies actively shape the lessons of the past in ways they find convenient than it is to say that they are shaped by them."[85] Snyder acknowledges in passing that the "blowback" of propaganda, the blurring of the line between "fact and fiction . . . sincere beliefs and tactical argument,"[86] entraps political leaders not only in their own confusions but in the political context that they helped create. But since this aside cuts against Snyder's rationalist interpretation of ideology, it remains one underdeveloped page in a long theoretical essay. Sociologists and cultural historians are likely to demur by insisting that "blowback is big."

Stephen Walt's theory of balance of threat shows a similar theoretical inclination.[87] As is true of Snyder's work, Walt's threat theory is not a minor modification of neorealism but a substantial departure from it. While Walt continues to subscribe to realism as an orienting framework, his emphasis on threat perception moves away from the systemic level and shifts analysis from material capabilities to ideational factors.[88] Walt views ideology as a variable that competes with others for explanatory power.[89]

---

85. Jack Snyder, *Myths of Empire: Domestic Politics and International Ambition* (Ithaca: Cornell University Press, 1991), pp. 17, 30.

86. Ibid., p. 41.

87. Stephen M. Walt, *The Origins of Alliances* (Ithaca: Cornell University Press, 1987).

88. Walt is very explicit in arguing that balancing in inter-Arab relations is atypical. While states typically "seek to counter threats by adding the power of another state to their own . . . in the Arab world the most important source of power has been the ability to manipulate one's own image and the image of one's rivals in the minds of other Arab elites" (ibid., p. 149).

89. In a second book, *Revolution and War* (Ithaca: Cornell University Press, 1996), Walt extends this analytical move from international threat perceptions to domestic threat perceptions. He argues that revolutions affect threat perceptions through miscalculation, hostility, perception of offensive power, and uncertainty—that is, through four different psychological mechanisms.

But balance-of-threat theorizing poses an obvious question about the importance of ideology in the threat perceptions of states. If one views ideology as a system of meaning that affects the definition of threat, then Walt's conclusions may warrant further investigation, for the cost calculations that states make when they weigh ideological solidarity against security concerns are not exogenous to their ideological affinities.[90]

James March and Johan Olsen, among others, have elaborated this view in an often neglected chapter of their much-cited book. Ideologies, norms, and identities do not simply serve instrumental purposes. March and Olsen argue that obligatory action contrasts with consequential action. Behavior is shaped not only by goals, alternatives, and rules of maximization or satisficing central to rationalist models of politics. Behavior is shaped also by roles and norms that define standards of appropriateness. Improvisation and strategic behavior are embedded in a social environment that constitutes the identity of the actors and their interests and that shapes the norms that also help to define their interests. "Political processes are as much concerned with managing interpretations and creating visions as they are with clarifying decisions. . . . We are led to a perspective that challenges the first premise of many theories of politics, the premise that life is organized around choice. Rather, we might observe that life is not only, or primarily, choice but also interpretation."[91]

---

90. For a critical discussion of Walt's use of correlational metaphors and ways of drawing conclusions, see Albert Yee, "The Causal Effects of Ideas Themselves and Policy Preferences: Behavioral, Institutional, and Discursive Formulations" (unpublished paper, Brown University, 1993), pp. 10–11, and Stephen Haggard, "Structuralism and Its Critics: Recent Progress in International Relations Theory," in Emanuel Adler and Beverly Crawford, eds., *Progress in Postwar International Relations*, pp. 420–22 (New York: Columbia University Press, 1991). For a more positive reading, see Gunther Hellmann, "Für eine problemorientierte Grundlagenforschung: Kritik und Perspektiven der Disziplin 'Internationale Beziehungen' in Deutschland" *Zeitschrift für Internationale Beziehungen* 1, no. 1 (June 1994): 82–83. Taken on Walt's terms, his analysis of ideology also fails to convince at times. He appears to be bent on arguing the case against the importance of ideology, especially for the superpowers, either by imposing excessively rigid definitional criteria or by coding decisions of cases that are not compelling. For example, as noted in Douglas J. MacDonald's review in *Journal of Politics* 51, no. 3 (August 1989): 795–98, Walt's restrictive definitional criteria of left-wing ideological adherence (p. 186) preclude coding the support of "united front" movements by the Soviet Union as alliances based on ideological considerations. And the ideologically close relations between the United States and Israel are simply argued away by referring to Israel as a "welfare-state theocracy" that has little ideological affinity with the United States (p. 200). Maybe so. But as Michael Barnett argues in this book, U.S.-Israeli relations became much more problematic in the late 1980s when some segments of the American public began to doubt that Israel was still behaving like an essentially like-minded parliamentary democracy.

91. James G. March and Johan P. Olsen, *Rediscovering Institutions: The Organizational Basis of Politics* (New York: Free Press, 1989), p. 51; March, "Decision-Making Perspective."

Applied to questions of national security, the work of Elizabeth Kier on strategic culture offers a compelling application of that general perspective.[92] In a landmark study, Barry Posen, for example, developed sophisticated arguments that link the preference of military organizations for offensive doctrines to the functional needs of military organizations—specifically their wish to control resources, to be autonomous from civilian interference, and to enhance the social prestige of military officers.[93] Kier has reexamined existing explanations of the choice of offensive and defensive military doctrines by military leaders, investigated fully the historical evidence, carefully evaluated the strengths and weaknesses of alternative explanations, and come to an unambiguous conclusion: military organizations do not have an inherent preference for offensive doctrines. One cannot deduce the interests of the military from either the functional needs of the military or the international balance of power. Instead, the political preferences for offensive or defensive doctrines of different branches of the military reflect organizational interests. And these must be understood within the context of specific organizational cultures, which are themselves nested in broader political-military cultures distinctive of the politics of different states.

A perspective that emphasizes obligatory action does not have to deny consequential action and the importance of the instrumental political use of norms and identities. For example, moral entrepreneurs who manipulate ideas, John Mueller and Ethan Nadelmann argue in different projects, have had important effects on how elites and mass publics view the institution of war and a variety of state policies combatting acts such as piracy, slavery, counterfeiting of national currencies, hijacking of aircraft, trafficking in women and children for purposes of prostitution, and trading in drugs.[94] As these examples make clear, empirical research on national security needs to evaluate the competing claims of both obligatory and consequentialist perspectives.

This book makes its main analytical move at the level of an orienting framework that privileges social factors. Contrasting analytical claims are

---

92. Kier, *Imagining War*.
93. Barry R. Posen, *The Sources of Military Doctrine: France, Britain, and Germany Between the World Wars* (Ithaca: Cornell University Press, 1984). See also Jack Snyder, *The Ideology of the Offensive: Military Decison Making and the Disasters of 1914* (Ithaca: Cornell University Press, 1984). I neglect Snyder's work here, since Kier replicates Posen's research on interwar Europe.
94. Mueller, *Quiet Cataclysm*; Ethan A. Nadelmann, "Global Prohibition Regimes: The Evolution of Norms in International Society," *International Organization* 44, no. 4 (Autumn 1990): 479–526.

best articulated in the form of specific hypotheses that are applied in particular empirical domains. This is the strategy that the empirical essays in this volume follow. It is on the ground of evidence that we have the best chance of intellectually engaging contrasting analytical perspectives that differ on questions of ontology, epistemology, and methodology.

For particular research questions in specific situations it may be sensible to conceive of states as actors with unproblematic identities that balance and bandwagon or conduct their political business in institutions that lower transaction costs. But for many research questions and in many situations we must capture additional factors to explain problematic aspects of national security policies.

The effort to test sociological, culture-based explanations against economic, interest-based explanations centers on identifying and describing problems overlooked by existing scholarship and specifying the social factors, here state identity and the cultural-institutional context, that shape conceptions of actor interest and behavior. Some essays in this book view the context of states and governments as more permeated by social facts than is typical of most scholarship on national security. Other essays focus on the problematic nature of the identity of states and governments. While the individual essays privilege one or the other aspect in their empirical research, the book as a whole makes both moves simultaneously. In this view the crucial question is not to establish whether interests prevail over identities and norms or whether identities and norms prevail over interests. What matters is how identities and norms influence the ways in which actors define their interests in the first place.

Essay 2 explicates more fully the theoretical approach, with its dual focus on cultural-institutional context and identity. It compares that approach to others in the analysis of international and domestic politics; it makes some basic conceptual distinctions; finally, drawing on the individual case studies as well as other literature, it reviews the effects of culture and identity on interests and national security policy.

Part 1 focuses on the cultural-institutional context in which states and governments define their interests and act. Dana Eyre and Mark Suchman analyze in essay 3 the effects that norms of military prowess have on some of the weapons procurement policies of states. Richard Price and Nina Tannenwald, in essay 4, analyze the historical evolution in norms of the non-use of chemical and nuclear weapons. In essay 5 Martha Finnemore examines the effects of changing norms on patterns of military intervention. She shows how shifts in understandings about the reasons to intervene and the means of intervening have changed the modalities of national security policies. In essay 6 Elizabeth Kier analyzes the effects of the organizational culture of the French military on the evolution of offensive and defensive military doctrine. Finally, in essay 7 Alastair Johnston argues that China's national security policy in the Maoist period resulted from a "hard" strategic culture of parabellum, a quintessentially constructed worldview, rather than from the condition of international anarchy. What unites these essays and sets them apart from related inquiries is their detailed attention to the effects of the cultural-institutional context on national security policies.

Part 2 analyzes how constructed, collective identities of political actors, such as states or governments, affect their interests and policies. In essay 8 Robert Herman traces the political process by which cosmopolitan reformers in the Soviet Union articulated and put into practice newly invented or rediscovered notions of a "Western" Soviet Union, thus helping to end the Cold War. Thomas Berger, in essay 9, deals with Germany and Japan as two instances in which collective identities have been deeply transformed by the effects of World War II in a political process marked by political contestation and historical contingency. In essay 10, Thomas Risse-Kappen examines the changing identities that help define changing security communities among liberal democracies in the North Atlantic area. And Michael Barnett, in essay 11, examines the effects of contested and changing identities on security policy, both in an Arab nation increasingly divided and between the United States and Israel.

The essays in parts 1 and 2 span domestic and international levels of analysis as well as national, regional, and global political contexts. They engage the present as well as the past. They deal with Western and non-Western states operating at different levels of development. But this diversity in empirical application conceals a unity of theoretical purpose. All these essays specify a political outcome or set of outcomes that is central to students of national security. And all of them either derive a plausible set of expectations from existing theories that do not address their question or offer a plausible explanation derived from existing analytical perspectives that they test against a preferred culture- or identity-based explanation.

The two essays in part 3 conclude the volume. In essay 12, Paul Kowert and Jeffrey Legro deal with the origins and consequences of norms and identities. Their analysis connects this book back to a set of intellectual concerns that distinguish a number of current approaches. In the interest of mapping directions for future work, they seek also to impose greater specification of variables and causal patterns. And they point to gaps and oversights in this book's approach and findings. Finally, essay 13 considers some recent realist and liberal writings that are trying to grapple with the issues of culture and identity raised in this book; it summarizes the approach, hypotheses, and main findings of the empirical essays and explores further some of the issues raised in them; it points to a broader research agenda for national security studies; and it concludes with a discussion of the implications of this book's perspective for the role of the United States in a changing world.

This book argues that we should not take for granted what needs to be explained: the sources and content of national security interests that states and governments pursue. A focus on political identity and the cultural-institutional context, this book claims, offers a promising avenue for elucidating the changing contours of national security policy.

2 • Norms, Identity, and Culture in National Security

*Ronald L. Jepperson, Alexander Wendt,
and Peter J. Katzenstein*

The analytical perspective of this book departs in two ways from dominant assumptions in contemporary national security studies. First, we argue that the security environments in which states are embedded are in important part cultural and institutional, rather than just material. This contrasts with the assumption made by neorealists and many students of the domestic sources of national security policy. In their views, international and domestic environments are largely devoid of cultural and institutional elements and therefore are best captured by materialist imagery like the balance of power or bureaucratic politics. Second, we argue that cultural environments affect not only the incentives for different kinds of state behavior but also the basic character of states—what we call state "identity." This contrasts with the prevailing assumption, made by neorealists and neoliberals

For their careful readings and critical comments of previous drafts we would like to thank the members of the project; the participants at the Social Science Research Council/MacArthur Workshops at the University of Minnesota and Stanford University in 1994; and Emanuel Adler, Pierre van den Berghe, Thomas Christensen, Alexander George, Lynn Eden, James Goldgeier, Peter Gourevitch, Ernst Haas, Peter Haas, Robert Hariman, Stanley Hoffmann, Christine Ingebritsen, Robert Keohane, Jonathan Kirshner, Atul Kohli, Friedrich Kratochwil, Charles Kupchan, David Laitin, Lisa Martin, John Meyer, Henry Nau, Judith Reppy, David Rowe, Heiner Schulz, David Skidmore, Richard Smoke, Jack Snyder, Dan Thomas, Janice Thomson, Stephen Walt, and two anonymous reviewers for Columbia University Press.

alike, that the defining actor properties are intrinsic to states, that is, "essential" to actors (rather than socially contingent), and exogenous to the environment. Although we believe these arguments apply to both the domestic and the international environments in which national security policy is made, we shall illustrate them at this point only with reference to the latter.

There are at least three layers to the international cultural environments in which national security policies are made. Commonly recognized in existing scholarship is the layer of formal institutions or security regimes: NATO, OSCE, WEU, arms control regimes like the NPT, CWC, SALT treaties, and the like. Less widely acknowledged is the existence of a world political culture as a second layer. It includes elements like rules of sovereignty and international law, norms for the proper enactment of sovereign statehood, standardized social and political technologies (such as organization theory and models of economic policy) carried by professional and consultancy networks, and a transnational political discourse carried by such international social movements as Amnesty International and Greenpeace. Finally, international patterns of amity and enmity have important cultural dimensions. In terms of material power, Canada and Cuba stand in roughly comparable positions relative to the United States. But while one is a threat, the other is an ally, a result, we believe, of ideational factors operating at the international level. In each case realists will try to reduce cultural effects to epiphenomena of the distribution of power; we argue that these effects have greater autonomy.

Our second argument refers to the effects of cultural environments on the identity, as opposed to just the behavior, of states. The term *identity* here is intended as a useful label, not as a signal of commitment to some exotic (presumably Parisian) social theory. Indeed, this concept has become a staple of mainstream social science, whether or not the term itself is actually used. Frederick Frey has written an underappreciated article on the problem of actor designation, which calls attention to the problems and importance of specifying who the actors are in a system.[1] Kenneth Waltz was implicitly talking about identity when he argued that anarchic structures tend to produce "like units."[2] Early on in the development of regime theory, Stephen Krasner[3] suggested that regimes could change state interests and, later, that

1. Frederick Frey, "The Problem of Actor Designation in Political Analysis," *Comparative Politics* 17, no. 2 (January 1985): 127–52.
2. Kenneth N. Waltz, *Theory of International Politics* (Reading, Mass.: Addison-Wesley, 1979), pp. 74–77.
3. Stephen D. Krasner, ed., *International Regimes* (Ithaca: Cornell University Press, 1983), pp. 362–64.

an "institutional" approach would problematize "the very nature of the actors: their endowments, utilities—preferences, capacities, resources, and identity."[4] And Robert Keohane,[5] too, has called for a "sociological" approach to state interests, in which transformations of interests become an important effect to be investigated. None of these scholars, however, has systematically pursued these insights; we attempt to do so here.[6]

More specifically, our argument envisions at least three effects that external cultural environments may have on state identities and thus on national security interests and policies. First, they may affect states' prospects for survival as entities in the first place. Just as Waltz argued that competitive material environments will "select out" states that do not adopt efficient organizational forms, so Robert Jackson[7] and David Strang[8] have argued that recognition of juridical sovereignty by the society of states has enabled weak states to survive when they otherwise might not. Second, environments may change the modal character of statehood in the system over

4. Stephen D. Krasner, "Sovereignty: An Institutional Perspective," *Comparative Political Studies* 21 (1988): 72.

5. Robert O. Keohane, "International Liberalism Reconsidered," in John Dunn, ed., *The Economic Limits to Modern Politics*, p. 183 (Cambridge: Cambridge University Press, 1990).

6. We are thus following the general line of argument suggested by John Ruggie's and Friedrich Kratochwil's writings during the last decade. See John Gerard Ruggie, "International Responses to Technology: Concepts and Trends," in "International Responses to Technology," special issue of *International Organization* 29, no. 3 (Summer 1975): 557–84; John G. Ruggie, "International Regimes, Transactions, and Change: Embedded Liberalism in the Postwar Economic Order," in Krasner, *International Regimes*, pp. 195–231; John G. Ruggie, "Continuity and Transformation in the World Polity: Toward a Neorealist Synthesis," *World Politics* 35, no. 2 (January 1983): 261–85; John G. Ruggie, "Multilateralism: The Anatomy of an Institution," in John G. Ruggie, ed., *Multilateralism Matters: The Theory and Praxis of an Institutional Form* (New York: Columbia University Press, 1993), pp. 3–47; John G. Ruggie, "Territoriality and Beyond: Problematizing Modernity in International Relations," *International Organization* 47, no. 1 (Winter 1993): 139–74; Friedrich V. Kratochwil, "The Protagorean Quest: Community, Justice, and the 'Oughts' and 'Musts' of International Politics," *International Journal* 43 (Spring 1988): 205–40; Friedrich V. Kratochwil, *Rules, Norms, and Decisions: On the Conditions of Practical and Legal Reasoning in International Relations and Domestic Affairs* (Cambridge: Cambridge University Press, 1989); Friedrich V. Kratochwil, "The Embarrassment of Changes: Neo-Realism as the Science of Realpolitik Without Politics," *Review of International Studies* 19 (1993): 63–80; Friedrich V. Kratochwil, "Norms Versus Numbers: Multilateralism and the Rationalist and Reflexivist Approaches to Institutions—A Unilateral Plea for Communicative Rationality," in Ruggie, *Multilateralism Matters*, pp. 443–74; Friedrich V. Kratochwil, "Is the Ship of Culture at Sea or Returning?" in Yosef Lapid and Friedrich V. Kratochwil, eds., *The Return of Culture and Identity in International Relations Analysis* (Boulder: Lynne Rienner, in press).

7. Robert Jackson, *Quasi-States: Sovereignty, International Relations, and the Third World* (Cambridge: Cambridge University Press, 1990).

8. David Strang, "Anomaly and Commonplace in European Political Expansion: Realist and Institutional Accounts," *International Organization* 45, no. 2 (Spring 1991): 143–62.

time. Today, in contrast to the late nineteenth century, it would be almost inconceivable for a country readily to vote to become a colony.[9] Relatedly, as late as the nineteenth century warfare was seen as a virtuous exercise of state power; today, while states are still organized to fight wars, changing international norms and domestic factors have "tamed" the aggressive impulses of many states, especially in the West, thus creating a disposition to see war as at best a necessary evil.[10] Finally, cultural environments may cause variation in the character of statehood within a given international system. The aftermath of World War II, for example, initiated a period of identity politics in both Germany and Japan, which generated "trading state" identities, as Thomas Berger shows in this volume. Similarly, unlike Britain, France maintained its commitment to the exchange rate mechanism of the European Monetary System (EMS) partly because it is a founding member—that is, because of its identity interests.[11] In each case a choice theoretic approach that treated the properties of state actors as exogenously given would fail to capture important effects of the external cultural environment on state identities, interests, and policies.

We develop this analytical perspective in the rest of this essay. What emerges is not a "theory" of national security so much as an orienting framework that highlights a set of effects and mechanisms that have been neglected in mainstream security studies. As such, this framework tells us about as much about the substance of world politics as does a materialist view of the international system or a choice theoretic assumption of exogenous interests. It offers a partial perspective, but one important for orienting our thinking about more specific phenomena.

9. Robert H. Jackson, "The Weight of Ideas in Decolonization: Normative Change in International Relations," in Judith Goldstein and Robert O. Keohane, eds., *Ideas and Foreign Policy: Beliefs, Institutions, and Political Change*, pp. 111–38 (Ithaca: Cornell University Press, 1993).

10. On changing attitudes toward war, see John Mueller, *Retreat from Doomsday: The Obsolescence of Major War* (New York: Basic Books, 1989); and James Lee Ray, "The Abolition of Slavery and the End of International War," *International Organization* 43, no. 3 (Summer 1989): 405–40. A distinguished military historian, John Keegan, concurs with the view that wars are not "natural" but "cultural." They are institutions of society that evolve. Keegan is "impressed by the evidence that mankind, wherever it has the option, is distancing itself from the institution of warfare. . . . War, it seems to me, after a lifetime of reading about the subject, mingling with men of war, visiting the sites of war and observing its effects, may well be ceasing to commend itself to human beings as a desirable or productive, let alone rational, means of reconciling their discontents" (John Keegan, *A History of Warfare* [New York: Knopf, 1993], p. 59). See also John Mueller, *Quiet Cataclysm: Reflections on the Recent Transformation of World Politics* (New York: Harper Collins, 1995), pp. 111–23.

11. David Cameron, "British Exit, German Voice, French Loyalty: Defection, Domination, and Cooperation in the 1992–93 ERM Crisis" (paper prepared for delivery at the 1993 annual meeting of the American Political Science Association, Washington, D.C., September 1993).

The next section of this essay sketches an intellectual map that conceptualizes international and domestic environments and their relationships to state identity. Subsequent sections locate prominent theoretical approaches in the field of national security on this map, in comparison to the approach of this book, pull together the book's main substantive arguments, and briefly discuss some methodological and metatheoretic issues. We conclude with some extensions of our analysis.

Analytical Context

The empirical essays in this volume focus on the ways in which norms, institutions, and other cultural features of domestic and international environments affect state security interests and policies. In pursuing this idea we do not claim that theories that do not do so are unhelpful or wrongheaded. The relationship between different lines of argument will vary from complementarity to competition to subsumption. One cannot prejudge the relative utility of different arguments apart from the specification of the problems that motivate the research in the first place. It is in this spirit that this volume departs from realism and liberalism as the dominant approaches in security studies.

Figure 2.1 provides a map for positioning the arguments of these essays relative to those of realism and liberalism.[12] The map is analytically general; we use it here to categorize domestic and international theories of national security.

One axis of the map (the x-axis) focuses on the relative cultural and institutional density of the environments in which actors move.[13] States can be conceived of as interacting with environments that range from having limited cultural and institutional content on the one hand to

---

12. The map is Wendt's idea; the conceptualization of this version, however, was developed jointly with Jepperson, who has produced a related but different map of social theories; see Ronald L. Jepperson, "Institutions, Institutional Effects, and Institutionalism," in Walter W. Powell and Paul J. DiMaggio, eds., *The New Institutionalism in Organizational Analysis*, pp. 143–63 (Chicago: University of Chicago Press, 1991). For further discussion of Wendt's own version, see Alexander Wendt, *Social Theory of International Politics* (Cambridge: Cambridge University Press, in press). Essays 1 and 13 in this volume provide some additional discussion of realist and liberal thought. In the interest of brevity we treat them here in a reified manner.

13. Throughout, we mean nothing special by *actors*. Typically, we are referring to governments or government elites. We treat *states* and *governments* largely as synonyms—sloppy practice for comparative politics, we realize, but this treatment is conventional in international relations. These shorthand references are not intended to anthropomorphize or reify actors.

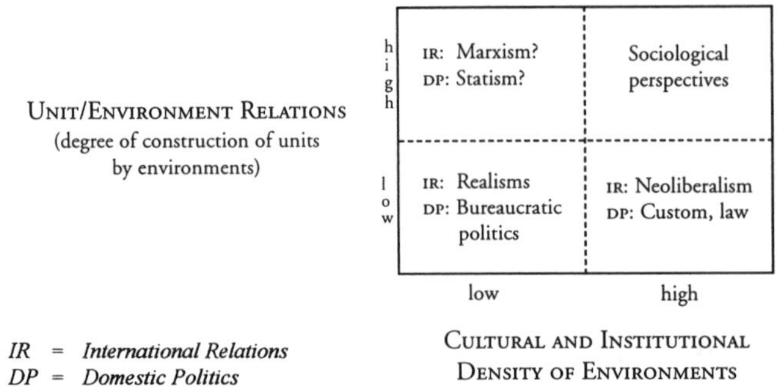

UNIT/ENVIRONMENT RELATIONS
(degree of construction of units
by environments)

	low	high
high	IR: Marxism? DP: Statism?	Sociological perspectives
low	IR: Realisms DP: Bureaucratic politics	IR: Neoliberalism DP: Custom, law

CULTURAL AND INSTITUTIONAL
DENSITY OF ENVIRONMENTS

IR = *International Relations*
DP = *Domestic Politics*

FIGURE 2.1 Theoretical Imageries

being thickly structured by cultural and institutional elements on the other.

At the low end of this continuum are theories that depict the environment in materialist terms. The analogy would be to ecology in the physical sciences. In international relations this is the view held by neorealists, who conceive environments in terms of a distribution of material (military and economic) capabilities. Materialists need not ignore cultural factors altogether. But they treat them as epiphenomenal or at least secondary, as a "superstructure" determined in the last instance by the material "base." This is probably the dominant view of state environments in security studies. Indeed, this view is so pervasive that even its critics, such as neoliberal institutionalists, typically refer to structure in material terms and then treat norms, rules, and institutions as mere "process."

At the high end of the x-axis are theories depicting environments as containing extensive cultural elements. Such theories might refer to the states system as an "anarchy" in the strict sense, that is, as lacking a world state. But they insist that even anarchies can be highly "social." What ultimately determines the behavior of actors within these anarchies is shared expectations and understandings that give specific meaning to material forces.[14]

---

14. It is important to note that while this more elaborated picture of structure is often associated with sociological analysis, it can be quite compatible with some versions of realism and rationalism. Paul Schroeder's critique of neorealism, for example, makes a move in this direction. See Paul W. Schroeder, *The Transformation of European Politics, 1763–1848* (Oxford: Oxford University Press, 1994); Paul W. Schroeder, "Neo-Realist Theory and International History: A Historian's View,"

When thinking about the relationship between theories located at opposing ends of this dimension, it is important to avoid two common misunderstandings. The first is assuming that materialist theories are necessarily about conflict and cultural ones are about cooperation. Although neorealism tends to predict conflict, Daniel Deudney's work on nuclear weapons[15] suggests that material forces may also lead to cooperation.[16] And conversely, although neoliberals tend to focus on cooperation, cultural explanations of conflict are equally possible, as Samuel Huntington's work on the "clash of civilizations" illustrates.[17] In this respect the perspective of this volume, and of social constructivism more generally, is like that of game theory; it is analytically neutral with respect to conflict and cooperation. In contrast to the work of regime theorists, the value of the arguments here does not depend on the extent to which states cooperate in security affairs. We argue that any general theory of national security, realist or otherwise, needs to accommodate both cooperation and coercion.

A second common misunderstanding in comparing theories along the x-axis is smuggling in unacknowledged cultural factors that do most of the explanatory work within ostensibly materialist theories. Alexander Wendt,[18] for example, has argued that neorealist arguments about the role

Security Studies (in press); Jack S. Levy, "The Theoretical Foundation of Paul W. Schroeder's International System," *The International History Review* 16, no. 4 (November 1994): 715–44. The same is true of game theoretic analyses that represent institutions as shared expectations or "common knowledge" that generates "focal points" in situations of strategic interaction; see David Kreps, "Corporate Culture and Economic Theory," in James Alt and Kenneth Shepsle, eds., *Perspectives on Positive Political Economy*, pp. 90–143 (Cambridge: Cambridge University Press, 1990); Judith Goldstein and Robert O. Keohane, "Ideas and Foreign Policy: An Analytical Framework," in Goldstein and Keohane, *Ideas and Foreign Policy*, p. 17; Arthur T. Denzau and Douglass C. North, "Shared Mental Models: Ideologies and Institutions," *Kyklos* 47, no. 1 (1994): 3–31; and John Kurt Jacobson, "Much Ado About Ideas: The Cognitive Factor in Economic Policy," *World Politics* 47, no. 2 (January 1995): 283–310. Similarly, Robert Axelrod and Robert O. Keohane note that the interstate "anarchy" they address is contained within an "international society"; see their essay "Achieving Cooperation Under Anarchy: Strategies and Institutions," in Kenneth A. Oye, ed., *Cooperation Under Anarchy*, p. 226 (Princeton: Princeton University Press, 1986). But this literature typically does not theorize this "society," suggesting at times that one does not need such theorization or that it is too difficult or unpromising to do so.

15. Daniel Deudney, "Dividing Realism: Structural Realism Versus Security Materialism on Nuclear Security and Proliferation," *Security Studies* 2, nos. 3–4 (Spring–Summer 1993): 7–37.

16. Put differently, realism does not equal materialism.

17. Samuel Huntington, "The Clash of Civilizations?" *Foreign Affairs* 72, no. 3 (Summer 1993): 22–49.

18. Alexander Wendt, "Anarchy Is What States Make of It: The Social Construction of Power Politics," *International Organization* 46, no. 2 (Spring 1992): 391–425.

of the distribution of power in world politics in fact trade on an implicit characterization of the background of shared expectations, a culture of fear and enmity. Whether or not neorealists in fact adopt such an explanatory strategy, however, it is important to disentangle claims about the effects of "brute" or generic material forces from claims about their effects that presuppose specific contingent cultural contexts. Relatedly, categories like "revisionist" or "status quo" power, when deployed in a realist explanation, often refer to social identities. To establish the validity of a materialist argument, one has to show that the material base *as such* governs a cultural superstructure.

An important consequence of both these points is that the use by states of material power and coercion in their security affairs in no way speaks to the validity of theories along the x-axis. Power is ubiquitous in social life, whether in the "coercive" sense of punishing and constraining behavior as emphasized by neorealists or in the "productive" sense of producing subjects as emphasized by students of culture. The issue that separates the contributions to this volume from mainstream security studies is therefore not the extent to which power and coercion are thought to matter in international life. In general the authors are just as attentive to coercion and force as neorealists are. The issue, rather, is whether the manifold uses and forms of power can be explained by material factors alone, or whether ideational and cultural factors are necessary to account for them. In the latter case it makes little sense to separate power and culture as distinct phenomena or causes: material power and coercion often derive their causal power from culture. This volume does not concede the study of conflict and war to neorealism, as if the latter provided a confirmed theoretical "baseline," to which cultural arguments merely add a few secondary variables. The issue is what accounts for power, not whether power is present.

The second line of argument of this book is represented by the y-axis. It focuses upon the relationship between actors, such as states, and their environments. This relationship is two-sided. It includes the impact of actors on their environments and the impact of environments on actors.[19] Specifically, this volume wants to draw attention to the significance of the latter. However, this intention does not stem from a belief that the effects of actors on environments are unimportant. On the contrary. The con-

19. Anthony Giddens, *The Constitution of Society* (Berkeley: University of California Press, 1984); Alexander Wendt, "The Agent-Structure Problem in International Relations Theory," *International Organization* 41, no. 3 (Summer 1987): 335–70.

tributors to this volume argue that agency and environment are mutually constitutive—in contrast with the primacy that the dominant realist and rationalist perspectives in international relations theory accord to the effects that actors have on environments. In this volume Richard Price and Nina Tannenwald, for example, illustrate such a constitutive relationship in the case of the non-use of chemical and nuclear weapons. Similarly, Berger's analysis suggests that the transformation in Germany's and Japan's collective identity affects the international environment.

In thinking about the effects of environments on actors it is useful to distinguish three kinds of effects, which correspond to progressively higher levels of "construction." First, environments might affect only the *behavior* of actors. Second, they might affect the contingent *properties* of actors (identities, interests, and capabilities).[20] Finally, environments might affect the *existence* of actors altogether. For example, in the case of individual human beings, the third effect concerns their bodies, the second whether these bodies become cashiers or corporate raiders, and the first whether or not the cashiers go on strike. Theories that call attention to lower-order construction effects may or may not stress higher ones. In this book we focus on the first and, especially, the second effects, usually taking the existence of states as given.

At the low end of this continuum are theories, such as rational choice and game theory, that depict the defining properties of actors as intrinsic and thus not generated by environments. Such theories may acknowledge a role for environmental structures in defining the opportunities and constraints facing actors, and thereby in conditioning the behavior of the latter via "price" effects,[21] but not in constructing actors themselves. Neoclassical economics, for instance, treats the preferences and capabilities of actors as exogenously given. Relatedly, Waltz[22] allows for what he calls "socialization" and "imitation" processes. But in so doing he envisions the shaping of the behavior of *pregiven* actors. He thus assumes that the processes determining the fundamental identity of states are exogenous to the states' environments, global or domestic.

---

20. The difference between these first two effects is partly captured by Robert Powell's useful distinction between "preferences over action" and "preferences over outcomes," though the actor properties in which we are interested go beyond preferences over outcomes to include identities and capabilities. See Robert Powell, "Anarchy in International Relations Theory: The Neorealist-Neoliberal Debate," *International Organization* 48, no. 2 (Spring 1994): 313–44.

21. George Stigler and Gary Becker, "De Gustibus non est Disputandum," *American Economic Review* 67, no. 2 (March 1977): 76–90.

22. Waltz, *Theory of International Politics*, pp. 74–77.

At the high end of the continuum are theories that treat unit properties as endogenous to the environment and, at the limit, assume that units have no essential intrinsic properties at all, a possibility that we neglect here. That someone has the identity (and associated interests) of a "student," for example, has no meaning outside of a particular institutional environment that also defines related identities, like "professor" (with its associated interests). A similar argument can be made about the identity of some states as "sovereign," which presupposes a system of mutual recognition from other states with certain competencies. In both cases the properties of an actor, as well as its behaviors, depend upon a specific social context. The identities that states project, and the interests that they pursue, can therefore be seen as partly constructed by their environments.

Theoretical Perspectives

Figure 2.1 provides a way of thinking about the relationship of this book to dominant approaches in security studies. Each approach represents different views about what environments consist of, and about how such environments affect actors—here, states. In this section we briefly characterize approaches to security studies in terms of this figure, dividing the review into international/systemic and domestic theories.[23] We should note that the two dimensions of figure 2.1 are continua, but for ease of exposition we discuss approaches by reference to the *quadrant* in which they fall.

International Politics

Few approaches fall cleanly in the upper-left quadrant. This combination is difficult to sustain. If actor properties are constructed, a dense cultural and institutional environment is normally implicated. But, nevertheless, there probably are a few representatives of this quadrant. Strands of neo-Marxism, especially world-systems theory, offer some examples. And Deudney's "security materialism" might also fall in this category.[24]

Since they insist on the determining effects of international structure, neorealists like Waltz[25] might also be located here. But it is not clear whether

---

23. We make no claim that figure 2.1 captures all significant differences among these traditions. And we are reasoning by illustration rather than canvassing the literature systematically.
24. Deudney, "Dividing Realism."
25. Waltz, *Theory of International Politics*.

such a classification is accurate. Waltz claims to derive state interests from an ecological argument about how the logic of anarchy produces "like units." His argument, however, takes the self-interested and sovereign character of states as given, and in practice his neorealist "structuralism" ends up focusing on how structure conditions the behavior of given state actors.[26] This interpretation is reinforced by his reliance on analogies from microeconomics, a discipline that treats actors' properties as exogenously given. Analytically, then, in neorealism states have largely unproblematic—that is, unvarying and acontextual—identities and interests.[27] In this view, neorealism might therefore more accurately be located in the lower-left quadrant of the map.

In fact, most mainstream strategic and deterrence theory and policy research fall in this quadrant. Actor identities are taken for granted, and material capabilities are considered the defining characteristic of environments. Game theoretic models are then typically used to analyze how material structure provides incentives for particular kinds of behavior. This perspective focuses on how to contain or manage given conflicts, neglecting strategies for solving them by transforming underlying identities and interests. The analytical problem of conflict management and order is thereby reduced to the problem of balancing or achieving cooperation between exogenously given competitors.

Scholars in the lower-right quadrant retain a rationalist approach to actor construction but attach considerably more importance to norms, institutions, and other cultural factors than do neorealists. This neoliberal school argues that norms and institutions matter both at the domestic level, where regime type is found to have an important effect on some domains of foreign policy behavior,[28] and at the systemic level, where international regimes change the incentives for state action.[29] They have conceptualized

---

26. Wendt, "Anarchy Is What States Make of It."

27. In his *Theory of International Politics*, pp. 74–77, Waltz does allow for "socialization" and "imitation" processes, but in so doing he envisions these primarily in terms of effects on behavior, thereby assuming that the processes determining the fundamental makeup or identity of states are exogenous to states' environments.

28. Michael Doyle, "Liberalism and World Politics," *American Political Science Review* 80, no. 4 (December 1986): 1151–69. Bruce Russett, *Grasping the Democratic Peace: Principles for a Post–Cold War World* (Princeton: Princeton University Press, 1993).

29. Krasner, *International Regimes*; Robert O. Keohane, *After Hegemony: Cooperation and Discord in the World Political Economy* (Princeton: Princeton University Press, 1984); Oye, *Cooperation Under Anarchy*. We are neglecting here very substantial differences between international and domestic versions of the liberal argument. For an important statement of some of these differences, see Andrew Moravcsik, "Liberalism and International Relations Theory" (unpublished paper, Harvard University, 1993).

the difference that norms make, for instance, in terms of their effects on the relative cost of specific forms of behavior—for example, through lowering transaction costs and reducing uncertainty about others' behavior. However, neoliberals have been relatively inattentive to varying constructions of actor identities on interests and policies. This contrasts with the keen interest of traditional realists in the effects of nationalism on state identity. Neoliberalism leaves that topic largely unexamined.[30]

In recent years theoretical disagreements between neorealists and neoliberals have constituted the core of mainstream international relations theory, which in turn has shaped security studies.[31] In terms of figure 2.1, these disagreements have occurred along the x-axis. While disputing the relative importance of material power versus norms and institutions, both approaches are committed to a rationalist view of the difference that structure makes. Structure merely affects behavior; it does not construct actor properties. Compared with earlier advances in international relations theory, this approach marks a substantial narrowing in analytical perspective. In the 1960s, for example, theorists of neofunctionalism and regional integration developed sophisticated approaches to investigating the effects of integration processes on actor properties.[32] These theories are precursors of current theoretical alternatives to neorealism and neoliberalism that can be found in the upper-right quadrant.[33] Since they differ greatly on impor-

---

30. Uday A. Mehta examines liberalism from this perspective in "Liberal Strategies of Exclusion," *Politics and Society* 18, no. 4 (1990): 427–54. This tendency is exemplified in Robert O. Keohane, Joseph S. Nye, and Stanley Hoffmann, eds., *After the Cold War: International Institutions and State Strategies in Europe, 1989–1991* (Cambridge: Harvard University Press, 1993).

31. Robert O. Keohane, ed., *Neorealism and Its Critics* (New York: Columbia University Press, 1986), pp. 90–143; Joseph S. Nye Jr., "Neorealism and Neoliberalism," *World Politics* 40, no. 2 (January 1988): 235–51; David Baldwin, ed., *Neorealism and Neoliberalism: The Contemporary Debate* (New York: Columbia University Press, 1993); Robert Powell, "Anarchy in International Relations Theory"; Emerson M. S. Niou and Peter C. Ordeshook, " 'Less Filling, Tastes Great': The Realist-Neoliberal Debate," *World Politics* 46, no. 2 (January 1994): 209–34.

32. Karl W. Deutsch et al., *Political Community and the North Atlantic Area: International Organization in the Light of Historical Experience* (Princeton: Princeton University Press, 1957); Ernst B. Haas, *Beyond the Nation-State: Functionalism and International Organization* (Stanford: Stanford University Press, 1964); Karl W. Deutsch et al., *France, Germany, and the Western Alliance: A Study of Elite Attitudes on European Integration and World Politics* (New York: Charles Scribner's Sons, 1967).

33. It is not entirely clear how to label these theories, given the confluence of different theoretical traditions that they represent. In "International Institutions: Two Approaches," *International Studies Quarterly* 32, no. 4 (December 1988): 379–96, Robert Keohane called some of them "reflectivist," but we find this appellation to be far too subjectivist in connotation, as well as analytically vague. The perspective represented in this volume is thoroughly structuralist rather than subjectivist. From our perspective it makes more sense to refer to research of this type as institutionalist or constructivist (or both). See, for example, Jepperson, "Institutions, Institutional Effects, and Institutionalism," and Wendt, *Social Theory of International Politics*.

tant issues of research practice, such alternatives should not be lumped together as representing one intellectual position. They offer instead a range of analytical perspectives that differ from realist and liberal variants of international relations theory.

The oldest stream of scholarship that might be positioned within this space, and to which subsequent traditions are partly indebted, is the Grotian tradition represented by Hedley Bull[34] and the English School.[35] From this perspective the international system is a "society" in which states, as a condition of their participation in the system, adhere to shared norms and rules in a variety of issue areas. Material power matters, but within a framework of normative expectations embedded in public and customary international law. Scholars in this tradition have not focused explicitly on how norms construct states with specific identities and interests. But sociological imagery is strong in their work; it is not a great leap from arguing that adherence to norms is a condition of participation in a society to arguing that states are constructed, partly or substantially, by these norms.

Perhaps the most fundamental institution in international society is sovereignty. It has become an important focus of a second body of scholarship, constructivism.[36] John Ruggie's important critique of Waltz[37] conceptualizes sovereignty as an institution that invests states with exclusive

34. Hedley Bull, *The Anarchical Society: A Study of Order in World Politics* (New York: Columbia University Press, 1977).

35. Hedley Bull and Adam Watson, eds., *The Expansion of International Society* (Oxford: Clarendon Press, 1984); Tony Evans and Peter Wilson, "Regime Theory and the English School of International Relations: A Comparison," *Millennium: Journal of International Studies* 21, no. 3 (1992): 329–51; Adam Watson, *The Evolution of International Society: A Comparative Historical Analysis* (London: Routledge, 1992); Barry Buzan, "From International System to International Society: Structural Realism and Regime Theory Meet the English School," *International Organization* 47, no. 3 (Summer 1993): 327–52; Ole Waever, "International Society: Theoretical Promises Unfulfilled?" *Cooperation and Conflict* 27, no. 1 (1992): 97–128.

36. For representative works, see Ruggie, "Multilateralism" and "Territoriality and Beyond." See also David Dessler, "What's at Stake in the Agent-Structure Debate?" *International Organization* 43, no. 3 (Summer 1989): 441–74; Kratochwil, *Rules, Norms, and Decisions*; Nicholas Onuf, *World of Our Making: Rules and Rule in Social Theory and International Relations* (Columbia: University of South Carolina Press, 1989); Emanuel Adler, "Cognitive Evolution: A Dynamic Approach for the Study of International Relations and Their Progress," in Emanuel Adler and Beverly Crawford, eds., *Progress in Postwar International Relations*, pp. 43–88 (New York: Columbia University Press, 1992); Emanuel Adler, "The Emergence of Cooperation: National Epistemic Communities and the International Evolution of the Idea of Nuclear Arms Control," *International Organization* 46, no. 1 (Winter 1992): 101–46; Peter Haas, ed., "Knowledge, Power, and International Policy Coordination," special issue of *International Organization* 46, no. 1 (Winter 1992); and Wendt, "Anarchy Is What States Make of It." Note that sovereignty is not the only form of identity in which constructivists are interested.

37. Ruggie, "Continuity and Transformation in the World Polity."

political authority in their territorial spaces, which he sees as crucial in the construction of state identity. By constituting states, and only states, with territorial rights, sovereignty determines what the basic political units of the system are. It thus defines also categories of "deviant" units, such as international trusteeships or safe zones, whose existence within the states system is thereby made problematic.[38] In addition to defining political identities, the institution of sovereignty also regulates state behavior through norms and practices of mutual recognition, nonintervention, and (state) self-determination—which in turn help reproduce state identities. These norms find expression in public international law, which communicates global agreements about how the society of states should operate. Such agreements matter. Sovereignty norms establish a largely "juridical statehood," for example, in Africa, which becomes a key political resource for these states within the interstate system.[39] And David Strang has shown that states externally recognized as sovereign show less movement between independent, dependent, and unrecognized statuses than do states not so recognized.[40]

Another body of scholarship, poststructural international relations theory, pursues a radical constructivist position. Beginning with the work of Richard Ashley,[41] poststructuralists have focused on how state identities are, down to their core, ongoing accomplishments of discursive practices. Crucial among these practices is foreign policy, which produces and reproduces the territorial boundaries that seem essential to the state.[42]

Neorealism's disregard of questions of identity formation, and classical realism's emphasis on the power-seeking interests of states as a function of human, rather than male, nature have given feminist critiques of realism a dual target. In the words of Ann Tickner, "in the name of universality, realists have constructed a worldview based on the experiences of certain men: it is therefore a worldview that offers us only a partial view of real-

---

38. Strang, "Anomaly and Commonplace in European Political Expansion."

39. Robert H. Jackson and Carl G. Rosberg, "Why Africa's Weak States Persist: The Empirical and the Juridical in Statehood," *World Politics* 35, no. 1 (October 1982): 1–24; Jackson, "The Weight of Ideas in Decolonization."

40. Strang, "Anomaly and Commonplace in European Political Expansion."

41. Richard K. Ashley, "The Poverty of Neorealism," *International Organization* 38, no. 2 (Spring 1984): 225–86; Richard K. Ashley, "The Geopolitics of Geopolitical Space," *Alternatives* 12, no. 4 (1987): 403–34.

42. David Campbell, *Writing Security: United States Foreign Policy and the Politics of Identity* (Minneapolis: University of Minnesota Press, 1992); R. B. J. Walker, *Inside/Outside: International Relations as Political Theory* (Cambridge: Cambridge University Press, 1993); Cynthia Weber, *Simulating Sovereignty* (Cambridge: Cambridge University Press, 1994).

ity."[43] In both of its incarnations, realism seeks to articulate objective and timeless laws—the will to power and the tendency to balance power—that feminist critics argue reflect a deeply gendered view of reality. Relativizing that view, feminist theory insists, is a crucial first step in eventually transforming it.[44]

Like feminism, a fourth theoretical perspective that fits into the upper-right quadrant also is not state-centric, and perhaps for that reason is not well known in international relations scholarship. This is the sociological research that John Meyer and his colleagues have done on the world polity.[45] This group has focused on the cultural and institutional foundations of *world* society as opposed to the society of *states*.[46] A parallel concern is quite natural to students of domestic affairs, who analyze the social embeddedness of states and markets as a crucial feature of national politics. And it resonates partly with theories of transnational relations that have informed international relations research during the last two decades.[47]

This body of empirical research has focused on a world political culture, carrying standardized models of statehood. The spread of democratic ideologies and market models provides obvious examples, along with the underlying consolidation of regional and even global ideologies of citizen-

---

43. J. Ann Tickner, *Gender in International Relations: Feminist Perspectives on Achieving Global Security* (New York: Columbia University Press, 1992), p. 30.

44. Rebecca Grant and Kathleen Newland, eds., *Gender and International Relations* (Bloomington: Indiana University Press, 1991); Spike Peterson, ed., *Gendered States: Feminist (Re)Vision of International Relations Theory* (Boulder: Lynne Rienner, 1992).

45. John W. Meyer, "The World Polity and the Authority of the Nation-State," in Albert Bergesen, ed., *Studies of the Modern World System*, pp. 109–37 (New York: Academic Press, 1980); George W. Thomas, John W. Meyer, Francisco O. Ramirez, and John Boli, *Institutional Structure: Constituting State, Society, and the Individual* (London: Sage, 1987); John W. Meyer, "Rationalized Environments," in W. Richard Scott and John W. Meyer, eds., *Institutional Environments and Organizations*, pp. 28–54 (Beverly Hills: Sage, 1994); and John W. Meyer, "The Changing Cultural Content of the Nation-State: A World Society Perspective," in George Steinmetz, ed., *New Approaches to the State in the Social Sciences* (Ithaca: Cornell University Press, 1996). We should note that work in the tradition of Gramsci, such as Robert W. Cox, *Production, Power, and World Order: Social Forces in the Making of History* (New York: Columbia University Press, 1987), and Stephen Gill, *American Hegemony and the Trilateral Commission* (New York: Cambridge University Press, 1990), also seeks to combine the analysis of structure, power, and ideas.

46. Buzan, "From International System to International Society."

47. Robert O. Keohane and Joseph S. Nye, eds., *Transnational Relations and World Politics* (Cambridge: Harvard University Press, 1972); Robert O. Keohane and Joseph S. Nye, *Power and Interdependence: World Politics in Transition* (Boston: Little, Brown, 1977); Thomas Risse-Kappen, ed., *Bringing Transnationalism Back In: Non-State Actors, Domestic Structures, and International Institutions* (Cambridge: Cambridge University Press, 1995).

ship and human rights.[48] Even states' military procurement is partly scripted in models of statehood that diffuse widely in the world system, as Dana Eyre and Mark Suchman argue in their essay in this volume. Adoption of such evolving world models has shown a weakening relationship over time with specific characteristics of particular states, which indicates conventionalization and in some instances even institutionalization at the global level.

This sociological literature, now well developed empirically,[49] has tracked a rapidly intensifying world institutional and discursive order, carried by an expanding range of "epistemic" communities[50] as well as intergovernmental and nongovernmental organizations. This line of argument does not describe any formal change in sovereignty, however, nor does it foresee any movement toward a global protostate.[51] Rather, the jurisdiction and agendas of states are increasingly worked out within a transnational context. Without reference to this standardizing world political culture, it is difficult to account for the high stability of the states system, as well as the decreasing variability of political forms and the rapid spread of political and social technologies within it.[52]

At the same time, new forms of global homogeneity and order also generate new forms of heterogeneity and disorder. "The insistence on heterogeneity and variety in an increasingly globalized world is . . . integral to globalization theory."[53] World society carries standardized oppositional ideologies that are usually selective reifications of elements of dominant world ideology. Thus authoritarian ideologies and experiments with state socialism in Third World settings in the 1960s, and the spread of Third

48. See Samuel Huntington, *The Third Wave: Democratization in the Late Twentieth Century* (Norman: University of Oklahoma Press, 1991) on democracy; Thomas J. Biersteker, "The Triumph of Neoclassical Economics in the Developing World," in James N. Rosenau and Ernst-Otto Czempiel, eds., *Governance Without Government: Order and Change in World Politics*, pp. 102–31 (Cambridge: Cambridge University Press, 1992) on market models; Francisco O. Ramirez and John W. Meyer, "The Institutionalization of Citizenship Principles and the National Incorporation of Women and Children, 1870–1990" (unpublished research proposal, Department of Sociology, Stanford University, 1992); John Boli, "Sovereignty from a World Polity Perspective" (unpublished paper, Department of Sociology, Emory University, Atlanta, 1993).
49. Consult the citations to studies in Meyer, "The Changing Cultural Content of the Nation-State." For a paper reviewing this research, see Martha Finnemore, "Norms, Culture, and World Politics: Insights from Sociology's Institutionalism," *International Organization* (in press).
50. Haas, "Knowledge, Power, and International Policy Coordination."
51. For an interesting argument that analyzes U.S. hegemony as a form of international governance from a moral perspective, see Lea Brilmayer, *American Hegemony: Political Morality in a One-Superpower World* (New Haven: Yale University Press, 1994).
52. Meyer, "The World Polity and the Authority of the Nation-State," and "The Changing Cultural Content of the Nation-State."
53. Roland Robertson, "Globalization Theory and Civilization Analysis," *Comparative Civilizations Review* 17 (1987): 22.

World demands for a New International Economic Order (NIEO) in the 1970s, both drew upon Western principles of justice.[54] Indeed, during the Cold War socialist models achieved (counter)hegemonic status in many Third World states, despite the absence of the standard preconditions for socialism. With the end of the Cold War it is conceivable that some strains of Islamic fundamentalism may assume a similar oppositional role. For as J. P. Nettl and Roland Robertson have argued, religion and societal ideologies may exercise stronger control functions over global society than do international law and industrialism.[55]

Domestic Politics

The differences in analytical perspective captured in figure 2.1 apply as much to theories of domestic politics as to those of international relations.[56] Thus, in their analyses of domestic politics, orthodox national security studies tend to adhere to the same materialist and rationalist perspective that characterizes realism at the international level. This work has taken two main forms: scrutiny of individual decision makers, often observed at times of crisis, and of bureaucratic organizations involved in the process of policy formulation and implementation. The theory of the state implicit in the former is the rational-state-as-actor model; the theory of politics implicit in the latter is bureaucratic pluralism or bureaucratic routinization.

Critics of deterrence have questioned these implicit theories by invoking in a variety of ways the cultural content of the environment, thus moving rightward along the x-axis. The cognitive and motivational biases impairing rationality that have attracted attention are, in this view, rooted not only in the information-processing proclivities of individuals but also in the operational codes, understandings, and worldviews shared by decision makers and diffused throughout society.[57] Similarly, Elizabeth Kier

54. Ronald Dore, "Unity and Diversity in Contemporary World Culture," in Bull and Watson, *The Expansion of International Society*, pp. 407–24.
55. J. P. Nettl and Roland Robertson, *International Systems and the Modernization of Societies: The Formation of National Goals and Attitudes* (London: Faber and Faber, 1968), p. 153; Roland Robertson, *Globalization: Social Theory and Global Culture* (London: Sage, 1992).
56. We are reviewing them here more briefly simply for reasons of economy.
57. Alexander George, "The 'Operational Code': A Neglected Approach to the Study of Political Leaders and Decision-Making," *International Studies Quarterly* 13 (June 1969): 190–222; Alexander L. George, "Ideology and International Relations: A Conceptual Analysis," *The Jerusalem Journal of International Relations* 9, no. 1 (1987): 1–21; Robert Jervis, *Perception and Misperception in International Politics* (Princeton: Princeton University Press, 1976); Richard Ned Lebow, *Between Peace and War: The Nature of International Crisis* (Baltimore: Johns Hopkins University Press, 1981); Richard Herrmann, *Perceptions and Behavior in Soviet Foreign Policy* (Pittsburgh: University of Pittsburgh Press, 1985).

and Alastair Johnston, in their respective essays in this volume, rely on studies of organizational and strategic cultures that criticize the lack of attention to cultural variables in the mainstream literatures on organizations and deterrence.[58]

To the extent that they focus on the effects of collective understandings (as embodied, for example, in ideologies and policy paradigms) rather than individual-level variables, these critics share much with recent writings in the fields of security studies, comparative political economy, and foreign policy analysis.[59] Although particular studies differ, they all pay attention to the institutionalization of ideas—in research institutes, schools of thought, laws, government bureaucracies—as a crucial determinant of policy. On this point the latter studies all belong to the "new institutionalism" in the analysis of domestic politics.

But the new institutionalism also has spurred debate about state identity, which moves one along the y-axis of figure 2.1, away from the origin. In the 1970s and 1980s, various forms of institutional analysis reemerged, providing powerful criticisms of the liberal and Marxist theories that regard the state as epiphenomenal.[60] Many realists were unmoved by these developments. If unitary state actors had to be disaggregated analytically, it was in terms of a plurality of bureaucratic and organizational actors. Other realists, however, embraced the return of an analytical perspective focusing on the state and looked for the enduring ideologies and world visions that motivate state action. Thus Stephen Krasner argued that American foreign policy was motivated by ideology rather than by the pursuit of a national interest more narrowly conceived.[61] But in the analysis

58. For a recent overview of the literature on organizational culture, see Frank R. Dobbin, "Cultural Models of Organization: The Social Construction of Rational Organizing Principles," in Diana Crane, ed., *Sociology of Culture: Emerging Theoretical Perspectives*, pp. 117–41 (Oxford: Blackwell, 1994). Alastair Iain Johnston's *Cultural Realism: Strategic Culture and Grand Strategy in Ming China* (Princeton: Princeton University Press, 1995) reviews the literature on strategic culture. See also his article "Thinking About Strategic Culture," *International Security* 19, no. 4 (Spring 1995): 32–64.

59. Peter Hall, *The Political Power of Economic Ideas: Keynesianism Across Nations* (Princeton: Princeton University Press, 1989); Haas, "Knowledge, Power, and International Policy Coordination"; Judith Goldstein, *Ideas, Interests, and American Trade Policy* (Ithaca: Cornell University Press, 1993); Charles A. Kupchan, *The Vulnerability of Empire* (Ithaca: Cornell University Press, 1994).

60. Peter Evans, Dietrich Rueschemeyer, and Theda Skocpol, eds., *Bringing the State Back In* (Cambridge: Cambridge University Press, 1985); James G. March and Johan P. Olsen, *Rediscovering Institutions: The Organizational Basis of Politics* (New York: Free Press, 1989); Sven Steinmo, Kathleen Thelen, and Frank Longstreth, *Structuring Politics: Historical Institutionalism in Comparative Analysis* (Cambridge: Cambridge University Press, 1992).

61. Stephen D. Krasner, *Defending the National Interest: Raw Materials Investments and U.S. Foreign Policy* (Princeton: Princeton University Press, 1978).

of domestic politics, the state remained for these observers a largely unitary actor, as it was in the analysis of international politics.

Some students of domestic politics, on the other hand, viewed the state in its relation to society. In their view the identity of the state and of social actors—for example, interest groups or political parties—could be understood only as mutually constitutive.[62] Conceiving of the state in relational terms and investigating the domestic sources of foreign policy focuses attention on the degree to which the identities of actors are constructed by state-society relations. Ideologies of social partnership, for example, helped define for the rich, small European states after World War II a set of political strategies that combined economic flexibility with political stability.[63] Furthermore, the relatively generous welfare policies associated with these political strategies are representative of moral and humanitarian concerns that have prompted foreign aid policies not easily explained in terms of narrow conceptions of economic self-interest.[64] Put differently, shared conceptions of identity appear to have had an important indirect effect on a number of policies.[65]

This brief review suggests a concluding observation about the pattern of theorizing in national security studies. In the case of international relations theorizing, one can discern a dominant arc of research. It starts in the lower-left quadrant with a materialist-rationalist neorealism, extends to

---

62. Peter J. Katzenstein, ed., *Between Power and Plenty: Foreign Economic Policies of Advanced Industrial States* (Madison: University of Wisconsin Press, 1978). Analogously, industrial sociology and social economics focus on the social context that envelops markets. "Industrial orders," writes Gary Herrigel, "have a relationship to agents within them that is analogous in some generic respects to the relation between a modern liberal constitution and its citizens" (Gary Herrigel, "Industry as a Form of Order: A Comparison of the Historical Development of the Machine Tool Industries in the United States and Germany," in J. Rogers Hollingsworth, Philippe C. Schmitter, and Wolfgang Streeck, eds., *Governing Capitalist Economies: Performance and Control of Economic Sectors*, p. 99 [New York: Oxford University Press, 1994]); Gary Herrigel, "Identities and Institutions: The Social Construction of Trade Unions in Nineteenth-Century Germany and the United States," *Studies in American Political Development* 7 (Fall 1993): 371–94; Frank Dobbin, *Forging Industrial Policy: The United States, Britain, and France in the Railway Age* (Cambridge: Cambridge University Press, 1994).

63. Peter J. Katzenstein, *Small States in World Markets: Industrial Policy in Europe* (Ithaca: Cornell University Press, 1985).

64. David Halloran Lumsdaine, *Moral Vision in International Politics: The Foreign Aid Regime, 1949–1989* (Princeton: Princeton University Press, 1993).

65. Relatedly, a substantial number of empirical studies suggest that democracies do not fight wars with one another. See Doyle, "Liberalism and World Politics"; Russett, *Grasping the Democratic Peace*; Randall Schweller, "Domestic Structure and Preventive War: Are Democracies More Pacific?" *World Politics* 44, no. 2 (January 1992): 235–69; and several articles and subsequent correspondence in *International Security* 19, no. 2 (Fall 1994), and 19, no. 4 (Spring 1995).

the right along the x-axis in the form of neoliberal regime theory, which adds more cultural imagery, and moves into the upper-right quadrant with constructivist theories that seek to link cultural structures to actor identities. One can also map the analysis of the domestic sources of national security policy along this arc, although with less clarity. Different intellectual currents have challenged two analytical positions that lie close to the origin: the bureaucratic politics paradigm and the presumption of rational, individual decision makers.

This volume (located in the upper-right quadrant) seeks to establish the fruitfulness of a sociological perspective on national security. As one moves away from the origin, one captures the two theoretical departures of this project: the imagined cultural and institutional density of states' environments increases, and so does the extent to which states' properties are constructed by these environments.

Arguments

Most of the essays in this volume feature *norms, culture,* or *identities* in causal arguments about national security policy. (We will clarify conceptualizations of these terms in the appropriate subsections below.) The main lines of argument advanced herein can be captured by a simple schema:[66]

Referring to the causal pathways summarized in figure 2.2, we outline five main types of arguments present in the substantive essays of this volume. (The numbers here correspond to the numbers labeling the pathways of the figure.)

1. Effects of norms (I). Cultural or institutional elements of states' environments—in this volume, most often norms—shape the national security interests or (directly) the security policies of states.

2. Effects of norms (II). Cultural or institutional elements of states' global or domestic environments—in this volume, most often norms—shape state identity.

3. Effects of identity (I). Variation in state identity, or changes in state identity, affect the national security interests or policies of states.

4. Effects of identity (II). Configurations of state identity affect interstate normative structures, such as regimes or security communities.

---

66. Figure 2.2 labels broad categories of causal construction effects. It is thus *not* a total causal model of state security activity. Specifically, since some actor properties are intrinsic, "identity" is not the only cause of "interest." Figure 2.2 is *not* in itself a "theory."

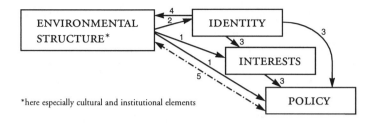

FIGURE 2.2 Lines of Argument

5. Recursivity. State policies both reproduce and reconstruct cultural and institutional structure.

The five essays in part 1 of this volume—by Eyre and Suchman, Price and Tannenwald, Finnemore, Kier, and Johnston—focus primarily on the cultural and institutional content of the environments in which states act. These essays give analytical priority, respectively, to norms of military prowess, the limited use of nuclear and chemical weapons, humanitarian intervention, and the organizational and strategic cultures of the military that define interests or affect policy directly. The four essays in part 2—by Herman, Berger, Risse-Kappen, and Barnett—highlight the contested construction or reconstruction of actor identities within environments. These essays problematize the notions of a "Western" Soviet Union, of a Japanese merchant state and a Europeanized Germany, of a security community of liberal democracies in the North Atlantic community, and of the tension between pan-Arabism and Arab statehood. Identities shape actor interests or state policy.

The essays differ in the details of their language and conceptualization, but they share a common idiom. They are cumulative in the challenge they pose to established analytical perspectives, and they illuminate how empirical analysis of cultural content and constructed identities can contribute to the study of national security. All essays specify one or more outcomes to be explained, compare alternative explanations, and stress the importance of agency and conflict in the construction of identity and the enactment of norms. All reach new and nontrivial conclusions regarding substantively important national security issues. The main lines of argument from the essays, in terms of the five main categories outlined above, appear below.[67]

_____

67. We occasionally add arguments and examples drawn from other sources.

1. *Cultural or institutional elements of states' environments—in this volume, most often norms—shape the national security interests or (directly) the security policies of states.* Many of the essays feature effects of norms. It has become more common to argue that, given constant interests, institutions change the transaction costs or information requirements for certain policies or that they change interests themselves. The essays in this volume build upon but broaden this insight, in ways that we will describe.

We should first mention that the essays employ the concept "norms" in a sociologically standard way. Norms are collective expectations about proper behavior for a given identity. (We will describe the concept "identity" momentarily.) Sometimes norms operate like rules defining (and thus "constituting") an identity—like the descriptors defining the basic characteristics of professorhood within a university, in relation to the other main identities found within that institution. These effects are "constitutive" because norms in these instances specify the actions that will cause relevant others to recognize and validate a particular identity and to respond to it appropriately.[68] In other instances, norms are "regulative" in their effect. They operate as standards for the proper enactment or deployment of a defined identity—like the standards defining what a properly conforming professor does in particular circumstances.

Thus norms either define ("constitute") identities in the first place (generating expectations about the proper portfolio of identities for a given context) or prescribe or proscribe ("regulate") behaviors for already constituted identities (generating expectations about how those identities will shape behavior in varying circumstances). Taken together, then, norms establish expectations about who the actors will be in a particular environment and about how these particular actors will behave.[69] With this conceptualization in mind, we proceed to arguments.

---

68. Francesca Cancian, *What Are Norms? A Study of Beliefs and Action in a Maya Community* (Cambridge: Cambridge University Press, 1975), pp. 137–38. Janice E. Thomson, "Norms in International Relations: A Conceptual Analysis," *International Journal of Group Tension* 23, no. 2 (1993): 67–83.

69. Norms may be "shared," or commonly held, across some distribution of actors in a system. Alternatively, however, norms may *not* be widely held by actors but may nevertheless be *collective* features of a system—either by being institutionalized (in procedures, formal rules, or law) or by being prominent in public discourse of a system. It is thus useful, following Emile Durkheim's fundamental discussion of types of social facts, to sustain a distinction between common (or shared or widely held) norms and collective ones, allowing for the possibility that some norms may be both common and collective. The now typical identification of norms as necessarily a "shared" social property is thus inappropriate. It builds subjectivist and aggregative imagery into the very conceptualization of norms. Instead, a distinction between collectively "prominent" or institutionalized

Price and Tannenwald show how models of "responsible" or "civilized" states are enacted and validated by upholding specific norms.[70] These norms constrain the use of some technologies for killing or incapacitating people in large numbers. Berger shows how Germany's and Japan's anti-militaristic norms have made it very difficult for their governments to adopt more-assertive national security policies since the end of the Cold War. Finnemore argues that nonwhite and non-Christian peoples can make claims for humanitarian military protection in the twentieth century in a way that was not conceivable in the nineteenth century. Humanitarian concerns have expanded and have shaped the interests and policies of states. Intervention now often occurs when geostrategic interests are absent or unclear, and when multilateral coalitions restrain the unilateral exercise of power.

Herman's analysis of Soviet foreign policy argues that the regime that emerged between the two superpowers during the era of detente articulated nascent norms—the avoidance of military force, the maintenance of strategic stability, and the legitimation of human rights—norms that shaped in demonstrable ways the definition of national interests advanced by liberal reformers within the USSR. Contesting definitions of security in the Soviet Union were tied to new interpretations of regime dynamics and U.S. debates by a significant sector of Soviet policy makers. These interpretive processes fostered a softening of the USSR's manichaean image of world order.[71]

The strength of the causal effects of norms varies. Norms fall on a continuum of strength, from mere discursive receptivity (as in the early years of American deterrence policy, discussed by Price and Tannenwald), through contested models (as revealed in Kier's contrasts of French, British, and German military doctrines in the interwar period), to reconstructed "common wisdom" (as in the eschewing of militarist policies in Japan and Germany that Berger discusses). Weak norms, as in the case of

---

norms and commonly "internalized" ones, with various "intersubjective" admixtures in between, is crucial for distinguishing between different types of norms and different types of normative effects. For a more extended discussion, see Ronald L. Jepperson and Ann Swidler, "What Properties of Culture Should We Measure?" *Poetics* 22 (1994): 359–71; Charles Taylor, "Interpretation and the Sciences of Man," *The Review of Metaphysics* 25 (1971): 3–51; and Wendt, *Social Theory of International Politics*, ch. 6.

70. See also Gerritt W. Gong, *The Standard of "Civilisation" in International Society* (Oxford: Oxford University Press, Clarendon Press, 1984).

71. Harald Müller, "The Internalization of Principles, Norms, and Rules by Governments: The Case of Security Regimes," in Volker Rittberger, ed., *Regime Theory and International Relations*, p. 384 (Oxford: Oxford University Press, Clarendon Press, 1993).

nuclear deterrence, and political ideologies, as in the case of the French military, have behavioral consequences neither as permissive as instrumental justifications nor as constraining as unthinking common sense.

Thus the presence of norms does not dictate compliance. Any new or emergent norm must compete with existing, perhaps countervailing, ones. This is a political process that implicates the relative power of international or domestic coalitions. But norms make new types of action possible, while neither guaranteeing action nor determining its results. Extending Finnemore's line of reasoning, one might argue that as norms become institutionalized, support for institutions may partly supplant adherence to norms as motivators of government behavior. It is plausible to argue, for instance, that the United States intervened in Somalia as much to make up for its own inaction in Bosnia and to show support for the UN as to alleviate human suffering in Somalia. A dramatic expansion in the scope of UN activities points in that direction.[72]

Other cultural effects. Some essays rather than invoking "norms" propose other "cultural" effects on the interests or national security policies of states. The use of the term *culture* in this volume also follows conventional sociological usage. While the authors who use the term vary in the details, they all invoke it as a broad label denoting collective models of nation-state authority or identity, represented in custom or law. As typically used (and as used here), *culture* refers both to a set of evaluative standards, such as norms or values, and to cognitive standards, such as rules or models defining what entities and actors exist in a system and how they operate and interrelate.[73]

For example, in their discussions here of domestic cultures, both Berger and Kier invoke country-specific models of (and discourse about) national identity and political organization. These models are constructed and con-

---

72. Taking 1988 as a baseline figure, by 1994 the number of Security Council resolutions adopted had increased from fifteen to seventy-eight; the number of disputes in which the UN was directly involved through preventive diplomacy or peacekeeping operations increased by a factor of three, as did the number of countries contributing military or police personnel. The UN budget for peacekeeping operations increased fifteen-fold, to $3.6 billion. The UN undertook election monitoring in twenty-one countries in 1994, as compared to none in 1988. And the number of sanctions imposed by the Security Council increased from one to seven. See Barbara Crossette, "U.N. Chief Chides Security Council on Military Missions," *New York Times,* January 6, 1995. Yet this expansion in UN activities has generated political contradictions and conflicts of its own, as is illustrated, for example, in the growing strength of the voices, especially in the U.S. Congress, favoring a unilateral approach in the United States. See John G. Ruggie, "Peacekeeping and U.S. Interests," *The Washington Quarterly* 17, no. 4 (1994): 175–84.

73. For further discussion of conceptual issues, see Jepperson and Swidler, "What Properties of Culture Should We Measure?"

tested by politicians, leaders of political movements, groups and parties, propagandists, lawyers, clerics, and even academics. Kier's analysis focuses on the military's organizational culture, but she also examines the broader domestic political culture. The French army in the interwar period did not, as many claim, inherently prefer an offensive military doctrine. Instead, given the constraints established in the domestic political arena, the French army's organizational culture fostered the adoption of a defensive doctrine. Other military organizations would not have responded the same way. In short, what the civilians and the military understand to be in their interest depends on the cultural context in which they operate.[74]

Kier's analysis focuses on the organizational culture of the military, which is nested in a broader domestic political culture. Berger's essay concentrates more directly on this broader setting, in his words the "politico-military culture." Price and Tannenwald in their essay follow recent trends in the field of science and technology studies and military technology,[75] arguing that even technologies of mass destruction are socially constructed. They concentrate on how political actors, in international, transnational, and national communities of discourse, contest different categories of weapons and thus contribute to the emergence and evolution of norms.[76]

Similarly, Jeffrey Legro turns to the military's organizational culture to explain why during World War II submarine attacks on merchant ships and aerial bombings of nonmilitary targets escalated beyond all restrictions, while the use of chemical weapons did not.[77] Dana Eyre and Mark Suchman's essay provides an international example. In referring to models

---

74. Two related research projects point in directions similar to that of Kier. See Jeffrey W. Legro, "Military Culture and Inadvertent Escalation in World War II," *International Security* 18, no. 4 (Spring 1994): 108–42; Jeffrey W. Legro, *Cooperation Under Fire: Anglo-German Restraint During World War II* (Ithaca: Cornell University Press, 1995); and Deborah D. Avant, "The Institutional Sources of Military Doctrine: Hegemons in Peripheral Wars," *International Studies Quarterly* 37, no. 4 (December 1993): 409–30. Avant's analysis of military doctrine relies on an institutional model that focuses on civil-military relations in Britain and the United States.
75. John Ellis, *The Social History of the Machine Gun* (Baltimore: Johns Hopkins University Press, 1975).
76. Their essay suggests that prohibitionary norms can be institutionalized either early or late; they can arise spontaneously in a diffuse manner in a national setting, or they can be created intentionally at the international level to become subsequently internalized in various states. Finally, norms can arise from dramatically different political sources: power politics in the case of nuclear weapons and moral opprobrium in the case of chemical weapons, also one of Robert W. McElroy's conclusions in *Morality and American Foreign Policy* (Princeton: Princeton University Press, 1992). One preliminary finding that the analysis of Price and Tannenwald suggests is that historical contingency in the emergence of norms deserves close attention and may be more important as a starting point of social processes than rationalist perspectives tend to assume.
77. Legro, "Military Culture and Inadvertent Escalation in World War II"; Legro, *Cooperation Under Fire.*

of military apparatuses and their world diffusion, they invoke what John Meyer has called a "more or less worldwide rationalistic culture," indicating "less a set of values and norms, and more a set of models defining the nature, purpose, resources, technologies, controls, and sovereignty of the proper nation state."[78] These models are politically constructed and contested within international organizations, transnational professions, the sciences and other "epistemic communities," social movement networks, and so forth.

2. Cultural or institutional elements of states' global or domestic environments—in this volume, most often norms—shape state identity. Cultural and institutional structure may also constitute or shape the basic identities of states, that is, the features of state "actorhood" or national identity. For example, in essay 3 Eyre and Suchman show how many states enact standardized models of statehood. Specifically, they analyze how many such states procure a standardized weapons portfolio, one related more to domestic display and international prestige than to the actual security threats that the states face. Analogously, Third World states draw upon other models of proper organization from UN agencies,[79] which helps to account for the extraordinary diffusion of social and political technologies within the world system. Similarly, the International Labor Organization (ILO) has been central in global standardization of some elements and practices of welfare states.[80]

Ideas of more or less legitimate state identities develop in world society, as do technologies of statehood. With the recent "third wave" of democratization, even authoritarian regimes now use the rhetorical and constitutional trappings of democracy.[81] Norms of racial equality that emerged from domestic debates over race relations eventually diffused globally through transnational politics and politicized South African apartheid.[82]

---

78. Meyer, "The Changing Cultural Content of the Nation-State," p. 2.

79. Connie McNeely, "Cultural Isomorphism Among Nation-States" (Ph.D. diss., Stanford University, 1989).

80. David Strang and Patricia Mei Yin Chang, "The International Labor Organization and the Welfare State: Institutional Effects on National Welfare Spending, 1960–80," *International Organization* 47, no. 2 (Spring 1993): 235–62.

81. Larry Diamond, Juan Linz, and Seymour Martin Lipset, *Democracy in Developing Countries* (Boulder: Lynne Rienner, 1988).

82. Zimbabwe's support for sanctions against South Africa illustrated the significance of this symbol, that country's high vulnerability to and dependence upon its neighbor state notwithstanding. Zimbabwe's identity interests—the import of enshrining racial equality for the identity of the new regime—trumped more narrowly defined security interests. See Audie Klotz, *Protesting Prejudice: Apartheid and the Politics of Norms in International Relations* (Ithaca: Cornell University Press, 1995).

Analogously, ideas about citizenship, developed in domestic contexts, were implicated in the process of decolonization.[83] In this volume, Herman discusses how Soviet reformers sought ways to reconstruct the Soviet Union as a more "normal" country and how they articulated contrasting radical "global" and more conventional "national" political visions. And Berger shows how the aftermath of World War II occasioned a period of identity politics in both Germany and Japan, in which global models of legitimate state and national identities affected the domestic political process of reconstructing identity. The institution of multilateralism has had a particularly powerful effect on Germany.[84]

The concept of "identity" thus functions as a crucial link between environmental structures and interests. The term comes from social psychology, where it refers to the images of individuality and distinctiveness ("selfhood") held and projected by an actor and formed (and modified over time) through relations with significant "others." Thus the term (by convention) references mutually constructed and evolving images of self and other.[85]

Appropriation of this idiom for the study of international relations may seem forced, since states obviously do not have immediately apparent equivalents to "selves." But nations do construct and project collective identities, and states operate as actors. A large literature on national identity and state sovereignty attests to this important aspect of international politics. We employ the language of "identity" to mark these variations. For the purposes of this project, more specifically, we employ "identity" as a label for the varying construction of nationhood and statehood. Thus we reference both (a) the nationally varying ideologies of collective distinctiveness and purpose ("nationhood" or nationalism, for short), and (b) country variation in state sovereignty, as it is enacted domestically and projected internationally ("statehood," for short).

This dimension of variation in statehood is less codified in the literature and requires a few words of further explication. We refer to two main

---

83. Jackson, "The Weight of Ideas in Decolonization."
84. Ruggie, "Multilateralism," pp. 8–9.
85. More precisely, identities come in two basic forms—those that are intrinsic to an actor (at least relative to a given social structure) and those that are relationally defined within a social structure. Being democratic, for example, is an intrinsic feature of the U.S. state relative to the structure of the international system. Being sovereign is a relational identity that exists only by virtue of intersubjective relationships at the systemic level. Put in the language of game theory, intrinsic identities are constituted exogenously to a game (though they might be reproduced or transformed through play of the game), whereas relational identities ("roles") are constituted by the game itself. In the latter case, part of what is "going on" in a game is the reproduction and/or transformation of identities.

forms of variation. First, the modal character of statehood varies over time *within* an international system, as well as varying *across* international systems. For instance, statehood in the contemporary West is arguably less militarist than statehood elsewhere and in earlier periods. Second, the kinds of statehood constructed within a given system also vary. For instance, the statehood of many African countries is more notably external and juridical than that found elsewhere.[86]

3. Variation in state identity, or changes in state identity, affect the national security interests or policies of states. Identities both generate and shape interests. Some interests, such as mere survival and minimal physical well-being, exist outside of specific social identities; they are relatively generic. But many national security interests depend on a particular construction of self-identity in relation to the conceived identity of others. This was certainly true during the Cold War. Actors often cannot decide what their interests are until they know what they are representing—"who they are"—which in turn depends on their social relationships. A case in point is the current ambiguity surrounding U.S. national interests after the Cold War. The collapse of the Soviet empire as a dominant "other" occasions instability in U.S. self-conception, and hence ambiguity in U.S. interests. The issue is considerably more pressing in Russia and several other successor states of the Soviet Union.

States can develop interests in enacting, sustaining, or developing a particular identity. For example, Price and Tannenwald (in essay 4) argue that a commitment to a "civilized" identity reinforced acceptance of norms defining chemical and nuclear weapons as illegitimate. And the wishes of American elites to present a pacific picture of the American nation facilitated the development of these norms.

Further, constancy in underlying identity helps to explain underlying

---

86. Jackson and Rosberg, "Why Africa's Weak States Persist." Why does one identity prevail over another one? To put a very complicated matter much too briefly, identities will be affected by the social density of transactions and communications, as well as by the power-dependency relations between actors. The greater the social density and actor dependency, the more the actors' identity will be wrapped up in and affected by that relationship. Small states, for example, are more affected in their identity by their relationship with regional hegemons than with global superpowers. Since social densities are typically much greater in domestic than in international politics, domestic identities normally carry more weight than international ones. If we view this question as a social process, we should look for reciprocity, or "reflected appraisals," in identity formation. In such dynamics actors learn to see themselves in the roles that other actors, especially powerful ones, attribute to them. For example, if states treat ("appraise") each other in threatening ways, they will come to internalize ("reflect") identities as "enemies." If more powerful states treat less powerful ones as "clients," weaker states will internalize that identity.

regularities in national security interests and policy. Thus Johnston argues in essay 7 that China's strategic culture in the Maoist period was based on a zero-sum view of the world, a division between "self" and "other" that generated specific strategic commitments. Classical Chinese conceptions were reinforced by contacts with the European state system: nationalism and Marxism-Leninism provided themes of class war and anti-imperialist war that could be grafted onto traditional constructions. Historical variations in the structural conditions of the Chinese empire do not account well for the constancy in strategic culture: the relation between "anarchy" and realpolitik depicted by neorealism, Johnston suggests, is in this case spurious. Rather, it is China's strategic culture that drives its realpolitik.

Correspondingly, change in identity can precipitate substantial change in interests that shape national security policy. Redefinition of Soviet identity, and of the U.S.-Soviet relationship, Herman argues, precipitated a new picture of Soviet interests. And the security dilemma of the Cold War was rooted, as Risse-Kappen demonstrates, in definitions of self and other that elites constructed politically in the late 1940s. In the current period, as multilateralism is "internalized" as a constitutive part of some states' identities, these states develop an interest in participating in and promoting it. As Berger shows, German state elites have sought to lock in a reconstructed German identity—pacified, democratic, and internationalist— by linking this identity to regional and multilateral institutions and identities. These processes are directly analogous to those of "self-binding"[87] and "character planning" conspicuous in personal identity.

Second, state policy or activity may be a direct enactment or reflection of identity politics. Postwar domestic battles in Germany and Japan over proper security policy were part of a broader political conflict over identity. In Germany, but not in Japan, these were open contests over the reconstruction and retelling of national history. Berger argues that the new constructions of national identity have little resemblance to the militarist visions driving these states before World War II. One might argue that identity reconstruction is more consolidated in Germany than in Japan precisely because of Germany's greater "self-entanglement" in regional and world institutions.[88] In any case, Berger's study shows how identity politics and change in collective identities can precipitate substantial change in state interest and policy.

87. Jon Elster, *Ulysses and the Sirens* (Cambridge: Cambridge University Press, 1984).
88. Peter J. Katzenstein, "Taming of Power: German Unification, 1989–1990," in Meredith Woo-Cumings and Michael Lorriaux, eds., *Past as Prelude: History in the Making of a New World Order*, pp. 59–82 (Boulder: Westview, 1993).

This argument has important implications for the post–Cold War era. The continuity in Germany's and Japan's security policy, Berger argues, must be attributed to their domestic politics of identity, rather than to discontinuity in the structure of the international system. Despite stark contrasts between China's hard realpolitik and Japan's and Germany's antimilitarist stance, analytically Berger's and Johnston's conclusions are isomorphic: China's strategic culture and Japan's and Germany's politico-military culture have stronger effects on national security policies than international structure does. Analogously, Kier shows that during the interwar years domestic, not international, conflict over the identity of the French state provided the setting in which the organizational culture of the French military caused the adoption of a defensive doctrine.

We have exemplified "identity interests" and "identity politics" as useful constructs for the analysis of states' national security interests and policy. Barnett's contribution to this volume suggests another contribution of the identity idiom. In his discussion of U.S.-Israeli relations, Barnett refers to the identity "crisis" that began in Israel in the late 1980s. It was rooted not in the dramatic changes in the international system but in the debates spurred by Israeli occupation policies in the West Bank. Israel was deeply divided between those defending a traditional conception of geostrategic security, even at the risk of losing the emotional support of the American public, and those favoring strategic retrenchment while strengthening the notion of Israel as a Western-style democracy. The peace offensive of the Rabin government illustrates that identity can trump geostrategy as a determinant of national security policy.[89]

4. Configurations of state identity affect interstate normative structures, such as regimes or security communities. The preceding section focused on the effects of constructed and contested state identities on national security interests or policy. One can also analyze how states seek to enact or institutionalize their identities (potentially shifting or multiple ones) in interstate normative structures, including regimes and security communities.

Risse-Kappen discusses how the formation of NATO both expressed the common identity of liberal democracies and reinforced an embryonic North Atlantic security community,[90] allowing for the development of new practices of collective defense, institutionalized over time in the NATO security regime. Specifically, he shows that an important aspect of that

89. See also Ian S. Lustick, *Unsettled States, Disputed Lands: Britain and Ireland, France and Algeria, Israel and the West Bank–Gaza* (Ithaca: Cornell University Press, 1993).
90. Deutsch et al., *Political Community and the North Atlantic Area.*

security community was the norm of multilateral consultation that clashed at times with the American urge for unilateral action. He argues further that this security community is persisting despite the evaporation of a common enemy, for it has come to embody norms of consultation, among others, that reinforce an acquired collective identity.[91] Also, proponents of European integration, believing that integration requires agreement, actively championed human rights ideologies, promoting an ideology in order to deepen European identity.[92]

Barnett similarly argues that shifts in models of Arab collective identity—specifically, an ongoing competition between pan-Arabism and state-centric models—have driven the search for normative structures to implement this identity. From this analytical vantage point, arguments that invoke the balance of threat as an explanation of alliance formation remain incomplete in their specification of causation, as long as they neglect variable and contested state identities as the main factor that defines for decision makers what constitutes a threat in the first place.[93]

5. *State policies both reproduce and reconstruct cultural and institutional structure.* The causal imagery captured in figure 2.2 represents a process. Cultural and institutional structures have no existence apart from the ongoing knowledgeable actions of actors.[94] This does not mean that such structures are reducible to such actions; it means that cultural and institutional structures cannot be divorced analytically from the processes by which they are continuously produced and reproduced and changed. Emanuel Adler,[95] for example, has analyzed how a particular political coalition of scientists close to the Kennedy administration helped establish the political practice of arms control for the United States, how that practice was exported, and how it eventually became institutionalized internationally.

---

91. The United States and the European members of NATO have been very careful not to risk the survival of NATO despite their deep differences over the war in Yugoslavia. Although Risse-Kappen stresses the primacy of domestic politics, his analysis is compatible with recent analyses of the institution of multilateralism; see Ruggie, "Multilateralism," and Alexander Wendt, "Collective Identity Formation and the International State," *American Political Science Review* 88, no. 2 (Summer 1994): 384–96.

92. Kathryn Sikkink, "The Power of Principled Ideas: Human Rights Policies in the United States and Western Europe," in Goldstein and Keohane, *Ideas and Foreign Policy*, pp. 139–70.

93. Stephen M. Walt, *The Origin of Alliances* (Ithaca: Cornell University Press, 1987); Stephen M. Walt, "Testing Theories of Alliance Formation: The Case of Southwest Asia," *International Organization* 42, no. 2 (Spring 1988): 275–316.

94. Giddens, *The Constitution of Society.*

95. Adler, "The Emergence of Cooperation."

Since this volume concentrates on invoking cultural and institutional elements as causes of national security policy, this recursive feature is less stressed in the substantive essays. But all of the authors take pains to avoid reifying cultural and institutional structures. All stress the contested construction and contested interpretation of such structures. Power and agency thus matter greatly. And all at least sketch some of the patterns of agency and microstructure upon which their macroscopic arguments depend.

For instance, Risse-Kappen, Berger, Barnett, and Herman all develop the recursive argument that states enacting a particular identity have profound effects on the structure of the international system to which they belong. The forging of an identity as a Western security community, for example, contradicts the expectation of Europe's quick return to nineteenth-century balance of power politics.[96] It predicts instead the continuation of institutional forms of security cooperation in NATO, the West European Union (WEU), the Organization for Security and Cooperation in Europe (OSCE), or some other multilateral forum. Germany's and Japan's identities as trading states have important consequences for the international security conditions in Europe and Asia.[97] The waxing and waning of pan-Arabism has had a profound effect on military alliances in the Middle East. And changes in Soviet identity and policy helped bring about the end of the Cold War.

In our insistence on documenting effects of norms and identities, we have unavoidably slighted important cognate topics. For instance, the essays do not offer detailed investigation of how cultural norms or constructed identities have effects. Ideas on this topic are scattered throughout the volume, but the topic itself does not receive concerted treatment.[98] And the essays do not present a sustained common argument about how

96. John Mearsheimer, "Back to the Future: Instability in Europe After the Cold War," *International Security* 15, no. 1 (1990): 5–56.

97. Katzenstein, "Taming of Power."

98. It is likely that greater attention to language will be important in specifying these effects. Language is neither an asset employed by given subjects nor an external constraint that is imposed on a subject. Rather it exemplifies the general social practices that form both social subjects and the objects to which they speak. There exists disparate work that engages this problem both inside and outside the field of ethnomethodology. See, for example, Francis A. Beer and Robert Hariman, "Realism and Rhetoric in International Relations," in Francis A. Beer and Robert Hariman, eds., *Post-Realism: The Rhetorical Turn in International Relations* (East Lansing, Mich.: Michigan State University Press, in press); Albert Yee, "The Causal Effects of Ideas Themselves and Policy Preferences: Behavioral, Institutional, and Discursive Formulations" (unpublished paper, Brown University, 1993); Hayward R. Alker, Jr., "Fairy Tales, Tragedies, and World Histories: Towards Interpretive Story Grammars as Possibilist World Models," *Behaviormetrika* 21 (1987): 1–28; and Deirdre Boden and Don H. Zimmermann, eds., *Talk and Social Structure: Studies in Ethnomethodology and Conversation Analysis* (Berkeley: University of California Press, 1991).

one detects a norm or when a prescription is sufficiently endorsed, conventionalized, or institutionalized to be considered normative. Discussion of these topics is important in future research and would certainly complement and extend the work produced here. But the arguments and causal effects that this essay and this book emphasize are freestanding without this further development.

In sum, the arguments developed in the empirical essays address the major pathways depicted in figure 2.2. The essays show that "norms," "identities," and "culture" matter. They impute, furthermore, a higher cultural and institutional content to environments than do the more materialist views informing, for example, neorealist explanations. Furthermore, the insistence on socially constructed and contested actor identities militates against the rationalist imagery informing most neorealist and neoliberal theories, which take identity as unproblematic. These lines of argument thus open avenues for further research that dominant theories so far have unduly neglected.

Methodological and Metatheoretic Matters
Methodological Nonissues

The departures of this volume are theoretical rather than methodological. This book neither advances nor depends upon any special methodology or epistemology. The arguments it advances are descriptive, or explanatory, or both. All of the essays start by problematizing a politically important outcome; they then develop their own line of argument in contrast with others. Many employ comparison across time or space, in ways now standard in social science. When they attempt explanation, they engage in "normal science," with its usual desiderata in mind.

Many of the essays make descriptive claims that seek in the first instance to document phenomena that have been insufficiently noticed, let alone analyzed. For example, Price and Tannenwald chart the emergence of norms with regard to non-use of nuclear and chemical weapons; Berger delimits changes in Japanese and German identities after World War II. Both are complex descriptive tasks. Many of the essays then go on to make a variety of explanatory claims positing causal effects either of identities or of the cultural/institutional content of global or domestic environments. Authors thus problematize features of national or international security often overlooked by dominant analytical approaches. And they posit causal effects typically left unexplored.

When the essays make explanatory arguments, they assume no special causal imagery. For example, in most of them, norms are invoked as context effects, affecting the interests that inform policy choices. Some essays make occasional references to "constitutive processes" of identity formation, invoking a set of processes whereby the specific identities of the acting units in a system are built up or altered.[99] In these instances, the analytical problem concerns the shape of identities that inform interests rather than, directly, behavior—a characteristic blind spot in the rationalist vision. But reference to "constitutive" processes invokes a category of substantive arguments and is more a theoretical than a methodological departure. Similarly, when essays deal with issues of "meaning" (for instance, when discussing contested interpretations of norms and identity), there is no commitment to any "subjectivism" in whatever sense. The authors in this volume are thoroughgoing structuralists: they are interested in how *structures* of constructed meaning, embodied in norms or identities, affect what states do.

These essays have a decidedly empirical bent to them. The evidence employed runs the gamut of statistical and interview data, as well as documentary sources. The authors have sought substantial comparative and historical variation and subjected it to intensive and varied empirical probes.

The empirical work amassed here does suggest that security scholars have occasionally been too narrow in their consideration of both topics and causal factors. This project tries to contribute to widening the scientific "phenomenology" of the national security field in both senses. Herman's and Berger's essays suggest two examples. During the 1970s and 1980s realists and liberals debated at great length competing models of hegemonic stability or decline for the United States. With the exception of the broader sociological literature, no similar attention was lavished on developments in the Soviet Union.[100] Yet it was developments in Soviet, not American, politics and the effects of U.S.-Soviet regimes that brought about the current revolution in world politics.[101] Detailed analysis of the

---

99. We neglect here to develop possible differences between constitutive and causal processes as conventionally understood. Most of the essays in this volume do not depend upon such further differentiation. See Wendt, *Social Theory*, for a discussion of this distinction and its implication.
100. Randall Collins, "The Future Decline of the Russian Empire," in *Weberian Sociological Theory*, pp. 186–212 (Cambridge: Cambridge University Press, 1986); Randall Collins, "Prediction in Macrosociology: The Case of the Soviet Collapse," *American Journal of Sociology* 100, no. 6 (May 1995): 1552–93. Immanuel Wallerstein, *Geopolitics and Geoculture: Essays on the Changing World System* (Cambridge: Cambridge University Press, 1991).
101. For a significant exception, see Valerie Bunce, "The Empire Strikes Back: The Transformation of the Eastern Bloc from a Soviet Asset to a Soviet Liability," *International Organization* 39, no. 1 (Winter 1985): 1–46.

military balance of power between the two superpowers overlooked aspects of reality that turned out to be of great significance. Similarly, the growth of Japanese and German power during the same period was not just constrained by their status as client states in an anarchic international system. Military defeat, occupation, and the political experience under the Pax Americana affected norms of appropriate behavior and conceptions of identity that help shape the current security situation in Asia and Europe.

Problematizing what others take for granted or even reify, such as the construction of state identity and interests, does not in and of itself involve any specific methodological imperatives. For instance, despite the concern in these essays with cultural forces, and hence implicitly or explicitly with "meanings," they do not depend exceptionally upon any specialized separate "interpretive methodology." For example, Price and Tannenwald's essay is in part about the emergence of structures that carry meaning—specifically, norms. It identifies the ways in which nuclear and chemical weapons have been delegitimated, placing emergent proscriptions in the context of larger legitimating discourse defining standards of appropriate conduct for "civilized" states. The empirical work here amounts to a form of "process tracing," whereby the development of the interpretive frames employed by actors is recounted in historical fashion. The "interpretations" at issue here are either explananda or causes in the world, rather than some specialized methodological approach or technique.

In stressing our methodological conventionalism we part company with those scholars who have pointed the way toward a sociological approach but who insist on the need for a special interpretive methodology—as do, for instance, Friedrich Kratochwil and John Ruggie, in an oft-cited article.[102] We note that neither author, either in this article or in subsequent writings, has explicated what such a methodology would entail in practice or provided an empirical exemplar representing concretely the kind of work he has in mind. Ruggie's illuminating recent work on sovereignty[103] is not especially interpretivist in any specific methodological sense. And the ways in which Kratochwil's substantive work[104] is and is not interpretivist are themselves not very clear. Moreover, the research practices of scholars like

102. Friedrich V. Kratochwil and John G. Ruggie, "International Organization: A State of the Art on an Art of the State," *International Organization* 40, no. 4 (Autumn 1986): 753–76.
103. Ruggie, "Multilateralism" and "Territoriality and Beyond."
104. Ray Koslowski and Friedrich V. Kratochwil, "Understanding Change in International Politics: The Soviet Empire's Demise and the International System," *International Organization* 48, no. 2 (Spring 1994): 215–48.

Ruggie, Kratochwil, and others identified with constructivist or interpretive approaches converge substantially with those advocated by mainstream scholars. We are not claiming that these research practices are identical in details. But methodological differences in practice appear to be small—or at least are not clearly conceptualized, specified, and articulated in the literature.[105] We suggest that the literature is prone to conflate substantive and theoretical differences with methodological ones, as if a theoretical departure necessarily depends upon some methodological uniqueness. It need not, and does not do so in this volume.

This methodological conventionalism matters to us. From today's perspective, for example, the methodological differences dividing "traditionalists" like Stanley Hoffmann from "behavioralists" like Karl Deutsch in the 1960s assumed disproportionate importance. In their actual studies, both scholars subscribed to different variants of the analytical perspective of historical sociology as the most productive means for understanding security issues in the middle of the twentieth century. Disagreements on secondary issues of methods, for example, should not short-circuit the incipient sociological turn among some realist and liberal scholars that essay 13 reviews briefly.

Relations Between Lines of Theorizing

Stressing that our intended departures are theoretical rather than methodological does, however, raise a more substantial issue: what is the relationship of the "cultural," "institutional," and "constructivist" arguments of this volume to those of realism and liberalism? The short answer is that there is no one a priori relationship to be assumed or found. Sometimes this volume's arguments supplement extant arguments; sometimes they compete with them; in some instances the intent would be to subsume realist or liberal arguments within a broader perspective. Although this listing is not exhaustive, the point is simple: one cannot prejudge the relationship between lines of argument; various relations are possible, and they have to be established theoretically and empirically, rather than assumed.

This matter merits a bit more development. The discussion of the various possible relationships between differing lines of argument seems

---

105. A recent book on methodology, for example, argues that "science . . . and interpretation are *not* fundamentally different endeavors aimed at divergent goals;" see Gary King, Robert O. Keohane, and Sidney Verba, *Designing Social Inquiry: Scientific Inference in Qualitative Research* (Princeton: Princeton University Press, 1994), p. 37; also pp. 34, 36, 84 n. 8.

impaired by the highly reified "paradigm"-talk common to contemporary analyses of international relations. Scholarly communities are quick to reify differing arguments as distinct and competing paradigms. Then scholars are prone to assume, often without much thought or argument, that differing arguments are in immediate and direct competition. Or they will resort to an additive view of theorizing, suggesting that newly suggested lines of argument at best add variables to a previously established explanatory model. These images are procrustean and facile.

We see the different arguments of this volume as having differing relationships to the arguments of realism and liberalism. In some cases one finds instances of direct competition. In these instances, an author has taken up an explanandum already addressed (or readily addressable) by extant arguments and has offered an alternative (more sociological) explanation. Kier's essay provides an excellent example. Kier develops a cultural explanation of French military doctrine that contradicts existing functional explanations favored by realists. The evidence suggests the superiority of her explanation over conventional ones. Eyre and Suchman's essay provides a second example of intentionally direct competition. They set up two distinct models of weapons acquisition and attempt to adjudicate them empirically. In this case, the empirical results are not clear-cut; both models receive some support, and thus the relative strength of the different explanatory approaches is not settled unambiguously. Johnston's essay provides a more complex instance of direct competition, as he attempts to subsume a realist argument within a broader cultural one. In Johnston's account, the continuities in China's strategic culture, not the changes in the international balance of power, offer the most compelling argument for marked continuities in China's definition of and response to security "threats."

In some cases the arguments of this volume are meant to supplement or complement more conventional arguments in the security field, rather than to displace, modify, or subsume them. The most straightforward, and commonly acknowledged, instance is when new arguments offer description and explanation of phenomena unaddressed by existing argumentation. In effect, the differing lines of arguments address different empirical domains; in principle their contributions are complementary, since the contributions are subject to eventual bridging and thus integration. For instance, Finnemore investigates humanitarian interventions, a domain left largely unexplored by realist and liberal analysis. Similarly, the non-use of chemical and nuclear weapons that Price and Tannenwald examine is a topic mostly overlooked or treated schematically in conventional deterrence theory with its heavy reliance on realist and rationalist imagery.

More-complex forms of complementarity also occur. One can imagine what might be called "stage-complementarity," whereby one argument covers one phase of a process, while another argument takes up the next phase.[106] Thus this project's focus on the problem of interest definition leaves virtually unattended problems of strategic interaction, a complementary process. An integrated analytical perspective of politics should have room for both. For example, sometimes the authors of these essays limit themselves to providing the front end, as it were, to largely realist arguments—trying to specify further the character of the actors involved in interaction and/or qualifying the character of the interests being pursued. Barnett, for example, argues that threat perceptions in the Arab world offer no more than a partial explanation of alliance patterns in the Middle East. For threat perceptions depend, in turn, on collective identities. Stage-complementarity does not mean, however, that only cultural and institutional arguments operate at the front end of a causal chain. Herman's analysis, for example, links dramatic changes in Soviet foreign policy and the end of the Cold War to the "New Thinking" of parts of the Soviet elite. In this case a realist argument offers a plausible starting point of a more fully specified causal chain. Adverse shifts in the relative capabilities of the Soviet Union may have been a major factor in how the reformers could install themselves in power in the first place.[107]

Alternatively, arguments can be nested within one another and become complementary in this sense. There are two main forms of nesting: (1) one argument provides foundations for another, as when microeconomics provides, at least in theory, foundations for macroeconomics; and (2) one argument provides conditions for another, as when Weberian institutionalism, in aspiration, describes and explains the conditions under which microeconomics obtains.[108] In this volume, the second form of nesting is

106. In the language of Robert Powell ("Anarchy in International Relations Theory"), this volume's analytical perspective complements neorealism's and neoliberalism's lack of a theory of "preferences over outcomes." Because problems of indeterminacy and incompleteness limit the claims that neorealism and neoliberalism can make concerning "preferences over actions," this volume's analytical perspective, at least potentially, might help us formulate stronger claims. We are indebted to Heiner Schulz for helping us sharpen our thinking on this point.

107. William C. Wohlforth, "Realism and the End of the Cold War," *International Security* 19, no. 3 (Winter 1994/95): 91–129.

108. Arthur Stinchcombe, "Review of Max Weber's *Economy and Society*," in Arthur Stinchcombe, *Stratification and Organization: Selected Papers*, pp. 282–89 (Cambridge: Cambridge University Press, 1986).

more likely, since the sociological (institutionalist and constructivist) thrust of the book's argument departs from the convention that nation-state actors are somehow contextless or ultimately "real." Eventually, these arguments should attempt to do two things. First, they should specify the institutional "scope conditions" under which realist interactions and liberal coordinations unfold.[109] And, second, they should characterize features of the role as actors (and interests) that states adopt when they compete and coordinate politically. Such arguments depart from weaker versions of "historical" institutionalisms by positing that the processes of institutional contextualization and construction are ongoing, rather than relegated to past epochal moments (such as the putative effects of the creation of the Westfalian state system on state sovereignty, or the effect of the Great Depression on a Keynesian consensus).[110]

In brief, competition is not the only possible analytical relationship between different lines of argument; various forms of complementarity, both immediate and more distant, are possible. Often metatheoretical assumptions afford too limited a picture of competition anyway. We are rarely in a position where differing arguments take the form of two (non-nested) regression models, with the same explananda ("dependent variables"), sitting side by side in two panels—with agreed-upon sets of goodness-of-fit statistics offering ready adjudication between them. Neither realism nor liberalism thus can reasonably be depicted as representing a baseline model against which all comers must be measured. For instance, one cannot simply assume that alternative lines of argument are properly depicted as merely "adding possible new variables" to an extant framework. Such a picture makes no allowance for reinterpretation of concepts given new arguments, or for transformation of original arguments given new ones, or for some other form of integration. Limiting the discussion of relations between lines of argument to a few comments about relative "explained variance" is a superficial and misleading appropriation of statistical imagery.[111]

---

109. Bernard P. Cohen, *Developing Sociological Knowledge*, 2d ed. (Chicago: Nelson Hall, 1989).

110. Michael R. Smith, *Power, Norms, and Inflation: A Skeptical Treatment* (New York: Aldine De Gruyter, 1992), pp. 253–59.

111. One cannot assume that alternative arguments are limited in effect to mopping up "unexplained variance" left behind by an extant argument. Such a suggestion is not only blatantly tendentious, it also prescribes a logical fallacy, best illustrated by referring to multiple regression analysis once more. As is well known, one cannot take the residuals from one regression model and then assess the import of a second set of explanatory variables by regressing these residuals on the new variables. In regression, one must allow for the possible intercorrelation of independent variables. Neglecting to do so will result in a form of specification error. The extension of this analogy to issues of explanation in general is direct.

In a world full of anomalies, realism is neither sufficiently established nor sufficiently precise to be treated as a sacrosanct "paradigm" to which other lines of argumentation must defer. Similarly, power-and-interest-based arguments should not be rendered as foundational, with other arguments relegated merely to providing ancillary modules. Such imagery is unwarranted. The end of the Cold War has reminded us once more how naked the emperor of international relations theory is.[112] It will take more than a couple of tailors to provide the necessary clothes.

Extension and Conclusion

So far this essay has treated realism and liberalism as broad orienting frameworks for the analysis of international relations; it has offered sociological institutionalism as an additional frame that also generates specific arguments about national security issues. But we can also consider theories of national security as part of the explananda of an institutionalist perspective.

In making this move, we treat different lines of academic theorizing as highly articulated versions of world cultural models.[113] Consider realism. Because states remain the predominant legitimated "actors" in the current world system, theories of national-security-in-international-anarchy remain dominant, building around world-cultural reifications of state sovereignty and actorhood. Realism thus frames the political discourse about national security. As more overt forms of international coordination have developed and become more prominent, an intellectual space has opened for the network, functional, and bargaining theories characteristic of neoliberalism.

As the world system changes, so does the way in which the domain of security is defined and conceptualized. For instance, as some types of state interaction have been reorganized into "regimes," the domain of security has been redefined in a correspondingly narrower fashion. International trade provides one example. As the multilateral coordination of trade conflicts has spread, trade has moved off the core agenda of national security scholars. Similarly, education systems were once core security concerns, because of their connection to military mobilization. Over time, the theories and practices of mass education have been reoriented around eco-

112. Baldwin, *Neorealism and Neoliberalism*.
113. We attempt to develop an argument suggested by John Meyer.

nomic development and domestic social concerns. Discussion of education on the world scene is now about human capital, not military strength. This second example shows the movement of national security issues into taken-for-granted conventions and beliefs—that is, into culture, rather than into regimes. Eugenics and population control provide a third example. Previously conceived as national security concerns, these issues were redefined over time as environmental and public health matters.

In these particular instances, the conceptualization of security has become more narrowly defined, after what had once been core national security issues were reorganized into regimes or into the taken-for-granted culture of the world system (e.g., into scientific discourse). Issues previously classified as national security have been reclassified as economics (as with trade) or as culture (as with education), or sometimes as simply disorder (as perhaps with terrorism, genocide, or international crime). Left behind is a more concentrated conceptualization of national security, one defined along realist lines. That is, if changing state practices transform national security issues into international regimes or world conventions or doctrines, then they are no longer coded as security matters. In this way realism continues to define the domain of national security—if in a rather tautological fashion.

Issues can also move in the other direction, from culture or regimes into security. A number of regimes are quite unstable, and the bargaining that they organize can readily spill back into more "anarchic" types of interstate relations, thus expanding the domain of national security. A number of weak regimes, like that concerning the non-use of nuclear weapons, operate in this way. Environmental issues present a parallel example. Some could easily shift from world scientific culture or transnational regimes into the domain of interstate conflict or bargaining. Consider also the renewed contestation of issues surrounding population migration and the associated problems of immigration policy. These issues have reemerged as deeply politicized from relatively taken-for-granted conventions of nationalism and citizenship. While such issues are not yet loci of substantial interstate tension, they have attracted the attention of some security scholars and could induce expansion in the conceptualization of security affairs.

The domain of national security theorizing thus evolves as issues flow between the interactions of states in "anarchic" settings, political bargaining in regimes, and conventions or doctrines relatively taken for granted in world culture. Over time, the domain of pure "anarchic" security politics, the realists' home domain, has probably narrowed somewhat, with the partial and fitful expansion of multilateral regimes and world society. Simultaneously, this security domain has intensified, with instances of "anarchic" conflict receiving intense scrutiny and problematization by their main world-cultural theorists, namely realists.

The security domain has been partly transformed in two other ways, changes that are now affecting security discourse. First, the state actors considered by security scholars have themselves been transformed by the reorganization of issues in the world system. Where military functions have attained more multilateral organization, most notably in Western Europe, state identity has been substantially pacified or tamed. Similarly, if less powerfully, as states are drawn more deeply into the world economy (with its attendant regimes, institutions, and associated doctrines of non–zero sum national development), state actorhood is partly reconstructed around less militarist lines. There is substantial regional variation in this process. It is a striking phenomenon in much of Latin America; in contrast, East Asia shows a picture of a more classic realist politics (and doctrines of common and benign economic development are, correspondingly, more weakly represented there). But it nevertheless remains notable that contemporary security discourse, even in Asia, no longer renders states inevitably as war machines locked into natural or routine Darwinian competition. "Lebensraum" is no longer assumed to be a desideratum of state identity.

Second, independent of the modal identity of states, it is clear that the security domain has become less exclusively an *interstate* realm: states' hegemony over security has partly eroded. States have undercut their own security by allowing (or promoting) a vast unregulated market in arms sales, feeding myriad civil wars and newly armed security-relevant "actors." Various mafias, narcotics cartels, crime syndicates, terrorist groups, and ethno-religious camps have proliferated and have attained regional and even global reach.

Thus while the interstate system, narrowly considered, is in some respects more pacified and ordered—some realists now consider it a "mature" anarchy[114]—the broader global system is not. Various dissipative forces could undermine or overwhelm existing forms of coordination or elements of world institutional and cultural structure. World crises could even give a new lease on life to traditional militarism in previously pacified states or regions. But that would not occur automatically or overnight. It

114. Barry Buzan, *People, States, and Fear*, 2d ed. (Boulder: Lynne Rienner, 1991), pp. 175–81.

would require highly visible and contested reconfigurations of state identities (even in countries like Japan or Germany, which have a substantial military apparatus). Conversely, it is notable that there has been a heightened reification of a world responsibility to respond to or manage collective threats. States more routinely organize interventions via multilateral regimes and justify such action in the name of a putatively existing or emerging world order, as Finnemore argues in her essay.

If one employs the above sociology of knowledge, it comes as no surprise that the analytical domain of "national security" has become less clearly defined and less canonically theorized. First, the realists' "anarchy" is now sufficiently embedded and penetrated that some core generalizations of realism—for example, the relationship between polarity and war—attenuate or break down. Second, the heightened reification of the "world" as an economy or society or physical environment expands the list of threats to security. Policy makers and scholars correspondingly call for a broadened conceptualization of the security field, or alternatively they demarcate entirely new fields outside traditional notions of national security (dealing, for example, with terrorism, genocide, or organized transnational crime).

The arguments of this book variously compete with, complement, and begin to contextualize those of realism and liberalism. We have represented realism's nation-state actor as a construction and reconstruction of evolving world and domestic social environments. And we see liberalism's functionalism as made possible in part by a broader evolving world society and culture. A developed institutionalist picture of the world system would describe the scope conditions under which realism and liberalism coexist. And it would also consider how realist and liberal theorizing is itself implicated in constructing and reconstructing the domain of international and national security.

Part · 1
Norms and National Security

3 • Status, Norms, and the Proliferation of Conventional Weapons: An Institutional Theory Approach

Dana P. Eyre and Mark C. Suchman

> *Namibia became the world's newest nation today as Africa's last colony celebrated the end of 75 years of South African rule. . . . South African soldiers lowered their country's banner for the final time just after midnight and Namibian troops hoisted the new blue, red and green flag of Namibia to a bugle fanfare. . . . Soldiers of the new Namibian army . . . marched briskly through the stadium to the beat of drums as officers bearing swords barked commands. About 25,000 spectators roared approval.*
>
> —Associated Press
> March 21, 1991

> *We cannot be an independent nation without an army of some sort.*
>
> —Sylvanus Olympio
> president of Togo, 1960–1966

In recent years, significant Third World militarization[1] has become a hallmark of the contemporary international order. Between 1973 and 1989 the total real military expenditures (in 1982 constant dollars) of developing countries increased from \$95.3 billion to an estimated \$220 billion, while arms imports grew an astounding 1,755 percent. Observing this trend and commenting on militarization in both the developed and the developing world, Peter Wallensteen, Johan Galtung, and Carlos Portales

---

Although many people have helped us in the course of this work, Victoria Alexander deserves special recognition for substantial effort during the formative period of this essay.

1. See Andrew L. Ross, "Dimensions of Militarization in the Third World," *Armed Forces and Society* 13 (1987): 561–78, and Robert L. West, "Problems of Third World National Security Expenditures" (paper presented at the United States Institute of Peace Conference on Conflict Resolution in the Post–Cold War World), for discussions of the term *militarization* and the scope and scale of modern militarization. Ross points out that frequent use of the term masks fundamental disagreements concerning its meaning. *Militarization* is used in this introductory paragraph to refer to a steady growth in the military potential of states. By using it in this sense, we follow the Stockholm International Peace Research Institute.

conclude that "ours is the age of militarization. . . . There is no doubt that the military formation is a major part of contemporary society."[2]

Although these trends have slowed somewhat in the past few years, they have not abated entirely.[3] And despite the relative slowing of proliferation, the overall magnitude of this arms buildup is in itself noteworthy. But it is the qualitative nature of these new arsenals rather than their growth rate that sets the current trend apart from its historical precursors. Since at least 1957 the global military buildup has been marked by a remarkable proliferation of "advanced" high-technology weaponry in the "developing" world. Today, twenty Third World countries possess or are developing ballistic missiles; at least a dozen are armed with more than a thousand main battle tanks; more than seventy have deployed advanced-capability supersonic fighter aircraft (at present there are approximately twenty thousand military aircraft in the developing world); and a similar number have fielded sophisticated offensive and defensive missile systems. Perhaps better known is the growing concern with weapons of mass destruction. Discussion about the causes and consequences of proliferation of these weapons in the developing world has reached a height not seen since the early atomic age. Regardless of the weapon system examined, however, the concern is the same: well-equipped "state of the art" militaries are no longer restricted to a few industrialized "core" powers; military development and economic development, it seems, have become decoupled.[4]

The primary aim of this essay is to develop and evaluate arguments con-

---

2. Peter Wallensteen, Johan Galtung, and Carlos Portales, *Global Militarization* (Boulder: Westview, 1985), p. xi.

3. Consider, for example, the growth of navies in Southeast Asia and the increasing attention given to submarines by many navies throughout the world.

4. Although the empirical focus of this essay is on "horizontal" proliferation (that is, the spread of weaponry of a given level of technological sophistication across countries), "vertical" proliferation (the development of weapons of increasing levels of technical sophistication) is of equal concern to the authors. The primary aim here is to develop and test general theories useful for understanding the dynamics of both vertical and horizontal proliferation. The choice to evaluate these theories empirically by examining horizontal proliferation in the "Two-Thirds World" is driven by analytical and methodological issues, not by theoretical claims concerning the uniqueness of the Two-Thirds World or by political concerns about the unique evils of horizontal proliferation. The research reported here focuses primarily on the determinants of conventional weapons proliferation in the states that won independence in the burst of decolonialization following the independence of Ghana in 1957. These ex-colonies began life as newly independent states with, for the most part, only modest military inheritances from their colonial governors. Their militaries were consequently relatively unformed. These states also lacked extensive military production capabilities, which required them to acquire weapons from beyond their borders, thus making the estimate of inventory levels somewhat easier. Together, these circumstances allow for the relatively complete tracing of their weapons acquisition histories.

cerning the spread of advanced conventional weaponry. In particular, the object here is to formulate a more theoretical and empirically tractable analysis of the role of "status" and "norms" in weapons proliferation. Traditionally, "status" or "norm" arguments about weapons proliferation are seldom systematically theorized and, when they are employed, are generally used in an ad hoc manner. Such factors are seen as playing only a residual role in the proliferation of weaponry; typically, "status" is the explanation given for a specific weapons acquisition when the acquisition can be attributed to no other factor. What is more important than the debate over the relative importance of such factors, however, is that "status" and "norm" arguments are seldom formulated in empirically testable ways, and seldom is evidence systematically developed for the role of status and norms in weapons proliferation. Our aim is to address this weakness and thereby to increase our ability to examine patterns of weapons proliferation through the development of a body of ideas that can support a less ad hoc approach.

We begin by reformulating existing arguments about the role of norms and status in weapons proliferation, using a sociological perspective known as institutional theory.[5] Through institutional theory, both weapons proliferation and the broader process of the worldwide spread of professional, technically oriented military organizations are interpreted as social (and not merely functional or military) phenomena. Weapons proliferation is shaped by the same forces that shape the development of other elements of the modern nation-state.[6] In contrast to this sociological approach, the

---

5. For a discussion of institutional theory and contemporary uses of the term *institution* within sociology, see Ronald L. Jepperson, "Institutions, Institutional Effects, and Institutionalism," in Walter W. Powell and Paul J. DiMaggio, eds., *The New Institutionalism in Organizational Analysis*, pp. 143–63 (Chicago: University of Chicago Press, 1991); and W. Richard Scott, *Institutions and Organizations* (Newbury Park, Calif.: Sage, 1995). For the foundational work in institutional theory, see John W. Meyer, John Boli, and George M. Thomas, "Ontology and Rationalization in the Western Cultural Account," in George M. Thomas, John W. Meyer, Francisco O. Ramirez, and John Boli, eds., *Institutional Structure: Constituting State, Society, and the Individual* (Newbury Park, Calif.: Sage, 1987); John W. Meyer and Brian Rowan, "Institutionalized Organizations: Formal Structure as Myth and Ceremony," *American Journal of Sociology* 83, no. 2 (1977): 340–63.

6. Charles Tilly, *Coercion, Capital, and European States* (Cambridge: Blackwell, 1990), pp. 2–3, and others have proposed distinguishing "national states" ("states governing multiple contiguous regions and their cities by means of a centralized, differentiated, and autonomous, structure") from "nation-states" ("state[s] whose people share a strong linguistic, religious, and symbolic identity"). This terminology usefully highlights the distinction between ethnic-cultural coherence and political autonomy. The phrase has not yet gained wide currency, however, and in the present discussion the distinction, while useful, is not of central theoretical importance for the processes examined. We therefore use the more common approach of employing *nation-state* to refer broadly to any sovereign entity that possesses territorial integrity and political independence and that enjoys international recognition as the collective representative of a discrete population.

existing literature has exhibited a tendency to treat militaries as unique organizations, to see them as fundamental—indeed, foundational—agents of the state, to take their existence for granted, and to explain their growth and development primarily through reference to technical and security concerns.[7] Such arguments see military strength as the bedrock on which nation-states are built. While these arguments have substantial merit, particularly in explaining the emergence of nation-states and militaries before this century, we shall develop here an alternative perspective, suggesting that modern militaries emerge as part of the more general, world-level *cultural* processes that have given rise to the modern nation-state.

In brief, we shall argue that militaries no longer build modern nations, but rather, the world political and social system builds modern nation-states, which in turn build modern militaries and procure modern weaponry. While the sociological vocabulary employed in this essay may strike some as a bit jargon-laden, the Namibian example should make the process analyzed herein quite clear. Namibia was brought into being by the modern world political and cultural system: drawing on taken-for-granted cultural models of appropriate political organization, United Nations efforts and the recognition of states throughout the world have constituted Namibia as a "state." As a symbol of its statehood, the incipient Namibian state created a flag and an army of more than a thousand soldiers. That the army was (and remains) essentially militarily insignificant when compared with those of its possible foes (e.g., South Africa or various armed factions in Angola) is irrelevant to its clearly significant symbolic role.[8]

Standard Explanations for the Proliferation of Weaponry

Three broad arguments are commonly made in efforts to understand the proliferation of the tools of military endeavor. We will label these the

---

7. Ibid.; Michael Mann, *States, War, and Capitalism: Studies in Political Sociology* (Cambridge: Blackwell, 1988).

8. The current Namibian military is approximately eight thousand strong and is in the process of acquiring several small patrol craft. These figures compare with Angolan military forces of approximately forty-five thousand (along with twenty thousand internal security police) and approximately forty thousand UNITA (National Union for the Total Independence of Angola) forces. In 1994, South Africa had armed forces of approximately sixty-seven thousand. The Namibian example, and our assertion of its problematic military utility, is, we realize, suggestive, not conclusive. We include it merely to remind readers of the central symbolic role played by militaries throughout the history of the nation-state, a role that persists even when actual military utility is exceptionally open to question.

superpower manipulation, national security, and factional interest arguments. Each stresses that weapons acquisition and military force structures are the result of rational calculation by actors in the pursuit of their own self-interest. All three of these explanations rest on a single paradigmatic image of human behavior. Described by James G. March as "consequential action" and by Jon Elster as rational choice, this approach sees behavior as guided by the determination of goals (or preferences), the assessment of alternatives available for action, and the mapping of alternatives to goals.[9] Alternatives are selected according to a decision rule—for example, maximize (or satisfice) goal attainment. Superpower manipulation or geopolitical arguments emphasize choice at the level of the major international powers; national security explanations, at the level of the individual nation-state; and factional interest approaches, at the level of subnational interests. Each argument will be briefly reviewed below; each argument leads to a set of at least partially unique empirical predictions concerning influences on the process of weapons proliferation. The particular hypotheses that we will investigate will be summarized after we discuss the three conventional approaches and the institutional theory alternative.

Superpower Manipulation

The proliferation of conventional weaponry and, more broadly, the militarization of the world system may be argued to be primarily the consequence of major power decisions and geopolitical concerns. Regional conflicts are seen as the playing out of superpower conflicts in alternative venues; weapons proliferation is driven not by (local) national needs or internal politics but by the global strategies of the U.S. and the USSR.[10] Superpower or geopolitical theorists differ among themselves with regard to the nature and origins of underlying superpower antagonisms. Thus, some attribute the structure of the international military order to fundamental geostrategic conflicts, while others focus on factional processes within the superpowers themselves and still others highlight action-reaction conflict spirals. For the purposes of this investigation, however, these debates are not central; whatever their view of the dynamics that drive

9. James G. March, "Decision-Making Perspective: Decisions in Organizations and Theories of Choice," in Andrew H. Van De Ven and William F. Joyce, eds., *Perspectives on Organization Design and Behavior*, pp. 205–44 (New York: Wiley, 1981); Jon Elster, *Nuts and Bolts for the Social Sciences* (Cambridge: Cambridge University Press, 1989).

10. For examples of superpower or geopolitical arguments, see Andrew J. Pierre, *The Global Politics of Arms Sales* (Princeton: Princeton University Press, 1982), or Graham T. Allison and Frederic A. Morris, "Armaments and Arms Control: Exploring the Determinants of Military Weapons," *Daedalus* 104 (1975): 99–129.

superpower policies, all geopolitical approaches concur in their emphasis on the active—indeed overwhelming—role of the superpowers in the militarization of the Third World.

National Security

Underlying most existing research on proliferation is the general assumption that strategic, operational, and tactical analysis governs force structure and weapons procurement decisions. Individual nations design a force structure to meet these needs. Decisions are made on the basis of rationally developed performance criteria and threat assessments, and nations are presumed to select a mix of weaponry that balances military benefits with purchase costs. Described by Graham T. Allison and Frederic Morris as the "prevailing simplification" in the weapons proliferation literature, the approach emphasizes that "weapons are the result of national strategic choice; government leaders select specific weapons and total force posture on the basis of precise calculations about national objectives, perceived threats, and strategic doctrine within the constraints of technology and budget." While the exact degree of precision in these calculations may be variable, the central argument is nonetheless clear: weapons procurement is driven by security needs.

Factional Interest

Contrasting with theories that focus on the value of weaponry to nations as a whole, factional or political theories view procurement as a reflection of competing internal interests. Thus the acquisition of a particular weapon is the product of a "procurement coalition" shaped by the self-interests of coalition participants. The military clearly is the primary group, with the most direct interest in weapons purchases.[11] Thomas Ohlson has suggested that military governments "by embracing doctrines which exaggerate the role of force and military preparedness and equate national development

---

11. Arguments about the role that procurement coalitions play in acquisition are most fully developed in examinations of American defense procurement; cf. Gordon Adams, *The Politics of Defense Contracting: The Iron Triangle* (New Brunswick, N.J.: Transaction Books, 1982), for examinations of "iron triangles." Although some similar work has been done on developing-world procurement processes (e.g., Nichole Ball, *Security and Economy in the Third World* [Princeton: Princeton University Press, 1988]; Stephanie G. Neuman, *Defense Planning in Less-Industrialized States* [Lexington, Mass.: Lexington Books, 1984]), it has concentrated on the defense planning and procurement processes of a few large states and does not provide the quantitatively oriented researcher with readily available cross-national and longitudinal indicators of procurement coalition power. Thus, despite the desirability of better-theorized arguments concerning Third World procurement coalitions, quantitative work is limited by the relatively crude indicators available.

with an expansion of national power, are likely to allocate larger sums to the armed forces than civilian-dominated governments."[12]

These three perspectives have generated a rich tradition of research in an effort to understand the dynamics underlying this worldwide trend in the post–World War II period.[13] This tradition has produced a theoretically elaborate and frequently fruitful collection of explanatory schema and numerous empirical studies, yet the dominant paradigms seem to have left the research community with a sense that something is missing. For example, Charles H. Anderton has noted:

> Much of the empirical arms race modeling literature represents an unsuccessful attempt to find fundamental "lawlike" arms race relationships. . . . The result has been an extremely large and growing literature . . . employing the most sophisticated empirical techniques, which has left us rather dry in terms of knowing more about arms races than we would otherwise know.[14]

Despite the dominance of the three perspectives within the arms trade literature, country- and region-level empirical examinations frequently find that these approaches perform poorly as predictors of actual weapons proliferation patterns. Confronting theory with data, observers frequently note the "widespread propensity to procure highly sophisticated, expensive weapon systems and technologies, despite well-known absorption handicaps, and to reject equally serviceable but cheaper and perhaps less sophisticated options that are readily available."[15] Explanations offered for this phenomenon tend to emphasize the inadequately rational nature of Third World military decision making rather than the potential inadequacies of the rational explanation. Rodney W. Jones and Steven A. Hildreth, for example, note the "superficial Third World knowledge of particular military systems" and also argue that "developing nations lack the analytical staffs necessary to assess the true military value of weapon tech-

12. Thomas Ohlson, ed., *Arms Transfer Limitations and Third World Security* (Oxford: Oxford University Press, 1988), p. xi.

13. Summarized in Edward J. Laurance, *The International Arms Trade* (New York: Macmillan, 1992); A. F. Mullins, *Born Arming: Development and Military Power in New States* (Stanford: Stanford University Press, 1987); Stephanie G. Neuman and Robert E. Harkavy, *Arms Transfers in the Modern World* (New York: Praeger, 1979); Robert E. Harkavy, *The Arms Trade and International Systems* (Cambridge, Mass.: Ballinger, 1975).

14. Charles H. Anderton, "Arms Race Modeling: Problems and Prospects," *Journal of Conflict Resolution* 33 (1989): 349.

15. Rodney W. Jones and Steven Hildreth, *Emerging Powers: Defense and Security in the Third World* (New York: Praeger, 1984), p. 65.

nologies or to determine how the new weapon can best be employed" and that "less developed countries are often unaware of significant military technologies that are and will be available to them at reasonable cost."[16]

Robert O'Connell argues that this situation is the "product of a fundamental misunderstanding of the intimate relationship between humans and their armaments."[17] Such a misunderstanding is almost inevitable given the tendency in the arms control literature to treat weapons merely as the tools of rationally developed policy; weapons are seen as technology "pure and simple" without independent meaning or significance. Dana Eyre, Mark Suchman, and Victoria Alexander have noted that students of arms control "must acknowledge what has become virtually a truism in other areas of sociology: that technology is never just technology, that every machine has a socially constructed meaning and a socially oriented objective and that the incidence and significance of technological developments can never be fully understood or predicted independently of their social context."[18] In this essay we investigate this "intimate relationship between humans and their arms" by identifying and examining factors that affect the adoption of a variety of individual weapon systems (e.g., supersonic aircraft, armored personnel carriers, or APCs) by nation-states in the Cold War period.

An Alternative Perspective: Obligatory Action and an Institutional Theory of Weapons Proliferation

We emphasize the argument that the spread of high-technology weaponry throughout the world is the result of more than rational policy or national security concerns. Reduced (for purposes of explication) to the simplest but strongest possible statement, weapons spread not because of a match between their technical capabilities and national security needs but because of the highly symbolic, normative nature of militaries and their weaponry. Weapons have proliferated because of the socially constructed meanings that have become associated with them. Highly technological militaries symbolize modernity, efficacy, and independence. Thus the spread of weapons is a process both driven and shaped by institutionalized normative

---

16. Ibid., pp. 5, 60–61.

17. Robert O'Connell, "Putting Weapons in Perspective," *Armed Forces and Society* 9 (1983): 441.

18. Dana P. Eyre, Mark C. Suchman, and Victoria D. Alexander, "Military Procurement as Rational Myth: Notes on the Social Construction of Weapons Proliferation" (paper presented at the 1986 annual meeting of the American Sociological Association).

structures linking militaries and their advanced weapons with sovereign status as a nation, with modernization, and with social legitimacy.[19] This argument, which can be labeled an "institutionalist" approach to arms transfers, emphasizes the role of world-level cultural models that "press all countries toward common objectives, forms, and practices"[20] and that therefore result in a notable degree of isomorphism in structures and practices among nation-states.

Consequential action (which lies at the core of traditional explanations for weapons proliferation) is not the only useful theory of human behavior. While a mythos of rationality may permeate much of Western culture, and the examination of international relations in particular, arguments emphasizing different mechanisms are common within sociology.[21] Central to social phenomenology, traditional role theory, and recent institutional approaches in sociology is an alternative perspective that James G. March terms "obligatory action."[22]

Obligatory action may be contrasted with consequential action. Behavior is explained not in terms of goals, alternatives, and decision rules such as maximization or satisficing (the vocabulary of consequential action) but through an emphasis on roles, norms, accounts (i.e., stories and explanations justifying particular actions) and definitions of appropriate action. Although the vocabulary of the obligatory action perspective may not be a central feature of modern American pop psychological discourse, social scientists should not ignore the value of the perspective. Viewed through the lens of obligatory action, the identity of an actor is profoundly social, and an actor's behavior is *explained by* the culturally constructed definition of the situation and of appropriate action within the situation. Through the perspective of obligatory action, the behavior of nation-states, and

---

19. We seek to develop arguments that provide a framework for systematically examining the impact of "normative" or "cultural" processes in the world military system. While we work within a well-established body of sociological thought (cited above), the application of these arguments to the examination of areas traditionally ceded to realist theory is new. We do this not in an effort toward an expansive sociological theoretical hegemony but in the spirit of Jon Elster's exposition of the process of "explanation by mechanism" (*Nuts and Bolts for the Social Sciences*). Elster argues that the first step in social science is the development of a "toolbox" of causal mechanisms, a set of "cogs and wheels" that can be assembled to provide explanations of specific events and facts. We seek not to replace other tools but to develop an alternative set of tools.
20. Connie McNeely, "Cultural Isomorphism Among Nation-States: The Role of International Organizations" (Ph.D. diss., Stanford University, 1989), p. 3.
21. For a discussion of the mythos of rationality in Western culture, see March, "Decision-Making Perspective," and Meyer and Rowen, "Institutionalized Organizations."
22. March, "Decision-Making Perspective."

people, can be seen as similar to the behavior of actors in a play, or players in a game. Their identity is constituted by the social system (for example, the identity of pitcher, or that of wife, is given meaning by the complex of behavioral rules associated with the role), and their behavior is guided by the "script" or the "playbook." Such arguments do not deny that individual actors are thoughtful or strategic; there is room for improvisation and creativity (neither people nor nation-states are mindless followers), but individual behavior is fundamentally shaped by the social structure surrounding the behavior. Indeed, actors themselves are constituted by the social system. Actors (be they organizations, persons, or nation-states) do not have social standing, or the ability to act within a social system, separate from the rules that both construct them and charter their actions. Within such a perspective the key question for understanding behavior is no longer "What are an actor's goals, alternatives, and decision rule?" but "How are roles, accounts, and rituals written, spread, and learned?"

Whatever the explanatory model chosen (consequential or obligatory), it is important not to reify the model. The concrete action of real people (and states) can be *explained* by alternative models, but the action itself is neither "consequential" nor "obligatory," "rational" nor "irrational"; rather, these ideas are the lenses that the analyst uses to understand action. Indeed, the ultimate purpose of constructing analytically distinct arguments is to enable us to combine these "nuts and bolts" in ways that are useful for the explanation of particular features of social life.

Within organizational theory and political sociology, "obligatory action" arguments are frequently labeled "institutionalist." Such arguments share three central assumptions: First, institutional theory sees society as more than a network of exchange relations and power-balancing efforts. Instead, institutionalists emphasize that the social world is a cultural system, structured by an evolving set of categorical prescriptions and proscriptions that define and delimit appropriate action. Second, institutional theory argues that since these cultural categories are practically taken for granted as lawful, actors rarely subject conforming behaviors to cost-benefit analysis—or do so only ritualistically.[23] In keeping with this outlook, institutionalists explain social life not by postulating goals and interests but by examining the mechanisms through which societal struc-

---

23. James G. March, "Ambiguity and Accounting: The Elusive Link Between Information and Decision Making," in *Decisions and Organizations*, pp. 384–408 (Cambridge: Blackwell, 1988); Martha S. Feldman and James G. March, "Information in Organizations as Signal and Symbol," *Administrative Sciences Quarterly* 26 (1981): 171–86.

tures and activities take on a rule-like or ritual status in the minds of participants. Thus, most institutional arguments focus on the ways in which apparently autonomous action reflects "higher-order constraints imposed by socially constructed realities."[24] Finally, institutional theory stresses that these normative "definitions of appropriateness" are not static but develop and change over time. Although cultural rules sometimes remain relatively static, this stability is the product of a dynamic process. Cultural definitions do not merely "originate" and then "spread"; rather, they should be thought of as in a constant process of evolution, perhaps akin to the process of speciation in the biological world.

Applied to international relations, these three features of institutional theory imply that nation-states are not autonomous, independent actors in pursuit of national interests within an anarchy, as realist theories assume. Most important, institutional theory emphasizes the central role of the larger world system in constituting the state as "carrier of collective value and purpose."[25] Indeed, it is this increasingly integrated global system of socially constructed rules that creates and legitimates nation-states as sovereign actors both in domestic affairs and on the international stage. It should be noted that institutional theories bear some similarity to perspectives in political science emphasizing the importance of regimes.[26] Both schools share conceptions of an international cultural or social system, and both emphasize a view of the world as more than an unstructured anarchy. But whereas systemic perspectives view global society as "order-providing"—that is, as a set of enforced constraints on behavior—institutionalist perspectives view the world system as "constitutive"—that is, as a set of fundamental definitions of legitimate actors and appropriate actions. To grossly oversimplify, within the systemic perspective, nations go to war in violation of international norms; within the institutional perspective, nations go to war because that is one of the actions their "charter" as a nation-state allows/instructs them to do. John Keegan, Donald Snow, and Martin Van Crevald offer sociologically informed historical analyses of the impact of social structure on warfare that are sympathetic to this approach.[27]

---

24. Jepperson, "Institutions, Institutional Effects, and Institutionalism."

25. George M. Thomas and Pat Lauderdale, "State Authority and National Welfare Programs in the World System Context," *Sociological Forum* 3 (1988): 383–99.

26. Hedley Bull, *The Anarchical Society: A Study of Order in World Politics* (New York: Columbia University Press 1977); Stephen D. Krasner, ed., *International Regimes* (Ithaca: Cornell University Press, 1983).

27. John Keegan, *A History of Warfare* (New York: Knopf, 1993); Donald M. Snow, *Distant Thunder* (New York: St. Martin's, 1993); and Martin Van Crevald, *The Transformation of War* (New York: Free Press, 1991).

Empirical examinations at the world-system level have generally emphasized the "remarkable degree of ideological and organizational convergence throughout the world,"[28] and most have concentrated on the three substantive areas: welfare systems, educational systems, and conceptions of citizenship.[29] This substantial body of empirical work has focused primarily on establishing the fruitfulness of the institutional perspective and on demonstrating the presence of isomorphism within the world system. Thomas and Lauderdale's examination of the worldwide spread of national welfare programs provides a useful example of work in this tradition.[30] Arguing against the assumption that nation-states adopt and expand welfare programs in response to functional needs (e.g., the argument that states have an unemployment insurance system because they have lots of unemployed workers who are hungry or politically active), the authors posit that "incorporation . . . into the world system reconstitutes the state as the carrier of collective value and purpose, . . . chartered with the responsibility for 'national welfare.' " Under such circumstances, welfare policies are not predicted by indicators of need; they are instead predicted by the extent of incorporation into the world polity. The basic pattern of the Thomas and Lauderdale study is typical of other institutional efforts, as are the empirical findings. Indicators of incorporation into the world system are found to predict the degree of adherence to international cultural norms chartering state action (here, the existence and extensiveness of social security programs). In contrast, indices of functional need for state action (for example, the percentage of elderly citizens in the population) fail to predict either the existence or the extent of governmental response. On the basis of these findings, Thomas and Lauderdale conclude that national policies establishing formal welfare programs are "best viewed as rituals of external legitimacy."[31]

As noted above, the institutional approach to the problem of proliferation developed herein will emphasize the role of the symbolic, normative

---

28. McNeely, "Cultural Isomorphism Among Nation-States;" p. 2.

29. For welfare, see Thomas and Lauderdale, "State Authority and National Welfare Programs in the World System Context"; for education, see Francisco O. Ramirez and John Boli, "Global Patterns of Educational Institutionalization" in Thomas et al., *Institutional Structure*, pp. 150–72. For citizenship, see Francisco O. Ramirez and Yasemin Soysal, "Women's Acquisition of the Franchise: An Event History Analysis" (paper presented at the 1989 annual meeting of the American Sociological Association).

30. Thomas and Lauderdale, "State Authority and National Welfare Programs in the World System Context."

31. Ibid., p. 393.

aspects of militaries and weaponry. Frequently, students of arms control recognize the potential significance of the processes described by institutional approaches, although generally employing words like *status* and *prestige*. Jones and Hildreth acknowledge that the drive to acquire high-technology weaponry may be a combination of inadequately rational decision-making systems and "a political compulsion to deploy systems as modern or sophisticated as a neighbor has."[32] Ohlson argues that "the armed forces, equipped with as modern weapons as possible, came to be regarded by many governments in the Third World as a symbol of unity and independence and as tangible evidence that the government intended to defend its sovereignty. The actual utility of these weapons . . . was often of secondary importance."[33] Examining the structure of European navies, Catherine M. Kelleher, Alden F. Mullins, and Richard C. Eichenberg found that the number of sea control vessels remained remarkably stable across all European states during the period 1960 to 1970. "The effects of constrained resources seem minimal. . . . Destroyers, frigates, corvettes, and (for a few states) carriers all seem to constitute an element of national prestige." Examining the force structures of individual countries, they argued that "in terms of traditional indicators, it seemed logical to predict the Netherlands and Italy would be prime candidates for our 'rational middle power'; yet their present naval profiles show few of the choices we hypothesized for [the model]. . . . It may well be the least powerful middle powers which are most attached to their symbols of 'equality.'"[34] While these findings are not conclusive (indeed, Kelleher, Mullins, and Eichenberg's study is one example of the use of prestige arguments when nothing else seems to fit), they clearly suggest that force structure is influenced by more than domestic politics and rational calculation of strategic need.

Despite apparent compatibility and the potential fruitfulness of an institutional approach to the study of the arms trade, existing examinations have tended to leave these nascent institutional arguments underdeveloped. For their part, institutional theorists have also have tended to skip the military in their empirical investigations of the world system. Yet the application of institutional arguments to the study of world militaries

---

32. Jones and Hildreth, *Emerging Powers*, p. 5.
33. Ohlson, *Arms Transfer Limitations and Third World Security*, p. 49.
34. Catherine M. Kelleher, Alden F. Mullins, Jr., and Richard C. Eichenberg, "The Structure of European Navies 1960—1977," in Oliver Veldman, ed., *The Future of West European Navies*, pp. 173–238 (The Hague: Den Helde, 1980).

should be uniquely fitting for at least two reasons. First, militarization, from an institutionalist perspective, may be seen not as a unique and especially problematic occurrence (except for the possible consequences) but as merely one additional facet of the larger, global system–wide trend toward isomorphism among nation-states that is the central empirical finding within institutional arguments. Second, failure to examine militaries from an institutionalist perspective is especially odd given the traditional, unique link between armed force and national sovereignty and the institutionalist concern for the construction of the nation-state as an actor. Michael Howard argues that, within the international system, "the military capability of a state is assumed to be [a] major element in its effectiveness as an actor in the international system."[35] This argument suggests that, far from being an aberrant event, the militarization of the Third World is inextricably linked with the extension of the nation-state system and the development of national sovereignty. Thus it can be argued that the developing world is militarized, not because of particular events or forces within or between developing world nation-states but because the developing world is made up of nation-states and one of the defining characteristics of the nation-state is the possession of a modern military.

From an institutional perspective, once a social object (say, a flag or a supersonic aircraft) is established as central to normative definitions of statehood (that is, once "being a nation" means, among other things, "having a flag" and "having a high-tech military"), the critical variable in the determination of acquisition of these objects is not the nation-state's functional requirement for the object but the degree of connection of the nation-state to the world system. In order to understand the "unprecedented proliferation of national flags in the post–World War II period," one does not look at the nation-state's functional need for a flag, or at the behavior of flag manufacturers. To understand flag proliferation, one must understand the cultural system that gives flags their unique meaning for nation-states. A nation-state "acquires" a flag because it is embedded in a normative system that gives the flag meaning. Thus, an institutional argument suggests that the proliferation of conventional weapons is profoundly shaped by an essentially "ritualistic" (in the sense of ritual as encapsulating meaning, not in the more common usage of habitual action devoid of meaning) belief in militaries and modern weaponry as distinguishing emblems of the modern nation-state. It follows that, if procure-

---

35. Michael Howard, "War and the Nation-State," *Daedalus* 108 (1979): 101.

ment results from immersion in such a normative system, then the pace of procurement should vary with the extent of the immersion.[36]

Institutional arguments are able to make comprehensible many otherwise problematic aspects of militaries and weapons proliferation. It is quite common for developing nations to maintain only a single "squadron" of four or five advanced aircraft—too few to offer any substantial strategic or tactical benefits in any but the rarest of circumstances, but enough to constitute a reasonable air show. Similarly, the symbolic nature of weaponry is almost certainly a significant part of the failure of the F-20 export fighter program, which was intended to provide a low-cost, high-reliability jet fighter designed specifically to meet the needs of newly industrialized countries. Despite having the "right stuff," it lacked the legitimating imprimature of USAF ownership and perished as unsalable. Institutional arguments must be better specified if a fuller understanding of the process is to be gained. Indeed, both Ann Swidler and Connie McNeely have noted that few investigations using institutional arguments have focused on the specification of the mechanisms by which isomorphism is produced; instead, they have focused primarily on establishing the fruitfulness of the institutionalist perspective and the existence of isomorphism within the world sys-

---

36. Some may object to the comparison of weapons and flags, arguing that flags are purely symbolic and weapons primarily or exclusively functional. We do not disagree with the observation that weapons have functional value. Guns, in fact, can be used to kill people. We do, however, disagree with the assumption that some social objects (e.g., flags) are purely symbolic and also with the a priori assumption that because some social objects (e.g., weapons) have a functional value, functional considerations must necessarily dominate the proliferation of those objects. First, it should be remembered that the actual utility of symbolically significant weaponry, such as a supersonic aircraft, is more open to question than weapons salespeople might acknowledge. This is particularly true in many developing-world strategic and tactical circumstances. Jet fighters, for example, are difficult to maintain and to employ effectively. Second, the a priori assessment of the relative functional value of military weaponry is often dependent on a complex set of assumptions that are themselves as much cultural theories of war as hard-earned, firsthand lessons of war. As a final complicating factor, the socially constructed nature of a "threat" should also be kept in mind. The nature and magnitude of a threat are shaped by perceptual processes and cultural assumptions, as well as military considerations. Thus, the degree to which a given weapon is seen as "functional" is dependent on threats and assessments of utility, both of which are socially constructed. The symbolic and the functional values of social objects cannot be simply separated or assessed. Carl Von Clausewitz, speaking of what he termed the "physical" and "moral" factors in war, noted: "One might say that the physical seem little more than the wooden hilt, while moral factors are the precious metal, the real weapon, the finely-honed blade" (*On War*, edited and translated by Michael Howard and Peter Paret [Princeton: Princeton University Press, 1984], p. 184). Again, we do not dispute the functionality of weapons. We merely point out that the assessment of "functionality" is more problematic than may be generally acknowledged and that one should begin the study of weapons proliferation with a question, rather than an assumption that one of these two tightly intertwined aspects necessarily dominates.

tem.[37] Although this investigation, which is designed to use institutional theory in a new empirical realm rather than to expand institutional theory, is marked by this limitation, we would now like to explore four directions in which institutional arguments can be developed: greater attention to the structure of the world system; systematic variation in the process of early and late adoption of an object; variation in the degree to which an object is given social meaning (or degree of institutionalization); and variation in the nature of an actor's identity. Although not all of these arguments will be empirically evaluated here, the effort is useful in the interest of giving a full picture of an institutional approach to proliferation.

Structure of the World System

Within the diffusion literature attention is paid both to the nature and degree of connectedness of the potential adopter and to the organization of the social system.[38] Institutional theory relying on empirical investigations have tended to assume an undifferentiated (or simply differentiated, e.g., core-periphery) world system, featuring only variations in the degree of connection of an individual state to the polity. However, Swidler usefully suggests that different "models of stateness may well be promulgated within subcommunities, based on language or colonial heritage, political divisions, etc."[39] This concern suggests an argument that the proliferation of high-technology weaponry should follow existing channels of international influence and communication. Variations in these channels should predict variations in patterns of weapons proliferation. For example, postcolonial relationships (e.g., the British Commonwealth) or regionally based alliance or cooperation organizations (e.g., the Organization of American States) may foster the development of variant models of stateness.

Few sociological investigations have systematically examined variations in the structure of the world cultural system. Anthony Giddens notes that current conceptions of the "world system" may exaggerate the level of integration of the system. The current world system may, he argues, be better characterized as being made up of a "global information system," a "nation-state system," a "world capitalist economy," and a "world military order."

---

37. Ann Swidler, "Culture in Action: Symbols and Strategies," *American Sociological Review* 51 (1987): 273–86; McNeely, "Cultural Isomorphism Among Nation-States."

38. Claude S. Fischer and Glenn R. Carroll, "Telephone and Automobile Diffusion in the United States, 1902–1937," *American Journal of Sociology* 93 (1988): 1153–78; J. S. Coleman, E. Katz, and H. Menzel, *Medical Innovation* (New York: Bobbs-Merrill, 1966); Lawrence A. Brown, *Innovation Diffusion: A New Perspective* (New York: Methuen, 1981).

39. Swidler, "Culture in Action."

"The world system exists," Giddens notes, but this "does not imply a single dominating dynamic in its development."[40] We see much value in this approach, and we would point out two major advantages. First, such a differentiated characterization allows for the formulation of arguments about the relationship between these systems, focusing, for example, on the degree to which conformity in one "sector" or "system" (e.g., education or the "global information system," using a measure of conformity such as that developed by McNeely)[41] predicts conformity in another sector (e.g., the "world military order"). Similarly, it should be possible, following the pattern of earlier institutional theories, to construct an indicator of connection to the world military system, using, for example, the number of military attachés sent abroad or the number of military-related treaties signed. It would then be possible to examine which indicator of connection was a better predictor of institutional conformity; significant improvement with the use of the indicator of connection to the world military system would suggest support for Giddens's arguments. Second, Giddens's framework implicitly challenges us to assess empirically the uniqueness of the dynamics of the world military system, rather than assuming that it must be dominated by either cultural processes or functional considerations.

Early/Late Adopters

Within the literature on institutional arguments at the organizational level, empirical research has "yielded the frequently replicated finding that early adoption (that is, adoption of an innovation soon after its introduction, before a large portion of the population at risk has adopted it) of organizational innovations is strongly predicted by technical or political attributes of adopters but that later diffusion is more poorly predicted by technical or political measures."[42] Pamela Tolbert and Lynne Zucker find that when civil service reforms are not required by the state, early adoption of civil service by cities is related to internal organizational requirements, with city characteristics predicting adoption, while late adoption is argued to be related to institutional definitions of legitimate structural form; empirically, they find that city characteristics no longer predict adoption.[43] The argu-

---

40. Anthony Giddens, *The Nation-State and Violence* (Berkeley: University of California Press, 1987), p. 276.
41. McNeely, "Cultural Isomorphism Among Nation-States."
42. Paul DiMaggio, "Interest and Agency in Institutional Theory," in Lynne G. Zucker, ed., *Institutional Patterns and Organizations: Culture and Environment* (Cambridge, Mass.: Ballinger, 1988), p. 6.
43. Pamela Tolbert and Lynne G. Zucker, "Institutional Sources of Change in the Formal Structure of Organizations: The Diffusion of Civil Service Reform, 1880–1935," *Administrative Sciences Quarterly* 28 (1983): 22–39.

ment may be restated more positively as: early adoption of an innovation will be predicted by "technical characteristics" of the adopter (reflecting the suitability of the innovation as a solution to a problem), while later adoption (after the "institutionalization" of the innovation) will no longer be predicted by technical characteristics and should be predicted by variables reflecting the degree to which the adopter is connected to the social system within which the innovation is institutionalized.

Degree of Institutionalization

If objects, such as flags, become, in Selznick's phrase, "infused with value," or institutionalized, it is reasonable to assume that different objects may vary in the degree to which they do so. A social object can vary in the degree to which it has been given meaning and has become part of, or linked to, a particular "taken for granted" image of social reality. The value given a particular object can vary across social systems. The most obvious example of this process is the value accorded small bits of ribbon. Within the military, these "bits of ribbon" are highly significant and full of meaning. In another social system, they may be mere insignificant and meaningless bits of ribbon. Within the modern world system, where sovereignty, modernity, and independence are the essence of our ideas about the nation-state, some weapons might reasonably be seen as highly institutionalized (or symbolically significant, e.g., supersonic aircraft), while others are less so (e.g., trucks, small arms). A given weapon's symbolic significance is dependent on the degree to which it is linked to cultural ideas and images of the nation-state; highly technological, visible, unique weapons are more effective at symbolizing independence than are mundane, unremarkable weapons. Thus, just as weapons can be thought to vary in technical capacity (e.g., "throw weight"—the capacity of a missile in terms of a weight/distance measure), so also can they be seen as varying in terms of institutional integration or "symbolic throw weight." Weapons that vary in this dimension should follow distinct patterns of diffusion; the diffusion of highly institutionalized weaponry should be influenced by linkage to the larger world system and by processes similar to those that shape the diffusion of other, highly institutionalized elements of the world system. The diffusion of weapons of a minimal degree of institutionalization (labeled by *The Economist* as "the tools of everyday slaughter") should be influenced primarily by consequential factors, including both strategic requirements and situational constraints.

One significant empirical task for institutional theory is to establish a means of systematically assessing the degree of symbolic significance for social objects. Establishing such a metric is difficult; for our purposes, however, variation in symbolic significance among weapons is relatively clear. Some weapons are commonly seen as highly loaded with meaning. Howard, looking at naval power at the beginning of the twentieth century, notes that "the Battleship was indeed a symbol of national pride and power of a unique kind; one even more appropriate to the industrial age than armies. It embodied at once the technological achievement of that nation as a whole, its world-wide reach and, with its huge guns, immense destructive power. It was a status symbol of universal validity, one which no nation conscious of its destiny could afford to do without."[44] In the post–World War II era, navies have not lost their symbolic significance; the evocative phrase "showing the flag" has not lost meaning, although the vehicles may have changed. Aircraft carriers may have taken pride of place in navies, their symbolic value equaling or exceeding that of battleships of old. Argentine reluctance to employ the aircraft carrier *Veintecinco de Mayo* in the Falklands war, for instance, suggests that the symbolic significance of the carrier exceeded its military utility. Aircraft have similarly significant roles; the rise of the symbolic significance of aircraft is captured in the contemporaneous labeling of the era from 1950 to 1970 as "the jet age." Although the 1990s are infrequently labeled as the jet age, the symbolic significance of aircraft has not been entirely eliminated. For example, the Slovenian Air Force held an air show in the spring of 1994, despite having fewer than five aircraft.[45]

Actor Identity

So far, world system–level empirical investigations employing institutional theory have tended to assume a single, undifferentiated identity for all nation-states: that of sovereign equals. It is reasonable to suspect, however, that there are variations in this basic identity. Clearly, a "superpower" is more than a mere nation-state; it is, within the military realm, a nation-state that—at a minimum—has nuclear weapons. Some nations (e.g.,

---

44. Howard, "War and the Nation-State," p. 104.
45. Others who have employed similar arguments acknowledging the symbolic significance of weaponry but examining distinct historical epochs include William H. McNeill (*The Pursuit of Power* [Chicago: University of Chicago Press, 1982]), who looked at the spread of chariots in the ancient world, and Richard A. Fletcher (*Moorish Spain* [London: Weidenfeld and Nicholson, 1992]), who examined the military structures of Moorish Spain.

India) have at times seemed actively to aspire to this differentiated status. Similarly, some states seem to aspire to a more local, but still differentiated, status as a "regional power"—for example, Nigeria or Argentina. Discussions of the spread of chemical and biological weapons have frequently featured the label "pariah state." While no state is likely to aspire, or even publicly acknowledge, such a label, labeling theory[46] offers potentially useful insights into the mechanisms through which such socially undesirable labels can shape behavior. Finally, it is reasonable to speculate that "microstates" (e.g., Kiribati, Nauru, St. Kitts, and Nevis) may very well view their identity as something other than a full nation-state.

Thus, some variation in the identity and behavior of nation-states may stem from variations on the basic concept of the nation-state in the world-level cultural model. But while world-level cultural concepts of the nation-state have a profound impact on the formation of specific states, identity as a nation-state is not constituted solely by world-level cultural processes. "Domestic" cultural definitions of nationhood and statehood interact with world-level cultural concepts of the nation-state to form the specific identity of individual nation-states and, in turn, to shape their behavior. Together, these two processes may account for substantial variation in the identity and behavior of individual nation-states. Clearly, the dynamics of identity formation for the nation-state require greater theoretical and empirical work. This discussion is adequate, however, to highlight the point that variations in national identity may shape variations in patterns of weapons acquisition.[47]

Hypotheses

Before turning to a summary of the hypotheses to be investigated, we should point out that there are strong reasons to anticipate robust period effects in the proliferation of conventional weaponry.[48] Most qualitative

---

46. Walter R. Gove, *The Labeling of Deviance*, 2d ed. (Newbury Park, Calif.: Sage, 1980).
47. This argument suggests the following hypothesis: elements of the nation-state that are more tightly tied to the local culture will exhibit more variation than elements of the state that are more loosely connected to the local culture and more tightly tied to the world-level cultural model. This argument neatly accounts for patterns of uniform isomorphism in world militaries as observed informally by the first author. Armies throughout the world exhibit substantial variation in the color, design, and symbols used on their uniforms. Navies, in contrast, seem to exhibit substantial uniform isomorphism. Most world navies have uniforms that vary little from the British Royal Navy scheme.
48. Laurance, *The International Arms Trade*.

literature on weapons proliferation suggests that the post–World War II era may be marked by three major periods: The immediate postwar and early Cold War period extended through approximately 1968. This period was marked by the relatively restrained aid policies of both superpowers. Weapons transfers were mostly outdated World War II–era equipment; the United States was still transferring World War II–era propeller-driven fighter aircraft to developing countries in the early 1960s. Beginning in the early 1960s and intensifying in the 1970s, the Soviet Union transferred large amounts of relatively "high-tech" equipment to independent and newly independent countries. The United States followed at a lag, and at a relatively reduced rate (with the obvious exception of transfers to a few key states, such as South Vietnam and Israel). This second period continued through the mid-1970s, when the burgeoning oil revenues fostered the development of an increasingly open arms "supermarket." In the third period, arms of increasing sophistication were available to any nation that had the cash, and to many that had only marginal credit. Marked by "let's make a deal" fervor, these black- and gray-market transfers pushed a large volume of weaponry into even the newest and least industrialized states.

The following hypotheses are suggested by the four arguments (superpower, national security, factional interest, institutional theory) reviewed above:

H1. Levels of conventional weaponry will be strongly shaped by patterns of alliance with the United States and the Soviet Union and will be less significantly shaped by local security considerations.

H2. Levels of conventional weaponry will be influenced primarily by the level of strategic military threat directly faced by a nation-state.

H2a. To the degree that national security arguments implicitly discount the role of "status" or "normative" processes or reduce them to residual effects (as described above), they also suggest that indicators of connection to the world system should not be consistently or powerfully related to weapons inventories.

H3. Military regimes will feature a higher level of conventional weaponry than will civilian regimes.

H4: Variation in levels of conventional weaponry will be predicted by variation in the level of connection of a nation-state to the global system. In developing this hypothesis, using the observation made above about variation in level of institutionalization for different weapon systems, we can add:

H4a. Inventory levels of noninstitutionalized weaponry (i.e., that with low symbolic significance, such as propeller aircraft or armored personnel carriers) will be influenced primarily by processes described by national security arguments.

H4b. Inventory levels of highly institutionalized weaponry (i.e., that with high symbolic significance, such as supersonic aircraft) will be influenced primarily by processes described by institutional arguments.[49]

Research Design, Data, and Methods of Analysis

Before proceeding to the details of the data and methods, we will comment briefly on the research design of the empirical investigation. Each of the arguments laid out above makes some claim to the accurate portrayal of some aspect of the growth of Third World militaries. A substantial number of empirical investigations have been conducted, including (1) examinations of broad patterns of international arms transfers, (2) studies of overall military expenditures at the country level, (3) efforts at understanding the growth of overall military capability, through the use of aggregate indicators of military capability, and (4) examinations of arms merchant behavior.[50] However, the dominant forms of empirical investigation have been the country- or region-focused case study and the econometrically flavored examination of levels of military spending. Each has a weakness. Country studies make the recognition of world-level processes difficult, while existing quantitative work, with its focus on sin-

---

49. Here we insert a brief confession of academic unworthiness, in order to reinforce the point we made earlier. The argument that objects that vary in their degree of symbolic significance should exhibit different patterns of diffusion within the world system is a reasonable extension of institutional theory. Developing means of assessing the symbolic significance remains an important task, one that we have not yet tackled. We proceed with this preliminary investigation based on the *assumption* that "high-tech" weaponry is emblematic of modern militaries and modern states. We believe that this assumption (and our current instantiation of it) is a reasonable starting point for empirical analysis. Moving beyond this assumption, through a theoretically informed, empirical assessment of symbolic significance, is an important future task. We also note, following the comments of one reviewer, that the ability to produce weaponry may also be symbolically significant. We agree and suggest that the arguments we have made would apply, mutatis mutandis.

50. Empirical investigations of the subject (summarized in Mullins, *Born Arming*; and Laurance, *The International Arms Trade*) have been conducted, including: (1) examinations of broad patterns of international arms transfers (e.g., Michael Klare, *The American Arms Supermarket* [Austin: University of Texas Press, 1984]), (2) studies of overall military expenditures at the country level (e.g., Robert E. Looney, *Third World Military Expenditure and Arms Production* [London: Macmillan, 1988]), (3) efforts at understanding the growth of overall military capability, through the use of aggregate indicators of military capability (e.g., Mullins, *Born Arming*).

gle indicators of military expenditure or capability, is, although sophisticated, perhaps too coarse-grained in its choice of dependent variables. Both sorts of analysis run the risk of obscuring potentially important aspects of the actual mechanics of proliferation. Relatively lacking thus far have been efforts to unpack the proliferation process and to conduct large-scale quantitative investigations of the spread of military organizational forms and individual weapon systems throughout the world. The preliminary work reported here is intended to fill this gap. In its more fine-grained view of the proliferation process, it will offer a view of the arms trade that has not been developed in existing studies. By its examination of the proliferation of individual weapon types, this investigation is designed to sharpen our understanding of the processes that drive the proliferation of weaponry in the developing world.

Measures and Indicators—Dependent Variables

Below, we will report results from the examination of a series of ordinary least squares cross-sectional regression models that evaluate the hypotheses discussed above. We have conducted a cross-sectional regression analysis of weapons inventories during the period from 1970 to 1990 (with 1970, 1980, and 1990 as target time points), using country-level weapons inventories (i.e., counts of weapons of various types possessed by a country) as dependent variables. Inventories of world militaries are drawn from a variety of published sources. The most significant are the International Institute for Strategic Studies' *The Military Balance*; the Stockholm International Peace Research Institute's *Arms Trade Registers* (covering 1950 to 1973) and *Arms Transfers to the Third World* (covering 1971 to 1985), and *Defense and Foreign Affairs Handbook.*[51] The data set used in the analyses reported for 1970, 1980, and 1990 (tables 3.1 and 3.2) for the developing world includes inventories for the states that became independent during the burst of decolonization following the independence of Ghana in 1957 through the mid-1980s. Not included are "microstates," those states with populations of fewer than about 750,000.[52] The analysis reported in table

---

51. International Institute for Strategic Studies, *The Military Balance 1993–1994* (London: Brassey's, 1993); Stockholm International Peace Research Institute, *The Arms Trade Registers* (Cambridge: MIT Press, 1975); and Stockholm International Peace Research Institute, *Arms Transfers to the Third World 1971–1985* (Cambridge: MIT Press, 1987).

52. We have chosen this population of states, and not included the microstates, for research design reasons. It can be argued that both acquisition of weaponry and IGO membership are prompted by a third variable, relative importance in world politics. Larger or "leader" states do more of both. This

3.3 covers *all* non-micro nation-states for which data were available in 1980. For both analyses, individual weapon systems inventories are aggregated into three basic categories: propeller-driven aircraft, supersonic aircraft, and armored personnel carriers. Propeller-driven aircraft include all ground-attack and transportation/utility aircraft in the military inventory, though most in this category are transportation aircraft. Supersonic aircraft include all aircraft in the military inventory identified as having supersonic capability, regardless of role. Armored personnel carriers include all armored vehicles, whether tracked or wheeled, designed for troop transportation. No differentiation is made between vehicles designed to be fought from and vehicles designed solely for transportation. Although these categories are somewhat crude and do not capture wide variations in the performance of weapon systems, they should adequately capture important similarities in the symbolic value of the weapon systems.

Measures and Indicators—Independent Variables

The independent variables used in this analysis are drawn primarily from the Data Bank on Political and Socioeconomic Development available from the Hoover Institution on War, Revolution, and Peace. This data bank provides more than three thousand economic, social, political, and cultural measures for 126 countries for the period 1950 to 1992. The majority of the data are drawn from United Nations or World Bank statistical sources.

Some of the common empirical indicators of connection used in institutional investigations are the nation-state's number of diplomatic representatives abroad and its number of memberships in international governmental organizations (e.g., United Nations, International Postal Union). The standard practice of most institutional theory empirical investigations is to use the number of *international governmental organization* (IGO) memberships as the indicator of connectedness to the world system. Strong theoretical and empirical justification exists for the routine use of this variable as an indicator of the degree of connection of a country to the

---

argument has some merit; but in restricting our primary population to developing-world states, we do not include those "core" states that are most important in world politics. While it still may be possible to argue that there is variation in importance in world politics within the population, the argument becomes less compelling. For similar reasons, not including microstates eliminates those states for which any but the most minor involvement in world politics would be a significant strain. Further empirical examination of this argument awaits a more sophisticated research effort.

world polity, with more memberships indicating a higher degree of connection.[53]

Measuring the relative political power of the military within a regime is a difficult task. While a number of somewhat successful efforts have been recorded, they have seldom been done both on a worldwide scale and over a significant period of time. Therefore, as a indicator of *type of regime* (Regime) we shall use the presence of a military officer as president, prime minister, or head of state. This is coded as a dummy variable and is admittedly a very rough indicator of military power within a government. We undertook a similar effort to examine the impact of authoritarian regimes as a part of the preliminary research effort, but the results paralleled those obtained by using the military regime indicator, and therefore we used the simpler military regime coding in R the final analyses.

Gross national product per capita (GNPPC), as measured in constant 1980 dollars, is used as an indicator of national development.

Obviously, constructing broadly applicable indicators of military threat is a difficult task. Perceived threat is shaped by a wide variety of factors that are unique to each potential conflict situation. Nonetheless, some widely applicable indicators can be identified; these fall into two broad classes, one based on strategic situation or potential threat and the other based on actual conflict experience. The *number of bordering countries* (Border) serves as a rough indicator of the potential for friction, while the fraction of a country's history spent at war, measured as the *number of years at war as a fraction of years of independence* (Years at War), captures a country's military experience. This indicator (drawn from Kidron and Smith)[54] and others include both international/cross-border wars and internal conflicts.[55]

Geopolitical alignment (Alignment) was used as an indicator of tie to the superpowers. Following Kidron and Smith, the general orientation of countries was assessed as pro-West, nonaligned, or pro-East.[56] This repre-

---

53. For example, see Thomas and Lauderdale, "State Authority and National Welfare Programs in the World System Context."

54. See Michael Kidron and Dan Smith, *The War Atlas: Armed Conflict—Armed Peace* (New York: Simon and Schuster, 1983).

55. While one might wish for a more individually tailored indicator of perceived threat, the conceptual and practical details involved in creating such an indicator are significant. Nonetheless, we stand by the use of the Years at War variable as a reasonable indicator of threat. Countries with a high level of involvement in warfare probably perceive greater threats than countries with long histories of peace.

56. Kidron and Smith, *The War Atlas*.

sents an assessment of a country's political allegiance and an effort to identify the state's main policy direction. It considers, but is not limited to, formal alliance or friendship pacts. In our preliminary efforts for this study, we used two dichotomous variables, one for alignment with the West, the other for alignment with the East, with "nonaligned" being the reference category. The dummy variable for West was not significant in any of the equations, and removing it from the equations did not alter the parameter estimates or substantive conclusions in any significant way. This does not, of course, mean that the West did not transfer arms to its allies; it means only that Western allies did not receive significantly more or fewer arms, overall, than did nonaligned nations. The West dummy variable is therefore not included in the final analyses. The Alignment variable is coded 0 for nonaligned or aligned with the West or 1 for aligned with the East/Soviet Union. For the examination of the world inventories of supersonic aircraft in 1980, an additional dichotomous variable was included to indicate membership in the *industrial core* (Core), either East or West, with 0 coded as outside of the core and 1 as a core member.

As appropriate, each variable is also identified by a suffix indicating the year the variable was measured (e.g., IGO82 indicates that the variable measures the number of international governmental organizations that a country belonged to in 1982). All dependent variables are measured in the year of the equation. Selection of appropriate lag times for independent variables is always a significant issue; however, for these analyses, variations in lag affected the relative significance of variables only modestly; for this investigation, a standard one-year lag was selected for purposes of simplicity. The exceptions to this are the IGO variables, which were available only for the years 1966, 1977, and 1982. This introduces an exceptionally long lag for the IGO variable in the 1990 equations, which should be expected therefore to attenuate the impact of the IGO variable on 1990 inventories.

Results

The three tables included in this essay present the results of a series of regression analyses. Table 3.1 covers analyses of weapons inventories of the newly independent states in 1980, Table 3.2 examines analyses of weapons inventories of the newly independent states in 1990, and Table 3.3 presents results of a regression analysis for inventories of supersonic aircraft for the entire world (again, minus microstates of under 750,000 population) for 1980. Tables 3.1 and 3.2 present the results for regressions of all of the independent variables on the three weapon systems categories: supersonic aircraft, propeller-driven aircraft, and armored personnel carriers. The tables show the number of cases and the R^2 for each of the individual equations. The coefficients reported below each R^2 are the standardized regression coefficients for each independent variable, along with their approximate significance levels.

Before turning to the tables, however, we must discuss the results of the 1970 equations. For all three of the equations the R^2 was exceptionally small and the equations were not significant. There were thirty-eight states in the 1970 analysis, and their inventory levels were relatively small. Few nation-states in the sample were more than ten years old, and most still featured militaries that resembled those left by the colonial powers. Because these units were designed primarily for colonial police missions, the military legacy left by the colonial powers was dominated by dismounted infantry formations and relatively low levels of equipment. In the case of Britain, this was a de facto policy; in the case of France, a formal policy was implemented to keep postcolonial militaries relatively small and internally oriented, with France sharing the external defense burden. Equipment deliveries from all sources to the newly independent states were relatively modest, and few, if any, states had developed any military industrial capacity at all.

Turning to the 1980 and 1990 equations, we find a very different pattern. All six equations are significant at or below the .01 level. The first

TABLE 3.1

Regression Results, Newly Independent States, Year =1980

Dependent Variable	Supersonic	Propeller Aircraft	Personnel Carriers
n =	57	57	57
R^2 =	.360	.360	.304
Years of War	.323**	.465**	.322**
Border	-.141	.325	-.145
IGO77	.390***	.079	.244**
CNPPC79	.101	.034	.130
Regime	.120	-.120	.210
Alignment	.355**	-.308**	.276*

Table shows standardized coefficient, with p values identified as follows:
*** = less than .01
** = less than .05
* = less than .1

finding that should be noted concerns the R^2 for the equations. Overall, the models fit the data reasonably well, with the 1990 equations seeming to fit slightly better on average. In both sets of equations, the Years at War variable is consistently significant and positive. In most of the equations it also has the largest standardized coefficient. The second threat indicator, Border, is not significant in any of the equations. Regime is also not significant in any equation. IGO is significant in five of the six equations in the 1980 and 1990 analyses; the only equation in which it is not significant is the 1980 propeller aircraft equation. Gross national product per capita (GNPPC) is not significant in any equation in the 1980 analysis but is significant in the supersonic aircraft and armored personnel carrier equations in the 1990 analysis. Finally, the Alignment variable is significant and positive in four of the six equations, significant and negative in the propeller aircraft 1980 equation, and not significant and negative in the 1990 propeller aircraft equation. In the 1980 world equation (table 3.3) we see a very similar pattern, with the Years at War, IGO, GNPPC, and Alignment variables positive and significant.

Comparing the findings with the hypotheses, we see first that the national security argument is strongly supported by the consistent positive effect of Years at War. In conjunction with the lack of significant effects by the Border variable, this result strongly suggests that countries should pay attention to their histories of conflict, and not to more abstract indicators of potential conflict, when making weapons acquisition decisions. In contrast with "hard" national security arguments, however, which tend to

TABLE 3.2

Regression Results, Newly Independent States, Year = 1990

Dependent Variable	Supersonic	Propeller Aircraft	Personnel Carriers
n =	57	57	57
R^2 =	.461	.362	.435
Years of War	.406***	.465**	.390***
Border	-.042	.064	.036
IGO82	.210*	.331**	.200*
GNPPC89	.288**	.059	.533***
Regime	.133	.050	.178
Alignment	.426***	-.060	.212*

Table shows standardized coefficient, with p values identified as follows:
*** = less than .01
** = less than .05
* = less than .1

employ cultural arguments as ad hoc explanations for idiosyncratic cases, the second notable finding is the consistent relationship between international governmental organization membership (IGO) and the number of weapons possessed by a country. This finding provides substantively significant support for institutionalist arguments. Indeed, it appears that international organizational membership is significantly related not merely to those weapons that were seen as highly symbolically significant (supersonic aircraft) but also to weapons that were seen as of lesser symbolic significance (armored personnel carriers). This finding can be interpreted as supporting a "strong" institutionalist argument. That is, at least for newly independent states, possession of any of the trappings of a modern military may be of symbolic significance.[57] It should be noted that the significance of the Years at War variable does not directly challenge institutionalist arguments, which do not deny the significance of functional factors. Rather, institutional arguments point out that functional requirements are responded to in socially structured ways: modern militaries are seen as the appropriate response to war (rather than other possible responses, including target hardening, civilian- or reserve-based defense, or prayer) because of the highly institutionalized linkage between the nation-state and the military.

The second major issue raised by these results concerns the assessment of the symbolic significance of various weapons. For our purposes, an a priori assumption was made: jets, supersonic aircraft, main battle tanks,

---

57. Our logic in making this assertion is as follows: Previous institutionalist empirical investigations (as noted above) have consistently found that IGO membership predicts adherence to world cultural models of statehood. The statement "the more a nation-state is connected to the larger world system, the more it follows the established cultural model of statehood" is strongly supported by empirical evidence (cf. Thomas et al., *Institutional Structure*). We have extended institutional theory through our arguments that social practices may vary in degree of institutionalization and that these variations should affect patterns of diffusion. In order to conduct a preliminary empirical evaluation of this extension, we have made an analytically necessary assumption: that supersonic aircraft have more symbolic significance than armored personnel carriers and propeller aircraft. As is often the case, the results were mixed. In 1980, IGO77 was significant in the equations for supersonic aircraft and personnel carriers but not in the equation of propeller aircraft. IGO82 was significant in all of the equations for 1990. These results can be interpreted as (a) disconfirming our extension of institutional theory, (b) disconfirming institutional arguments in general, or (c) disconfirming our analytic assumption but being generally in accord with institutional theory. We have chosen (c) because the overall pattern of our results strongly resembles patterns of results in other institutionalist investigations and because we realize that our initial analytic assumption is just that, an initial assumption. It is grounded in a plausible argument, but it remains an auxiliary assumption rather than a theoretically justified, empirically assessed position. Mechanization, it is equally plausible to argue, may be symbolically equivalent (for armies) to high-performance aircraft (for air forces).

and (for later analysis) large naval vessels were assumed to be weapons of high symbolic significance. The results discussed above, and conversations with foreign military trainers, have suggested that many elements of the modern military system may have substantial symbolic significance. Devising a means for systematically assessing the symbolic significance of weaponry remains an important task. The level of technological sophistication involved in a weapon system is clearly one variable that contributes to symbolic value. But the visibility of a weapon may also have much to do with its symbolic value. We are currently proceeding with a study on demonstration effects by examining the proliferation of Exocet missiles after the Falkland Islands war. The results of this preliminary empirical work make it clear that development of a theoretically justified assessment of symbolic significance is a central research task.

The lack of significance of the Regime variable is interesting but not inexplicable. Military regimes may indeed spend more on military budgets and not buy more military hardware. Budgets may very well go to salaries and personal comfort rather than to organizational capability. While we cannot discount the possibility that military power within the nation-state may more profoundly shape procurement patterns—although the effect may be masked by the admittedly crude measure of military power—we can with some safety assume that this effect is not the primary motor driving weapons proliferation.

The Alignment variable shows that a strong connection to the Soviet Union has a substantial impact on force structure: the average state connected to the Soviet Union in 1980 had approximately twelve more supersonic aircraft and one hundred more armored personnel carriers than the average nonaligned/West-aligned state. In 1990 the effect was similar: aligned states had approximately twenty-five more supersonic aircraft and ninety more armored personnel carriers than the reference group. The negative effect of alignment in the propeller equation is interesting. The average Soviet-aligned state has about six fewer propeller aircraft than the reference group. This result may reflect a propensity on the part of the Soviet Union to transfer helicopters rather than propeller aircraft: in equations (not reported in the tables) for helicopter inventories, the alignment variable is positive and significant, with the average aligned state having five to six more helicopters. Again, it should be noted that the absence of an effect for alignment with the West does not mean lack of Western transfers; it suggests instead a lack of differentiation in Western transfers.

The pattern of significance for the GNPPC variable is interesting. Although insignificant in the 1980 emerging-nation equations, it is significant and positive in two of the three 1990 emerging-nation equations and in the 1980 world equations as well. This outcome may reflect the dynamics of an aggressive marketing effort by major suppliers in the middle period of the arms supermarket. During this rather frenzied time, suppliers may very well have hung out signs that said, in effect, "Credit is no object. Your good name (as a country) is your credit." Certainly this effect was seen in bank loan patterns, as the credit-refinancing crunch of the late 1980s demonstrated. The 1990 equations may reflect the impact of this tightening credit, with propeller aircraft (which have much broader utility and generally much cheaper prices) the only exception.

Before closing, we should review the significance of the 1980 world equation. The world equation includes 138 nation-states, all the countries of the world except for the microstates. The Core variable has a significant effect, and core nations have more supersonic aircraft than noncore nations, but the effects of other variables in the equation are similar to their effects in the developing-world equations. This outcome suggests that the effect captured by the IGO variable is relatively robust and is not unique to the developing world or to the formation of new militaries in newly independent states.

In this essay we have tried to do two things. First, we have summarized a theoretical approach capable of moving beyond the ad hoc nature of existing arguments about the role of status and norms in weapons proliferation.

TABLE 3.3

Regression Results, World, Year =1980	
Dependent Variable	LSSAC80
n=	138
$R^2 =$	.502
Log Years of War	.330***
Border	.147
IGO77	.256***
GNPPC79	.264***
Regime	.067
Alignment	.247***
Core	.207*

Table shows standardized coefficient,
with p values identified as follows:
*** = less than .01
** = less than .05
* = less than .1

Institutional theory provides a vocabulary and a research tradition comparable in sophistication and structure to existing theoretical approaches to weapons proliferation. Second, we have conducted a preliminary empirical investigation employing these arguments. We have argued that the acquisition of modern weaponry, like the acquisition of a flag, is at least in part a product of world-level cultural definitions of the modern nation-state. The results reviewed above provide some modest, tentative support for our arguments. The theoretical structure of institutional theory, the empirical research informed by it in other substantive areas, and the initial empirical results presented here suggest that institutional theory offers significant insights into the process of weapons proliferation.

In the remainder of this essay we would like to look beyond our initial results and discuss directions for further work. We suggest that this effort be approached not as a process of adjudication, pitting theory against theory in some intellectual version of a World Wrestling Federation loser-leaves-town-winner-takes-all grudge match, but as a process of dialogue, framing more-sophisticated and -nuanced arguments in order to capture important variations in social processes. Weapons proliferation is a complex phenomenon that is unlikely to be explained fully by any single theoretical vocabulary. Theoretical rivalry serves understanding only if it later builds to theoretical synthesis. We have elsewhere laid out suggestions for this process.[58] Here we wish to focus our attention on the development of institutional theory and empirical analysis.

As a first step, we note that the arguments we have laid out have not specified the mechanisms of influence upon which institutional processes are dependent. How is it that world-level cultural models shape the acquisition behaviors of particular nation-states? Full explication of these mechanisms is beyond the scope of this essay; it is, however, possible at least to suggest some mechanisms that may serve to carry cultural expectations into the nation-state.

Institutional theory has attended to this issue. When examining the growth and development of the nation-state, institutional theory has primarily emphasized the role of international organizations as "teachers of norms."[59] For example, McNeely notes that international organizations

---

58. Mark C. Suchman and Dana P. Eyre, "Military Procurement as Rational Myth: Notes on the Social Construction of Weapons Proliferation," *Sociological Forum* 7 (1992): 137–61.

59. Martha Finnemore, "Restraining State Violence: The International Red Cross as a Teacher of Humanitarian Norms" (paper prepared for delivery at the 1992 annual meeting of the American Political Science Association).

such as the UN serve to convey a wide variety of expectations to member states, and Finnemore also traces the powerful role played by UNESCO in the establishment of national science policy boards.[60] But this organizational- or regime-based mechanism is clearly absent in the world military system. With the exception of NATO and the Warsaw Pact, the world military system has no formal international organization or regime with a significant standardizing effect. Thus, while the International Organization for Lappish Culture and Reindeer Husbandry may have the effect of standardizing the forms and practices of reindeer husbandry, no similar organization exists to account for similarity of form and practice in modern military organizations.

Institutional theory, however, when examining the role of cultural processes at the organizational level, has emphasized an additional set of cultural carriers. At this level the role of professional processes in both the emergence and the spread of organizational forms is significant. For example, Meyer and others examine the role of professional processes in educational organizations, Scott looks at these processes in mental health organizations, and DiMaggio examines the construction and spread of the modern American art museum.[61]

While the exact role of professional processes in the emergence and spread of organizational forms varies in each case, all share a common set of elements, including the development of a unique professional identity, the development of a theorized body of knowledge, the development of professional organizations, increases in the density of intraorganizational contacts between professionals, increases in the flow of organization, and the emergence of a collective definition of the field.[62] Students of military sociology and civil-military relations will recognize that this is the story of the development of the professional officer corps in the early modern era. But while the story of the emergence of the professional officer within the

---

60. McNeely, "Cultural Isomorphism Among Nation-States"; Martha Finnemore, "Science, the State, and International Society (Ph.D. diss., Stanford University, 1991).
61. See, for example, John W. Meyer and W. Richard Scott, with the assistance of Brian Rowan and Terrence E. Deal, *Organizational Environments: Ritual and Rationality* (Newbury Park, Calif.: Sage, 1983), for examinations of the role of professional processes in educational organizations; W. Richard Scott, "The Organization of Medical Care Services: Toward an Integrated Theoretical Model," *Medical Care Review* 59 (1993): 271–302, for a discussion of the role of these processes in mental health organizations; and Paul DiMaggio, "Constructing an Organizational Field as a Professional Project: U.S. Art Museums, 1920–1940," in Powell and DiMaggio, *The New Institutionalism in Organizational Analysis*, pp. 267–92, for a discussion of the growth of art museums.
62. DiMaggio, "Constructing an Organizational Field as a Professional Project."

nation-state is familiar, the story of the development of transnational connections within the military profession is less well known.

Our study of this process is in the early stages, but it is sufficiently well developed to outline these linkages. There are at least two key sets of linkages between military professionals that cross national boundaries. The first is the exchange of liaison officers and observers and the development of exchange officers in military schools. While this process has been carried out between developed nations at a relatively modest pace for at least a hundred years, the international exchange of officers has picked up substantially in the post–World War II era. For example, the United States Army's Command and General Staff College usually has students from some fifty to sixty nations attending its courses in any given year. Attendance at military schools in the developed world is very common for military officers from the developing world; indeed, even during the Cold War some Third World officers had the no doubt stimulating and unusual experience of attending both American and Soviet, or American and Chinese, military courses.

The second major set of linkages is the development of an international defense literature. While some of this material is the product of official defense establishments (for example, some U.S. Army professional journals have Spanish editions), the largest part of it is of commercial origin. *Jane's Defense Weekly, Aviation Week and Space Technology*, and *Flight* are but a few examples of this substantial body of literature. Thus, to a degree that may be unexpected by those who assume that security considerations restrict the flow of defense information across borders, the military profession is marked internationally by many of the same features that other professions exhibit. It seems therefore that many of the same carriers responsible for the transmission of cultural definitions of appropriate behavior in other organizational sectors are also present within the military sector.

Empirical investigation of these arguments needs to proceed along several lines. Along with the development of more-sophisticated quantitative indicators of critical concepts, quantitative work needs to be done employing more-sophisticated techniques, such as event history analysis and sequence analysis.[63] Case study methods also promise insight into the processes described by institutional theory. In particular, case studies offer

---

63. For event history analysis, see Nancy Brandon Tuma and Michael T. Hannan, *Social Dynamics: Models and Methods* (Orlando: Academic Press, 1984); for sequence analysis, see Andrew Abbott and Alexandra Hrycak, "Measuring Resemblance in Sequence Data: An Optimal Matching Analysis of Musicians' Careers," *American Journal of Sociology* 96, no. 1 (1990): 144–85.

the ability to assess the degree and nature of connection between states and the larger world culture. The utility of the case study is not unlimited, however. Case studies of individual weapons acquisition processes by individual countries fall victim to the problem noted above: myopic focus on individual cases means that world-level processes are seen only as distant blurs, if at all.

In summary, we have reviewed thinking about the role of status and norms in the proliferation of weaponry. Using institutional theory, we have reformulated these arguments in a way that allows for quantitative empirical evaluation, and, briefly, we have suggested some mechanisms through which cultural models may be transmitted. The results of this effort offer substantial insight into the role of normative processes in weapons proliferation. Norms, we suggest, do not directly cause the acquisition of a particular weapon. Nation-states do not buy particular weapons exclusively to enhance their prestige. Rather, the creation of a military and the acquisition of the basic "tools of the trade" both confer and confirm the central cultural construct of "statehood" wihin the modern world system. The more a nation interacts with this larger cultural environment, the more it tends to assert and authenticate its sovereign status with the ultimate symbol of nationhood, a military.

4 • Norms and Deterrence: The Nuclear and Chemical Weapons Taboos

Richard Price and Nina Tannenwald

The concept of deterrence has been central to traditional international security studies. Deterrence has been invoked as the primary explanation for two central phenomena of twentieth-century international relations—the non-use of nuclear weapons and the non-use of chemical weapons. Yet, upon closer examination, it becomes clear that the conventional notion of deterrence—based on a rationalist account—does not by itself adequately account for the practice of non-use of these weapons. Instead, a significant normative element must be taken into account in explaining why these weapons have remained unused. Moreover, closer examination also reveals that rationalist explanations for the development of these norms themselves are indeterminate at best or mistaken at worst.

This essay offers an alternative view on deterrence and the non-use of nuclear and chemical weapons, one that highlights the socially constructed nature of deterrence and deterrent weapons. We argue that in order to fully account for why these weapons have remained unused, we

For their helpful comments and criticisms, we would like to thank the participants in the conferences at Cornell, Minnesota, and Stanford, and especially Judith Goldstein, Ronald Jepperson, Peter Katzenstein, Jeffrey Legro, Diana Richards, Scott Sagan, Alexander Wendt, and the late Richard Smoke.

must problematize, not assume, their status as deterrent weapons. The patterns of non-use of these weapons cannot be fully understood without taking into account the development of prohibitionary norms that shaped these weapons as unacceptable "weapons of mass destruction." Moreover, we argue that constructivist accounts are needed to redress gaps or mistakes in existing explanations for the origins and development of these norms.

The discussion presented here consists of four parts. It begins with a critique of the traditional conception of deterrence—a realist explanation that assumes that states are unified rational actors acting on the basis of exogenously given self-interest. We argue that the explanatory power of this conception in accounting for "non-use" is severely limited by its ultimate indeterminacy: it is impossible to know "what deters" or why a practice of non-use has arisen without investigating the normative context in which actor identities and interests are defined. Thus it is not that realist deterrence theory is entirely wrong so much as it is uninterested in the kinds of questions necessary for a full understanding of the phenomenon of the non-use of nuclear and chemical weapons. Positing deterrence as an unproblematic variable elides the question of how certain weapons have been defined as deterrent weapons whereas other weapons have not.

We then suggest social constructivist approaches that problematize the issue of non-use, the nature of the technology and weapons involved, and the notion of actor self-interest upon which traditional deterrence theory is based. The genealogical approach to the chemical weapons (cw) taboo and the social construction of nuclear deterrence both argue that in order to understand the anomalous status and patterns of non-use of chemical and nuclear weapons, it is necessary to understand how particular social and cultural meanings become attached to certain kinds of weapons, how these normative understandings arise historically through actor practices and interpretations thereof, and how they shape actors' conceptions of their interests and identities.

The second and third sections of the essay then suggest how these two constructivist perspectives, respectively, illuminate the two empirical cases—chemical and nuclear. These cases provide a useful comparison, since their domains of analysis are somewhat different. The cw taboo originated largely at the systemic level, while the nuclear taboo arose domestically, principally (although not entirely) in the United States and was then diffused transnationally. These sections highlight how the different conceptual puzzles opened up by these approaches result in a more complete account of the origins and roles of norms in international relations. They briefly sketch the historical development of the respective non-use norms, describe how they enter into an account of the non-use of these weapons, and then suggest several ways these norms have affected the substance of international politics. If anarchy and self-help are "what states make of it," then these non-use norms have constrained self-help by delegitimating certain kinds of military technologies.[1] More broadly, if the "structure" of the international system is understood to include both material and ideational elements, then these norms have come to play a significant role in structuring a certain kind of hierarchical world order in the post–Cold War era.[2]

The final section of the essay evaluates some of the similarities and differences in the two cases with respect to the origins and role of prohibitionary norms in international politics. It summarizes a constructivist perspective on norms, clarifying the relationship between our argument and alternative explanations, as well as how these norms matter and where they came from. It seeks to demonstrate why explanations involving norms are not simply a matter of accounting for "residual variance."

The Social Construction of Deterrence
Explaining Non-use

Deterrence theory, which draws on realist assumptions of unitary state actors and exogenously given interests, focuses its analytical attention on the use of retaliatory threats of force to deter attack.[3] Deterrence is defined as dissuading an adversary from doing something it otherwise would want to do (and which is perceived as threatening) through threats of unacceptable costs. The analytical power of rational deterrence theory derives from a set of simplifying assumptions about how states seek to maximize

---

1. Alexander Wendt, "Anarchy Is What States Make of It: The Social Construction of Power Politics," *International Organization* 46, no. 2 (Spring 1992): 391–425.
2. For constructivist arguments regarding the structure of the international system, see Wendt, "Anarchy Is What States Make of It"; also see David Dessler, "What's at Stake in the Agent-Structure Debate?" *International Organization* 43, no. 3 (Summer 1989): 441–74.
3. Rational deterrence theory posits three basic requirements for deterring an adversary: credible capabilities, a clearly communicated threat, and a credible willingness to carry out the threat. See William Kaufman, "The Requirements of Deterrence," in William Kaufman, ed., *Military Policy and National Security*, p. 19 (Princeton: Princeton University Press, 1956).

their utility. Most deterrence theorists stress a strong material cost-benefit logic to deterrence and a strong rationalism.[4]

The logic of deterrence has been invoked as a primary explanation of the non-use of both nuclear and chemical weapons. As the argument goes, the non-use of these weapons is due substantially to fear of retaliation in kind. They are self-evidently so horrifying and/or destructive that actors acting on the basis of rational self-interest would naturally be deterred from employing them, for fear of the overwhelming devastation that nuclear or chemical retaliation would bring. This parsimonious account provides the dominant explanation for the non-use of nuclear weapons by the superpowers during the Cold War and is often cited as the most important immediate factor in explaining the non-use of cw.[5]

Yet, explanations from deterrence are insufficient by themselves to explain the non-use of either chemical or nuclear weapons. For example, they cannot account for significant cases of the non-use of either weapon when there was no threat of retaliation in kind. For cw, the Spanish Civil War, the Korean War, the French in Indochina and Algeria, the Vietnam War, and the Soviet intervention in Afghanistan are prominent cases. Even during the violence of World War II, cw were not employed in situations where they offered a clear military advantage. To cite but one example, the U.S. did not employ gas warfare against the Japanese, even though there was no threat of retaliation and cw would have been enormously effective against Japanese forces entrenched in the tunnels and caves of the Pacific Islands.

Likewise, a deterrence explanation cannot account for why nuclear weapons were not used by the United States during the first ten years of the nuclear era, when the U.S. possessed a virtual monopoly on nuclear weapons and fear of retaliation was not a dominant concern. In the late 1940s and early 1950s, the United States faced crises in Berlin, Korea, Quemoy and Matsu, and Dien Bien Phu. Yet, despite a perceived weak-

---

4. The best discussion in support of rational deterrence theory is Christopher Aachen and Duncan Snidal, "Rational Deterrence Theory and Comparative Case Studies," *World Politics* 41, no. 2 (January 1989): 143–69. Deterrence theory has at its core rational choice theory, to which it adds a set of assumptions about the nature of strategic actors. Useful discussions are Daniel Little, "Rational Choice Theory," in Daniel Little, *Varieties of Social Explanation*, pp. 39–67 (Boulder: Westview, 1991), and Patrick M. Morgan, *Deterrence: A Conceptual Analysis*, vol. 40, Sage Library of Social Research (Beverly Hills, Calif.: Sage, 1977), pp. 77–100.

5. See, for example, Robert Jervis, *The Meaning of the Nuclear Revolution* (Ithaca: Cornell University Press, 1989); Albert Carnesale et al., *Living with Nuclear Weapons* (Cambridge: Harvard University Press, 1983); and McGeorge Bundy, *Danger and Survival: Choices About the Bomb in the First Fifty Years* (New York: Random House, 1988). On the cw case, see n. 9 below.

ness in U.S conventional military capabilities and a military strategy that relied increasingly upon nuclear weapons, U.S. leaders did not use nuclear weapons during these crises. Later, in the 1991 Persian Gulf war, U.S. officials effectively ruled out use of nuclear weapons against a nonnuclear Iraq, even though a small nuclear weapon could have been militarily effective on the desert battlefield.[6]

Several additional factors suggest why a traditional deterrence explanation is inadequate and raise the issue of the role of normative taboos in shaping the practice of non-use of these weapons. Here the deficiencies in the scholarship on the chemical and nuclear cases diverge somewhat: the literature on cw recognizes that a deterrent explanation alone is inadequate but does not fully explore the mutually constitutive operation of the normative status of cw and its successful definition as a deterrent weapon. In contrast, the nuclear literature by and large finds the deterrence explanation satisfactory. In both cases, however, the acceptance of "deterrence" as more or less unproblematic leads to a slighting of the role of other factors—in particular, normative ones—in shaping the patterns of non-use.

For cw, World War II offers the most studied and spectacular case of non-use, and it is widely recognized in the literature that the avoidance of chemical warfare cannot be attributed solely to deterrence.[7] Indeed, there is a virtual consensus in this literature that attributes this non-event to three major factors:

> The two sides warned each other not to use chemical weapons at the risk of strong retaliatory action in kind; a general feeling of abhorrence on the part of governments for the use of CB weapons, reinforced by the pressure of public opinion and the constraining influence of the Geneva Protocol; and actual unpreparedness within the military forces for the use of these weapons.[8]

---

6. The handful of public calls for U.S. use of tactical nuclear weapons during the Persian Gulf war specifically invoked the 1945 precedent of saving American lives. Mirroring earlier arguments that were employed to justify the use of atomic weapons against Japan, some of the advocates of U.S. nuclear use against Iraqi troops went even further, underscoring the potential savings in lives on *both* sides of the battlefield if the United States used nuclear weapons. See, for example, physicist Lawrence Cranberg's "Tactical Nukes in Iraq: An Option That Could Ultimately Save Lives," *New York City Tribune*, November 20, 1990; Congressman Dan Burton on *Crossfire*, January 11, 1991; John Barry, "The Nuclear Option: Thinking the Unthinkable," *Newsweek*, January 14, 1991, pp. 16–17.

7. Referring to the non-use of cw between the Western Allies and the Axis powers during World War II is not to ignore that cw was employed by Japan in its campaigns in China and that the Germans used gas in their concentration camps.

8. Stockholm International Peace Research Institute (hereafter SIPRI), *The Problem of Chemical and Biological Warfare*, vol. 4, *CB Disarmament Negotiations, 1920–1970* (Stockholm: Almqvist and Wiksell, 1971), p. 21.

It is of signal importance to note that while some authors have privileged individual factors over others for different stages and aspects of the story, none of the major studies has dismissed the prohibitionary norm as irrelevant in the overall explanatory equation.[9] Thus while it has been argued that legal and moral restraints were not central in immediately affecting decisions to avoid using cw,[10] the same authors recognize that the unpreparedness of the military establishments cannot be taken as an unproblematic variable but has to be explained itself. It is here that normative and legal opposition to cw takes pride of place in explaining why cw were not used in World War II, as these restraints were crucial in preventing the assimilation of cw as a standard weapon of war.[11]

On this basis alone, the normative opposition to cw cannot be dismissed as peripheral in preventing the use of cw in World War II. An even stronger case can be made, however, for the impact of the taboo in preventing the use of cw. Just as the literature recognizes that the variable of military preparedness itself has to be explained, it is argued here that the variable of deterrence—the status of cw as a deterrent weapon—also has to be problematized. Why would the fear of retaliatory cw attacks be any more robust a restraint than the fear of other horribly destructive methods of warfare such as incendiary bombing raids or submarine attacks on civilian shipping? If we are to avoid merely begging the question of why a special dread of retaliation operated with respect to cw, we need to understand how the discursive practices of statesmen served to set cw apart as a

9. See Frederic J. Brown, *Chemical Warfare: A Study in Constraints* (Princeton: Princeton University Press, 1968); SIPRI, *The Problem of Chemical and Biological Warfare*, vol. 1, *The Rise of CB Weapons* (Stockholm: Almqvist and Wiksell, 1971); SIPRI, *The Problem of Chemical and Biological Warfare*, vol. 5, *The Prevention of CBW* (Stockholm: Almqvist and Wiksell, 1971); Kenneth Adelman, "Chemical Weapons: Restoring the Taboo," *Orbis 30*, no. 3 (Fall 1986): 444; Susan Wright, "The Military and the New Biology," *Bulletin of the Atomic Scientists* 41, no. 5 (May 1985): 10; and John Ellis van Courtland Moon, "Chemical Warfare: A Forgotten Lesson," *Bulletin of the Atomic Scientists* 45, no. 6 (August 1989): 40–43.

10. SIPRI, *The Rise of CB Weapons*, p. 321; Brown, *Chemical Warfare*, p. 296.

11. SIPRI, *The Rise of CB Weapons*, pp. 334, 322; Brown, *Chemical Warfare*, pp. 293, 295. A number of factors have been identified as contributing to the failure of military establishments to be adequately prepared for chemical warfare in the years leading up to World War II: the uncertain military value of cw, the resistance of tradition-bound military cultures, the extra logistical burden of cw, and so on. Jeffrey W. Legro offers an organizational culture explanation in his richly researched *Cooperation Under Fire: Anglo-German Restraint During World War II* (Ithaca: Cornell University Press, 1995).

Similar kinds of resistance often accompany new weapons technologies, but rarely do they result in total abstinence from using such weapons. The argument here is that what made such factors politically decisive in retarding the acceptance of cw—and thus ultimately prevented their use in World War II—was the existence of a stigma against cw.

symbolic threshold of acute political importance and defined cw as a weapon *that might not be used.*

In sum, the odium attached to cw is indispensable in accounting for their non-use. In the absence of a normative discourse that ostracized and politicized the use of cw as unacceptable, illegal, and reprehensible, a strong counterfactual case could be made for the possibility or even the probability that these weapons eventually would have been assimilated into military arsenals and their use would have proceeded as an uncontroversial and unpoliticized standard practice of warfare.

The nuclear case, in contrast, is in some ways a "harder" case for challenging traditional deterrence theory than that of chemical weapons because it is widely felt that the tremendous destructive power of thermonuclear weapons *does* render them qualitatively different from other weapons (and therefore makes them "natural" deterrent weapons). Also, in contrast to the chemical case, the U.S. military establishment has been fully prepared to use nuclear weapons.

Nevertheless, while a special dread of nuclear weapons may be easier to understand, the opprobrium attached to them—as with cw—does not follow purely "rationally" or logically from the nature of the technology. Use of the atomic bomb by the U.S. on Hiroshima and Nagasaki in 1945 (which caused less destruction than the firestorms in Tokyo a few months earlier) was widely supported in the United States, and moral arguments were invoked as justification.[12] It was only later, when the development of thermonuclear weapons appeared to clearly violate any previously existing conceptions of proportionate weapons, that a normative stigma against nuclear use emerged. But why did the nuclear taboo then come to apply equally to *all* nuclear weapons, small and large, tactical as well as strategic, irrespective of utility considerations? Why did subsequent efforts to pursue such things as "peaceful nuclear explosions" fail, despite the latter's peaceful and practical applications? Or, to take another angle, why have nuclear weapons, supposedly fearsome deterrent weapons, *not* deterred some conventional attacks by nonnuclear states against nuclear states or allies of nuclear states?[13]

---

12. See Paul Boyer, *By the Bomb's Early Light: American Thought and Culture at the Dawn of the Atomic Age* (New York: Pantheon, 1985).

13. China attacked U.S. forces during the Korean War, North Vietnamese forces attacked U.S. forces in Vietnam, Egypt attacked Israel in 1973, Argentina attacked British forces over the Falklands in 1982, and most recently, Iraq attacked Israel and U.S. bases in Saudi Arabia in the Persian Gulf war.

A rational deterrence explanation for nuclear non-use, while capturing some broad outlines of the Cold War nuclear experience, also glosses dangerously over the historical record. In doing so it tends to lend an impression of inevitability to the nuclear non-use tradition that is far from warranted. As military historians remind us, the enormous destructive capability of weapons and the prospect of retaliation cannot be assumed to give rise automatically to rational self-interested avoidance-of-use behavior on the part of actors; such assumptions have failed more often than not in the past. The parsimonious explanation for nuclear non-use obscures the variety of reasons that the bomb did not get used on different occasions, not all of which are "normative," to be sure, but not all of which qualify as "deterrent" either. These include concerns about lack of military effectiveness of bombs, shortage of bombs, disagreement over policy options, public and allied opinion, moral concerns, and, especially, contingency. However, as we discuss further in the fourth section of this essay, clear distinctions between "normative" and "nonnormative" concerns may in actuality be difficult to make. In sum, the overall "pattern of caution" with regard to nuclear use in the postwar era does not mean that in each individual case of nuclear crisis, decision makers were cautious.[14]

In fact, the picture over time of nuclear non-use by the United States suggests a significant role for a normative element in undergirding emerging perceptions of nuclear weapons as lacking in military utility. U.S. restraint with regard to nuclear use was in part a matter of chance, in part a matter of deterrence, but was also shaped in part by emerging American perceptions of nuclear weapons as "disproportionate" (a profoundly normative concern), a view that increasingly clashed with U.S. leaders' perceptions of America's moral identity. Even a "realist" such as John Lewis Gaddis concludes at the end of his examination of nuclear non-use during the early postwar period that moral considerations may have played a significant role.[15]

Explaining the Taboos

Both the nuclear and the cw taboos are norms that matter in international politics. The odium attached to the use of these weapons is indis-

---

14. This is made clear by Richard Betts's careful survey of cases of Cold War nuclear crises in *Nuclear Blackmail and Nuclear Balance* (Washington, D.C.: Brookings Institution, 1987).
15. John Lewis Gaddis, "The Origins of Self-Deterrence: The United States and the Non-use of Nuclear Weapons, 1945–1958," in *The Long Peace: Inquiries into the History of the Cold War*, pp. 104–46 (Oxford: Oxford University Press, 1987).

pensable in explaining their non-use. In addition, these taboos are phenomena that themselves cannot be reduced to the assumptions of deterrence theory. The problem with deterrence theory is not that its logic has never operated in the case of chemical and nuclear weapons but that it does not address the question of how a particular weapon comes to be defined in deterrent terms whereas other weapons do not or that of how actor "interests" with respect to use or non-use come to be defined. How is it that a prohibitive fear of CW has operated over and above the fear of other powerful means of destruction, some of which are accorded the legitimacy of "conventional" weapons despite their capability to wreak more havoc than CW can? Similarly, how have nuclear weapons been defined alternatively as moral or immoral weapons, and how have perceptions of them been shaped such that all uses of nuclear weapons are unacceptable? How did American decision makers come to define their interests with regard to nuclear use? How have both chemical and nuclear weapons been ostracized apart from other weapons as an unacceptable practice of warfare? What do these prohibitions mean for the practice of international politics?

Just as rationalist explanations for the non-use of nuclear and chemical weapons are not fully satisfactory, neither do rationalist explanations for the norms themselves suffice to accommodate some of the peculiarities involved in the origins and operations of these taboos. The argument is often made that CW have not been used, and a norm of non-use has developed, because CW are perceived as being of marginal military utility. While there is a long controversy over the question of utility of CW (because of complications such as wind conditions, logistical burdens, and so forth), this controversy has never been definitively resolved—there has never been unanimous agreement that the use of CW would not be advantageous in certain circumstances. In short, the argument that the CW taboo arose from the lack of utility of CW is not empirically sustainable, as CW have been favorably assessed by military establishments on many occasions.[16]

A second kind of argument also draws upon the intrinsic characteris-

---

16. For example, during World War II, tests were done in the U.S. to determine the effectiveness of using CW against Japanese forces barricaded in the caves and tunnels of the Pacific islands. Even the most cautious assessments of those tests concluded that CW would be effective, while some argued that the tests demonstrated that "gas is the most promising of all weapons for overcoming cave defenses" (John Ellis van Courtland Moon, "Project SPHINX: The Question of the Use of Gas in the Planned Invasion of Japan," *Journal of Strategic Studies* 12, no. 3 [September 1989]: 303–23). See also Richard Price, "A Genealogy of the Chemical Weapons Taboo" (Ph.D diss., Cornell University, 1994).

tics of CW to explain their anomalous status. Michael Mandelbaum has offered an account of the stigma against CW in the course of a comparison between the status of nuclear weapons and that of CW. But while he purports to provide an argument based on cultural and institutional restraints, in the end his case rests on the implausible argument that the opposition to CW is a genetic aversion rooted in human chromosomes.[17] His argument fails because, like arguments that ascribe the norm to the lack of utility of CW, it is premised on the assumption that there must be a rational reason for the taboo that can be deduced from the essential features of these weapons.

Likewise, it is often pointed out that while the United States did contemplate using nuclear weapons on several occasions, it never faced a situation in which its vital interests were at stake. The intended point is that the real "hard test" case for a constraining norm never materialized. This may be true, but it misses what is interesting here, which is precisely that historically, *despite* the fact that nuclear weapons are indeed qualitatively different, U.S. leaders on various occasions contemplated their use in cases of less than overwhelming national interest. This situation provides telling contrast with today's widely shared assumption that nuclear use could be morally contemplated only in the direst of circumstances (if at all). The historical comparison reminds us that the revolutionary nature of the weapons was not evident to all.

Further, the particular domestic sources of the nuclear taboo—a democratic United States—were crucial in shaping interpretations of these weapons as unusable. While a rationalist account may tell some of the nuclear story, ignoring questions about identity and thus taking interests as given leaves rational deterrence theory fundamentally unable to explain the criteria for "deterrence"—that is, what goes into leaders' calculations of "unacceptable costs." For similar reasons, rationalist regime theory, because it neglects identity, may offer an inadequate account of norms. With its ahistorical approach, rationalist regime theory has little to say about the origins and evolution of norms and practices that cannot be conceived as simply the rational calculation of the national interest.[18]

---

17. See his *Nuclear Revolution* (Cambridge: Cambridge University Press, 1981), pp. 39, 48.

18. As noted by Robert Keohane, "International Institutions: Two Approaches," in Robert Keohane, *International Institutions and State Power: Essays in International Relations Theory*, pp. 158–79 (Boulder: Westview, 1989). To cite but one example, the U.S. was the dominant force behind interwar efforts to proscribe CW, even though it was recognized that the country would be giving up a material advantage with such a prohibition. See the remarks of the Navy Board in U.S. Senate, *Disarmament and Security: A Collection of Documents, 1919–55* (Washington, D.C.: Government Printing Office, 1956), p. 701.

Actually, both the nuclear and the CW taboos resist the parsimonious explanations offered by rationalist approaches. It is precisely the widely recognized anomaly that taboos may embody an "irrational" attitude toward technology—a norm that defies the realist dictum that only useless weapons are banned—that makes the origins and persistence of these norms such an intriguing puzzle.

For these reasons, it is clear that an account of the chemical and nuclear taboos requires an investigation into the meanings and social practices that have constituted these norms. As James Johnson argues, moral decision making must be understood as "essentially historical in character, an attempt to find continuity between present and past, and not an ahistorical activity of the rational mind."[19] That is, the nature of the question plays to the strengths of constructivist approaches to norms. Such approaches are provided by the genealogical method, on the one hand, and a "social construction of deterrence" approach, on the other. The differences in the two approaches lie in the primary analytical focus: the genealogical approach focuses on understanding how norms are constituted through social and discursive practices and how these discourses normalize or delegitimate forms of behavior; the social construction of deterrence perspective emphasizes the relationship between norms, identities, and interests and provides a causal explanation of how the norm affects outcomes. As will be made clear, these two approaches offer complementary methods of analyzing norms.

The genealogical method, a mode of analysis articulated by Friedrich Nietzsche and popularized more recently by Michel Foucault, is particularly appropriate for shedding light on the case of the CW taboo, for several reasons.[20] Not only is it a method specifically concerned with the origins and operations of moral discourses, but it also emphasizes the role that contingency and chance play in the constitution of moral institutions. As will be discussed below, such fortuitous factors played a major role in the origins and development of the prohibition against the use of CW. In addition, the genealogy is a constructivist approach and is thus well suited to the contention of this essay that the CW taboo is a political construction that cannot be adequately explained solely by virtue of the intrinsic qualities of CW.

19. James Turner Johnson, *Just War Tradition and the Restraint of War: A Moral and Historical Inquiry* (Princeton: Princeton University Press, 1981), p. x.
20. See Friedrich Nietzsche, *On the Genealogy of Morals*, trans. Walter Kaufmann and R. J. Hollingdale (New York: Vintage Books, 1989); and Michel Foucault, "Nietzsche, Genealogy, History," in Paul Rabinow, ed., *The Foucault Reader*, pp. 76–100 (New York: Pantheon, 1984).

Besides remedying the deficiencies of rationalist approaches by historicizing moral institutions, this study of the CW taboo draws upon the genealogical method through its analytic focus on moral discourses. Discourses produce and legitimate certain behaviors and conditions of life as "normal" and, conversely, construct categories that themselves make a cluster of practices and understandings seem inconceivable or illegitimate.

Prohibitionary norms in this sense do not merely restrain behavior but are implicated in the productive process of constituting identities as well: actors have images of themselves as agents who do or don't do certain sorts of things. Unlike some approaches, which seek to distance the study of norms from power, then, the genealogy in this way implicates norms in hierarchical relations of domination and resistance. Drawing upon these insights of the genealogy illuminates aspects of the origins, functions, and development of the CW taboo that have gone underanalyzed in the literature. All of this results in a better appreciation of the sources and robustness of this remarkable success in banning a weapon of war.

A social constructivist perspective on deterrence also problematizes the social and historical construction of deterrence, but that approach takes as its analytical focus the interaction between norms and the constitution of identities and interests of the actors involved. It holds that in order to determine "what deters," the identity and interests of actors have to be investigated. A social constructivist approach is explicitly interested in the relationships among norms, interests, and outcomes but conceives of norms very differently from the way a rationalist account does. In a rationalist view, norms constrain exogenously given self-interest and behavior or lead to recalculations of self-interest. In the constructivist view—developed primarily in the sociological literature—norms shape conceptualizations of interests through the social construction of identities.[21] Actors conform to norms in order to validate social identities, and it is in the process of validating identities that interests are constituted. Thus both the creation, and reproduction, of norms and their salience for actors are inseparable from the social constitution of actors' identities.

Both of these approaches open up sets of questions different from those that are typically posed by the dominant approaches in international rela-

---

21. Francesca Cancian, *What Are Norms? A Study of Beliefs and Action in a Maya Community* (Cambridge: Cambridge University Press, 1975), p. 137; Peter L. Berger and Thomas Luckmann, *The Social Construction of Reality* (New York: Anchor Books, 1966), part 3, pp. 129–84; Alexander Wendt, "State Autonomy and Structural Change in International Relations Theory" (unpublished manuscript, Yale University, December 1992).

tions scholarship, and it is this problematic that is required for an adequate account of these weapons taboos and their influence on outcomes. What set nuclear and chemical weapons as categories apart from other methods of warfare in the first place? How were nuclear and chemical weapons defined and delegitimated as a special category of "nonconventional" weapons, and what features of these weapons were regarded as critical in regarding them as unacceptable weapons? How did actors come to define their interests with regard to these weapons, and how were their identities validated in the construction and strengthening of these norms? Have the meanings of the taboos changed over time, and what are the implications of such discursive transformations for the robustness of the taboos? In the following two sections, we suggest how the genealogical and social constructivist perspectives illuminate the two cases by showing that deterrence and non-use cannot be adequately explained on a purely rationalist basis, but rather require attention to the elements of identity, contingency, and the socially constructed nature of weapons taboos.

The Chemical Weapons Taboo

In this short space it is not possible to address at each point every alternative explanation for each issue and event relevant to the development of the CW taboo and the non-use of CW. Instead, the account that follows is designed to illustrate the contributions of a genealogical analysis by filling in neglected gaps in the CW story and redressing key errors. First, and in opposition to essentialist explanations and arguments from utility, the contingency involved in the political construction of the CW taboo is examined to underline the difficulties of a straightforward rationalist accounting of its origins and development. Second, the development of the contested features of the moral discourse are traced in an effort to gauge the robustness of the norm. Third, it is argued that a better understanding of the meaning and significance of violations of the CW taboo is gained when it is recognized that this taboo is implicated in the hierarchical operation of ordering war and international relations according to a discourse that characterizes nations as "civilized" and "uncivilized."

Contingency

Rather than being viewed as simply the inevitable result of the objective qualities of chemical weapons, as is often supposed, the CW taboo is better

understood as a political construction that owes much to a series of fortuitous events. International law first proscribed chemical warfare at the
Hague Conference of 1899, which banned the use of asphyxiating shells
even though no such weapon had yet been developed. This prohibition
was accepted by delegates to the conference largely because it was not
believed to have much significance. In fact, however, the Hague Declaration subsequently proved to be of no small importance. As will be seen
below, later prohibitions against CW—culminating in the Geneva Protocol
of 1925—were made possible on the basis of the understanding that these
bans represented not the creation of a new norm but only the reaffirmation of the norm embodied in the Hague Declaration. In the absence of
the Hague Declaration, it is unlikely that agreement would have been
reached on interwar efforts to proscribe CW.[22]

If such an understanding made agreement on a renewed CW prohibition
possible, efforts to proscribe CW might not even have been on the international agenda at all except for an interwar hysteria over CW generated by
the overzealous propaganda efforts of the chemical industry lobby and the
gas warfare lobby. Especially in the U.S. and Britain, a massive campaign
made "totally irresponsible . . . exaggerations of new weapons developments" in order to secure chemical tariffs and the survival of chemical warfare departments.[23] The fearful scenarios of future danger that these lob-
bies constructed around the issue of CW were so effective because they
encountered no opposition until it was too late: the same dialogue of dread
was being inscripted by the opponents of gas warfare.[24] Hence, the image
of CW that was constructed was far out of proportion to the actual danger
they represented at the time, as many have noted.[25] Indeed, of all the

---

22. For example, the Geneva Protocol was the product of a conference on the traffic in arms; it
decided that it did not have the competence to create a new norm against CW. The protocol was
actually enunciated as only a reaffirmation of an existing norm meant as a transitory measure until a
future conference on CW could be held.

23. Brown, *Chemical Warfare*, p. 180.

24. The turnaround in assessments of gas warfare by these propagandists was remarkable. In contrast
to earlier warnings of the catastrophic potential of CW, see the revised assessments by members of
the U.S. Chemical Warfare Service in *New York Times*, September 10, 1926, p. 6, and November 26,
1926, p. 12. One can imagine the contempt with which, in a moment of unsurpassed irony, the
president of the American Chemical Society declared that the widespread feeling against gas was the
result of hysteria and propaganda (*New York Times*, December 11, 1926, p. 3).

25. "To anyone who was prepared to consider the potentialities of CW dispassionately, it would have
been clear that the chemical threat did not differ markedly from that posed by high-explosive
weapons. Against well-equipped and well-disciplined troops, the chemical weapons of the time
would never be overwhelming; if anything, their efficacy had declined since 1918" (SIPRI, *The Rise of*

recent technological innovations in offensive warfare, CW are the one weapon that is most susceptible to defensive measures, a fact that makes the image of CW as a special threat all the more intriguing.

This depiction of CW eventually backfired on those seeking to promote CW preparedness, for it led to renewed efforts to prohibit CW. The first major effort was at the Washington Naval Conference of 1921–1922. At this gathering, U.S. Secretary of State Charles Evans Hughes pushed through an absolute prohibition on any first use of CW, despite the unanimous recommendations of a subcommittee of experts that CW be treated the same as any other weapon. According to the subcommittee, "the only limitation practicable is wholly to prohibit the use of gases against cities and other large bodies of noncombatants in the same manner as high explosives may be limited."[26] While Hughes was prepared to accept the same kinds of limitations on CW as on other weapons if his resolution had encountered stiff opposition,[27] his proposal for an absolute ban was accepted as Article V of the Washington Treaty.

Its acceptance was made possible by the belief of the delegates at the conference that such a prohibition was neither nothing new nor anything terribly important. On the one hand, they saw it as merely reaffirming previous bans—the Hague Declaration, whose violation during World War I left little confidence in such treaties, and Article 171 of the Versailles Treaty, which itself cited the previous outlawing of CW as its basis and in any case was essentially an anti-German provision of a dictated peace. Furthermore, it was believed that such a treaty was not very important, since it would not prevent preparations for chemical warfare. Even though the Washington Treaty never came into effect,[28] the clause banning CW lived on in the sense that it served directly as the basis and even the rationale for the Geneva Protocol of 1925, which in turn has operated as the focal point of the CW norm for almost seventy years.[29]

CB Weapons, p. 247). See also *Times* (London) editorial of April 3, 1923, p. 7; and L. F. Haber, *The Poisonous Cloud* (Oxford: Clarendon Press, 1986), pp. 288, 307, and 317. By 1927, a *New York Times* editorial (February 16, 1927, p. 22) had dismissed the exaggerated fears of CW as "sheer romancing," noting that the previous war had demonstrated that high explosives were far more destructive.

26. U.S. Department of State, *Conference on the Limitation of Armament* (Washington, D.C.: U.S. Government Printing Office, 1922), p. 730.

27. Charles E. Hughes, "Possible Gains," in *Proceedings of the American Society of International Law*, pp. 1–2 (Washington, D.C.: American Society of International Law, 1927).

28. The treaty did not come into effect—the French failed to ratify it because of their opposition to provisions regarding submarines.

29. At least until 1992, when agreement was reached on the Chemical Weapons Convention.

In genealogical fashion, an institutional tradition prohibiting cw came to be invoked as its own justification, in such a way as to obscure the fortuitous ancestry of the taboo. The cw taboo was reborn from the ashes of World War I not simply as a technologically determined and self-interested reaction to a prohibitively costly new means of warfare but also as a political construction whose institutionalization has in turn helped to politically legitimate the definition of cw as a practice beyond the pale of civilized nations.

Defining Features

An important aspect of the cw taboo that is brought out by the genealogical tracing of discourses concerns the features of the taboo that have been regarded as essential in defining cw as unacceptable. When the Germans initiated the use of lethal chlorine gas from cylinders in the trenches of World War I, they defended this use of cw by arguing that it was no more cruel than shattering soldiers to bits with guns and howitzers. In taking this position, the Germans directly challenged the presumption of the cw prohibition that cw were an especially inhumane method of warfare. This contestation of the very core of the cw prohibition became even more prominent in the U.S. Senate during the ratification hearings for the Geneva Protocol. Typical of such a position was the contention of Senator David Reed that the cw ban would prevent the U.S.

> from using gas against the next savage race with which we find ourselves in war, and would compel us to blow them up, or stab them with bayonets, or riddle them and sprinkle them with shrapnel, or puncture them with machine-gun bullets, instead of blinding them for an hour or so until we could disarm them. That is the "humanity" that is attempted to be worked out by the Geneva Protocol.[30]

Because the humanitarian core of the cw taboo has over time become increasingly unacceptable to question, such sentiments strike most contemporary observers as rather unsettling. To bring this out more starkly, the above developments can be compared to attitudes toward cw during the most recent use of cw, the Iran-Iraq war of the 1980s. Iraq did not even admit to the use of cw until the last year of the war. Even then, Iraq's leaders stated that they supported the general rule prohibiting the use of cw; Iraq justified the use of cw as the "right to defend itself and protect

---

30. See *Congressional Record*, 69th Cong., 2d sess., 1927, 68, pt. 1:150.

its territorial integrity and its homeland."[31] One need not attribute too much credence to Iraq's claims to abide by the cw norm to notice that something significant had not occurred: a reopening of what has over time become the humanitarian core of the cw norm. Similar to the Italians in their war against Ethiopia in 1935–1936, the Iraqis made no attempt to legitimate their use of cw on the basis of the alleged humanitarian qualities of cw.

This closure of direct challenges to the humanitarian definition of cw as a particularly odious means of warfare is indicative of a gradual strengthening of the taboo over time. Indeed, while it may seem that the opposition of many Arab nations to the Chemical Weapons Convention[32] represents a fundamental challenge to the anti-cw norm, it will be argued below that this contestation in fact positively depends on cw's being ostracized as a terror weapon of last resort, though now in its more recent incarnation as a "weapon of mass destruction."

Domination and Resistance: Weapons of Mass Destruction

A significant manifestation of the cw prohibition has been its operation in the hierarchical ordering of relations of domination in the international system. This feature of the taboo is most evident in the characterization of cw as weapons of the weak and the taboo's role in the disciplining discourse of civilized conduct of international society.

The Hague Declaration established a discriminatory regime insofar as its language stipulated that the ban against asphyxiating shells was "only binding on the Contracting Powers in the case of war between two or more of them." Furthermore, the declaration stated that "it shall cease to be binding from the time when, in a war between the Contracting Powers, one of the belligerents shall be joined by a non-Contracting Power." Those contracting powers were the nations that would count as the members of an emerging society of civilized states. That is, one of the qualifications for gaining the status of a civilized nation was to participate in the regulation of warfare that began among the European society of states in the mid-

---

31. "Paper Interviews 'Aziz on Kurds, Other Issues," Kuwait AL-QABAS in Arabic, October 31, 1988, Foreign Broadcast Information Service (hereafter *FBIS*), November 2, 1988, p. 27; and "WAKH Reports Khayrallah 15 September Press Conference," Manama WAKH in Arabic, 15 September 1988 *FBIS*, September 16, 1988, pp. 23–24.
32. The Chemical Weapons Convention (cwc), which opened for signature in January 1993, prohibits the possession, production, and transfer of cw. At the time of writing, 159 states have signed the cwc.

nineteenth century.[33] As such, the origins of the cw taboo were implicated in exclusionary practices that distinguished between civilized and uncivilized areas of the globe.

The symbolic connection of cw with standards of civilized conduct has made it more difficult for advanced nations to employ these weapons against each other as just another unremarkable, unpoliticized, and standard means of warfare. At the same time, however, it has also played a part in undermining the taboo in "uncivilized" areas. The invocation of the disciplining discourse of civilization operated during the two most significant violations of the cw taboo since World War I: their use against Ethiopia by Italy in 1935–1936 and during the Iran-Iraq war of the 1980s.

The use of cw against Ethiopia led some to expect—and fear—that their employment would be a matter of course during World War II.[34] For others, however, the assessment was different: war among the industrialized nations of Europe was a different matter than conflicts involving less technologically advanced areas, such as the colonies.[35] The surprising lack of gas warfare during World War II can thus be understood as part of a process by which the conduct of war among "civilized" nations was demarcated from that involving "uncivilized" nations. As one author has put it, a standard view of world affairs after Versailles was that the arenas of European war and colonial war might well have been separable.[36] And the use of cw might have been less unacceptable in one arena than in the other.

This phenomenon of differentiation in the acceptability of forms of

---

33. The rise of the society of states is associated with the work of Hedley Bull and Adam Watson. See in particular Bull's *Anarchical Society: A Study of Order in World Politics* (New York: Columbia University Press, 1977); Hedley Bull and Adam Watson, eds., *The Expansion of International Society* (Oxford: Clarendon Press, 1984); and also Gerritt W. Gong, *The Standard of "Civilisation" in International Society* (Oxford: Clarendon Press, 1984).

34. See, e.g., Anthony Eden's impassioned speech reported in *New York Times*, April 21, 1936, p. 18.

35. For example, the U.S. military "denied that there were any lessons to be learned from the use of gas as a weapon of opportunity against a totally unprepared enemy in a colonial war" (Brown, *Chemical Warfare*, p. 145). For a similar German assessment, see Rolf-Dieter Müller, "World Power Status Through the Use of Poison Gas? German Preparations for Chemical Warfare, 1919–1945," in Wilhelm Deist, ed., *The German Military in the Age of Total War*, pp. 183, 189 (Warwickshire: Berg Publishers, 1985).

36. George Quester, *Deterrence Before Hiroshima: The Airpower Background of Modern Strategy* (New York: John Wiley, 1966), p. 78. Thus while reports of Japan's use of cw against the Chinese were ignored, even the suggestion that cw was being contemplated in Spain drew preemptory attention from Britain. The use of tear gas by government forces was reported, and the insurgents claimed that they, too, had gas but "refuse to break the international law which forbids its use" (*Times* [London], August 19, 1936, p. 10). In response, Britain sent its diplomats to investigate these allegations and convey the grave consequences that might follow from the use of gas even in reprisal (*Times* [London], September 8, 1936, p. 12).

warfare has received recent articulation by a number of authors, most forcefully perhaps by John Mueller. For Mueller, major war—war among developed states—has been subject to a gradual obsolescence that has not occurred in other areas of the globe.[37] The occasional ruptures of the CW taboo reflect the understanding that modern warfare between industrialized powers is a qualitatively different situation than war involving an "uncivilized" country.[38] Such was the argument of the Italians, who contended that the "Ethiopians have repeatedly shown she is not worthy of the rank of a civilized nation."[39]

This disciplining discourse of identity has not issued solely from the developed world, however. In a July 1988 statement defending the use of CW, Iraqi foreign minister Tariq Aziz ventured to argue: "There are different views on this matter from different angles. You are living on a civilized continent. You are living on a peaceful continent."[40] CW were indeed a symbol of unacceptable violence—at least among "civilized" countries.

A related manifestation of the disciplining aspect of the CW discourse has been the characterization of CW as weapons of the weak. To be sure, the designation of CW as the "poor man's atomic bomb" has condescending overtones, but recently this characterization has been turned on its head. The link between chemical and nuclear weapons established by the terminology of CW as the poor man's atomic bomb has been appropriated by some nations in the developing world—the Arab nations in particular—by situating it within a broader discourse of "weapons of mass destruction."

For the industrialized world, the category of weapons of mass destruction has served as the touchstone for efforts to curb the proliferation of

---

37. John Mueller, *Retreat from Doomsday: The Obsolescence of Major War* (New York: Basic Books, 1989). Similarly, Francis Fukuyama has drawn a sharp distinction between the behavior of the Third World and the industrial democracies—the historical and posthistorical parts of the world. He argues that the rules of the latter are different from those of the former and that it is only in the historical world that the old rules of power politics continue to apply (Francis Fukuyama, *The End of History and the Last Man* [New York: Free Press, 1992]). See also James Goldgeier and Michael McFaul, "A Tale of Two Worlds: Core and Periphery in the Post–Cold War Era," *International Organization* 46, no. 2 (Spring 1992): 467–91; and Michael Doyle's finding that democracies do not fight wars against each other in "Kant, Liberal Legacies, and Foreign Affairs," parts 1 and 2, *Philosophy and Public Affairs* 12 (Summer and Fall 1983): 205–35 and 323–53.

38. And as Michael Adas has demonstrated, it was the level of technological sophistication—rather than race, religion, morality, or other factors—that served as the chief standard by which the West judged the degree of civilization of other societies. See his exhaustive account in *Machines as the Measure of Men* (Ithaca: Cornell University Press, 1989).

39. *Giornale d'Italia*, as reported in *New York Times*, July 4, 1935, p. 1. See also Amy Gurowitz, "The Expansion of International Society and the Effects of Norms" (unpublished paper, 1993).

40. *New York Times*, July 2, 1988, p. A3.

advanced weapon systems in the Third World. The Arab world, however, has appropriated this discourse in a manner that has made explicit the double standard in the antiproliferation designs of the industrialized world: while the Third World is prevented from acquiring deterrents such as nuclear or chemical weapons, the Western powers are permitted to retain their weapons of mass destruction—conventional and otherwise— as legitimate tools of diplomacy.[41] Israel's undeclared nuclear arsenal is a particular concern in this strategy of linkage, and it is on these grounds of eliminating all weapons of mass destruction that the opposition of some nations to the Chemical Weapons Convention is centered.

This appropriation of the mass destruction discourse is a remarkable example of the kind of interpretive reversal that Nietzsche and Foucault had in mind in their writings on moral discourses. As Foucault wrote, "The successes of history belong to those who are capable of seizing these rules, to replace those who had used them, to disguise themselves so as to pervert them, invert their meaning, and redirect them against those who had initially imposed them."[42]

The important point to note for the purposes of this essay is the effects of this usurpation on the illegitimacy of cw. First, it is to be noted that framing unacceptable weapons in terms of the "weapons of mass destruction" discourse invites the question of why other enormously destructive "conventional" weapons are not included in this category. On that level, the overall thrust of the weapons discourse has been to try to expand the definition of unacceptable weapons rather than to restrict or abolish it.[43]

---

41. As one author has remarked, "The major nations' unwillingness to eliminate their nuclear weapons while resisting further chemical (and nuclear) proliferation is seen in some Third World nations as the height of hypocrisy. It sends a message that 'the lesser nations aren't mature enough for the most powerful of military capabilities' " (Victor A. Utgoff, "Neutralizing the Value of Chemical Weapons: A Strong Supplement to Chemical Weapons Arms Control," in Joachim Krause, ed., *Security Implications of a Global Weapons Ban*, p. 97 [Boulder: Westview, 1991]). See also Geoffrey Kemp, "The Arms Race After the Iran-Iraq War," in Efraim Karsh, ed., *The Iran-Iraq War*, pp. 269–79 (New York: St. Martin's, 1989). He argues that "many countries in the Near East and South Asia express a profound irritation at what they perceive to be selective Western outrage over the use of chemicals. They believe that the United States, having failed to prevent India, Pakistan and Israel from building nuclear weapons is now trying to deny them the very weapons that provide some sort of counter balance to nuclear devices" (p. 277).

42. Foucault, "Nietzsche, Genealogy, History," pp. 85–86.

43. This is not to say, however, that the view has not been expressed privately in the developing world—though not in official public discourse—that to die by chemical weapons is neither more nor less horrible than to die by bullet or flame. See, e.g., the testimony of Brad Roberts in U.S. Congress, *Chemical Warfare: Arms Control and Nonproliferation* (Washington, D.C.: U.S. Government Printing Office, 1984), pp. 60–61.

Second, while the linkage to nuclear weapons conceivably could serve to justify the possession of cw as a deterrent, the linkage to nuclear weapons has not legitimated the actual *use* of cw. If anything, the taboo against using nuclear weapons is in all likelihood stronger and more universal than the taboo against using cw. Thus the effect of linking cw to nuclear weapons has been to further remove cw from the arsenal of standard and acceptable means of warfare.

The argument here is that this shift in the site of contestation of the norm—from earlier debates over the alleged humanitarian benefits of chemical weapons to contemporary efforts to extend the nonproliferation regime of weapons of mass destruction—is indicative of the consolidation of the taboo over time. Not only is the resistance to the transformation of the norm from use to possession restricted to a small group of nations, but the main thrust of this resistance has not been to challenge the unacceptability of using cw so much as it has been to question the legitimacy of possessing other weapons of mass destruction, including the definition of what counts as such a weapon.

The Non-use of Nuclear Weapons

The analysis of the nuclear case offered here focuses initially on the non-use of nuclear weapons by the United States but then broadens its scope to examine, as in the chemical case, the global implications of the norm for non-use and its world-ordering impact. The "social construction of deterrence" perspective problematizes nuclear "deterrence" and seeks to determine on what grounds the United States was deterred. Why did President Truman agonize after World War II over the possibility of nuclear use again against a nonnuclear adversary while President Eisenhower actively considered nuclear use against allies of a nuclear-armed adversary, for example? Why were only a few nuclear weapons considered enough to deter in the early years while in later years "deterrence" was defined as requiring a much higher level of damage? What goes into the definition of "unacceptable costs"?

These kinds of questions highlight the relevance of a constructivist account that investigates how U.S. interests and identity were defined with respect to nuclear weapons and nuclear use. The account that follows emphasizes several features of the origins and operation of the nuclear non-use norm and its impact on outcomes. First is the nature of the initial precedent set by nuclear use on Hiroshima and Nagasaki, which provides a point of contrast for later developments. Second is the role of both practice and contingency in the development of the non-use norm and the nonlinear process by which it developed. Third is the way normative concerns that were linked with American identity reinforced emerging perceptions of lack of military utility of nuclear weapons on the part of American decision makers. Fourth, and finally, is the role the non-use norm has come to play in the selective delegitimation of nuclear weapons.

Parts of the constructivist account of nuclear non-use are complementary to a rationalist account (when fear of retaliation genuinely holds), and parts offer an alternative to the deterrence argument (when fear of retaliation is not prominent and other factors, including moral repugnance and the perceived illegitimacy of nuclear weapons, play a significant role). In all cases, however, a constructivist account is necessary to get at "what deters" and how/why deterrence "works."

The Initial Precedent: Hiroshima and Nagasaki—from Seamless Web to Utter Discontinuity

The first point to emphasize is the precedent that World War II created of a seamless web between nuclear and conventional bombing and between "tactical" and "strategic" bombing. It was only later that thresholds were created between the two. As historians have noted, the atomic attacks on Japan represented a continuation of—not a rupture with—wartime bombing strategy.[44] While the attacks on Hiroshima and Nagasaki were carried out with new and revolutionary weapons, they simply culminated an effort by American strategic air power to decimate almost every important city in Japan through firebombing. Nuclear weapons provided a more effective means of carrying out a strategy that was already widely and vigorously pursued through conventional bombing, and "it was not thought that any irreversible threshold had been crossed."[45] In fact, conventional bombing *intensified* after the nuclear attacks, and the heaviest conven-

---

44. See Ronald Schaffer, *Wings of Judgment: American Bombing in World War II* (New York: Oxford University Press, 1985); and Michael S. Sherry, *The Rise of American Air Power: The Creation of Armageddon* (New Haven: Yale University Press, 1987).

45. Sheldon Cohen, *Arms and Judgment: Law, Morality, and the Conduct of War in the Twentieth Century* (Boulder: Westview, 1989), p. 91. It is important to note that while this view was shared by important segments of the military and political leadership, it was not the view of many of the scientists who had worked on the bomb, such as Robert Oppenheimer, who had a better appreciation of the revolutionary significance of the weapon. As the postwar period unfolded, the debate was precisely about whether nuclear weapons were revolutionary or not. Einstein's famous phrase "everything has changed except our way of thinking" indicates that both sides are right here.

tional bombing of the war *followed* Hiroshima and Nagasaki.[46] General Leslie Groves, head of the Manhattan Project, wanted to drop as many nuclear bombs on Japan as were ready.[47] Plans were discussed for dropping a third atomic bomb in late August if Japan did not surrender; after news of the scale of the destruction at Hiroshima and Nagasaki, President Truman was reluctant to do so, but he began to think he might have to. Recent research reveals that General George Marshall, Army Chief of Staff, briefly explored the tactical use of atomic bombs in connection with plans for the possible invasion of Japan at the end of the war.[48]

These facts emphasize the continuity of atomic weapons with existing military strategy and plans. George Quester highlights this continuity, noting that the kind of thinking we tend to associate largely with nuclear weapons existed *before* 1945 with regard to strategic (conventional) bombing: "Modern terms such as 'deterrence,' 'tacit agreement' or 'balance of terror' show up often in the literature, coupled with descriptions of war scenarios every bit as awesome as a nuclear holocaust."[49] Thus the label of "weapons of mass destruction" cannot be said to be simply a straightforward designation of objective features.

Contingency, Iteration, and Principled Belief

While the notion that nuclear weapons ought to remain unused after Hiroshima and Nagasaki dates from the immediate postwar period,[50] its

46. On August 14 and 15, a 1,014-plane mission, the largest of the war, staged a fourteen-hour bombing attack on six Japanese cities, dropping six thousand tons of conventional explosives. This was *after* Radio Tokyo had broadcast Japanese acceptance of American terms (but before the message had reached Washington through official channels). According to the U.S. Air Force official history of the war, Air Force Chief of Staff Hap Arnold "wanted as big a finale as possible" (quoted in Leon V. Sigal, *Fighting to a Finish: The Politics of War Termination in the United States and Japan, 1945* [Ithaca: Cornell University Press, 1988], p. 254). New York Times, "Superforts Stage 6-Target Wind-Up," August 15, 1945, p. 8; Gar Alperovitz, *Atomic Diplomacy: Hiroshima and Potsdam*, 2d ed. (New York: Penguin, 1985), p. 26.
47. Sigal, *Fighting to a Finish*, p. 207.
48. See Barton J. Bernstein, "Eclipsed by Hiroshima and Nagasaki: Early Thinking About Tactical Nuclear Weapons," *International Security* 15, no. 4 (Spring 1991): 149–73.
49. Quester, *Deterrence Before Hiroshima*, pp. 1–2.
50. The very first resolution of the new United Nations General Assembly adopted unanimously as a goal "the control of atomic energy to the extent necessary to ensure its use only for peaceful purposes" (UN GA Resolution 1[I], January 24, 1946). In a long paper in the fall of 1949 opposing development of the hydrogen bomb, George Kennan urged U.S. leaders to reconsider their commitment to the principle of nuclear first use, expressing strong aversion to that option (John Newhouse, *War and Peace in the Nuclear Age* [New York: Knopf, 1989], p. 77). This suggestion was not well received by Dean Acheson, who suggested that Kennan could go and preach his "Quaker gospel" somewhere else (David S. McLellen, *Dean Acheson: The State Department Years* [New York: Dodd, Mead, 1976], p. 176).
Starting in 1946, the Soviet Union regularly proposed that the use of nuclear weapons be prohibited, as a first step toward a comprehensive program of disarmament.

realization in practice and its transformation from a notion of prudence and, for some, moral belief into a collective, normative understanding was a matter of a gradual historical process. During the early period of the Cold War, little consensus existed on the nature of nuclear weapons, their military or political uses, how they should be controlled or managed, or whether they should, or would, be used again. But as the United States became increasingly vulnerable to Soviet nuclear attack, especially after the development of thermonuclear weapons and advanced delivery capabilities by both sides in the mid-1950s, the perception that strategic nuclear weapons could have no meaningful uses increased. However, the development of tactical nuclear weapons combined with the increased prospect of retaliation gave rise to a temporary interest in limited nuclear wars and the possible creation of various kinds of "thresholds."

It was thus only gradually during the postwar period that nuclear weapons acquired their status as unacceptable weapons and that the no-first-use taboo emerged and the utter discontinuity between nuclear weapons of all kinds and conventional weapons was established. But this development was neither linear nor inevitable; rather, it owes much to the combined workings of contingency and the iterated practice of non-use over time, as well as to self-conscious efforts on the part of some to foster a normative stigma. For example, President Truman, though he had been the one who actually dropped the bomb, expressed great horror at the possibility of having to do so again. His administration spent considerable energy pursuing the Baruch Plan for international control of atomic weapons at the UN, and Truman established the precedent of civilian control over nuclear weapons, thus signaling their special status.[51] The Eisenhower administration, however, subsequently attempted to reverse earlier efforts at setting nuclear weapons apart as something "different." It is useful to speculate on the counterfactual situation—that had Eisenhower preceded Truman as president, postwar nuclear history might have looked quite different.

The Impact of the Norm

While conventional deterrence theory takes interests as given, from the constructivist perspective the issue is how normative considerations, identities, and interests regarding nuclear use mutually shaped each other and

---

51. Gaddis, "The Origins of Self-Deterrence"; Gregg Herken, *The Winning Weapon: The Atomic Bomb in the Cold War* (New York: Knopf, 1980); Lawrence Freedman, *The Evolution of Nuclear Strategy*, 2d ed. (New York: St. Martin's, 1989).

hence influenced outcomes. The Korean War provides a good example of how an emerging "taboo" against initiating use of nuclear weapons influenced American leaders. In the 1950s, the emerging non-use norm entered decision making instrumentally in the form of a "cost" (public opinion against the first use of nuclear weapons), which top decision makers initially sought to appease, while disagreeing with it themselves. When President Eisenhower and Secretary of State John Foster Dulles came into office, tactical nuclear weapons had recently become available, and they actively sought to make these weapons "usable," i.e., to make them like any other weapon. Their attempts reveal the normative stigma against nuclear weapons that was already beginning to emerge. Policy discussions during the spring of 1953 on how to end the Korean War suggest that Eisenhower and Dulles were more preoccupied by the constraint on nuclear use imposed by negative public opinion than by any more material concern.[52]

Over time, a central element of the definition of nuclear weapons was that they were disproportionately lethal, and this aspect came to clash with U.S. leaders' perceptions of the United States as a moral country that took seriously the traditional laws of armed conflict, such as proportion in the use of force and the avoidance of killing noncombatants. During the crisis over Quemoy and Matsu in 1958, several State Department officials who thought Dulles was too enthusiastic about seeking out opportunities for use of tactical nuclear weapons produced some estimates showing how many civilians would be killed on the islands by a U.S. tactical nuclear attack on Chinese forces. There is some reason to believe that this dampened Dulles's ardor for the nuclear option; in any case, the issue was disproportionate destruction of civilians—a normative concern—not fear of retaliation.[53]

In contrast to the chemical case, in which chemical weapons were not

---

52. See the records of discussions in *Foreign Relations of the United States*, 1952–1954, vol. 15, *Korea*, part 1, pp. 721–1151, and part 2, pp. 1152–446; and vol. 2, *National Security Affairs*, part 1, pp. 202–464.
53. C. Gerard Smith, who was close to Dulles and who was the director of Policy Planning at the time, recalled in an interview the attempt to disabuse Dulles of the notion that using nuclear weapons on military targets adjacent to the islands would not cause a large number of civilian deaths. Dulles was "being tempted by an activist group in the Pentagon that wanted to take out the artillery batteries at Amoy that were shelling the islands." Smith called in some weapons specialists from the Pentagon and asked them to estimate the civilian casualties that any such limited nuclear strike would produce. They estimated about 186,000 civilian casualties. Said Smith, "I never heard another word about it after that" (Newhouse, *War and Peace in the Nuclear Age*, p. 126).

well integrated into the military establishment, nuclear weapons have been the central element of U.S. military plans since the late 1940s.[54] This information raises the question of the location of the nuclear non-use norm. As it emerged, it was held primarily by the top civilian leadership and by the public, but not by the military as an institution. However, even the U.S. military and NATO have over time moved away from the "early first use" plans of the early Cold War years toward what many have argued is a de facto no-first-use position. Normative development tends to proceed neither linearly nor necessarily coherently: norms can (and often do) develop even in the face of seemingly contradictory behavior.[55] As the non-use norm continues to strengthen, one would expect to see it increasingly reflected in operational plans that downgrade the role of nuclear weapons.[56]

Though the U.S. was the only country ever to have used nuclear weapons in warfare, American leaders later came to define nuclear use as contrary to Americans' perception of themselves. As one high-level official reportedly said of the nuclear option during the 1991 Persian Gulf war, "We just don't do things like that."[57] This unwillingness to consider nuclear options in the war against Iraq, where no fear of retaliation existed, provides telling contrast to Hiroshima and Nagasaki. A non-use norm has ruled out any serious consideration of nuclear use in places where small nuclear weapons might have been useful—to bomb bridges or dams in the Vietnam War, for example, or in the Gulf war for use on massed Iraqi troops—wars that were otherwise highly destructive.[58] The drive to create "smart" bombs and other high-tech options so that leaders will not have to resort to nuclear weapons is indicative of the special status of nuclear

---

54. The Single Integrated Operations Plan (SIOP) is the main operational statement of U.S. plans for using nuclear weapons in the event of a Soviet attack. For a concise history of SIOP, see David Alan Rosenberg, "The Origins of Overkill: Nuclear Weapons and American Strategy, 1945–1960," *International Security* 7, no. 4 (Spring 1983): 3–71.

55. An example is the decolonization/self-determination norm. See the discussion in Thomas Franck, *The Power of Legitimacy Among Nations* (Oxford: Oxford University Press, 1990), pp. 153–74.

56. In the nuclear case, the fact that the decision to use nuclear weapons rests with the president creates a significant gap between what the military has plans for and what the president might actually do. The historical record suggests that presidential thinking about nuclear weapons has been relatively independent of developments in strategic planning in the military. See Freedman, *The Evolution of Nuclear Strategy*, and Betts, *Nuclear Blackmail and Nuclear Balance*.

57. Author interview, Office of Policy Planning, State Department, March 6, 1992.

58. A Pentagon physicist calculated during the war that the conventional ordnance dropped on Iraq per week averaged the equivalent of a one-kiloton nuclear bomb (author interview, Pentagon, Washington, D.C., March 5, 1992).

weapons. Whereas nuclear weapons were once relied upon in order to avoid spending money on conventional forces, the nuclear non-use norm now propels the building of high-tech conventional arsenals that are more politically "usable."

But with the convergence in destructive power of small nuclear weapons and advanced conventional weapons, the traditional threshold between nuclear and conventional technology may become increasingly blurred. Fuel-air explosives provide a case in point. During the Gulf war, coalition military leaders first worried about Iraq's possible use of fuel-air explosives and then used such weapons themselves at the end of the war against Iraqi forces. Military officials described the weapons as capable of delivering a devastating blast similar to a small nuclear explosion over an area several miles wide.[59] Unlike chemical and biological weapons, fuel-air explosives are blast-effect weapons and there is no ready defense against them. Official and private statements on why the United States would not need to resort to nuclear weapons in the Gulf war generally echoed the theme that the coalition could create equivalent damage with conventional forces without the moral "downside" of using nuclear weapons. The destructiveness of nuclear weapons per se was not a prominent feature of the reasoning.[60]

The strength of the nuclear taboo and the odium attached to nuclear weapons as weapons of mass destruction render unusable all nuclear weapons, even though certain kinds or uses of nuclear weapons could, from the perspective of just war theory, conceivably be justified. The feature of

59. Fuel-air explosives (FAEs) are among the most lethal of the new generation of high-tech weapons. They are a kind of gas bomb involving two detonations. Fuel dispersed in the air is ignited and detonates, creating a huge fireball and an invisible shock wave, which officials have described as similar to a tactical nuclear weapon. It spreads rapidly across a wide area and is capable of flattening buildings, destroying aircraft, knocking down oil rigs, and killing troops. According to Pentagon estimates, at peak efficiency FAEs have destructive effects ten times more powerful than conventional explosives of the same size (Douglas Frantz and Melissa Healy, "Iraqi Bomb Gives Nuke-Type Blast, Pentagon Says," *Los Angeles Times*, October 5, 1990, p. 18).

60. That is, the reasoning was not "Nuclear weapons are too destructive" but rather "We now have weapons that are as destructive as nuclear weapons." According to one commentator, nuclear use by the United States would be highly unlikely because "it has conventional weapons equivalent to very small nuclear weapons" (Juan J. White, "U.S. Forces Probably Have 500 N-Arms in Gulf," *USA Today*, November 30, 1990, p. 10). An analyst who studied nuclear warfare for the Air Force said, "Today we've got conventional weapons that approach the effectiveness of the old nuclear stuff. We can dig out those Iraqi bunkers more effectively with guided 2000-pound bombs than with tactical nuclear weapons—and without the moral downside" (David Wood, *Minneapolis Star-Tribune*, February 10, 1991, p. 15). Said a former assistant secretary of defense, "Militarily you don't need them in terms of the damage you want to inflict on Iraq" (Lawrence Korb, quoted in Lee Michael Katz and Richard Latture, "Nuke Threat Always Implied," *USA Today*, February 8, 1991).

nuclear weapons at the core of the taboo—their disproportionate nature—may change with advancing technology. As scattered proponents of tactical nuclear use during the Gulf war argued, in some circumstances the use of very small, accurate "micronukes" with low yields could minimize disproportionate destruction and avoid the killing of noncombatants.[61] The capability must be juxtaposed against the coalition's destruction of the Iraqi electric and water infrastructure during the Gulf war, which caused vast numbers of civilian deaths from infectious diseases and the lack of food, water, and medical care.[62] Such an attack erodes the moral claims against the killing of noncombatants, which are the traditional basis for objection to nuclear weapons. Thus the nuclear taboo may have "permissive effects"—permitting other weapons and practices that, while avoiding the stigma of nuclear means, accomplish equivalent ends of destructiveness.

The Non-use Norm and World Order

As suggested in the discussion of the cw taboo, both the chemical and the nuclear prohibitionary norms have become instruments for structuring certain kinds of status hierarchies in the international system, thus becom-

---

61. The most outspoken exhortations for nuclear use during the Gulf war came from Representative Dan Burton (R-Ind.) and physicist Sam Cohen, the "father of the neutron bomb." Burton argued that use of tactical nuclear weapons would save American lives (Dan Burton, "Tactical Nuclear Weapons Could Save Lives," *USA Today*, February 13, 1991, p. 10). Cohen urged the use of neutron artillery shells to attack Iraqi armored columns. He endorsed nuclear weapons as a more discriminating and effective weapon; see Sam Cohen, "Use Neutron Bomb on Iraqis?" *Los Angeles Times*, August 18, 1990. To dismiss such people as crackpots only reinforces the general perception of these notions as "beyond the pale" or "unthinkable" today. Despite the fact that both of them sought to justify nuclear use in just-war terms of proportionate destruction and saving lives, their views prompted outrage among other editorialists, opinion makers and security experts. See, for example, Mary McGrory, "Chilling Talk of Using Nukes," *Washington Post*, February 14, 1991, p. A2; Leslie Gelb, "Gas, Germs, and Nukes," *New York Times*, January 30, 1991; Joseph Nye, "Nuclear Restraint—Now and Later," *Boston Globe*, February 21, 1991, p. 13; Ellen Goodman, "The Nuke-em Brigade," *Boston Globe*, February 14, 1991, p. 31.

For a discussion of "micronukes," see Thomas W. Dowler and Joseph S. Howard II, "Countering the Threat of the Well-Armed Tyrant: A Modest Proposal for Small Nuclear Weapons," *Strategic Review* 19, no. 4 (Fall 1991): 34–39.

62. A special UN report on the immediate postwar situation in Iraq stated that the conflict had wrought "near-apocalyptic results upon the economic infrastructure . . . Iraq has been relegated to a pre-industrial age" (*Report to the Secretary-General on Humanitarian Needs in Kuwait and Iraq in the Immediate Post-Crisis Environment*, UN Security Council Document S/22366 [March 1991]). Various study teams concluded that this resulted in large numbers of civilian deaths well beyond the end of the war. One epidemiological report estimated more than 46,900 excess deaths among children between January and August 1991; see Alberto Ascherio et al., "Effect of the Gulf War on Infant and Child Mortality in Iraq," *New England Journal of Medicine* 327, no. 13 (September 24, 1992), pp. 931–36. More generally, see H. Jack Geiger, "Bomb Now, Die Later: The Consequences of

ing, in effect, "world order" norms. This development is particularly interesting in the nuclear case because of the patently asymmetrical application of varying nuclear prohibitionary norms to different categories of states and because of the remarkably widespread—if ultimately fragile—acceptance of the legitimacy of this asymmetry.

In the post–Cold War era, nuclear proliferation has replaced superpower conflict as the major potential threat to the tradition of non-use. The links between non-use and nonproliferation are best understood in terms of the differing—and sometimes tenuous—degrees of legitimacy that the international community appears to attach to different aspects of nuclear weapons—use, acquisition, possession, and deterrence—and the ambivalence toward such weapons that this attitude ultimately reflects.[63] These various nuclear taboos apply unequally to states—only the great powers may legitimately possess nuclear weapons, for example—and provide mechanisms for the international community to differentiate the status and legitimacy of the various states. Compliance with the appropriate nuclear norms reinforces the identity of states and their status as legitimate members of the international community and/or as a certain kind of state (responsible, civilized, etc.).

The non-use norm, for example, provides the basis for justifying asymmetrical rights and statuses between nuclear and nonnuclear powers. On one hand, the non-use norm has the effect of legitimating and stabilizing the practice of deterrence between the superpowers. Stable nuclear deterrence could not be taken for granted at the end of the 1950s; up to 1962, U.S.-Soviet relations were unstable because there was as yet no expected process by which they were conducted and there were few shared norms. After 1962, deterrence was stabilized by a host of arms control agreements that embodied a variety of shared understandings about nuclear weapons and were based implicitly on the expectation that nuclear weapons should not be used.[64] These made the process predictable and legitimated the

Infrastructure Destruction for Iraqi Civilians in the Gulf War," in John O'Loughlin, Tom Meyer, and Edward Greenberg, eds., *War and Its Consequences: Lessons from the Persian Gulf Conflict* (New York: Harper Collins, 1994); Barton Gellman, "Allied Air War Struck Broadly in Iraq," *Washington Post*, June 23, 1991, pp. A1, A16; and Michael Walzer, "Justice and Injustice in the Gulf War," in David E. Decosse, ed., *But Was It Just? Reflections on the Morality of the Persian Gulf War*, pp. 1–17 (New York: Doubleday, 1992).

63. An eloquent discussion of the role of legitimacy in the international community is Franck, *The Power of Legitimacy Among Nations*.

64. The 1972 Anti-Ballistic Missile (ABM) Treaty between the United States and the Soviet Union is the clearest and most important institutionalized expression of a non-use presumption. In its banning of missile defenses against nuclear weapons, the ABM Treaty reflects a shared understanding that nuclear weapons should not be used.

concept and practice of deterrence as the appropriate form of superpower political competition.

On the other hand, nuclear deterrence is a practice reserved for the superpowers, and the non-use norm at the same time serves to justify the illegitimacy of the acquisition of nuclear weapons by the majority of the world. This relationship between non-use of nuclear weapons and "nonacquisition" is explicitly embodied in the Nuclear Non-Proliferation Treaty and in various commitments by the nuclear powers not to use nuclear weapons against nonnuclear powers who are parties to the treaty.[65]

Norms, Constructivism, and Explanation

In the final section, we briefly compare and contrast the two cases, with the aims of drawing out some generalizations and also clarifying more specifically a constructivist conception of the role of norms. Specifically, we summarize and assess the contribution of our cases with respect to three questions: (1) What are alternative explanations of non-use? (2) How do these norms matter (what were their effects)? (3) Where did these norms come from (why is rationalism insufficient)? Consideration of these questions helps to illuminate the basic constructivist argument about norms and how they work, in particular why and how it is not merely a matter of explaining "residual variance."

The Two Cases Compared

The chemical and nuclear cases present a number of interesting similarities and differences with respect to the origins and role of norms. While both are highly specific norms, the nuclear non-use norm was initially *uninstitutionalized* (in fact, "use" is what was institutionalized), while the anti-CW norm was *institutionalized* from its earliest origins.[66] In the nuclear case, the de facto norm arose first, and only later did it begin to become institutionalized in bilateral and multilateral security and arms control agreements. Unlike the case of the chemical taboo, there is as yet no specifically *legal*

---

65. Lawrence Scheinman, "The Non-Proliferation Treaty: On the Road to 1995," *IAEA Bulletin* 34, no. 1 (1992): 33–40.
66. By *institutionalized* we mean explicitly or implicitly expressed in treaties, agreements, or documents with corresponding operationalization in some way in state practices. These are all obviously matters of degree.

prohibition against the use of nuclear weapons.[67] This process contrasts with that depicted by the dominant approach to norms in the international relations literature (i.e., rationalist regime theory), which tends to focus on how norms are created in the process of negotiating institutions (a process that may be more characteristic of political economy than of security issues). In contrast, the anti-cw norm is not only *institutionalized*, but the fact that it was institutionalized before the development of modern chemical weapons is perhaps the single most outstanding feature that explains how cw have been so successfully ostracized. Finally, the nuclear non-use norm is probably stronger and more widespread than the chemical taboo, despite the fact that it is largely a de facto norm.

These cases also raise the issue of the relationship between national and international norms. The nuclear case focuses on how a norm arose in a *national context* (that of the United States) and then was subsequently diffused more broadly, while the chemical case involves a norm that was created *at the international level* and then diffused into national policies.[68] Both of these analyses could, in theory, be broadened to look at the rise of these non-use norms globally (though this is not to claim that they are universal), the various processes by which this rise occurred, and the way these norms now shape actors' perceptions of their identities and interests. We have suggested how they both constitute part of a larger explanation concerning the rise of international society and efforts to regulate the destructiveness of warfare among "civilized" states. It was because of such concerns that cw (especially) and, later, nuclear arms control and disarmament were placed on the international agenda in the first place.

---

67. Although resolutions and prohibitions passed in the United Nations General Assembly and other international forums have repeatedly proclaimed use of nuclear weapons to be illegal, the United States and other nuclear powers have consistently voted against them. Up through the 1950s, legal scholars were themselves divided over the legality of nuclear weapons use. Today, although there is probably some agreement that certain kinds of uses of nuclear weapons are illegal under traditional laws of armed conflict, there is by no means agreement that all use of nuclear weapons is illegal. The difficulty of coming to conclusions about the legality of nuclear weapons makes it more useful to think about their status in terms of the notion of legitimacy. For a history of legal interpretations of nuclear weapons, see Elliott L. Meyrowitz, *Prohibition of Nuclear Weapons: The Relevance of International Law* (Dobbs Ferry, N.Y.: Transnational Publishers, 1990). The first U.S. statement on the *legality* of nuclear use appeared in 1955.

68. Much of international norm creation has probably taken the first route, as the history of international law suggests. For example, revolutionary regimes such as France, America, and the Soviet Union injected new values and norms into the international state system. See David Armstrong, *Revolution and World Order: The Revolutionary State in International Society* (Oxford: Oxford University Press, 1993).

The single most important effect of these taboos, however, is that the delegitimation of these weapons constrains the practice of self-help in the international state system. Military technologies that might be useful under some circumstances are successfully proscribed. This phenomenon belies the realist view—captured in the sayings "war is hell" and "in time of war law is silent"—that everything is permitted in warfare. Rather, the existence of prohibitionary norms reveals that war is rarely absolute; instead, it displays features of a social institution.[69] National leaders are forced to seek or develop alternative technologies for use in war or defense—or else risk being classified as acting outside the bounds of "civilized" international society. "Society," not anarchy, is the source of constraining and permissive effects.

In sum, these stories suggest that the path of normative development can be highly varied. They suggest that prohibitionary norms can be institutionalized early or late, that they can arise from different sources—from power politics, moral opprobrium, and/or domestic politics—and that they can arise either in a national context and be diffused more broadly or at the international level. They also suggest that norms may arise more or less spontaneously or as the result of intentional efforts. Finally, they point to the important role of historical contingency in normative development, highlighting the often nonlinear, contingent, and contradictory features of this process.

Alternative Explanations

Why were the weapons not used? We have argued that the development of prohibitionary norms was a necessary condition for the limited use of nuclear and chemical weapons. Without these taboos, the patterns of use would likely have looked quite different. In short, there would have been more use. In order to explicate more precisely the nature of this claim, we show below how it relates to possible alternative explanations.

Several alternative explanations could be put forth. The most skeptical is the occasionally cited argument that nuclear and chemical weapons were not very useful and hence states did not use them. In this view—a classic realist argument—norms are simply frosting on the cake. They merely prohibit what states did not want to do anyway. States possessed alterna-

---

69. For further discussion of this issue, see Michael Howard, George, J. Andreopoulos, and Mark R. Shulman, eds., *The Laws of War: Constraints on Warfare in the Western World* (New Haven: Yale University Press, 1994); and Geoffrey Best, *War and Law Since 1945* (New York: Clarendon Press, 1994).

tives (namely, conventional weapons) and therefore did not need to use nuclear or chemical weapons.

This view is easy to reject on both empirical and conceptual grounds. Both of these weapons were clearly viewed as useful weapons for a range of circumstances and were, in fact, used, with great effect.[70] The U.S. nuclear arsenal was initially developed as a more desirable, "more-bang-for-the-buck" alternative to a more expensive conventional force (a relationship that has since been reversed because of the nuclear taboo). Since the advent of thermonuclear weapons, there has never been any real doubt about the military effectiveness of nuclear weapons or their potential for terror. Even as some U.S. political leaders began to question privately the utility of nuclear weapons, others, especially in the military, continued to view tactical nuclear weapons as militarily useful.[71] If anything, the history of nuclear weapons is a history of unresolved disputes over their utility, which continued into the 1990–1991 Gulf war.

Similarly, we noted earlier that in the case of chemical weapons there has always been an unresolved debate over their utility, because of limitations such as dependence on weather conditions. There are, however, undeniable instances in the historical record in which it was recognized that cw would have been enormously useful from a military standpoint— Dunkirk, D day, and U.S. operations against the Japanese in the Pacific islands, to cite just a few examples.

Beyond the empirical inaccuracy of the claim, however, the very fact that the supposed lack of "utility" is put forth as a reason for non-use despite the historical record demonstrates a key constructivist contention. "Utility," like "rationality," can be read back into history to tell a compelling story, but it is not at all obvious that such "reasons" were decisive, nor is it clear how they developed in the first place. In fact, the rationalist argument often imposes a backward teleology: because these weapons were not used, it is assumed they could not have been very useful, and that

---

70. Nuclear weapons were tremendously useful at Hiroshima and Nagasaki. Tactical nuclear weapons, especially, have been viewed as useful for both deterrent and war-fighting purposes. Not only were chemical weapons used on a massive scale during World War I, but an important British assessment done after the war took it as a "foregone conclusion" that gas "will be used in the future" because no *successful* weapon had ever been abandoned (Haber, *The Poisonous Cloud*, p. 293).

71. During the Vietnam War, the U.S. Joint Chiefs of Staff repeatedly suggested that nuclear weapons might be needed to keep China out of the war. Nuclear attacks would have a "far greater probability of forcing China" to stop an attack than would a U.S. conventional response (Robert S. McNamara, *In Retrospect: The Tragedy and Lessons of Vietnam* [New York: Times Books, 1995], p. 111).

is therefore taken to be the reason for non-use. Our taken-for-granted beliefs today that these weapons are not "useful" must not obscure the fact that they have been viewed as quite useful to accomplish specific military tasks, and those same technological capabilities remain.[72] If, indeed, states did not find them "useful," the more fundamental question is *why* states did not think they were useful, which we maintain had quite a bit to do with the existence of taboos.

A second line of alternative argument would accept the view that these weapons possess utility but would identify a set of "non-norms" reasons as to why they did not get used. That is, there may be reasons for non-use that have nothing to do with norms.[73] These could include, for example, fear of immediate retaliation, fear of longer-term military consequences, public and international opinion constraints, lack of organizational readiness, and so on. This perspective would suggest setting up a "test" between a "norms" explanation and a "non-norms" explanation. The analytical goal would be to establish what proportion of the "outcomes" is explained by "norms" and what proportion is explained by other factors. Neoliberal institutionalism takes this approach, a view quite sympathetic to the role of norms.

We entirely agree that these factors enter into an account of non-use for both of these weapons, though to varying degrees (for example, "lack of organizational readiness" does not apply to nuclear weapons). However, the problem with framing the question as such is that these supposed non-norms factors may *not* in fact be independent variables. They may only become politically salient because of the prior existence of a taboo or norm, however strong or weak. For example, while "lack of organizational readiness" in chemical warfare is not entirely reducible to normative disdain for cw, we show that such constraints were unlikely to have been decisive in the absence of more-politicized sources of restraint issuing directly from the cw taboo.

This point gets to the heart of a constructivist perspective on norms. Viewing norms as capturing the "residual variance," while consistent with a standard treatment of variables, misses the core of constructivism. Constructivism does not view the world in terms of discretely existing independent variables whose independent effect on variance can be measured

---

72. The utility of "mininukes" in contemporary scenarios is discussed in Dowler and Howard, "Countering the Threat"; and Thomas F. Ramos, "The Future of Theater Nuclear Forces," *Strategic Review* 19, no. 4 (Fall 1991): 41–47.
73. We thank Scott Sagan for his suggestions on this question.

according to the logic of statistics. This was, after all, Friedrich Kratochwil and John Ruggie's critique of treating norms as variables.[74] Instead, certain issues, events, possibilities may matter—they become meaningful—only in the context of a norm. Thus a distinction between "norms" and "non-norms" explanations may in some instances risk becoming a false dichotomy. For example, to argue that nuclear and chemical weapons were not used because alternatives were available obscures the fact that alternatives would not even have been sought in the first place if these weapons had been seen as just another uncontroversial weapon, like grenades or artillery shells. What counts as a concern is shaped by the normative context.

Norms structure realms of possibilities; they do not determine outcomes. Attaching a percentage figure to the effects of the norms versus the effects of other factors may be one way to think about norms and outcomes. But we think this approach is inaccurate, because, as our cases show, other factors (e.g., cost/benefits of use versus non-use) become politicized and relevant only in the context of a prohibitionary norm that adds force to such factors. It was the combination of these factors at historical junctures that mattered, and without the norm, the combination would not have been as potent. That doesn't mean that the norm did all the work itself, nor does it mean that the norm is simply residual.

The bottom line is that these taboos were a necessary condition—in the sense that we describe above—for the pattern of non-use of these weapons, but they alone were not the single, all-powerful "variable."

How These Norms Matter

It is important to underscore that norms are quite marginal in the existing deterrence literature and that we are asking about a dimension of analysis that receives little attention in the standard treatments. Because we are telling a "norms story," it is easy to assume that we must be making a case for the all-determining effects of all-powerful norms. We do not claim these taboos are truly "taken-for-granted" norms—that is, fully developed, robust intersubjective structures of the type that are the focus of some interpretive theorists.[75] They are rather contested norms-in-process that

---

74. Friedrich Kratochwil and John Gerard Ruggie, "International Organization: A State of the Art on an Art of the State," *International Organization* 40, no. 4 (Autumn 1986): 753–75.
75. Charles Taylor, "Interpretation and the Sciences of Man," in Paul Rabinow and William Sullivan, eds., *Interpretive Social Science: A Second Look*, pp. 33–81 (Berkeley: University of California Press, 1987).

have on occasion but not always exhibited the quality of an unthinking context (more true for nuclear than chemical weapons).

Our case studies illustrate a number of ways in which norms work. As we have stated, they structure realms of possibilities and create "options" that would not have been self-evident in the absence of a norm.[76] But they need not be wholly "taken for granted" to count. We have also indicated the way they operate instrumentally—for example, as public opinion constraints on leaders in the case of nuclear weapons and as a source of bargaining leverage in the global nonproliferation regime for Arab states in the case of cw.

These stories also are not just tales of two taboos in isolation. As we show, they are firmly embedded in deeper, "civilizational" normative structures. While the taboos themselves may be "in process," the higher-order discourses and world-order norms we refer to—of value-neutral technology and "civilization"—possess the kind of taken-for-grantedness of a norm as intersubjective context.

For example, how do we account for the fact that the anti-cw norm is sometimes obeyed, sometimes violated? Deterrence arguments underscore that since World War I the only use of cw has been against a foe that did not have a cw retaliatory capability. But explaining patterns of use and non-use via fear of retaliation fails to account for myriad situations in which no fear of retaliation existed and cw still were not used. To make sense of these practices, we need to take account of the higher-order norm of "civilization," which castigates users of cw as unfit for membership in civilized international society. This normative discourse structures new contexts of the realm of acceptable practice. It does not determine outcomes but makes certain practices acceptable or illegitimate. Without the cw taboo, there would not have been such otherwise unexplainable variation—cw would simply have been used whenever appropriate without controversy.

Likewise, without the normative inhibition on nuclear use it would be difficult to explain why the Soviet Union did not resort to nuclear weapons to avoid a costly and humiliating defeat in Afghanistan, why Britain did not use nuclear weapons in the Falklands, why Israel did not

---

76. Even punishment or ostracism for violation of a norm only becomes a possibility that would not exist in the absence of the norm. The norm itself does not determine the reaction but sets the context for how use is interpreted. Murder is seen as a violation, but a murderer sometimes gets off with a year in jail, sometimes gets the electric chair. The norm proscribing murder itself does not determine these outcomes, but they would not be understandable if such a norm were not present.

use them on Egypt in 1973, or the United States in the Gulf war—all cases in which the adversary could not retaliate in kind. It is also essential to making sense of the perceived illegitimacy of even benign uses of nuclear explosions, such as for blasting new riverbeds in northern Russia or harbors in developing countries. In remarking on the blanket perception of nuclear weapons as "evil," Thomas Schelling has noted the "virtually universal rejection" by American arms controllers and energy-policy analysts in the 1970s of a proposal to create an ecologically clean source of electrical energy that would have detonated tiny thermonuclear bombs in underground caverns to generate steam. As Schelling commented, "I have seen this idea unanimously dismissed without argument, as if the objections were too obvious to require articulation." The view was simply that "even 'good' thermonuclear explosions are bad and should be kept that way."[77]

In sum, norms can work in a variety of ways and have a variety of effects. We highlight constraining, permissive, and constitutive effects of these taboos. They may manifest differing degrees of embeddedness or taken-for-grantedness. Norms can justify action or the lack thereof. They can work instrumentally, for example, out of fear of punishments (sanctions, costs) or the constraints imposed by domestic or international public opinion (this is consistent with a rationalist formulation). Norms also have permissive or enabling effects, permitting alternatives through both focusing and obscuring effects. They may also have constitutive effects—as we suggest with regard to the larger discourse of "civilization" and identity. Here they work because of conceptions of "who we are"—certain kinds of people just do or do not do certain things. Finally, they can be such a taken-for-granted part of "context" that they are not consciously considered at all.

Constructivism's contribution is that it evokes the "context" effects of norms. It rejects the dichotomy of norms versus interests/material factors. Material factors by themselves are not all there is; their meaning depends on how they are interpreted. We have shown that even in the hardest cases, such as nuclear weapons—in which material factors should be so overwhelming—it would be impossible to tell an entirely non-norms story about these non-use events.

Origins of Norms

A final issue is how we account for the existence of these taboos in the first place. As we have outlined above, the conventional explanation is a ratio-

---

77. Thomas Schelling, "The Role of Nuclear Weapons" (unpublished manuscript, February 1993), pp. 11–12.

nalist, functionalist one. It accepts the genuine usefulness of the taboos but argues that they reflect a straightforward utility function. These taboos and the resultant self-restraint are in the interests of states, and this explains both their origins and why people continue to observe them.[78]

We have two lines of response to this explanation. First, as we argue, a rationalist account of the origins of these taboos is either wrong (cw) or incomplete (nw) on empirical grounds. For cw, the essentialist reasoning as exhibited by Mandelbaum cannot account for the taboo, and the argument from utility does not hold up. For nuclear weapons, the rationality argument, which dominates the literature, is important but underspecified and insufficient. It misses the fact that luck, contingency, iterated behavior, and moral concerns all went into changing interpretations of "interests" and the calculation of "rational" costs and benefits. Further, simply attributing abhorrence to nuclear weapons does not account for the changing context (such that they were not seen as prohibitively abhorrent during World War II but they were afterward).

This leads us to our second point, which is that a rationalist account is ultimately indeterminate. Saying that the origins of the taboos are rationally based begs the question of what gets to count as rational and why. Once taboos of self-restraint exist, it may well be functional to uphold them (for either instrumental or constitutive reasons). But our question is the prior one of what constitutes "functional" or "rational." We can imagine, for example, other taboos that would be very "functional" but that don't exist—taboos on war, handguns, cigarettes, missiles, etc. For example, it would have been very functional indeed for the belligerents in World War I to forsake the senseless slaughter of the trenches by "mutually deterring" each other from using machine guns. But they did not. Thus perhaps a weakness of our research design is that we do not study noncases of taboos, which might make clearer our point that there is nothing inevitable about the existence of these taboos, even though they might seem so self-evidently rational in retrospect.[79]

Ultimately, it must be admitted, a rational story can be told about virtually any outcome in retrospect. But honest inquiry recognizes that ratio-

---

78. This functional, interest-based explanation would argue that non-use of weapons of mass destruction is entirely consistent with a rationalist interpretation, especially if extended to include the somewhat long-term "rationality" of making norms and institutions worth preserving.

79. Causal inference and the study of norms are entirely compatible, but the substantive interests of researcher and research design may not be. In our case we have chosen a subject matter that is meaningful politically but nevertheless violates dictums to study null cases. This is a problem for all empirical research, however.

nalism, like any theoretical perspective, has both uses and limits; constructivism's contributions lie in probing the latter. It may well be that rationalism has theorized about norms and culture, i.e., instrumentally, and has explained them with rational choice arguments. We show other kinds of effects, and we demonstrate that these taboos developed for other reasons as well. We are not giving a story about "irrationality," but one about what counts as rational. A rational deterrence argument is thus not necessarily incompatible with the more complex "taboo" argument. Constructivism asks a different set of questions and attempts to fill in the gaps that rationalist approaches leave unexplained.

From the perspective of what counts as theory in international relations, our theoretical claims are modest. Our aims are more descriptive than theoretical, at least insofar as the focus on origins goes. We do draw on our case studies to suggest a number of generalizations regarding normative development and effects. But we make no claim to the kind of grand theory of international politics that overturns realist or liberal theory. Rather, the goal is to convince deterrence and rational choice theorists of the incompleteness of their arguments, not to defeat them in some epic Lakatosian battle as if only one can exist and the other must perish.

In conclusion, readers might wish to imagine what the world might be like if the taboos vanished—namely, if the use of these weapons came to seem "normal." This is an image of the future that practically everyone finds utterly horrible to contemplate. Perhaps taboos can thus be conceived of as providing images of "implicit possible futures." They implicitly contain or communicate a subconscious human awareness or vision of a terrible state of affairs that could come to pass if the future develops in a certain way.[80]

Such a thought experiment suggests the meaningfulness of these taboos. Our insistence on historical contingency and luck reminds us that while there are no iron laws of history here, even a world arranged according to human constructions has its limits.

---

80. We thank the late Richard Smoke for this provocative idea.

5 · Constructing Norms of Humanitarian Intervention

Martha Finnemore

Since the end of the Cold War, states have increasingly come under pressure to intervene militarily and, in fact, *have* intervened militarily to protect citizens other than their own from humanitarian disasters. Recent efforts to enforce protected areas for Kurds and no-fly zones over Shiites in Iraq, efforts to alleviate starvation and establish some kind of political order in Somalia, the huge UN military effort to disarm parties and rebuild a state in Cambodia, and to some extent even the military actions to bring humanitarian relief in Bosnia are all instances of military action whose primary goal is not territorial or strategic but humanitarian.

Realist and liberal theories do not provide good explanations for this behavior. The interests that these theories impute to states are geostrategic and/or economic, yet many or most of these interventions occur in states of negligible geostrategic or economic importance to the interveners. Thus, no obvious national interest is at stake for the states bearing the bur-

This essay benefited from comments by Michel Girard, James Goldgeier, Richard Hermann, Peter Katzenstein, Elizabeth Kier, Stephen Krasner, Joseph Lepgold, James Lee Ray, Henry Shue, Nina Tannenwald, Stephen Walt, Alexander Wendt, two anonymous reviewers for Columbia University Press, and the participants at the third Social Science Research Council/MacArthur Workshop at Stanford University, October 1994. Research assistance and insightful comments by Darel Paul are gratefully acknowledged.

den of the military intervention in most if not all of these cases. Somalia is perhaps the clearest example of military action undertaken in a state of little or no strategic or economic importance to the principal intervener. Similarly, the states that played central roles in the UN military action in Cambodia were, with the exception of China, not states that had any obvious geostrategic interests there by 1989; China, which did have a geostragetic interest, bore little of the burden of intervening. Realism and liberalism offer powerful explanations for the Persian Gulf war but have little to say about the extension of that war to Kurdish and Shiite protection through the enforcement of UN Resolution 688. The United States, France, and Britain have been allowing abuse of the Kurds for centuries. Why they should start caring about them now is not clear.

The recent pattern of humanitarian interventions raises the issue of what interests intervening states could possibly be pursuing. In most of these cases, the intervention targets are insignificant by any usual measure of geostrategic or economic interest. Why, then, do states intervene?

This essay argues that the pattern of intervention cannot be understood apart from the changing normative context in which it occurs. Normative context is important because it shapes conceptions of interest. Standard analytic assumptions about states and other actors pursuing their interests tend to leave the sources of interests vague or unspecified. The contention here is that international normative context shapes the interests of international actors and does so in both systematic and systemic ways. Unlike psychological variables that operate at the individual level, norms can be systemic-level variables in both origin and effects.[1] Because they are *inter*subjective, rather than merely subjective, widely held norms are not idiosyncratic in their effects. Instead, they leave broad patterns of the sort that social science strives to explain.

In this essay I examine the role of humanitarian norms in shaping patterns of humanitarian military intervention over the past 150 years.[2] I

1. One could have subsystemic normative contexts as well, as illustrated by several essays in this volume.
2. The term *military intervention* in this essay refers to the deploying of military forces by a foreign power or powers for the purpose of controlling domestic policies or political arrangements in the target state in ways that clearly violate sovereignty. *Humanitarian intervention* is used to mean military intervention with the goal of protecting the lives and welfare of foreign civilians.
Note that interventions to protect a state's *own* nationals from abuse are excluded from this analysis. Such intervention was once categorized as humanitarian by international legal scholars, but it does not present the same intellectual puzzles about interests, since protecting one's own nationals is clearly connected to conventional understandings of national interest. Further, scholars of interna-

show that shifts in intervention behavior correspond with changes in normative standards articulated by states concerning appropriate ends and means of military intervention. Specifically, normative understandings about which human beings merit military protection and about the way in which such protection must be implemented have changed, and state behavior has changed accordingly. This broad correlation establishes the norms explanation as plausible. The failure of alternative explanations to account for changing patterns of intervention behavior increases the credibility of the norms approach. I conclude with a discussion of ways to move beyond this plausibility probe.

The analysis proceeds in five parts. The first shows that realist and liberal approaches to international politics do not explain humanitarian intervention as a practice, much less change in that practice over time, because of their exogenous and static treatment of interests. A constructivist approach that attends to the role of international norms can remedy this by allowing us to problematize interests and their change over time. The next section examines humanitarian action in the nineteenth century. It shows that humanitarian action and even intervention on behalf of Christians being threatened or mistreated by the Ottoman Turks were carried out occasionally throughout the nineteenth century. However, only Christians appear to be deserving targets of humanitarian intervention; mistreatment of other groups does not evoke similar concern.

The third section investigates the expansion of this definition of "humanity" by examining efforts to abolish slavery, the slave trade, and colonization. Protection of nonwhite non-Christians did become a motivation for military action by states, especially Great Britain, in the early nineteenth century, when efforts to stop the slave trade began in earnest. But the scope of this humanitarian action was limited. Britain acted to stop commerce in slaves on the high seas; she did not intervene militarily to protect them inside other states or to abolish slavery as a domestic institution of property rights. It was not until decolonization that this redefinition of "humanity" in more universal terms (not just Christians, not just whites) was consolidated.

----

tional law are increasingly making the distinction that I make here and reserving the term *humanitarian intervention* for military protection of foreign citizens, as I do, to follow changing state practice. See Anthony Clark Arend and Robert J. Beck, *International Law and the Use of Force: Beyond the UN Charter Paradigm* (New York: Routledge, 1993), esp. ch. 8; and Fernando Tesón, *Humanitarian Intervention: An Inquiry Into Law and Morality* (Dobbs Ferry, N.Y.: Transnational Publishers, 1988).

The fourth section briefly reviews humanitarian intervention as a state practice since 1945, paying particular attention to the multilateral and institutional requirements that have evolved for humanitarian intervention. Contemporary multilateralism differs qualitatively from previous modes of joint state action and has important implications for the planning and execution of humanitarian interventions. The essay concludes by outlining questions about the role and origins of norms that are not treated here but could be addressed in future research.

Using Norms to Understand International Politics

Humanitarian intervention looks odd from conventional perspectives on international political behavior because it does not conform to the conceptions of interest that they specify. Realists would expect to see some geostrategic or political advantage to be gained by intervening states. Neoliberals might emphasize economic or trade advantages for interveners.

As I discussed in the introduction, it is difficult to identify the advantage for the intervener in most post-1989 cases. The 1989 U.S. action in Somalia is a clear case of intervention without obvious interests. Economically Somalia was insignificant to the United States. Security interests are also hard to find. The U.S. had voluntarily given up its base at Berbera in Somalia because advances in communications and aircraft technology made it obsolete for the communications and refueling purposes it once served. Further, the U.S. intervention in that country was not carried out in a way that would have furthered strategic interests. If the U.S. had truly had designs on Somalia, it should have welcomed the role of disarming the clans. It did not. The U.S. resisted UN pressures to "pacify" the country as part of its mission. In fact, U.S. officials were clearly and consistently interested not in controlling any part of Somalia but in getting out of the country as soon as possible—sooner, indeed, than the UN would have liked. The fact that some administration officials opposed the Somalia intervention on precisely the grounds that no vital U.S. interest was involved underscores the realists' problem.

Intervention to reconstruct Cambodia presents similar anomalies. The country is economically insignificant to the interveners and, with the end of the Cold War, was strategically significant to none of the five on the UN Security Council except China, which bore very little of the intervention burden. Indeed, U.S. involvement appears to have been motivated by domestic opposition to the return of the Khmers Rouges on moral grounds—another anomaly for these approaches—rather than by geopolitical or economic interests.

Liberals of a more classical and Kantian type might argue that these interventions have been motivated by an interest in promoting democracy and liberal values. After all, the UN's political blueprint for reconstructing these states is a liberal one. But such arguments also run afoul of the evidence. The U.S. consistently refused to take on the state-building and democratization mission in Somalia that liberal arguments would have expected to be at the heart of U.S. efforts. Similarly, the UN stopped short of authorizing an overthrow of Saddam Hussein in Iraq even when it was militarily possible and supported by many in the U.S. armed forces. The UN, and especially the U.S., have emphasized the humanitarian rather than the democratizing nature of these interventions, both rhetorically and in their actions on the ground.

None of these realist or liberal approaches provides an answer to the question, What interests are intervening states pursuing? In part this is a problem of theoretical focus. Realism and most liberals do not investigate interests; they assume them. Interests are givens in these approaches and need to be specified before analysis can begin. In this case, however, the problem is also substantive. The geostrategic and economic interests specified by these approaches appear to be wrong.

Investigating interests requires a different kind of theoretical approach. Attention to international norms and the way they structure interests in coordinated ways across the international system provides such an approach. Further, a norms approach addresses an issue obscured by approaches that treat interests exogenously: it focuses attention on the ways in which interests change. Since norms are socially constructed, they evolve with changes in social interaction. Understanding this normative evolution and the changing interests it creates is a major focus of a constructivist research program and of this analysis.

A constructivist approach does not deny that power and interest are important. They are. Rather, it asks a different and prior set of questions: it asks what interests *are*, and it investigates the ends to which and the means by which power will be used. The answers to these questions are not simply idiosyncratic and unique to each actor. The social nature of international politics creates normative understandings among actors that, in turn, coordinate values, expectations, and behavior. Because norms make similar behavioral claims on dissimilar actors, they create coordinated patterns of behavior that we can study and about which we can theorize.[3]

Before beginning the analysis, let me clarify the relationship postulated here among norms, interests, and actions. In this essay I understand norms to shape interests and interests to shape action. Neither connection is determinative. Factors other than norms may shape interests, and certainly no single norm or norm set is likely to shape a state's interests on any given issue. In turn, factors other than state interests, most obviously power constraints, shape behavior and outcomes. Thus, the connection assumed here between norms and action is one in which norms create permissive conditions for action but do not determine action. Changing norms may change state interests and create new interests (in this case, interests in protecting non-European non-Christians and in doing so multilaterally through an international organization). But the fact that states are now interested in these issues does not guarantee pursuit of these interests over all others on all occasions. New or changed norms enable new or different behaviors; they do not ensure such behaviors.

I should also offer a rationale for examining justifications for intervention as an indicator of norms and norm change. The conventional wisdom is that justifications are mere fig leaves behind which states hide their less savory and more self-interested reasons for actions. Motivation is what matters; justification is not important.

It is true that justification does not equal motivation. Humanitarian justifications have been used to disguise baser motives in more than one intervention. More frequently, motives for intervention are mixed; humanitarian motives may be genuine but may be only one part of a larger constellation of motivations driving state action.[4] Untangling precise

3. For a more extended discussion, see Martha Finnemore, *Defining National Interests in International Society* (Ithaca: Cornell University Press, 1996), ch. 1. There is not space here to discuss the various sociological and psychological links between norms and behavior. For one set of sociological arguments, see Walter W. Powell and Paul J. DiMaggio, eds., *The New Institutionalism in Organizational Analysis* (Chicago: University of Chicago Press, 1991). For a somewhat different view, see James G. March and Johan P. Olsen, *Rediscovering Institutions: The Organizational Basis of Politics* (New York: Free Press, 1989). For psychological arguments, see Henri Tajfel, *Human Groups and Social Categories: Studies in Social Psychology* (Cambridge: Cambridge University Press, 1981).
4. The U.S. intervention in Grenada is one such case, in which humanitarian justifications were offered (and widely rejected) for action of doubtful humanitarian motivation. See discussion in Tesón, *Humanitarian Intervention*, pp. 188–200. The Spanish-American War is a slightly different case, in which the U.S. offered humanitarian justifications as part of what were genuinely very complex motives for intervention. See Marc Trachtenberg, "Intervention in Historical Perspective," in Laura Reed and Carl Kaysen, eds., *Emerging Norms of Justified Intervention*, pp. 15–36 (Cambridge, Mass.: Committee on International Security Studies, American Academy of Arts and Sciences, 1993).

motivations for intervention is difficult and would be impossible in an essay of this length and historical breadth.

The focus here is justification, and for the purposes of this study justification *is* important because it speaks directly to normative context. When states justify their interventions, they are drawing on and articulating shared values and expectations held by other decision makers and other publics in other states. It is literally an attempt to connect one's actions to standards of justice or, perhaps more generically, to standards of appropriate and acceptable behavior. Thus through an examination of justifications we can begin to piece together what those internationally held standards are and how they may change over time.

My aim here is to establish the plausibility and utility of norms as an explanation for international behavior. States may violate international norms and standards of right conduct that they themselves articulate. But they do not always—or even often—do so. Aggregate behavior over long periods shows patterns that correspond to notions of right conduct over time. As shared understandings about who is "human" and about how intervention to protect those people must be carried out change, behavior shifts accordingly in ways not correlated with standard conceptions of interests.

We can investigate these changes by comparing humanitarian intervention practice in the nineteenth century with that of the twentieth century. The analysis is instructive in a number of ways. First, the analysis shows that humanitarian justifications for state action and state use of force are not new.

Second, the analysis shows that while humanitarian justifications for action have been important for centuries, the content and application of those justifications have changed over time. Specifically, states' perceptions of *which* human beings merit intervention has changed. I treat this not as a change of *identity*, as other essays in the volume use that term, but as a change of *identification*. Nonwhite non-Christians always knew they were human. What changed was perceptions of Europeans about them. People in Western states began to identify with non-Western populations during the twentieth century, with profound political consequences, for human-

---

It should also be noted that humanitarian justifications are often *not* offered by states that might legitimately claim them. Tanzania's invasion against Amin's Uganda and Vietnam's invasion of Pol Pot's Cambodia were both justified on security grounds. India initially offered humanitarian reasons for her 1971 intervention after massacres in East Pakistan but quickly dropped those in favor of self-defense and security justifications. See discussion below.

itarian intervention, among other things. Perhaps one could argue that the identity of the Western states changed, but I am not sure how one would characterize or operationalize such a change. Certainly Western states have not taken on an identity of "humanitarian state." Far too many inhumane acts have been committed by these states in this century to make such a characterization credible—nor do Western states themselves proclaim any such identity. Besides, these states were "humanitarian" on their own terms in the nineteenth century. What has changed is not the fact of the humanitarian behavior but its focus. Identification emphasizes the affective relationships between actors rather than the characteristics of a single actor.[5] Further, identification is an ordinal concept, allowing for degrees of affect as well as changes in the focus of affect. Identification—of Western Europeans with Greeks and of Russians with their fellow Slavs—existed in the nineteenth century. The task is to explain how and why this identification expanded to other groups.

Third, the analysis highlights contestation over these normative justifications and links it to change. Ironically, while norms are inherently consensual (they exist only as convergent expectations or intersubjective understandings), they evolve in part through challenges to that consensus. Some challenges succeed, some fail. The analysis traces the challenges posed by humanitarian claims, noting where they succeed and where they have failed. It also points to instances of continued contestation, even over norms that appear to be gaining wider acceptance. Humanitarian norms have risen in prominence, but their acceptance is still limited and contested; certainly there are many forms of intervention, particularly unilateral intervention, that apparently cannot be justified even by humanitarian norms.

Fourth, the analysis relates evolving humanitarian intervention norms to other normative changes over the past century. When humanitarian intervention is viewed in a broader normative context, it becomes clear that changes in this particular norm are only one manifestation of the changes in a larger set of humanitarian norms that have become more visible and more powerful in the past fifty or one hundred years. Particularly prominent among these changing norms are the norms of decolonization and self-determination, which involved a redefinition and universalization of "humanity" for Europeans that changed the evolution of sovereignty and of humanitarian discourse (both of which are essential components of human-

---

5. Obviously, single-actor characteristics may be defined in relation to or by comparison with those of others, but identification makes affective relationship central in ways that identity does not.

itarian intervention). Thus mutually reinforcing and consistent norms appear to strengthen each other; success in one area (such as decolonization) strengthens and legitimates claims in logically and morally related norms (such as human rights and humanitarian intervention). The relationship identified between decolonization and humanitarian intervention suggests the importance of viewing norms not as individual "things" floating atomistically in some international social space but rather as part of a highly structured social context. It may make more sense to think of a fabric of interlocking and interwoven norms rather than individual norms of this or that—as current scholarship, my own included, has been inclined to do.[6]

Finally, the analysis emphasizes the structuring and organization of the international normative context. Examination of humanitarian norms and intervention suggests that norm institutionalization, by which I mean the way norms become embedded in international organizations and institutions, is critical to patterns of norm evolution. Institutionalization of these norms or norm-bundles in international organizations (such as the UN) further increases the power and elaboration of the normative claims.

Humanitarian Intervention in the Nineteenth Century

Before the twentieth century virtually all instances of military intervention to protect people other than the intervener's own nationals involved protection of Christians from the Ottoman Turks.[7] In at least four instances

---

6. The intellectual orientation of the regimes literature probably had much to do with this atomized treatment of norms. Norms were incorporated as a definitional part of regimes, but regimes were always conceived of as pertaining to individual issue areas. Scholars wrote about norms pertaining to specific issues without addressing either the larger context in which these norms exist or the ways in which they may be related one to another.

Arguments about interrelationships among norms and the nature of an overarching social normative structure have been made by both sociological institutionalists like John Meyer and, to a lesser extent, English School scholars like Gerrit Gong, in his discussion of standards of "civilization." See George Thomas, John Meyer, Francisco Ramirez, and John Boli, eds., *Institutional Structure: Constituting State, Society, and the Individual* (Newbury Park, Calif.: Sage, 1987), esp. ch. 1; also Gerrit Gong, *The Standard of "Civilisation" in International Society* (Oxford: Clarendon Press, 1984). For an extended discussion of normative fabrics and social structures, see Finnemore, *Defining National Interests in International Society*.

7. Intervention in the Boxer Rebellion in China (1898–1900) is an interesting related case. I omit it from the analysis here because the primary goal of the intervenors was to protect their own nationals, not the Chinese. But the intervention did have the happy result of protecting a large number of mostly Christian Chinese from slaughter.

during the nineteenth century, European states used humanitarian claims to influence Balkan policy in ways that would have required states to use force—in the Greek War for Independence (1821–1827); in the Lebanon/Syria conflict of 1860–1861; during the Bulgarian agitation of 1876–1878; and in response to the Armenian massacres (1894–1917). Although full-scale military intervention did not result in all these instances, the claims made and their effects on policy in the other cases shed light on the evolution and influence of humanitarian claims during this period.

Greek War for Independence (1821–1827)

Russia took an immediate interest in the Greek insurrection and threatened to use force against the Turks as early as the first year of the war. Part of her motivation was geostrategic: Russia had been pursuing a general strategy of weakening the Ottomans and consolidating control in the Balkans for years. But the justifications that Russia offered were largely humanitarian. Russia had long seen herself as the defender of Orthodox Christians under Turkish rule. Atrocities such as the wholesale massacres of Christians and the sale of women into slavery, coupled with the sultan's order to seize the Venerable Patriarch of the Orthodox Church after mass on Easter morning and hang him and three archbishops, then have the bodies thrown into the Bosporus, formed the centerpiece of Russia's complaints against the Turks and the justification of her threats of force.[8]

Other European powers, with the exception of France, opposed intervention largely because they were concerned that weakening Turkey would

---

8. J. A. R. Marriott, *The Eastern Question: An Historical Study in European Diplomacy* (Oxford: Clarendon Press, 1917), pp. 183–85. There were plenty of atrocities on both sides in this conflict. Many of the early Turkish massacres were in response to previous insurgent massacres of Muslims at Morea and elsewhere in April 1821. For example, Greek Christians massacred approximately eight thousand Turkish Muslims in the town of Tripolitza in 1821. In all, about twenty thousand Muslims were massacred during the war in Greece without causing the great powers concern. Since, under the law of the Ottoman Empire, the patriarch of Constantinople was responsible for the good behavior of his flock, his execution was viewed as justified. See Eric Carlton, *Massacres: An Historical Perspective* (Aldershot, Hants, Eng.: Scolar Press, 1994), p. 82; Marriott, *The Eastern Question*, p. 183; *Cambridge Modern History* (New York: Macmillan, 1911), 10:178–83.

Atrocities continued throughout the five-plus years of the conflict and fueled the Russian claims. Perhaps the most sensational of these were the atrocities committed by Egyptian troops under Ibrahim when they arrived to quell the Greek insurrection in 1825 for the sultan (to whom they were vassals). Egyptian troops began a process of wholesale extermination of the Greek populace, apparently aimed at recolonization of the area by Muslims. This fresh round of horrors was cited by European powers as the reason for their final press toward a solution.

strengthen Russia.[9] Although the governments of Europe seemed little affected by these atrocities, significant segments of their publics were. A philhellenic movement spread throughout Europe, especially in the more democratic societies of Britain, France, and parts of Germany. The movement drew on two popular sentiments: the European identification with the classical Hellenic tradition and the appeal of Christians oppressed by the infidel. Philhellenic aid societies in Western Europe sent large sums of money and even volunteers to Greece during the war.[10]

Russian threats of unilateral action against the sultan eventually forced the British to become involved, and in 1827 the two powers, together with Charles X of France in his capacity as "Most Christian King," sent an armada that roundly defeated Ibrahim at Navarino in October 1827.

It would be hard to argue that humanitarian considerations were decisive in this intervention; geostrategic factors were far too important. However, the episode does bear on the evolution of humanitarian norms is several ways.

First, it illustrates the circumscribed definition of who was "human" in the nineteenth-century conception of that term. The massacre of Christians was a humanitarian disaster; the massacre of Muslims was not. This was true regardless of the fact that the initial atrocities of the war were committed by the Christian insurgents (admittedly after years of harsh Ottoman rule). The initial Christian uprising at Morea "might well have been allowed to burn itself out 'beyond the pale of civilization'"; it was only the wide-scale and very visible atrocities against Christians that put the events on the agenda of major powers.[11]

Second, intervening states, particularly Russia and France, placed humanitarian but also religious reasons at the center of their continued calls for intervention and application of force. As will be seen in other cases from the nineteenth century, religion seems to be important in both motivating humanitarian action and defining who is human. Notions about Christian charity supported general humanitarian impulses, but specific religious identifications had the effect of privileging certain people over others. In this case Christians generally were privileged over Muslims.

---

9. France had a long-standing protective arrangement with Eastern Christians, described below, and had consistently favored armed intervention (*Cambridge Modern History*, 10:193).

10. William St. Clair, *That Greece Might Still Be Free* (London: Oxford University Press, 1972), p. 81; C. W. Crawley, *The Question of Greek Independence* (New York: Howard Fertig, 1973), p. 1; *Cambridge Modern History*, 10:180.

11. *Cambridge Modern History*, 10:178–79.

Elsewhere, as later in Armenia and Bulgaria, denominational differences within Christianity appear to be important both in motivating action and in restraining it.

Third, the intervention was multilateral. The reasons in this case were largely geostrategic (restraining Russia from temptation to use this intervention for other purposes), but, as subsequent discussion will show, multilateralism as a characteristic of legitimate intervention becomes increasingly important.

Fourth, mass publics were involved. It is not clear that they influenced policy making as strongly as they would in the second half of the century, but foreign civilians did become involved both financially and militarily on behalf of the Greeks. Indeed, it was a British Captain Hastings who commanded the Greek flotilla that destroyed a Turkish squadron off Salona and provoked the ultimate use of force at Navarino.[12]

Lebanon/Syria (1860–1861)

In May 1860 conflict between Druze and Maronite populations broke out in what is now Lebanon but at the time was Syria under Ottoman rule. Initial rioting became wholesale massacre of Maronites, first by the Druze and later by Turkish troops.

The conflict sparked outrage in the French popular press. As early as 1250, Louis IX had signed a charter with the Maronite Christians in the Levant guaranteeing protection as if they were French subjects and, in effect, making them part of the French nation.[13] Since then, France had styled itself as the "protector" of Latin Christians in the Levant.[14]

Napoleon III thus eagerly supported military intervention in the region, at least in part to placate "outraged Catholic opinion" at home.[15] Russia was also eager to intervene, and Britain became involved in the intervention to prevent France and Russia from using the incident to expand.[16]

On August 3, 1860, the six great powers (Austria, France, Britain, Prussia, Russia, and Turkey) signed a protocol authorizing the dispatch of

---

12. Ibid., p. 196.
13. R. W. Seton-Watson, *Britain in Europe, 1789 to 1914* (New York: Macmillan, 1937), p. 419; also Trachtenberg, "Intervention in Historical Perspective," p. 23.
14. Seton-Watson, *Britain in Europe*, pp. 419–20; Trachtenberg, "Intervention in Historical Perspective," p. 23.
15. Seton-Watson, *Britain in Europe*, p. 421.
16. Ibid., p. 420.

twelve thousand European troops to the region to aid the sultan in stopping violence and establishing order. A letter from French foreign minister Thouvenal to the French ambassador in Turkey stressed that "the object of the mission is to assist stopping, by prompt and energetic measures, the effusion of blood, and [to put] an end to the outrages committed against Christians, which cannot remain unpunished." The protocol further emphasized the lack of strategic and political ambitions of the powers acting in this matter.[17]

France supplied half the twelve thousand troops immediately and dispatched them in August 1860. The other states sent token warships and high-ranking officers but no ground troops, which meant that in the end the six thousand French troops were the sum total of the intervention force.

The French forces received high marks for their humanitarian conduct while they were in the region, helping villagers to rebuild homes and farms. They left when agreement was reached for Christian representation in the government.[18]

This case repeats many of the features of the Greek intervention. Again, saving Christians was central to the justification for intervention. Public opinion seems to have had some impact, this time on the vigor with which Napoleon pursued an interventionist policy. The multilateral character of the intervention is somewhat less clear, however. There was multilateral consultation and agreement on the intervention plan, but the execution of that plan was essentially unilateral.

The Bulgarian Agitation (1876–1878)

In May 1876 Ottoman troops massacred unarmed and poorly organized agitators in Bulgaria. A British government investigation put the number killed at twelve thousand, with fifty-nine villages destroyed and an entire church full of people set ablaze after they had already surrendered to Turkish soldiers. The investigation confirmed that Turkish soldiers and officers were promoted and decorated rather than punished for these actions.[19]

---

17. Louis B. Sohn and Thomas Buergenthal, *International Protection of Human Rights* (Indianapolis: Bobbs-Merrill, 1973), pp. 156–60.
18. A. L. Tiwabi, *A Modern History of Syria* (London: Macmillan, 1969), p. 131; Seton-Watson, *Britain in Europe*, p. 421.
19. Mason Whiting Tyler, *The European Powers and the Near East, 1875–1908* (Minneapolis: University of Minnesota Press, 1925), p. 66 n.; Seton-Watson, *Britain in Europe*, pp. 519–20; Marriott, *The Eastern Question*, pp. 291–92; *Cambridge Modern History*, 12:384.

Accounts of the atrocities, gathered by American missionaries and sent to British reporters, began appearing in British newspapers in mid-June. The reports inflamed public opinion, and protest meetings were organized around the country, particularly in the north, where W. T. Stead and his paper, the *Northern Echo*, were a focus of agitation.[20]

The result was a split in British politics. Prime Minister Disraeli publicly refused to change British policy of support for Turkey over the matter, stating that British material interests outweighed the lives of Bulgarians.[21] However, Lord Derby, the Conservative foreign secretary, telegraphed Constantinople that "any renewal of the outrages would be more fatal to the Porte than the loss of a battle."[22] More important, former prime minister Gladstone came out of retirement to oppose Disraeli on the issue, making the Bulgarian atrocities the centerpiece of his anti-Disraeli campaign.[23]

While Gladstone found a great deal of support in various public circles, he did not have similar success in government. The issue barely affected British policy. Disraeli was forced to carry out the investigation mentioned above, and he did offer proposals for internal Turkish reforms to protect minorities—proposals that were rejected by Russia as being too timid.[24]

Russia was the only state to intervene in the wake of the Bulgarian massacres. The 1856 treaty that ended the Crimean War was supposed to protect Christians under Ottoman rule. Russia justified her threats of force on the basis of Turkey's violation of these humanitarian guarantees. In March 1877 the great powers issued a protocol reiterating demands for the protection of Christians in the Ottoman Empire that had been guaranteed in the 1856 treaty. After Constantinople rejected the protocol, Russia declared war in April 1877. She easily defeated the Ottoman troops and signed the Treaty of San Stefano, which created a large, independent Bulgarian state—an arrangement that was drastically revised by the Congress of Berlin.

As in the previous cases, saving Christians was an essential feature of this incident, and Gladstone and Russia's justifications for action were

---

20. Seton-Watson, *Britain in Europe*, p. 519.
21. Mercia MacDermott, *A History of Bulgaria, 1393–1885* (New York: Praeger, 1962), p. 280.
22. *Cambridge Modern History*, 12:384.
23. Tyler, *European Powers and the Near East*, p. 70. Gladstone even published a pamphlet on the subject, *The Bulgarian Horrors and the Question of the East*, which sold more than 200,000 copies; Seton-Watson, *Britain in Europe*, p. 519; Marriott, *The Eastern Question*, p. 293.
24. MacDermott, *A History of Bulgaria*, p. 277; Tyler, *European Powers and the Near East*, p. 21.

framed in that way. But military action in this case was not multilateral.[25] Perhaps the most remarkable feature of this episode is its demonstration of the strength of public opinion and the media. While they were not able to change British policy they were able to make adherence to that policy much more difficult for Disraeli in domestic terms.

Armenia (1894–1917)

The Armenian case offers some interesting insights into the scope of Christianity requiring defense by European powers in the last century. Unlike the Orthodox Christians in Greece and Bulgaria and the Maronites in Syria, the Armenian Christians had no European champion. The Armenian Church was not in communion with the Orthodox Church, hence Armenian appeals had never resonated in Russia; the Armenians were not portrayed as "brothers" to the Russians, as were the Bulgarians and other Orthodox Slavs. Similarly, no non-Orthodox European state had ever offered protection or had historical ties as the French did with the Maronites. Thus some of the justifications that were offered for intervention in other cases were lacking in the Armenian case.

The fact that the Armenians were Christians, albeit of a different kind, does seem to have had some influence on policy. The Treaty of Berlin explicitly bound the sultan to carry out internal political reforms to protect Armenians, but the nature, timing, and monitoring of these provisions were left vague and were never enforced. The Congress of Berlin ignored an Armenian petition for an arrangement similar to that set up in Lebanon following the Maronite massacres (a Christian governor under Ottoman rule). Gladstone took up the matter in 1880 when he came back to power but dropped it when Bismarck voiced opposition.[26] The wave of massacres against Armenians beginning in 1894 was far worse than any of the other atrocities examined here, in terms of both the number killed and the brutality of their executions. Nine hundred people were killed, and twenty-four villages burned in the Sassum massacres in August 1894. After this, the intensity increased. Between fifty thousand and seventy thousand people were killed in 1895. In 1896 the massacres moved into the capital,

---

25. Arguably, too, the action was not intervention, since the Russians actually declared war. Since the war aims involved reconfiguring internal Ottoman arrangements of rule, however, the incident seems to have properties sufficiently similar to those of intervention to merit consideration in this study.

26. *Cambridge Modern History*, 12:415–17; Marriott, *The Eastern Question*, pp. 349–51.

Constantinople, where on August 28–29, six thousand Armenians were killed.[27]

These events were well known and highly publicized in Europe.[28] Gladstone came out of retirement yet again to denounce the Turks and called Abd-ul-Hamid the "Great Assassin." French writers denounced him as "the Red Sultan." The European powers demanded an inquiry assisted by Europeans, which submitted to European governments and the press extensive documentation of "horrors unutterable, unspeakable, unimaginable by the mind of man."[29] Public opinion pressed for intervention, and both Britain and France used humanitarian justifications to threaten force. But neither acted. Germany by this time was a force to be reckoned with, and the kaiser was courting Turkey. Russia was nervous about nationalist aspirations in the Balkans in general and had no special affection for the Armenians, as noted above. The combined opposition of Germany and Russia made the price of intervention higher than either the British or the French were willing to pay.[30]

These four episodes are suggestive in several ways. First, humanitarian justifications for uses of force and threats of force are not new in the twentieth century.

Second, humanitarian action was rarely taken when it jeopardized other stated goals or interests of a state. Humanitarians were sometimes able to mount considerable pressure on policy makers to act contrary to stated geostrategic interests, as in the case of Disraeli and the Bulgarian agitation, but they never succeeded. Humanitarian claims did, however, provide states with new or intensified interests in an area and new reasons to act where none had existed previously. Without the massacre of Maronites in Syria, France would almost certainly not have intervened. Further, she left after her humanitarian mission was accomplished and did not stay on to pursue other geostrategic goals, as some states had feared she would. It is less clear whether there would have been intervention in the Greek war for

27. Of course, these events late in the nineteenth century were only the tip of the iceberg. More than a million Armenians were killed by Turks during World War I, but the war environment obviates discussions of military intervention for the purposes of this essay.
28. Indeed, there were many firsthand European accounts of the Constantinople massacres, since execution gangs even forced their way into the houses of foreigners to execute Armenian servants (*Cambridge Modern History*, 12:417).
29. Quotation is from Lord Rosebery, as cited in *Cambridge History of British Foreign Policy*, 3:234.
30. *Cambridge Modern History*, 12:417–18; Sohn and Buergenthal, *International Protection of Human Rights*, p. 181.

independence without humanitarian justifications for such interventions. Russia certainly had other reasons to intervene, but she was also probably the state with the highest level of identification with the Orthodox Christian victims of these massacres. Whether the former would have been sufficient for intervention without the latter is impossible to know. Once Russia did intervene, the British certainly had an interest in restraining Russian activities in the area and joining the intervention. At the same time Britain had consistently articulated a strong doctrine of nonintervention. It may be that humanitarian claims made by important sectors of domestic opinion were necessary to override this doctrine, but it would be impossible to be certain.

Third, humanitarian action could be taken in a variety of forms. Action could be multilateral, as in the case of Greek independence. It could be unilateral, as when Russia intervened in Bulgaria. Action might also be some mixture of the two, as in Lebanon/Syria, where several states planned the intervention but execution was essentially unilateral. As will be shown below, this variety of forms for intervention shrinks over time. Specifically, the unilateral option for either planning or executing humanitarian intervention appears to have disappeared in the twentieth century.

Fourth, interveners identified with the victims of humanitarian disasters in some important *and exclusive* way. At a minimum, the victims to be protected by intervention were Christians; there were no instances of European powers' considering intervention to protect non-Christians. Pogroms against Jews did not provoke intervention. Neither did Russian massacres of Turks in Central Asia in the 1860s.[31] Neither did mass killings in China during the Taipings rebellion against the Manchus.[32] Neither did mass killings by colonial rulers in their colonies.[33] Neither did massacres of Native Americans in the United States. Often there was some more specific identification or social tie between intervener and intervened, as between the Orthodox Slav Russians and Orthodox Slav Bul-

---

31. For more on this, see Stanford J. Shaw and Ezel Kural Shaw, *History of the Ottoman Empire and Modern Turkey*, vol. 2, *Reform, Revolution, and Republic: The Rise of Modern Turkey* (Cambridge: Cambridge University Press, 1977).

32. Christopher Hibbert, *The Dragon Wakes: China and the West, 1793–1911* (Newton Abbot, Devon, Eng.: Readers Union, 1971). Hibbert estimates that the three-day massacre in Nanking alone killed more than 100,000 people (p. 303).

33. In one of the more egregious incidents of this kind, the Germans killed sixty-five thousand indigenous inhabitants of German Southwest Africa (Namibia) in 1904. See Barbara Harff, "The Etiology of Genocides," in Isidor Wallimann and Michael N. Dobkowski, eds., *Genocide and the Modern Age: Etiology and Case Studies of Mass Death*, pp. 46, 56 (New York: Greenwood, 1987).

garians. In fact, the Armenian case suggests, lack of such an intensified identification may contribute to inaction.

The Expansion of "Humanity" and Sovereignty

This last feature of nineteenth-century intervention, the ways in which interveners identify with victims to determine who is an appropriate or compelling candidate for intervention, changed dramatically over the twentieth century as the "humanity" deserving of protection by military intervention became universalized.[34] The seeds of this change lie in the nineteenth century, however, with efforts to end slavery and the slave trade. With the abolition of slavery in the nineteenth century and decolonization in the twentieth, a new set of norms was consolidated that universalized "humanity" and endowed it with rights, among them self-determination, which came to be equated with sovereign statehood. These processes are obviously complex and cannot be treated adequately here. What follows is a brief discussion showing how these larger normative developments contributed to the evolution of humanitarian intervention norms.[35]

Abolition of Slavery and the Slave Trade

The abolition of slavery and the slave trade in the nineteenth century was an essential part of the universalization of "humanity." European states generally accepted and legalized these practices in the seventeenth and eighteenth centuries, but by the nineteenth century the same states proclaimed them "repugnant to the principles of humanity and universal

---

34. The expansion of conceptions of humanity is also relevant to the development of international human rights and has been discussed by international legal scholars interested in such issues. See, for example, Louis Henkin, *The Age of Rights* (New York: Columbia University Press, 1990), ch. 1. The legal literature on international human rights, however, does not attend to the connection emphasized here between these expanding notions of humanity and the international use of organized military force.

35. One might argue that the current plight of the Bosnian Muslims suggests that "humanity" is not as universal as we would like to think. They, after all, are Muslims being slaughtered by Christians, and the Christian West is standing by. Countering this would be the case of Somalia, where the West *did* intervene to save a largely Muslim population. I would argue that the explanation for different intervention behaviors in these cases does not lie in humanitarian norms. Strong normative claims to intervene have been made in both cases and have met with different results, for old-fashioned geostrategic reasons. As is discussed elsewhere in this essay, humanitarian norms create only permissive conditions for intervention. They create an "interest" in intervention where none existed. They do not eliminate other competing interests, such as political or strategic interests.

morality."[36] Human beings previously viewed as beyond the edge of humanity—as, in fact, property—came to be viewed as human, and with that status came certain, albeit minimal, privileges and protections.[37] Further, military force was used by states, especially Britain, to suppress the slave trade. Britain succeeded in having the slave trade labeled as piracy, thus enabling her to seize and board ships sailing under non-British flags that were suspected of carrying contraband slaves.[38]

While this is in some ways an important case of a state using force to promote humanitarian ends, the way the British framed and justified their actions also says something about the limits of humanitarian claims in the early to mid-nineteenth century. First, the British limited their military action to abolishing the trade in slaves, not slavery itself. There was no military intervention on behalf of Africans as there was on behalf of Christians. While the British public and many political figures contributed to a climate of international opinion that viewed slavery with increasing distaste, the abolition of slavery as a domestic institution of property rights was accomplished in each state where it had previously been legal without military intervention by other states.[39] Further, the British government's strategy for ending the slave trade was to have such trafficking labeled as piracy, thus making the slaves "contraband," i.e., still property. The government justified its actions on the basis of maritime rights governing commerce. Slavery and slaveholding themselves did not provoke the same reaction as Ottoman abuse of Christians did.

---

36. The quotation comes from the Eight Power Declaration concerning the universal abolition of the trade in Negroes, signed February 8, 1815, by Britain, France, Spain, Sweden, Austria, Prussia, Russia, and Portugal (as quoted in Leslie Bethell, *The Abolition of the Brazilian Slave Trade* [Cambridge: Cambridge University Press, 1970], p. 14).

37. I do not mean to minimize the abuses suffered by freed slaves after emancipation, as Europeans tried in various ways to subvert the emancipation guarantees. I only wish to stress that emancipation entailed formal guarantees of a minimal kind (e.g., freedom against forced labor, freedom of movement) and that subversion was now necessary if whites were to obtain what had previously been available through overt methods.

38. Bethell, *Abolition of Brazilian Slave Trade*, ch. 1. In 1850 Britain went so far as to fire on and board ships in Brazilian ports to enforce antislave trafficking treaties (ibid., pp. 329–31). One might argue that such action was a violation of sovereignty and thus qualified as military intervention, but if so, it was intervention of a very peripheral kind.

39. The United States is a possible exception. One could argue that the North intervened militarily in the South to abolish slavery. Such an argument would presume that (a) there were ever two separate states such that the North's action could be understood as "intervention," rather than civil war and (b) abolishing slavery rather than maintaining the Union was the primary reason for the North's initial action. Both assumptions are open to serious question. (The Emancipation Proclamation was not signed until 1863, when the war was already half over.) Thus, while the case is suggestive of the growing power of a broader conception of "humanity," I do not treat it in this analysis.

This may be because the perpetrators of the humanitarian violations were "civilized" Christian nations (as opposed to the infidel Turks).[40] Another reason was probably that the targets of these humanitarian violations were black Africans, not "fellow Christians" or "brother Slavs." It thus appears that by the 1830s black Africans had become sufficiently "human" that enslaving them was illegal inside Europe, but enslaving them outside Europe was only distasteful. One could keep them enslaved if one kept them at home, within domestic borders. Abuse of Africans did not merit military intervention inside another state.

Colonization, Decolonization, and Self-determination

Justifications for both colonization and decolonization also offer interesting lenses through which to examine changing humanitarian norms and changing understandings of who is "human." Both processes—colonization and its undoing—were justified, at least in part, in humanitarian terms, but the understanding of what constituted humanity was different in the two episodes in ways that bear on the current investigation of humanitarian intervention norms.

The vast economic literature on colonization often overlooks the strong moral dimension perceived and articulated by many of the colonizers. Colonization was a crusade. It would bring the benefits of civilization to the "dark" reaches of the earth. It was a sacred trust, it was the white man's burden, it was mandated by God that these Europeans go out into unknown (to them) parts of the globe, bringing what they understood to be a better way of life to the inhabitants. Colonization for the missionaries and those driven by social conscience was a humanitarian mission of huge proportions and consequently of huge importance.

Colonialism's humanitarian mission was of a particular kind, however: it was to "civilize" the non-European parts of the world—to bring the "benefits" of European social, political, economic, and cultural arrangements to Asia, Africa, and the Americas. Until these peoples were "civilized," they were savages, barbarians, something less than human. Thus in an important sense the core of the colonial humanitarian mission was to *create* humanity where none had previously existed. Non-Europeans became human in European eyes by becoming Christian, by adopting European-style structures of property rights, by adopting European-style

---

40. For an extended treatment of the importance of the categories *civilized* and *barbarian* on state behavior in the nineteenth century, see Gong, *The Standard of "Civilisation" in International Society*.

territorial political arrangements, by entering the growing European-based international economy.[41]

Decolonization also had strong humanitarian justifications.[42] By the mid-twentieth century, however, normative understandings about humanity had shifted. Humanity was no longer something one could create by bringing savages to civilization. Rather, humanity was inherent in individual human beings. It had become universalized and was not culturally dependent, as it has been in earlier centuries. Asians and Africans were now viewed as having human "rights," and among those rights was the right to determine their own political future—the right to self-determination.

There is not space here to investigate in detail the origins of decolonization and accompanying human rights norms. I would, however, like to highlight three features of the decolonization process that bear on the evolution of humanitarian intervention.[43] First, as international legal scholars have long noted, logical coherence among norms greatly enhances their legitimacy and power.[44] Decolonization norms benefited greatly from their logical kinship with core European norms about human equality. As liberal norms about the "natural" rights of man spread and gained

41. Gerrit Gong provides a much more extensive discussion of what "civilization" meant to Europeans from an international legal perspective (see ibid.). Uday Mehta investigates the philosophical underpinnings of colonialism in Lockean liberalism and the strategies aimed at the systematic political exclusion of culturally dissimilar colonized peoples by liberals professing universal freedom and rights. One of these strategies was civilizational infantilization; treating peoples in India, for example, like children allowed liberals to exclude them from political participation and, at the same time, justified extensive tutelage in European social conventions in the name of civilizing them and preparing them for liberal political life. See Uday S. Mehta, "Liberal Strategies of Exclusion," *Politics and Society* 18 (1990): 427–54.

Of necessity, this very abbreviated picture of colonialism obscures the enormous variety in European views of what they were doing. Some social reformers and missionaries no doubt had much more generous notions of the "humanity" of the non-Europeans with whom they came in contact and treated them with respect. In the view of some more-racist participants in the colonialist project, no amount of Christian piety or Europeanization would ever raise these non-Europeans up to a level of humanity comparable to that of Europeans. My goal in this sketch is to emphasize the effort to create humanity so that connections with decolonization can be seen.

42. To reiterate, I am making no claims about the causes of decolonization. These causes were obviously complex and have been treated extensively in the vast literature on the subject. I argue only that humanitarian norms were central in the justification for decolonization.

43. Neta Crawford makes similar but not identical arguments in "Decolonization as an International Norm: The Evolution of Practices, Arguments, and Beliefs," in Reed and Kaysen, *Emerging Norms of Justified Intervention*, pp. 37–61.

44. For an excellent exposition, see Thomas M. Franck, *The Power of Legitimacy Among Nations* (New York: Oxford University Press, 1990), esp. ch. 10.

power within Europe, they influenced Europe's relationship with non-European peoples in important ways. The egalitarian social movements sweeping the European West in the eighteenth and nineteenth centuries were justified with universal truths about the nature and equality of human beings. These notions were then exported to the non-European world as part of the civilizing mission of colonialism. Once people begin to believe, at least in principle, in human equality, there is no logical limit to the expansion of human rights and self-determination.[45]

The logical expansion of these arguments fueled attacks on both slavery and colonization. Slavery, more blatantly a violation of these emerging European norms, came under attack first. Demands for decolonization came more slowly and had to contend with the counterclaims for the beneficial humanitarian effects of European rule. In both cases, former slaves and Western-educated colonial elites were instrumental in change. Having been "civilized" and Europeanized, they were able to use Europe's own norms against these institutions. These people undermined the social legitimacy of both slaveholders and colonizers not simply by being exemplars of "human" non-Europeans but also by contributing to the arguments undercutting the legitimacy of slavery and colonialism within a European framework of proclaimed human equality.

Although logic alone is not the reason that slavery and colonialism were abolished, there does appear to be some need for logical consistency in normative structures. Changes in core normative structure (in this case, changes toward recognition of human equality *within* Europe) tended to promote and facilitate associated normative changes elsewhere in society. Mutually reinforcing and logically consistent norms appear to be harder to attack and to have an advantage in the normative contestations that go on in social life. Thus, logic internal to the norms shapes their development and consequently social change.

Second, as Neta Crawford and others have noted, formal international organizations, particularly the United Nations, played a significant role in the decolonization process and the consolidation of anticolonialism norms. The self-determination norms laid out in the charter, the trusteeship system it set up, and the one-state-one-vote voting structure that gave majority power to weak, often formerly colonized states, all contributed to

---

45. Crawford, "Decolonization as an International Norm," p. 53. David Lumsdaine makes a similar point about the expanding internal logic of domestic welfare arguments that led to the creation of the foreign aid regime in *Moral Vision in International Politics: The Foreign Aid Regime, 1949–1989* (Princeton: Princeton University Press, 1993).

an international legal, organizational, and normative environment that made colonial practices increasingly illegitimate and difficult to carry out.[46]

Third, decolonization enshrined the notion of political self-determination as a basic human right associated with a now universal humanity. Political self-determination, in turn, meant sovereign statehood. Once sovereign statehood became associated with human rights, intervention, particularly unilateral intervention, became more difficult to justify. Unilateral intervention certainly still occurs, but, as will be seen below, it cannot now be justified even by high-minded humanitarian claims.

Humanitarian Intervention Since 1945

Unlike humanitarian intervention practices in the nineteenth century, virtually all of the instances in which claims of humanitarian intervention have been made in the post-1945 period concern military action on behalf of non-Christians and/or non-Europeans. In that sense, the universalizing of the "humanity" that might be worth protecting seems to have widened in accordance with the normative changes described above.

What is interesting in these cases is that states that might legitimately have claimed humanitarian justifications for their intervention did not do so. India's intervention in East Pakistan in the wake of Muslim massacres of Hindus, Tanzania's intervention in Uganda toppling the Idi Amin regime, Vietnam's intervention in Cambodia ousting the Khmers Rouges—in every case intervening states could have justified their actions with strong humanitarian claims. None did. In fact, India initially claimed humanitarian justifications but quickly retracted them. Why?

The argument here is that this reluctance stems not from norms about what is "humanitarian" but from norms about legitimate intervention. While the scope of who qualifies as human has widened enormously and the range of humanitarian activities that states routinely undertake has expanded,[47] norms about intervention have also changed, albeit less dras-

---

46. Even veto power on the Security Council could not protect colonial powers from the decolonizing trend, as the Suez incident in 1956 made clear to Britain and France. See Thomas Risse-Kappen's discussion of that case in essay 10 of this volume.

47. See, for example, Lumsdaine's excellent discussion of the rise and expansion of foreign aid in *Moral Vision in International Politics*. See also the discussion of humanitarian intercession in Sohn and Buergenthal, *International Protection of Human Rights*.

tically. Humanitarian military intervention now must be *multilateral* to be legitimate.

As we saw in the nineteenth century, multilateralism is not new; it has often characterized humanitarian military action. But states in the nineteenth century still invoked humanitarian justifications, even when intervention was unilateral (for example, Russia in Bulgaria during the 1870s and, in part, France in Lebanon). That has not happened in the twentieth century. Without multilateralism, states will not and apparently cannot claim humanitarian justification.[48]

Multilateralism had (and has) important advantages for states. It increases the transparency of each state's actions to others and so reassures states that opportunities for adventurism and expansion will not be used. Unilateral military intervention, even for humanitarian objectives, is viewed with suspicion; it is too easily subverted to serve less disinterested ends of the intervener. Further, multilateralism can be a way of sharing costs, and thus it can be cheaper for states than unilateral action.

Multilateralism carries with it significant costs of its own, however. Cooperation and coordination problems involved in such action have been examined in detail by political scientists and can make it difficult to sustain.[49] Perhaps more important, multilateral action requires sacrifice of power and control over the intervention. Further, it may seriously compromise the military effectiveness of those operations, as recent debates over command and control in UN military operations suggest.

---

48. One interesting exception that proves the rule is the U.S. claim of humanitarian justification for its intervention in Grenada. First, the human beings to be protected by the intervention were not Grenadans but U.S. nationals. Protecting one's own nationals can still be construed as protecting national interests and is therefore not anomalous or analytically interesting in the way that state action to protect nationals of *other* states is. Second, the humanitarian justification offered by the United States was widely rejected in the international community, underscoring the point made here that unilateral humanitarian intervention is generally treated with suspicion by states. See the discussions in Tesón, *Humanitarian Intervention*, pp. 188–200; and Arend and Beck, *International Law and the Use of Force*, pp. 126–28.

The apparent illegitimacy of unilateral humanitarian intervention is probably related to two broad issues that cannot be treated in this limited space—namely, the expansion of multilateralism as a practice and the strengthening of juridical sovereignty norms, especially among weak states. On multilateralism, see John G. Ruggie, ed., *Multilateralism Matters: The Theory and Praxis of an Institutional Form* (New York: Columbia University Press, 1993). Concerning the strengthening of sovereignty norms among weak states, see Stephen D. Krasner, *Structural Conflict* (Berkeley: University of California Press, 1985).

49. Significantly, those who are more optimistic about solving these problems and about the utility of multilateral action rely on norms to overcome the problems. Norms are an essential part of both regimes and multilateralism in the two touchstone volumes on these topics. See Stephen D. Krasner, ed., *International Regimes* (Ithaca: Cornell University Press, 1983), and Ruggie, *Multilateralism Matters*.

There are no obvious efficiency reasons for states to prefer either multilateral or unilateral intervention to achieve humanitarian ends. Each has advantages and disadvantages. The choice depends in large part on perceptions about the political acceptability and political costs of each, which, in turn, depend on normative context. As will be discussed below, multilateralism in the twentieth century has become institutionalized in ways that make unilateral intervention, particularly intervention not justified as self-defense, unacceptably costly.

The next two sections of the paper compare post–World War II interventions in situations of humanitarian disaster with nineteenth-century practice to illustrate these points. The first section provides a brief overview of unilateral intervention in the post-1945 period in which humanitarian justification could have been claimed to illustrate and elaborate these points but was not. Following that is an even briefer discussion of recent multilateral humanitarian actions that contrast with the previous unilateral cases.[50]

Unilateral Intervention in Humanitarian Disasters

India in East Pakistan (1971)

Pakistan had been under military rule by West Pakistani officials since partition. When the first free elections were held in November 1970, the Awami League won 167 out of 169 parliamentary seats reserved for East Pakistan in the National Assembly. The Awami League had not urged political independence for the East during the elections, but it did run on a list of demands concerning one-person-one-vote political representation and increased economic autonomy for the east. The government in West Pakistan viewed the Awami electoral victory as a threat. In the wake of these electoral results, the government in Islamabad decided to postpone the convening of the new National Assembly indefinitely, and in March 1971 the West Pakistani army started indiscriminately killing unarmed civilians, raping women, burning homes, and looting or destroying property. At least one million people were killed, and millions more fled across the border into India.[51] Following months of tension, border incidents,

---

50. These synopses are drawn in large part from Tesón, *Humanitarian Intervention*, ch. 8; Michael Akehurst, "Humanitarian Intervention," in Hedley Bull, ed., *Intervention in World Politics*, pp. 95–118 (Oxford: Clarendon Press, 1984); and Arend and Beck, *International Law and the Use of Force*, ch. 8.

51. Estimates of the number of refugees vary wildly. The Pakistani government put the number at two million; the Indian government claimed ten million. Independent estimates have ranged from five to nine million. See Tesón, *Humanitarian Intervention*, p. 182, including n. 163, for discussion.

and increased pressure from the influx of refugees, India sent troops into East Pakistan. After twelve days the Pakistani army surrendered at Dacca, and the new state of Bangladesh was established.

As in many of the nineteenth-century cases, the intervener here had an array of geopolitical interests. Humanitarian concerns were not the only reason or even, perhaps, the most important reason to intervene. It is, however, a case in which intervention could have been *justified* in humanitarian terms, and initially the Indian representatives in both the General Assembly and the Security Council did articulate such a justification.[52] These arguments were widely rejected by other states, including many with no particular interest in politics on the subcontinent. States as diverse as Argentina, Tunisia, China, Saudi Arabia, and the U.S. all responded to India's claims by arguing that principles of sovereignty and noninterference should take precedence and that India had no right to meddle in what they all viewed as an "internal matter." In response to this rejection of her claims, India retracted her humanitarian justifications, choosing instead to rely on self-defense to justify her actions.[53]

Tanzania in Uganda (1979).

This episode began as a straightforward territorial dispute. In the autumn of 1978 Ugandan troops invaded and occupied the Kagera salient—territory between the Uganda-Tanzania border and the Kagera River in Tanzania.[54] On November 1 Idi Amin announced annexation of the territory. Julius Nyerere considered the annexation tantamount to an act of war and on November 15 launched an offensive from the south bank of the Kagera River. Amin, fearing defeat, offered to withdraw from the occupied territories if Nyerere would promise to cease support for Ugandan dissidents and not to attempt to overthrow his government. Nyerere refused and made explicit his intention to help dissidents topple the Amin regime. In January 1979 Tanzanian troops crossed into Uganda, and by April Tanzanian troops, joined by some Ugandan rebel groups, had occupied Kampala and installed a new government headed by Yusef Lule.

---

52. See ibid., p. 186 n. 187, for the text of a General Assembly speech by the Indian representative articulating this justification. See also Akehurst, "Humanitarian Intervention," p. 96.

53. Akehurst concludes that India actually had prior statements concerning humanitarian justifications deleted from the Official Record of the UN (Akehurst, "Humanitarian Intervention," pp. 96–97).

54. Amin attempted to justify this move by claiming that Tanzania had previously invaded Ugandan territory.

As in the previous case, there were nonhumanitarian reasons to intervene, but if territorial issues were the only ones that mattered, the Tanzanians could have either stopped at the border, having evicted Ugandan forces, or pushed them back into Uganda short of Kampala. The explicit statement of intent to topple the regime seems out of proportion to the low-level territorial squabble. Fernando Tesón makes a strong case that Nyerere's intense dislike of Amin's regime and its practices influenced the scale of the response. Nyerere had already publicly called Amin a murder and refused to sit with him on the Authority of the East African Community.[55] Tesón also presents strong evidence that the lack of support or material help for Uganda in this intervention from the UN, the OAU, or any state besides Libya suggests tacit international acceptance of what would otherwise be universally condemned as international aggression because of the human rights record of the target state.[56]

Despite evidence of humanitarian motivations, Tanzania never claimed humanitarian justification. In fact, Tanzania went out of her way to minimize responsibility for the felicitous humanitarian outcome of her actions, saying only that she was acting in response to Amin's invasion and that her actions just happened to coincide with a revolt against Amin inside Uganda. When Sudan and Nigeria criticized Tanzania for interfering in another state's internal affairs in violation of the OAU charter, it was the new Ugandan regime that invoked humanitarian justifications for Tanzania's actions. It criticized the critics, arguing that members of the OAU should not "hide behind the formula of non-intervention when human rights are blatantly being violated."[57]

Vietnam in Cambodia (1979)

In 1975 the Chinese-backed Khmers Rouges took power in Cambodia and launched a policy of internal "purification" entailing the atrocities and genocide now made famous by the 1984 movie *The Killing Fields*. This regime, under the leadership of Pol Pot, was also aggressively anti-Vietnamese and engaged in a number of border incursions during the late 1970s. Determined to end this border activity, the Vietnamese and an anti–Pol Pot army of exiled Cambodians invaded the country in December 1978 and by January 1979 had routed the Khmers Rouges and

---

55. Tesón, *Humanitarian Intervention*, p. 164.
56. Ibid., pp. 164–67.
57. As quoted in Akehurst, "Humanitarian Intervention," p. 99.

installed a sympathetic government under the name People's Republic of Kampuchea (PRK).

Again, humanitarian considerations may not have been central to Vietnam's decision to intervene, but humanitarian justifications would seem to have offered some political cover to the internationally unpopular Vietnamese regime. Like Tanzania, however, Vietnam made no appeal to humanitarian justifications. Instead, its leaders argued that they were only helping the Cambodian people achieve self-determination against the neocolonial regime of Pol Pot, which had been "the product of the hegemonistic and expansionist policy of the Peking authorities."[58] Even if Vietnam *had* offered humanitarian justifications for intervention, indications are that these would have been rejected by other states. In their condemnations of Vietnam's action, a number of states mentioned Pol Pot's appalling human rights violations but said nonetheless that these violations did not entitle Vietnam to intervene. During the UN debate, no state spoke in favor of the existence of a right to unilateral humanitarian intervention, and several states—Greece, the Netherlands, Yugoslavia, and India—that had previously supported humanitarian intervention arguments in the UN voted for the resolution condemning Vietnam.[59]

Multilateral Intervention in Humanitarian Disasters

To be legitimate, humanitarian intervention must be multilateral. The Cold War made such multilateral efforts politically difficult to orchestrate, but since 1989 several large-scale interventions have been carried out claiming humanitarian justifications as their primary raison d'être. All have been multilateral. Most visible among these have been:

- the U.S., British, and French efforts to protect Kurdish and Shiite populations inside Iraq following the Gulf War;
- the UNTAC mission to end civil war and reestablish a democratic political order in Cambodia;
- the large-scale UN effort to end starvation and construct a democratic state in Somalia; and
- current, albeit limited, efforts by UN and NATO troops to protect civilian, especially Muslim, populations from primarily Serbian forces in Bosnia.

---

58. As quoted in ibid., p. 97 n. 17.
59. One reason for the virtual absence of humanitarian arguments in this case, as compared with the Tanzanian case, may have been the way in which the intervention was conducted. Tanzania exerted much less control over the kind of regime that replaced Amin, making the subsequent Ugandan regime's defense of Tanzania's actions as "liberation" less implausible than were Vietnam's claims that it, too, was helping to liberate Cambodia by installing a puppet regime that answered to Hanoi.

While these efforts have attracted varying amounts of criticism concerning their effectiveness, they have received little or no criticism of their legitimacy. Further, and unlike their nineteenth-century counterparts, all have been organized through standing international organizations—most often the United Nations. Indeed, the UN charter has provided the framework in which much of the normative contestation over intervention practices has occurred since 1945. Specifically, the charter enshrines two principles that at times, and perhaps increasingly, conflict. On the one hand, article 2 enshrines states' sovereign rights as the organizing principle of the international system. The corollary for intervention is a near absolute rule of nonintervention. On the other hand, article 1 of the charter emphasizes promoting respect for human rights and justice as a fundamental mission of the organization, and subsequent UN actions (adoption of the Universal Declaration of Human Rights, among them) have strengthened these claims. Gross humanitarian abuses by states against their own citizens of the kinds discussed in this essay bring these two central principles into conflict.

The humanitarian intervention norms that have evolved within these conflicting principles appear to allow intervention in cases of humanitarian disaster and abuse, but with at least two caveats. First, they are permissive norms only. They do not require intervention, as the cases of Burundi, Sudan, and other states make clear. Second, they place strict requirements on the ways in which intervention, if employed, may be carried out: Humanitarian intervention must be multilateral if states are to accept it as legitimate and genuinely humanitarian. Further, it must be organized under UN auspices or with explicit UN consent. If at all possible, the intervention force should be composed according to UN procedures, meaning that intervening forces must include some number of troops from "disinterested" states, usually midlevel powers outside the region of conflict—another dimension of multilateralism not found in nineteenth-century practice.

Contemporary multilateralism thus differs from the multilateral action of the nineteenth century. The latter was what John Ruggie might call "quantitative" multilateralism and only thinly so.[60] Nineteenth-century multilateralism was strategic. States intervened together to keep an eye on each other and discourage adventurism or exploitation of the situation for nonhumanitarian gains. Multilateralism was driven by shared fears and

---

60. John G. Ruggie, "Multilateralism: The Anatomy of an Institution," in Ruggie, *Multilateralism Matters*, p. 6.

perceived threats, not by shared norms and principles. States did not even coordinate and collaborate extensively to achieve their goals. Military deployments in the nineteenth century may have been contemporaneous, but they were largely separate; there was virtually no joint planning or coordination of operations. This follows logically from the nature of multilateralism, since strategic surveillance of one's partners is not a shared goal but a private one.

Recent interventions exhibit much more of what Ruggie calls the "qualitative dimension" of multilateralism. They are organized according to and in defense of "generalized principles" of international responsibility and the use of military force, many of which are codified in the United Nations charter, declarations, and standard operating procedures. These emphasize international responsibilities for ensuring human rights and justice and dictate appropriate means of intervening, such as the necessity of obtaining Security Council authorization for action. The difference between contemporary and nineteenth-century multilateralism also appears at the operational level. The Greek intervention was multilateral only in the sense that more than one state had forces in the area at the same time. There was little joint planning and no integration of forces from different states. By contrast, contemporary multilateralism requires extensive joint planning and force integration. UN norms require that intervening forces be composed not just of troops from more than one state but of troops from disinterested states, preferably not great powers—precisely the opposite nineteenth-century multilateral practice.

Contemporary multilateralism is political and normative, not strategic. It is shaped by shared notions about when the use of force is legitimate and appropriate. Contemporary legitimacy criteria for the use of force, in turn, derive from these shared principles, articulated most often through the un, about consultation and coordination with other states before acting and about multinational composition of forces. U.S. interventions in Somalia and Haiti were not made multilateral because the U.S. needed the involvement of other states for military or strategic reasons. The U.S. was capable of supplying the forces necessary and, in fact, did supply the lion's share of the forces. No other great power was particularly worried about U.S. opportunism in these areas, and so none joined the action for surveillance reasons. These interventions were multilateral for political and normative reasons. For these operations to be legitimate and politically acceptable, the U.S. needed UN authorization and international participation. Whereas Russia, France, and Britain tolerated each other's presence in the operation to save Christians from the infidel Turk, the U.S. had to beg other states to join it for a humanitarian operation in Haiti.

Multilateral norms create political benefits for conformance and costs for nonconforming action. They create, in part, the structure of incentives facing states. Realists or neoliberal institutionalists might argue that in the contemporary world, multilateral behavior is efficient and unproblematically self-interested because multilateralism helps to generate political support both domestically and internationally for intervention. But this argument only begs the question, *Why* is multilateralism necessary to generate political support? It was not necessary in the nineteenth century. Indeed, multilateralism as currently practiced was inconceivable in the nineteenth century. As was discussed earlier, there is nothing about the logic of multilateralism itself that makes it clearly superior to unilateral action. Each has advantages and costs to states, and the costs of multilateral intervention have become abundantly clear in recent UN operations. One testament to the power of these multilateral norms is that states adhere to them even when they know that doing so compromises the effectiveness of the mission. Criticisms of the UN's ineffectiveness for military operations are widespread. The fact that UN involvement continues to be an essential feature of these operations despite the UN's apparent lack of military competence underscores the power of multilateral norms.[61]

Realist and neoliberal approaches cannot address changing requirements for political legitimacy like those reflected in changing multilateral practice any more than they can explain the "interest" prompting humanitarian intervention and its change over time. A century ago, protecting nonwhite non-Christians was not an "interest" of Western states, certainly not one that could prompt the deployment of troops. Similarly, a century ago states saw no interest in multilateral authorization, coordination, force integration, and use of troops from "disinterested" states. The argument of this essay is that these interests and incentives have been constituted socially through state practice and the evolution of shared norms by which states act.

---

61. Contemporary multilateralism is not, therefore, "better" or more efficient and effective than the nineteenth-century brand. My argument is only that it is different. This difference in multilateralism poses a particular challenge to neoliberal institutionalists. Those scholars have sophisticated arguments about why international cooperation should be robust and about why it might vary across issue-areas. They cannot, however, explain these qualitative changes in multilateralism, nor can they explain changes in the amount of multilateral activity over time, without appealing to exogenous variables (such as changes in markets or technology).

Humanitarian intervention is not new. It has, however, changed over time in some systemic and important ways. First, the definition of who qualifies as human and therefore as deserving of humanitarian protection by foreign governments has changed. Whereas in the nineteenth century European Christians were the sole focus of humanitarian intervention, this focus has been expanded and universalized such that by the late twentieth century all human beings are treated as equally deserving in the international normative discourse. In fact, states are very sensitive to charges that they are "normatively backward" and still privately harbor distinctions. When Boutros Boutros-Ghali, shortly after becoming secretary-general, charged that powerful states were attending to disasters in white, European Bosnia at the expense of nonwhite, African Somalia, the U.S. and other states became defensive, refocused attention, and ultimately launched a full-scale intervention in the latter but not the former.

Second, while humanitarian intervention in the nineteenth century was frequently multilateral, it was not necessarily so. Russia, for example, claimed humanitarian justifications for its intervention in Bulgaria in the 1870s; France was similarly allowed to intervene unilaterally, with no companion force to guard against adventurism. These claims were not contested, much less rejected, by other states, as the claims of India, Tanzania, and Vietnam were (or would have been, had they made such claims) a century later, despite the fact that Russia, at least, had nonhumanitarian motives to intervene. By the twentieth century, not only does multilateralism appear to be necessary to claim humanitarian justifications but sanction by the United Nations or some other formal organization is also required. The U.S., Britain, and France, for example, went out of their way to find authority in UN resolutions for their protection of Kurds in Iraq.

The foregoing account also illustrates that these changes have come about through continual contestation over norms related to humanitarian intervention. The abolition of slavery, of the slave trade, and of colonization were all highly visible, often very violent, international contests about norms. Over time some norms won, others lost. The result was that by the second half of the twentieth century norms about who was "human" had changed, expanding the population deserving of humanitarian protection. At the same time norms about multilateral action had been strengthened, making multilateralism not just attractive but imperative.

Finally, I have argued here that the international normative fabric has become increasingly institutionalized in formal international organizations, particularly the United Nations. As recent action in Iraq suggests, action in concert with others is not enough to confer legitimacy on intervention actions. States also actively seek authorization from the United Nations and restrain their actions to conform to that authorization (as the U.S. did in not going to Baghdad during the Gulf war).[62] International organizations such as the UN play an important role in both arbitrating normative claims and structuring the normative discourse over colonialism, sovereignty, and humanitarian issues.[63]

Changes in norms create only permissive conditions for changes in international political behavior. One important task of future research will be to define more specifically the conditions under which certain kinds of norms might prevail or fail in influencing action. A related task will be to clarify the mechanisms whereby norms are created, changed, and exercise their influence. I have suggested a few of these here—public opinion, the media, international institutions. More detailed study of individual cases is needed to clarify the role of each of these mechanisms. Finally, the way in which normative claims are related to power capabilities deserves attention. The traditional Gramscian view would argue that these are coterminous; the international normative structure is created by and serves the most powerful. Humanitarian action generally, and humanitarian intervention specifically, do not obviously serve the powerful. The expansion of humanitarian intervention practices since the last century suggests that the relationship between norms and power may not be so simple.

---

62. Inis Claude's classic discussion of this collective legitimation function of the UN is well worth a second reading in the current political environment; see Inis L. Claude Jr., "Collective Legitimization as a Political Function of the United Nations," *International Organization* 20, no. 3 (Summer 1966): 367–79.

63. For more on the role of IOs in creating and disseminating norms, see Martha Finnemore, "International Organizations as Teachers of Norms: The United Nations Educational, Scientific, and Cultural Organization and Science Policy," *International Organization* 47, no. 4 (Autumn 1993): 599–628.

6 • Culture and French Military Doctrine Before World War II

Elizabeth Kier

When war broke out in May 1940, the French army found itself saddled with a highly defensive doctrine that was incapable of breaking the German assault. France used the interwar period to bolster its military and was well prepared to fight a war against Germany—but only if Hitler fought the war on French terms. As a result, few defeats were as rapid or as devastating as the May–June campaign in Western Europe. Making sense of the French defeat as well as the more general question of the origins of choices between offensive and defensive military doctrines requires casting aside traditional theoretical approaches. Neither the civilians nor the military behaves as hypothesized by structural or functional analyses. Instead, changes in military doctrine are best understood from a cultural perspective.

First, dominant domestic political actors hold assumptions about the military's role in society, and these beliefs guide civilian decisions that often affect doctrinal developments. Restricting the sources of military

I would like to thank Jonathan Mercer, Scott Sagan, Kathyrn Sikkink, Jack Snyder, Stephen Walt, and two anonymous readers for Columbia University Press for their thoughtful comments and criticism. A more detailed version of some of the arguments presented in this essay appears in Elizabeth Kier, "Culture and Military Doctrine: France Between the Wars," *International Security* 19, no. 4 (Spring 1995): 65–93.

doctrine to the calculations of balance of power politics inadequately depicts the influence of civilian policy makers and the external environment. Civilians address their concerns about the domestic distribution of power before they consider the structure of the international system. Second, military organizations differ in how they view their world and the proper conduct of their mission, and these organizational cultures determine the myriad preferences of such organizations. We should not assume that most military organizations, most of the time, prefer offensive military doctrines; a functional view of the interests of military organizations fails to capture the variety in organizational behavior. What the military perceives to be in its interest is a function of its culture. In short, by accounting for policy makers' cultural environment, we can better explain choices between offensive and defensive military doctrines.

By focusing on the ways in which culture affects the formation of military doctrine, this essay endorses this volume's general lesson on the importance of sociological approaches to understanding international security questions. Culture may be an effective tool in the hands of political entrepreneurs, but an acknowledgment of culture's instrumental role does not require a denial of its causal one. Unlike rationalists who take interests as given, this essay explores the ways in which culture and the meanings that actors attach to certain policies shape actors' interests. Independent exigencies such as the distribution of power, geographic factors, or technological discoveries are important, but culture is not merely derivative of functional demands or structural imperatives. Culture has (relative) causal autonomy.

Making the case that culture is important to explaining choices between offensive and defensive military doctrines requires taking three steps. Since the origins of military doctrine have already received sophisticated attention from scholars in a rationalist tradition, I first summarize and critique their work. Then, having highlighted some of the limitations of this more conventional work, I set out my argument, outlining how culture affects civilian and, especially, military decisions about doctrinal developments. The final section uses the case of the French army during the 1920s and 1930s to illustrate the power of a culturalist approach.[1]

---

1. This essay is based on a larger study of doctrinal developments in the British and French army and air force during the 1920s and 1930s. For a discussion of the case selection, see Elizabeth L. Kier, *Imagining War: French and British Military Doctrine Between the Wars* (Princeton: Princeton University Press, in press).

Alternative Explanations

Barry Posen and Jack Snyder's pioneering work on military doctrine uses structural and functional arguments to explain choices between offensive and defensive military doctrines.[2] Although these scholars disagree on the role of domestic politics and the explanatory weight of organizational factors, they agree on two important points. Both see the international system as providing accurate cues for civilian intervention in doctrinal developments. While Snyder argues that it is the civilians' absence that allows the military to adopt its self-serving doctrine, Posen accords an active role to civilians, arguing that as the international system becomes more threatening, civilians intervene in doctrinal developments in accordance with systemic imperatives. The civilians are painted as the champions of the national interest and the principal architects of well-integrated military plans.

In contrast, the military is portrayed as choosing doctrines that serve its parochial interests, not national objectives. These scholars argue that military organizations use the adoption of offensive doctrines to further their quest for greater resources, certainty, autonomy, and prestige. For example, Posen argues that the greater complexity involved in the execution of offensive doctrines justifies increased expenditures, and Snyder claims that quick, decisive, and offensive campaigns enhance the army's prestige and self-image. According to a functional logic, these beneficial consequences cause this behavior. Discounting the imperatives of the international system, the military adopts the offensive doctrine that corresponds to its functional needs.

The Civilians' International Vision

The argument that civilian intervention in doctrinal developments corresponds to the international system has weak theoretical and empirical foundations; it exaggerates the power of systemic imperatives and misses

---

2. Barry R. Posen, *The Sources of Military Doctrine: France, Britain, and Germany Between the World Wars* (Ithaca: Cornell University Press, 1984); and Jack Snyder, *The Ideology of the Offensive: Military Decision Making and the Disasters of 1914* (Ithaca: Cornell University Press, 1984). Also see Stephen Van Evera, "The Causes of War" (Ph.D. diss., University of California, Berkeley, 1984), esp. pp. 206–398. The quantity and quality of scholarship that Posen's, Snyder's, and Van Evera's work has generated testifies to the power of their ideas. See especially Deborah D. Avant, *Political Institutions and Military Change: Lessons from Peripheral Wars* (Ithaca: Cornell University Press, 1994); and Kimberly Marten Zisk, *Engaging the Enemy: Organization Theory and Soviet Military Innovations, 1955–1991* (Princeton: Princeton University Press, 1993).

the focus of civilian concerns. This is true even in an easy case for balance of power theory, such as France during the 1920s and 1930s. If there is any example where the international system should determine a state's doctrinal orientation, this is it. French policy makers understood the nature of the threat that they faced and devoted extensive resources to ensuring France's security. The objective international requirements were neither misperceived nor seemingly not addressed. France had spent twenty years preparing for the German assault.

As compelling as the international system was, it cannot account for doctrinal developments in France. And in general, the international system does not provide determinate explanations for choices between offensive and defensive doctrines.[3] Although revisionist states require offensive doctrines, both offensive and defensive doctrines can defend a status quo state, and states often ignore alliance commitments that require offensive capabilities. Most important, a state's relative power is indeterminate of doctrinal choice.

Throughout the interwar period, French policy makers understood France's weakness relative to Germany. In the 1920s Paris argued that France had to strike out offensively and win quickly. Engaging in a long war of attrition, the reasoning went, could only result in the eventual triumph of Germany's superior economic strength and industrial mobilization. An official report in the early 1920s explained that "an offensive conception was the only one that would permit us to compensate for the inescapable causes of our weakness which result from the inferiority of our population and industrial strength."[4] France's relative weakness required an offensive orientation.

This argument was turned on its head a decade later. Now, it seemed, France must stay on the defensive in the opening battles of a conflict with Germany and throw all its resources into defeating the initial German assault. France's only hope, it was now argued, was that the initial resistance to a German offensive would provide the necessary time for the injection of allied assistance. France could only win a long war. In other words, France's relative weakness led to support for an offensive orientation in the 1920s and a defensive doctrine in the 1930s. French policy

---

3. Unlike Waltz, who refined balance of power theory to explain why balances recur, Posen uses balance of power theory to explain specific states' military doctrines; see Kenneth N. Waltz, *Theory of International Politics* (Reading, Mass.: Addison-Wesley, 1979).

4. Quoted in Paul-Émile Tournoux, *Haut commandement, gouvernement et défense des frontières du Nord et de l'Est (1919–1939)* (Paris: Nouvelles Editions Latines, 1960), p. 334.

makers were not misguided, nor did they misunderstand France's strategic position. Either an offensive or a defensive posture is a sensible response to the systemic demands of a relatively weak state.

The indeterminacy of the external environment makes clear why dramatic doctrinal shifts occur in the absence of systemic variation, or why changes in the structure of the international system do not lead to shifts in states' doctrinal orientations. For example, although both the French and the British armies shifted from offensive to defensive doctrines from 1914 to 1939, conditions in the international system remained relatively static from one period to the next. Similarly, although India's strategic position changed dramatically upon independence in 1947, it was not until the early 1980s that the Indian army began to shed the doctrinal orientation of its British predecessor.[5]

Realists might dismiss the above critique of the indeterminacy of the external environment by arguing that France's position in the international system changed between the 1920s and the 1930s; it is this shift in the distribution of power that explains doctrinal developments. After all, Germany had virtually no army in the 1920s. There seems to be a powerful correlation between German power and French doctrine. Germany is relatively weak in the 1920s and the French army has an offensive orientation; Germany is strong in the 1930s and the French army has a defensive doctrine.

This argument cannot be sustained. It did not take German rearmament for the French to worry about German power. The French sought to use the Versailles negotiations to harness German power, and France's Eastern diplomacy during the 1920s discredits any notion that it took Hitler's rise to power and German rearmament to wake the French up to the potential threat on their doorstep. More important, France switched to a defensive doctrine five years before Hitler's seizure of power, seven years before the reinstatement of conscription, eight years before the remilitarization of the Rhineland. . . . It was in 1929 that the French war plans became unabashedly defensive—before Hitler came to power and German rearmament began. There is not a correlation between French doctrine and German power: the French army switched to a defensive doctrine *long before* Germany had begun to rearm.

---

5. Ravi Rikhye, *The War That Never Was: The Story of India's Strategic Failures* (Delhi: Chanakya Publications, 1988), p. 23; Colonel Gurdial Singh, "Let Us Reorganize Our Logistical Services," *Journal of the United Service Institution of India* 111/463 (January–March 1981), p. 64.

Even if this timing had not been off, the correlation would be unsupported by process-tracing.[6] When France switched to a defensive doctrine in the late 1920s, the French army repeatedly and explicitly linked the change to the government's decision to reduce the length of conscription. The French army did not connect the rise of German power with the adoption of a defensive doctrine. There is neither correlation or causation between German power and French doctrine.

Barry Posen provides a sophisticated defense of the ability of balance of power theory to explain French army doctrine during the interwar period. Posen argues that because of France's relative weakness, French policy makers focused on external balancing—in particular, on gaining British support to allow France to "pass the buck." This required, according to Posen, the adoption of a defensive doctrine in order to avoid appearing bellicose in British eyes.[7]

Though logically compelling, this argument is empirically problematic. The French did seek Britain as an alliance partner, but we are provided with no evidence that the political repercussions of an offensive doctrine concerned Paris or London, or that the French were motivated by a desire to avoid antagonizing Britain. Across a whole spectrum of issues, France was more than willing to court British displeasure. On an economic front, the French attempted to exploit their ability to undermine the international monetary regime and to weaken its leader, Great Britain.[8] In foreign policy, the British were far from pleased with French behavior during the Chanak crisis and the occupation of the Ruhr. And in military policy, French war plans were explicitly designed to draw Germany into Belgium in order to threaten the security of the British Isles. This is hardly an action of a state seeking British approval. Also, if French policy makers desired a defensive doctrine in order to present a reassuring image to their British allies, why did French war plans continue to be offensive until 1929?

In addition, if external balancing took precedence, French recognition of British reluctance to make a continental commitment should have encouraged France to seek alternative sources of assistance. French policy makers could have ensured that France had the military capabilities to

6. Alexander George and Timothy J. McKeown, "Case Studies and Theories of Organizational Decision-Making," *Advances in Information Processing in Organizations* 2 (1985): 34–41.

7. Posen, *Sources of Military Doctrine*, pp. 105–40.

8. Jonathan Kirshner, *Currency and Coercion: The Political Economy of International Monetary Power* (Princeton: Princeton University Press, 1995), ch. 5.

honor alliance commitments in Eastern Europe or formed a military alliance with the Soviets. France did neither.

Finally, there is little support for the claim that French policy makers sought to "pass the buck" through external balancing. To the contrary, there is evidence that French civilians strongly objected to such an idea. During a meeting of the Superior Council of War in December 1927, one of the military officers remarked that France could aid itself only with the help of allies. The (civilian) minister of defense quickly responded that such a remark was extremely serious, useless, and dangerous.[9] France did of course seek allied support, but to accuse French policy makers of buck-passing slights the substantial financial resources that French defense spending consumed throughout the interwar period—even during periods of economic crisis and left-wing governments.[10]

Contrary to what one would expect from balance of power theory, much of civilian behavior in France during the 1930s seemed immune to the quickening pace of international events. Many of Hitler's policies severely compromised France's security system, but French civilians did little to realign French army doctrine with the new strategic realities. For example, even though French policy makers recognized that the Belgian declaration of neutrality and the German remilitarization of the Rhineland weakened France's strategic position, these moves met little response from Paris. After the German invasion of Poland and in an attempt to maintain morale during the "phony war," the French command took the dramatic action of instructing the troops to plant rosebushes around the Maginot Line.[11] The rosebushes were planted, but General Charles de Gaulle's calls for the creation of an armored force capable of offensive strikes were ignored.

By establishing constraints, civilian decisions affect doctrinal developments, but civilians rarely participate actively in the formation of army doctrine. During the 1920s and 1930s, French civilians deferred to the military on questions of doctrine.[12] Their British counterparts did like-

---

9. Service Historique de l'Armée de Terre (SHAT), 1 N 20, "Résumé succinct des séances du Conseil Supérieur de la Guerre (CSG)," December 14, 1927.

10. For example, see Robert Allan Doughty, *The Seeds of Disaster: The Development of French Army Doctrine, 1919–1939* (Hamden, Conn.: Archon Books, 1985), p. 183; and Robert Frankenstein, "A Propos des Aspects Financiers du Réarmement Français (1935–1939)," *Revue d'histoire de la deuxième guerre mondiale* 102 (April 1976): 2–9.

11. Serge Berstein, *La France des années 30* (Paris: Armand Colin, 1988), p. 164.

12. See Jeffrey Johnstone Clark, "Military Technology in Republican France: The Evolution of the French Armored Force, 1917–1940" (Ph.D. diss., Duke University, 1968), p. 178; and Henri Michel, *Le Procès de Riom* (Paris: Albin Michel, 1979), p. 220.

wise; neither the British cabinet nor the parliament concerned itself with army doctrine.[13] In fact, civilian intervention can be counterproductive to doctrinal change. Given the state of civil-military relations in France during the 1930s, civilian intervention in doctrinal developments was probably the best way to guarantee that a change would *not* occur. In 1936 de Gaulle sought the aid of a parliamentarian, Paul Reynaud, in his quest for the adoption of an offensive doctrine. As a result, de Gaulle's reputation within the army plummeted, and as Edward Pognon explains, "Rare, very rare are those among his comrades who were not scandalized by his appeal to a politician."[14] The following year, the High Command, seeking to demonstrate displeasure with de Gaulle's ideas and his appeal to civilian intervention, dropped him from the promotion list.[15] Far from fostering doctrinal innovation, civilian intervention frustrated de Gaulle's efforts.

This does not mean that civilian decisions are not important to doctrinal developments. They frequently are. But the proposition that civilians intervene in doctrinal developments in accordance with systemic imperatives is more problematic than it first appears to be. The international system is indeterminate, civilians infrequently intervene, and most important, civilian decisions constraining doctrinal developments are rarely in response to the structure of the international system. Instead, military doctrine frequently corresponds to policy makers' concerns about the distribution of power domestically.

The Military's Parochial Interests

According to a functional argument, offensive doctrines are powerful tools in a military organization's pursuit of greater resources, autonomy, and prestige. The pursuit of these goals, however, is largely indeterminate of choices between offensive and defensive military doctrines. Even if these goals could be fulfilled only with an offensive doctrine, military organizations often forfeit the attainment of them. This pattern holds true even in the case of the preference for greater resources. Furthermore, without civilian prompting, military organizations ostracize those officers who advo-

13. Brian Bond, *British Military Policy Between the Two World Wars* (Oxford: Clarendon Press, 1980), p. 41; Franklyn Arthur Johnson, *Defence by Committee: The British Committee of Imperial Defence, 1885–1959* (London: Oxford University Press, 1960), pp. 12–13; and Norman Henry Gibbs, "British Strategic Doctrine, 1918–1938," in Michael Howard, ed., *The Theory and Practice of War*, p. 187 (New York: Praeger, 1966).
14. Edward Pognon, *DeGaulle et l'armée* (Paris: Librarie Plon, 1976), p. 95.
15. Brian Crozier, *De Gaulle: The Warrior* (London: Eyre Methuen, 1973), p. 74.

cate a more offensive orientation and willingly and dogmatically endorse defensive doctrines.

Although Posen and Snyder argue that the preference for the reduction of uncertainty encourages the adoption of offensive doctrines, defensive doctrines can also structure the battlefield and reduce the need to improvise. An integral aspect of the French army's excessively defensive doctrine before World War II was the concept that the French termed the *methodical battle*. Instead of allowing for initiative and flexibility, *la bataille conduite* ensured tightly controlled operations in which all units adhered to strictly scheduled timetables. As a German officer explained, "French tactics are essentially characterized by a systematization which seeks to anticipate and account for any eventuality in the smallest detail."[16] The French army's *defensive* doctrine maximized the centralization of command and reduced spontaneity to a minimum.

Similarly, military organizations use both offensive and defensive doctrines to insulate themselves from civilian interference. The French army's endorsement of a defensive doctrine after 1929 is partly attributable to its being part of a larger package that allowed the army to retain what it most treasured—a small (and relatively autonomous) professional force. With the exception of the air force, there is a weak connection between autonomy and offensive doctrines. Civilians, and especially those in the foreign office, would be more likely to interfere in military planning if these operations included offensive strikes into a foreign country. Civilians are not likely to take a hands-off approach if their armed forces are invading a neighboring country.[17] Air forces have exploited strategic bombing (an offensive doctrine) to ensure their independence. During the 1920s and 1930s, both the French and the British air forces used an offensive doctrine in their efforts to obtain institutional autonomy. But the extent to which each service manipulated its doctrinal preferences to defeat the army and navy attack on its independence does not correspond to the expectations of a functional perspective. While the French air force fought bitterly and unsuccessfully for its independence, French airmen only halfheartedly endorsed the offensive doctrine that, according to a functional argument, could have furthered

16. Quoted in Alvin D. Coox, "French Military Doctrine, 1919–1939: Concepts of Ground and Aerial Warfare" (Ph.D. diss., Harvard University, 1951), p. 108. Although for different reasons, Posen argues that the French army adopted a defensive doctrine because it would reduce uncertainty (Posen, *Sources of Military Doctrine*, p. 118).
17. I thank Scott Sagan for this point.

their quest for autonomy.[18] In contrast, the Royal Air Force (RAF) gained institutional autonomy relatively easily but remained enamored of strategic bombing long after it had cemented its independent status as the third service.

Even when military organizations could gain greater resources, autonomy, or prestige through the adoption of an offensive doctrine, they often fail to do so. This is true even in such easy cases for a functional analysis as the French and British armies during the interwar period. Throughout the 1920s and 1930s, the British army was starved for resources and was the lowest (financial) priority among the British armed services. The army command was familiar with the concept of offensive mechanized warfare and had even led its development during the 1920s. British civilians did not intervene in doctrinal decisions or advocate the adoption of a defensive doctrine. In short, the British army had the (functional) need, the freedom, and the knowledge to advocate the adoption of an offensive doctrine in order to increase its modest budgetary allocation. It is hard to imagine a military organization better positioned to behave as hypothesized by a functional analysis. Nevertheless, the British army ignored this opportunity and adopted a defensive doctrine.

Similarly, throughout the 1930s, the French army had access to the ideas of mechanized warfare and freedom from civilian interference. Unlike the British army, it was not on a strict budgetary diet—the functional need for an offensive doctrine was less compelling. However, the French army's desire for autonomy from the civilians could hardly have been more extreme. With the recurrent instability of the Third Republic, the rise of the Left, and the outbreak of the Spanish Civil War, the army became increasingly fearful and distrustful of the republic. If military organizations seek autonomy through the adoption of an offensive doctrine, we should see it here. The French army had the (functional) need, the money, the ideas, and freedom from civilian intervention. Nevertheless, instead of adopting an offensive doctrine in order to increase its independence from the government, the French army became dogmatically committed to a defensive doctrine.

Still more surprising from a functionalist perspective is the budgetary behavior of the French and British military during the interwar period. In

---

18. Pascal Vennesson, *L'Institutionnalisation de l'armée de l'air en France* (Paris: Presses de la fondation nationale des sciences politiques, 1996, in press); Pascal Vennesson, "Institution and Airpower: The Making of the French Air Force," *Journal of Strategic Studies* 18, no. 1 (March 1995): 36–67.

1936, for example, the Popular Front government concluded that the budget request from the Chief of the French General Staff, General Maurice Gamelin, was insufficient. Léon Blum and Edouard Daladier augmented Gamelin's request for nine billion francs with an additional five billion francs![19] All three British services show a similar budgetary modesty that baffles a conventional evaluation of organizational interests. The British army ignored the financial benefits that adoption of an offensive doctrine could have brought. In fact, although all three British services suffered from a lack of financial support, it was the civilians that consistently prodded the military chiefs to submit larger budget requests.

When leading military and civilian decision makers met in the mid-1930s to plan British rearmament, the RAF submitted modest budget requests, arousing the ire of the Foreign Office, which felt that the RAF was underestimating the strength of the Luftwaffe.[20] The air staff retorted that the Foreign Office was placing too much emphasis on the threat of a German air attack, and the programs eventually adopted exceeded what the services themselves considered necessary.[21] This reluctance to submit excessive, or in the Foreign Office's view, adequate budget requests, was equally true of the Royal Navy, leading one participant to comment that he found it "curious how, all throughout, the Chiefs of Staff have been the moderating influence."[22]

The generalization that military organizations prefer offensive doctrines cannot explain why some military organizations adopt, and at times dogmatically embrace, defensive doctrines. They do this on their own initiative, without civilian prodding, and despite adequate knowledge of and resources for the development of an offensive doctrine. In the French case, the civilians did not intervene in doctrinal developments to force a defensive doctrine down the throats of the reluctant high command. Similarly,

---

19. Robert Frankenstein, "A Propos des aspects financiers du réarmement français," *Revue d'histoire de la deuxième guerre mondiale* 102 (April 1976): 7; Georges LeFranc, *Histoire du Front Populaire, 1934–1939* (Paris: Payot, 1965), p. 392.

20. Brian Bond and Williamson Murray, "The British Armed Forces," in Allan R. Millett and Williamson Murray, eds., *Military Effectiveness*, vol. 2, *The Interwar Period* (Boston: Allen and Unwin, 1988); Michael Howard, *The Continental Commitment: The Dilemma of British Defence Policy in the Era of the Two World Wars* (London: Maurice Temple Smith, 1972), p. 106; and Wesley K. Wark, *The Ultimate Enemy: British Intelligence and Nazi Germany* (Oxford: Oxford University Press, 1986), pp. 47, 56.

21. Uri Bialer, *The Shadow of the Bomber: The Fear of Air Attack and British Politics, 1932–1939* (London: Royal Historical Society, 1980), pp. 58–68.

22. Quoted in Wark, *The Ultimate Enemy*, p. 29. Also see Brian Bond, *Liddell Hart: A Study of His Military Thought* (New Brunswick, N.J.: Rutgers University Press, 1977), p. 67.

the British army marginalized those officers advocating the offensive use of massed tanks. This does not mean that military organizations prefer defensive doctrines or that organizational goals do not drive military choices. Instead, what the military perceives to be in its interest is a function of its culture.

Legacy of Verdun

The lessons of World War I seem to explain why a functional explanation cannot account for French doctrine. According to this argument, the 1920s and 1930s were an exceptional period: emerging from the carnage of the Great War, the subjective offense/defense balance was so skewed that an otherwise accurate generalization—that military organizations prefer offensive doctrines—appears to be incorrect. Given the French army's doctrine in 1939, it seems plausible that the leadership of the French army, marked by the bloody experiences of World War I, had prepared for a rematch of the previous war. Devastated by the disastrous results of the *offense à outrance*, and influenced in particular by the battle for Verdun, the French officer corps had learned their lesson and prepared to fight the next war behind the reinforced concrete of the Maginot Line.

Although this is the most popular explanation of the origins of the French army's defensive doctrine, this argument fails to recognize the considerable debate in the French army in the decade following the signing of the Versailles Treaty.[23] The French army eventually adopted a doctrine reminiscent of the trench warfare in World War I, but this was not the only lesson available, nor the only alternative considered. The extent to which offensive options were not only considered but also endorsed becomes clear by examining the debate about the potential use of fortifications, the war plans, and the discussions about the future of mechanization.

Within months of the armistice's signing, the French military elite began debating the potential use of prepared positions, in particular whether the fortifications would serve offensive or defensive functions.[24] While Marshal Pétain and others argued that fortifications were primarily defensive, Generals Berthelot, Debeney, Fillomeau, Foch, Guillemaut, Joffre, and Mangin were the primary partisans of an offensive use of fortifications. Concerned that too great an emphasis on fortifications might cripple the French army,

23. For example, see Alistair Horne, *The Price of Glory: Verdun 1916* (London: Macmillan, 1962), pp. 2, 336.
24. For the most comprehensive account of the development of the Maginot Line, see Tournoux, *Défense des frontières*.

they argued that fortified regions should serve as centers of resistance to facilitate offensive actions. For example, Ferdinand Foch estimated that Philippe Pétain's attempt to guarantee the inviolability of the frontiers was a dangerous step. For him, "assuring the inviolability of the territory is not the army's most important goal. . . . Establishing a Wall of China would pledge ourselves to defeat." Similarly, Maxime Weygand argued that fortifications should be used to economize forces such that a greater portion of the troops could strike offensively into Germany.[25]

The controversy between these two schools of thought continued throughout the 1920s. In a meeting of the Superior Council of War in 1926, Generals Guillemaut, Berthelot, and Fillomeau attacked Pétain's proposal. Supported by Joseph Joffre and Eugéne Debeney, General Guillemaut insisted that it would be dangerous to place greater importance on fortifications than on the equipment that would allow the prepared positions to be used as points of maneuver.[26] Foch agreed: "If we don't have the tool, it will not be the umbrella that will protect the country."[27] Guillemaut also spoke out strongly against Pétain's conceptions:

> The Wall of France is a dream financially speaking, and from the military point of view can be a danger. It could lead us to subordinate all war plans. . . . It would be better to build a strong army capable of going on the offensive. Whatever money is remaining—if any does remain—could be used to construct fortifications that would serve as a base of departure.[28]

In their view, fortifications should be used to facilitate offensive actions and to avoid a repetition of the static defense of World War I.[29]

This debate continued for almost a decade, and this prolongation, according to a leading historian of the Maginot Line, is indicative of the "markedly offensive spirit of the French high command."[30] Pétain's conception of a continuous frontier eventually won out, but the debate over the fortifications and the earlier official endorsement of offensive uses belies the notion that the French officer corps left World War I convinced that only a defensive doctrine was possible.

---

25. Eugene Carrias, *La Pensée militaire française* (Presses Universitaires de France, 1960), p. 330.

26. SHAT, 1 N 20, "Résumé succinct des séances du CSG," December 14 and 15, 1926.

27. Ibid., July 2, 1927.

28. Quoted in Jean-Baptiste Duroselle, *La Décadence, 1932–1939* (Paris: Imprimerie nationale, 1979), p. 244.

29. Judith M. Hughes, *To the Maginot Line: The Politics of French Military Preparations in the 1920s* (Cambridge: Harvard University Press, 1971), p. 200.

30. Tournoux, *Défense des frontières*, p. 36.

The discussions about the potential of mechanized warfare further reveal the extent to which the French army was open to offensive possibilities in the aftermath of World War I. Just as there was no consensus among the military leaders over how best to use fortifications, there was also considerable disagreement in the 1920s about the optimum use of armor. While some officers advocated the development of independent tank units that could take advantage of the speed and maneuverability of this new technology, other officers argued that tanks should be assigned to fill traditional roles of support for the infantry in defensive operations.[31]

The war plans of the 1920s are additional evidence that the lessons of World War I did not determine French military thinking: these plans officially endorsed offensive operations. If a conflict with Germany occurred, the French intended to bring the battle to Germany and divide the country in two.[32] In a letter to the minister of defense in 1925, a French officer explains French intentions: "We must therefore, and at any price, have at our disposal at the beginning of a conflict offensive forces capable of decisive strikes into Germany such that Germany will be required to maintain the mass of her forces in the face of us and to fight on her territory."[33] Increasingly defensive plans later superseded these offensive plans, but the initial reaction to the threat of a resurgent Germany was once again to plan offensive strikes beyond the French frontier.

This is not to downplay the impact of the slaughter of World War I on the collective memory in France. It is only to argue that the French army did not leave World War I convinced that only a defensive doctrine was possible. Other lessons and interpretations were available and endorsed by important and influential sectors of the French army. As the lessons of World War I took on heroic proportions, however, it became increasingly difficult to remember that the Great War's defensive lessons were not the only ones available or supported.

---

31. One author estimated that in the early 1920s, two-thirds of the articles in professional military journals endorsed mechanized warfare. See, for example, Captain Fernand-Charles Grazin, "Essai d'emploi d'autos mitrilleuses sur chenilles aux manoeuvres de la Sarre," *Revue de cavalerie* 3 (1923); and Col. Jean Alphonse Louis Flavigny, "Manoeuvres de la 4e division de cavalerie en Rhénanie en 1928," *Revue de cavalerie* 9 (1929).

32. Anthony Adamthwaite, *France and the Coming of the Second World War, 1936–1939* (London: Frank Cass and Company, 1977), p. 24; Jean Doise and Maurice Vaisse, *Diplomatie et outil militaire, 1871–1969* (Paris: Imprimerie nationale, 1987), pp. 269, 276; and General André Laffargue, *Justice pour ceux de 1940* (Limoges: Charles Lavauzelle, 1952), p. 91; Tournoux, *Défense des frontières*, pp. 332–35.

33. SHAT, l N 27, file 3, "Rapports de présentation du CSG," March 9, 1925.

The lessons of history are multiple, and they frequently inform policy making only after a particular policy has been adopted. They are not necessarily the origin of the policy itself. In other words, the French army adopted a defensive doctrine in the interwar years *not* because of the trench warfare of World War I but for different reasons. Once this defensive orientation had been chosen, history began to be read and used in a particular way to justify or bolster the chosen policy or institution. As Jack Snyder has aptly stated in his study of the myths of empires, "Statesmen and society actively shape the lessons of the past in ways that they find convenient, more than they are shaped by them."[34]

The Cultural Roots of Doctrinal Decisions

Some may think it foolish to argue that the conditions in the international system do not determine doctrinal developments by influencing the decisions made by civilian policy makers. If military doctrine, which is designed to defeat an adversary's armed forces, is not determined by the international system, one might reasonably ask what would be. I argue that it is counterintuitive to assume that military policy would respond only to the objective conditions in the international arena. Military doctrine is about state survival, but military policy is also about the allocation of power *within* society. After all, what could be more politicized than questions about who within the state has the support and control of the armed services? Designing military policy requires first and foremost that policy makers address their concerns about the distribution of power at the domestic level.

I expect fewer objections to the argument that implies that military organizations, constrained by their own culture, ignore international imperatives. It is commonly argued that military organizations pursue their parochial interests. Accurate explanations of military doctrine require an understanding of the often conflicting perspectives held by military organizations. Deducing preferences from functional characteristics is too general and too imprecise. Understanding the variation in organizational behavior requires an analysis of cultural characteristics and how these shape choices between offensive and defensive doctrines.

---

34. Jack Snyder, *Myths of Empire: Domestic Politics and International Ambition* (Ithaca: Cornell University Press, 1991), p. 30.

Domestic Politics and Military Doctrine

The military plays a pivotal role in the state-building process, and this experience informs policy makers' views of military policy. The creation or stabilization of every state requires that a bargain be struck over the control of the military. For example, the United States Constitution ensured that the individual states would retain control of the militia and that Congress would control defense expenditures. The British Parliament, forever worried that a strong standing army would once again threaten English liberties, has refused to allow the military to become independent of legislative control. The critical divide in France was not between the national and the local levels, as in the United States, or Parliament and the Crown, as in England; instead, it reflected class divisions. The conservative, industrial, and landowning classes felt that only a professional army could ensure social stability and the preservation of the status quo, while the Left and the Republicans stressed that only a conscript army could guarantee republican liberties.

In other words, civilian choices in military policy often reflect fears about the distribution of power within the state, not the structure of the international system. These concerns often become institutionalized and shape decision makers' views of military policy. In many instances, they persist past their objective relevance so that when civilians make decisions about military policy, their perceived interests cannot be disentangled from their country's experience with the armed services and the role that it played in securing a particular distribution of power within the state.

To capture the role of domestic politics in choices between offensive and defensive military doctrines, I focus on *political military subcultures*— that is, civilian policy makers' beliefs about the role of armed force in the domestic arena. What is the perception of the role of the military in society? Do domestic political actors fear the latent force in particular military organizations? Should the armed services reflect the society at large, or are they viewed as separate and insular organizations? The questions focus on the importance of force in domestic politics; the answers usually originate in each state's experience with the military in the state-building process.

The way the civilians view the military varies from state to state. In some countries, all important political actors share the same view of the military. This was the case for Great Britain in the 1920s and 1930s, when there was general agreement across the political spectrum about the role of the armed forces in society. When only one subculture exists, this set of ideas and values can best be understood as approaching common sense: it constrains behavior by establishing what is "natural" and makes other patterns of behavior unimaginable. In other countries, as we will see in the case of France during the same period, there are several competing conceptions. In these cases, the competing subcultures more closely approximate ideologies: they provide explicit, self-conscious guidelines for action.[35]

The presence of one or several subcultures also affects the extent to which civilian intervention in doctrinal developments corresponds to systemic imperatives. If there is more than one subculture, civilian decisions are more likely to respond to domestic considerations. Civilians are first and foremost concerned with securing the preferred domestic distribution of power. In contrast, with a consensual subculture, the civilians will not be consumed by domestic battles over military policy, and as a result their decisions are more likely to reflect the external environment.

The Organizational Culture of the Military

Encouraged in part by the economic success of Japanese companies, organizational theorists began studying how the *culture of an organization* affects organizational behavior and decisions.[36] Although analysts have adopted different definitions, I define organizational culture as the set of basic assumptions, values, norms, beliefs, and formal knowledge that shapes collective understandings. The culture of an organization shapes its members' perceptions and affects what they notice and how they interpret it; it screens out some parts of "reality" while magnifying others.

Organizations' perceptions of their world frame and constrain the decision-making process. This is particularly true of military organizations. Few institutions devote as many resources to the assimilation of their members as does the military. The emphasis on ceremony and tradition, and the development of a common language and an esprit de corps, testify to the strength of the military's organizational culture.

The culture of a military organization is the collection of ideas and

35. I am indebted in this discussion to Ann Swidler's article "Culture in Action: Symbols and Strategies," *American Sociological Review* 51, no. 2 (April 1986): 273–86.

36. For useful discussions of organizational culture, see Terrence E. Deal and Allen A. Kennedy, *Corporate Cultures* (Reading, Mass.: Addison-Wesley, 1982); Andrew Pettigrew, "On Studying Organizational Cultures," *Administrative Science Quarterly* 24 (December 1979): 570–82; Edgar Schien, "Coming to a New Awareness of Organizational Culture," *Sloan Management Review* 25, no. 2 (Winter 1984): 3–6. For an application of this concept to security studies, see Jeffrey W. Legro, *Cooperation Under Fire: Anglo-German Restraint During World War II* (Ithaca: Cornell University Press, 1995).

beliefs about armed force—both its conduct and its relationship to the wider society. The components of the military's culture can be divided into those values and attitudes relevant to its relationship with its external environment—both international and domestic—and those characteristics internal to the organization. For example, is war a question of courage and morale or has the steel and firepower of the modern age fundamentally altered its nature? What skills or formation does the officer corps value—does it model its behavior after the modern-day business manager or the warrior and heroic leader?

Military culture does not mean *military mind*; it does not refer to a general set of values and attitudes that all militaries share. All military organizations can be classified according to a basic set of components, but they do not all share the same mixture of values and attitudes. Nor is this an argument about strategic culture.[37] Organizational culture refers to the collectively held beliefs within a particular military organization, not to the beliefs held by civilian policy makers. Finally, organizational culture is not the primordial notion sometimes found in analyses of strategic culture; the military's organizational culture is not equivalent to the national character. The military's culture may reflect some aspects of the civilian society's culture, but that is not necessarily the case. The military's powerful assimilation processes can displace the influence of the civilian society.

Determining the culture of a military organization requires an extensive reading of archival, historical, and other public documents. Curricula at military academies, training manuals, personal histories of officers, internal communications in the armed services, and the leading military journals should all be examined. It is also important to look for who or what is considered deviant or taboo in the culture and what it is about these beliefs that conflicts with the organization's culture.

Making sense of the interests that military organizations bring to doctrinal decisions requires understanding the cultural context within which these decisions are made. Not all militaries share the same collection of ideas about armed force, and these beliefs shape how the organization responds to changes in its external environment.

Focusing exclusively on either domestic politics or the military's organizational culture provides neither a necessary nor a sufficient explanation of choices between offensive and defensive doctrines. Military doctrine is

---

37. For example, see Alastair I. Johnston, *Cultural Realism: Strategic Culture and Grand Strategy in Chinese History* (Princeton: Princeton University Press, 1995).

the product of two things. First, domestic politics sets constraints—for example, the length of conscription or the type of army—but these constraints do not in themselves determine doctrine. Second, the military's organizational culture must work within these constraints. The organizational culture is the intervening variable between domestic constraints and military doctrine.

In cases where there is only one political military subculture—that is, when there is consensus across the political spectrum on the role of armed force—the organizational culture dominates doctrinal developments. In Britain, the civilian consensus on the role of the military in society meant that the army's and the air force's cultures took on primary significance in explaining their doctrinal orientation in the 1920s and 1930s. Domestic politics still establishes constraints, but these are less direct than in conflictual polities. Civilian decisions are also more likely to reflect the external environment.

In other cases, decisions made by domestic political actors severely limit the organization's perception of its available options. For example, in France during the interwar period, the civilian decision to reduce the length of conscription to one year dramatically constrained what the French army thought was possible. Another military organization might have reacted differently to the reduction in the length of conscription, but given the French army's organizational culture, the high command felt that it had no choice but to adopt a defensive doctrine. In short, a civilian decision when coupled with the distinctive culture of the French army yielded a particular type of doctrine. Both civilian decisions and the military's organizational culture are important, and their interaction must be taken into account. Political decisions set constraints, but rarely do they determine outcomes. Likewise, the organizational culture alone does not explain the change in doctrine. There must be some change in the external environment of the organization—primarily as a result of domestic politics—to which the organizational culture reacts.

The Cultural Roots of French Doctrine

As ill-suited to the external threat as the French army's doctrine may have been, it corresponded well to domestic political battles and the French army's organizational culture. Since the mid-nineteenth century the Left and Right had fought over the organizational form of the army. While the

Right demanded a professional army that, in its view, could ensure domestic order and stability, the Left feared that a professional army would do the bidding of the reactionary segments of society. To the Left, only militia or reserve forces could guarantee the survival of the French Republic.

In 1928 the Left and Republican forces reduced the term of conscription to one year. The army resisted this decision, but once it had been made, the high command had no choice but to design a doctrine within that constraint. The leeway that the French army had cannot, however, be determined objectively; not all military organizations would respond similarly to the need to work with short-term conscripts. Despite evidence to the contrary, French officers could imagine only a professional army executing an offensive doctrine: in their view, only years of service could endow a soldier with the necessary skills for offensive warfare.

In sum, when deciding on the organizational structure of the army, French policy makers responded to domestic, not international, factors. The reduction in the term of conscription to one year addressed the Left's fear of domestic threats, not its concern about German capabilities. The army reacted to this decision within the constraints of its organizational culture. Instead of demonstrating a preference for offensive doctrines, the French army chose a defensive doctrine.

Competing Political Military Subcultures

Much has been written on the instability of the Third Republic, a dreary picture of one cabinet after another giving way to some equally powerless coalition. Yet it was not the fragility of the French government that established the framework for French doctrine; instead, it was the competition between contending political forces with conflicting political military subcultures. Within months of the signing of the armistice, the old political struggle over the organizational form of the army reemerged.

Since the French Revolution, and especially in the latter half of the nineteenth century, the organizational structure of the army had become one of the primary arenas of conflict between two major factions in French politics. While the Right sought a professional army comprising long-service soldiers, the Left advocated a national army founded on short-term conscripts in the form of either a militia or a force highly dependent on reserves.

In the Left's view, it was imperative that the army not be a separate caste, isolated from society and imbued with military values.[38] If the army could retain the conscript for several years, it would be able to elicit passive obedience and to use this force for domestic repression. It was only by eliminating the professional army that the threat to French democracy would diminish.

The Left believed that the army must reflect society and society's values in order to be able to defend the entire country (rather than only a particular class). For the Left, the less time spent in the barracks, the better; the conscript needed to be under the colors just long enough to learn the requisite military skills. Everything must be done to avoid the development of a corporate spirit potentially at odds with the republic. In early 1934 Léon Blum, the leader of the Socialist Party, expressed his fear of long-serving soldiers:

> History teaches very clearly that collective feelings develop in professional armies. They are the army of a corps, while waiting to become the army of a leader. Isolated from the surrounding life, compressed and focused on itself by training, customs, and discipline, the army establishes within the nation an enclosed enclave. . . . Public duty is replaced by hierarchical obedience. National solidarity is replaced by professional solidarity.[39]

Whether the military was a militia force or a mixed army heavily dependent on the mobilization of reserves, the leftist ideal required a short term of service that would, in the Left's view, harness the repressive designs of the reactionary part of French society.[40] During parliamentary debates in the early 1920s over the length of conscription, a radical socialist declared, "It is necessary that France have the army of its policies; but I don't want France to carry out the policies of her army."[41]

In contrast, the French Right demanded the retention of a professional army. Just like the Left, the Right felt that the number of years that the soldier served in the ranks determined whether or not the army could be relied upon to maintain the status quo. In a domestic crisis, only soldiers

---

38. Classic texts that embody the political military subculture of French Left include Jean Jaurès, *L'armée nouvelle* (Paris: Editions Sociales, 1977); and J. Monteilhet, *Les Institutions militaires de la France* (Paris: Felix Alcan, 1932).

39. Léon Blum, "A bas l'armée de métier!" *Le Populaire*, December 1, 1934.

40. On the Left's view of reserves, see Adrien Roux, *Gardons le service de deux ans* (Paris: Librarie Positiviste, 1912), pp. 6–7; and General Percin, *La Guerre et la nation armée* (Paris: Ligue des Droits de l'Homme et du Citoyen), pp. 7–13.

41. Quoted in Edouard Bonnefous, *Histoire politique de la Troisième République*, vol. 3, *L'après-guerre* (Paris: Presses Universitaires de France, 1968), p. 311.

toughened by many years of strict discipline could be depended upon to guarantee social stability and the preservation of law and order. Creating citizen-soldiers would only, in the Right's view, strengthen the revolutionary forces in society. In the nineteenth century Louis Adolphe Thiers declared that he did not want "obligatory military service which will enflame passions and put a rifle on the shoulder of all the socialists; I want a professional army, solid, disciplined, and capable of eliciting respect at home and abroad."[42]

Whereas the Left sought to avoid a deep divide between the army and society by minimizing the length of conscription, the Right wanted to keep the conscript under arms for at least two years. The Right agreed that a shorter military service was sufficient to train soldiers, but more time was needed to create the necessary *obéissance passive*.[43] Before Parliament, Horace de Choiseul explained this process: "A soldier that has served for one year has learned without doubt to use his weapons, but he has not learned to obey; his character has not been subjugated, his will has not been broken; he has not yet become what makes an army strong: passive obedience."[44] For the Right, a long term of service would allow the officer corps to instill an esprit de corps in the troops and thus detach the allegiance of the men from the society at large and forge a collective identity that would unquestionably follow the orders of the commanders.

Remembering the workers' revolt in 1848 and hardened by their experience during the Commune, the Right felt that one of the army's chief tasks was to preserve peace at home. As the Germans were approaching Paris in 1940, General Weygand revealingly declared, "Ah! If only I could be sure the Germans would leave me the necessary forces to maintain order!"[45]

In short, although French policy makers were acutely aware of their position in the international system, it was their perception of domestic rather than international threats that shaped the pivotal decision about the French army's organizational structure. A collection of center and left-

---

42. Quoted in J. Monteilhet, "L'avènement de la nation armée," *Revue des études Napoléoniennes* (September–October 1918): 51.

43. General Jules L. Lewal, *Contre le service de deux ans* (Paris: Librairie Militaire de Baudoin, 1895), pp. 46. 51–52, 77; Richard D. Challener, *The French Theory of the Nation in Arms, 1866–1939* (New York: Columbia University Press, 1955), pp. 85–87; Claude Croubois, *L'Officier français des origines à nos jours* (St-Jean-d'Angely: Editions Bordessoules, 1987), p. 304; and Monteilhet, *Institutions militaires*, pp. 166, 169.

44. Quoted in Monteilhet, *Institutions militaires*, p. 166.

45. Quoted in Crozier, *De Gaulle*, p. 97.

wing parties captured Parliament in 1924 and within three years adopted a series of legislation that established the organizational structure of the army that France took to war in 1939. The Left's agenda had finally triumphed: the length of conscription was reduced to one year. The reason for the Left's rejection of the longer service had nothing to do with Germany, Britain, or the Eastern allies. As Léon Blum warned, a longer term of service would "be a danger for republican liberties, that is to say for *domestic* peace."[46]

These choices reflected interests, but we can understand these interests only by understanding the meanings that actors attributed to the choices. We often cannot understand what an actor will view as in its interest without first understanding the cultural connotations of a particular policy. We cannot assume that all left-wing parties, like the French in the 1920s, fear a professional army or that all right-wing parties do not want a conscript army. The types of armies that the British and French Left imagined to be in their interests were opposite. For the French Left, conscription expressed community spirit, equality, and most important, insurance against the growth of a praetorian guard. For the British Left, conscription attacked individual liberty and was a tool of continental imperialism.

There is nothing inherent in a conscript or militia army that makes it a force for the Left. The very social forces that opposed reliance on a conscript army in France (the Right) mobilized in support of this system in both England and the United States.[47] Likewise, while the French Left liked militia forces, the American Left feared them, and with good reason. Although militias in the United States had been in decline since the 1820s, they underwent a dramatic revival in the late 1870s, especially after the great railroad strike of 1877. Strikebreaking became the militia's main function, and states with large working-class populations took the lead in the militia's revival.[48] In fact, in 1892 Samuel Gompers declared that "membership in a labor organization and a militia at one and the same time is inconsistent and incompatible."[49]

In the early part of this century, the American Left bitterly attacked pro-

46. Emphasis added. Léon Blum, "A bas l'armée de métier!" *Le populaire*, December 1, 1934.

47. John Whiteclay Chambers, "Conscripting for Colossus: The Progressive Era and the Origins of the Modern Military Draft in the United States in World War I," in Peter Karsten, ed., *The Military in America: From the Colonial Era to the Present*, pp. 277–81 (New York: Free Press, 1980).

48. Barton C. Hacker, "The United States Army as a National Police Force: The Federal Policing of Labor Disputes, 1877–1898," *Military Affairs* 33, no. 2 (April 1969): 259.

49. Stephen Skrowronek, *Building a New American State: The Expansion of National Administrative Capacities, 1877–1920* (Cambridge: Cambridge University Press, 1982), p. 105.

posals for national service and instead advocated the creation of a well-equipped and volunteer professional force. What the U.S. Left supported, the French Left opposed (and the French Right supported). Similar social-economic positions do not necessarily mean similar policy positions across national boundaries. To make sense of these choices, we must understand the meanings attached to policies, that is, we must examine the relevant cultures.

The Army's Culture and the Meaning of Conscription

The French army objected to the shorter length of service, but once it had been adopted, the army was obliged to design a doctrine around that decision. It is because the French army had a choice that the importance of the army's culture becomes clear. A shorter length of service did not require the adoption of a defensive doctrine. It was a conceptual barrier that stood in the way of the adoption or, more accurately, that prevented a continuation of an offensive orientation after 1928.

An offensive doctrine was objectively possible. The French army did not suffer from a lack of financial support; the requisite material for armored warfare could have been acquired. Nor was it unaware of offensive alternatives. The French army was well versed on doctrinal developments in Germany, as well as having its own advocates of mechanized warfare. De Gaulle's campaign in the 1930s is the most renowned but not the only attempt by a French officer to persuade the French army of the potential of massed armor. Nor did French civilians demand a defensive doctrine or actively participate in the formation of army doctrine. Even construction of the Maginot Line left open offensive possibilities. As discussed above, the fortifications were initially conceived to support offensive operations. The French army had the money, ideas, and freedom to adopt an offensive doctrine, but it instead chose a defensive doctrine. Its organizational culture would not allow otherwise.

It was conceptually impossible for the French army to conceive of the execution of an offensive doctrine with short-term conscripts. To the French officer, one-year conscripts were good for only one thing—a defensive doctrine. In the army's view "young troops" could only be engaged "methodically"; they could not handle sophisticated technology or new methods of warfare, and they could not exhibit the élan necessary for offensive actions. To most French officers, a one-year term of conscription reduced the army to marginal value. In discussing the annual intake of conscripts, General Debeney explained that these "men are far from having the solidity of professional soldiers since they have only done six to eleven months of service. . . . In effect, this mass of reservists will only be good for the second echelon."[50] Similarly, General Weygand commented on the technical capabilities of short-term conscripts: "The professional army is able to use certain material. . . . A militia, to the contrary, will be incapable of manipulating modern material."[51]

Although Pétain is frequently blamed for infusing the French army with a defensive spirit, he was explicit in arguing that it was the presence of the *nation armée* that made it inconceivable to initiate a war against Germany with a strategic offensive. Pétain stated that "the professional army is above all an offensive instrument."[52] With only short-term conscripts, General Henri Mordacq explained, "it was absolutely impossible to give our contingents an instruction responding to the demands of modern warfare."[53] The vice president of the Superior Council of War and inspector general of the army, General Weygand, agreed about the marginal value of the French conscript army:

> The character and the possibilities of the French army were profoundly modified the day that France adopted military service of less than two years. . . . Because of its organizational structure, today's army [1932] is much weaker and less prepared to fight than the army in 1914. . . . This army has been reduced to the lowest level possible to permit France's security.[54]

In sum, short-term conscripts, who represented only quantity, could not be entrusted with offensive operations.

This rejection of the value of short-term conscripts or reserves was not shared by all armies or based on the experiences of the French army. The French officers had plenty of opportunities to see that short-term conscripts could be used effectively in offensive operations. France's defeat in 1870 by a quantitatively superior army based on universal military service should have alerted French military leaders to a potential source of power that they had previously dismissed. Yet, before World War I, while Joffre

50. General Eugène Debeney, "Armée nationale ou armée de métier?" *Revue politique et parlementaire* (May 10, 1933): 214.

51. Ministère des affaires étrangères, *Documents diplomatiques français, 1932–1939*, vol. 1, no. 1 (Paris: Imprimerie nationale, 1964), p. 568.

52. Philippe Pétain, preface to General Chauvineau, *Une invasion est-elle encore possible?* (Paris: Editions Berger-Levrault, 1940), pp. vii–xii.

53. General Henri Mordacq, *La défense nationale en danger* (Paris: Les editions de France, 1938), p. 2.

54. SHAT, 1 N 42, file 2, Etat-major Maxime Weygand, CSG, "Rapport sur l'état de l'armée," May 1932.

was declaring that "under no circumstances will we absorb the reserve formations in the active units," the German army was stating that "reserve troops will be employed in the same way as the active troops."[55] In addition, during the initial battles of World War I, the German army had successfully used reserve formations in offensive operations. Since it was Napoleon who first took advantage of this new form of military organization, this persistence of the link between professional armies and offensive operations in the organizational culture of the French army is all the more surprising. By Napoleon's mastery of the war of masses, the French army had conquered all of Europe.

General de Gaulle's advocacy of an offensive doctrine in the 1930s may raise questions about this argument. Here we have a French officer, assimilated into the culture of the French army yet calling for the adoption of an offensive doctrine *subsequent* to the reduction in the length of conscription. This seems to suggest that the reduction in the length of conscription was not as important as I claim. Yet a closer look at de Gaulle's campaign illustrates both the strength of the French army's culture and the importance of domestic politics.

In *Vers l'armée de métier*, de Gaulle called for the creation of a professional army and the adoption of an offensive doctrine. Intending it as an addition to and not a substitute for the mass conscript army, de Gaulle advocated the establishment of seven armored divisions composed of 100,000 soldiers serving a six-year tour of duty. De Gaulle envisioned that these highly mobile divisions would be capable of immediate action into enemy territory and would return the offensive to the battlefield.[56]

De Gaulle was convinced that the defense and ultimate *grandeur* of France depended on the adoption of a new offensive doctrine, yet he endorsed these offensive operations only if they were coupled to a force of professionals serving *six years* of military service. As a product of the organizational culture of the French army, de Gaulle could not imagine entrusting young, unseasoned troops with the tasks involved in mechanized warfare. Only professional soldiers possessed the skill and training to implement lightning attacks by armored units. De Gaulle stuck with this proposal even though he was well aware of the political hurdles to the creation of a professional force of long-serving soldiers.

---

55. Jean Feller, *Le dossier de l'armée française: la guerre de "cinquante ans, 1914–1962"* (Paris: Librairie Academique Perrin, 1966), p. 65.
56. Charles DeGaulle, *Vers l'armée de métier* (Paris: Editions Berger-Levrault, 1944).

The reception that de Gaulle's ideas received in the French army further reveals the linking of a professional army with an offensive doctrine in the organizational culture of the French army. The high command was not persuaded. One of the primary reasons for its rejection of de Gaulle's ideas was that the creation of the specialized corps would, in the command's view, cut the army in two.[57] The officer corps could not imagine that the conscript army could implement this new offensive warfare. To adopt this doctrine would, in their minds, inevitably mean draining many of the army's professionals from the conscript army, and the latter, stripped of its professional officers, would have little if any combat value. The French officer corps could only accept the whole package of de Gaulle's ideas; separating the offensive doctrine from the professional army was inconceivable. These concepts were to be implemented either by a professional army or not at all.

De Gaulle's campaign also reveals the impact of domestic politics and especially the political military subculture of the French Left. The Left was not, to say the least, pleased with de Gaulle's proposals for a professional army. The fear of the domestic ramifications—and not whether these ideas were most suited to repel a German attack—emerges time and again in the leftist press and in parliamentary debate. For example, an article in *L'Esprit* states explicitly the reason for his opposition to de Gaulle's ideas: "This leader, having collected in his hand all the armed force of the country, multiplied indefinitely by the technological possibilities, having in hand hired killers, each of which possesses all the aptitudes of murder and all the extraordinary instruments to kill—when will this leader then march on Paris?"[58] Similarly, Edouard Daladier, the leader of the Radical Socialist Party, worried that a professional army might be "more dangerous than one might believe for the security of our nation."[59] Not surprisingly, de Gaulle's ideas received a different reception from the Right and the extreme Right.[60]

Even though the international environment had become dramatically

57. For example, see General Eugène Debeney, "Encore l'armée de métier," *Revue des deux mondes* (July 15, 1935): 285–90.

58. Jacques Lefrancq and Leo Moulin, "Dialogue sur l'armée de la classe 15 à la classe 25," *Esprit* 32 (May 1935).

59. Quoted in Pierre Hoff, *Les programmes d'armement de 1919 à 1938* (Vincennes: Service historique de l'armée de terre, 1982), p. 157.

60. Ladislas Mysyrowicz, *Anatomie d'une défaite* (Laussane: Editions de l'age d'homme, 1973), pp. 237–38; Alois Schumacher, *La politique de sécurité française face à l'Allemagne: Les controverse de l'opinion française entre 1932 et 1935* (Frankfurt: Peter Lang, 1978), p. 213.

more threatening, the domestic political divide persisted. Domestic considerations again determined the army's organizational structure. Once this constraint was set, the French army could imagine only one possibility. De Gaulle and the French army were incapable of decoupling offensive concepts from a professional army, yet the insistence on a professional force doomed de Gaulle's efforts because such a force was politically impossible. The French were trapped: the Left would not accept a professional army, and the army could not envision an offensive doctrine without one.

Culture's Sources

This essay does not directly address the origins of military culture.[61] However, before arguing that cultural factors have relative autonomy, it is important to address two potential sources of cultural factors.

First, one must show that the cultural beliefs are sincere. For example, how can we know that the French army really believed that short-term conscripts and a defensive doctrine were inseparable? Could this belief have been instrumental and so all consequence and not cause? Some of the best evidence comes from the French army's estimate of the German army before World War I. The French army's belief that conscript forces could not undertake offensive actions prevented its leaders from believing—despite intelligence reports—that the Germans would attack with the forces that they did. Because they could not imagine short-term conscripts leading offensive operations, the French army dismissed intelligence reports showing that the Germans would use "young troops" in the front lines. This misreading of the situation caused the French army to underestimate the strength of the German offensive by twenty corps, that is, by at least 680,000 soldiers![62] Whatever the outcome of the future battle, the French army's belief in the relative incompetence of short-term conscripts was not in its interest; it is not in the military's interest to underestimate the strength of opposing forces.

One can make a similar argument about de Gaulle. He was convinced that defending France depended on the adoption of an offensive doctrine. He also knew that the creation of a professional force was politically impossible. Yet he continued to advocate the coupling of an offensive doc-

---

61. For an extended discussion of the origins of military cultures, see Kier, *Imagining War*.
62. On the size of the German corps, see Girard Lindsay McEntree, *Military History of the World War* (New York: Scribner's, 1937), p. 33; Philip Neame, *German Strategy in the Great War* (London: Arnold, 1923), appendixes 1 and 2, pp. 123–27.

trine with a professional army. If de Gaulle's estimation of the value of short-term conscripts had been insincere, he would have dropped it in order to pursue what he felt was in France's national interest—an offensive doctrine.

The second thing that one must demonstrate about the origins of the culture is that it is not simply a reflection of structural conditions. We must see that individuals or groups sharing the same situational constraints reach different conclusions. We already saw the various ways in which the Left evaluates conscription. We also saw that the German and French armies have different evaluations of the value of reserve or conscript forces. The contrasting positions of the French and British delegations at the Versailles negotiations is another example. Both countries shared the same objective interest for the same context: reducing the military threat posed by Germany. France proposed that Germany rely solely on a conscript army. A French officer wrote that it "would be better to let Germany have a relatively numerous army, without seriously trained officers than a smaller army of well-tried, proven officers that Germany will have and which I fear she will know how to make use of."[63] Britain reached the opposite conclusion. David Lloyd George worried that with a conscript army "Germany will train 200,000 men each year, or two million in ten years. Why make a gift to them of a system which in fifteen to twenty years will give Germany millions of trained soldiers?"[64] He insisted that only the imposition of a professional army would harness German military power.[65] Both countries sought to contain Germany's offensive potential, but they proposed opposite prescriptions.

This essay is not a call for the wholesale adoption of cultural analyses. Structural and functional analyses are valuable tools in understanding international politics. Indeed, the normative and political rationale for pursuing this question stems from a structural constraint. It is only because offensive military postures are structural impediments to cooperative relations among states that the question of the determinants of

---

63. Quoted in Pierre Miquel, *La paix de Versailles et l'opinion publique française* (Paris: Flammarion, 1972), p. 258. Also see Ministère des affaires étrangères, *Documents diplomatiques française, 1932–1939*, vol. 1, no. 1 (Paris: Imprimerie nationale, 1969), p. 569.

64. Quoted in Miquel, *Paix de Versailles*, p. 256.

65. Bertrand de Jouvenel, "Le service militaire obligatoire. . . . Est-il une institution de gauche?" *La Voix*, February 9, 1930, p. 8; and Pertinax (pseud. André Géraud), "Le désarmement radical de l'Allemagne est décidé," *Echo de Paris*, March 11, 1919.

choices between offensive and defensive doctrines is important.[66] Nevertheless, functional and structural analyses cannot adequately explain choices between offensive and defensive military doctrines. We must understand the civilians' political military subculture and the military's organizational culture in order to explain choices between offensive and defensive doctrines.

While structural and functional accounts of the origins of military doctrine are parsimonious and generalizable, they also appear to be wrong. In contrast, this alternative account better explains why militaries end up with the doctrines they do. With the formation of new states and the reorganization of their military forces in the post–Cold War world, we want to encourage these states to adopt defensive doctrines. Neither looking to the international system nor relying on civilian oversight is likely to have much of a payoff. Instead, to intervene effectively in doctrinal developments, we need to understand the politics of military policy and the constraints of the military's culture.

---

66. For discussions and debate about the destabilizing effects of offensive military doctrines, see Robert Jervis, "Cooperation Under the Security Dilemma," *World Politics* 30, no. 2 (January 1978): 167–214; Van Evera, "The Causes of War"; and numerous articles in Steven E. Miller and Sean Lynn-Jones, eds., *Military Strategy and the Origins of the First World War* (Princeton: Princeton University Press, 1991).

7 • Cultural Realism and Strategy in Maoist China

Alastair Iain Johnston

Where does realpolitik behavior come from? Classical realists might attribute states' preferences for unilateral, competitive, coercive strategies to human nature, greed, a hardwired desire to maximize power. Neorealists have attributed it to the uncertainty generated by anarchy, mediated by different distributions of material capabilities. Both explanations are unsatisfactory because both have difficulty accounting for the considerable volume and consequentiality of non-realpolitik behavior. Some scholars have recognized this and have conceded that non-realpolitik, "deviant" behavior is more likely a product of cooperative ideas or institutions, but at the same time they have reaffirmed that "nondeviant," realpolitik behavior remains best explained by the key causal variables in their respective versions of realism. To some extent, those with a constructivist and ideational theoretical bent have unwittingly reinforced the hegemony of realist theory in the realm of realpolitik behavior, precisely by focusing on non-realpolitik behavior. It is critical, then, that constructivists and their

I would like to thank the following people for their comments and criticisms of this essay: Peter Katzenstein and other participants in the Social Science Research Council/MacArthur Project, as well as outside commentators at the three project workshops; members of the Olin Institute National Security seminar, and Thomas Christensen, Dale Copeland, Robert Keohane, Kenneth Lieberthal, and Stephen Walt. They are blameless for any shoddy analysis or errors of fact.

fellow travelers take up the challenge and see how far ideational arguments can go in accounting for realpolitik behavior.[1]

This essay is an initial attempt to do just that through an analysis of the China case. Essentially I argue that China has historically exhibited a relatively consistent hard realpolitik or *parabellum* strategic culture that has persisted across different structural contexts into the Maoist period (and beyond).[2] Chinese decision makers have internalized this strategic culture such that China's strategic behavior exhibits a preference for offensive uses of force, mediated by a keen sensitivity to relative capabilities. These preferences are often a reasonably accurate guide to strategic behavior. The persistence of an ideationally based hard realpolitik, however, suggests that structural accounts of realpolitik behavior are incomplete, precisely because this empirically observable cultural realpolitik has persisted across vastly different interstate systems, regime types, levels of technology, and types of threat. And it persists into the post-Mao period at a time when objectively and subjectively China's threat environment is the most benign in several decades. Since I have already looked at the presence and effects of this realpolitik strategic culture in traditional China,[3] in this essay I examine Maoist China, with some reference to the ancient past, to determine the degree of continuity in Chinese realpolitik.

Mainstream realist theorists react to these claims by arguing that cultural realpolitik is epiphenomenal, a product, say, of the logic of anarchy. The realist retort, however, rests at different times on three problematic claims: (1) only deviant, non-realpolitik behavior may be ideational in origin, but, by implication, nondeviant behavior is not explained by ideational variables; (2) realist theory, whether classical or structural, makes determinate predictions about state strategies in the absence of some ideational interpretation of the meaning of material capabilities; (3) realpolitik ideology is epiphenomenal. An analysis of Chinese realpolitik, however, challenges these claims, or at least shows that they are too weak to dismiss cultural realism as a third, ideationally rooted, explanation for realpolitik behavior.

The essay begins with a quick summary of the content of traditional

---

1. Alexander Wendt has recently articulated the importance for constructivist approaches of taking on this "hard case" of realpolitik behavior. See his "Constructing International Politics: A Response to Mearsheimer," *International Security* 20, no. 1 (Summer 1995).

2. *Parabellum* comes from the realpolitician's axiom "si pacem, parabellum" (if you want peace, then prepare for war). This parallels a Chinese idiom, "ju an si wei, wu bei you huan" (while residing in peace, think about dangers; without military preparations there will calamity).

3. Alastair Iain Johnston, *Cultural Realism: Strategic Culture and Grand Strategy in Chinese History* (Princeton: Princeton University Press, 1995).

Chinese strategic culture and then moves on to a discussion of the conceptual and methodological issues involved in rigorously analyzing ideational sources of strategic choice. It then applies this discussion to the analysis of Maoist strategic culture and Chinese conflict management behavior in the post-1949 period. Since traditional Chinese and Maoist strategic cultures make predictions about behavior similar to those made by a determinate structural realpolitik model, the Chinese case raises critical questions about ideational versus structural explanations of strategic choice. In the last section I examine these questions, arguing that a structural realpolitik model can in fact be subsumed within an ideational realpolitik strategic culture, that the latter is not epiphenomenal. At the very least, structure cannot account for Chinese realpolitik.

Why China?

China poses interesting problems for the analysis of ideational influences on strategic choice. Many have assumed that the China case should turn up evidence for cross-cultural differences in strategic thought and practice. In other words, China could be a hard case for hypotheses derived from the Western strategic experience or a relatively easy case for culturally and historically contingent explanations. Practically all the scholars, Chinese or Western, who have studied Chinese strategic thought have argued that the Chinese have persistently exhibited what are essentially nonrealist predispositions. According to standard interpretations, from the core notions of this strategic thought we should expect that as a political actor becomes stronger in relative terms it becomes less, not more, coercive, seeking to induce potential adversaries to submit by magnanimously offering them legitimacy or material wealth. Those who have not studied the Chinese case, but who have tended to rely on this literature to make the claim that ideational and cultural sources of strategic choice do matter, consequently have tended to reinforce this perception of the "China difference."[4] China, then, could be a crucial case both for those who would privilege anarchical structures and self-help behavior and for those who would privilege

4. Barry Gill, "The Hegemonic Tradition in East Asia: A Historical Perspective," in Stephen Gill, ed., *Gramsci, Historical Materialism, and International Relations*, p. 195 (Cambridge: Cambridge University Press, 1993); Justin Rosenberg, "Secret Origins of the State: The Structural Basis of *Raison d'etat*," *Review of International Studies* 18 (1992): 132; John A. Vasquez, *The War Puzzle* (Cambridge: Cambridge University Press, 1993), p. 116.

norms, cultures, ideas, and other shared, socially constructed, ideational influences on strategic behavior.

A closer look at the Chinese case, however, suggests a more complex picture.[5] The short of it is, the Chinese strategic tradition does not embody only one set of clear strategic preferences. Rather, there are at least two different strategic cultures. One, derived from what can be called a Confucian-Mencian paradigm, places nonviolent, accommodationist grand strategies before violent defensive or offensive ones in a ranking of strategic choices. This preference ranking is associated in the core texts in Chinese strategy with language that reflects the Confucian-Mencian stress on "benevolent," "righteous," and "virtuous" government as a basis of security. This language casts military force as "inauspicious," to be used only under "unavoidable circumstances," and stresses the submission of the enemy without the resort to force.[6]

The other set of strategic preferences comes from what could be called a parabellum, or hard realpolitik, paradigm, which generally places offensive strategies before static defense and accommodationist strategies; at the violent end of the spectrum, the preference for offensive actions depends on the "softness" or the "hardness" of the realpolitik axioms in a particular text. This paradigm reflects a set of characterizations of the external environment as dangerous, adversaries as dispositionally threatening, and conflict as zero-sum, in which the application of violence is ultimately required to deal with threats. Moreover, this paradigm explicitly embodies a key decision axiom—the notion of *quan bian*—which stresses absolute flexibility and a conscious sensitivity to changing relative capabilities. The more this balance is favorable, the more advantageous it is to adopted offensive coercive strategies; the less favorable, the more advantageous it is

---

5 The following section draws from Johnston, *Cultural Realism*.

6. Confucius (551–479 B.C.) was a philosopher of ancient China whose teachings (and their interpretations) became the basis of the predominant orthodoxy in political and moral thought in China. Mencius (390?–305? B.C.) was one of the more influential interpreters of Confucius' thought. At the risk of oversimplifying a complex body of thought, on questions of war and peace Confucianism stressed that external security rested on a ruler's ability to provide for the material and moral needs of his people through virtuous personal conduct and enlightened policies. This way, the people of the realm would be content with their lot, and potential enemies would willingly submit to partake of the ruler's magnanimity. Moral education was sufficient to transform potential enemies into willing and submissive allies. Confucius did not oppose military preparations, though he downplayed their role in the security of the state. Mencius, in particular, pushed Confucian ideas in a more extreme direction, arguing that a virtuous ruler had no need to use military force because he could have no enemies. It is highly questionable, however, whether this orthodoxy exercised much restraint on operational strategic thought and practice in Chinese history. See ibid.

to adopted defensive or accommodationist strategies to buy time until the balance shifts again.

These two sets of preferences, however, do not stand as two separate but equal strategic cultures. Rather, the Confucian-Mencian language represents an idealized discourse. None of the ancient texts on strategy that I examined (with one exception) devotes very much space to any detailed, concrete application of Confucian-Mencian concepts of security. Moreover, a number of the texts, along with some historical commentaries and annotations, implicitly or explicitly relegate these vague strategic axioms to indistinct golden ages of sage kings and legendary rulers, thus suggesting the historical and strategic irrelevance of these axioms. Finally, critical security concepts in the Confucian-Mencian paradigm are causally disconnected from, or only indirectly related to, the defeat of the adversary or the security of the state. Contrary, then, to most of the Chinese and Western literature on Chinese strategic thought, traditional China's operational strategic culture exhibited marked hard realpolitik tendencies.

The predominance of the hard realpolitik, parabellum strategic culture seems confirmed by the fact that much of the strategic practice in imperial China reflected these realpolitik preferences. My analysis of the Ming dynasty (1368–1644), for instance, indicates that realpolitik decision axioms showed up in the cognitive maps of key strategists during the Ming dynasty as they debated how to deal with the Mongol threat from north and west of China. Empirically, Chinese strategic choices tended to reflect this decision calculus to the extent that in periods of clear military advantage the Ming tended to act more aggressively toward Mongols than in periods when the relative capabilities shifted out of Ming favor. Indeed, Ming strategists tended to argue explicitly that static defensive and accommodationist strategies (e.g., peace treaties) were temporary fixes, rather than culturally preferred ways of dealing with external threats. This calculus is similar to that discovered by Paul Forage in his detailed historical analysis of the Northern Song dynasty's (A.D. 960–1127) strategy toward the Xi Xia "barbarians" along the northern border in the eleventh century.[7]

These conclusions are based only on an analysis of Chinese strategic culture before China's integration into the European/global state system in the twentieth century and before the importation into China of "Western" lib-

---

7. Paul Forage, "The Struggle for the Northwestern Frontier and the Consequences for the Northern Song" (paper presented at the annual conference of the Association of Asian Studies, Boston, March 1994).

eral democratic and Marxist-Leninist ideologies. Does this parabellum strategic culture persist across this transition? To telegraph the findings of this essay, Maoist strategic culture does indeed represent continuity with the past, reinforced by modern Chinese nationalist and Marxist-Leninist influences on strategic preferences. The evidence suggests, as well, that China's conflict management behavior after 1949 has been generally consistent with hard realpolitik strategic axioms. The fact that these axioms have persisted into the 1980s and 1990s when China has become increasingly integrated into international economic institutions and when its threat environment is the most benign since 1949 (a phenomenon that neither neoliberal nor neorealist approaches can comfortably account for) suggests that China's realpolitik behavior is ideationally rooted. As I will suggest at the end of the essay, this possibility raises complicated conceptual and methodological questions in explaining where realpolitik behavior comes from.

Some Conceptual and Methodological Issues

To date, many of those who have explicitly used the term *strategic culture* have tended to define it in ways that make it unfalsifiable and untestable. Especially egregious in this regard is what could be called the first (and most influential) generation of studies in strategic culture.[8] Definitionally,

---

8. I concentrate on the first generation here because it is this work that has tended to dominate the literature. The first generation, which emerged in the early 1980s, focused for the most part on trying to explain why the Soviets and the Americans apparently thought differently about strategy in the nuclear age. Borrowing from Snyder's work on strategic culture and Soviet limited nuclear war doctrine, authors such as Gray, Lord, and Jones all argued in some form or another that these differences were caused by unique variations in deeply rooted historical experience, political culture, and geography among other macroenvironmental variables. See Jack L. Snyder, *The Soviet Strategic Culture: Implications for Nuclear Options*, Rand R-2154-AF (Santa Monica, Calif.: RAND Corporation, 1977); Colin Gray, "National Styles in Strategy: The American Example," *International Security* 6, no. 2 (1981): 21–47; Colin Gray, *Nuclear Strategy and National Style* (Lanham, Md.: Hamilton Press, 1986); Carnes Lord, "American Strategic Culture," *Comparative Strategy* 5, no. 3 (1985): 269–93; David R. Jones, "Soviet Strategic Culture," in Carl G. Jacobsen, ed., *Strategic Power: USA/USSR*, pp. 35–49 (New York: St. Martin's, 1990). The second generation refers to a small number of studies that appeared mostly in the mid-1980s and focused on strategic culture as a kind of Gramscian discourse designed to reinforce the policy hegemony of strategists. See Bradley Klein, "Hegemony and Strategic Culture: American Power Projection and Alliance Defence Politics," *Review of International Studies* 14 (1988): 133–48; Robin Luckham, "Armament Culture," *Alternatives* 10, no. 1 (1984): 1–44. The third generation broadly includes work emerging in the 1990s that has focused on using culture, norms, and ideas as explanations for behavior. This literature is the most rigorous in conceptualization and methodology, but it is too new to have had much of an impact on the analysis of "strategic culture" in mainstream security studies. See Jeffrey W. Legro,

this literature subsumed both thought and action within the concept of strategic culture, leaving the mechanically deterministic implication that strategic thought led consistently to one type of behavior.[9] The literature also tended to include everything from technology to geography to ideology to past patterns of behavior in an amorphous concept of strategic culture, even though those variables could stand as separate, even conflicting, explanations for strategic choice. This left little conceptual space for nonstrategic culture explanations of behavior. As a result, the work took on a mechanistically deterministic hue and concluded that there were obvious and easy differences in the strategic cultures of different states.

Methodologically, there was little explication of, let alone agreement on, the process of observing a strategic culture. The literature is unclear about the sources one should look to for representations of strategic culture, the analytical methods one should use to sort out deep structures in strategic thought from symbolic or instrumental elements, how strategic culture is transmitted through time, and how it affects behavior.

We need, then, to construct a more rigorous concept of strategic culture that specifies its scope and content, the objects of analysis, the historical periods from which these are drawn, and the methods for deriving strategic culture from these objects. Then it is necessary to explicate a research strategy that can credibly measure the effects of strategic culture on the process of making strategic choices.

I have explored these issues elsewhere,[10] but briefly put, the research strategy should involve three steps. The first is to come up with a definition of strategic culture that is falsifiable. The second is to test for the presence of strategic culture in the formative "texts" of a particular society's strategic traditions. The third is to test for the effect of strategic culture on behavior.

As for the first step, paraphrasing heavily from Clifford Geertz's definition of religion,[11] I define strategic culture as an integrated system of symbols (i.e., causal axioms, languages, analogies, metaphors, etc.) that acts to establish pervasive and long-lasting strategic preferences by formulating concepts of the role and efficacy of military force in interstate political affairs, and by clothing these conceptions with such an aura of factuality that the strategic preferences seem uniquely realistic and efficacious.

Cooperation Under Fire: Anglo-German Restraint During World War II (Ithaca: Cornell University Press, 1995); and the essays in this volume by Elizabeth Kier, and Nina Tannenwald and Richard Price. For a detailed discussion of the three generations of work on strategic culture, see Johnston, *Cultural Realism*.

9. See Gray, "National Styles in Strategy," and Gray, *Nuclear Strategy and National Style*.
10. Johnston, *Cultural Realism*, ch. 2.
11. Clifford Geertz, *The Interpretation of Cultures* (New York: Basic Books, 1973), p. 90.

Specifically, strategic culture as a "system of symbols" comprises two parts. The first consists of basic assumptions about the orderliness of the strategic environment, that is, about the role of war in human affairs (whether it is aberrant or inevitable), about the nature of the adversary and the threat it poses (zero-sum or variable sum), and about the efficacy of the use of force (the ability to control outcomes and eliminate threats and the conditions under which it is useful to employ force). Together these make up the central paradigm of a strategic culture (figure 7.1).[12]

The second part of strategic culture consists of assumptions at a more operational level, about what strategic options are the most efficacious for dealing with the threat environment as defined by the central paradigm. It is at this second level that strategic culture begins to affect behavior directly. Thus the essential components or empirical referents of a strategic culture will appear in the form of a limited, ranked set of grand strategic preferences that are consistent across the objects of analysis and persistent across time.[13] They are not, therefore, necessarily responsive to changes in noncultural variables such as technology, threat, or organization. At the high end of the three dimensions we should expect strategic preferences to reflect a hard realpolitik central paradigm, that is, to show a preference for offensive over defensive over accommodationist strategies.[14] At the low end we should expect the opposite preference ranking, consistent with an idealpolitik central paradigm.[15]

---

12. Here I rely on Taber's notion of a dominant paradigm as a collection of heuristics used "to guide the selection of problem-solving strategies for some specifiable period of time. Individual leaders may or may not be aware of the influence of a dominant paradigm on strategic choice" (Charles Taber, "Modern War Learning: A Markov Model" [paper presented at the Midwestern Political Science Association Conference, Chicago, 1987], p. 4). There are similarities here with operational codes and belief systems, except that strategic culture analysis focuses more squarely on historically rooted and collectively shared, rather than individual, belief systems.

13. See also Wildavsky's "cultural theory of preference formation" in Aaron Wildavsky, "Choosing Preferences by Constructing Institutions: A Cultural Theory of Preference Formation," *American Political Science Review* 81, no. 1 (1987): 3–20.

14. Lebow argues, for instance, that acceptance of the inevitability of war leads to preferences for preventive and/or preemptive strategies, since if war is inevitable, it makes sense to act before the enemy does. See Richard Ned Lebow, *Between Peace and War: The Nature of International Crisis* (Baltimore: Johns Hopkins University Press, 1987), pp. 254–63. See also Snyder on the "cult of the offensive"; Jack L. Snyder, *The Ideology of the Offensive: Military Decision Making and the Disasters of 1914* (Ithaca: Cornell University Press, 1984), pp. 17, 39, 199.

15. A belief that war is an aberrant or at least a preventable event in human affairs ought to be associated with a non-zero-sum view of the adversary. If conflicts are in the main negotiable, then presumably the enemy has a price short of one's own capitulation. If this is the case, then ceteris paribus highly coercive, violent strategies—which entail severe economic and political costs—would seem to be strategies of last resort, since trade-offs and logrolling opportunities appear more cost-effective in *managing* (as opposed to *eliminating*) the threat.

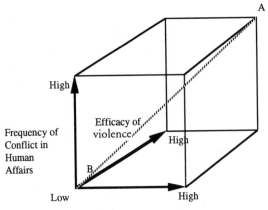

Zero-Sum Nature of Conflict

A = hard realpolitik (or parabellum)
B = idealpolitik

FIGURE 7.1 The Central Paradigm

I use *ranked* preferences instead a simple menu of strategic options because if different societies have different strategic cultures they ought to put different weights on these choices—that is, rank them differently. Ranked preferences allow for testing for consistency in strategic culture within systems and thus for differences between systems.[16] This approach also provides a concept of strategic culture that is falsifiable. If preference rankings are not consistent across objects of analysis across time, then a single strategic culture can be said not to exist. Additionally, I use strategic preferences that are ranked because that approach should yield, ceteris paribus, explicit predictions about behavior, thus making it more possible to distinguish a strategic culture model of choice from other models.

The next step in this research design is to test for the presence of a strategic culture by testing for the congruence between the strategic preference rankings across the cultural objects of analysis (or "texts"). This requires first determining what are the "artifacts" in which one expects to find a culturally based set of ranked strategic preferences. In principle, there could be a large variety, including the writings and debates of strate-

16. David J. Elkins and Richard E. B. Simeon, "A Cause in Search of Its Effect, or What Does Political Culture Explain," *Comparative Politics* 11 (1979): 133.

gists, military leaders, and "national security elites," or war plans, or even images of war and peace in various media.[17]

Fortunately, in the study of China one does not have to be too arbitrary in sampling these objects of analysis. In my work on traditional China, I used a set of texts—the *Seven Military Classics*—which together formed the core of Chinese strategic thought and military education from the eleventh century on, though some of the texts had existed individually since 500 B.C.[18] In the study of Maoist strategic culture, Mao's own writings form the obvious sampling base. For this study I have chosen a handful of texts from different periods in Mao's life when he faced different strategic contexts. The assumption here is that if there is indeed a persistent Maoist strategic culture, the central paradigm and related strategic preferences should be consistent across these different texts, across time and different strategic contexts.[19]

---

17. For a list, see Luckham, "Armament Culture," tables 2 and 3. See also Kier's list (essay 6 in this volume), which includes curriculum from military schools, training manuals, journals, languages, symbols, taboos, etc. Legro, in *Cooperation Under Fire*, examines planning documents, regulations, military exercises, and memoirs.

18. These texts on statecraft, strategy, and tactics are still read and studied in the professional military education systems in Taiwan and the People's Republic of China. Sun Zi's *The Art of War* is one of the seven texts. For the only English translation of the complete set, see Ralph Sawyer, trans., *The Seven Military Classics of Ancient China* (Boulder: Westview, 1993).

19. Given the importance of sampling those texts that are most likely to capture the strategic culture(s) in a society, doesn't this sampling of one individual's works on strategy virtually guarantee that I will find congruence in preference rankings across texts? How can the ideas and axioms of an individual constitute a collectively shared, hence socially constituted, strategic culture? These are legitimate concerns. I have a couple of responses. First, to the extent that we are interested in explaining behavior, it makes sense to look for the presence of a strategic culture in the work of those who play a key role in decision making. As recent scholarship underscores, Mao was essentially in charge of Chinese foreign policy making at the strategic and even tactical levels from 1949 on. See Thomas J. Christensen, *Useful Adversaries: Grand Strategy, Domestic Mobilization, and Sino-American Conflict, 1947–1958* (Princeton: Princeton University Press, in press); Robert Ross, *The United States and China: Negotiating for Cooperation, 1969–1989* (Palo Alto: Stanford University Press, 1995); Chen Jian, *China's Road to the Korean War* (New York: Columbia University Press, 1994). Second, given Mao's dominance of the policy process in China, coupled with his personality cult, Mao's "thought" formed the core of ideological socialization in China. To the extent that decision makers in China were exposed to antecedent strategic axioms on the basis of which they may or may not have made decisions, these axioms came largely from Mao. Given the special circumstances of strategic decision making in Maoist China, there is no easy way around the question of whether Maoist strategic culture was collectively shared. I would argue, however, that given the absence of any substantial contestation of Maoist strategic axioms during *and* after his life, the term *Maoist strategic culture* is still valid. That Maoist strategic axioms persisted after Mao died and after most of his economic, political, and cultural legacies were dismantled under Deng Xiaoping suggests that the strategic and military legacy was accepted and internalized by Chinese decision makers. There are literally scores of books on Mao's strategic and foreign policies that have been published in recent

Having chosen the objects of analysis, the next question is, How should one extract the central elements of a strategic culture, if indeed one exists? Here I rely primarily on a modified form of cognitive mapping supplemented by symbolic analysis. Cognitive mapping seems appropriate because the researcher is interested in what the texts appear to be telling a strategist about what to do, how to rank options, and thus how to make choices. Causal judgments are a key step as decision makers reason about how certain types of behavior will affect their environment in such a way as to secure basic foreign policy goals.[20] Cognitive mapping is precisely a technique for uncovering causal linkages between certain behavioral axioms and their estimated behavioral effect.[21]

As for symbolic analysis, the literature on cultural analysis in anthropology and organizational studies suggests that symbols (e.g., analogies, metaphors, key words, idioms) are the vehicles through which cultural forms (e.g., shared rules, axioms, preferences) are manifested empirically, such that culture can be communicated, learned, or debated.[22] From a symbolic perspective, then, strategic culture may be reflected by symbols about the role of force in human affairs, about the efficacy of certain strategies, and hence about what sorts of strategies are better than others.

The third stage in research involves analyzing the relationship between strategic culture and behavior. Here one has to trace the presence of a strategic culture from the objects of analysis up to the strategic assumptions of key decision makers in the historical period of interest. Since Mao

years. See Foundation for International Strategic Studies, ed., *Huan qiu tong ci liang re: yi dai ling xiumen de guoji zhanlue sixiang* [Global contradictions: A generation of leaders and their international strategic thought] (Beijing: Central Documents Publishing House, 1993); and Gu Yan, "Duli zizhu shi Mao Zedong waijiao sixiang de linghun" [Independence is the soul of Mao Zedong's foreign policy thinking], *Shijie jingji yu zhengzhi* [World economics and politics], no. 2 (1994): 30–33.

20. David Dessler, "Notions of Rationality in Conflict Decision-Making" (paper presented at the annual conference of the International Studies Association, Anaheim, Calif., 1986), pp. 18–19; see also Judith Goldstein and Robert O. Keohane, "Ideas and Foreign Policy: An Analytical Framework," in Judith Goldstein and Robert O. Keohane, eds., *Ideas and Foreign Policy: Beliefs, Institutions, and Political Change*, p. 13 (Ithaca: Cornell University Press, 1993).

21. Robert Axelrod, ed., *Structure of Decision: The Cognitive Maps of Political Elites* (Princeton: Princeton University Press, 1976).

22. See, for example, Charles D. Elder and Roger W. Cobb, *The Political Uses of Symbols* (New York: Longman, 1983), p. 28; Lowell Dittmer, "Political Culture and Political Symbolism," *World Politics* 29 (1977): 577, 579; Lance Bennett, "Perception and Cognition: An Information-Processing Framework for Politics," in *Handbook of Political Behavior* (New York: Plenum, 1981), 1:76; Earl R. MacCormac, *A Cognitive Theory of Metaphor* (Cambridge: MIT Press, 1985), pp. 23–24; Yuen Foong Khong, *Analogies at War: Korea, Munich, Dien Bien Phu, and the Vietnam Decisions of 1965* (Princeton: Princeton University Press, 1992), p. 10.

was the key decision maker in post-1949 China until his death in 1976, I look at the possible influences and parallels between traditional strategic culture and Mao's strategic decision axioms.

The next substep, then, is to test for the effects of decision makers' preference rankings on politico-military behavior. Here the primary methodological issue is how to conceptualize the relationship between culture and behavior. In essence, the research problem at this stage is to control for the effects of culturally exogenous variables. This is not a clear-cut process. There are a number of ways of conceptualizing the relationships between strategic culture and other exogenous independent variables.[23] The key issue is how to measure the effects of a constant or slow-to-change variable on outcomes that are supposed to vary (strategic choice). My preference is to treat strategic culture as a consistent set of ranked preferences that persists across time and across strategic contexts. Decision makers are sensitive to structural or exogenous conditions (i.e., relative capabilities) in a culturally unique way, such that interaction may (though it need not) yield unique predictions. This conceptualization allows one to consider strategic culture as a constant that, in interaction with a structural intervening variable, creates variation in the overall independent inputs into strategic choice.[24] One can then test the influence of strategic culture against noncultural variables.

But this then raises the obvious question: What alternative models are "out there" against which a strategic culture model can be tested? At first glance, the most obvious competitive model would be a structural realpolitik model. One version of this model posits that states' decision makers generally share an undifferentiated interest in expanding the influence of the state. Given that interest, states will expand as long as their resources allow, since greater relative capabilities increase the probability of success of expansion.[25] This structural realpolitik model

---

23. These are explored in Johnston, *Cultural Realism*, ch. 2.

24. One of the criticisms that structuralists sometimes level at those who work with cultural variables is that a constant, like culture, cannot explain change in state behavior. This charge fundamentally misunderstands the constructivist argument: ideas as independent variables are useful only because they interpret or give meaning to material facts. Thus changes in relative capabilities, for instance, mean something different to a realpolitician concerned about relative gains in a competitive world than they do to a liberal concerned about absolute gains. Variation in the predictions of cultural models comes from changes in the relevant material environment; the implications of these changes, however, depend on the content of the ideational constant. So constructivists should have no trouble using a structural intervening variable to make determinate predictions.

25. Readers will note that this foreign policy offshoot of structural realism assumes that states prefer to maximize power, not simply to seek mere survival. This assumption is not uncontroversial, but

would therefore predict that as a state consolidates and mobilizes resources it will adopt increasingly coercive strategies. The state will become more, not less, belligerent.[26] As the relative power capabilities decline, the state turns to less offensively coercive, more static defensive strategies, and from there to more accommodating strategies as temporary fixes for disadvantageous conditions. One could pit this model against a strategic culture model as long as the latter made distinctive predictions about strategic choice, or as long as some form of critical experiment could be set up to test for additional sets of predictions if the initial sets were similar.

As I have suggested, however, China's hard realpolitik strategic culture does not make predictions that are unambiguously different from this more determinate version of structural realpolitik. Yet the ideational explanation should not be dropped simply on the grounds of parsimony; to do so in the absence of some sort of critical test would be to make an important theoretical choice for aesthetic reasons. Moreover, to do so would be to accept the logical fallacy that ideational models can explain only non-realpolitik "deviant" behavior and that "nondeviant" realpolitik behavior is not ideationally rooted. As I will argue, because of its inadequacy in accounting for the persistence of cultural realpolitik axioms, structural realpolitik should be abandoned as the "null" hypothesis. This choice does not mean abandoning competitive hypothesis testing, but it does suggest that the most logical alternative models to cultural realpolitik are themselves ideational in nature. More of this later.

---

without it realist models of strategic choice become indeterminate, just as economic expected utility approaches to decision making become indeterminate, or harder to model, without the use of money as the basis of the utility function. See Mancur Olson, "Toward a Unified View of Economics and the Other Social Sciences," in James E. Alt and Kenneth A. Shepsle, eds., *Perspectives on Positive Political Economy*, p. 218 (Cambridge: Cambridge University Press, 1992). If survival is the goal of states, one might expect a range of grand strategic preferences—from "defensive" expansionism in the name of the status quo, to static defense or deterrence strategies. On the other hand, if the expansion of influence and power is the primary goal of states, it makes less sense for them to rely solely on defensive or deterrence strategies. Thus the latter assumption about state interests leads to more determinant predictions about strategic behavior. In essence, to make structural realist models determinate, one has to plug in assumptions about state interests that are more commonly found in classical realist literature. This is essentially why Mearsheimer's version of neorealism is more determinate than most. See John J. Mearsheimer, "The False Promise of International Institutions," *International Security* 19, no. 3 (Winter 1994/95): 9–11.

26. John A. Vasquez, "Capability, Types of War, Peace," *Western Political Science Quarterly* 39, no. 2 (1986): 321; John A. Vasquez, "Foreign Policy Learning and War," in Charles Hermann, Charles W. Kegley Jr., and James N. Rosenau, eds., *New Directions in the Study of Foreign Policy* (Boston: Unwin Hyman, 1987), pp. 367–68.

The Maoist Central Paradigm

As I suggested above, strategic culture provides answers to the three broad interrelated questions in the central paradigm, and from this paradigm should flow logically connected strategic preferences about how to deal with threats to security. Traditional Chinese strategic thought tended to provide answers toward the hard parabellum end of these three dimensions. Operationally, therefore, the strategic preference ranking tended to place offensive strategies above defensive and defensive above accommodationist. Where does Maoist strategic thought fit along these three dimensions?

The Nature of Conflict

Mao's writings are nothing if not paeans to the constancy of conflict and struggle in human affairs. The starting point is Mao's theory of contradictions.[27] While scholars debate whether Mao was simply inheriting traditional Chinese concepts of the dualism of existence or Hegelian dialectics through Marx, Engels, and Lenin, or was fusing the two, most agree that for Mao contradictions were the driving force of all natural and human activity.[28] The resolution of contradictions within a thing was the fundamental source of its transformation and development. Conflict between contradictory elements drove nature and history. The resolution of one contradiction led to the creation of or superordination of another contradiction. Balance or the stability of equilibria in natural and social phenomena was relative, imbalance was absolute. For Mao, conflict didn't require a solution, it *was* the solution to political problems. Hence politics and international affairs were processes by which contradictions—whether

---

27. Mao Zedong, "On Contradiction," [1937], *Selected Works of Mao Zedong* (Beijing: Foreign Languages Press, 1965), 1:311–47; Gao Tiejun, "Mao Zedong guofang xiandai hua sixiang chu tan" [A preliminary discussion of Mao Zedong's thinking on national defense modernization], *Junshi lishi yanjiu* [Studies in military history], no. 3 (1987): 61; Liu Chunjian, *Shenqi de qi he: Mao Zedong Deng Xiaoping yu Zhongguo chuantong wenhua* [A mystical unity: Mao Zedong, Deng Xiaoping, and China's traditional culture] (Shanxi: People's Publishing House, 1992); John Bryant Starr, *Continuing the Revolution: The Political Thought of Mao* (Princeton: Princeton University Press, 1979).
28. We know that from an early age, before he endorsed Marxism-Leninism, Mao accepted the notion that all phenomena comprise contradictory elements that create a process of constant change. In his marginal notes on a book about ethics that he read in 1917–1918 in his mid-twenties, Mao commented, "There is no life and death, only change. If this thing grows, that thing is eliminated. Life is not only life, and death is not only extermination. Merely a change" (Mao Zedong, " 'Lunli xue yuan li' pi zhu" [1917] [Critical comments on the Tenets of Ethics], in *Mao Zedong zao qi wen gao* [Mao Zedong's early writings] [Hunan: People's Publishing House, 1990], p. 200).

230 Alastair Iain Johnston

between classes or states—were resolved through conflict, leading to the emergence of new contradictions.

In Mao's view, conflict in human affairs was not only inevitable but also desirable. Harmony was transitory and undesirable. He came to this conclusion well before he had accepted Marxist-Leninist normative arguments that class conflict was central to historical progress. In his late teens he—like many from his nationalistic generation—had come to believe that China's political weakness in the face of imperialism was not just analogous to but was also a product of the physical weakness of the Chinese people. His class notes, written when he was a student in Changsha, indicate that he accepted the view that people who were lazy, indolent, and weak could not progress; they would fall behind, decline, and die. Likewise, states that were lazy, indolent, and weak would fall behind other states, decline, and be exterminated by others. People and states needed to struggle; they required a spirit of vitality and vigor.[29] Here one finds parallels to the social Darwinism arguments, made by nineteenth-century European nationalists, holding that extended periods of peace atrophy the physical capabilities and will of the state.[30] But there are parallels as well in traditional Chinese strategic thought and practice. Ming dynasty strategists, for instance, also lamented that prolonged peace led to the decline in military preparedness and will that in turn encouraged Mongol enemies to exploit this weakness.[31]

This notion that conflict was ubiquitous and inevitable dovetailed with Mao's embrace of Marxism-Leninism in his late twenties. Class contradictions compelled history forward, and the resolution of class contradictions was an inherently conflictual process, aimed fundamentally at the elimination of the adversary. His analogy for politics seemed to summarize these axioms: "Politics is bloodless warfare. Warfare is bloody politics."[32]

---

29. Mao Zedong, "Jiang tang lu" [1913] [Class notes], in *Mao Zedong zao qi wen gao*, p. 585; Lucian Pye, *Mao Tse-tung: The Man in the Leader* (New York: Basic Books, 1976).

30. See, for instance, the writings of Heinriche von Treitschke, *Selection from Treitschke's Lectures on Politics*, trans. Adolf Hausrath (London: Gowans and Gray, 1914), and his *Politics*, trans. Blanche Dugdale and Torben de Bille (New York: Macmillan, 1916). As Frank Dikotter implies, however, it is more likely that Mao was influenced by Spencerian notions of organic intergroup competition as interpreted by Yan Fu. Darwin's work was not completely translated into Chinese until 1919. Instead, among early-twentieth-century Chinese intellectuals Herbert Spencer was one of the most influential European thinkers on the struggle between social groups; see Frank Dikotter, *The Discourse of Race in Modern China* (Stanford: Stanford University Press, 1993), p. 104.

31. See Johnston, *Cultural Realism*.

32. He Taiyou and Zhang Zhongliang, *Mao Zedong Zhanfa* [Mao Zedong's Art of War] (Beijing: National Defense University Press, 1988), p. 11. See also Lan Shuchen, "Mao Zedong junshi sixiang yu zhongguo chuantong wenhua" [Mao Zedong's military thought and China's traditional culture], *Junshi lishi yanjiu* [Studies in military history], no. 3 (1987): 69.

The Nature of the Enemy

In ancient Chinese strategic thought, the nature of the enemy was defined by the concept of righteous war (*yi zhan*). Generally the concept meant "sending forth armor and weapons in order to punish the unrighteous," namely, those who bullied weaker states, killed their own people, insulted other states, and otherwise rebelled against the established political and social order. In the face of unrighteous behavior, the violent destruction of the enemy was both necessary and desirable.[33] Within this context the ends justified the means: once the ends of war were deemed righteous, then actions that in another context could be unrighteous (i.e., invasion and killing) were infused with moral intent.[34] Since the adversary was a threat to the moral political order, the contest was explicitly zero-sum: the enemy could not be won over but had to be destroyed.[35]

Like the ancient Chinese, Mao also developed a concept of righteous or

33. On righteous war, see Zeng Zhen, *Tang Tai Zong, Li Wei Gong wen dui jin zhu jin yi* [Contemporary translation and annotation of the "Dialogues of Tang Tai Zong and Li Wei Gong"] (Taibei: Commercial Press, 1986), p. 12; Lin Pinshi, *Lu Shi Chun Qiu jin yi jin zhu* [Contemporary translation and annotation of the "Lu shi chun qiu"] (Taibei: Commercial Press, 1986), p. 188; Shi Zimei, *Shi shi qi shu jiang yi* [Shi Zimei's teaching materials on the Seven Military Classics], Riben wen jiu san nian ed. (1222; Taibei: Taiwan National Museum), 31:9b and 34:17a; Niu Hongen and Qiu Shaohua, *Xian Qin zhu zi junshi lun yi zhu* [Translation and annotation of military essays by Pre-Qin scholars] (Beijing: Military Sciences Press, 1985), 1:397; Liu Yin, *Si Ma Fa zhi jie* [Commentary on the "Si Ma Fa"] (Taibei: Shijian Press, 1955), ch. 1.

34. There are parallels with Machiavelli's view of morality and war: "Morality in Machiavelli's usage is entirely instrumental: it is part of a prince's arsenal to be used to greater or lesser effect. In no sense does it restrain state behavior—nor should one expect it to do so because the state in Machiavelli's treatment is beyond such restraint" (Michael Joseph Smith, *Realist Thought from Weber to Kissinger* [Baton Rouge: Louisiana State University Press, 1986], p. 10). For a fuller discussion, see Johnston, *Cultural Realism*, ch. 3.

35. See Liu Yin [SKQS], *Huang Shi Gong San Lue zhi jie* [Commentary on Huang Shi Gong's Three Strategies] [Si Ku Quan Shu version] (Taibei: Commercial Press, 1983–1985), p. 726.103; see also Shi, *Shi shi qi shu jiang yi*, 36.7b, and Lin, *Lu Shi Chun Qiu*, pp. 211, 217. The demonization of an unrighteous adversary—and the corollary that any and all means of eliminating this enemy are legitimate—is described well by modern-day attribution theory. The adversary's behavior is seen as dispositional, while one's own behavior is circumstantial. This construct creates "an image of the situation for personal and public consumption that releases the subject from moral inhibitions and allows the subject to deal with the threat or opportunity without restraint" (Richard Herrmann, "The Empirical Challenge of the Cognitive Revolution: A Strategy for Drawing Inferences About Perceptions," *International Studies Quarterly* 32 [1988]: 183, 185). See also Thomas Hart, "Cognitive Paradigms in the Arms Race: Deterrence, Detente, and the 'Fundamental Error' of Attribution," *Conflict and Cooperation* 3 (1978): 150; John E. Mack, "The Enemy System," in Vamik D. Volkan, Demetrios A. Julius, and Joseph V. Montville, eds., *The Psychodynamics of International Relations*, vol. 1, *Concepts and Theories* (Lexington, Mass.: Lexington Books, 1990), pp. 60–61; Howard F. Stein, "The Indispensable Enemy and American-Soviet Relations," in ibid., p. 82; J. Richard Eiser and D. van der Pligt, *Attitudes and Decisions* (London: Routledge, 1988), pp. 45–66.

just war in which the enemy was defined as dispositionally apt to threaten one's own fundamental values as a class or state. For Mao, just wars were wars conducted by oppressed classes or nations. Unjust wars were those undertaken by oppressors, whether classes or nations. Hence, conflicts between oppressed and oppressor were zero-sum in nature. Under these circumstances, any and all strategies and tactics were acceptable. Well before he embraced Marx, Mao criticized Song Rang Gong of the Spring and Autumn period for his moral chivalry. Later, in a major work on strategy titled *On Protracted War*, Mao repeated this critique that in a just war strategy and tactics are questions of methods, not morality.[36]

Applied to politics, Mao's theory of contradictions complemented the zero-sum conceptualization of the enemy inherent in his vision of just war. Mao divided contradictions into two sets of categories: principal and secondary, antagonistic and nonantagonistic. He saw the principal contradiction in any particular phenomenon as playing the "leading and decisive role."[37] The secondary contradiction played a subordinate role and did not immediately drive the development of a phenomenon. Once the principal contradiction was resolved, however, the secondary contradiction could turn into the new principal one. He developed the notion of antagonistic and nonantagonistic contradictions to resolve the problem of conflict within socialist parties and societies. If contradictions embodied all things, then even after socialist societies had abolished class society, contradictions had to exist. These contradictions, Mao argued, were nonantagonistic, in the sense that their resolution did not necessitate the violent eradication of the adversary required by antagonistic contradictions. Nonantagonistic contradictions existed "among the people," that is, within and between progressive classes and social groups remaining inside a socialist movement or state.

In combination, these types of contradictions created a two-by-two matrix (figure 7.2). Contradictions in the first cell were those in which conflict was inherently zero-sum and thus could be resolved only by eliminating the adversary. There could be no compromises with actors in this cell, except for very strict tactical purposes designed to weaken the enemy.

---

36. Song Rang Gong, a ruler of a state during the Spring and Autumn period in the seventh century B.C., was defeated after he refused to attack a vulnerable enemy force as it crossed a river. He argued that it was immoral to attack before the enemy had fully formed up. For his chivalry he suffered a defeat and the opprobrium of later generations of "realist" strategists. See also Lan, "Mao Zedong junshi sixiang," p. 68.

37. Mao, "On Contradiction," p. 322.

	Principal	Secondary
Antagonistic	1	2
Nonantagonistic	3	4

FIGURE 7.2 Mao's Typology of Contradictions

Contradictions in the second cell were temporarily subordinate to the resolution of the principal contradiction. Actors in this cell could be temporary allies, with whom one could form a united front but against whom one also prepared for inevitable conflict.[38] Actors in the third cell were those with whom the resolution of conflict required not their elimination but rather their transformation (e.g., through political education). Contradictions within this cell were primarily within one's own in-group, not between an in-group and an out-group. Actors in the fourth cell were the least threatening to one's security or well-being and constituted the most credible political allies.

The question is, How did an actor get put in the first cell in Maoist strategic thought? What was the threshold of threatening behavior beyond which the conflict was defined as antagonistic and principal? It is hard to answer this question with much precision. In effect, it asks, Where on the first two dimensions of the central paradigm does one put Mao in relation to other texts in China's strategic tradition? In the traditional texts on strategy, the threshold beyond which a conflict is defined as zero-sum varied somewhat from text to text.

As a Marxist-Leninist, Mao drew upon his class analysis to provide this threshold, and it appears to have been quite low, perhaps lower than that

---

38. Mao's essay "On Policy" is a good example of how to deal with an actor in the second cell. In it he argues for a united front with the GMD even in the face of increased anti-Communist actions by the CCP's erstwhile anti-Japanese allies. The essay was re-released in the early 1970s to justify the necessity of rapprochement with the U.S. in the face of a growing Soviet threat. See Mao Zedong, "On Policy" [1940], in *Selected Works of Mao Zedong*, 2:441–49.

of the traditional texts. In principle, all oppressive classes belonged at some point in cell 1, depending on the immediate political problem (e.g., the overthrow of the nationalists or the consolidation of political control in the new China). As a Chinese nationalist, Mao could easily put all major powers (whether socialist or capitalist) in cell 1, depending again on the strategic problem at hand (e.g., facing American imperialism in the 1960s or Soviet social imperialism in the 1970s).

In sum, according to Mao's strategic thought, at some point in the development of contradictions between two adversaries this relationship would enter the realm of the principal antagonistic contradiction. At that point the nature of the conflict with the enemy became zero-sum, and negotiation, compromise, logrolling, and suasion were essentially ruled out. One could venture, then, that Maoist thought defined most class-based disputes and all threats to Chinese territorial and political integrity as inherently zero-sum conflicts.

The Role of Violence

Given the ubiquitousness of contradictions and conflict in human affairs and given also a zero-sum conceptualization of the adversary inherent in the process of resolving antagonistic contradictions, it is not surprising that Mao placed a great deal of stock in violence or in the employment of overwhelming force to eliminate adversaries. Thus superior force was a key ingredient in the forward march of history. This principle held between oppressed and oppressor states as well. For Mao, there was both a strong ideological and pragmatic acceptance that violence inhered in human social processes and that preparations for and the use of violence were essential for self-preservation and self-development. In Mao's view war was the highest form of struggle, the most efficacious means of resolving antagonistic contradictions among classes and states.[39] Mao accepted Clausewitz's notion that war was a continuation of politics by other means, but he did not accept the potential restraints that this axiom placed on the scale or conduct of war. If the nature of politics was the struggle between

---

39. This did not mean that Mao advocated the wholesale slaughter of enemy forces or political enemies. Annihilation required the elimination of the enemy's military power. This could entail the application of such overwhelming military force that enemy forces capitulated en masse. What Mao opposed was attrition, whereby enemy forces would be routed or bloodied such that they could still fight another day. As he remarked, "Injuring all of a man's ten fingers is not as effective as chopping off one, and routing ten enemy divisions is not as effective as annihilating one of them" (Mao Zedong, "Problems of Strategy in China's Revolutionary War" [1936], *Selected Works of Mao Zedong*, 1:248).

the just and the unjust, then just war was a valid continuation of politics. And given that the unjust enemy was unlikely to be satisfied with the mere political resolution of conflict, then just war was not a last resort.[40] Force did not come at the end of a process of political give-and-take that had stalemated, leaving no other choice but coercion. The use of force depended wholly on whether the adversary capitulated. Since class and national enemies were not predisposed to capitulate short of the use of force, violence was in all likelihood a necessary part of the process of dealing with threats.[41]

Mao came to this conclusion at an early age, though somewhat tentatively. In his notes from his school days in Changsha, for example, he recorded that those without strong power could not complete their tasks or be successful, whatever their endeavors.[42] Despite this, as late as mid-1919 he was reluctant to endorse fully violent revolution in China, arguing in one essay that radical change that used "power politics" to overthrow power politics would only result in more of the same.[43] The radicalization of Chinese intellectuals during the May Fourth movement in 1919, however, pushed Mao to embrace Marxism-Leninism in 1920 and 1921 and to embrace, intellectually at least, the role of violence in social transfor-

---

40. Lan, "Mao Zedong junshi sixiang," p. 69, and He and Zhang, *Mao Zedong Zhanfa*, p. 11. It is often suggested that Mao came to Clausewitz through Lenin. This may indeed have been Mao's first exposure to the notion of war as a continuation of politics, but recent new materials on Mao suggest that Mao also studied Clausewitz directly, beginning in the spring of 1938. He even organized a Clausewitz study group joined by other Party military leaders. This sparked a small "Clausewitz fever" in the Communist base area at Yenan over the next couple of years as translations and commentaries on "On War" appeared in the Communist press. See Sun Baoyi, ed., *Mao Zedong de du shu shengya* [The book reading life of Mao Zedong] (Beijing: Knowledge Press, 1993), pp. 79–80.
41. This is consistent with the ancient Chinese notion of "using the military instrument only under unavoidable circumstances" (*bu de yi er yong bing*). Whether or not these circumstances were avoidable depended wholly on the enemy. Since the environment was, in the main, conflictual, and since the conflict with the enemy was, in the main, zero-sum, the likelihood that force would have to be used frequently was quite high. For a good contemporary example of this type of argument, see Mao's discussion of the use of coercion against Taiwan under unavoidable circumstances. See Mao Zedong, "Dui Zhonggong ba da zhengzhi baogao gao de pi yu he xiugai" [Comments on and revisions of the draft political report to the 8th Congress of the CCP] [1956], in *Jianguo yilai Mao Zedong wen gao, 1956–1957* [Mao Zedong's manuscripts since the founding of the nation] (Beijing: Central Documents Publishing House, 1992), 6:142–43. The PLA marshal Nie Rongzhen argued in a speech to leading cadres in military industry in 1963, "Whether we fight or not is definitely not up to us. We are not the general staff of imperialism" (Nie Rongzhen, "Zai jun gong lingdao ganbu huiyishang de jianghua" [1963], in Nie Rongzhen, *Nie Rongzhen junshi wenxuan* [Selected military works of Nie Rongzhen] [Beijing: Liberation Army Press, 1992], p. 497).
42. Mao, "Jiang tang lu," p. 585.
43. Mao Zedong, "Min zhong de da lian he—yi" [The great alliance of the masses—1] [1919], in *Mao Zedong zao qi wen gao*, pp. 293, 341.

mation. In 1926, after a lengthy investigation of the radicalizing peasant movement in Hunan, he came to believe that armed uprising was the only way to resolve principal antagonistic contradictions. Subsequently he stressed that when carrying out a revolution one had to use "blade against blade, and rifle against rifle," because class enemies were not going to submit voluntarily.[44]

For Mao, then, the causal relationship between military power and security was straightforward. As he remarked in reference to a perceived threat that the U.S. might intervene in the Chinese civil war to defend the collapsing Guomintang (GMD) regime, "The stronger and more resolute the power of the people's revolution the lower the possibilities that the United States will directly interfere militarily."[45] Mao was not referring here abstractly to the revolutionary enthusiasm, cohesion, or organization of Chinese people; he was referring to the military power of the Chinese Communist Party (CCP).

To get a more systematic handle on the role of military force in the achievement of security, it would be instructive to take a closer look at the cause-effect relationships and symbolic content in Mao's writings on strategy and statecraft.

Problems of Strategy in China's Revolutionary War (1936)

According to the cause-effect relationships in this text (figure 7.3), victory over the adversary depended on variety of inputs or "causes." Among these were the effective use of intelligence to spot the enemy's weak points (211.5.1)[46] and then the use of military force to attack those points (e.g.,

---

44. Song Shilun, *Mao Zedong junshi sixiang de xingcheng ji qi fazhan* [The formation and development of Mao Zedong's military thought] (Beijing: Military Sciences Press, 1984), pp. 9–16; see also Mao Zedong, "Zhengquan shi you qiang ganzizhong qu de de" [Political power is obtained from the barrel of a gun] [1927], in Mao Zedong, *Mao Zedong junshi wen xuan (neibu ben)* [Selected military essays of Mao Zedong (internal edition)] (Beijing: Liberation Army Press, 1981), p. 4.

45. Mao Zedong, "Muqian xingshi he dang zai yi jiu si jiu nian de ren wu" [The present situation and the Party's tasks for 1949] [1949], in Mao, *Mao Zedong junshi wen xuan*, p. 328.

46. A word about notation. The first numeral refers to the page number of the text, the next refers to the paragraph number, and the last to the assigned number of the cause-effect relationship found in that paragraph. The cause-effect statements were entered into a simple database program that allowed me to search for particular effects or particular causes using key words. In each text the cause and effect concepts were collapsed and clustered into self-evident categories, and I tried to keep these categories as consistent as possible across texts. For each causal argument, I have listed only a couple of representative cause-effect statements here, rather than providing notation for each of the 810 cause-effect statements relating to security, statecraft, strategy, and tactics that I coded. On coding, see Margaret Tucker Wrightson, "The Documentary Coding Method," in Axelrod, *Structure of Decision.* My own coding adapted and simplified some of her procedures.

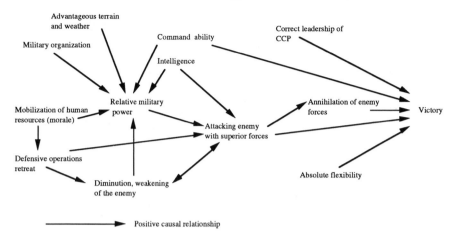

FIGURE 7.3 Cognitive Map of "Problems of Strategy in China's Revolutionary War"

184.2.4; 201.1.1; 224.2.1); immediate retreat after achieving tactical victory, followed by a second attack (232.1.2); the concentration of superior military force (e.g., 199.1.4; 233.2.1; 238.1.1); and the annihilation, as opposed to the mere routing, of enemy forces (e.g., 202.2.2; 224.2.1; 248.3.2). Victory was also a function of a commander's abilities, in particular his understanding that war was the highest form of resolving contradictions (180.1.3), and his subjective ability to understand the objective limitations on the use of force (e.g., 188.1.2; 190.2.4; 232.1.3). Absolute flexibility was also critical for victory. A strategist must be able to act according to circumstances and demonstrate tactical flexibility (e.g., 184.1.2; 232.1.1). Other causes of victory included flexible borrowing from the military experiences of other states (180:5.2; 181.2.10) and the correct military and political leadership of the CCP (e.g., 192.1.2; 194.1.3).

Defensive operations were also sources of victory, but only as temporary stages in the offensive application of force. In one cause-effect relationship, Mao linked the loss of territory from retreat to victory over the enemy, but it is clear from the context that this strategy involved trading space for time and then using that time to create conditions advantageous for the attack by, say, tiring the enemy or forcing it to make mistakes that then could be exploited (e.g., 217.3.9; 221.1.2; 232.1.2; 234.4.3). Indeed, defensive operations were the first operational step in defeating the enemy. A defensive retreat in the face of an enemy offensive, or the use of positional defense of key points alongside mobile warfare, led to the defeat of enemies in a civil war (207.4.4; 217.3.8) and more generally to military util-

ity (e.g., 199.4.2; 215.3.2; 242.2.1). Defense also had instrumental political value. It lulled the enemy politically (207.4.5), and in just wars it
could rally conservative or "backward" elements in society around one's
cause (207.4.6). But a defensive retreat was only a prelude to the shift to
the strategic offensive. Passive defense or pure defense reduced the scope
for initiative (234.4.1). "Active defense"—defense for the purposes of
counterattacking and taking the offense—had positive utility and was a
source of victory (e.g., 207.3.1; 233.1.6; 234.2.1).

As for the ability to attack the enemy with overwhelming superiority,
this was rooted in the fighting power of the military, which in turn was
dependent on popular support, advantageous terrain and weather, military
organization, and the confidence and experience of cadres and commanders (e.g., 206.3.1; 206.5.1; 212.2.2; 222.4.3; 223.2.4). Favorable
changes in relative power, then, led to an increasing ability to concentrate
superior military forces for offensive operations (e.g., 199.1.6; 202.4.1;
208.4.1; 215.5.1; 248.4.1). In other words, the relationship between the
human element (e.g., morale, popular political support, etc.) and military
victory was indirect, mediated by the ability to apply superior armed force
against a weakening enemy.

A couple of points are worth mentioning here. First, it is clear that this
text does not advocate passive defense (e.g., retreat or static defense) as a
permanent, effective means of dealing with an external threat. Rather, it
develops the notion of active defense, whereby in an initial period of
strategic weakness one relies on retreats, hoping to "lure the enemy in
deep" or wear it down through small counteroffensives within the context
of strategic defense. Once the relative balance of power—here an amalgam
of human and material variables—begins to shift in one's favor, one should
go on the attack. The end point of this attack is the strategic annihilation
of the enemy's ability to wage war. The entire process—from strategic
defense to strategic offense—is called *active defense*. This terminology is
dictated by an instrumental need to frame one's own actions as entirely
defensive and just, a position that is important for winning popular support and sympathy.[47] The term *active defense* is probably important at a
deeper symbolic level as well: the concept of just war requires that the

---

47. As Mao wrote, "With the slogan of defending the revolutionary base areas and defending China,
we can rally the overwhelming majority of the people to fight with one heart and one mind, because
we are the oppressed and the victims of aggression. In every just war the defensive not only has a
lulling effect on politically alien elements, it also makes possible the rallying of the backward sections of the masses" (Mao Zedong "Problems of Strategy in China's Revolutionary War" [1936],
Selected Works of Mao Zedong, 1:207).

enemy's threatening actions be defined as dispositional rather than situational, hence morally beyond the pale. Thus the enemy's nature is to threaten; one's own is to defend.

Second, the text stresses that strategists must exercise patience and absolute flexibility at the tactical and strategic levels, what Mao called the "flexible application of principles according to circumstances" (*an zhao qing Kuang huo yong yuan ze*).[48] The shift from the strategic defensive to the strategic offensive should come only when conditions are ripe—namely, when the relative balance of composite capabilities shifts in one's favor. A strategist has varying degrees of control over when and how this shift occurs. Part of the process involves actively wearing the enemy down militarily. It also involves "conserving one's own strength," avoiding decisive engagements, building one's own military capabilities, and seeking out political and military allies. In both cases, however, the key is to remain flexible enough to exploit opportunity when shifting from the strategic defensive to the strategic offensive. This flexibility axiom parallels the notion of *quan bian* found in ancient texts on strategy and statecraft. Absolute flexibility was at the core of the strategic advice in traditional China. As a Warring States text, the *Si Ma Fa* summarized it nicely: "As for war, it is [a question of] expedient assessment" (*zhan zhe quan bian ye*).[49] A Ming dynasty (1368–1644) text put it best: "As for the way of employing the military instrument there should be no constant form in either attacking or defending; there should be no constant rules for either dispersing or uniting forces; there should be no constant time period when one is in motion or at rest; there should be no constant directional momentum, either when extending or retracting [one's forces]."[50]

Mao was quite at home with this type of thinking. One could not be bound by one set of methods (e.g., strategic defensive) when the annihilation of the enemy required the adoption of another set (e.g., strategic offensive). And the strategic offensive required superior capabilities. It is not entirely accurate, then, to characterize Mao's strategic thought as only stressing "using weakness to overcome strength" (*yi ruo sheng qiang*) by

---

48. Ibid., p. 187. There are a slew of cause-effect relationships in the text in which the cause concept is some formulation of the notion of absolute flexibility or the exploitation of changing circumstances and the effect is military utility or military victory. See, for example, 184.2.6; 187.4.1; 190.2.5; 191.1.6; 205.3.4; 240.7.1.

49. Liu, *Si Ma Fa zhi jie*, p. 33.

50. Academy of Military Sciences, eds., *Tou Bi Fu Tan* (Beijing: Academy of Military Sciences Press, 1984), p. 87.

dint of superior morale or political mobilization.[51] Mao outlined a process—active defense—by which an *initially* weak military entity could acquire the human and material resources for eventually defeating an *initially* stronger military entity. But the defeat, or annihilation, of that enemy entity at the tactical and finally the strategic level required military superiority. In other words, a humanly richer but materially impoverished military force could not defeat a materially superior enemy. At the moment of defeat the "just" side would have to have superior human *and* material capabilities. I will come back to this point shortly in the discussion of Mao's Moscow speech in 1957.

On the New Stage (1938)

This short essay (figure 7.4) on the creation of an anti-Japanese united front with the GMD is essentially a discussion of how to handle secondary antagonistic contradictions, the second cell in figure 7.2. Mao readily moved the conflict with the GMD from cell 1 to cell 2, as Japanese imperialism became the primary threat to Chinese national development in the 1930s. The causal arguments in this essay were straightforward: Japanese imperialism threatened the survival of all classes in the Chinese nation. Hence the security of the state was an "effect" of the defeat of the enemy's "savage and protracted" warfare (191.1.3). Cooperation with the GMD was

---

51. This is a common characterization found in both Chinese and Western analyses of Mao's thought. See, for instance, Ralph Powell, "Maoist Military Doctrines," *Asian Survey* (1964): 239; Zhang Shuguang, *Deterrence and Strategic Culture: Chinese-American Confrontations, 1949–1958* (Ithaca: Cornell University Press, 1992), p. 278; Lin Chongpin, *China's Nuclear Weapons Strategy* (Lexington, Mass.: Lexington Books, 1988), p. 24; Ellis Joffe, *The Chinese Army After Mao* (Cambridge: Harvard University Press, 1987), p. 4. Unfortunately the discussion of the role of the "human" element in Mao's thought has missed some of the subtlety in his writings. To be sure, for Mao a highly motivated population or military was preferable to a poorly motivated one. The question is why he argued this. I would suggest that his de-emphasis on material capabilities—technology, weaponry, and so on—was a part of a strategy for mobilizing morale under conditions of relative military weakness. Mao believed that in the face of strength it made sense to appear cavalier and unafraid so as to combat fatalism on one's own side and to make the enemy think twice about the wisdom of unleashing a conflict over which it might have little control. It is also clear that one reason that Mao stressed the application of massively overwhelming numerical superiority was that in the face of a technologically superior enemy, only a quantitatively superior force could concentrate quantitatively superior technological capabilities. Mao was no strategic Luddite; he did not believe that a military should deliberately eschew technological modernization or the development of superior capabilities. Rather, the human element and technology had synergistic multiplier effects on each other. Christensen makes the important argument that one of the key goals of the Great Leap Forward in the late 1950s was to mobilize the Chinese economy to produce more advanced military technology to match (eventually) the capabilities of other major powers; see Christensen, *Useful Adversaries*; see also Song, *Mao Zedong junshi sixiang*, pp. 214–15.

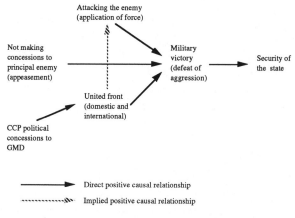

FIGURE 7.4 Cognitive Map of "On the New Stage"

causally connected to the defeat of Japanese imperialism (e.g., 179.2.7), as was the application of violence ("the barrel of the gun") (190.2.1), though from context it seems clear that the former runs through the latter to lead to victory.[52] Indeed, there was a feedback relationship between the united front and the Japanese invasion, such that the latter compelled the former to develop, while the former would lead to the defeat of the latter.

The development of the united front, in turn, required that the CCP make political concessions to the GMD, such as refraining from expanding CCP-controlled territory and from organizing secret cells within the GMD (e.g., 185.1.3; 187.3.1; 188.3.1). United front activities were not to be limited to the GMD, however. Mao also argued that alliances with other states opposed to Japanese imperialism were, in a general sense, of great utility (191.1.1; 191.1.2). Concessions with the secondary contradiction were, of course, permissible. Concessions in the face of the primary contradiction, however, were politically and militarily disastrous and would assist the enemy's aggression (e.g., 193.1.1; 193.2.9). Mao used the initial Allied reaction to Hitler as an analogy. The unwillingness of the democracies to sanction aggressor states, and their endorsement of the policy of appeasement, were equivalent to assisting aggression.

Despite the focus on the united front, in this essay the defeat of the principal adversary also ultimately required the use of force. The united front within China, and between China and other anti-fascist states,

---

52. Mao did concede, consistent with his notion of absolute flexibility, that when a state lacked sufficient power it should avoid direct battle with larger states and instead adopt "ingenious methods" and stratagems (192.1.5).

would create superior capabilities to apply in the contest with fascism. Concessions toward or bargaining with the principal enemy were anathema and would only encourage aggression. These cause-effect relationships do not differ much from those set forth in the essay on strategy in China's revolutionary war. Rather this text focuses on one part of the process of creating superior power capabilities to deal with a zero-sum conflict.

The Present Situation and Our Tasks (1947)

This text (figure 7.5) outlines the strategy for the final overthrow of the GMD and the establishment of a new state. As in the other texts, here also victory over the adversary is the result of varied causes, but they boil down to two: political mobilization and the offensive use of superior military power. As for the former, popular political support and rigorous political work inside and outside the People's Liberation Army (PLA) are both "causes" of victory over the GMD (159.1.4; 161.2.6). While the text links these two factors directly to victory in China's revolutionary war, comparatively little time is spent in the text expanding on this causal relationship. It is not unreasonable to view it as in fact indirect, with political mobilization being an input into the ability of the PLA to defeat the adversary militarily.

By far the most attention is paid to the military process of defeating the adversary. Here victory is a function of putting the GMD on the defensive

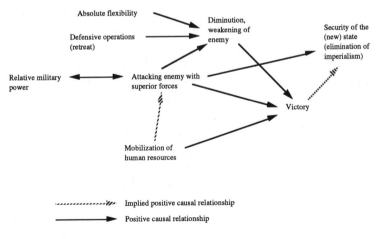

FIGURE 7.5 Cognitive Map of "The Present Situation and Our Tasks"

militarily through the application of people's war (157.1.6; 161.2.3) and through being absolutely superior in every specific campaign even though strategically inferior (160.1.15). In other words, relative capabilities matter. Advantages in relative capabilities allow the PLA to attack, to shift from the defensive to the offensive against the enemy, attacking dispersed, isolated enemy forces first, crushing the enemy with a combination of frontal and flank attacks, and then attacking concentrated and strong forces second (e.g., 160.1.2–13). The causal paths lead directly from these actions to the defeat of the enemy, as well as to the elimination of imperialist influence in China (157.1.5; 160.1.14). The failure of the CCP/PLA to oppose the GMD with military means leads directly to the forfeiting of China's future (158.1.1; 158.1.2).

In addition to being direct causes of the enemy's defeat, offensive operations lead to the diminution of the enemy's ability to fight. Specifically, offensive operations are causally linked to the destruction of the enemy's plans to take the war into CCP territory (157.1.2), pushing the enemy onto the defensive (157.1.1; 157.1.3), liberating territory (159.2.1), and improving the PLA's relative ability to operate successfully against other enemy forces (160.1.12). Strategic flexibility—namely, the ability to abandon strategically disadvantageous points—fuels the enemy's underestimation of PLA strength (161.2.6), which in turn leads to the defeat of the enemy (162.1.1).

Mao's Moscow Conference Speech (1957)

This speech (figure 7.6) to the Moscow Conference of Communist Parties in November 1957 was not a work on strategy proper. Rather it was a broader discussion of statecraft and the role of power capabilities in general in the achievement of strategic goals. In particular, Mao focused on the sources of the socialist bloc's strength, arguing that it was rooted in three things. One was the foreign policy crises facing imperialism—such as the Suez crisis, setbacks for U.S. influence in Africa and Asia, China's victory in the Korean War—all of which were indicative of the weakening strategic influence of Western imperialism. These crises were a direct cause of the East Wind's (socialism's) prevailing over the West Wind (imperialism) (e.g., 117.3.1;119.3.1).

A second set of causes for the socialist bloc's strength had to do with industrial and military capabilities. Here Mao argued that the bloc's emerging technological superiority (e.g., the Soviet Union's *Sputnik* launch, increases in steel production) would lead to the East Wind's prevailing over the West Wind (117.6.1; 118.1.2; 118.1.3; 118.2.5). This

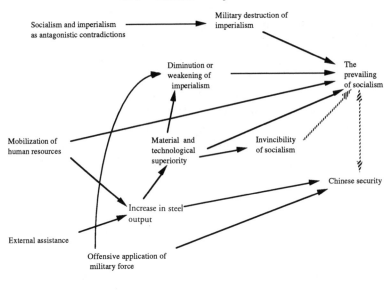

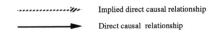

FIGURE 7.6 Cognitive Map of "The Moscow Speech"

superiority was a cause of the West's political-psychological weakening (116.2.1) and contributed to socialism's global surge. In other words, socialism's material superiority, translated into political and military strength, would lead to socialism's prevailing over imperialism (119.6.2).[53]

Finally, Mao hinted that the military destruction of imperialism was also causally related to socialism's victory. Even in nuclear war, he argued, an atomic attack by imperialism would lead to retaliation by socialism (118.4.1; 118.4.2), which in turn would lead to the destruction of imperialism and the triumph of socialism (119.1.1; 119.1.4; 119.1.5). Short of nuclear war launched by "maniacs" in the imperialist camp, the invincibility of socialism would deter imperialism from fighting and would lead to everlasting peace (118.3.2; 118.3.3; 119.1.7).

53. Here, as elsewhere in his works, Mao was not constrained by a narrow consistency. He also argued that the basic factor leading to socialism's victory was the desire or will of the people, the human factor (119.7.1). At the same time, however, the speech stressed the causal importance of steel production, the stuff of industrial and military power, in the superiority of socialism. Mao was at this time apparently quite influenced by Stalin's views on economics, which took steel as the "key link" in the development of socialism. I thank Thomas Christensen for this last point.

As for China, Mao was also quite clear about the basis of its security. One factor was increased steel production (118.2.3; 118.2.6), which in turn was a product of Soviet assistance and the Chinese people's willingness to exert themselves for this goal (118.2.1). Another was its military prowess, as demonstrated in the defeat of the GMD (116.4.1; 116.4.2), the victory in the Korean War (117.2.1), and the American unwillingness to send forces to aid the French in Vietnam. As for the cause of military victory, the strategy was a piecemeal one, to destroy the enemy one by one (120.2.8). Offensive military actions were also causally related to compelling the enemy to compromise or capitulate (117.2.4). In other words, a military hard line against the Americans and/or their allies appeared to have desirable political effects.

The speech also provided evidence of Mao's consistent zero-sum conceptualization of adversaries. For him, the maintenance of an uncompromising strategic objective while flexibly blending compromises and struggle at the tactical level is a correct strategy when dealing with a zero-sum conflict (e.g., 122.3.1; 122.2.5). When two sides are unable to accommodate each other, the struggle or contradiction is inherently antagonistic, and those conditions must lead to the overthrow of the adversary. Socialism and imperialism exist absolutely exclusively of each other, and resolution of this contradiction leads invariably to the collapse of imperialism (122.2.2; 122.2.4).

A couple of observations about the patterns in these cognitive maps are in order here. First, in all the maps the management of the security *problematique* requires most directly the military defeat of the adversary. In one of the texts—Mao's Moscow speech—there is an alternative route, namely, socialism's technological and material (hence military) superiority, but it is not clear why that alone might lead to the destruction of imperialism. Mao hints that this superiority will deter imperialism from attacking socialism, giving time for the internal contradictions within the imperialist camp and its spheres of influence to cause its implosion. In any case, superior military power is clearly a critical causal element in the defeat of an adversary and the achievement of key political goals. When circumstances require the application of this superior military power, offensive uses of force are causally linked to military success. Defensive operations are only a temporary and early stage in the application of violence, and by themselves they are inadequate for achieving desirable political ends. The so-called human element is only one input into this process of applying superior military force offensively. Relative material power counts, and in fact determines military success.[54] Most of the texts also highlight a concept of absolute strategic flexibility that along with the concept of just war lifts any a priori moral or political boundaries on the means by which the enemy is defeated.

A second general observation is that none of these causal relationships is inconsistent with the cognitive maps in traditional Chinese texts on strategy. Like these ancient texts, Mao's texts are essentially deeply structured around a parabellum or hard realpolitik central paradigm. The key question is, then, to what extent was Mao directly socialized in this traditional strategic culture? Unfortunately, on this point the evidence is rather spotty. The issue is also complicated by the fact that by the 1920s Mao had been exposed to Leninist and Clausewitzian ideas about statecraft and strategy. A case can be made that these traditions also embodied a parabellum central paradigm, hence the difficulty in separating out the effects of traditional Chinese influences.

We do have evidence, however, that Mao had read at least some of ancient texts on strategy as early as 1913, well before he had any contact with Clausewitz's or Lenin's works.[55] One of his school notes from 1913 seems to paraphrase a key passage in the *Si Ma Fa* to the effect that it is legitimate to "kill people in order to give life to people" (*sha ren yi sheng ren*)—that is, destroy an enemy in order to achieve a greater good.[56] This position is consistent with the absolute flexibility axiom at the core of Chinese conceptions of just war, and it embodies an obvious instrumentalism in conceptualizing the role of force. Later on, in his more mature works on strategy, Mao echoes again this axiom: "Whoever wants to seize state power and intends to preserve it must have a strong military. . . . We are for the abolition of war, we do not want war. But only through war can we

---

54. Mao uses a couple of historical analogies to make this point. In "Problems of Strategy in China's Revolutionary War," he cites the example of the states of Lu and Qi in the Spring and Autumn period of the Zhou dynasty (twelfth century B.C. to third century B.C.) to illustrate the axiom "When the enemy tires, we attack" (p. 211). In an essay on strategy against Japan, he uses the analogy of "Relieving the state of Chao by attacking the state of Wei" to argue that if the enemy's forces were diverted elsewhere, then an offensive deep inside enemy territory where it was weakest was a legitimate strategy (Mao, "Problems of Strategy in Guerrilla War Against Japan" [1938], in *Selected Works of Mao Zedong*, 2:104).

55. Open Chinese sources do not mention this early exposure. Sun suggests only that during the revolutionary wars against the GMD Mao read Sun Zi over several times, along with another Warring States text, *Guan Zi*. From *Guan Zi*, Mao is said to have absorbed the principle of attacking the enemy's weak points first and avoiding his strong points. See Sun, *Mao Zedong de du shu shengya*, pp. 78–79; and Lan, "Mao Zedong junshi sixiang," p. 66.

56. Mao, "Jiang tang lu," pp. 595–96.

abolish war, and if we want to get rid of the gun we must take up the gun."[57]

The occasional references to *Sun Zi* in Mao's later works all focus on the notion of absolute flexibility. Two of the four references in "Problems of Strategy in China's Revolutionary War" and in "On Protracted War" are to Sun Zi's axiom "Know the enemy and know yourself and in one hundred battles you will not be in danger," one refers to avoiding the enemy when it is stronger and attacking it when it weakens, and one refers to deception, or displaying a false "form" to the enemy. Arguably, all four references relate to gauging the nature of changing circumstances and exploiting these strategic opportunities.

As for other influences from works on traditional Chinese military history, we also know Mao was an avid reader of popular histories and novels set in the Warring States (475–221 B.C.) and Three Kingdoms period (220 B.C.–A.D. 280). These stories tended to stress the righteous use of force, often by militarily inferior groups. Operationally many of the accounts stressed ingenious political and military stratagems and hence were instrumental in creating the myth that Chinese strategic tradition stressed minimally violent solutions to security problems—but these were usually preludes to the application of offensive violence.

What Mao seems to have most clearly rejected was the minimal violence notion in Sun Zi that one could "not fight and subdue the enemy." After he emerged as the chief strategist for the CCP in the 1930s, Mao was apparently tutored on traditional Chinese strategic thought by Guo Huaruo, who until the mid-1980s was the CCP's most authoritative interpreter and annotator of Sun Zi's *Art of War*. Guo stressed that from a Marxist-Leninist perspective the notion of "not fighting and subduing the enemy"—the core of the conventional interpretation of Sun Zi—was unMarxist, since class enemies could not be credibly defeated without the application of violence.[58] This axiom was dismissed as "idealist" (*wei xin zhu yi*). In this instance, traditional Chinese texts were mediated by Marxist-Leninist arguments, but it is possible that Mao was receptive to this interpretation, given his socialization in the popular novels and histories.

---

57. Mao Zedong, "Zhanzheng he zhanlue wenti" [Problems of war and strategy] [1938], in *Mao Zedong xuanji*, p. 512 (Beijing: People's Press, 1967).

58. Interview with researchers at the Academy of Military Sciences, Beijing, March 1991; Guo Huaruo, " 'Sun Zi yi zhu' qian yan" [Preface to "Translation and annotation of *Sun Zi*"] [1983], in Gua Huaruo, *Guo Huaruo junshi lunwen xuanji* [Guo Huaruo's selected essays on military affairs] (Beijing: Liberation Army Press, 1989), p. 427.

In sum, while the evidence is scattered, it does seem that Mao was exposed to elements of the parabellum tradition in Chinese strategy thought before he was introduced to Clausewitzian and Leninist variations of parabellum. The net result of Mao's socialization in these three traditions was, arguably, a mutual reinforcement of the hard realpolitik tendencies in his strategic thought.

Strategic Preference Rankings

Since the Maoist and traditional Chinese texts share the parabellum central paradigm, we should also expect them to share the grand strategic preference rankings derived from that paradigm. That is, the Mao texts should embody a preference for offensive operations over static defense, and static defense should be preferred to accommodationist strategies.[59] It is clear from the cognitive maps that Mao believed that final victory over an adversary in a zero-sum conflict required the offensive application of superior military force to annihilate rather than merely deter the enemy. The process of getting to this point, however, is a little complicated and obscured by the political language that Mao used to clothe his offensive preferences.

Starting from the least-preferred strategy, Mao's concept of principal antagonistic contradictions, and his notion of just war, ruled out the possibility of long-term cooperation or accommodation with an enemy. The goal of political struggles was to "preserve oneself and annihilate the enemy." It was unlikely, in Mao's view, that the other side in a "principal antagonistic contradiction" would willingly submit, or bargain away its existence.

As for static defensive strategies, Mao labeled these *passive defense* (*xiao ji fang yu*) or *pure defense* (*dan chun fang yu*), to contrast them with his preferred strategy of "active defense." Passive defense, he argued, involved methods essentially for blocking or obstructing an enemy who was on the offensive. These strategies were of only limited value for holding territory temporarily while other forces engaged in offensive operations within the

---

59. I have discussed the congruence in preference rankings across the *Seven Military Classics* elsewhere (Johnston, *Cultural Realism*, ch. 4). Suffice it to say that there is not perfect statistical congruence across all seven texts. Depending on how the preferences of a couple of the more ambiguous texts are inferred, the coefficient of congruence (Kendal's W) ranges from .39 to .43. The former is significant at the 0.09 level, the latter at the 0.05 level. This moderate consistency is in large measure attributable to the effects of one text's preference rankings—the *San Lue*. This text, in contrast to the other six, places more emphasis on the Confucian-Mencian central paradigm. Consequently, it tends to prefer accommodationist and defensive strategies over clearly offensive ones.

context of the strategic defense. Passive defense put one in a reactive position and tended to force the dispersal and weakening of one's military power.[60] Mobile defense—the tactical offense within strategic defense—was designed to create the conditions ripe for a shift to the strategic offensive.

Mao argued, then, that superior military forces applied offensively were decisive in defeating an adversary. In one specific discussion of the final push to defeat the GMD in the late 1940s, he wrote that ideally the annihilation of the enemy required accumulating 3:1 or 4:1 numerical superiority.[61] Thus the shift to the offensive depended on relative capabilities: when these were advantageous, the just side should apply offensive violence to annihilate the enemy's war-making ability. Any other strategy, then, whether defensive or accommodationist, was contingent and should be adopted only when relative capabilities could not guarantee the successful offensive use of force.[62]

This preference for the offense was qualified, however, in two ways. Politically Mao stressed that offensive uses of force, whether at the level of operational strategy or grand strategy, should be named *active defense*. While just wars were not defensive ones, in the sense that the just side could declare war or initiate violence, they should nonetheless be called defensive. For one thing the term *active defense* was more politically palatable; it could be used in arousing righteous indignation among masses and soldiers or to attract sympathetic support from external sources.[63] Just

---

60. Liao Guoliang, Li Shishun, and Xu Yan, *Mao Zedong junshi sixiang fazhan shi* [The history of the development of Mao Zedong's military thought] (Beijing: Liberation Army Press, 1991), p. 450.
61. Mao Zedong, "Gei di yi canmie yu gei di yi canmie xing da ji bixu tongshi zhuzhong" [We must pay simultaneous attention to annihilating the enemy and attacking him with annihilating effects] [1947], in *Mao Zedong junshi wen xuan*, p. 314.
62. Interestingly, Chinese sources indicate that Mao's decision in 1948 to shift to the strategic offensive in the war with the GMD came as material conditions were shifting clearly in the CCP's favor. In 1946 the ratio of regular GMD to CCP troops stood at 3.5:1. By 1948 this figure had dropped to 1.3:1, but of these the CCP's first-line forces outnumbered the GMD's first-line forces by a ratio of 1:0.62. See Song, *Mao Zedong junshi sixiang*, pp. 190–91.
63. For a good explication of Mao's doctrine of active defense and the political uses of "defense," see Peng Dehuai's report to the National Defense Commission in July 1957; Peng Dehuai, "Junshi jianshe gaikuang" [The general situation in military construction] [1957], in *Peng Dehuai junshi wenxuan* [Selected military works of Peng Dehuai] (Beijing: Central Documents Publishing House, 1988), pp. 588–91. See also Song, *Mao Zedong junshi sixiang*, pp. 166–208. The deliberate use of "defense" to describe a doctrine that allowed, indeed required, offensive operations points to another similarity between Maoist and traditional Chinese strategic cultures, namely, the presence of a distinct symbolic discourse disconnected from operational decision rules. While Maoist Chinese strategic culture and behavior exhibited parabellum tendencies, it was clothed in the rhetoric of people's war. In principle the doctrine of people's war is quintessentially defensive—an attacking enemy should be "lured in deep" into Chinese territory and enveloped by an armed population and a

wars were also a legitimate response to what we would now call "structural violence." The source of conflict was the existence of an oppressor class or an oppressor nation(s). The oppressor was acting offensively, in that ultimately if it were not for the existence of this oppressor there would be no fundamental contradiction requiring the use of force for its resolution.[64]

Operationally, the offensive use of force was qualified by a preference against a first strike out of the blue. Instead Mao evidently preferred an offensive "second strike" (*hou fa zhi ren*).[65] Again, the reasoning was both political and military. To strike the enemy, particularly its territory, first, without specific provocation would be to give it the sympathy of world opinion and would tar the just side with the politically damaging label of *aggressor*.[66]

Militarily, Mao's version of a second strike offensive was designed to compel the enemy to move first, thus allowing an opportunity to gauge its intentions and capabilities. One could thereby ascertain the enemy's weak points, and attacks on these points, not first strikes per se, were decisive in conflict.[67] There are, in fact, parallels here to the strategic calculus in the traditional Chinese texts. The Sun Zi text speaks of "first putting oneself in an undefeatable position" and waiting for the enemy to put itself in a defeatable position. In other words, whether at the grand strategic or the operational level

mobile professional military. I would argue that people's war per se did not reflect Mao's most preferred strategy, in that he believed defensive strategies were only one stage in a broader process of shifting to the offensive. Indeed, in practice, at no time in the post-1949 period did the PRC fight a people's war. The PLA's use of force was invariably at or beyond China's borders. For a more detailed discussion of the hypothesized roles of the symbolic discourse in strategic decision making, see Johnston, *Cultural Realism*, ch. 5.

64. Wang Sanxin, *Mao Zedong junshi sixiang yanjiu* [Studies in Mao Zedong's military thought] (Beijing: National Defense University Press, 1988), p. 24.

65. This did not exclude the initiation of violence when it appeared that conflict was imminent. In the parlance, Mao eschewed preventive war but not preemptive war. In his view, China's initial offensive in the Korean War was a second strike because the initial basis of conflict had been established by the U.S. presence on Taiwan and its threatening operations on the Korean peninsula; see Song, *Mao Zedong junshi sixiang*, p. 222. Similarly, according to a recent analysis, China's operations against Vietnam in 1979 were militarily offensive but politically defensive. "Concerning the counter-aggression nature of the national revolutionary warfare, a strategic counterattack carries the implications of a strategic offensive. From a political perspective, it makes more sense and is more advantageous not to call it 'attack' but to call it a 'counterattack.' For example, the February 1979 self-defense counterattack against Vietnam, from the perspective of military operations, we adopted offensive actions, but the essence of this type of offense was a self-defense counterattack" (Zhang Jing and Yao Yanjin, *Jiji fangyu zhanlue qianshuo* [An introduction to the active defense strategy] [Beijing: Liberation Army Press, 1985], p. 137).

66. See Peng, "Junshi jianshe gaikuang," pp. 588–91.

67. Ibid.

of strategy, defense and offense were linked. One waited to see how the enemy moved, while one's own strategic posture of apparent immobility and obscurity concealed one's capabilities and intentions. Once the enemy revealed its disposition, its weaknesses and strengths, then one shifted to the offensive, striking at the enemy's "empty" (*xu*) points and disarming it. One could use limited amounts of force to provoke the adversary into a definitive move. Defensive strategies established the parameters within which the enemy had to operate and thus allowed oneself to retain the initiative.

If the above characterization of the central paradigm and related strategic preferences in Mao's thought is accurate, then what sorts of expectations should we have about Chinese strategic behavior under Mao? First, we would expect the use of force to be framed politically as defensive and just, whether or not China initiated violence. This is not an unusual expectation; most states develop some symbolic language to frame behavior in culturally acceptable terms. We would also expect the Chinese to initiate force after establishing that conflict is imminent, given the disposition of the enemy and the zero-sum nature of the conflict. In other words, initiation would come after Chinese decision makers have concluded that force is "unavoidable." There ought to be a low threshold establishing when an adversary's moves indicate that conflict is inevitable. That is, once it has been determined that conflict is zero-sum, we should expect the Chinese leadership to initiate larger-scale conflicts, and given the premium placed on military initiative, we should also expect China to resort to force in these types of conflicts. In other words, there should be an observable tendency to link more isolated threats to a broader challenge to the fundamental values of the state. To the extent that there are gradations in the severity of this threat to the fundamental values of the state, severe threats will require the military annihilation of the enemy's capacity to continue to challenge China. We should expect too that in a general conflict situation, Chinese coercive behavior should be positively related to advantageous changes in relative military capabilities. In other words, once in a conflict situation, advantageous shifts in relative capabilities should be a necessary cause of the initiation of force.

Chinese Conflict Behavior

How well does Chinese conflict behavior after 1949 fit the expectations that follow from the Maoist variant of the parabellum strategic culture?

The first observation is that, of all the major powers, the PRC has been quite prone to use force in foreign policy crises. According to the data set on foreign policy crises generated by Jonathan Brecher, Michael Wilkenfeld, and Sheila Rosen, the PRC has been involved in eleven foreign policy crises through 1985 and has resorted to violence in eight (72 percent), proportionally more than the other major powers in the twentieth century. Comparable figures for the U.S., the USSR, and the UK from 1927 to 1985 are 18 percent, 27 percent, and 12 percent, respectively. And according to these researchers, the Chinese use of violence has been what they label "high intensity," involving "serious clashes" or "full-scale war."[68]

Second, these conflicts were all located along China's borders. Territorial disputes were thus crucial drivers in most of these crises. According to the Brecher and Wilkenfeld data set, in comparison with other major powers China was more likely to use violence in a dispute over territorial issues, employing it as a key conflict management technique in 80 percent of such crises ($N = 5$). For the U.S., the figure was 0 percent ($N = 11$); the USSR, 20 percent ($N = 10$); Britain, 8.3 percent ($N = 12$); France, 27.3 percent ($N = 11$); India, 33.3 percent ($N = 3$); and for all actors in the data set, 23.5 percent ($N = 281$). Chinese decision makers tended to see territorial disputes as high-value conflicts, partly because of a historical sensitivity to threats to the territorial integrity of the state.[69]

The definition of high-value, zero-sum conflicts was not limited to territorial issues, however. There seems to have been a tendency for Chinese leaders to define even political/diplomatic crises as high threat and to view force as a legitimate response. China used violence as the major response in 66.7 percent of the crises involving political/diplomatic issues ($N = 3$); the comparable statistic for all actors is 18.1 percent ($N = 127$). This would suggest that Chinese leaders were more apt to view a wide range of disputes in zero-sum terms, thus establishing a low threshold for determining what conflicts constituted a clear threat to the security of the state.[70] Obviously these comparisons need to be handled with care. Given

---

68. Jonathan Wilkenfeld, Michael Brecher, and Sheila Rosen, *Crises in the Twentieth Century: Handbook on Foreign Policy Crises* (New York: Pergamon, 1988), 2:161.
69. On the crucial role of territorial disputes in the outbreak of interstate war, see Vasquez, *The War Puzzle*.
70. The finding that the Chinese have been more crisis-prone than many other states would suggest, logically, that we should not expect the realpolitik strategic cultures of these other major powers to be as "hard" as that of the Chinese. Since I have not done a cross-national study of strategic cultures, I can't show this empirically. That China, compared to other states, appears to be more willing to consider political/diplomatic crises to be high-threat situations indirectly suggests, however, that many other states would not rank as high as it does on estimates of the inherent zero-sum nature of the strategic environment. This is a testable hypothesis.

the small *N* of Chinese cases, a relatively small number of new cases in which Chinese behavior deviated from past trends could very quickly change the percentages. The data are, nonetheless, suggestive, particularly since the behavior is consistent with the hard realpolitik ideational structure behind Maoist understandings of conflict.[71]

The sparse anecdotal evidence we have of the Chinese decision-making process is consistent with the aggregate data. In most cases when China used force, the "threat" was considered high and the issue at hand tended to be a zero-sum one. In the Korean War case, for instance, before resorting to force Mao argued that not only did American military actions in the peninsula threaten China's industrial base in Manchuria but also domestic counterrevolutionaries could take advantage of an extended war with the U.S. to undermine the *CCP*'s tenuous political control of the mainland.[72] In the first Quemoy-Matsu crisis of 1954–1955, Mao viewed the imminent conclusion of the U.S.-Taiwan Mutual Defense Treaty as a two-pronged threat: one prong was the security threat posed by a formalized American military presence in a number of bilateral security arrangements around China's periphery; the other was the possibility that formal bilateral security relations between Taiwan and the U.S. might encourage the U.S. and other states to make a de facto endorsement of the concept of two Chinas, an outcome that Mao considered a threat to Chinese territorial integrity.[73] The Sino-Indian border crisis of 1962 was a "conventional"

---

71. Indeed, in almost every variable relating to the type and scope of states' responses to a foreign policy crisis in the Brecher, Wilkenfeld, and Rosen data set, the Chinese cases indicate a higher level of militarized behavior than one finds in the population of states as a whole. (1) In 56.5% of foreign policy crises triggered by nonmilitary events, states as a whole responded with nonmilitary responses (*N* = 216). In 9.7% of the cases of a nonmilitary trigger, states responded with a violent response. In 0% of China's foreign policy crises triggered by nonmilitary events, China responded with nonviolent responses (*N* = 2). In 50% of the cases of a nonmilitary trigger, China responded with a violent response. (2) In 42.3% of foreign policy crises categorized as military-security-territory related, states as a whole responded with a nonmilitary response (*N* = 281). In 20% of China's cases categorized as military-security-territory related, China responded with a nonmilitary response (*N* = 5). (3) In 10% of foreign policy crises categorized as military-security-territory related, states used violence as the preeminent response (*N* = 281). In 40% of China's crises categorized as military-security-territory related, China used violence as the preeminent response. (4) In 11% of foreign policy crises categorized as political-diplomatic related, states used violence as the preeminent response (*N* = 127). In 33.3% of China's crises categorized as political-diplomatic, China used violence as the preeminent response.

72. Thomas J. Christensen, "Threats, Assurances, and the Last Chance for Peace: The Lessons of Mao's Korean War Telegrams," *International Security* 17, no. 1 (1992): 122–57; Zhou Enlai, "Kang Mei huan Chao, baowei heping" [Resist America, Support Korean, protect peace] [950], in Zhou Enlai, *Zhou Enlai Xuanji* [Selected writings of Zhou Enlai] (Beijing: People's Publishing House, 1984), pp. 50–54.

73. Thomas Stolper, *China, Taiwan, and the Offshore Islands* (Armonk: M. E. Sharpe, 1985); Zhang, *Deterrence and Strategic Culture*, pp. 193–99.

zero-sum territorial dispute, but it came at a time of severe economic dislocation, in the wake of the Great Leap Forward and shortly after another "invasion" scare from Taiwan. Thus the urgency of preserving China's territorial integrity was accentuated by the sense of domestic economic and political crisis in China. There is some controversy about who initiated the Ussuri clashes with the USSR in 1969 and even less certainty about the decision process on the Chinese side. But one plausible argument is that in the face of a very real concern that China might be the next on the Brezhnev Doctrine list, Mao initiated conflict to signal to the Soviets that China was a risk-acceptant player and that any subsequent Soviet use of force would carry high costs for Moscow as well. To the extent that the Chinese had the Czechoslovakian case in mind, the issues at stake in this conflict—China's territorial integrity and political survival—were high-value ones as well.

Third, the Chinese have also been quite willing to initiate violence in disputes. In the Brecher and Wilkenfeld data, China initiated violence in 62.5 percent of those crises in which it ended up using violence ($N = 8$). To be sure, coding initiators in conflicts is an exceedingly difficult task, since it is sometimes hard to tell when a crisis or dispute began and which side was defending the status quo. Nonetheless, the Brecher and Wilkenfeld data are consistent with a rough estimate of Chinese initiation based on a preliminary version of the Correlates of War militarized dispute data. These data suggest that of the seventeen cases of militarized disputes in which the PRC has been involved with the USSR through 1985, China probably initiated the dispute in eleven cases (65 percent). In seven of these eleven cases, the issue for China was either a perceived threat to Chinese territorial claims or an attempt by Beijing to modify territorial boundaries, a finding that is again consistent with the Brecher and Wilkenfeld data.[74]

Fourth, Chinese conflict behavior has tended to be sensitive to changing relative capabilities in ways that are consistent with a hard realpolitik strategic calculus. In other words, as in the Ming period, *once in a conflictual situation*, there seems to have been a correlation between an advantageous shift in relative capabilities and the *PRC*'s initiation of hostile actions along a scale of violence. The question is, How did the Chinese or

---

74. The secondary literature about China's military disputes also suggests that the Chinese began large-scale military operations against the target in most of these cases. See Christensen, "Threats, Assurances, and the Last Chance for Peace; Harlan Jencks, "China's Punitive War on Vietnam: A Military Assessment," *Asian Survey* 19, no. 8 (August 1979): 568–84; Gerald Segal, *Defending China* (London: Oxford University Press, 1985).

Mao determine relative capabilities? On the one hand, Mao often incorporated quite subjective measures about who was on the "defensive" and who was on the "offensive" in his assessment of the relative strengths of the U.S., the USSR, and China. On the other hand, Mao was also quite sensitive to relative material capabilities. A very strong theme running through his Moscow speeches in the fall of 1957, a year before the second Quemoy-Matsu crisis, was that the Soviet Union's technological breakthroughs, coupled with the rapid industrial growth rates in the socialist camp, translated into strategic power.[75]

It is not unreasonable to assume, then, that Mao used fairly rough estimates of relative industrial and military power to determine whether China had more or fewer capabilities with which to assert its interests in conflict situations. For the moment I will use the ratio of the percent shares of major power capabilities as a rough indicator of relative power. Very preliminary findings indicate, for instance, that in all three foreign policy crises with the U.S. (Korea, Quemoy-Matsu 1954–1955, Quemoy-Matsu 1958) the U.S.-PRC power ratio had shifted in China's direction over the previous year. In the two foreign policy crises involving the USSR (the Ussuri River crisis of 1969 and the Chinese invasion of Vietnam in 1979) the USSR-PRC power ratio shifted in China's direction.[76] In the one

---

75. Mao Zedong, "Speech of 18 November 1957" [1957], in Michael Schoenhals, "Mao Zedong: Speeches at the 1957 'Moscow Conference,'" *Journal of Communist Studies* 2, no. 2 (June 1986): 115–24; Zhang, *Deterrence and Strategic Culture*, p. 229. Christensen argues that at that point Mao did not really believe socialism was prevailing over imperialism in material capabilities terms. Rather, the "East Wind" statements were projections of a future state of affairs if current technological and industrial trends continued. Moreover, Mao's upbeat pronouncements were part of a pep talk to the socialist camp in order to deflate the threatening nature of U.S. imperialism. See Christensen, *Useful Adversaries*. I think the evidence on this point is somewhat murky. To be sure, Mao believed that a certain bravado in the face of the adversary was necessary to rally popular morale and prevent fatalism and pacifism. This is in part what he meant by "despising the enemy strategically." On the other hand, in his November 1957 speeches he clearly puts socialism's material superiority in the present tense (Mao, "Mao Zedong: Speeches," p. 118). Later, in November 1958 after the Quemoy-Matsu crisis, Mao again disparaged imperialism's strength, remarking, "All evidence proves that imperialism adopts a defensive stance and has not undertaken the slightest offensive" (cited in Allen S. Whiting, "Mao, China, and the Cold War," in Yonosuke Nagai and Akira Iriye, eds., *The Origins of the Cold War in Asia*, p. 260 [New York: Columbia University Press, 1977]).
76. In the U.S.-PRC cases the U.S.-PRC power ratio shifted from 2.58:1 to 2.33:1 in 1949–1950, from 2.11:1 to 1.91:1 in 1953–1954, and from 1.68:1 to 1.4:1 in 1957–1958. In the USSR-PRC cases, the Soviet-Chinese power ratio shifted from 1.21:1 to 1.13:1 in 1968–1969 and from 1.2:1 to 1.16:1 in 1978–1979. The capabilities data come from the Correlates of War major powers capabilities data set. The percent shares are on a world base. These data are suggestive only; the shifts in ratios are quite small in some instances (though these can translate into substantial raw power resources). In some cases, however, these data do reflect Mao's unambiguous subjective calculation of whether the superpower involved was on the defensive or on the offensive.

China-U.S. crisis that did not lead to violence (Taiwan, summer 1962), China's relative power ratio with the U.S. declined.[77] These are crises in the Brecher, Wilkenfeld, and Rosen data set in which China initiated direct military conflict with the adversary. This does not mean that an improvement in relative capabilities inexorably led to the initiation of conflict. Indeed, there are a number of dyad years in Chinese-U.S. and Chinese-Soviet relations, for instance, where such an improvement occurred and there was no military conflict. Rather, a favorable change in relative capabilities appears to have been a necessary but not sufficient condition. That is, without such a change, it appears that there would not have been any conflict. Given such a change, in the absence of a foreign policy crisis military conflict is not inevitable. But in the universe of cases of foreign policy crises, an advantageous shift in relative capabilities did accompany the initiation of violence.

Problems of Analysis

A couple of conclusions can be drawn at this point about traditional Chinese and Maoist strategic culture. First, the predominant Chinese strategic tradition does not differ radically from key elements in the Western realpolitik tradition. Indeed, the Chinese case might be classified as a hard realpolitik one, sharing many of the same basic tenets about the nature of the enemy and the efficacy of violence with advocates of nuclear war fighting on both sides in the Cold War or late-nineteenth-century social Darwinian nationalists.[78] It is characterized by positions at the high end of the three dimensions that make up the central paradigm of a strategic culture. From these central assumptions flows a preference for offensive and/or preemptive strategies in dealing with threats.

Second, the Chinese case suggests that strategic culture is not a trivial variable in the analysis of strategic behavior. There is, at least in the Chinese case, a long-term, deeply rooted persistent and relatively consistent set of assumptions about the strategic environment and about the best means for dealing with it. Moreover, these assumptions appear to have a nontrivial influence on grand strategic choice in several different historical

---

77. The U.S.-PRC power ratio increased from 1.74:1 in 1960 to 1.84.1 in 1961.

78. See Martin Wight, *International Theory: The Three Traditions*, ed. Gabriele Wight and Brian Porter (Leicester: Leicester University Press, 1991), for a discussion of realpolitik as one of the three Western traditions in international relations.

periods. These parabellum assumptions have persisted across different state systems in Chinese history—from the anarchical Warring States period, to the hierarchical imperial Chinese state system, to the increasingly interdependent post–Cold War period. In the 1980s and 1990s, even as China's economy has become increasingly integrated into the global economy, even as international economic institutions play an increasing role in directing China's development strategies, and even as China faces the most benign threat environment since 1949, hard realpolitik decision rules continue to dominate the Chinese leadership's approach to foreign policy and security affairs. Chinese approaches to global issues such as arms control, the environment, and human rights are still dominated by defection and freeriding decision rules. Chinese leaders openly admit that China's development goal is "a rich state and a strong army" (*fu guo qiang bing*).

These conclusions raise a host of complex implications and questions about the nature of strategic culture and its influence on behavior. The crux of these problems is, as should be apparent, that the predictions from a hard realpolitik model of Chinese strategic culture are similar to those from what could conventionally be called a structural realpolitik model. This situation poses obvious difficulties for any competitive hypothesis testing. Indeed, neorealists might immediately ask what the point is in constructing a strategic culture model of realpolitik when an "old-fashioned" realist model without reference to strategic culture might do just as well.[79] Their argument would be that Chinese realpolitik strategic culture is epiphenomenal, not causal, a function of anarchical structures. I think this is a premature judgment. There are two broad kinds of responses to this charge.

The first is to admit that these two models make similar predictions and then to set up critical tests. A relatively useful test of realpolitik strategic culture is to look for periods in Chinese history in which, controlling for structural change, one could identify fluctuations in the strength of the strategic culture. If strategic choice were consistent with these variations (e.g., the absence or weakness of an identifiable realpolitik strategic culture correlated with accommodationist strategies even when conditions favored the use of force against an adversary), then the case for cultural realism would obviously be stronger.

---

79. This was a point made by Stephen Walt in his comments on this book project at the American Political Science Association meeting in New York, September 1994.

There is suggestive evidence that this was the case in the Ming dynasty. Proportionately most "events" (e.g., years in which relative power favored the Ming and in which the Ming launched offensives) occurred in the first quarter of the dynasty, when *overall* structural conditions favored the Ming. Proportionately, however, during this period one was also more likely to see "nonevents" (e.g., years in which relative power favored the Ming and in which the Ming did not launch offensives). In general, the first quarter was a period in which Ming emperors were engaged in legitimating their dynastic rule. Part of that process involved issuing statements affirming the more benign Confucian approach to security. It is possible that in these microperiods Ming rulers, facing a relatively benign threat environment and concerned about establishing an image of a magnanimous rule, endorsed a degree of restraint in strategic choice. A more fine-tuned test, then, would be to look in more detail at each of these years of non-events and compare the strength of the parabellum calculus in the decision process for the years in which offensives were launched. To the extent that the strength of the parabellum axioms varied in the predicted direction across these two types of cases, one could make firmer conclusions about the effects of cultural versus structural realpolitik.

In the PRC case, we would need evidence that in those foreign policy crises in which China did not resort to force hard realpolitik axioms were not as prominent. Unfortunately we are working with a very small number of cases. There is one instance in which China did not resort to force immediately in the face of threat to a high-value territorial security issue— namely, the U.S. decision in June 1950 to use the Seventh Fleet in the Taiwan straits to prevent a Communist invasion of Taiwan. Mao clearly considered this a major challenge to his plans to liberate the rest of China and another major threat, given the war in Korea. Yet the absence of an immediate Chinese violent response was the result not of a softening of Mao's hard realpolitik worldview but of his inability to do anything about the problem in the short run. This inaction is consistent with both a structural and an ideational realpolitik that is sensitive to relative capabilities. This case, then, does not offer a conclusive test of the two models. Overall, the kind of test outlined above may be relatively hard to set up, since there has been very little fluctuation in the hegemony of the hard realpolitik strategic culture, particularly in the post-1949 period.

A second test might be a cross-national one. Here one would look for cases in which one could plausibly argue that the hard realpolitik paradigm was replaced by a different strategic culture, cases in which changes in relative capabilities have not led to the coercive opportunism that one finds in Chinese history. My argument has been that the hard realpolitik strategic culture is a prism through which changes in relative capabilities are interpreted. Absent this paradigm, and changes in relative capabilities should mean something different.[80] In this respect, liberal democratic zones of peace, based on shared identities, provide intriguing evidence. The argument is that shared identities reduce in-group exclusivity, hence the group values the "other" more. Since each side knows that it prefers accommodation and negotiation, and since each side believes that this is the case for the other, the central assumptions of the parabellum paradigm become hard to maintain. Thus the high measures on the three dimensions of the central paradigm should move dramatically toward low measures. Military conflict is not seen as imminent, conflict is not considered zero-sum, and violence is not considered efficacious. Accommodationist strategies are therefore more preferred than offensive ones, regardless of changes in relative capabilities. As a result, advantages in relative capabilities are not exploited, and disadvantages are not feared. Since the parabellum paradigm does not pervade decision makers' perceptions when they are dealing with other democracies, changes in relative capabilities should not have the same effect as on states with parabellum strategic cultures. The absence of war itself, and the virtual absence of militarized disputes, even as the relative capabilities of these states have changed or remained imbalanced, suggests, then, that there is no relationship between structural changes and violent conflict among liberal democracies.[81] Such a finding would be consistent with absence of the parabellum paradigm.

Since I am not using the absence of war (the dependent variable) to posit the absence of parabellum (the independent variable), this is not a tautological argument. Rather, I am using a shared democratic identity to posit the absence of parabellum. If the absence of the parabellum strategic culture correlates with the absence of coercive exploitation of advantages in changing relative capabilities among democracies, then it seems reasonable to conclude that the presence of a parabellum strategic culture in China is

80. In this respect, China's realpolitik strategic culture is not merely permissive, since it specifies exactly how one should react under different material conditions. Absent this realpolitik and we should expect very different reactions to similar measures of the material variables.

81. Bruce Russett, *Grasping the Democratic Peace: Principles for a Post–Cold War World* (Princeton: Princeton University Press, 1993); Bruce Bueno de Mesquita and David Lalman, *War and Reason: Domestic and International Imperatives* (New Haven: Yale University Press, 1992); Randall L. Schweller, "Domestic Structure and Preventive War: Are Democracies More Pacific?" *World Politics* 44 (1992): 250–51.

correlated with the coercive exploitation of these advantages. Needless to say, a structural realpolitik model could not account for the relative absence of realpolitik interpretations of changing material capabilities in democratic security communities. Thus there is no logical reason to expect it to account for the presence of realpolitik interpretations in nondemocracies.

This brings me to a final test, one designed to see whether the content of China's strategic culture remained relatively stable over time as structure changed. If this were the case, then the charge of epiphenomenality would not stand. To be sure, the formative period for this realpolitik strategic culture was, arguably, the Spring and Autumn and Warring States periods (770–221 B.C.), a time when politics among the feudal states of central China were characterized by anarchical multipolar relations. But realpolitik axioms persisted across the rise of unipolar imperial states interacting with weaker nomadic tribal states (e.g., early Han dynasty from the mid-second to the mid-first century B.C., the Tang dynasty of the early seventh century B.C., the Ming dynasty in the mid- through late fifteenth century, when it was the largest empire in the world). And these persisted during periods of weak dynastic or imperial control when relations between Chinese and non-Chinese states, or among Chinese states, were bipolar or multipolar (e.g., the Three Kingdoms period (A.D. 220–280), the Northern and Southern dynasties period (A.D. 420–581), and the Northern and Southern Song period (A.D. 960–1279).[82] These different systems cannot all be legitimately considered the same anarchical type even though, strictly speaking, in each there was no supreme authority regulating relations among the key actors. To argue that they were the same type of system would be to ignore the effects of the vast power differentials across these systems on actors' perceptions of their options. It would mean ascribing to the mere absence of supreme authority such a deterministic

---

82. On the Spring and Autumn interstate system, see Richard L. Walker, *The Multi-State System of Ancient China* (Hamden, Conn.: Shoe String Press, 1953). On the Han, see Yu Ying-shih, "Han Foreign Relations," in Denis Twitchett and Michael Loewe, eds., *The Cambridge History of China*, vol. 1, *The Ch'in and Han Empires, 221 B.C.–A.D. 220* (New York: Cambridge University Press, 1986); and Thomas J. Barfield, *The Perilous Frontier: Nomadic Empires and China* (Cambridge: Blackwell, 1989). On the Tang, see ibid. On the Five Dynasties, see Edmund Worthy, "Diplomacy for Survival: Domestic and Foreign Relations of the Wu Yueh, 907–978," in Morris Rossabi, ed., *China Among Equals: The Middle Kingdom and Its Neighbors, 10th–14th Centuries* (Berkeley: University of California Press, 1983). On the Song, see Forage, "The Struggle for the Northwestern Frontier"; and Wang Gungwu, "The Rhetoric of a Lesser Empire: Early Sung Relations with Its Neighbors," in Rossabi, *China Among Equals*. And on the Ming, see Arthur Waldron, *The Great Wall of China: From History to Myth* (Cambridge: Cambridge University Press, 1990); and Johnston, *Cultural Realism*.

effect that relative power becomes unimportant. Structural realists can't have it both ways—they cannot sometimes argue that anarchy is the most important variable determining states' strategic choices and other times argue that power distributions are the most crucial.[83] Indeed, one could argue that in lopsided unipolar imperial systems one ought to expect some dramatic variation from realpolitik behavior, since even though the system is anarchic in the strict definition of the term, the empire's survival is not threatened by weak, disunited tribes along the periphery. Massively asymmetric relative capabilities would suggest that the empire could afford to ignore or buy off these low-level threats.[84] Yet, in the Chinese case at least, Chinese empires, especially at peak periods of power, often exhibited an offensive, coercive behavior rooted in a perception of adversaries as implacably hostile and threatening to the very survival of the system and in a distrust of the long-term efficacy of accommodationist strategies.

In short, that this hard realpolitik calculus undergirded the strategic decision making in the unipolar imperial state system during the peak periods of Ming power in the fifteenth century (periods when the Ming was most aggressive in its efforts to exterminate the Mongol threat, for instance) and in the multipolar and bipolar "anarchical" state systems in which twentieth-century China was situated suggests that its persistence is

---

83. This is where Fischer's critique of Kratochwil's analysis of the feudal system runs into problems. See Markus Fischer, "Feudal Europe: Discourse and Practice," *International Organization* 46, no. 2 (Spring 1992). The feudal and Westphalian systems, like the unipolar imperial and multipolar state systems in China, cannot both be usefully classified as similarly anarchical. This stripped-down definition of anarchy implies that all historical "state" systems have been anarchical, from imperial, unipolar systems to sovereignist, multipolar systems, because even in the former there is no overarching authority governing relations between the empire and smaller states and tribes. As Mueller implies, this kind of conceptual stretching reduces the utility of the concept; see John Mueller, "The Impact of Ideas on Grand Strategy," in Richard N. Rosecrance and Arthur A. Stein, eds., *The Domestic Bases of Grand Strategy*, pp. 48–62 (Ithaca: Cornell University Press, 1993).

84. Some realists will argue that the key link between anarchy and realpolitik behavior is uncertainty about the intentions and capabilities of others. This leads states to fear that others will exploit them and thereby threaten their survival, hence their reliance on self-help measures. So regardless whether the system is uni-, bi-, or multipolar, or some form of mixed-actor system, these are all technically anarchical, hence they all produce realpolitik behavior. Yet presumably fear is a variable—that is, it varies as uncertainty varies. Not all anarchical systems ought to produce the same degree of uncertainty and fear. Indeed, the more asymmetrical the distribution of power—e.g., the more the system resembles a unipolar imperial system—the less the imperial state needs to worry about the capabilities other states have (even if their intentions remain constant), and thus it can be more certain about its ability to survive in the face of external threats. One therefore ought to see less "self-help" realpolitik behavior on the part of the empire the more powerful and system-dominant it becomes. If one does not, this suggests that neither anarchy nor the (asymmetrical) distribution of power variables explains the persistence of realpolitik impulses.

related not to particular distributions of power or to different kinds of anarchical state structures but to the transmission of a particular strategic culture. In Mao's case socialization in the parabellum strategic culture came both from exposure to some of its elements in traditional texts military strategy and history as well as from Leninist and Clausewitzian ideas. Hence there is at least some evidence that *realpolitik* axioms developed and persisted across different structural contexts.

But a second broad way to deal with the neorealists' charge of epiphenomenality is to argue that, if anything, it is the effects of structure that are epiphenomenal to realpolitik strategic culture. The argument that one has to set up a critical test between a material structural and an ideational model of realpolitik rests on the assumption that these two make predictions about behavior that are causally independent of each other: in one model, strategic culture interacts with changing relative capabilities to produce behavior; in the other, according to neorealists, changing relative capabilities alone explains behavior. But when neorealists make this latter link between capabilities and behavior, they in fact require an assumption about the meaning or implications of this change for state survival. The problem is, the basis of this assumption for neorealism is not clear.[85] For some neorealists the answer is simple: anarchy is the primary cause of states' interests and preferences over actions because in conditions of uncertainty about the intentions of others, one's own security is assured ultimately only with sufficient military capabilities arrayed on one's own side (by either internal or external balancing). Thus under conditions of anarchy states will tend to interpret disadvantageous shifts in relative capabilities as threatening and dangerous.[86]

---

85. Indeed, the construction of an "old-fashioned" realist model is not as unproblematic as structural realists might assume, as a whole generation of excellent literature by scholars trained in neorealist analysis has shown. See Stephen M. Walt, *The Origins of Alliances* (Ithaca: Cornell University Press, 1987); and Jack Snyder, *Myths of Empire: Domestic Politics and International Ambition* (Ithaca: Cornell University Press, 1991). On the problems that realism has conceptualizing the relationship between structure and behavior, see Alexander Wendt, "Anarchy Is What States Make of It: The Social Construction of Power Politics," *International Organization* 46, no. 2 (Spring 1992): 391–425; Fareed Zakaria, "Realism and Domestic Politics: A Review Essay," *International Security* 17, no. 1 (Summer 1992): 177–99; Randall L. Schweller, "Neorealism's Status Quo Bias: Bringing the Revisionist State Back In" (paper presented at the National Security Seminar, Olin Institute for Strategic Studies, Harvard University, November 1993); and Robert Powell, "Anarchy in International Relations Theory: The Neorealist-Neoliberal Debate," *International Organization* 48, no. 2 (Spring 1994): 313–44.

86. In this sense, anarchy for structural realists is analogous to norms, identities, ideas, and cultures for some constructivists. To the extent that these are constant they cannot in and of themselves explain variation in behavior. But both require the intervention of changing material variables to provide variation in the composite independent variable. For the former, fear, bred from anarchy,

Yet for other neorealists, the relationship between anarchy and realpolitik is in fact not coterminus. This is because their argument contains a normative element that if states wish to survive in anarchy they have to think in realpolitik ways; otherwise they lose. Since there are losers in anarchy (and I don't think their proportion has diminished over time, as the selection argument would predict), then one has to assume there are states that don't act on these assumptions about interests and capabilities, and hence that there is at least some choice in the matter. As some neorealists will agree, the only way that changing relative capabilities—structure—can explain behavior is if decision makers think these changes matter for the security of the state. That is, states or state elites provide the realpolitik meaning of changes in structure. This meaning depends on how states conceive their interests.

So the question is, Where does this particular realpolitik interpretation of interests come from? Some neorealists are happy to acknowledge that these interests, and the process by which states interpret changes in relative capabilities in the light of these interests, are *assumptions* and are not endogenous to structures per se. At some level the empirical validity of these assumptions is important to neorealism. But of greater importance is that these assumptions are made in the first place. The *way* in which these assumptions are correct—in other words, where decision makers get these tendencies to interpret changes in relative capabilities in realpolitik ways—is of still lesser importance. Of course, this failure to problematize the interpretation of relative capabilities opens the door to the constructivist argument that, to the extent that neorealism has no well-defined theory of where state interests or preferences over actions come from, just as long as these interests are realpolitik ones and are present in anarchical structures, it is quite possible that empirically these interests and preferences come from realpolitik strategic cultures, independent of structure.

For other neorealists, the source of these realpolitik interpretations of changes in relative capabilities is anarchy.[87] Anarchy produces uncertainty, and uncertainty produces fear of being exploited. It is fear that gives mean-

---

provides a particular interpretation of the meaning of these changes. For the latter, the interpretation depends on the content of the ideational constant. Realpolitik strategic cultures will give these changes a realpolitik hue; non-realpolitik strategic cultures, a non-realpolitik hue. Structural realists, however, will only predict realpolitik interpretations because anarchy can only breed uncertainty and fear. Thus they mispredict a great deal of non-realpolitik behavior in the world. This suggests that anarchy, then, does not have the determining effect on interpretations of relative capabilities, and thus, by definition, cannot account for the realpolitik behavior either.

87. Mearsheimer, "The False Promise of International Institutions," pp. 9–10.

ing to a change in power distributions. But empirically we know that there is considerable variation in the levels of fear. France has reacted very differently to the unification of Germany in the 1990s than it did to the same process in the 1860s. Western Europe of the 1990s, as a democratic security community of sovereign states, reacts to relative capabilities changes among them in very different ways than it has in the past. So anarchy, a constant, cannot account for dramatic variation in levels of fear. Thus anarchy cannot account for realpolitik interpretations of changes in relative capabilities.

If this is the case, then the initial puzzle above does not require a critical test, since all the Chinese case does is provide empirical evidence that structural realism's assumptions about state preferences are rooted in realpolitik strategic cultures. These two models, then, are not competing ones. Rather, structural realpolitik can be subsumed within the cultural realpolitik model. Indeed, cultural realpolitik is necessary to save structural realpolitik from the embarrassment that its assumptions may be wrong. If this is the case, then, the standard juxtaposition of norms versus interests or structural/rational versus ideational models is a false one. If what we have come to know as structural realism rests on the empirical presence of cultural or ideational realism, then realpolitik behavior is ideationally based, just as behavior that deviates from realpolitik behavior has ideational roots as well. This makes sense to those who consider interests and preferences to be socially constructed. There can be no interests that are not socially constructed, hence there can be no interests that are not rooted in ideational cues for ordering the environment. Thus one simply cannot conceive of interests' being rooted outside of ideas (e.g., in structural anarchy) or pitted against them.

This conclusion is not particularly good news for many realists. While it suggests that there is an empirical basis for the assumption in neorealism that states can tend to interpret the constraints of structures in realist ways, it also suggests that this empirical basis is independent of structure. In other words, if cultural realism provides the content for one of the key assumptions of structural realism, and if this content is independent of structure (to the extent that it inhabits decision makers' perceptions *and* persists across different structural contexts), then realpolitik behavior is independent of structure. Cultural realism saves structural realism the embarrassment of being empirically wrong about how states "think" but in doing so suggests that structure cannot cause realpolitik behavior.

This conclusion raises a problem for research methodology. It suggests, as Jackson rightly puts it, that ideas and interests should not be juxtaposed against each other because both are "concepts and therefore ideas" and because both can exist independent of anarchical structures.[88] If this is the case, we then have to explain what exactly is the relationship between ideas, norms, cultures on the one hand, and structure on the other. While most scholars who take the "autonomous power of ideas" seriously would concur with the importance of this question, they come up with at least three different conceptualizations of the relationship between ideas and structure. One view is that material structure does in fact produce determinate predictions about behavior but that these are often wrong because ideas, norms, and culture sometimes mediate and thus skew the impact of structure on the decision-making processes. Scholars who start from this assumption thus explore cases that "deviate" from a neorealist prediction. Their conceptualization could be portrayed as in figure 7.7.[89]

A second view sees neorealist structures producing indeterminate predictions, providing limited possibilities and choices, which are then decided upon through the mediation of ideas, norms, and culture (see figure 7.8). Ideas finalize interests and preferences.[90] In both conceptualizations, structure is implicitly or explicitly given enough content independent of ideas to produce behavioral predictions.

But a complete rejection of the ideas-interests dichotomy leads to a third conceptualization. Here ideas, norms, and culture generate structures—anarchical ones if the "strategic culture" is essentially a realpolitik one and institutionalized ones if the strategic culture is essentially an idealpolitik one. Behavior flows from structures, but these are given content and meaning by the ideational precursors. The behavior reinforces the ideational base upon which the super-"structure" rests (figure 7.9).

Of course, this still begs the question, raised in Wendt's important arti-

---

88. Robert H. Jackson, "The Weight of Ideas in Decolonization: Normative Change in International Relations," in Goldstein and Keohane, *Ideas and Foreign Policy*, pp. 112–13.

89. Goldstein and Keohane implicitly accept this conceptualization when they suggest that the way to test for the influence of ideas on behavior is to test the null hypothesis that behavior conforms to "egoistic interests in the context of power realities" (Goldstein and Keohane, "Ideas and Foreign Policy," p. 26). Their approach seems to me to be contradictory. On the one hand, they recognize that most material-interest arguments are indeterminate because of the problem of multiple equilibria and uncertainty. This is precisely why, they argue, ideational factors are important (e.g., in establishing focal points, for instance). But on the other hand, they insist that one has to construct an interest maximization null hypothesis to show that ideas are not epiphenomenal.

90. G. John Ikenberry, "Creating Yesterday's New World Order: Keynsian 'New Thinking' and the Anglo-American Postwar Settlement," in Goldstein and Keohane, *Ideas and Foreign Policy.* p. 59.

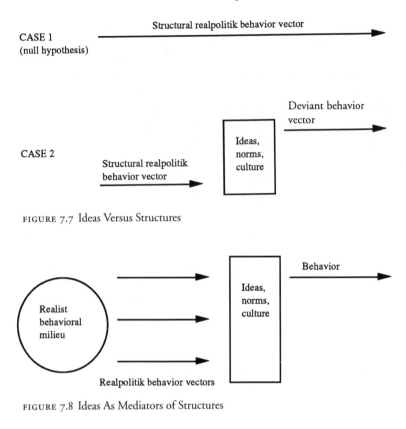

FIGURE 7.7 Ideas Versus Structures

FIGURE 7.8 Ideas As Mediators of Structures

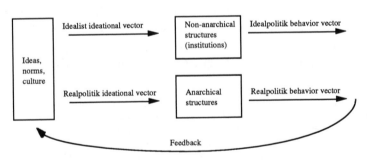

FIGURE 7.9 Ideas Generating Structures

cle,[91] Where do these ideational bases come from and why do certain ideational and behavioral vectors appear at different times? In trying to explain where in the process of social interaction the disposition to identify other states as potential enemies against whom one should be prepared to use force developed, Wendt ventures that the emergence of a predatory state might teach other states to act in competitive power-political ways, though he fails to identify where a predatory state might come from. I am in no position to comment about the primordial origins of hard realpolitik strategic cultures, but I am willing to argue that their presence is a precondition for realpolitik behavior.[92] The parabellum strategic culture— this learned resignation that disputes are settled through violence—may be one of the key ideational links in the chain leading from the appearance of interstate grievances to war.[93]

This does not necessarily mean that a cultural realpolitik model of strategic choice must be universally, cross-culturally valid or indeed constantly valid within one society across time. If this "style" of strategic choice is cultural in the sense that only those who "learn" it are likely to act along parabellum lines, then the Chinese case leaves open the theoretical and empirical possibility that other decision makers may not share hard realpolitik assumptions. The China case, then, underscores Vasquez's contention that realpolitik is "historically contingent and confined to certain issue areas" and Wendt's argument that structural anarchy is not the

---

91. Wendt, "Anarchy Is What States Makes of It."

92. A fruitful direction may be to examine the relationship between the formation of in-groups and out-groups, the requirements for legitimating power structures within the in-group, and the devaluation of the out-group. If the out-group is viewed as dispositionally likely to act in devalued ways, then the shift from viewing an out-group as being somewhat suspect to seeing it as a hardcore enemy is a shift in degree, not kind. In-groups are predisposed to view out-groups as potential adversaries, and this provides the ideational basis for realpolitik behavior. Variation in the strength of in-group/out-group differences and changes in the composition of the in-group will explain variation in strength of realpolitik ideas and axioms and hence in realpolitik behavior directed at other actors. See Donald T. Campbell and Robert A. Levine, "Ethno-centrism and Intergroup Relations," in Robert Abelson et al., eds., *Theories of Cognitive Consistency: A Sourcebook*, pp. 551–64 (Chicago: Rand McNally, 1968); Murray Edelman, *Political Language: Words That Succeed and Policies That Fail* (New York: Academic Press, 1977); Ernest G. Bormann, "Symbolic Convergence: Organizational Communication and Culture," in Linda L. Putnam and Michael E. Pacanowsky, eds., *Communication and Organizations: An Interpretative Approach*, pp. 99–122 (Beverly Hills: Sage, 1983); Jonathan Mercer, "Anarchy and Identity," *International Organization* 49, no. 2 (1995): 229–52; Daniel Druckman, "Nationalism, Patriotism, and Group Loyalty: A Social Psychological Perspective," *Mershon International Studies Review* 38, supp. 1 (1994): 47–48; and Marc Ross, *The Culture of Conflict: Interpretations and Interests in Comparative Perpective* (New Haven: Yale University Press, 1993), pp. 11–12, 40.

93. Vasquez, *The War Puzzle*, p. 113.

cause of self-help behavior. The test is to find a "system or issue area" characterized by non-parabellum or non-realpolitik behavior.[94] At the moment, as I noted above, perhaps the best case for the argument that not all "successful" states act in realpolitik ways is the existence of the democratic security community or zone of peace, a community of sovereign states that in their interaction have abandoned the assumptions of the parabellum paradigm.[95]

The China case leads us to think harder about the ideational roots of realpolitik behavior. China is a critical case both for those who accept the independent causal effect of ideational variables and for those who don't. The former, constructivists and institutionalists alike, have tended to use ideational arguments to explain behavior that deviates from "standard" realist expectations. They will have to develop ideational explanations for "nondeviant" behavior in order to present a truly competitive challenge to dominant structural approaches. Chinese strategic behavior is a place to start. The latter will have to show why China's cultural realpolitik is not causal but epiphenomenal, despite its persistence across very different exogenous conditions. I don't think they can do it, for the reasons I've outlined here. In short, China is a hard case for both approaches, but it is the analysis of hard cases that drives theory forward.

---

94. John A. Vasquez, *The Power of Power Politics: A Critique* (New Brunswick, N.J.: Rutgers University Press, 1983), p. 216; Vasquez, *The War Puzzle*, p. 89.

95. Evidence for the presence of non-parabellum strategic cultures and behavior suggests that the null hypothesis for a cultural *realpolitik* model is not structural realism but cultural liberalism, or cultural institutionalism, or some formal model that aggregates domestic political preferences, themselves ideationally rooted. If structural realism is incomplete without ideational assumptions about interests, then it is not really an alternative to a cultural *realpolitik* model. In other words, any competitive hypothesis testing of a parabellum strategic culture model should be done with other ideational models, not against structural realism. This conclusion suggests that many of those involved in the "norms, ideas, and culture" project are right to reject the ideas-interest dichotomy in favor of an ideas-ideas dichotomy.

Part • 2
Identity and National Security

8 · Identity, Norms, and National Security: The Soviet Foreign Policy Revolution and the End of the Cold War

Robert G. Herman

Tensions arising from Russia's recent pursuit of a less reflexively pro-Western foreign policy, coupled with President Boris Yeltsin's unsettling warnings of a looming "cold peace," tempt us to forget the extraordinary change in the nature of Moscow's relations with the advanced industrial democracies since the mid-1980s. The debate over the future direction of Russia domestically and internationally is inextricably linked to the ongoing, spirited argument over the origins of the end of the Cold War. This essay joins the debate in offering an alternative analytical framework to explain the tectonic shift in Soviet foreign and military policy.

The advent of "New Thinking" (*novoye mishleniye*)[1] accompanying

The author would like to thank the participants at the three Social Science Research Council/MacArthur Workshops for illuminating discussions and helpful comments. I am also indebted to Peter Katzenstein, David Holloway, Stephen Walt, and two anonymous reviewers for their suggestions and insightful comments. I gratefully acknowledge the support of the Brookings Institution and the Social Science Research Council.

1. The term *New Thinking* became shorthand for the ensemble of insights, concepts, initiatives, and practices that the USSR's international strategy comprised in the Gorbachev era. While the precise content of New Thinking changed over time, the new approach rested on three core ideas. First, the existence of the "security dilemma," wherein measures taken by one side to enhance its security are invariably perceived by a would-be rival as undermining its own, means that security must be mutual or common and cannot be pursued unilaterally. Second, resort to force or threats of force is neither

the accession to power of Mikhail Gorbachev brought about the end of the Cold War and created the conditions for a durable East-West peace. Both the depth and the breadth of this change, from the unilateral steps to reduce and restructure military forces to give them a less offensive cast to the rejection of force to maintain communist domination in Eastern Europe and to prevent the dissolution of the Soviet Union itself, went far beyond what conventional international relations theories can accommodate as well as what knowledgeable area specialists imagined was possible.[2]

This essay contends that reigning realist and liberal explanations cannot adequately account for New Thinking's revolutionary character, which made the transformation of superpower relations possible. If policy outcomes represent the final phase in a causal sequence, the principal contribution of realism lies at the front end, in identifying structural constraints on political actors. However, even here realism's preoccupation with material capabilities produces a reified view of structures that does not capture the multiple dimensions (e.g., political, ideological, moral) of the USSR's systemic crisis. Liberal approaches provide a richer context and greater explanatory power for foreign policy moderation in the early Gorbachev era, allowing us to move further along the causal chain. Yet they, like their realist competitors, either marginalize or ignore altogether the social

---

an efficacious nor a legitimate way to resolve interstate conflicts. To ameliorate the security dilemma and the pressures propelling states to eschew diplomatic solutions, strategies of reassurance must replace or at least supplement those based on deterrence threats. And last, class values should be subordinated to "universal human values." Adoption of this idea amounted to a repudiation of Marxism-Leninism's Manichaean worldview of irreconcilable interests between capitalism and socialism and thus paved the way for a new international order based on shared values. On the content of New Thinking, see Matthew Evangelista, "The New Soviet Approach to Security," *World Policy Journal* 3, no. 4 (Fall 1986):561–99; Elizabeth Kridl Valkenier, "New Thinking About the Third World," *World Policy Journal* 4, no. 4 (Fall 1987): 651–74; Bruce Parrott, "Soviet National Security Policy Under Gorbachev," *Problems of Communism* 37, no. 6 (November/December 1988): 1–36; Robert Legvold, "The Revolution in Soviet Foreign Policy," *Foreign Affairs* 68, no. 1 (Winter 1989): 82–98; and Raymond Garthoff, *Deterrence and the Revolution in Soviet Military Doctrine* (Washington, D.C.: Brookings Institution, 1990).

2. The debate over the end of the Cold War continues to engage the intellectual and emotional energies of scholars. Among important recent works are Richard Ned Lebow and Thomas Risse-Kappen, eds., *International Relations Theory and the End of the Cold War* (New York: Columbia University Press, 1995); William Wohlforth, "Realism and the End of the Cold War," *International Security* 19, no. 3 (Winter 1994/95): 91–129; Matthew Evangelista, *Taming the Bear: Transnational Relations and the Demise of the Soviet Threat*, forthcoming; Raymond Garthoff, *The Great Transition: American-Soviet Relations and the End of the Cold War* (Washington, D.C.: Brookings Institution, 1994); John Lewis Gaddis, "International Relations Theory and the End of the Cold War," *International Security* 17, no. 3 (Winter 1992/93): 5–58; and Jack Snyder, *Myths of Empire: Domestic Politics and International Ambition* (Ithaca: Cornell University Press, 1991).

processes that spawned the core ideas of mature New Thinking and helped bring them to policy fruition.

The ideas and identity framework developed here both complements and challenges realist and liberal paradigms. It builds on some of their powerful insights while pointing to analytical shortcomings and blind spots, posing different questions and proffering a new, more compelling explanation for changes in state behavior.

Most scholars and policy makers have interpreted the shift in Soviet foreign policy as a tactical adjustment necessitated by internationally or domestically generated imperatives rather than as a genuine reconceptualization of interests grounded in new collective understandings about the dynamics of world politics and in actors' evolving identities. The first view, which privileges material capabilities, unquestionably sheds light on sources of moderation in Soviet international policy, particularly the generally modest changes enacted during the early stages of Gorbachev's tenure. Its narrowly drawn, materialist conception of interests, however, misses the cultural-institutional context that shaped the ways in which future Soviet decision makers understood the policy implications of the USSR's economic and political plight. Only the second interpretation, with its emphasis on collective ideational constructs, can account for the revolutionary path followed once proponents of radical foreign policy reform triumphed over their moderate rivals.[3]

The two accounts are not necessarily mutually exclusive, but integrating them requires explication of the complex interaction of ideational and material structures in influencing state behavior. Such eclectic theorizing can be accommodated far better by an explanation that does not take interests as given and fixed.

The central argument advanced here is that the momentous turn in Soviet international policy was the product of cognitive evolution and policy entrepreneurship by networks of Western-oriented in-system reformers coincident with the coming to power of a leadership committed to change and receptive to new ideas for solving the country's formidable problems.[4] These expert communities comprised in part liberal interna-

---

3. In distinguishing between moderate and radical perspectives among foreign policy reformers, I draw generously on the work of Franklyn Griffiths. His article "The Sources of American Conduct: Soviet Perspectives and Their Policy Implications," *International Security* 9, no. 2 (Fall 1984): 3–50, offers a useful typology that loosely informs my own categories.
4. Research for this project included interviews with dozens of specialists from institutes under the Soviet Academy of Sciences as well as with senior state and party *apparatchiks*, many from the Central Committee's International Department (CCID) and the Ministry of Foreign Affairs (MFA). I also

tional affairs specialists (or *mezhdunarodniki*) from a few research institutes of the Academy of Sciences together with a small cadre of like-minded officials in the party and state apparat.[5]

Having helped to lay the conceptual groundwork for the East-West rapprochement of the early 1970s, liberal specialists were spurred by its early successes and subsequent demise to question the basic assumptions undergirding the Brezhnev Politburo's coercive approach to detente. In seeking to strengthen and expand the norms embedded in this nascent security regime, they developed new understandings about cause-and-effect relationships in international politics and the nature of security in the contemporary age.[6] Determined to reverse the self-defeating ways of Kremlin foreign and military policy, liberal specialists espoused jettisoning Marxist-Leninist ideology as a guide for defining state interests and advocated conciliatory measures designed to soften would-be adversaries' perception of hostile Soviet intentions. This "conciliatory realpolitik" perspective was the common baseline for virtually all foreign policy reformers and closely resembled the moderate strand of New Thinking prevalent in the early Gorbachev years.

But the radical course on which the Soviet regime embarked beginning in late 1987 and early 1988 and that led directly to the cessation of the Cold War was the work of a subgroup of specialists who promoted a new political order based in part on principles governing relations among the

---

worked in the CPSU Central Committee Archives and gained access to previously classified memoranda (*zapiski*) prepared by institute analysts for the leadership. The potential problems with interviews are well known. I took several steps to ensure that the oral testimony used in my analysis was reliable, including corroboration based on other independent accounts, interlocutors' published writings, and the aforementioned classified documents, which provided analysts with greater latitude to express critical views. And while the majority of interviewees were committed New Thinkers, my discussions extended to moderate and conservative opponents, some of whom occupied important posts in the government.

5. Three social science institutes figure most prominently in my research: World Economy and International Relations (IMEMO), USA and Canada (ISKAN), and Economics of the World Socialist System (IEMSS). This troika formed the bulwark of revisionist scholarship and provided many of the intellectual shock troops in the New Thinking army. For a more in-depth discussion of the early histories of these institutes, see Jeff Checkel, "Organizational Behavior, Social Scientists, and Soviet Foreign Policymaking" (Ph.D. diss., Massachusetts Institute of Technology, 1991); Neil Malcolm, *Soviet Political Scientists and American Politics* (New York: St. Martin's Press, 1984); Georgi Arbatov, *The System: An Insider's Life in Soviet Politics* (New York: Times Books, 1992); and Oded Eran, *Mezhdunarodniki: An Assessment of Professional Expertise in the Making of Soviet Third World Policy* (Tel Aviv: Turtle Dove, 1979).

6. In this paper norms are defined as collective beliefs that regulate the behavior and identity of actors.

Western democracies and within those societies.[7] Some of these principles were transmitted to Soviet reformers through transnational contacts with liberal-Left counterparts in the West that flourished in the 1970s and survived detente's precipitous decline.[8]

Other central elements of New Thinking (e.g., the relationship between peace and socialism and between class values and "values common to all mankind") were indigenous, often the product of ongoing debate within the socialist bloc. The fact of Soviet hegemony in Eastern Europe blurred the distinction between international and domestic policy and helps to explain why foreign policy radicals, virtually all of whom came to political consciousness as anti-Stalinist reformers, were equally committed to fundamental changes in the way Soviet society was organized. In this respect, the end of the Cold War is directly linked to the collapse of communism and the long-standing struggle of in-system reformers to realize an alternative socialist future.

Propelled by a vision of the USSR as a democratic and peaceable member of the international community and touting "values common to all mankind," these "idealists" sought to eliminate the underlying causes of East-West conflict. Conceiving of the Soviet Union in this new identity rendered obsolete the two-camp view of the world that formed the core of Marxist-Leninist ideology.[9] This change, in turn, enabled the two sides to transcend their decades-long confrontation rather than simply mute the rivalry—which had been the extent of Soviet aims since the Khrushchev era.

The contest between advocates of these two discrete yet closely linked perspectives formed part of the political-intellectual milieu in which Soviet foreign policy was forged in the mid- to late 1980s. As discussed in the concluding section, this battle over the content of New Thinking also goes far in explaining elements of both continuity and change between the Gorbachev and Yeltsin governments.

---

7. Finer lines demarcating Europeanists and Atlanticists have been drawn by Western scholars, including Hannes Adomeit, "Capitalist Contradictions and Soviet Policy," *Problems of Communism* 33, no. 3 (May/June 1984): 1–18.

8. See Thomas Risse-Kappen, "Ideas Do Not Float Freely: Transnational Coalitions, Domestic Structures, and the End of the Cold War," *International Organization* 48, no. 2 (Spring 1994): 185–214; Evangelista, *Taming the Bear*; and Robert G. Herman, "Ideas, Identity, and the Redefinition of Interests: The Political and Intellectual Origins of the Soviet Foreign Policy Revolution" (Ph.D. diss., Cornell University, 1995).

9. The deideologization of Soviet foreign policy in the Gorbachev period has been well documented (e.g., see Stephen Kull, *Burying Lenin: The Revolution in Soviet Ideology and Foreign Policy* [Boulder: Westview, 1992]), but few works examine the identity basis of this change.

Realist and Liberal Explanations

Realist and liberal explanations capture some of the factors and processes that contributed to the change in Soviet international policy in the Gorbachev era. The former tend to emphasize adverse changes in material conditions in inducing states to modify their behavior. Some realist explanations stress imperial overstretch[10] or Moscow's deteriorating geostrategic position in the wake of American military resurgence and demonstrated military-technological prowess in the Reagan years.[11] Companion arguments focus on economic stagnation[12] and the requirements of advanced industrial production and the need to integrate into the global economy to reap the benefits of the scientific-technological revolution.[13]

That material circumstances, both international and domestic, affect the intellectual evolution and policy choices of political decision makers is not in dispute, though the nature of the interaction between the material and the ideational worlds remains undertheorized. Scholars have shown, for instance, that periods of crisis can both stimulate new ideas and create a demand for them,[14] particularly when accompanied by political succes-

---

10. Paul Kennedy, *The Rise and Fall of the Great Powers: Economic Change and Military Conflict from 1500 to 2000* (New York: Random House, 1987), pp. 488–514. Valerie Bunce predicted that the growing burden of the USSR's empire in Eastern Europe would force the Soviet leadership to deregulate the bloc; see "The Empire Strikes Back: The Transformation of the Eastern Bloc from a Soviet Asset to a Soviet Liability," *International Organization* 39, no. 1 (Winter 1985): 1–46.

11. For a sophisticated form of the argument, see John Lewis Gaddis, "Hanging Tough Paid Off," *Bulletin of the Atomic Scientists* 45 (January 1989): 11–14. Subscribers to the "Peace Through Strength" thesis, mostly conservative analysts, credit the Reagan-era military buildup (especially the threat posed by the Strategic Defense Initiative) and bellicose strategy with forcing Moscow to adopt New Thinking and end the Cold War on Western terms. This account mirrors the dominant explanation in Soviet policy circles for U.S. interest in a relaxation of tensions in the late 1960s. Proponents of this interpretation of recent history contended that a shift in the correlation of forces in favor of socialism, most significantly Moscow's attaining strategic parity, compelled Washington to seek accommodation with its chief adversary.

12. See, for example, Coit Blacker, *Hostage to Revolution: Gorbachev and Soviet Security Policy, 1985–1991* (New York: Council on Foreign Relations Press, 1993), esp. Introduction and ch. 5; and Stephen Meyer, "Sources and Prospects of Gorbachev's New Political Thinking on Security," *International Security* 13, no. 2 (Fall 1988): 124–63.

13. Daniel Deudney and G. John Ikenberry, "Soviet Reform and the End of the Cold War: Explaining Large-Scale Historical Change," *Review of International Studies* 17 (Summer 1991): 225–50. Specialists at IMEMO and IEMSS offered similar conclusions in classified reports prepared throughout the 1970s. Some analysts also recognized the need to transfer resources from military to civilian production.

14. For example, Peter Hall, *The Political Power of Economic Ideas: Keynesianism Across Nations* (Princeton: Princeton University Press, 1989); Kathryn Sikkink, *Ideas and Institutions: Developmentalism in Brazil and Argentina* (Ithaca: Cornell University Press, 1993); and Judith Goldstein and Robert O. Keohane, "Ideas and Foreign Policy: An Analytical Framework," in Judith Goldstein and Robert O. Keohane, eds., *Ideas and Foreign Policy: Beliefs, Institutions, and Political Change*, pp. 3–30 (Ithaca: Cornell University Press, 1993).

sion. Historically, incoming regimes have tended to be more receptive to new ideas,[15] multiplying the opportunities for policy entrepreneurship. In the Soviet Union, the combination of economic decline and unfavorable changes in the global correlation of forces increased the probability of reformers' coming to power in the first place[16] and continued to influence the thinking of the Gorbachev regime in the ensuing years. Policy is not made in a vacuum. The saliency of the New Thinking critique and alternative strategy had much to do with the severity of the problems that the country was facing.

But how a political leadership will respond to the strategic environment is indeterminate; it depends at least in part on how decision makers understand the world[17] and how they interpret the frequently ambiguous lessons of history.[18] Virtually the same confluence of internal and external pressures that purportedly compelled the adoption of New Thinking had been present since the late stages of the Brezhnev regime without any significant changes in policy until 1985 and the arrival of the Gorbachev circle.[19] Moreover, Gorbachev's rivals for power offered a different diagnosis of and cure for the country's ailments, and reformers themselves

---

15. Valerie Bunce, *Do New Leaders Make a Difference?* (Princeton: Princeton University Press, 1981).

16. Wohlforth, "Realism and the End of the Cold War."

17. The literature on perception, belief systems, constitutive processes, etc., as applied to state behavior is enormous. I cite here only some of the works that I used for this study: Joseph S. Nye, Jr., "Nuclear Learning and U.S.-Soviet Security Regimes," *International Security* 41, no. 3 (Summer 1987): 371–402; Ernst B. Haas, *When Knowledge Is Power* (Berkeley: University of California Press, 1990); Emanuel Adler, "Cognitive Evolution: A Dynamic Approach for the Study of International Relations and Their Progress," in Emanuel Adler and Beverly Crawford, eds., *Progress in Postwar International Relations* (New York: Columbia University Press, 1991); Philip Tetlock, "Learning in U.S. and Soviet Foreign Policy: In Search of an Elusive Concept," in George Breslauer and Philip Tetlock, eds., *Learning in U.S. and Soviet Foreign Policy*, pp. 20–61 (Boulder: Westview, 1991); Friedrich Kratochwil and John Gerard Ruggie, "International Organization: A State of the Art on an Art of the State," *International Organization* 40, no. 4 (Autumn 1986): 753–75; and Alexander Wendt, "Anarchy Is What States Make of It: The Social Construction of Power Politics," *International Organization* 46, no. 2 (Spring 1992): 391–425. The classic work on belief systems remains Milton Rokeach, *The Open and Closed Mind* (New York: Basic Books, 1960).

18. See Ernest May, *"Lessons" of the Past: The Use and Misuse of History in American Foreign Policy* (New York: Oxford University Press, 1973), and Robert Jervis, *Perception and Misperception in International Politics* (Princeton: Princeton University Press, 1976).

19. Domestically, the Brezhnev, Andropov, and Chernenko regimes either ignored the gathering crisis or instituted cosmetic reforms that would do little to address systemic deficiencies. In foreign policy, contrary to the popular view that the U.S./West vanquished the USSR, forcing it to pursue accommodation, these regimes responded to the West's confrontational strategy with their own more bellicose posture. Strained relations also made it extremely difficult for nascent New Thinkers to express their views, even in classified sources. See Herman, "Ideas, Identity, and the Redefinition of Interests."

could not agree on either the nature of the problem or the prospective solution.

The point is that permissive structural conditions did not make New Thinking, particularly in its full-blown form, inevitable. Alternative strategies existed, and any satisfactory explanation for Soviet international policy in the mid- to late 1980s must deal with that reality. To what degree those strategies offered viable long-term solutions to the country's myriad problems is of less consequence than the fact that each commanded identifiable constituencies in the Soviet political establishment and thus constituted credible rivals to New Thinking. At the time of the death of Konstantin Chernenko, chairman of the Communist Party of the Soviet Union (CPSU), the foreign policy course that the world would come to know as New Thinking was not advocated by any of the contenders for power, including Gorbachev.

Options ranged from carrying on Chernenko's approach of muddling through domestically and internationally to heeding the hard-liners' call for mobilizing resources to repel the Reagan administration onslaught. Also in the policy mix were those who could be called "economic modernizers" of varying inclinations. They supported moderating Moscow's foreign policy to permit domestic economic renovation. Some proponents viewed this as a temporary arrangement to buy time to retool the defense-industrial complex for the inevitable long-term rivalry with the capitalist powers. Others hoped that a milder version of the Brezhnev-Gromyko international strategy would ratchet down the East-West military competition and yield a sustainable detente relationship. The USSR might have taken any one of these paths in 1985, and even after the selection of Gorbachev—known more as a talented technocrat than as an ardent reformer—the country was not fated to travel the New Thinking road. Realism cannot provide the sharper analytical tools needed to explain why (or how) a particular policy option prevails.

Nor does realism (or liberalism, for that matter) necessarily generate unambiguous predictions about state action. Employing realist assumptions regarding the material basis of state interests to predict the foreign policy behavior of a beleaguered USSR in the early to mid-1980s yields two rather contradictory outcomes. On the one hand, Soviet decision makers could, as William Wohlforth contends they did, respond rationally to perceptions of relative decline by retrenching, thereby trying to allay Western fears and encourage NATO to adopt a less hard-line anti-Soviet posture.[20]

20. Wohlforth, "Realism and the End of the Cold War."

On the other hand, a Soviet leadership attempting to balance against a heightened Western threat might just as rationally decide to resist this external pressure forcefully by exacting the sacrifices deemed necessary to match NATO's aggressive stance or, in an extreme and all but unimaginable case, launch a preventive war.[21]

To sum up, while identifying the set of constraints and incentives with which decision makers have to contend, realist explanations are underdetermining with respect to policy outcomes. In the case of Soviet international behavior in the period under discussion, even accepting that realism points to the increased possibility of reformers' coming to power, it cannot adequately account for the vast *scope* and radical *content* of the changes undertaken by the Gorbachev regime.

Having treated states' interests as given—rationally derived from the anarchic nature of and distribution of capabilities within the international system—realist arguments preclude any meaningful role for human reflection or political-ideological contention in (re)shaping actors' conception of interests.[22] At the same time, realism's view of the material world as largely devoid of ideational content leads proponents to miss the importance of the existence of successful nonsocialist models of social organization and economic development (e.g., the prosperity of the West and great promise of the "Asian tigers") as well as norms of "civilized nations" in making up part of the strategic environment in which Soviet interests were defined.[23]

By ignoring the process of cognitive evolution and the ways in which collective understandings of cause-and-effect relationships and shared values are diffused through the political system, these explanations reduce the New Thinking revolution to a mechanical act of rational adaptation to adverse changes in material circumstances.[24] The Soviet leadership

21. Many power transition theories predict that declining hegemons will go to war to preserve their international position. See Robert Gilpin, *War and Change in World Politics* (New York: Cambridge University Press, 1981).

22. See Richard Ashley, "The Poverty of Neorealism," *International Organization* 38, no. 2 (Spring 1984): 225–86; and Adler, "Cognitive Evolution."

23. My thanks to David Holloway for this insightful point.

24. This view of learning-induced policy change does not even meet the criteria of "simple" or "tactical" learning in which decision makers devise more efficient strategies for pursuing unchanged goals; see Nye, "Nuclear Learning and U.S.-Soviet Security Regimes." Kenneth Oye offers a sophisticated realist argument that tries to show how the external environment is endogenized and can be read as incorporating a cognitive dimension. He contends that "international environmental characteristics—specifically the development of nuclear weapons and the subsequent long central systemic peace—were a significant permissive cause of the political and economic liberalization within the Soviet Union" ("Explaining the End of the Cold War: Morphological and Behavioral Adaptations to the Nuclear Peace," in Lebow and Risse-Kappen, *International Relations Theory and the End of the Cold War*, p. 58).

"learned" only in the sense that like any firm in microeconomic theory, it had to conform to the dictates of the strategic environment if it was to survive.[25] This account bears little resemblance to the intellectual and political processes whereby Soviet interests were redefined in the Gorbachev era.

The liberal paradigm is better equipped to incorporate the cognitive and political processes that produced the turn in Soviet international behavior. Scholars advancing a variety of liberal explanations centered on ideas,[26] learning,[27] international regimes,[28] transnational linkages,[29] and the social consequences of the modernization process;[30] all either argue outright or allow for the possibility that changes in Moscow's foreign policy were the result of new conceptions of state interests. Each of these factors has causal significance, and several are integrated into the alternative framework outlined in the next section.

What these liberal explanations have in common is that they challenge realism's austere view of international politics.[31] Liberal institutionalist approaches, for example, point to the set of rules that states have devised (or customs they have formalized) to regulate behavior and facilitate coop-

25. As Jeffrey W. Legro points out, neorealist theorists do acknowledge a role for political socialization whereby states are brought into conformity with system norms, but their emphasis is on punishment/reward for unacceptable/acceptable behavior, a process more aptly described as simple adaptation; see "Strategy Under Anarchy" (draft paper for Norms and National Security Workshop, Cornell University, February 1993).

26. Jeff Checkel, "Ideas, Institutions, and the Gorbachev Foreign Policy Revolution," *World Politics* 45 (January 1993): 271–300; Douglas Blum, "The Soviet Foreign Policy Belief System: Beliefs, Politics, and Foreign Policy Outcomes," *International Studies Quarterly* 37 (1993); Allen Lynch, *The Soviet Study of International Relations* (New York: Cambridge University Press, 1987); and Goldstein and Keohane, *Ideas and Foreign Policy.*

27. Breslauer and Tetlock, *Learning in U.S. and Soviet Foreign Policy;* Robert Legvold, "Soviet Learning in the 1980s," in ibid.; Janice Gross Stein, "Political Learning by Doing: Gorbachev As Uncommitted Thinker and Motivated Learner," *International Organization* 48, no. 2 (Spring 1994): 155–84; and Nye, "Nuclear Learning and U.S.-Soviet Security Regimes."

28. Alexander George, Philip Farley, and Alexander Dallin, eds., *U.S.-Soviet Security Cooperation: Achievements, Failures, Lessons* (New York: Oxford University Press, 1988); Nye, "Nuclear Learning and U.S.-Soviet Security Regimes," and Herman, "Ideas, Identity, and the Redefinition of Interests." Also see Garthoff, *The Great Transition.*

29. Risse-Kappen, "Ideas Do Not Float Freely," and Evangelista, *Taming the Bear.*

30. A strong case for the modernization explanation, focusing on the emergence of a younger, more educated, and reform-minded generation, is Moshe Lewin, *The Gorbachev Phenomenon: An Historical Interpretation* (Berkeley: University of California Press, 1988). For a variant employing social coalition analysis, see Jack Snyder, "The Gorbachev Revolution: A Waning of Soviet Expansionism?" *International Security* 12, no. 3 (Winter 1987/88): 93–131.

31. Hedley Bull, *The Anarchical Society: A Study of Order in World Politics* (New York: Columbia University Press, 1977).

eration.[32] Frequently these rules are institutionalized in the form of international regimes. Regime theorists acknowledge that institutions that were initially based on states' rational cost-benefit calculations can over time alter actors' conception of interests.[33] One way that regimes accomplish this is by facilitating learning, usually through strategic interaction.[34] I will show that this was the case with Soviet foreign policy reformers, who came to see in detente's extant rules of prudential superpower behavior the potential for a more far-reaching East-West accommodation.

Whereas realists deny or greatly downplay the causal effect of such regime-embedded regulatory norms on actor behavior, several variants of liberalism accord these ideational phenomena independent explanatory power. To the extent that New Thinkers' alternative conception of Soviet interests was derived from the regulatory principles loosely codified in the detente regime of the 1970s, a cognitive-institutionalist framework accounts for considerable policy innovation in the Gorbachev period. But the decision makers who determined the content of Soviet policy in the late 1980s were driven by a vision of the USSR that went far beyond that embodied in the regulatory norms of superpower rapprochement.

Neither the realist nor even the aforementioned liberal approach can account for the New Thinking revolution in its conceptual and applied-policy totality. The most likely policy trajectory derived from the logic of a combination of realist and liberal assumptions approximates conciliatory realpolitik. An incoming Soviet regime alert to the country's declining position could be expected to pare down its overseas commitments, pursue modest arms reduction accords as a way to cut military expenditures and reduce the West's sense of threat, seek an expansion of East-West trade and technical cooperation, and generally try to recast itself in the image of a kinder, gentler superpower rival. This was the program judged by the vast majority of in-system reformers to be necessary to redress the USSR's most pressing domestic difficulties and international setbacks.[35]

---

32. Joseph S. Nye, Jr., "Neorealism and Neoliberalism," *World Politics* 40, no. 2 (January 1988): 235–51; and Robert Keohane, "International Institutions: Two Approaches," *International Studies Quarterly* 32, no. 4 (December 1988): 379–96. While acknowledging that the international realm is by definition anarchic, liberals reject the depiction of interstate politics as a Hobbesian, self-help world.
33. Stephen Krasner, "Regimes and the Limits of Realism: Regimes as Autonomous Variables" in Stephen Krasner, ed., *International Regimes* (Ithaca: Cornell University Press, 1983).
34. Nye, "Nuclear Learning and U.S.-Soviet Security Regimes."
35. This "detente-plus" strategy seems close to what at least some of Gorbachev's Politburo selectors had in mind. See Yegor Ligachev, *Inside Gorbachev's Kremlin* (New York: Random House, 1993); also author's interviews with Gorbachev advisers A. Yakovlev, G. Shakhnazarov, V. Zagladin, A. Chernyaev, and others.

But in moving unilaterally to reduce its military forces and give them a defensive character, in actively pressing for peaceful resolution of protracted Third World conflicts, and in tolerating the collapse of fraternal allies in Eastern Europe—for four decades considered the indispensable bulwark against Western aggression—the Gorbachev leadership's fully developed New Thinking strategy trumped conciliatory realpolitik.

The differences in the two policy approaches stem not from varying assessments of the gravity of the Soviet problematique but from different underlying assumptions and motivating forces. Idealists parted company with purveyors of a more cautious brand of New Thinking akin to conciliatory realpolitik in rejecting a view of East-West relations as inherently conflictive—if not ideologically, then geostrategically. Similarly, radical reformers were not content to ameliorate the security dilemma; they were determined to transcend it altogether, through strategies based on reassurance rather than deterrence threats and, more ambitiously, through the transformation of the Soviet Union into a democratic society integrated into the Western community of nations. And whereas proponents of a conciliatory realpolitik course lauded its amorality and pursuit of decidedly traditional state interests (after decades of Marxist-Leninist ideology as the guiding principle), idealists were driven by a normative vision that defined Soviet interests in wholly new ways.

To reject categorically the use of force to maintain the Soviet Union's security shield in Eastern Europe and then to preserve the USSR itself is inexplicable in realist terms. No Soviet regime, regardless of the perceived urgency of the country's economic plight or its faltering geostrategic position, would take steps that it thought would jeopardize the physical security of the state. The Gorbachev cohort was no exception. What allowed it to pursue a strategy utterly unthinkable to its predecessors was its fundamentally different understanding of the nature of the threat.

In coming to hold an altogether different vision of the USSR and its relations with the outside world, the Gorbachev regime's idealist cohort was confident that a transformed Soviet Union would render the Cold War confrontation an artifact of history. It is the pivotal significance of this identity dimension for explaining the revolutionary course in Soviet foreign policy in the late 1980s that eludes both realist and liberal approaches.

An Ideas and Identity Framework

Taking ideational phenomena seriously as independent variables in influencing actors' definitions of interests requires a systematic exploration of intellectual evolution within the Soviet policy elite and the political process whereby new strategic prescriptions[36] carried by in-system reformers became state policy.

The alternative conceptual framework developed here seeks to incorporate identity and domestic politics into a social cognitive perspective. Following Judith Goldstein and Robert Keohane, I accord explanatory autonomy to collectively held ideas but refine their approach in showing the constitutive effects of norms on actor behavior.[37] Identity is the link between norms and interests that motivate behavior. The idealist conception of Soviet interests that determined the content of New Thinking in the mid- to late Gorbachev period was championed by in-system reformers who identified with the principles governing relations among Western democratic states and between said governments and their respective polities.

I modify the framework offered by Goldstein and Keohane by unpacking their concept of principled beliefs to distinguish between regulatory and constitutive principles. Both assert claims on behavior, though the latter do so much more strongly. Regime theory tends to give short shrift to constitutive norms. Perhaps for most instances of policy revision, and certainly for changes in Soviet international practice in the first years of the Gorbachev era, regulatory norms suffice to explain the attending modification in decision makers' conception of state interests. In the case of the sweeping redefinition of interests that yielded the radical variant of New Thinking, constitutive norms of identity were the principal motor force.

For many liberal scholars, cognitive evolutionary processes are central to the discussion of the effects of norms on behavior, whether constitu-

---

36. The strategic prescriptions advanced by New Thinkers incorporated both causal ideas and principled beliefs, suggesting that the dichotomy proposed by Goldstein and Keohane (*Ideas and Foreign Policy*) needs further refinement. I am grateful to Thomas Risse-Kappen for calling this point to my attention.

37. On the constitutive effects of norms, see Friedrich Kratochwil, *Rules, Norms, and Decisions: On the Conditions of Practical and Legal Reasoning in International Relations and Domestic Affairs* (Cambridge: Cambridge University Press, 1989).

tive or regulatory. While there is no single approach to learning,[38] the distinction drawn by Joseph Nye and others between "simple" and "complex" learning is helpful for explaining the magnitude of foreign policy change in the Gorbachev years.[39] In the former, policy adjustments constitute a more efficient matching of means and ends—tactical adaptation that leaves fundamental assumptions unquestioned and unchanged. Complex learning, in contrast, involves intellectual deliberation in which decision makers' interests may be redefined in light of new understandings about cause-and-effect relationships.[40] By this definition, both regulatory and constitutive norms are linked analytically to complex learning through their effects on actors' conceptions of interest. There is no analytical or methodological reason why changes in actor identity cannot be incorporated into cognitive evolutionary approaches premised on complex learning.

I employ the concept of specialist networks[41] to explicate two distinct

---

38. As Philip Tetlock observes, there is not even agreement on the definition of the term; see "Learning in U.S. and Soviet Foreign Policy"; also see Jack Levy, "Learning and Foreign Policy: Sweeping a Conceptual Minefield," *International Organization* 48, no. 2 (Spring 1994): 279–312.

39. Nye, "Nuclear Learning and U.S.-Soviet Security Regimes," and Legvold, "Soviet Learning in the 1980s."

40. Haas, *When Knowledge Is Power.* According to Legvold ("Soviet Learning"), change at the level of fundamental beliefs can occur either gradually through "exposure to more testing instances," in which case a richer, more differentiated representation of reality results from the accumulation of greater knowledge, or suddenly, when the schema with which a person makes sense of the world crumbles under the onslaught of disconfirming experiences. In either case, decision makers demonstrate increased "cognitive differentiation and integration of thought and capacity for self-reflection." Also see Lloyd Etheredge, *Can Governments Learn?* (New York: Pergamon Press, 1985).

41. I have deliberately eschewed the term *epistemic communities* because the networks of reform-minded specialists examined here do not fit the decidedly technical knowledge-based criteria employed by the concept's most prominent theoreticians, including Peter M. Haas (ed., *Knowledge, Power, and International Policy Coordination,* special issue, *International Organization* 46, no. 1 [Winter 1992]). The Soviet networks overwhelmingly comprised social scientists from different disciplines who shared a roughly common worldview rather than common expertise. Identifiable subgroups also came to share certain values commitments. Recent works on the USSR/Russia that employ some variant of specialist communities in an attempt to link expert knowledge to policy outcomes include Evangelista, *Taming the Bear;* Checkel, "Ideas, Institutions, and the Gorbachev Foreign Policy Revolution"; Emanuel Adler, "The Emergence of Cooperation: National Epistemic Communities and the International Evolution of the Idea of Nuclear Arms Control," *International Organization* 46, no. 1 (Winter 1992): 101–46; Sarah Mendelson, "Internal Battles and External Wars: Politics, Learning, and the Soviet Withdrawal from Afghanistan," *World Politics* 45, no. 3 (April 1993): 327–60; and Herman, "Ideas, Identity, and the Redefinition of Interests." An example of a non-Soviet case in which specialists' shared values are the motive force is Kathryn Sikkink, "Human Rights and Principled Issue-Networks," *International Organization* 47, no. 3 (Summer 1993): 411–41.

but interrelated processes: (1) social construction[42] of the ideas/ideology[43] and identities that gave New Thinking its radical orientation and (2) political contention/selection, or how these shared conceptions became the basis of state policy in the late 1980s. The use of specialist networks provides the leverage to overcome two major shortcomings of the cognitive approaches that form the core of my argument. First, I do not see learning as an act of individual cognition that can be aggregated to generate insights about state or institutional behavior. Cognitive evolution is a social process.[44] New Thinking was a collaborative effort, the result of intellectual give-and-take within these expert groups.[45] I integrate identity formation into the cognitive framework by emphasizing the collectivity. Identity norms make much more powerful claims on behavior than do the causal beliefs and schemata that are the central focus of most learning approaches. In addition, building identity norms into cognitive approaches corrects bias of the latter toward the diffusion of technical knowledge at the expense of values and principles.

The second relevant shortcoming of learning explanations is that they are frequently divorced from politics and questions of power.[46] Specialist networks quite literally provide the bridge between the emergence of new ideas and identities and their prospective adoption by the political leadership. Which conception of Soviet national interests would prevail was largely a function of political struggle between competing groupings within the elite.

---

42. Proponents of constructivist approaches problematize the notion of structure; what matters is not so much objective conditions but how actors understand them. For many constructivists, this is largely a function of self-conception or identity, which in turn shapes definitions of interests. State behavior becomes intelligible only by examining such collective ideational phenomena; see Wendt, "Anarchy Is What States Make of It."

43. New Thinking can be viewed as an alternative ideology to Marxism-Leninism. For the purposes of this study I define ideology as a coherent set of interrelated ideas containing causal inferences about means-ends relationships, value judgments about those ends, and a guide to action for attaining them. Two classic works on Soviet ideology are Robert C. Tucker, *The Soviet Political Mind* (New York: Praeger, 1963) and Nathan Leites, *A Study of Bolshevism* (New York: Free Press, 1953).

44. Ernst B. Haas, "Collective Learning: Some Theoretical Speculations," in Breslauer and Tetlock, *Learning in U.S. and Soviet Foreign Policy*, pp. 62–99; and Albert Bandura, *Social Learning Theory* (Englewood Cliffs, N.J: Prentice Hall, 1977).

45. In our interviews, liberal specialists cited discussions with colleagues, including Western counterparts, as playing a crucial role in their intellectual evolution. Key decision makers such as Gorbachev and Shevardnadze likewise credit formal and informal sessions with these experts as influencing their thinking.

46. Checkel, "Ideas, Institutions, and the Gorbachev Foreign Policy Revolution," Mendelson, "Internal Battles and External Wars"; and Haas, *When Knowledge Is Power.*

As other scholars have made considerable headway in correcting the apolitical nature of most cognitive approaches, my primary aim in this essay is to demonstrate the impact of collective identity norms on actor behavior.

Incorporating constitutive norms of identity into existing cognitive explanations for Soviet foreign policy change allows me to differentiate between the conciliatory realpolitik and idealist perspectives within the New Thinking camp. This distinction has largely escaped students of contemporary Soviet/Russian affairs despite its importance in explaining the evolution of Soviet policy during the Gorbachev years and after.

The conciliatory realpolitik perspective was the dominant outlook among progressive detractors of the Brezhnev leadership's handling of foreign affairs. Proponents criticized the regime's approach on the grounds that its unilateralist and ideology-driven strategy was eroding rather than advancing traditional state interests defined in terms of military security and economic well-being. Soviet practice was self-defeating, having unnecessarily antagonized the West and squandered precious resources with little to show in return. For many, though by no means all, of the reformers who subscribed to this line of thinking, the problem was not the goals of Soviet policy but the means employed to attain them. In this sense, envisaged changes in Kremlin international policy did not reflect a full-fledged reconceptualization of interests.

In contrast, the idealist outlook claimed a much smaller following and was only just emerging in the late 1970s and early 1980s, although it too had its rudimentary precursors. Proponents of this perspective conceived of Soviet interests in ways unrecognizable to realist practitioners of traditional great power politics and even to liberal institutionalists. In addition to promoting a strategy of reassurance to reverse the arms race and eradicate the political sources of military conflict, they sought to inject normative criteria into the formulation and conduct of foreign policy.[47]

Idealists embodied a new identity that held out the possibility of transcending the East-West divide. They viewed Soviet national interests in the context of global problems and values common to all mankind. For them, the failure of the Brezhnev-Gromyko approach resided in both its skewed representation of international political reality and its flawed

---

47. Reflecting on the lessons of the Chernobyl disaster regarding Moscow's less-than-forthcoming initial reports to the international community, by then former foreign minister Shevardnadze wrote, "It tore the blindfold from our eyes and persuaded us that politics and morals could not diverge. We had to gauge our politics constantly by moral criteria" (*The Future Belongs to Freedom* [New York: Free Press, 1991], pp. 175–76).

vision of how the world and the Soviet Union *ought* to be. Genuine peace, according to idealists, could be achieved only on the basis of a common identity. To this end, they envisioned the USSR's joining the community of advanced industrial democracies whose relationships were governed by norms of reciprocity and non-use of force. The Cold War would wither away, its sustaining logic having vanished.

In practice, idealist and conciliatory realpolitik perspectives were not so easily distinguishable. They are best thought of as two ends of a spectrum, with the vast majority of foreign policy reformers distributed along the continuum. Thus the purveyors of New Thinking simultaneously held elements of both worldviews, the precise admixture of which changed over time. This is why it is possible to find inconsistencies in their policy positions, starting with Mikhail Gorbachev, whose thinking underwent considerable evolution during his six years in power.[48]

The existence of contending factions within the reformer camp is also one of the reasons the idealist version of New Thinking took a few years after Gorbachev was chosen general secretary to become state policy.[49] Proponents of foreign policy reform, including top decision makers, held divergent views about the source of the problem and the nature of the prospective solution. In the absence of an agreed-upon blueprint, the initial New Thinking vision articulated by Gorbachev was predictably an amalgam of themes and concepts, some of which even resonated with foreign policy conservatives.[50] It was sufficiently vague to permit political forces with relatively moderate agendas to claim allegiance to a common ideal even as they strived to head off any radical change.[51] For his part,

---

48. This conclusion is based on my reading of Gorbachev's extensive writings and speeches, a large secondary literature, and interviews with senior Gorbachev advisers such as A. Yakovlev, A. Chernyaev, G. Shakhnazarov, and Ye. Velikhov.

49. The faint outlines of the idealist agenda were visible in statements from the April 1985 Central Committee plenum. They became more deeply etched in Gorbachev's report to the Twenty-seventh Party Congress (February 1986) and even more so in his speech before the Nineteenth All-Union Party Conference in the summer of 1988.

50. Gorbachev's much-heralded report to the Twenty-seventh Party Congress was far from a New Thinking manifesto. While the speech contained some significant revisions in Soviet thought, it also offered a generous dose of well-worn Marxist-Leninist polemics about capitalism's inherent militarism and imperialistic tendencies.

51. Most notable was the struggle pitting civilian defense specialists and their party/government allies against the military. The debate grew in intensity as the leadership pursued more radical measures. See Blacker, *Hostage to Revolution*, esp. pp. 144–82; Garthoff, *Deterrence and the Revolution in Soviet Military Doctrine*; Michael McGwire, *Perestroika and Soviet National Security* (Washington, D.C.: Brookings Institution, 1991); Parrott, "Soviet National Security Under Gorbachev"; and articles in Timothy Colton and Thane Gustafson, eds., *Soldiers and the Soviet State: Civil-Military*

Gorbachev remained open to the arguments of advocates of both the conciliatory realpolitik and the idealist perspectives, ultimately siding with the
latter.[52]

The focus of the empirical section of this essay is the neglected idealist
outlook because it is here that we find the newly minted identity and attendant normative commitments that gave New Thinking its transformative
character and made possible the peaceful end of the East-West conflict. As
I have shown, existing liberal explanations that emphasize cognitive evolution can account for many important policy revisions undertaken by the
Gorbachev regime. In doing so, they persuasively demonstrate that ideas
promoted by in-system reformers exerted independent influence on Soviet
behavior, effectively rebuffing realists' materialist conception of interests,
which views ideas solely in instrumental terms[53] (i.e., used by Kremlin
decision makers to justify or make palatable changes necessary for domestic restructuring).[54] But in order to account for New Thinking's idealist
incarnation, which in effect deprived the West of its Cold War enemy,
these liberal approaches must be supplemented with a collective identity
dimension.

The Empirical Case
Origins of New Thinking's Idealist Variant

The ideas and identity that gave New Thinking its revolutionary content
had historical antecedents going back to the Khrushchev era and the

Relations from Brezhnev to Gorbachev (Princeton: Princeton University Press, 1990). The battle to
define New Thinking was also a prominent theme in many of the interviews that I conducted. On
this point, also see two pseudo-memoirs: G. Arbatov, *The System*, and E. Shevardnadze, *The Future
Belongs to Freedom*.

52. A number of Gorbachev's top advisers expressed to me that he came to power with a fairly
sophisticated grasp of broad foreign policy issues and was intent on demilitarizing East-West relations. But he also retained vestiges of "old thinking" about the nature of capitalism, which partly
explains the cautious nature of early Soviet overtures compared to later initiatives. Whether Gorbachev learned, and if so how, remains a matter of debate. See Stein, "Political Learning by Doing."

53. Even liberal macrohistorical and domestic political explanations that accord a role to ideas/beliefs tend to view
them instrumentally. See Snyder, *Myths of Empire*; Deudney and Ikenberry, "Soviet Reform and the End of the
Cold War"; and Mendelson, "Internal Battles and External Wars."

54. There is a parallel here to glasnost and democratization. Many commentators have rightly
pointed out the instrumental character of the democratic turn: reforms would create pressure for
change from below, bring the intelligentsia on board the perestroika bandwagon, help to weaken a
bureaucratic structure hostile to reform, and allow for richer debate to correct past mistakes. On
several occasions, the leadership spoke of democratic reforms as an indispensable companion to

beginnings of de-Stalinization. They have been documented elsewhere and need not be examined here.[55] But one cannot draw a straight line from Khrushchev-inspired reformers—the self-described "children of the Twentieth Party Congress"—to purveyors of the idealist strand of New Thinking almost three decades later, even though in some cases they were same people.[56] Getting to that point required some conceptual leaps that many proved unable or unwilling to make. Those who did underwent a profound evolution that led them to repudiate fundamental axioms of Marxism-Leninism that they had once taken to be true.

It was as a result of both the early success and the disillusioning demise of 1970s superpower rapprochement that liberal *mezhdunarodniki* began to challenge the underlying assumptions of the Brezhnev regime's coercive detente strategy and to formulate an alternative approach. Detractors rejected both the prevailing conception of peaceful coexistence as a form of class struggle and the dominant interpretation of Western accommodationist policies as being compelled by a shift in the "correlation of forces" in favor of socialism. Their conclusion that Western cooperative behavior was in part dispositional rather than wholly circumstantial pointed to the need for more-conciliatory Soviet policies that could be expected to strengthen the hand of "realistic-minded" circles in the elite and thereby elicit Western reciprocity.

With the expansion of East-West detente, liberal reformers were less inclined to view capitalist states as inherently aggressive or to accept the notion of irreconcilable interests between the two social systems. Buoyed by detente's promising early returns, some of these specialists saw the pos-

perestroika. But it is also the case that for many reformers greater individual freedom and steps toward some form of popular rule were goals in themselves, not merely a means to aid perestroika. In-system liberals such as Fydor Burlatsky, Georgi Shakhnazarov, Andrei Grachev, Vitaly Korotich, and others believed strongly in the need for a multiparty system and the rule of law. For them the time had come for the USSR to join the ranks of the democratic states (though not necessarily to emulate the capitalist economic system of those states).

55. See William Zimmerman, *Soviet Perspectives on International Relations, 1956–1967* (Princeton: Princeton University Press, 1969); Lynch, *The Soviet Study of International Relations*; Franklyn Griffiths, "Image, Politics, and Learning in Soviet Behavior Towards the United States" (Ph.D diss., Columbia University, 1972); Checkel, "Ideas, Institutions, and the Gorbachev Foreign Policy Revolution"; Lewin, *The Gorbachev Phenomenon*; and Robert English, "Russia Views the West: The Intellectual and Political Origins of Soviet New Thinking" (Ph.D. diss., Princeton University, 1995).

56. One of the most influential of the early liberal specialist networks was the group of consultants assembled around then Central Committee secretary Yuri Andropov in the early to mid-1960s. The members were Fydor Burlatsky, Georgi Shakhnazarov, Georgi Arbatov, Oleg Bogomolov, Aleksandr Bovin, and Gennadi Gerasimov. Remarkably, all went on to play important roles in the New Thinking drama.

290 · Robert G. Herman

sibility that superpower rapproche-ment could bring about the restructuring of international relations and with it the prospect of eliminating the risk of armed conflict between the two blocs.[57]

The hope of radically recasting East-West relations was most evident in the distinction drawn by Soviet commentators between "negative peace" and "positive peace." The former refers to the absence of war because of mutual deterrence, while the latter connotes a state of pacific relations in which the root causes of conflict have been eliminated. The conceptual link between the ideas of positive peace and the restructuring of international relations on the one hand and the idealist strand of New Thinking on the other is unmistakable.[58] What enabled these ideas to survive the downturn in relations only to reappear in modified form in the Gorbachev era was their partial codification in the series of East-West agreements that collectively composed detente.

The institutionalization of nuclear arms control in the form of the 1972 Anti-Ballistic Missile Treaty, which banned nationwide missile defense systems, and the Strategic Arms Limitations Treaty of the same year, which placed ceilings on offensive weapons, together with accords aimed at regulating superpower rivalry in the Third World (Basic Principles Agreement, BPA) and ratifying the postwar political settlement in Europe (the 1975 Helsinki Accords) constituted a nascent security regime. Embedded in the regime were fledgling norms of behavior that shaped the identity of would-be radical New Thinkers. These diffuse norms represented an attempt to articulate shared aspirations as well as to codify formally extant practices.[59]

---

57. Nikolai Lebedev, "The Struggle of the USSR for the Restructuring of International Relations," *Mezhdunarodnaia zhizn'* 12 (December 1975); and V. Kortunov, "The Relaxation of Tensions and the Struggle of Ideas in Contemporary International Relations," *Voprosy istorii KPSS* 10 (October 1975). Both are cited in Raymond Garthoff, *Detente and Confrontation: American-Soviet Relations from Nixon to Reagan*, rev. ed. (Washington, D.C.: Brookings Institution, 1994), pp. 64 and 49, respectively.

58. Nor is it surprising. The purveyors of these ideas in those two time periods were often the same people. See V. Petrovsky, "The Struggle of the USSR for Detente in the Seventies," *Novaya i noveiyshaya istoriya* 1 (January/February 1981); and D. Tomashevsky, "Na puti k korennoi perestroike mezhdunarodnykh otnoshenii" [Toward a radical restructuring of international relations], *MEiMO* 1 (January 1975): 3–13.

59. See George, Farley, and Dallin, *U.S.-Soviet Security Cooperation*; Garthoff, *Detente and Confrontation*; Nye, "Nuclear Learning and U.S.-Soviet Security Regimes"; Harald Müller, "The Internalization of Principles, Norms, and Rules by Governments: The Case of Security Regimes," in Volker Rittberger, ed., *Regime Theory and International Relations*, pp. 361–88 (Oxford: Oxford University Press, Clarendon Press, 1993); and Genreikh Trofimenko, "SSSR-SSHA: Mirnoe sosushchestvovanie kak norma vzaimootnoshenii" [USSR-USA: Peaceful coexistence as a norm of mutual relations], *SShA* 2 (February 1974): 3–17.

Regrettably, neither Moscow nor Washington was prepared to countenance the potentially far-reaching implications of the ABM Treaty or the BPA.[60] That all changed when the Gorbachev regime placed reasonable sufficiency and finite deterrence on the policy agenda[61] and made good on its pledge to seek political solutions to festering regional conflicts in Afghanistan, Cambodia, Angola, and elsewhere in the developing world.[62]

The Basic Principles Agreement was especially relevant to the emergence of the idealist outlook in the Gorbachev years. The accord was destined to become a casualty of continuous superpower efforts to shape political outcomes in the Third World for unilateral advantage.[63] But for liberal *mezhdunarodniki* analyzing the reasons for the demise of detente, the accord came to be viewed as a stillborn attempt to create a regime premised on nonintervention and nonresort to force. What the two sides initially regarded as a commonsense and self-interested way to constrain provocative behavior was later endowed with normative significance by New Thinkers whose vision of the USSR precluded the expansionist and militaristic Kremlin strategies they now concluded had helped destroy detente.[64] They recognized the transformative but wasted potential of the BPA. The problem, according to these foreign policy revisionists, was not that superpower detente had been overambitious. To the contrary, detente had been too timid; it had neglected to address the root causes of the Cold

---

60. Despite the failure to grasp these implications, a strong case can still be made that the ABM Treaty, by codifying mutual vulnerability, helped to turn the practice of non-use of nuclear weapons into an international norm on which New Thinkers would later build. The first part of the argument is put forward by Nina Tannenwald, "Dogs That Don't Bark: The United States, the Role of Norms, and the Non-Use of Nuclear Weapons Since 1945" (Ph.D. diss., Cornell University, 1995).

61. This was first done in Gorbachev's January 1986 proposal to eliminate all nuclear weapons by the year 2000. The text of the plan appeared in *International Affairs* 3 (March 1986).

62. On changes in Soviet Third World policy, see Valkenier, "New Thinking About the Third World"; Jerry Hough, *The Struggle for the Third World: Soviet Debates and American Options* (Washington, D.C.: Brookings Institution, 1986); and Mark Katz, *Gorbachev's Military Policy in the Third World* (New York: Praeger, 1989).

63. One of the best treatments of the demise of the BPA and of detente in general is Garthoff, *Detente and Confrontation*. Also see Harry Gelman, *The Brezhnev Politburo and the Decline of Detente* (Ithaca: Cornell University Press, 1984).

64. New Thinkers were not suggesting that the U.S. had lived up to its commitments under the BPA. However, Georgi Arbatov and other liberal Americanists did point out that important segments of the U.S. foreign policy establishment had opposed the war in Vietnam and were taking steps to prevent such imperialist interventions in the future (e.g., the War Powers Act). This, they argued, would render superpower military involvement in the periphery anachronistic.

War conflict, thereby forgoing any chance to move from managed rivalry to full-fledged collaboration.[65]

The human rights provisions of the Helsinki Accords similarly affected the ideational evolution of would-be idealists, albeit indirectly, by giving rise to a network of committed activists in the USSR and Eastern Europe.[66] Their courageous efforts, while more or less successfully suppressed by the various communist governments, did not go unnoticed by Soviet liberal reformers, anti-Stalinists all, who could condemn the dissidents' confrontational tactics but could no longer deny the validity of their simple message about the regime's harsh repression and the absence of basic freedoms. Dissidents such as Andrei Sakharov, together with Western transnational partners whose unwavering support for human rights *and* detente bolstered their credibility in the eyes of Soviet in-system reformers, confronted these liberal reformers with the dark reality of the regime of which they were very much a part.[67]

The response by liberal *mezhdunarodniki* to the crash in East-West relations was largely confined to revisionist scholarship on international relations theory, although some specific regime policies were criticized by institute experts and specialists in the apparat.[68] The Institute of World

---

65. Among the most forceful proponents of this view was Aleksei Arbatov, head of IMEMO's arms control and disarmament section. This analysis of the failure of detente was shared by a number of younger specialists then at ISKAN, among them Andrei Kortunov and Sergei Karaganov. One of their more interesting conclusions was a retrospective appreciation of the Carter administration's early efforts to push beyond the modest rapprochement of the early 1970s, most notably in the area of nuclear arms control and resolving Third World conflicts.

66. I am grateful to Daniel Thomas for his comments on the role of the Helsinki Accords and the CSCE process more generally with respect to the birth and/or strengthening of human rights movements throughout the communist bloc. How ironic that an agreement designed to stabilize Europe by codifying postwar arrangements would contribute to the collapse of communist power and the birth of democratic successor states. It did so by empowering small groups of human rights campaigners whose activities helped to erode the legitimacy of the various regimes.

67. This is the composite picture to emerge from numerous interviews with Soviet reformers. Without trying to portray themselves as having always been secretly in agreement with Sakharov and other regime opponents, several liberal specialists recounted how the dissidents' very visible activities speeded their own recognition that repression and denial of individual rights remained endemic to the Soviet system. The ambivalence that many in-system reformers felt toward the dissidents is apparent in Georgi Arbatov's memoir, *The System.*

68. The two policy decisions that drew the most fire were the intervention in Afghanistan and the reflexive modernization of medium-range nuclear missiles targeted on Western Europe—the SS-20 debacle. Critics were still circumspect in expressing their views, but there is little question that these two actions were regarded by most foreign policy reformers as egregious mistakes and, more important, as symptomatic of the flawed assumptions on which the USSR's overall international strategy rested. Oleg Bogomolov, director of the Institute of Economics of the World Socialist System, circulated one of the few pointed attacks; see "Afghanistan As Seen in 1980," *Moscow News* 30, July 30–August 6, 1988.

Economy and International Relations (IMEMO) took the lead in promoting an analysis that emphasized states rather than classes as the principal actors on the world stage, accelerating interdependence, the primacy of nonclass values, the role of nonmaterial factors (e.g., domestic politics, culture, individual leaders' worldviews) in determining states' interests, and implicitly, a more benign view of capitalism.[69] All of these themes were to become central tenets of the USSR's new course, having been conveyed to future CPSU chairman Gorbachev through institute director Aleksandr Yakovlev (the reformist former Central Committee secretary banished to Canada to be Soviet ambassador and brought back to Moscow in 1983 at Gorbachev's behest to take the helm of IMEMO) and his successor Yevgeny Primakov.

Joining IMEMO analysts in this self-conscious attempt to purge Soviet foreign policy of its ideological underpinnings were like-minded colleagues at the Institute of the United States and Canada (ISKAN), the Institute of Economics of the World Socialist System (IEMSS), and other Academy of Sciences think tanks, together with sympathetic experts in the government and party bureaucracy. With growing temerity they advanced cogent critiques of Soviet international strategy despite the stifling impact on foreign policy–related discourse of the burgeoning conflict with the West.

As alluded to earlier, many of the international security and arms control concepts associated with New Thinking were originally developed by peace scholars and other liberal-Left experts in the West and transmitted to pro-reform *mezhdunarodniki* and aspiring civilian defense analysts in the USSR through transnational networks.[70] None of these linkages proved more important than the membership of ISKAN director Georgi Arbatov on the Independent Commission on Disarmament and Security Issues chaired by Olaf Palme.[71] Under the tutelage of West German arms control expert and prominent Social Democratic Party official Egon Bahr, the influential Arbatov became a convert to common security[72] and his insti-

---

69. Checkel, "Ideas, Institutions, and the Gorbachev Foreign Policy Revolution." Among the relevant articles appearing in the institute's journal were Oleg Bikov, "Leninskaya politika mira i yeyo voploshcheniye v deyatel'nosti KPSS" [Lenin's peace policy and its implementation in the activities of the CPSU], *MEiMO* 3 (March 1984); and V. Lukov and D. Tomashevsky, "Interesy chelovechestva i mirovaya politika" [Human interests and world politics], *MEiMO* 4 (April 1985).
70. Evangelista, *Taming the Bear*, and Risse-Kappen, "Ideas Do Not Float Freely."
71. The commission's final report was published under the title *Common Security: A Blueprint for Survival* (New York: Simon and Schuster, 1982).
72. Author's interview with Arbatov and several ISKAN analysts.

tute became the entrepreneurial source of proposals for asymmetrical cuts in nuclear and conventional arms and for nonoffensive-force postures later taken up by Gorbachev.[73]

Other transnational links that influenced Soviet security policy included Soviet specialists' contacts with European alternative defense proponents such as Danish physicist Anders Boserup (through Pugwash Conference working groups)[74] and Academy of Sciences vice president and Gorbachev adviser Yevgeny Velikhov's participation in joint projects with U.S. arms control experts.[75] The fact that these Western specialists were critical of their own governments' policies as well as those of the USSR enhanced their standing with Soviet interlocutors.

Yet even more important than the contribution of transnational networks to the eclipse of the image of the West as implacably hostile and to the diffusion of knowledge about mitigating the pernicious effects of the security dilemma was the role of these specialists in the identity evolution of Soviet in-system reformers. During the heyday of detente, the Brezhnev regime did its best to insulate Soviet society from subversive bourgeois liberal ideas. Still, through transnational contacts, progressive *mezhdunarodniki* were exposed to Western conceptions of human rights and sensitized to the flaws in the Soviet system by staunchly pro-detente counterparts in

---

73. ISKAN defense specialists such as Andrei Kokoshin, Valentin Larionov, Andrei Kortunov, and Sergei Karaganov turned out increasingly ambitious proposals for reducing and restructuring Soviet nuclear and conventional forces. Their contributions and those of other pro-reform specialists to New Thinking were cited by Anatoly Dobrynin, the longtime ambassador to the United States, appointed by Gorbachev to head the Central Committee International Department. "For a Nuclear-Free World As We Approach the Twenty-first Century," *Kommunist* 9 (June 1986). Also see Pat Litherland, "Gorbachev and Arms Control: Civilian Experts and Soviet Policy," Peace Research Report 12, University of Bradford (UK), November 1986.

74. The Soviet ambassador to Copenhagen in the mid-1980s, Lev Mendelevich, took an active interest in Boserup's work. After Mendelevich was appointed head of the Foreign Ministry's Evaluation and Planning Directorate, he brought to bear some of the scientist's ideas. According to my interviews with former high-ranking Foreign Ministry officials Georgi Kornienko and Viktor Komplektov, a few months before Gorbachev's historic December 1988 UN speech announcing unilateral force cuts and modest restructuring, Boserup was brought in to meet with senior staffers to discuss issues related to nonprovocative defense. On the contribution of Pugwash to East-West relations in this period, see Joseph Rotblat and V. I. Goldanskii, eds., *Global Problems and Common Security: Annals of Pugwash 1988* (Berlin: Springer-Verlag, 1989).

75. Author's interview. Velikhov chaired the Committee of Soviet Scientists for Peace, Against the Nuclear Threat, which lobbied the regime not to match the U.S. SDI program but to rely on cheaper, less-destabilizing countermeasures. Velikhov willingly credits discussions with Western counterparts, particularly the members of the American Academy of Sciences arms control working group (SISAC) for imparting knowledge on the finer points of nuclear strategy and persuading him on the wisdom of the superpowers' adopting a minimum deterrent posture and banning nuclear tests.

the U.S. and Western Europe.[76] They also witnessed the advantages of pacific international partnership, political pluralism and democratic governance, and the establishment of the rule of law.

Many of these specialists had the opportunity to travel to the West and, in the case of ISKAN postgraduates, to spend several months working in the U.S. at the embassy in Washington or at the UN mission in New York. Firsthand experience with the West did not necessarily send liberal reformers rushing to try to replicate on Soviet soil a free-market system and democratic political institutions. But by their own admission it instilled in them an abiding appreciation for the numerous strengths of these societies and purged them of many deeply ingrained myths and stereotypes about capitalism.[77]

Contact with the West gave Soviet reformers a new lens through which to view their own society: the stifling repression, pervasive secrecy, lagging living standards, and adversarial relationship with every non-communist country on the Eurasian landmass. By the late 1970s a number of in-system regime critics, already firmly ensconced in the Westernizer camp, were making the transition from anti-Stalinist reformers to democratic socialists and in some cases, to social democrats.[78] Direct and indirect exposure to the West may have helped Soviet reformers to comprehend the magnitude of the USSR's systemic crisis, but, far more important, this contact influenced the content of the program that they formulated and then proceeded to implement once they gained power.

Liberal reformers who developed this new identity decreasingly defined the Western threat in broad political-ideological terms. The adversary, as they saw it, was the bellicose strategy pursued by right-wing hawks in the West (and the provocative Soviet policies that helped generate support for it), not the democratic capitalist system per se (some of the founding principles of which this cadre of Soviet reformers now accepted).

The intervention in Afghanistan was a pivotal event in the identity evo-

---

76. On the diffusion of Western values to Russia/USSR, see Frederick Starr, "The Changing Nature of Change in the USSR," in Seweryn Bialer and Michael Mandelbaum, eds., *Gorbachev's Russia and American Foreign Policy*, pp. 3–35 (Boulder: Westview, 1988).

77. Author's interviews with liberal *institutchiki*, particularly those who had spent time in the West when in their twenties.

78. This progression is admittedly difficult to track because fledgling democrats in the policy establishment were not prepared to jeopardize their positions by openly attacking the foundations of the Soviet political system. Still, among the ranks of the reformers was a smaller group whom, I later learned through extensive interviewing, colleagues credited with having held Western-oriented views regarding a multiparty system, individual rights, an independent judiciary, etc. There was no definitive consensus, but prominent names most frequently mentioned included Georgi Shakhnazarov, Vitaly Korotich, Fydor Burlatsky, Aleksandr Bovin, and Andrei Grachev.

lution of liberal *mezhdunarodniki*.[79] Foreign policy reformers saw their unprecedented admission of Kremlin complicity in the fall of detente give way to a more profound critique of Soviet international behavior. Beyond conventional arguments that intervention would prove politically costly (e.g., deal a deathblow to an already ailing detente) and militarily ineffective, some of these specialists saw the introduction of Soviet troops as a violation of international law governing the resort to force and the sanctity of interstate borders.[80] In essence, they were rejecting the Brezhnev Doctrine, a position that they articulated with greater force a few years later in connection with the rise of the Solidarity trade union movement in Poland and the possibility of armed Soviet intervention.[81]

It was becoming clear to a growing number of reformers that the USSR could not take its place among the world's "civilized nations" if it insisted on violating at home and abroad the norms of behavior governing Western democratic regimes' treatment of their own citizens and relations between member states of that community.[82] It is the significance of this identity-derived normative dimension in molding the ultimate character

79. This was one of my most definitive findings, based on interviews with Soviet scholars, party and government officials, journalists, etc.

80. Shevardnadze was one of the first to give public voice to this position (and then only after three years as foreign minister) with his extraordinary admission that the USSR had "violated the norms of proper behavior." Some specialists (e.g., Vladimir Lukin, Aleksandr Bovin) had made similar arguments years earlier at the time of the Warsaw Pact's intervention in Czechoslovakia to crush the reformist regime of Alexander Dubcek. A number of *zapiski* written during the 1970s, mostly by experts at IEMSS, indirectly attacked the so-called Brezhnev Doctrine. Also see Bogomolov, "Afghanistan as Seen in 1980."

81. The Institute of Economics of the World Socialist System (IEMSS) worked diligently in *zapiski* and in conversations between director Bogomolov and key decision makers, including KGB chief Andropov, to persuade the Soviet leadership that the political crisis accompanying the rise of Solidarity could be resolved without resort to force. Secret reports prepared by institute experts emphasized the popular support enjoyed by the illegal labor union and also pointed out, using carefully crafted language, that armed intervention would do irreparable harm to East-West relations. Analyst Yevgeny Ambartsumov went further still, arguing that the Polish crisis was rooted in contradictions inherent in socialism and was not a product of imperialist subversion as the Kremlin claimed—a stand for which he was punished by the authorities.

82. A similar but less starkly moral argument was advanced by Yakovlev. A staunch opponent of the invasion, he felt strongly that the withdrawal of Soviet troops from Afghanistan was the linchpin of any possible shift in East-West relations because the intervention seemed to corroborate the West's basest fears about Soviet intentions. According to colleagues, Georgi Arbatov made a similar case in suggesting that such armed intervention by the great powers had become anachronistic, citing the popular and elite-level backlash against the U.S. involvement in Vietnam. This line of reasoning flowed from an earlier book in which he contended that in the age of nuclear deterrence armed force was of diminishing utility: *Ideologicheskaya bor'ba v sovremennykh mezhdunarodnykh otnosheni-yakh* [The ideological struggle in contemporary international relations] (Moscow: Politizdat, 1970).

of the Gorbachev foreign policy revolution that is beyond the reach of realist and liberal explanations.

The vision of Soviet society and the USSR's relationship to the outside world that united moderate and radical reformers is conveyed in the term *normal country*. Virtually every New Thinker I interviewed or who has spoken or written on the topic has invoked it to describe his or her hopes for the nation. And while not all of them meant precisely the same thing, the general notion was not difficult to discern. At the most elemental level it meant removing the "absurdity and irrationality" that was everyday life.[83] In the economic sphere, that translated to the necessity of a system with rational incentives that produced food and consumer goods in sufficient quantities that citizens would not suffer the indignity of perpetual lines. In the political sphere it meant once and for all throwing off the yoke of Stalinism and moving in the direction of democratic governance (i.e., respect for individual rights, establishment of the rule of law, competitive elections).[84] With respect to interstate relations, becoming a normal country required abandoning Marxism-Leninism as a guide for defining state interests and pursuing either an enlightened realpolitik dedicated to advancing traditional security goals or, alternatively, a foreign policy based on the norms and principles associated with the bolder version of New Thinking.

Ideas reflecting both the amoral realpolitik perspective and its fledgling idealist competitor started to reach those who later would wield political power in the Gorbachev era. Dispirited by the failure of successive regimes to take remedial steps to redress economic and political stagnation and to repair the dangerous rift in superpower relations,[85]

---

83. The phrase is Vladimir Petrovsky's, but it accurately expressed the view of the vast majority of the reformers I interviewed.

84. There is a caveat. Among the reformers were those I've termed "economic modernizers," who sought technocratic solutions to the Soviet Union's problems and were either agnostic about or hostile to corresponding political reforms. Two members of this school of thought were Nikolai Ogarkov and Sergei Akhromeyev, successive heads of the military's general staff. They reasoned that without structural changes in the economy the USSR would be unable to compete militarily with the technologically advanced capitalist powers in the coming decades. Like-minded commentators praised the path taken by China and South Korea, authoritarian states that had enjoyed stunning rates of growth in harnessing the scientific-technological revolution. For the most part, Soviet economic modernizers envisaged the state as continuing to play the dominant role in economic reconstruction, thereby putting them at odds with proponents of greater decentralization of decision-making authority closer to Western capitalist models.

85. The hardest blow came with Yuri Andropov. A pragmatic conservative whose long-standing contact with liberal reformers and early admission of serious domestic and foreign policy problems gave rise to expectations for meaningful change, he proved incapable of seeing that the causes of the Soviet Union's predicament were systemic.

nascent New Thinkers nevertheless were determined not to abandon their cause. They refined their critique, circulated heterodox views on contemporary international relations, and cultivated support among certain members of the leadership, most notably Mikhail Gorbachev, who by 1983 had become a major force on the Politburo and Andropov's heir apparent.

Examination of relevant CPSU and individual institute archives reveals that by this time Gorbachev was already on the receiving end of secret *zapiski* from progressive specialists. While generally avoiding assessments of specific Soviet actions (with the exception of the Afghanistan intervention and deployment of SS-20s), these analysts succeeded in raising first-order questions about the USSR's overall international strategy. There was also a collection of more than a hundred white papers written during Andropov's tenure by experts from an array of disciplines on the full panoply of problems confronting the USSR. They were done at the behest of Politburo member Gorbachev with the help of Nikolai Ryzhkov, head of the Central Committee's Economic Department. A few years later, addressing a group of sympathetic intellectuals to encourage them to redouble their efforts in the struggle for reform, Gorbachev publicly confirmed the existence of the white papers. Recalling his earlier frank conversations with many of the authors, Gorbachev stated: "The results of these discussions and their analyses formed the basis for the decisions of the April [1985] plenum and the first steps thereafter."[86]

In addition to his close personal relationship with Yakovlev, who provided a window onto innovative work being done at IMEMO, the future general secretary had contact with a range of other prominent liberal thinkers. Among them were ISKAN director Arbatov, Political Science Association chief Georgi Shakhnazarov, journal (*Ogonek*) editor Vitaly Korotich, head of the Institute of Economics and Industrial Organization Abel Aganbegyan, and senior staffers from the International Department of the Central Committee Secretariat. Gorbachev's practice of seeking out experts and engaging them in wide-ranging discussions became institutionalized once he was elevated to the *CPSU* chairmanship. He empowered pro-reform specialists to fill in his sparse vision,[87] which at that point more closely resembled conciliatory realpolitik than its incipient idealist rival.

86. "To Build Up the Intellectual Potential of Restructuring," *Pravda*, January 7, 1989; and *FBIS-SOV*, January 9, 1989, pp. 52–64.
87. Personal interviews with Yakovlev, Chernyaev, G. Arbatov, Bogomolov, Shakhnazarov, Oleg Grinevsky, Zagladin, and others.

The New Thinking Revolution

During the Gorbachev period Soviet international policy evolved from a comparatively modest set of initiatives aimed at ratcheting down the East-West confrontation to a daring program for completely revamping the USSR's relations with the West and the rest of the world. Focusing on Moscow's Eastern Europe strategy and on Soviet military doctrine and arms control practices, I show that profound changes in these areas reflected the success of purveyors of the idealist variant of New Thinking. Capitalizing on the failure of the early Gorbachev line to elicit reciprocal Western restraint, radicalized *mezhdunarodniki* persuaded Kremlin decision makers to embrace their analysis and policy prescriptions. Elements of the idealist version of New Thinking were incorporated into leadership statements and initiatives from the outset of Gorbachev's tenure as CPSU chairman, although it became the dominant perspective in Soviet policy only in 1988–1989.[88] Beginning with the plan to eliminate nuclear weapons by the year 2000 and the general secretary's "Political Report to the Twenty-seventh Party Congress" and culminating in Gorbachev's historic December 1988 speech at the United Nations and decision to tolerate the collapse of successive communist regimes in Eastern Europe, Soviet interests were redefined, consistent with the rival vision of the Soviet Union put forward by radical specialists.

Contrary to the view of realist-minded skeptics in the West that Moscow was trying to make virtue of necessity by cloaking an unavoidable redirection of international policy in noble language, the New Thinking course pursued by the Gorbachev Politburo starting about late 1987 was the product of decades-long intellectual evolution that was influenced but not determined by material factors. It embodied both new understandings about how the world works and normative judgments about how it should. What initially looked to suspicious NATO governments like a straightforward case of survival-driven adaptive behavior cleverly packaged to portray the USSR as the champion of inspiring, high-minded ideals was nothing less than a long-time-in-the-making metamorphosis of intellect and conscience.[89]

---

88. Translating ambitious ideas into concrete policy would take time. The new leadership first had to consolidate its position, which it did beginning with an enormous turnover of personnel at the upper echelons of the party and state apparat. See Thane Gustafson and Dawn Mann, "Gorbachev's First Year: Building Power and Authority," *Problems of Communism* 35, no. 3 (May/June 1986): 1–19; Jerry Hough, "Gorbachev Consolidating Power," *Problems of Communism* 36, no. 4 (July/August 1987): 21–43; and Parrott, "Soviet National Security Under Gorbachev."

89. The West's initial response to Gorbachev's New Thinking was far from uniform. It ranged from outright dismissal by Reagan administration hawks to varying degrees of enthusiasm in the German elite, including some in the conservative Kohl government; see Risse-Kappen, "Ideas Do Not Float Freely."

Arms Control and Military Doctrine

The drastic changes in Soviet defense policy that paved the way for the end of the Cold War rivalry were not on the incoming regime's original agenda. The new team in the Kremlin hoped to alter the perilous trajectory of superpower relations through renewed summit meetings and a number of modest arms control concessions (e.g., a freeze on the deployment of SS-20 missiles and a temporary moratorium on nuclear tests)[90] designed to convey a more moderate strategy and greater flexibility at the bargaining table.

At the same time, evidence of radical inclinations at the highest levels was not hard to find. Dismissed in the West as another in a long line of transparently propagandistic Soviet disarmament ploys designed to play to world public opinion, the January 1986 proposal for a nuclear-free world gave every indication of being a serious initiative. It differed from past grandiose pronouncements both in laying out a specific, sequential approach to reductions and, more important, in demonstrating an understanding of the nuclear revolution and the dangerous fallacy of a unilateral path to security. According to Vladimir Petrovsky, a respected international relations theorist and practitioner who helped draft the documents that became the basis of the proposal, the plan also captured Gorbachev's personal commitment to disarmament on ethical as well as on economic and security grounds.[91] In statements aimed at explaining Moscow's thinking on contemporary international relations, the Soviet leader frequently expressed doubts about the morality of nuclear deterrence. It was a view he shared with Ronald Reagan and one that led them to flirt with a pact to eliminate strategic nuclear arms at the Reykjavik summit.[92]

The vigorously contested report to the party convocation in February

90. The West was quick to dismiss both steps as propaganda gambits rather than good faith overtures. In the case of the unilateral halt to nuclear testing, NATO governments did not appreciate the political capital expended by Gorbachev to override the intense objections of the military establishment. Accounts of the military's opposition are based on interviews with officials who participated in high-level policy meetings, including Yevgeny Velikhov, Oleg Grinevsky, and Aleksandr Yakovlev.
91. Author's interview. Gorbachev's personal foreign policy adviser, Anatoly Chernyaev, similarly stressed to me the significance of the "moral dimensions" of the revolution in Soviet international policy, citing both the desire to eradicate nuclear weapons and the commitment to forgo armed force in favor of negotiated agreements in Eastern Europe and in the developing world.
92. For an account of the summit proceedings, including the controversy over this elusive disarmament agreement, see Don Oberdorfer, *The Turn: From Cold War to a New Era, 1983–1990: The United States and the Soviet Union* (New York: Poseidon, 1991).

1986[93] provided further evidence that radical New Thinkers were already influencing Politburo policy debates.[94] Reiterating earlier statements about the need for new approaches in Soviet international praxis, Gorbachev embraced common security and endorsed the principles of reasonable sufficiency and nonprovocative defense that were already being promoted by maverick civilian analysts—albeit cautiously, given the strong taboo on public discussion of questions related to strategy and force posture.

The general secretary's declared intentions and some meaningful doctrinal modifications (e.g., a shift in the official goal from war-fighting to war prevention) notwithstanding,[95] actual Soviet military policy changed relatively little in the early Gorbachev years. A major obstacle was the military high command, which persisted in trying to define reasonable sufficiency and nonoffensive defense in such a way as to deflect efforts to overhaul the armed forces and thereby safeguard its institutional autonomy.[96] Nor was a political leadership that continued to harbor doubts about U.S. objectives ready to translate those abstract concepts into bold, concrete arms control measures.

93. "Central Committee of the CPSU Political Report to the Twenty-seventh Party Congress," *Kommunist* 5 (March 1986). According to interviews with participants in the drafting sessions and related discussions, including A. Yakovlev, G. Arbatov, V. Zagladin, and A. Grachev, there was intense infighting over the portions of the report dealing with foreign and military policy. One of the major battles concerned the war in Afghanistan. A preliminary draft contained an explicit call for the withdrawal of Soviet troops, but the final version was watered down considerably.

94. While the document did not abandon the notion of rivalry between the two social systems, it did transcend the USSR's signature zero-sum view of international politics, summed up in the perennial Russian question "kto - kogo?" or Who prevails over whom? Similarly, in discussing economic interdependence, "global problems affecting all of humanity," and the primacy of nonclass values, the Gorbachev team was unceremoniously jettisoning Marxism-Leninism's Manichaean worldview, which had structured Soviet thinking since the Bolshevik Revolution. The USSR was casting aside its historically self-regarding view of the world in affirming a global commonality of interests. One measure of the Kremlin's earnestness was the alacrity with which it moved to bolster the effectiveness of international institutions, most prominently the United Nations, by deepening multilateral cooperation.

95. Garthoff, *Deterrence and the Revolution in Soviet Military Doctrine*, esp. pp. 101–8. In May 1987 at a meeting of Warsaw Pact defense ministers, it was announced that defensive operations would henceforth be the primary means to repel aggression. They also proposed that the two blocs reduce their forces to levels that would preclude the capability to mount offensive operations; see "On the Military Doctrine of the Member States of the Warsaw Pact," *Pravda*, May 30, 1987.

96. Contrary to civilian experts' conception of New Thinking, in which the USSR would escape the parity trap by restructuring its forces based on the notion of sufficiency, Defense Minister Dmitri Yazov held fast to the view that "military strategic parity remains the decisive factor in preventing war at the present time." Yazov amplified on his views in *Na strazhe sotsializma i mira* [On guard for socialism and peace] (Moscow: Voyenizdat, 1987).

The turning point came when Moscow moved to de-link a prospective agreement to ban all land-based intermediate range nuclear missiles from the impasse over the proposed American Star Wars antimissile system and reductions in the superpower strategic nuclear arsenals. Gorbachev attributed the decision to lobbying by civilian defense experts[97] and discussions with foreign intellectual and cultural figures gathered in Moscow in February 1987 for a conference titled "For a World Without Nuclear Weapons, for Humanity's Survival."[98]

Acceptance of the previously vilified "zero option" was the first crucial step toward implementation of the agenda formulated by radical New Thinkers. It reflected a substantial redefinition of Soviet security interests and marked a dramatic departure from past policy. The treaty's ban on an entire category of newly deployed nuclear weapons required deeply asymmetrical cuts in Soviet forces. Eager to extend glasnost to the secretive military establishment, the Soviet leader agreed to unprecedented intrusive verification provisions.[99] In the stroke of a pen, Gorbachev and his allies had confounded Western forecasters and Soviet foreign policy moderates alike.[100]

The accord proved empowering for ardent reformers because it was tantamount to official admission that the original deployment of SS-20s—

---

97. Following the near-momentous meeting in Reykjavik, a group of experts met with Gorbachev to persuade him to seek a separate deal on INF. Meanwhile, institute specialists wrote a number of *zapiski* urging the Soviet leader to take the lead to alter the course of East-West relations. One, which was prepared by IEMSS and, Yakovlev confirmed, discussed by members of the Politburo ("Thoughts on the Agenda of the Upcoming Session of the Political Consultative Commission of the Warsaw Pact," March 2, 1987), outlined with unusual bluntness the need for the USSR to dismantle the Soviet threat to Western Europe through unilateral and negotiated reductions in military forces and the adoption of a strictly defensive posture.

98. M. S. Gorbachev, *Perestroika: New Thinking for Our Country and the World* (New York: Harper and Row, 1987), p. 153.

99. Soviet support for intrusive on-site inspections was first evidenced in the 1986 Stockholm Agreement of the Conference on Security and Cooperation in Europe. Gorbachev was eager to demonstrate Moscow's greater openness for two reasons. First, he and his civilian advisers knew that excessive secrecy had been extremely counterproductive, since it lent credence to Western hawks' assessments of Soviet intentions. As Foreign Minister Shevardnadze observed, comprehensive verification measures were vital to promote trust and "a norm of political reliability."

Second, they believed that openness was a hallmark of democratic systems and a practice that the "new" Soviet Union should emulate. My thanks to Ann Florini for her comments on emerging norms of transparency in international arms control.

100. Soviet moderates were not necessarily opposed to the INF Treaty. Most were firmly supportive of efforts to control the arms race. However, they distrusted the Reagan administration and were concerned about establishing a precedent of asymmetrical reductions in Soviet forces; author's interviews with high-ranking Foreign Ministry officials Georgi Kornienko, Viktor Komplektov, Mikhail Zamyatin, and others.

and by extension much of Moscow's international security policy—had been fatally flawed. In acceding to the Western demand that it scrap its most modern medium-range missiles, the Soviet regime showed it was coming to terms with the USSR's role in detente's collapse, an analysis proffered by radicalized *mezhdunarodniki* in support of their more benign view of capitalist states. These specialists responded to the Intermediate Range Nuclear Forces (INF) accord by intensifying their efforts on behalf of increasingly far-reaching measures to overhaul Soviet defense strategy and force structure.[101]

In the months following conclusion of the accord, articles by emboldened civilian defense analysts began to appear in several publications. With growing confidence, these commentators advanced proposals to extend to strategic nuclear and conventional forces the conceptual breakthrough that sealed the INF deal and in so doing gave content to often amorphous New Thinking proclamations. The battle for the hearts and minds of the Gorbachev leadership to determine which version of New Thinking would prevail had entered a decisive and openly contentious phase.[102]

The intellectual work, political battling, and "lobbying" by radical civilian defense specialists was rewarded when Gorbachev announced before the UN that Moscow would reduce troop levels by five hundred thousand within two years and would destroy ten thousand tanks, eighty-five hun-

---

101. Gorbachev's speech on the occasion of the seventieth anniversary of the October Revolution provided further stimulus in signaling a more permissive attitude on the part of the leadership toward critical, public examination of foreign policy issues past and present; "October and Restructuring: The Revolution Goes On," *Kommunist* 17 (December 1987), speech delivered at a special joint session of the Central Committee and Supreme Soviet, November 2, 1987.

102. In the spring of 1988, Aleksei Arbatov, the IMEMO defense analyst who by virtue of director Yevgeny Primakov's close relationship with Gorbachev and his own links to the Foreign Ministry had lines to top decision makers, published a comprehensive two-part article in the institute's journal ("Deep Reductions in Strategic Arms," *MEiMO* 4 and 5 [April and May 1988]; reprinted in Steve Hirsch, ed., *MEiMO: New Soviet Voices on Foreign and Economic Policy*, pp. 435–52 and 453–70 [Washington, D.C.: Bureau of National Affairs, 1989]). Arbatov outlined deep cuts in superpower nuclear arsenals and implicitly argued for greater flexibility by Moscow in ongoing negotiations. A few months later, Arbatov upped the ante. He directly contradicted the military and challenged the political leadership in arguing that reasonable sufficiency did not mean the USSR should endeavor to preserve nuclear parity. Contending that the West was pursuing a competitive strategy of embroiling the Soviet Union in a resource-depleting arms race, Arbatov insisted that the USSR should "proceed on the principle of reasonable sufficiency and drop out of the West-imposed race for parity" ("Parity and Reasonable Sufficiency," *International Affairs* 10 [October 1988]: 75–86. A number of specialists offered parallel prescriptions for conventional forces. Among the most influential was Andrei Kokoshin; see A. Kokoshin and V. Larionov, "The Confrontation of Conventional Forces in the Context of Ensuring Strategic Stability," *MEiMO* 6 (June 1988): 23–30.

dred artillery systems, and eight hundred combat aircraft. He pledged to demobilize six Soviet divisions stationed in Czechoslovakia, Hungary, and East Germany and said that remaining divisions would be reorganized and "given a different structure from today's, which will become unambiguously defensive after the removal of a large number of their tanks." Assault landing and river-crossing forces were also to be withdrawn.[103] It was not so much the magnitude of the reductions that drew Western attention as the stunning shift from an offensive to a defensive military posture and the retreat from traditional Russian/Soviet conceptions of security that these unilateral moves represented.

Gorbachev's UN speech had the hoped-for impact, propelling the U.S. and the USSR to dismantle the military confrontation that had defined their relationship for four decades. Having taken up the agenda urged by radical civilian defense experts, Gorbachev steered the superpowers toward a series of sweeping agreements that transformed the security situation on the European continent and advanced the cause of global peace and security. In less than three years East and West concluded the strategic nuclear arms reduction treaty (START I) and the conventional forces in Europe accord (CFE Treaty) and made substantial progress on eliminating chemical weapons and on follow-on cuts in the strategic arsenals.

The reconceptualization of Soviet security interests that made these agreements possible reflected a new collective identity in which a critical core of the Soviet leadership no longer viewed the West as the "other." When Gorbachev, Shevardnadze, and others spoke of depriving the West of an enemy, they were not only alluding to the possibility of the USSR's unilaterally dropping out of the arms race; they were expressing aspirations of joining the community of democratic states. They now understood that even significant disarmament accords would not suffice to overcome the East-West divide. Only a common identity would permit the two sides to transform their relationship, because at its core the Cold War was a political-ideological conflict, especially for the U.S., with its own Manichaean worldview and messianic impulse "to make the world safe for democracy." This is why, in addition to Soviet behavior abroad, the regime's policies at home and within the bloc would determine whether Moscow and the West would move beyond rapprochement to genuine partnership.

---

103. Blacker, *Hostage to Revolution*, p. 80.

Eastern Europe

That the complete revamping of Soviet arms control strategy was informed by broader idealist commitments pertaining to the non-use of force in interstate relations and the fostering of conditions of "positive peace" is easier to discern in the context of Moscow's policy toward Eastern Europe.

Well acquainted with the large body of revisionist scholarship strongly suggesting a loosening of Soviet hegemonic control,[104] the Gorbachev cohort came to power convinced of the need for a more permissive and outright supportive stance toward pro-reform elements in Eastern Europe.[105] Addressing the Twenty-seventh Party Congress, the general secretary signaled the onset of a policy to "deregulate" the bloc[106] when he observed that "unity has nothing in common with uniformity" or "with interference by some parties in the affairs of others." The official death of the Brezhnev Doctrine was still more than three years away, but the leadership was clearly hinting that Moscow would not impose its will on Eastern European allies and certainly would not do so through force.

As part of the move to relax the USSR's four-decade iron grip on the bloc, Gorbachev actively encouraged Warsaw Pact governments to emulate Moscow in introducing greater liberalization in economic and political life. The result was to energize Eastern European reformers and antagonize Stalinist stalwarts such as East German chief Eric Honecker, but there were as yet few signs of the coming cataclysm and every reason for the Kremlin's confidence that it could control the pace of events.

A number of specialists at IEMSS and elsewhere who provided the intellectual and political support for Moscow's more benign stance sought broader changes in the USSR's relationship with fraternal socialist allies. They were motivated as much by normative qualms about an empire held together by force as by pragmatic considerations revolving around the desire to ease the economic burden posed by the bloc.[107] The contrast

104. Foremost among the relevant books and reports was the classified Zvezda project on which progressive specialists from ISKAN, IMEMO, and IEMSS collaborated with colleagues from the respective Academy of Sciences institutes of the various Warsaw Pact nations. The comprehensive report consisted of five volumes issued over several years, beginning in the mid-1970s.
105. Author's interviews with Yakovlev, Shakhnazarov, Zagladin, Bogomolov, and Chernyaev.
106. See Valerie Bunce, "Soviet Decline as a Regional Hegemon: Gorbachev and Eastern Europe," *Eastern European Politics and Societies* 3 (Spring 1989): 235–67.
107. Throughout the 1970s and early 1980s, IEMSS analysts were touting reform experiments in Eastern Europe, most notably in Hungary, whose leader, Janos Kadar, was a personal friend of institute director Bogomolov. In secret *zapiski* and classified reports, including the comprehensive

between NATO's Kantian security community and the Warsaw Pact had not been lost on liberal *mezhdunarodniki*, many of whom envisioned a socialist commonwealth bound together by shared principles rather than by imposed dogmas and the omnipresent threat of Soviet intervention.[108] These specialists found important allies within the regime's top echelons, including Foreign Minister Shevardnadze and senior Gorbachev advisers Georgi Shakhnazarov and Anatoly Chernyaev.

The Gorbachev leadership came under growing pressure from reformers to launch bolder initiatives in both domestic and foreign affairs. In the summer of 1988 two major gatherings, the Nineteenth All-Union CPSU Conference[109] and a meeting of influential experts at the Foreign Ministry,[110] propelled Soviet reforms in a more radical direction.[111] Policy toward Eastern Europe was no exception. Authoritative statements in support of the principle of noninterference in allies' affairs were now more frequent and less equivocal and were given added credence by the multilateral accord providing for the withdrawal of Soviet troops from Afghanistan.

The cuts in Soviet military forces stationed on the territory of Pact

---

Zvezda project series, IEMSS pushed for greater autonomy for the Warsaw Pact allies. One of the most radical specialists was Vyacheslav Dashichev, who by 1987–1988 was advocating an end to Soviet hegemony in Eastern Europe and later was among the first commentators to call for the reunified German state to be integrated into NATO.

108. This was the general vision held out in most of the entries in the Zvezda project series, particularly numbers II, "Countries of the Socialist Commonwealth and the Restructuring of International Relations" (1979), and IV, "Concrete Problems in the Policies of Countries of the Socialist Commonwealth in Relations with Developed Capitalist States in the 1980s" (1984).

109. Michel Tatu, "The Nineteenth Party Conference," *Problems of Communism* 37 (May/August 1988): 1–15; and "Resolutions of the Nineteenth All-Union CPSU Conference," *Kommunist* 10 (July 1988).

110. This extraordinary conference witnessed some of the most candid attacks yet on Soviet international policy, past and present. It began with Shevardnadze's keynote address, in which he all but disowned the Brezhnev Doctrine and called for a constitutional mechanism providing for the use of force outside Soviet borders. For Shevardnadze's speech and excerpts from conference proceedings, see "Scientific and Practical Conference at the Ministry of Foreign Affairs," *International Affairs* 10 (October 1988): 3–35.

111. After the Gorbachev regime's modest first phase of reform, roughly April 1985 to late 1987, failed to produce the anticipated turnaround in the economy or in relations with the West, Gorbachev and his allies pushed through a more radical program. The plan was approved at the Nineteenth All-Union Party Conference in June 1988. On the undulations in the reform process, see Anders Aslund, *Gorbachev's Struggle for Economic Reform* (Ithaca: Cornell University Press, 1989, 1991); and Richard Sakwa, *Gorbachev and His Reforms, 1985–1990* (Englewood Cliffs, N.J.: Prentice-Hall, 1991).

states outlined in Gorbachev's watershed address to the UN[112] were a powerful expression of Kremlin intentions toward Eastern Europe as well as the NATO states. The implicit removal of the threat of Soviet force to crush challenges to communist authority was followed by a series of fateful decisions by the Gorbachev hierarchy that indirectly fomented popular upheaval and hastened the collapse of all the Warsaw Pact regimes.[113]

With Poland already making the transition to a non–communist led government and the East German regime under siege, the Gorbachev cohort showed it was true to its professed principles. During a trip to Helsinki in October 1989, the Soviet leader all but declared the Brezhnev Doctrine formally dead,[114] stating that "the USSR does not have the moral or political right" to interfere in the affairs of its Warsaw Pact allies. He ordered Soviet troops based in the German Democratic Republic (GDR) (East Germany) not to participate in the suppression of antigovernment demonstrations threatening to topple the regime. The Berlin Wall was breached, and the communists were soon ousted. The same fate befell their comrades throughout the bloc by year's end. Near-total control over territory deemed absolutely essential to Soviet security for four decades had been relinquished without firing a shot. In the final analysis, Moscow may well have been a "hostage to revolution,"[115] but it was a revolution

112. The announcement of unilateral force reductions in support of a defensive military posture was only one element of the Soviet leader's sweeping exposition of the idealist variant of New Thinking. Speaking passionately about the need to humanize and de-ideologize international relations, Gorbachev said, "Our idea is a world community of states based on the rule of law which also make their foreign policy activity subordinate to the law." He went on to discuss the "revolutionary transformation" under way in the USSR in which "under the badge of democratization, restructuring has now encompassed politics, the economy, spiritual life, and ideology" (M. S. Gorbachev's speech at the UN Organization, *Pravda*, December 8, 1988). Here was the head of the world's first socialist state and frequent pariah telling the international community that the Soviet Union was reinventing itself based on the principles and ideals that had provided the original inspiration for the UN. Gorbachev advisers Yakovlev, Shakhnazarov, Chernyaev, and especially Petrovsky vigorously conveyed to me this last point.

113. Kremlin actions included pressure on Polish Communist Party bosses to cooperate in the transfer of power to a new non-communist-led government headed by Solidarity intellectual Tadeusz Mazowiecki; preapproval of Hungary's decision to open its borders with Austria, allowing thousands of East German "tourists" to flee; and Gorbachev personally urging Eric Honecker's beleaguered successor, Egon Krenz, to open up the GDR's borders. See Ronald Asmus, J. F. Brown, and Keith Crane, *Soviet Foreign Policy and the Revolutions of 1989 in Eastern Europe* (Santa Monica, Calif.: RAND Corporation, 1991).

114. Government spokesperson Gennadi Gerasimov half-jokingly hailed the arrival of the "Sinatra Doctrine," in which Warsaw Pact states were free to do things their own way.

115. The term and the complementary analysis belong to Coit Blacker, *Hostage to Revolution.*

largely of its own making and one that the Gorbachev leadership consciously declined to derail when opportunities to do so still existed.

If the Gorbachev leadership had not intended to preside over the collapse of the Soviet position in Eastern Europe, why would it have made such feeble attempts to avert that outcome, given the bloc's overwhelming strategic value in Soviet security assessments? The answer is closely related to the idealist identity that was taking hold among the Gorbachev cohort and the attending redefinition of Soviet interests and external threats.[116]

Moscow's benevolent response to the revolutions of 1989 reflected the goal of radical New Thinkers that the USSR take its place among the world's advanced industrialized nations not on the basis of its military prowess—the path pursued by each of Gorbachev's predecessors—but on that of shared principles and a common identity. What would it mean for an aspiring democratic Russia to move to suppress nonviolent popular democratic movements in Eastern Europe and how could such a country expect to join the community of Western states?[117] Gorbachev and his chief allies were committed to a Soviet Union rooted in that community, and they made clear their readiness to expose Soviet society to the influence of Western ideas, values, institutions, and culture.[118]

---

116. While Gorbachev and Shevardnadze felt strongly that the Bush administration was not moving fast enough to consummate a prospective post–Cold War partnership, they did not see U.S./NATO as the fierce threat they had previously. Specifically regarding the issue of the West and turmoil in Eastern Europe, Bush's efforts to reassure Moscow that the U.S. would do nothing to exploit the USSR's potential vulnerability were another factor in the Soviet decision to permit the collapse of its security buffer. On the role of U.S. reassurance, see Michael Beschloss and Strobe Talbott, *At the Highest Levels: The Inside Story of the End of the Cold War* (New York: Little, Brown, 1993).

117. It is beyond the scope of this paper, but a parallel argument about Soviet identity and rejection of force in Eastern Europe could be made concerning the dissolution of the USSR itself. The decision not to use force to keep the Soviet Union together in the aftermath of the failed coup in August 1991 went to the core of the Gorbachev cohort's conception of self and of the nation. As Shevardnadze explained to his American counterpart, James Baker, following the first explosion of separatist-related unrest (April 1989 in Tbilisi): "If we were to use force then it would be the end of perestroika. We would have failed. It would be the end of any hope for the future, the end of everything we're trying to do, which is to create a new system based on humane values. If force is used, it will mean that the enemies of perestroika have triumphed. We would be no better than the people who came before us. We cannot go back" (cited in Beschloss and Talbott, *At the Highest Levels*, p. 96).

118. Writing in the journal *International Affairs*, Andrei Kolosovsky, then an assistant deputy minister for foreign affairs, eloquently drew the connection between shared values and security: "Much is being said today about the affirmation of the priority of universal values in world politics as one of the ways to build a secure world. For us, this slogan means we are stating our readiness to accept anew the values of European civilization, many of which we vigorously rejected over the past seventy years, alluding to class interests. . . . Discarding democratic traditions and norms of morality developed in the depths of Western civilization over centuries led to a lag in development and had serious consequences for people's lives and freedom" ("Risk Zones in the Third World," *International Affairs* 8 [August 1989]: 39–49).

When Gorbachev had first invoked the image of a "common European home" during his visit to London in December 1984, his vision of a demilitarized continent was based on the continued existence of two political systems. By 1989 the "common home" phrase expressed the desire to create a new "European" (i.e., Atlantic to the Urals) security order based on a common identity made possible by the political and, to a lesser degree, economic reformation under way in the USSR.[119] The Soviet leadership had come to appreciate that although disarmament accords and adoption of defensive military postures could ameliorate the security dilemma, only a common identity provided the basis for "positive peace" in which nations forswear (and cannot even fathom) resort to force or the threat of force as a means to resolve disputes.[120] Significantly, Gorbachev's call for a USSR integrated into Asia, first made in his 1986 Vladivostok speech, never invoked visions of shared values and identity as had analogous statements on the common European home.[121]

The point of the foregoing analysis of the relationship between identity evolution on the one hand and Soviet arms control strategy and policy toward Eastern Europe on the other is not to claim that purveyors of the idealist variant of New Thinking became Gandhian pacifists and Jeffersonian democrats. They did not, as the body of their statements, writings, and actions attests. But neither were they the same individuals who in their formative years viewed the world through the prism of Marxism-Leninism and continued to believe in its central tenets as a guide for Soviet international policy. Particularly the older cohort of reformers—

---

119. Shevardnadze put it this way: "Universal security cannot be dependably safeguarded as long as nations reject common humanist values and common respect for human rights."

120. The need to transform the East-West relationship from one of cooperative-competitive coexistence to partnership (i.e., detente to entente) was a core tenet of the idealist perspective. See Shevardnadze, *The Future Belongs to Freedom*, and assorted articles by Soviet authors in a Soviet-American collaborative volume sponsored by the Beyond War Foundation: Anatoly Gromyko and Martin Hellman, eds., *Breakthrough: Emerging New Thinking* (New York: Walker, 1988).

121. The Western orientation of the Gorbachev cohort is a major reason that the so-called Chinese model was rejected for the Soviet Union, even though it appeared to hold great promise for making the transition from a centrally planned economy to a free-market one. They were committed to political reform, which they judged to be incompatible with the Chinese path, particularly after the massacre in Tiananmen Square—shortly after Gorbachev's visit to Beijing brought cheers of "Gorby, Gorby" from pro-democracy students. Repudiation of the Chinese model was tied to the question of Soviet identity in another way that had little to do with principles and values. In the eyes of the Soviet leadership, the USSR was a superpower and an advanced industrial state that should look to its equal-stature Western competitor for useful techniques and practices rather than to a great power wanna-be like China.

the children of the Twentieth Party Congress—who came to power with Gorbachev, underwent tremendous changes in their thinking about the world, about Soviet society, and about themselves over a period of many years.[122] This evolution was inextricably tied to changes in collective identity that, while greatly influenced by the transmission of Western ideas and principles, were essentially homegrown. It was nurtured in an oppressive system that denied its citizens basic political and civil rights and failed to provide anything more than a meager material existence and in a foreign policy that made hostile encirclement a self-fulfilling prophecy.

There is little question that foreign policy reformers, both liberal and radical, did not intend to bring about a precipitous decline in Soviet international influence, to say nothing of the disintegration of the USSR. On the contrary, they wanted to arrest the Soviet Union's accelerating internal decline and to preserve the country's status as a prime actor in world affairs. But how the idealist contingent defined being a great power varied markedly with historical Soviet understandings (as well as with extant Western ones). Reflecting on the theme of greatness and responding to the accusations of his vociferous detractors about his having engineered the USSR's loss of power and prestige, Foreign Minister Eduard Shevardnadze poignantly stated:

> The belief that we are a great country and that we should be respected for this is deeply ingrained in me, as in everyone. But great in what? Territory? Population? Quantity of arms? Or the people's troubles? The individual's lack of rights? In what do we, who have virtually the highest infant mortality rate on our planet, take pride? It is not easy to answer the questions: Who are you and who do you wish to be? A country which is feared or a country which is respected? A country of power or a country of kindness?[123]

As Shevardnadze's questions illustrate, foreign policy radicals, of which he was definitely one, had a very different conception of what it meant to be a great power, a conception bound up with changing notions of Soviet national identity. These specialists were confident that if the Gorbachev government pursued the enlightened policies that they prescribed, the USSR could return to a position of visionary leadership in the international

---

122. Glimpses into these personal, intellectual, and philosophical journeys can be seen in Stephen F. Cohen and Katrina vanden Heuvel, *Voices of Glasnost: Interviews with Gorbachev's Reformers* (New York: Norton, 1989). My argument also draws heavily on my own extensive interviews.

123. "Shevardnadze Addresses the Foreign Ministry," *FBIS-SOV*, April 26, 1990, cited in Oberdorfer, *The Turn*, p. 438.

community. As the birthplace and tireless promoter of New Thinking, the USSR would be in the vanguard of the movement to construct a peaceful and prosperous new world order.

In this way there was a profound link to the ideals of the great October Revolution. Gorbachev's invocation of the Leninist legacy was not so much a bid to garner legitimacy for a regime moving to dismantle a system erected by the founding father as it was an attempt to redeem the promise of the revolution.[124] Retaining its character as a socialist state was probably less important than reclaiming the mantle of international political leadership. For idealists, it was not enough that their country be a normal country. They entertained grander ambitions of transforming the Soviet Union, which, they reasoned, would in turn alter the fundamental nature of postwar international politics.[125] As New Thinking idealists had hoped, the radical course finally adopted by the Gorbachev regime brought tribute from around the world and made Moscow the center of revolutionary praxis, thereby reaffirming the country's singular destiny. This sense of mission was and remains central to the Soviet/Russian national identity.

Back to the Future?

In this essay I have attempted to show that the revolutionary elements of Soviet New Thinking that ushered in the end of the Cold War were the product of a profound reconceptualization of state interests. This redefinition of interests was rooted in new collective understandings about causal relationships in international politics and in regulatory and constitutive norms that spawned a vision of a democratic Soviet Union in full partnership with the Western powers.

The ideas and identity framework developed here both complements and challenges realist and liberal approaches in offering, it is argued, a more compelling explanation for the transformative character of Soviet foreign policy in the mid- to late Gorbachev era. Beyond being able to account for the radical turn in Kremlin arms control strategy and the pacific response to the revolutions in Eastern Europe and independence

---

124. Craig Nation presents a similar view in *Black Earth, Red Star: A History of Soviet Security Policy, 1917–1991* (Ithaca: Cornell University Press, 1992), pp. 323–24.
125. Few radical reformers anticipated that ending the Cold War and altering the basic shape of world politics would prove far easier than transforming the Soviet Union.

movements in various then Soviet republics, it also helps to explain why the Soviet Union under Gorbachev rejected the "Asian path" of economic development as unsuitable for the USSR.[126] In this regard, the ideas and identity framework speaks to both Russia's past and its future.

It does not follow from my explanation for the end of the Cold War that Russia would continue to pursue an entirely cooperative and arguably deferential foreign policy or that Kremlin decision makers would continue to view the nation's interests as fully congruent with those of its former adversaries. To the contrary, the framework presented here strongly suggests that the future direction of post-Soviet Russian international policy was and remains very much in question and that the long-run prospects for radical New Thinking were, for reasons elaborated below, never especially encouraging.

For realists who see burgeoning strains in U.S.-Russian relations—whether stemming from Moscow's hegemonic behavior in the "near abroad," its brutal war against the breakaway Chechen Republic, or its sale of nuclear technology to Iran—as confirming the inevitability of a return to great power rivalry following an aberrant honeymoon, Russia's growing assertiveness would seem to confound the expectations of realist theory. If, as realists insist, New Thinking was a rational response to dire circumstances, how can they account for the Yeltsin government's increasingly nationalist course at a time when Russia is far weaker in both relative and absolute terms than in the late 1980s? Similarly, if Moscow's recent behavior does herald a return to more traditional Soviet/Russian patterns, thereby rendering late-Gorbachev-era New Thinking a historical anomaly, it is powerful evidence that state interests cannot be deduced from material capabilities.

To the extent that Russian rhetoric and actions in the international

---

126. The cold reception accorded the Asian model by the Gorbachev leadership raises the important but frequently neglected question of why certain ideas lose. For realists, the defeat of the Asian option would be attributed to its projected failure to advance the material interests of influential segments of the political establishment. This is an unconvincing explanation because the statist paths pursued with such encouraging results by several developing countries in Asia would seem to hold considerable attraction for a Soviet leadership committed to economic reconstruction but still uneasy about scrapping the central planning apparatus. The ideas and identity framework suggests that whether an idea generates a politically consequential constituency depends on more than the material concerns of its addressing actors. As stated elsewhere in this paper, the Chinese or East Asian model lost in Soviet debates largely because key elements of the Gorbachev regime viewed it—perhaps erroneously—as incompatible with democratic political reform, particularly in the wake of the Chinese government's brutal crackdown on the democracy movement. In short, the values content of ideas can matter enormously in the competition for supremacy.

sphere reflect the exigencies of post-Soviet domestic politics, the driving force behind Moscow's behavior is beyond the reach of dominant (neo)realist structural explanations. In contrast, the ideas and identity framework, with its imperfect attempt to integrate politics and collective ideational constructs, makes intelligible Russia's ambivalent—partly cooperative, partly combative—stance toward the West.

The battle waged by opponents and supporters of New Thinking is part of a larger struggle over Soviet identity in the modern world—a struggle with roots deep in the Russian past.[127] For centuries, Slavophiles and Westernizers armed with their competing visions have fought for the soul of Russia.[128] What kind of society and what kind of country did Russia aspire to be?

Those questions must still be answered as the Russian Federation charts its foreign policy future. Many factors will determine which course Russia pursues in its relations with the outside world.[129] The contest between advocates of the conciliatory realpolitik and idealist variants of New Thinking (later joined by stridently nationalist voices at the extremes of the political spectrum) remains relevant for understanding the Yeltsin government's flirtation with a more assertive international posture and for the longer-term evolution of Russian policy. Present-day policy debates in the political elite and increasingly in the general public reflect the ongoing struggle over the meaning and content of Russian national identity, which was only temporarily settled in the late Gorbachev era.[130]

The idealist view of the world and the USSR's place in it never commanded the support of a majority of foreign policy reformers even after Gorbachev sided with the radicals. Opposition from hard-liners was constant and continues to the present. What changed was the addition to the opposition ranks of moderate reformers who welcomed the initial revi-

127. See James Billington, *The Icon and the Axe: An Interpretive History of Russian Culture* (New York: Knopf, 1966).

128. Refinements in the Slavophile-Westernizer typology have been numerous. One that seems particularly relevant today centers on a third general perspective that some have termed *Eurasianist*. Proponents see the country's geographical location as a compelling metaphor for Russia, and they advocate borrowing from East and West to form a unique hybrid. See S. Neil MacFarlane, "Russia, the West, and European Security," *Survival* 35, no. 3 (Autumn 1993): 3–25.

129. See Aleksei Arbatov, "Russia's Foreign Policy Alternatives," *International Security* 18, no. 2 (Fall 1993): 5–43.

130. See Sergei Stankevich, "Russia in Search of Itself," *National Interest* 28 (Summer 1992): 47–51; and MacFarlane, "Russia, the West, and European Security."

sions in Soviet strategy, then watched with alarm as radicals comman-deered the policy process.[131]

Eduard Shevardnadze, one of the most forceful proponents of the rad-ical agenda, was also among the first casualties of the backlash against what was seen as the "naive idealism" of the USSR's international course.[132] The embattled foreign minister resigned under a barrage of criticism for kow-towing to the West and betraying Soviet interests (e.g., supporting the anti-Iraq coalition in the Persian Gulf war, permitting German unification and the new state's incorporation into NATO, bowing before the Interna-tional Monetary Fund's demands for painful structural reforms). Detrac-tors also attacked unilateral force reductions and the abandoning of long-time allies while disparaging New Thinking tenets such as universal human values and the diminished utility and dubious morality of armed force in the modern era.

More recently, former foreign policy reformers have joined extremists on the Right and Left in demanding a more forceful posture toward the states of the former Soviet Union, either to quell bloody ethnic conflicts along the Russian border or to prevent discrimination against Russian minorities living there.[133]

Bowing to pressure, President Yeltsin and Foreign Minister Andrei Kozyrev, at first content to continue the course that they inherited, began to take a harder—or at least a less overtly pro-Western—line. This has been manifested in the not-so-surreptitious intervention by Russian units in the Georgian civil war, delayed troop withdrawals from former Baltic republics, support for "brother Slavs" in the Bosnian war, and sometimes bitter complaints about Russia's treatment as a junior partner in its post–Cold War relations with onetime foes.

Moscow's recent decision to join the Partnership for Peace (after press-ing vigorously but unsuccessfully for full NATO membership or some spe-

131. Western policy makers did not appreciate the fact of divisions within the New Thinker camp. Interviews conducted by the author beginning in 1990 revealed growing anti-idealist sentiment among foreign policy moderates. One of the most outspoken of these commentators has been for-mer IEMSS analyst and former chairman of the Congress of Peoples Deputies Foreign Affairs Com-mittee Yevgeny Ambartsumov, who has written widely on the need for a less pro-Western policy orientation.
132. David Remnick's *Lenin's Tomb: The Last Days of the Soviet Empire* (New York: Random House, 1993) contains interviews with critics of the accommodationist line pursued by Gorbachev and then Yeltsin.
133. A recent work on Russian policy toward some of the newly independent states is Karen Daw-isha and Bruce Parrott, *Russia and the New States of Eurasia: The Politics of Upheaval* (New York: Cambridge University Press, 1994).

cial status to distinguish Russia from other new partners) suggests that those who see Russia's future as a democratic and capitalist nation firmly anchored in the West retain the upper hand. But whether this once and sure-to-be-future great power will continue to cast its lot with the West will depend in large measure on which among the competing national identities emerges as the most salient.

Western leverage over Russia's choice and its future evolution is modest, and pronouncements to the contrary run the risk of generating the kind of unrealistic expectations that doomed detente in the 1970s and already have a Republican-controlled Congress moving to slash U.S. aid to Moscow. Efforts to integrate Russia into the constellation of international institutions and emerging regional security architecture can help to blunt historical Russian suspicion that the Western powers harbor malevolent intentions and seek to exploit Moscow's weakened position. Decision makers in Western capitals have not been sufficiently sensitive to the multiple traumas—disorienting political and economic transformation at home and collapse of power and prestige abroad—that beset present-day Russia.

There is no simple causal nexus between U.S./Western action and Soviet behavior. In the early 1980s external Western pressure may have helped undermine the legitimacy of the old guard, but only because liberal reformers were ready and able to make a compelling case that Western belligerence was not immutable and was in part a response to threatening Soviet behavior. A similar Western strategy today would likely ensure Russia's nationalist turn.[134] At a minimum, the ideas and identity framework elaborated in this essay can provide scholars and policy makers with an improved set of tools with which to assay the often neglected complex social processes that shape the ways in which states define their interests.

---

134. Just as New Thinking was not the inevitable outcome of Soviet decline, those who see a nationalist turn in Russian foreign policy as a foregone conclusion misjudge the degree of support for such a shift. While there exists in Russia a widely shared sense of dismay and resentment regarding the country's diminished role and influence in international affairs, there is no popular groundswell in favor of an aggressive anti-Western or expansionist strategy. For instance, surveys show that citizens want Russia to maintain a firm hand in dealing with the new independent states (especially over the treatment of ethnic Russians) but have little interest in reconstituting the Soviet Union. Surveys also reveal that whatever Russians' disappointment or anger toward the West (e.g., over the failure of assistance to prevent tumbling living standards), relatively few view the West as a threat. The situation is not dissimilar in the domestic sphere, where the common wisdom has Russians ready to give up political freedoms for the security of the old days. Yet despite the hardships associated with the transition to a market economy that have given rise to a nostalgia for the certainties of the past, they do not seek a return to the Stalinist system that produced those certainties.

Having illuminated these processes and suggested a causal sequence that takes us from systemic crisis to recognition to political and ideological contestation and finally to foreign policy outcomes, the ideas and identity framework would appear to be a promising candidate for comparative crossnational research. Only further empirical study will tell.

9 • Norms, Identity, and National Security in Germany and Japan

Thomas U. Berger

For nearly half a century Germany and Japan have pursued remarkably consistent national security policies that deemphasize military instruments as a means of achieving national objectives. They have continued to adhere to these policies despite dramatic changes in their security environments and steady growth in their relative power. Since the 1950s many outside analysts have predicted that these two nations will inevitably assume a larger defense and national security role. Yet, contrary to these predictions, not only have Germany and Japan failed to assume a more independent defense posture, but they have also been slow to assume a larger security role within the context of multilateral institutions, such as the UN, NATO, or the more limited bilateral context of the U.S.-Japanese Security Treaty.

This behavior is anomalous from the perspective of neorealism and neoliberalism, which see state behavior as being driven by the rational responses of state actors to pressures emanating from their international environments. While these two schools differ in the way they specify international structure, both perspectives would predict greater German and Japanese responsiveness to the changes in the international system than has in fact occurred. Instead of increasing their political-military power, as neorealist perspectives suggest they would, Germany and Japan have done precisely the opposite. Although it may be argued that the two nations have developed formidable military establishments, their ability to act independently of their allies has been sharply circumscribed by the types of weapon systems that they have acquired, by the kinds of missions that their forces train for, and by various institutional limitations placed on their armed forces. Despite demands periodically placed upon them by the United States and other allies, Germany and Japan have resisted pressures to expand their global military roles. This aversion to acting more independently might at first seem to be consistent with the predictions of neoliberalism. But Germany's and Japan's timidity in assuming greater military responsibilities within the framework of international institutions opens them up to the charge of free riding and threatens to undermine the very security regimes upon which they have come to depend.

This essay will argue that an adequate explanation of German and Japanese antimilitarism requires us to look beyond international structures and examine the domestic cultural-institutional context in which defense policy is made. The central thesis is that Germany and Japan, as a result of their historical experiences and the way in which those experiences were interpreted by domestic political actors, have developed beliefs and values that make them peculiarly reluctant to resort to the use of military force. During the immediate postwar period of 1945 to 1960, these beliefs and values became institutionalized in the German and Japanese political systems in various ways, both formal and informal, and are now integral parts of their countries' post-1945 national identities. Together they constitute unique political-military cultures that lead Germany and Japan to choose certain responses to their respective international environments, responses that might differ from those of other states in identical situations. Although the end of the Cold War has fundamentally transformed the two nations' security environments, their approaches to national security have changed only minimally. While some further evolution is likely, the pace of change is glacial and the direction in which they are likely to evolve cannot be deduced from objective, external factors alone. Rapid changes in Germany's and Japan's cultures of antimilitarism are likely only if they are challenged by a major external shock—for instance, a direct military attack on German or Japanese population centers or a collapse of their alliances with the United States and the West combined with the emergence of new security threats.

The argument will be structured as follows: After examining the shortcomings of purely structural approaches to explaining German and Japanese antimilitarism, I shall briefly explicate my use of the concept of political-military culture. I shall then examine first the development of these two cultures in the immediate postwar period and subsequently during the Cold War. Finally, I will examine the persistence of these two cultures of antimilitarism since 1989.

The purpose of this exercise is not to "disprove" structural approaches to analyzing state behavior. Unlike much of the literature on strategic culture, this essay will underline how noncultural factors can, under certain circumstances, shape the evolution of culture. At the same time, however, cultural forces have a significant impact on how states respond to the structural conditions (the distribution of economic and military power, the density of international institutions) under which they operate. While the relationship between culture and structure may be dialectical, without factoring in cultural and ideological variables we cannot achieve an adequate understanding of foreign outcomes or even make the most guarded predictions about future state behavior.

Deficiencies of Structural Accounts

The development of postwar German and Japanese national security policies, particularly since the end of the Cold War, poses a number of thorny problems for both neorealist and neoliberal theories of state behavior. The two nations' profound reluctance to assume larger military roles, either independently or in a multilateral setting, raises questions about the domestic origins of state preferences and their perceptions of the international system that cannot be answered by perspectives that focus solely on a state's position in the international system.

Realism offers a convincing explanation of the origins of German and Japanese defense and national security policies in the post-1945 period and provides important insights on the structural forces that helped shape German and Japanese security policy during the Cold War. Defeated in World War II and occupied by the United States, Germany and Japan found that their policy makers had little room to maneuver during the early postwar years. Since the two nations were dependent on the United States for both their security and their prosperity, the costs of not joining the Western alliance system would have been prohibitive and would have posed unacceptable risks from the perspective of the leaders of the time.

Differences in the two nations' geopolitical positions also help explain

320 • *Thomas U. Berger*

why they adopted very different approaches to their alliances. Faced with a formidable Soviet military threat on its borders and fearful that the United States might abandon Western Europe, Germany sought to extract from its allies as clear a commitment to its security as it could. In return for such guarantees, German leaders were willing to pay a considerable price in national autonomy. In contrast, Japan, as an island nation relatively insulated from immediate military threat, was primarily concerned that too close an alliance with the United States might entangle it in bloody regional conflicts like Korea and Vietnam. Consequently Japan preferred to maintain a high degree of military autonomy within the context of its purely bilateral security arrangement with the United States.[1]

Finally, a realist analysis of German and Japanese foreign policies would emphasize the two nations' security relationship with the United States to explain their relatively low military expenditures during the Cold War. In effect, the United States provided them with a free ride on security, allowing them to concentrate their national energies on increasing their economic strength. From the perspective of 1990, this strategy seems to have proved itself a brilliant success, as Germany and Japan emerged from the Cold War with arguably the world's strongest economies, while the United States and the Soviet Union appeared exhausted after forty years of political-military competition.

The shortcomings of a purely realist analysis, however, become more apparent when we try to examine the foreign policies of the two countries after they reemerged as major powers in the 1960s and 1970s. Contrary to so-called aggressive variants of neorealism, which see states as power maximizers, Germany and Japan did not seek to develop military capabilities commensurate with their burgeoning economic power.[2] On the contrary, they were profoundly ambivalent about any increase in military power, even when the opportunity was thrust upon them—for example, during the debate over the creation of a multilateral nuclear force (MLF) as part of

---

1. On the contrasting implications for alliance relations of fears of entanglement and of abandonment, see Michael Mandelbaum, *The Nuclear Revolution* (New York: Cambridge University Press, 1981), ch. 6.
2. See John J. Mearsheimer, "Back to the Future," *International Security* 15, no. 1 (Summer 1990): 5–56; Christopher Layne, "The Unipolar Illusion: Why New Great Powers Will Rise," *International Security* 17, no. 4 (Spring 1993), esp. pp. 41–45; and Kenneth N. Waltz, "The Emerging Structure of International Politics," *International Security* 18, no. 2 (Fall 1993): 44–79. A number of Japanese experts make similar arguments; see Chalmers Johnson, "Rethinking Asia," *National Interest* 32 (Summer 1993): 20–28. Perhaps the most widely known representation of this view is George Friedman and Meredith Lebard, *The Coming War with Japan* (New York: St. Martin's, 1992).

NATO in the 1960s.[3] Likewise, many Japanese leaders in the fifties and six-ties, including Prime Ministers Kishi Nobusuke and Sato Eisaku, sup-ported American requests for Japan's assumption of a greater regional role in containing Communism and would gladly have increased Japanese mil-itary capabilities, but they were sharply constrained by domestic political pressures.

Even from a more moderate realist point of view that sees states as secu-rity optimizers that balance against potential threats rather than as power maximizers, it would have appeared perfectly rational for Germany and Japan to have sought to acquire greater independent military capabilities, including, if not their own nuclear *force de frappe*, at least joint control over allied nuclear forces stationed in their own territory.[4] German and U.S. interests had diverged sharply over such issues as Berlin and detente, while in Asia new security threats, including a highly ideological, nuclear-armed People's Republic of China, had emerged in Asia. Moreover, with the Soviet acquisition of the capability to reach targets in the United States, the doctrine of extended deterrence had become highly problematic.[5]

That such a *force de frappe* was a real possibility from the perspective of the time is reflected by U.S. willingness to supply Germany with theater nuclear weapons in the late 1950s and American fears in the 1960s that without something like MLF Germany was very likely to develop its own nuclear forces.[6] Similarly, in the late 1960s Japanese policy makers pri-vately reviewed the possibility of developing a nuclear capability, while in public a fierce debate broke out over whether Japan should shift to an "autonomous defense" (*jishubōei*) stance.[7] Ultimately, German and Japan-ese decision makers chose not to acquire such capabilities for a variety of reasons, including fears of triggering regional arms races. Yet there were

---

3. See Catherine M. Kelleher, *Germany and the Politics of Nuclear Weapons* (New York: Columbia University Press, 1975), chs. 7, 9, and 10.

4. Leading examples of this sort of approach include Barry R. Posen, *The Sources of Military Doc-trine: France, Britain, and Germany Between the World Wars* (Ithaca: Cornell University Press, 1984); and Stephen M. Walt, *The Origins of Alliances* (Ithaca: Cornell University Press, 1987).

5. See Earl C. Ravenal, "NATO: The Tides of Discontent," University of California Institute of International Affairs, Policy Papers in International Affairs, no. 23 (Berkeley, 1985), pp. 12–13.

6. John Mearsheimer's recent argument that the United States should seek to ensure that Germany acquires nuclear weapons in an orderly, nondestabilizing fashion, is in this sense perfectly consistent with earlier American policy initiatives. See Kelleher, *Germany and the Politics of Nuclear Weapons*, pp. 180–81.

7. Recently key documents have been released to the public in Japan that revealed that the Defense Agency, on instructions from Prime Minister Satō Eisaku, had investigated the possibility of Japan's acquiring its own *force de frappe*. See *Mainichi*, August 1, 1994, p. 1.

good, realist reasons for them to have gone in the other direction as well. Tipping the balance in both cases—but especially in Japan—were the domestic political costs that would have been associated with taking such measures.

Realist difficulties in accounting for German and Japanese behavior have increased since the end of the Cold War. The end of the East-West confrontation has considerably enlarged the two nations' room for maneuver and heightened their relative stature in the international system. Nonetheless, neither Germany nor Japan has sought to take advantage of the new opportunities by increasing military capabilities. On the contrary, both nations have reduced their armed forces in the wake of the Cold War—significantly so in the German case—and have deliberately eschewed new military responsibilities even when they were thrust upon them, as during the Gulf war.

At the start of the Gulf crisis, German and Japanese leaders and security policy experts believed that it was vital that their forces participate directly in the allied war effort in the Gulf. They feared that in the event of heavy U.S. casualties, Germany and Japan would run the risk of triggering an isolationist backlash in the United States, undermining the international security order on which both countries have come to depend. In other words, the rational free rider would have found the dispatch of a small number of forces of the Gulf—if not on the scale of Britain or France, then at least on a par with Italy or Belgium—a worthwhile investment to ensure that the free ride would continue. The force of domestic antimilitary sentiments, however, ruled out taking even minimal military measures.[8]

In certain respects, recent German and Japanese behavior poses less of a problem for neoliberals, who maintain that a variety of international structural changes are diminishing the pressures toward military competition—notably the spread of liberal democracy, growing economic interdependence, the proliferation of international institutions, and social and technological developments that greatly increase the costs of war while reducing the benefits. Neoliberal scholars such as Richard Rosecrance, John Goodman, and Jeffrey Anderson have viewed German and Japanese national security policies as a confirmation of their positions. Even some

8. Conversations with Motoo Shiina, spring 1991, and Professor Satō Seizaburō, summer 1992. See also Thomas Kielinger, "The Gulf War and Consequences from the German Point of View," *Aussenpolitik* 42, no. 2: 241–50, and the interview with Wolfgang Schäuble in *Der Spiegel*, no. 4, January 25, 1993, p. 20.

former traditional realists, such as Edward Luttwak, see in Germany and Japan evidence that the world is moving from an era of geopolitics to a new age of geoeconomics. German and Japanese antimilitarism, from this perspective, is not an aberration of the international norm but rather a harbinger of things to come; in the future, adherents of this view argue, other nations are likely to behave more like Germany and Japan in security matters.[9]

In contrast to the realist perspective, however, neoliberals have difficulty accounting for the origins of German and Japanese antimilitarism, important elements of which had clearly developed before causal factors stressed by liberals had an opportunity to have much of an effect. Moreover, neoliberals find it difficult to explain the depth of German and Japanese antimilitarism compared to that of other countries that find themselves in similar structural positions. War is unpopular in liberal democracies the world over, and there are many other advanced industrial societies similarly embedded in the global network of international institutions and dependent on access to foreign markets and resources. Yet no other nations display as intense a sense of antimilitarism as do Germany and Japan.

Here again, the Gulf war provides us with the best recent example. German and Japanese interests in the Gulf war were certainly no less than those of other American allies; in fact, given the dependence of these countries on the United States for security, their interests were arguably much greater. Yet not only were the Germans and Japanese far less active than the British and French—who, one could plausibly maintain, as members of the Security Council have reputations as great military powers to uphold—but they seemed timid compared to even the Italians, Dutch, and Belgians, all of whom dispatched to the Gulf precisely the kind of symbolic military forces that pragmatists in the German and Japanese defense and foreign ministries were urging their governments to send.

Finally, neither the neorealist nor the neoliberal perspective addresses the issue of national identity and the way in which the definition of national identity in turn shapes the national interest. The importance of

---

9. See Richard Rosecrance, *The Rise of the Trading State: Commerce and Conquest in the Modern World* (New York: Basic Books, 1986); Jeffrey J. Anderson and John B. Goodman, "Mars or Minerva: A United Germany in a Post–Cold War Europe," in Robert O. Keohane, Joseph S. Nye, and Stanley Hoffmann, eds., *After the Cold War: International Institutions and State Strategies in Europe, 1989–1991*, pp. 23–63 (Cambridge: Harvard University Press, 1993); and Edward Luttwak, "From Geopolitics to Geo-Economics," *National Interest*, no. 20 (Summer 1990): 17–23.

national identity is particularly apparent in the case of Germany during the Cold War because of its peculiar status as a divided nation. For nearly half a century, German policy makers on both the Left and the Right pursued the dream of national reunification, even though the economic and diplomatic costs of pursuing relations with Eastern Europe were considerable and international realities made their quest seem increasingly quixotic. Nonetheless, even in the 1970s and 1980s, after the Germans reconciled themselves with their fate as a divided nation, the dream of national unity lived on, and no German politician could afford to abandon a definition of national identity that committed the nation to pursuing that dream. That identity, and the definition of national interest that it produced, cannot be understood using systemic approaches that simply treat states as unitary, independent actors.[10]

National identity, however, is a static variable. For while German national identity survived the nation's half-century-long partition, it underwent at the same time a profound transformation. Whereas in the pre-1945 era German statesmen and intellectuals had emphasized Germany's unique path of development, *Der deutsche Sonderweg* between East and West, during the 1950s and 1960s Germany redefined itself as part of a larger, nascent European community of nations bound together by common values and interests. This commitment to integration with the rest of Western Europe fundamentally altered the way in which national interest was calculated. As a result, once reunification was achieved, Germany further reduced its national sovereignty by accelerating the European integration process through the treaty of Maastricht. To achieve this objective, Germany agreed to sacrifice the German mark and support the creation of a European central bank, even though it thereby relinquished a major source of power and influence in a way that neither neorealism nor neoliberalism can easily account for.

---

10. Traditionally, realists have shown a keen appreciation of the effects of nationalism on international politics. For the most part, however, they treat its existence as a given and do not even attempt to explain its origins or the reasons for the intensity or forms that nationalist sentiments assume at different points in time, thus rendering their use of nationalism post hoc. See Hans Morgenthau, *Politics Among Nations: The Struggle for Power and Peace*, 5th ed. (New York: Knopf, 1978), esp. pp. 337–47. For more recent efforts to analyze nationalist sentiments from a basically realist perspective, see Jack Snyder, *Myths of Empire: Domestic Politics and International Ambition* (Ithaca: Cornell University Press, 1992), and Stephen Van Evera, "Hypotheses on Nationalism and War," *International Security* 18, no. 4 (Spring 1994): 3–39. Both Snyder and Van Evera, however, have departed significantly from the core proposals of systemic realism, adopting approaches that come perilously close to certain variants of constructivism.

In short, both neorealism and neoliberalism identify important systemic factors that sharply constrained German and Japanese policy makers during the early Cold War period and provided incentives for pursuing more moderate policies thereafter. By themselves, however, international structures are underdetermining. While pressures from the international system may influence state actors like Germany and Japan, the signals that it sends are ambiguous, even contradictory, and a multiplicity of plausible solutions is available. Under such circumstances states are likely to be guided in their decision making by their own internal sets of preferences and beliefs about the international system.[11] To argue that simply because German and Japanese policy proved successful in the end meant that this was the only rational course of action open to those nations is to commit the same sort of post hoc fallacy that cultural explanations are often accused of. What is needed at this point is a model of how these beliefs and values may have come into existence and why they continue to persist across generational boundaries.

The Concept of Political-Military Culture

Common to all theories of culture is the notion that human behavior is guided by socially shared and transmitted ideas and beliefs.[12] Cultures as such comprise beliefs about the way the world is—including at the most basic level beliefs that define the individual's and the group's identities—and ideas about the way the world ought to be.[13] Political culture refers to those cultural beliefs and values that shape a given society's orientations toward politics.[14] Political-military culture in turn refers to the subset of the larger political culture that influences how members of a given society

---

11. A similar argument is made with regard to the role of ideas in international relations by Geoffrey Garret and Barry Weingast, "Ideas, Interest, and Institutions: Constructing the European Community's Internal Market," in Judith Goldstein and Robert O. Keohane, eds., *Ideas and Foreign Policy: Beliefs, Institutions, and Political Change*, pp. 173–206 (Ithaca: Cornell University Press, 1993).

12. For an excellent yet succinct summary of the main features of a cultural theory of action, see Harry Eckstein, "A Culturalist Theory of Political Change," in Eckstein, *Regarding Politics: Essays on Political Theory, Stability, and Change*, pp. 267–71 (Berkeley: University of California Press, 1992).

13. For an interesting discussion of the relationship between national identity and national interest, see William Bloom, *Personal Identity, National Identity, and International Relations* (New York: Cambridge University Press, 1990), esp. ch. 4; and Alexander Wendt, "Anarchy Is What States Make of It: The Social Construction of Power Politics," *International Organization* 46, no. 2 (Spring 1992): 391–425.

14. The classic formulation of the concept of political culture can be found in Gabriel Almond and Sydney Verba, *The Civic Culture* (Boston: Little, Brown, 1965), pp. 11–14.

view national security, the military as an institution, and the use of force in international relations.

Although influenced by the real world, cultures (including political-military cultures) are not merely subjective reflections of objective reality. Two individuals or groups with different cultural backgrounds are likely to behave differently even when confronted with identical situations. For example, if French or American policy makers found themselves in geostrategic positions similar to Japan's or Germany's, they might be expected to behave in a very different way than their German and Japanese counterparts do because they come from cultural backgrounds with very different norms and values regarding the military and the use of force.

Cultures—and by extension political-military cultures—are not static entities hovering above society, directing behavior while they themselves remain immune to social, economic, and political forces. They are transmitted through the often imperfect mechanisms of primary and secondary socialization and are under constant pressure from both external developments and internal contradictions.[15] Cognitive beliefs about the world are constantly tested by actual events. While failures and surprises can be reinterpreted so that they do not contradict existing norms and beliefs, they also create pressures that can lead to a reevaluation and modification of the culture. In extreme cases, if a culture totally fails to meet the expectations of its members, large-scale defections to other cultural systems are likely to result.[16] The collapse of Communism may serve as a case in point.

Such adaptation, however, is neither quick nor easy. Simple, instrumental beliefs can be discarded easily. More-abstract or emotionally laden beliefs and values that make up the core of a culture (such as a preference for democracy or belief in monotheism) are more resistant to change.[17] Ordinarily such change takes place slowly and incrementally. Occasionally more rapid change in core beliefs and values occurs, but only after they have been thoroughly discredited and the society is under great strain. Individuals and groups are then forced to reexamine their old beliefs and seek new ways of making sense of the world and new solutions to the prob-

---

15. For an example of the kind of internal contradictions that may emerge out of a culture over time, see Daniel Bell, *The Cultural Contradictions of Capitalism* (New York: Basic Books, 1976).

16. Michael Thompson, Richard Ellis, and Aaron Wildavsky, *Cultural Theory* (Boulder: Westview, 1990), ch. 5.

17. For more on the process of social learning, see Milton Rokeach, *The Open and Closed Mind* (New York: Basic Books, 1960); Lloyd Etheridge, *Can Governments Learn?* (New York: Pergamon, 1985); and Ernst Haas, "Why Collaborate? Issue Linkage and International Relations," *World Politics* 32, no. 3 (April 1980): 357–405.

lems confronting them. Such rapid and fundamental change tends to be accompanied by psychological distress and is broadly similar to Thomas Kuhn's description of paradigm shifts in the natural sciences.[18]

The reexamination of the core beliefs and values of a particular nation is a complicated affair. At any one time there exists a multiplicity of political actors—motivated by their own distinctive experiences and interests—who seek to establish their understandings as binding for the rest of the society. In pluralistic political systems, however, usually no one group is able to impose its views on the rest. In order to pursue their agenda, political actors are compelled to enter into debates and negotiations with other groups, making compromises and concessions along the way. These compromises, however, have to be legitimated, both internally within the group and externally in the rest of society. Such legitimations often involve a reinterpretation of past events, current conditions, and future goals. In this way, politics is a question not only of who gets what but of who persuades whom in an ongoing negotiation of reality.

At first such compromises are precarious. Political actors are keenly aware of their arbitrary and artificial nature, and many may hope to reverse the agreed-upon compromises at the earliest possible opportunity. Once agreed upon, however, these negotiated realities are typically institutionalized in the political system and cannot be easily changed even if there is a shift in the balance of power among the different political actors. Decision-making rules, such as the requirement of a two-thirds majority to revise a constitution, may create high barriers to the reversal of agreed-upon policies, while the credibility of leaders may be damaged by a constant shifting of positions. Moreover, over time the legitimations offered on behalf of these compromises—particularly if they are perceived as successful—are reified and become what Emile Durkheim called "social facts."[19] Subsequent generations of decision makers come to take for granted these legitimations and the beliefs and values on which they are based. What may have been an ad hoc response to historical necessities at one time becomes hallowed social truth at another. These legitimations thus become part of the political culture of the nation and can have a lasting impact on state behavior long after the circumstances that gave birth to them have passed.

18. Thomas Kuhn, *The Structure of Scientific Revolutions*, 2d ed. (Chicago: University of Chicago Press, 1970).
19. Emile Durkheim, *The Rules of the Sociological Method*, trans. Sarah A. Solovay and John D. Mueller, ed. George E. G. Catlin (Chicago: University of Chicago Press, 1938), pp. 1061–62.

The study of the political-military culture of an entire nation requires a detailed, multilayered research strategy, involving three central empirical tasks. First, it is necessary to investigate the original set of historical experiences that define how a given society views the military, national security, and the use of force, paying careful attention to the interpretation of these events among different groups in the society. Second, one needs to examine the political process through which actual security policy was made and how particular decisions were subsequently legitimated. In this context it is important to define the essential features of both the political-military culture and the security policy associated with it at a *particular point in time*. Third, it is necessary to examine the evolution of both the political-military culture and defense policies over time, monitoring how they evolved in response to historical events.

Such a longitudinal analysis allows us to escape the trap of deriving culture from behavior, which leads to the kind of tautological, ad hoc reasoning of which cultural analysis is often accused.[20] While in practice it is nearly impossible to separate culture from behavior, for analytical purposes it is possible to disaggregate policy behavior and the meanings that political actors and the general public attach to those policies, as reflected in public opinion polls, parliamentary debates, books and articles written by opinion leaders, newspaper editorials, and so forth. This procedure allows us to judge the degree of consistency between behavior and expressed beliefs and values over time. If culture (in this case, political-military culture) changes without any corresponding shift in behavior, there are grounds to question the posited relationship between the two. Likewise, if behavior changes without any change in the expressed beliefs and values that have been associated with earlier policies, then again we have reason to doubt that the two factors influence one another. In other words, expressed cultural beliefs and values should develop in tandem with behavior—in this case defense and national security policy. When there is a disjuncture between the two, an appropriate degree of tension should be observable in the political system.

According to the model of cultural change explicated above, under normal circumstances culture should change only incrementally in response to ordinary historical events such as shifts in the balance of power or the

20. See Brian Barry, *Sociologists, Economists, and Democracy* (London: Collier-Macmillan, 1970); and Carole Pateman, "Political Culture, Political Structures, and Political Change," *British Journal of Sociology* 1, no. 3 (July 1971): 291–306.

formation of international institutions. When major new policy initiatives violating existing norms and values are proposed, resistance in the form of demonstrations, political confrontations, and changes in government should be observable. If major changes occur without generating such resistance, then the presumed relationship between political-military culture and defense policy can be considered to have been falsified.

In this sense, political-military culture often acts as a source of inertia in policy making, at least in the short run. At the same time, how nations choose to behave can have significant, system-level effects in the long run as well, especially if they are important actors like Germany and Japan. For example, isolationism in the United States before 1941 significantly delayed the American entry into World War II, creating a window of opportunity in which the Axis powers could have achieved military victory. While from a structural realist point of view the only significant difference would have been that Western Europe would have been organized under the aegis of a Nazi German rather than a democratic American hegemon, the character of the international system would have been profoundly different.[21]

The Origins of the New Political-Military Cultures

To a remarkable degree, the political-military cultures of Germany and Japan continue to be shaped and guided by the ideological and political battles of the late forties and fifties. During this critical formative period the foundations of the postwar German and Japanese approaches to security were put in place. The creation of the new German and Japanese defense establishments was not merely a technocratic exercise in obtaining maximum security at minimal price, nor were they merely the products of a pluralistic bargaining process between interest groups concerned with maximizing their share of societal resources. Rather, the German and Japanese defense debates of the 1950s revolved around much more fundamental questions of national identity, the definition of the national interest and of the kind of political, economic, and social systems that the two nations should adopt. In the course of these debates, basic decisions regarding defense and national security became inextricably intertwined with the new national identities of postwar Germany and Japan.

---

21. For a similar type of argument, see John Gerard Ruggie, "Multilateralism: The Anatomy of an Institution," in Ruggie, ed., *Multilateralism Matters: The Theory and Praxis of an Institutional Form* (New York: Columbia University Press, 1993), pp. 24–31.

Perhaps the most important fact to be noted in any analysis of postwar German and Japanese thinking about defense and national security is the degree to which it represented a radical departure from the dominant historical patterns. Prewar Germany and Japan had been quintessential militarist societies.[22] The armed forces had played a pivotal role in the formation of the modern German and Japanese states, and their status as great military powers was central to their national self-understandings. In Germany, it was the Prussian army that had fulfilled the nineteenth-century nationalist dream of unifying the German nation. In Japan, governments since the Meiji restoration of 1868 legitimated their rule by depicting themselves as the defenders of the nation and the sacred Imperial institution from predatory Western powers. As a result, the German and Japanese military establishments wielded tremendous political influence and enjoyed high social prestige in the prewar period.[23]

The disastrous defeat in World War II dealt a lethal blow, both materially and spiritually, to these highly militaristic political-military cultures. Both nations suffered enormous physical losses. More than six million Germans and three million Japanese perished between 1939 and 1945. By the time the fighting ended, their cities had been reduced to rubble, their economies had collapsed, and their populations were saved from starvation only by the massive infusion of Western aid. Perhaps more important than the material losses were the psychological ones. The German and Japanese armies had failed to fulfill the missions that had been their principle sources of legitimacy. In Germany, instead of unifying all German-speakers, the war ended in national partition and dismemberment. In Japan, the military was blamed for having recklessly dragged the country into a disastrous war that ended in the first occupation of Japan in recorded history and left the emperor at the mercy of foreign conquerors.

In the wake of these disasters the popular mood was one of disillusionment with nationalist ambitions and a rejection of the prewar military ethos. These sentiments by themselves, however, were insufficient to effect a lasting transformation of German and Japanese political-military cultures. In the past, other countries—including post–World War I Ger-

---

22. See Volker R. Berghan, *Militarism: The History of an International Debate, 1861–1979* (Cambridge: Cambridge University Press, 1981).

23. On the political influence of the military in prewar Germany, see Gordon Craig, *The Politics of the Prussian Army*, rev. ed. (New York: Oxford University Press, 1964); Geoff Eley, *Reshaping the German Right: Radical Nationalism and Political Change After Bismarck* (New Haven: Yale University Press, 1980). On Japan, see Richard J. Smethurst, *A Social Basis for Japanese Militarism: The Army and the Rural Community* (Berkeley: University of California Press, 1974).

many—had suffered defeats of comparable magnitude and exhibited similarly powerful moods of war weariness without developing lasting antimilitary cultures. Alongside the natural pacifism of two defeated peoples there also lurked feelings of fear and resentment of the victorious Allied powers. There remained as well a host of issues—including most important questions of territory—that potentially could have become catalysts for new aggressively irredentist movements.

The dimensions of the defeat, however, did create windows of opportunity after 1945 during which general societal attitudes toward the military and the use of force became unusually malleable. Two sets of actors—the American occupation authorities and the new German and Japanese democratic elites—played key roles in reinforcing and institutionalizing the antimilitary sentiments that appeared in the wake of the war.

For the American occupation authorities, demilitarization was both a physical and a psychological project. Not only did the occupation forces demobilize and dismantle the vast German and Japanese war machines, but they also worked hard to impress upon the German and Japanese people that theirs had been a moral as well as a military defeat. The political and military leaders of the wartime regimes were put on trial for war crimes; books and passages in school texts deemed to be militaristic were expunged from the curriculum; and the German and Japanese populations were bombarded with antimilitary propaganda that was almost as fierce as the wartime propaganda that preceded it.[24]

At least as critical to the ultimate demilitarization of Germany and Japan were the efforts of their own political elites, on both the Left and the Right. The left-wing labor unions and socialist/social-democratic movements, the traditional enemies of the military in the prewar period, were naturally opposed to seeing their old political rivals reestablished. The main centrist and right-of-center political formations, organized under the Christian Democrats led by Konrad Adenauer in Germany and the Liberals under Yoshida Shigeru in Japan, were deeply suspicious of the armed forces and blamed them for the failure of party democracy in the 1930s. Although less critical of the military than the Left, men like Adenauer and Yoshida were determined to prevent the armed forces from playing the kind of political role that they had before 1945. Even archconservatives,

---

24. On the American efforts in Japan, see Meirion Harries and Susie Harries, *Sheathing the Sword: The Demilitarization of Postwar Japan* (New York: Macmillan, 1987). On Germany, see Lucius Clay, *Decision in Germany* (Garden City, N.Y.: Doubleday, 1950); and Howard Zink, *The United States in Germany, 1944–1951* (New York: Van Nostrand, 1957).

such as later defense minister Franz Josef Strauss, declared themselves vehemently opposed to the military and militarism.[25]

When the basic institutions of the postwar German and Japanese democratic systems were put into place in the late 1940s, the dominant political forces were committed to the eradication of the old military ethos. At the same time, democratization took place in an international environment in which pressures for German and Japanese rearmament remained muted and the international community was primarily concerned with preventing the reemergence of a German or Japanese military threat. German and Japanese leaders emphasized the degree to which the new political systems differed from the old and antimilitarist values were institutionally anchored in the new democratic political systems. The most prominent of these new institutions were to be found in the new constitutions of the two countries; Japan's article 9, which forbade the maintenance of military forces or war-fighting material, and article 87a of the German Basic Law, which prohibits waging wars of aggression.

The emergence of the Cold War, and especially the outbreak of the Korean War, soon compelled Germany and Japan to reconsider their antimilitary postures. Under pressure from the United States and worried by the threat of Communism, German and Japanese leaders felt they had no choice but to reverse, at least partially, the antimilitary policies that had been implemented over the past five years.

This change in direction, however, clashed with the powerful popular mood of antimilitarism, and throughout the 1950s West German and Japanese politics were dominated by fierce domestic struggles over the defense issue. In both nations this debate was in good measure also a debate over the future of the German and Japanese economic and social systems. The Left—backed by the trade unions and large segments of the intelligentsia—feared that joining the American-led alliance would lock them into the Western capitalist system and hamper their efforts to achieve more far-reaching, socialist reform in their respective societies. The Right—supported by business interests and traditionally conservative sectors of society such as the church and agriculture—hoped for precisely the opposite.

Ultimately pro-Western, right-of-center coalitions won the day in both countries, aided by improving economic conditions and the considerable

25. See Ōtake Hideo, *Saigumbi to Nashyonarizumu* (Tokyo: Chūōkōshinsho, 1989); and Hans-Peter Schwarz, *Adenauer: Der Aufstieg, 1876–1952* (Stuttgart: Deutsche-Verlags-Anstalt, 1986).

benefits afforded by U.S. patronage.[26] Their left-wing rivals, hampered by inept Soviet diplomacy, were unable to translate popular sympathy for neutrality into victories at the ballot box. More-conservative forces, which favored large-scale, unrestricted rearmament and a more independent policy stance, enjoyed little popular support. Even in Japan, where conservative, prodefense leaders like Hatoyama Ichiro and Kishi Nobosuke came into power, the far Right's influence on policy and the popular debate on defense remained relatively marginal.

Although the supporters of alliance and rearmament achieved their chief objectives, they were compelled to make a number of important concessions in order to reassure the public and the opposition forces—as well as neighboring countries—that there would be no reversion to militarism. Consequently, rearmament took place on a limited scale and at a relatively cautious pace. The new German Bundeswehr and Japanese Self Defense Forces (SDF) were placed under strict regimes of civilian control, and great care was taken to underline their purely defensive nature. Both countries forswore the acquisition of certain categories of weapons systems—most notably weapons of mass destruction—and both the Federal Republic and Japan passed legislation prohibiting the dispatch of their forces beyond their own territory, or—in the German case—outside of the area covered by NATO.[27]

During this formative period, when German and Japanese attitudes toward their military were in flux and their room for maneuvering decidedly limited, geopolitical forces had a powerful influence on the development of the two countries' defense policies. In particular, contrasting German fears of abandonment and Japanese fears of entanglement led to very different, almost inverse patterns of alliance relations. Faced with a clear and present danger in the Soviet Union, Germany chose to integrate itself as tightly as possible with its allies through an impressive array of overlapping multilateral institutions, including NATO, the European Community, and the West European Union. In contrast, Japan, confronted with a

---

26. On the considerable influence that the United States wielded in German and Japanese politics, as well as the extensive benefits it could provide in terms of aid and access to the newly emerging international trading system, see Hans Jürgen Grabbe, *Unionspartei, Sozialdemokratie, und die Vereinigten Staaten von Amerika, 1946–1966* (Düsseldorf: Droste Verlag, 1983); and Akaneya Tatsuo, "Saikeikoku taigu o motomete," in Watanabe Akio, ed., *Sengo Nihon no Taigaiseisaku*, pp. 108–34 (Tokyo: Yuhikaku, 1985).

27. See Paul B. Stares, *The Restrictions on the Forces of the Federal Republic of Germany* (Washington, D.C.: Brookings Institution, 1991); and *Bōei Handobukku*, 1989 ed. (Tokyo: Asagumo Shimbunsha, 1989), pp. 425–26. Certain ambiguities did remain. For example, the Japanese armed forces planned to acquire the ability to defend merchant shipping well beyond Japan's territorial waters in the event of hostilities.

much lower level of external threat and fearful that it might be dragged into destructive regional conflicts like Korea and Vietnam, declined various American proposals for regional security arrangements and remained relatively isolated from its neighbors.

Yet even in this period, domestic political and historical factors played an important role in certain aspects of the two nations' defense policies, most notably in the area of civil-military relations. In the modern era both nations have had their share of problems with maintaining control over the armed forces. The German Reichswehr under General Kurt von Schleicher played a key role in bringing Adolf Hitler to power, while the Japanese militarists had progressively taken control of the Japanese government through a decade-long series of coups, assassinations, and engineered military emergencies. This historical background served to greatly sharpen the dilemma of how to reconcile democratic institutions with the military establishment. Although Germany and Japan faced problems that were structurally almost identical, they adopted virtually the opposite strategies for maintaining control over their armed forces.

In the German case memories were still fresh of how the Reichswehr— a small, highly professional force of military men with political views far to the right of those of German society as a whole—had been instrumental in the demise of the Weimar Republic. From the point of view of many German political and military leaders, the key issue was how to integrate the new armed forces into society and ensure that they not become a collecting point for extreme Right views. The solution that they found relied principally on two mechanisms: the reintroduction of universal military service and the institutionalization of the doctrine of *innere Führung* (internal leadership), designed to infuse the armed forces with a democratic ethos and to protect the civil rights of recruits.[28]

In Japan, on the other hand, the Imperial Army had been a mass-based organization with powerful social and political foundations. The militarists had used its informal network of contacts to bolster the extensive formal privileges granted to the armed forces under the Meiji constitution. As a result, it was not altogether surprising that the last thing that Japan's postwar political leaders wanted to do was to create a military establishment that was thoroughly integrated into society. While some efforts were made to indoctrinate the military with a democratic ethos, the basic postwar Japanese strategy for controlling the military was to isolate it politically and

---

28. The best English-language source on West German civil-military relations is Donald Abenheim, *Reforging the Iron Cross* (Princeton: Princeton University Press, 1988).

socially. The armed forces were placed under a tight system of both internal and external bureaucratic controls, and their uniformed personnel were carefully monitored by the civilian overseers in charge of the Japanese Defense Agency. The agency itself occupied a very subordinate position within the Japanese bureaucratic hierarchy, and many of its key departments, including finance and procurements, were effectively under the control of other ministries, The idea of military conscription, although favored by some military men, never even reached the political agenda in Japan.[29]

The highly polarized character of the Japanese political system in the 1950s and 1960s further reinforced the isolation of the armed forces. The presence of extremely conservative figures in the ruling coalition (Prime Minister Kishi had been munitions minister under General Tōjō Hideki and was a signatory of the declaration of war on the United States) and the readiness of much of the Japanese Left to accept Soviet propaganda at face value created an ideological gulf between the government and the opposition that was far wider than in West Germany. Cooperation between government and opposition was almost unknown.[30] Without even a minimal consensus on defense, and faced with deep public antipathy toward the armed forces, the Japanese government was compelled to place the armed forces under an evolving system of legislative constraints in order to reassure the public (and indeed, many members of the government itself) that the military establishment was not becoming too powerful to control.

In the Federal Republic, despite the bitter polemical battles between the Christian Democrats and the Socialists, the opposition was willing to cooperate with the government on key defense legislation in order to help shape national policy.[31] As a result, the Bundeswehr enjoyed far greater

29. For a brief overview of postwar Japanese civil-military relations, see Leonard A. Humphreys, "The Japanese Military Tradition," in James H. Buck, ed., *The Modern Japanese Military System*, pp. 21–40 (Beverly Hills: Sage, 1975). See also Hirose Katsuya, *Kanryō to Gunjin: Bunmin tōsei no Genkai* (Tokyo: Iwanami Shoten, 1989). On external bureaucratic controls, see Peter J. Katzenstein and Nobuo Okawara, *Japan's National Security: Structures, Norms, and Policy Responses in a Changing World*, Cornell East Asia Series no. 58 (Ithaca: Cornell University Press, 1993).

30. On the Left's fears of the government's intentions, see Ōtake Hideo, *Saigumbi to Nashyonarizumu*. On the gullibility of the Japanese Left, see Kojima Ryō, *Hangarii Jiken to Nihon: 1956 Shisōteki Kōsatsu* (Tokyo: Chūōkōronsha, 1987).

31. An important factor that reinforced the polarization of the Japanese political system was the presence of the Communist Party, which competed with the Socialists for left-wing votes. In West Germany, on the other hand, the Communist Party was banned in 1951, making it easier for the SPD to move to the right on defense and other issues. When an alternative to the left of the SPD—the Greens—emerged in the 1970s pressure built for the party to shift to the left. See Josef Joffe, *The Limited Partnership: Europe, the United States, and the Burdens of Alliance* (Cambridge, Mass.: Ballinger, 1987).

political legitimacy than did the Self Defense Forces, and the German military, while far from popular and much criticized, was not regarded with nearly the same degree of suspicion.

During the 1950s German and Japanese security policy makers were unusually sensitive to the various forces—both domestic and international—present in the policy-making environment. In the course of the policy-making process, however, new institutional structures were created that insulated defense policy from the domestic and international pressures. Some of these structures were legal in nature, such as the restrictions placed on the German and Japanese armed forces by their interpretations of the constitutions. Others were more bureaucratic-organizational, such as the office of the *Wehrbeauftragte* (a special independent commissioner charged with overseeing *innere Führung* in the Bundeswehr). Once installed, these formal institutions could not easily be discarded, and therefore they locked the further evolution of policy into fixed paths of development.[32]

Other structures were ideological in character, including the beliefs and values used to legitimate the new national security policies and institutions. Central to these legitimations were new definitions of the German and Japanese national identities. In West Germany, Adenauer and other proponents of the Western alliance argued that for a hundred years democracy in Germany had been crippled by the cross-pressures generated by its geographical and cultural location between East and West. This ambivalence, they maintained, had spawned the aggressive hypernationalism of the prewar period that had proved so destructive. To contain the demons of nationalism, Adenauer and others argued, Germany had to bind itself into a network of transatlantic and Western European institutions. Economic and military alignment with the West was thus not merely a strategy for maximizing the national interest; it was a decision to resolve a centuries-old identity crisis and to anchor the nation firmly in Western civilization and thus support the values of liberal democracy.[33]

In a similar way Prime Minister Yoshida Shigeru provided his countrymen with a vision of Japan as a "merchant nation" (*shonin kokka*), a country that concentrated on economic development while eschewing the pur-

---

32. On the concept of path-dependent development, see Douglas C. North, *Institutions, Institutional Development, and Economic Performance* (New York: Cambridge University Press, 1990), esp. ch. 11.

33. Hans-Peter Schwarz, *Die gezähmten Deutschen* (Stuttgart: Deutsche-Verlags-Anstalt, 1985).

suit of military power. With this slogan Yoshida subverted the Left's own vision of Japan as a "peace nation," a nation dedicated to the pacifist ideals of the Japanese constitution, by linking antimilitarism to the decidedly nonleftist desire for commercial gain. Also unlike the Left, Yoshida and other centrists looked to the capitalist West rather than the socialist East for the model of development that Japan should emulate. They argued that alliance with the United States was the price that Japan had to pay for entering the global community of prosperous modern powers. The military side of the relationship, as opposed to the commercial one, was carefully deemphasized.[34]

Potentially, these legitimations could have been used to support very different policies. There is nothing about the notion of Germany as a part of the West that intrinsically required it to indoctrinate its armed forces with democratic values (no other member of NATO has a comparable policy). Nor does Japan's collective identity as a merchant nation a priori bar it from dispatching forces overseas. *Innere Führung* and the highly restrictive ban on the overseas dispatch of forces were the products of the constellations of political forces dominant in Germany and Japan in the 1950s. Likewise, Germany's decision to integrate itself into the West, and Japan's determination to stay aloof from regional security affairs were logical responses to the particular external pressures that the two countries experienced. Once made, however, these decisions were tied to the new national identities by the German and Japanese governments, which had to justify their policies to their highly critical public. In this way policies were invested with a symbolic value that linked them to the core values of the new German political-military culture and made them quite resistant to change.

Over the course of the next thirty years, these cultures and patterns of behavior would be frequently challenged. Domestically, there existed powerful rival visions of national identity and policy agendas that were promoted by parties on both the Left and the Right. Internationally, the evolving East-West relationship and shifts in the balance of power were to generate pressures for change as well. Nonetheless, a basic set of beliefs and values, along with associated patterns of defense behavior, can be identified as existing around 1960 and can be summarized briefly as follows.

In the following sections we will trace the subsequent evolution of German and Japanese defense and national security policies and the debates

---

34. Kenneth B. Pyle, *The Japanese Question: Power and Purpose in a New Era* (Washington, D.C.: AEI Press, 1992).

TABLE 9.1

Core Elements of the German and Japanese Approaches to National Security

	National Identity	Alliance Relations	Force Structure	Civil-military Relations
Japan	1. Japan as a merchant nation that concentrates on economic development while foregoing the pursuit of political-military power	1. Passive dependence on the U.S. for military security, but no entanglement in U.S. strategy	1. Non-nuclear, non-aggressive 2. Territorial defense role	1. Tight bureaucratic control of Self Defense Forces 2. Few connections between the military and nationalism
Germany	1. Germany as a member of a larger community of Western nations. Nationalism contained through multi-lateral ties	1. Active engagement in alliance structures as a means of achieving political, military and security objectives	1. Non-nuclear, non-aggressive 2. Operations restricted to within the NATO area	1. Democratization of the armed forces through *innere Führung* 2. Maintenance of an open military through universal male conscription

surrounding them. In the process we will analyze the extent to which Germany and Japan deviated from the norms, values, and patterns of behavior established during the critical early years after the war.

The Evolution of the Two Political-Military Cultures

Public opinion surveys from the sixties and seventies reveal a marked increase in West German and Japanese popular support for the institutional pillars of the new approaches to defense and national security, including their alliances with the United States, political and economic integration with the West, and the new armed forces. Whereas in 1960 a substantial minority of the population in Japan (32 percent) supported neutrality over alignment with the United States (44 percent), by 1978 backing for the West had increased to 49 percent, while support for neutrality declined to 25 percent.[35] In West Germany popular support for the military alliance with the United States rose as well, albeit not quite as dramatically as in Japan. In 1961, for example, 42 percent were still for neutrality, against 40 percent for alliance with the West, by 1975 proalliance attitudes had risen to 48 percent versus 38 percent.[36] Support for integration with Western Europe increased similarly during this period. Although in 1965 a large majority of West Germans (69 percent) still said that given a choice they would prefer reunification over integration with Europe, by 1973 the balance had shifted dramatically, with 65 percent preferring European integration over German reunification.[37]

In both countries external factors may have contributed to this shift in attitudes. The end of the Vietnam War and detente reduced Japanese fears of entanglement, and Ostpolitik removed some of the chief obstacles to a solution—albeit a far from satisfactory one—for the problem of national partition. While these external events may have facilitated the consolida-

---

35. Question: Should Japan join the Free World, the Communist camp, or be neutral?

Year	Communist World (percent)	Be Neutral (percent)	Free World (percent)
1960	1	32	44
1963	1	28	45
1966	1	31	41
1969	2	30	44
1972	2	34	37
1975	2	29	41
1978	2	25	49
1980	2	25	55

Adapted from Etō Shinkichi and Yamamoto Yoshinobu, *Sōgoanzenhoshō to Mirai no Sentaku* (Tokyo: Kodansha, 1991), p. 23.

36. Question: In your opinion, what would be better foreign policy: Should we continue to ally ourselves with the United States or should we try to be neutral, for example, like Switzerland?

Year	Neutral (percent)	Ally with the U.S. (percent)	DK/Undecided (percent)
1961	42	40	18
1965	37	46	17
1969	38	44	18
1973	42	41	17
1974	38	51	11
1975	36	48	16
1981	31	55	14

From Berthold Meyer, *Der Bürger und seine Sicherheit* (Frankfurt: Campus Verlag, 1983), p. 217, table 3.2.2.1.

37. At the same time, support for German reunification remained very high. There were important generational differences, however, with younger Germans showing markedly less interest in reunification than their elders. See Elisabeth Noelle-Neumann, ed., *Jahrbuch* (Institut für Demoskopie, Allensbach, 1976), p. 83.

tion process, once the consensus was in place, further changes did not lead to a reversal. Even after the Cold War reintensified in the late 1970s and the first half of the 1980s, support for the basic security institutions remained high in both countries.[38]

Support for nonmilitary means of ensuring national security also grew steadily. In Germany after 1973 public support for Ostpolitik continued to increase even as superpower relations deteriorated. In 1973, 49 percent of those surveyed felt that Ostpolitik had been worthwhile, and 29 percent did not. By January 1980, the level of support had increased to 51 percent versus 28 percent, and the vast majority of West Germans supported the further promotion of detente—74 percent versus 17 percent.[39]

Although there was far less emphasis on dialogue with the Soviet Union or other potential enemies in Japan, there was evidence of strong popular preferences for relying on nonmilitary instruments for national security. A 1972 *Yomiuri* newspaper survey revealed that only 6 percent of the respondents thought military power was a very effective means of defending the nation, while 32 percent thought it was somewhat effective and 14 percent thought it was totally ineffective. In contrast, 32 percent thought that economic instruments (foreign aid, trade, and so forth) were very effective ways of maintaining national security, and 43 percent thought that they were somewhat effective. Respondents rated diplomatic negotiations, maintaining a high standard of living and international exchanges all as more effective than military power as ways of ensuring national security.[40]

Expressions of elite opinion as well gravitated toward greater support of the existing approach to defense and national security, especially in Japan. Whereas in the 1950s Japanese intellectuals and the media overwhelmingly backed the Left's proposals for unarmed neutrality, during the 1960s and 1970s increasing numbers of intellectuals came out in favor of the government's policy of alignment with the West and maintenance of a minimal defense establishment. At the forefront of this movement was a new generation of scholars such as Kosaka Masataka and Nagai Yonosuke,

---

38. The peace movement and the acrimonious West German debate over the NATO decision to deploy a new generation of intermediate-range missiles caused some temporary shifts, but overall the impact was almost surprisingly limited. See Hans Rattinger, "The Federal Republic of Germany: Much Ado About (Almost) Nothing," in Hans Rattinger and Gregory Flynn, eds., *The Public and Atlantic Defense*, pp. 101–73 (Totowa, N.J.: Rowman and Allanhead, 1985).

39. Meyer, *Der Bürger und seine Sicherheit*, p. 255, table 6.7.8.

40. *Gekkan Yoron Chōsa*, July 1972, cited in Akio Watanabe, "Japanese Public Opinion and Foreign Affairs," in Robert A. Scalapino, ed., *The Foreign Policy of Modern Japan*, pp. 105–45 (Berkeley: University of California Press, 1977), p. 115.

who provided new, more sophisticated rationales for Japan's postwar approach to national security and were increasingly enlisted by the Japanese government to serve on panels to study defense and foreign policy issues.[41]

During the early 1980s this trend accelerated, as reflected by *Yomiuri's* shift to a prodefense editorial line and the increased willingness of Japanese companies to produce weapons. At the same time, the public defense debate went from being a battle between the pacifist Left and the proalliance Center to a struggle between centrists and a resurgent, nationalist anti-American Right that favored a major military buildup and a more independent approach to foreign policy.[42]

Whereas in Japan the shift in the overall spectrum of political opinion among elites was toward the Right and Center, in West Germany elite opinion shifted in the opposite direction, toward the Left. In the late 1960s support for detente grew dramatically in the face of stubborn resistance by the CDU (Christian Democratic Union) government to closer ties with Eastern Europe. The student movement and the issue of coming to terms with the atrocities of the Nazi era added a powerful emotional dimension to the new policy of Ostpolitik announced by Chancellor Willy Brandt in 1969, making the new diplomatic policy as much a matter of strengthening democracy and atoning for the past as of pursuing German national interests. These moves reinforced and further institutionalized the antimilitary character of West German political-military culture. Consequently, massive demonstrations broke out in Germany when in the late 1970s and 1980s NATO governments, including German chancellors Helmut Schmidt and Helmut Kohl, sought to counter growing Soviet military strength by deploying a new generation of theater nuclear forces.[43]

The positions of political parties mirrored shifts in popular and elite attitudes. In West Germany during the late 1950s the Social Democrats

41. See Komiya Ryutarō, "Uerubeki Migi Senkai," *Gendai Keizai* 6 (Spring 1979): 71–84. For more on the employment of Japanese intellectuals in the Japanese policy-making process, see Frank Schwartz, "Of Fairy Cloaks and Familiar Talk: The Politics of Consultation," in Gary D. Allinson and Yasunori Sone, eds., *The Political Dynamics of Contemporary Japan*, pp. 217–41 (Ithaca: Cornell University Press, 1993).

42. See Umemoto Tetsuya, *Arms and Alliance in Japanese Public Opinion* (Ph.D. diss., Princeton University, 1985). Characteristic of the new right-wing literature was Shimizu Ikutarō, *Nihon yo Kokka o Tare!: Kaku no Sentaku* (Tokyo: Bungeishunju, 1980).

43. See Jeffrey Herf, *War by Other Means: Soviet Power, West German Resistance, and the Battle over the Euromissiles* (New York: Free Press, 1991).

(SPD) shifted decisively toward accepting NATO and integration with the West.[44] Even in the late 1980s, after the SPD partially reversed itself on national security in response to the emergence of the far left-wing Green Party and a new, more radical generation within the party, the Social Democrats refrained from calling for withdrawal from NATO. Indeed, whereas in the 1950s the SPD had bitterly opposed NATO and integration with Western Europe, in the 1980s it came out in favor of greater European integration in the hope that a united Europe could provide a counterweight to the United States and preserve detente.[45] For its part, the CDU came to accept Ostpolitik and detente in the 1980s, conducting its own mini-detente with the German Democratic Republic even at the height of the U.S.-Soviet confrontation of the early to mid-1980s.[46] Despite the enormous controversy surrounding defense issues in West Germany during the 1980s, on a deeper level consensus on national security actually grew.

On the whole, shifts in Japan tended to be less dramatic than in West Germany. Nonetheless, over the course of the 1970s and 1980s the Socialist opposition to the government's national security policies became less virulent than it had been in the 1950s. An important factor in this trend was the Socialists' efforts to court the so-called middle-of-the-road parties (the Democratic Socialist Party and the Clean Government Party), which were more supportive of the Self Defense Forces and the alliance with the United States and which were prepared to compromise with the government in order to pass new defense legislation.[47] Although there remained right-wingers in the LDP (Liberal Democratic Party) who wanted to see Japan become a "normal nation" by assuming a larger and more independent military role, they were held in check by the party's centrist mainstream.[48]

44. See Gordon D. Drummond, *The German Social Democrats in Opposition, 1949–1960* (Norman: University of Oklahoma Press, 1982).
45. Berthold Meyer, *Die Parteien der BRD und die sicherheitspolitische Zusammenarbeit in Europa* (Frankfurt am Main: Hessische Stiftung für Friedens und Konflikt Forschung, Bericht 2, 1987), ch. 3.
46. See Clay Clemens, *Reluctant Realists* (Durham: Duke University Press, 1989).
47. See Umemoto Tetsuya, *Arms and Alliance in Japanese Public Opinion*, esp. pp. 175–80; and Horie Tadashi and Ikei Masaru, *Nihon no Seitō to Gaikō Seisaku* (Tokyo: Keiō Tsūshin, 1980), chs. 2 and 3.
48. Typical of the centrists' ability to check the Right was the way in which they foiled Nakasone's efforts to link increasing defense spending above one percent of the GNP with a rekindling of Japanese nationalism. See Kaminishi Akio, *GNP 1% Waku* (Tokyo: Kadokawa Bunko, 1986); and Akasaka Shintarō, "1% Waku de Tsumazuita Nakasone Shushō," *Bungeishunju* (January 1986): 178–82.

As in Germany, the defense debate of the 1980s revealed that the growing consensus was no longer confined to a shift toward the center in the *distribution* among the different subcultures; a deeper transformation was taking place in the contents of the beliefs that they proposed. Whereas in the past, Japanese rightists had hoped to use the defense issue to spark a new debate on national identity and Japan's global mission, during the 1980s right-wing ideologues like Ishihara Shintaro and Eto Jun increasingly chose to focus on trade issues instead in order to inflame nationalist passions.[49] In effect, the Right accepted the centrist position that Japan's strength lay in its role as a merchant nation.

Behind this shift in the terms of the political debate was a broader intellectual transformation of the ways in which Japan's new national identity was related to its past. Borrowing ideas from the popular analysis of Japanese culture known as *nihonjinron* (the theory of Japanese-ness), more and more influential Japanese came to accept the argument that because Japan had never been subjected to successive waves of foreign invasion as had Europe and mainland Asia, conflict had always tended to be of a more limited nature than elsewhere in the world. This historical insularity is alleged to have made the Japanese people inherently inept at power politics, while at the same time strengthening their inclination toward harmony and cooperation.[50] The conclusions that centrists—and, increasingly, right-wing figures as well—draw from this analysis jibes well with Japan's overall strategy as a "merchant nation"—namely, to recognize its relative weakness as a military power, rely on "warrior nations" like the United States to come to its aid, and concentrate its energies on the areas in which it enjoys a comparative advantage: trade, technology, and economic growth.

In sum, there is little doubt that the political-military cultures of Germany and Japan shifted in significant ways during the course of the Cold War in response to international events and domestic political developments. These shifts, however, on the whole led to a greater consensus in favor of the antimilitary policies that had been established in the 1950s. Efforts to move in the opposite direction triggered considerable domestic political turmoil. In West Germany the development of Ostpolitik was

---

49. See Ishihara Shintarō, *The Japan That Can Say "No": The New U.S.-Japanese Relations Card* (New York: Simon and Schuster, 1991); and Etō Jun, *Nichibei Sensō wa owatte inai: Shukkumei no Taiketsu—Sono Genzai, Kako, Mirai* (Tokyo: Nesco Books, 1986).

50. Sophisticated versions of this argument can be found in Amaya Naohirō, "Shoninkoku Nihon Tedai no Kurigoto," *Bungeishunju* (March 1980); and Okazaki Hisahiko, *Senryakuteki Kangaekatta to wa Nani ka* (Tokyo: Chūōkōshinsho, 1983), pp. 9–13, 24–26.

accompanied by intense infighting within the CDU and the coming to power of the SPD. Likewise, the decision to deploy new intermediate-range nuclear weapons in the early 1980s triggered mass demonstrations and another change in government. In a similar fashion, the Japanese student movement and the debates over the return of Okinawa (then still occupied by the United States) fueled intense political controversy in Japan. Various conservative defense initiatives, such as Prime Minister Fukuda Takeo's efforts in 1978 to pass new legislation enabling the Self Defense Forces to respond to a military emergency, generated so much political resistance that they had to be greatly modified or abandoned.[51]

The end of the Cold War has sparked new controversy over national security in Germany and Japan, and there are clear signs that popular and elite attitudes toward defense are continuing to evolve. The main focal point of the new defense debate of the 1990s is whether and in what form Germany and Japan should participate in international peacekeeping missions. During the Gulf war German and Japanese public opinion, despite negative views of Saddam Hussein, showed overwhelming opposition to direct involvement in the war.[52] German and Japanese elite views were similarly divided over how to respond to the crisis, with the Left generally opposed to involvement, the Right supporting a limited show of force, and the Center waffling somewhere in between.[53]

Since the Gulf war public opinion has slowly coalesced in favor of some degree of limited military participation in international affairs, accompanied by perhaps the most intensive debate of national security issues in these two countries since the 1950s. Public opinion polls show cautious popular approval of the limited forays into peacekeeping in Cambodia and Somalia. Media treatment of these operations has been largely favorable. The trend toward increased consensus received a boost in Japan when Socialist Matsuyma Tomiichi became prime minister in coalition with the conservative Liberal Democrats and announced that his party would partially reverse its

51. See Ötake Hideo, *Nihon no Boei to Kokunai Seiji* (Tokyo: Sanichi Shobo, 1983), pp. 26–100.

52. In Japan a mere 10% supported SDF dispatch with no limitations, and even among LDP supporters opponents of dispatch outnumbered proponents 41% to 14.9%; *Nikkei*, October 15, 1990. In Germany in January 1991, 71% of all German-supported allied actions, but only 20% would have supported Bundeswehr participation in the campaign; *Der Spiegel* 5, January 28, 1991, pp. 32–36. See also *Der Spiegel* 11, March 11, 1991, p. 36.

53. For an overview of the Japanese debate, see Ito Kenichi, "The Japanese State of Mind: Deliberations on the Gulf Crisis," *Journal of Japanese Studies* 17, no. 2 (Summer 1991); on Germany, see Michael J. Inacker, *Unter Ausschluß der Öffentlichkeit: Die Deutschen in der Golfallianz* (Bonn: Bouvier Verlag, 1991). For a brief overview of the German intellectual debate at the time, see Cora Stephan, "An der deutschen Heimatfront," *Der Spiegel* 10, March 4, 1991.

long-standing policy of opposition to the Self Defense Forces and the alliance with the United States.[54] In Germany the Federal Constitutional Court ruled in favor of the government, decreeing that the Bundeswehr could indeed participate in military operations, including combat missions, outside of the NATO area, providing it received parliamentary approval and these operations were conducted in a multilateral framework.[55]

These developments, while significant, do not represent fundamental deviations from the political-military cultures of the Cold War. Despite its enhanced position of power in the center of Europe, and despite various, often serious disagreements with its European allies over such issues as Bosnia, the Uruguay round, or the expansion of NATO into central Europe, Germany remains committed to deepening its integration with the West and pursuing a policy of reassurance vis-á-vis its neighbors to the East. Japan for its part, prefers to overlook simmering regional threats in North Korea and China and continues to insist that it will make only nonmilitary contributions to the international order. While there is slow evolution—as there has been during much of the Cold War—there is no fundamental shift in direction, either toward greater defense autonomy or toward the assumption of a leadership role on security issues in a multilateral context.

The Evolution of German and Japanese Security Policies

Accompanying the changes in German and Japanese political-military cultures there were also shifts in their national security policies, as one would expect if there is a causal relationship between the two. Moreover, when those shifts ran against the established antimilitary cultures, they were accompanied—as predicted earlier—by intense domestic political debate and controversy. For analytical purposes it is useful to distinguish three different aspects of national security policy: alliance politics, force structure and mission, and civil-military relations.

Alliance Politics

German and Japanese alliance policies changed in two major ways during the Cold War: U.S.-Japanese military ties were intensified in the late 1970s and 1980s, and West Germany tried to achieve closer relations with

54. See *Yomiuri*, July 9, 1994, pp. 1 and 2.
55. See the *Frankfurter Allgemeine Zeitung*, July 15, 1994, pp. 1 and 2.

the Soviet Union and Eastern Europe, beginning in the late 1960s. In West Germany the primary impulse for Ostpolitik came from a deep-rooted desire to hammer out a modus vivendi with the Soviet Union that would decrease the threat of war and increase contact with the East German population. Such geostrategic considerations and nationalist aspirations alone need not have led to a far-reaching series of agreements on trade and security.[56] The Republic of South Korea, for instance, has endured national partition and the threat of war for an even longer period than West Germany did, without engaging in a comparable diplomatic campaign. In addition, the student movement of the late 1960s and the desire to atone for Germany's crimes during the Nazi period made a moral imperative out of a diplomatic initiative and lent the Ostpolitik policies of Willy Brandt and Egon Bahr a dynamic that went well beyond the satisfaction of immediate German national interests.

After immensely difficult negotiations and fierce parliamentary battles (the Brandt government survived a no-confidence measure by a mere two votes), in 1971 the West German government signed a series of agreements with its Eastern neighbors, including the Soviet Union and the East German regime. These agreements covered a wide range of issues, the most important of which were increased economic and diplomatic ties, the status of Berlin, and humanitarian contacts between the two German states.[57] Thereafter, the West German government continued to pursue closer ties with the East, becoming the primary sponsor of the CSCE (Conference on Security and Cooperation in Europe), which led to the signing of the Helsinki Accords in 1975.[58] Even during the bitterest period of U.S.-Soviet confrontation in the early 1980s, the Federal Republic continued to pursue relations with the East despite widespread American and Western apprehensions that Germany was heading down the path toward neutralism.[59]

---

56. On this point the author is indebted to conversations with Victor Cha on the evolution of the dialogue between North and South Koreas. Relations between Taiwan and China also contrast sharply with the German case.

57. For what is still one of the best overviews of the politics leading up to the Eastern Treaties, see William E. Griffith, *The Ostpolitik of the Federal Republic of Germany* (Cambridge: MIT Press, 1978), esp. ch. 5.

58. See Jonathan Dean, *Watershed in Europe* (Lexington, Mass.: Lexington Books, 1987); and Vjotech Mastny, *Helsinki, Human Rights, and European Security* (Durham: Duke University Press, 1986).

59. See Clay Clemens, *Reluctant Realists*. For a sampling of the fears that this policy caused abroad, see Christopher Layne, "Deutschland über Alles," *New Republic* (September 1987); and Eberhard Schulz and Peter Danylow, eds., *Bewegung in die deutsche Frage? Die ausländischen Besorgnisse über die Entwicklung in den beiden deutschen Staaten* (Bonn: Deutsche Gesellschaft für auswärtige Politik, 1985).

In the case of Japan, the initial impetus toward greater military cooperation with the United States came in the mid-1970s, as American power in the Pacific appeared to decline after Vietnam while that of the Soviet Union increased. These developments led to a stormy debate within the LDP over whether Japan should assume a more active, independent stance on defense even while retaining its security links with the United States, a position known as *jishubōei*.[60] After much deliberation and internal squabbling, the ruling party leaders and bureaucrats, alarmed by the nationalist rhetoric of the *jishubōei* camp and signs of growing anxiety abroad, chose to strengthen Japan's alliance with the United States instead. Over the next few years, the government laid the groundwork for closer cooperation between the two nations' armed forces, culminating in the 1978 Guidelines on U.S.-Japanese Defense Cooperation. Thereafter contacts between the Self Defense Forces and the U.S. military increased sharply. Japanese naval forces were dispatched abroad on training missions, and American and Japanese military planners began formal discussions on how they might react to a military crisis in the Far East. These trends accelerated further in the early 1980s, especially under the conservative Nakasone administration, which opened the door for joint weapons research and development and increased Japan's commitment to containing the Soviet Union.[61]

In short, the changes in German and Japanese elite and public attitudes toward defense mirrored actual shifts in policy. In West Germany the Left's objective of establishing at least a limited security partnership with Eastern Europe was realized, while in Japan the Right's long-sought-after goal of strengthening the armed forces through closer ties to the United States was finally achieved. These were important shifts in policy that had been encouraged—though not dictated—by changes in the international environment, but whose implementation was delayed for years until the requisite domestic political support could be mustered. In West Germany the CDU was able to resist the trend toward detente for nearly a decade. In Japan it took more than five years after the end of the Vietnam War before an internal consensus in favor of closer ties to the United States could be formed.

These changes in policy did not imply, however, that the basic German and Japanese alliance strategies had been abandoned. Both countries

---

60. See Ōtake, *Nihon no Boei to Kokunai Seiji*, chs. 1–3.
61. See Chuma Kiyofuku, *Saigumbi no Seijigaku* (Tokyo: Chishikisha, 1985), pp. 45–94.

remained dependent on the United States for military security, and efforts either to establish an independent defense posture (as called for by Naka-sone and the advocates of *jishubōei*) or to abandon NATO (as demanded by the Greens and the left wing of the SPD) had been emphatically denied. Germany remained tightly integrated into the NATO command structure and continued to seek to reach its foreign policy objectives primarily through multilateral institutions. Germany also continued to be one of the prime proponents of deepening the European Community—if anything, German unification even accelerated this trend—while at the same time integrating itself even more thoroughly into new NATO institutions such as the Nuclear Planning Group.[62]

Japan, on the other hand, maintained relatively looser ties with the United States. Even after 1978 there was no joint command structure, only a coordinating office to be set up in the event of an emergency. Despite Nakasone's sometimes belligerent rhetoric (he once described Japan as an "unsinkable aircraft carrier" ready to repel Soviet aggression), it remained uncertain whether Japanese forces would assist the United States except in the event of a direct Soviet attack.

Since the end of the Cold War there has been some shift toward increased regionalism in both countries, but the basic patterns of behavior remain consistent with the core values established in the 1950s. In Europe, in keeping with its traditional strategy of integrating itself, Germany has deepened both its European and its Atlantic multilateral military commitment, turning the French-German brigade into a corps and promoting the creation of multinational forces inside NATO to which the alliance's most combat-ready forces will be allocated.[63] Germany has also been the chief promoter of expanding the alliance eastward while offering the Soviet Union various forms of reassurance that such moves are not directed against it, but rather are designed to gradually pull the entire region into a peaceful, multinational security order.

Japan, like Germany, remains wedded to its close military relationship with the United States. At the same time, it also has begun to foster a security dialogue with neighboring countries in East Asia. Nonetheless, Japan's

---

62. See Dieter Mahncke, *Nukleare Mitwirkung: Die Bundesrepublik in der Atlantischen Allianz* (Berlin: de Gruyter, 1972).

63. See Thomas-Durrell Young, *Franco-German Security Accommodation: Illusion of Agreement* (Carlisle, Pa: U.S. Army War College, Strategic Studies Institute, 1993); Hilmar Linnenkamp, "The Security Policy of the New Germany," in Paul B. Stares, ed., *The New Germany and the New Europe* (Washington, D.C.: Brookings Institution, 1992), pp. 98–100; and Wolfgang Schlör, *German Security Policy*, Adelphi Paper 277 (London: IISS-Brassey's, June 1993), pp. 30, 58–59.

efforts in this direction remain tentative. Although with the end of the Cold War the strategic positions that Germany and Japan now occupy have become quite similar with respect to the risks of entanglement versus the dangers of abandonment, the Japanese political-military culture still has not adjusted to its changed external environment. The fear of entanglement continues to loom large in Japanese politics. Perhaps more important, whereas German leaders are able to justify their policies through reference to Germany's membership in a larger community of Western values, similar arguments with respect to the commonalities between Japan and the United States or Japan and the rest of Asia fail to have similar domestic resonance.

Force Structure and Mission

During the Cold War, West Germany's and Japan's decisions to continue to rely on the United States for external security implied that, at least to a limited extent, they had to follow the U.S. lead on security issues. As the United States redoubled its efforts to contain growing Soviet military strength in the late 1970s and 1980s, Germany and Japan were compelled to follow suit, expanding and modernizing their armed forces and adopting military missions and force postures that in certain respects appeared to signal a departure from their earlier policies. To many West German critics, the deployment of a new generation of intermediate nuclear forces (INF) and the Kohl government's willingness to support President Ronald Reagan's Strategic Defense Initiative (SDI) signified German acceptance of new, highly belligerent nuclear doctrines.[64] Fears that German foreign policy was being remilitarized were further reinforced by the Bundeswehr's adoption of the American doctrine of Follow-on Forward Attack (FOFA), which foresaw deep strikes into Eastern Europe in order to disrupt a Soviet assault.

Likewise, in Japan, Prime Minister Suzuki Zentaro's pledge to defend his nation's sea lanes of communication for up to a thousand nautical miles from the Japanese mainland appeared to mark a dramatic expansion of the SDF's traditional territorial defense role. Similarly, the overturning of the one-percent-of-GNP limit on defense spending was interpreted by many as a sign that the Japanese government was moving beyond its minimalist approach to spending and preparing to embark on a major arms buildup.[65]

---

64. See Hans Günter Brauch, ed., *Star Wars and European Defense* (New York: St. Martin's, 1987).
65. On the sea lanes issue, see Chuma Kiyofuku, *Saigumbi no Seijigaku*, pp. 107–24; on Japanese defense spending, see Joseph P. Keddell, Jr., *The Politics of Defense in Japan: Managing Internal and External Pressures* (Armonk: M. E. Sharpe, 1993), ch. 3.

Yet on closer inspection, many of these apparent departures prove far less significant that they were made out to be. The primary purpose of deploying the INF missiles was not to develop the ability to launch a decapitating first strike but rather to reinforce the credibility of the American nuclear guarantee in an era of increasing Soviet power.[66] Moreover, consistent with the pattern of behavior that had already been established in the 1950s, Germany continued to seek accommodation even as it strengthened deterrence by linking the INF deployments to new arms control initiatives.[67]

Similarly, Kohl's endorsement of SDI was motivated more by the desire to demonstrate solidarity with the United States than to help establish military dominance over the Soviet Union. Within the German government even prodefense conservatives, such as Manfred Wörner, were uneasy about SDI, fearing that if it were realized it might prove destabilizing. Consequently, Chancellor Kohl made his support of SDI even as a *research* program contingent on further progress in the area of arms control.[68] German support for American plans for a conventional defense of Europe was similarly lukewarm, and for the most part Germany paid only lip service to these new doctrines and did not actually implement them. The concrete impact of these policies on actual German force structures and defense planning was on the whole rather minimal.[69]

The Japanese commitment to defending its sea lanes was also a highly political statement with little concrete military impact. The Japanese Self Defense Forces had long planned to patrol Japan's sea lanes of communication in order to assure the continued flow of oil and other vital raw materials. Yet the Maritime Self Defense Forces had little hope of accomplishing this mission on their own, and Suzuki's announcement did little to change that state of affairs. Indeed, it seems that the policy owed more to domestic political intrigues than to geostrategic exigencies. There is

---

66. See Helmut Schmidt, *Menschen und Mächte* (Berlin: Siedler. 1987), p. 92; and Wolfram Hanrieder, *Germany, America, and Europe* (New Haven: Yale University Press, 1989), pp. 110–11.

67. See Helga Haftendorn, *Sicherheit und Entspannung* (Baden-Baden: Nomos Verlag, 1986), pp. 250–51.

68. Christian Hacke, *Weltmacht wider Willen* (Stuttgart: Ernst Klett, 1988), pp. 334–41; Ernst-Otto Czempiel, "SDI and NATO: The Case of the Federal Republic of Germany," in Sanford Lakoff and Randy Willoughby, eds., *Strategic Defense and the Western Alliance*, pp. 147–64 (Lexington, Mass.: Lexington Books, 1987).

69. See the comments by General Inspector of the Bundeswehr Klaus Naumann on the prospects for a conventional defense of Western Europe in Naumann, "The Forces and the Future," in Stephen S. Szabo, *The Bundeswehr and Western Security* (London: Macmillan, 1990), p. 174.

considerable evidence that Suzuki never intended to expand Japan's military obligations in the first place but enemies inside the government had tricked him into making the statement in order to embarrass him.[70]

Other defense initiatives also increased Japan's dependence on the United States. In the event of a Soviet attack, Japanese defense planners envisioned, Japanese forces would serve as the conventional "shield," protecting the American forces, which would act as a military "spear," launching attacks on Soviet forces in the Far East. Consequently there was a heavy emphasis on acquiring basically defensive weapons systems, such as improved antisubmarine warfare capabilities and air defense systems. Little effort was made to acquire greater force projection capabilities, and Japan eschewed obtaining weapons systems that might be construed as being offensive in character, such as aerial refueling capacity or helicopter carriers. Japanese forces also continued to adhere to a territorial defense role. During the first Gulf crisis, in 1987, many Japanese foreign policy experts thought that it would be in Japan's interests to dispatch at least minesweepers to the region to demonstrate support for the United States and to nudge public opinion toward acceptance of a broader role for the SDF. Once again, however, pressures from within the ruling party vetoed such a move.[71]

West German defense spending patterns from the mid-1970s to the mid-1980s reflected this relatively low level of interest in expanding military capabilities. While the defense budgets of both countries continued to grow and their capabilities increased as a result of force modernization, defense spending as a percentage of GNP grew only marginally in Japan and actually declined in Germany. And this at a time when East-West tensions were at their highest since the Cuban missile crisis and conservative, prodefense governments were in office in both countries.

With the decline of the Soviet threat after the Cold War, both Germany and Japan have significantly reduced their armed forces and their defense budgets. This is particularly true of Germany, which has reduced its army to 370,000 and greatly slowed the pace of force modernization.[72] Since Japanese forces started from a much lower baseline, pressures for force

---

70. See Chuma Kiyofuku, *Saigumbi no Seijigaku*, pp. 110–12; Keddell, *The Politics of Defense in Japan*, pp. 112–18; interview with highly placed officials in the Japanese Foreign Ministry, Tokyo, October 1988.

71. See *Asahi*, July 7, 1987, evening ed., p. 1; *Asahi*, September 5, 1987, p. 3; *Japan Times*, October 8, 1987, p. 1; and Gotoda Masaharu, *Seiji to wa Nanika* (Tokyo: Kodansha, 1988), p. 172.

72. Schlör, *German Security Policy*, pp. 40–43; and Linnenkamp, "The Security Policy of the New Germany," pp. 95–96.

TABLE 9.2

Defense Spending as a percentage of GNP, 1975–1986			
	1975	1980	1986
United States	6.0	5.1	6.7
Germany	3.7	3.3	3.1
Japan	0.9	0.9	1.0

Source: Simon Duke, *The Burdensharing Debate*
(New York: St. Martin's, 1993), p. 116.

reduction have not been as great. Nonetheless, there, too, defense spending has decreased, reaching its lowest level of increase—0.7 percent—in more than thirty years.

Both armed forces continue to modernize, albeit slowly. The only significant change has been in the definition of their mission, which since the Gulf war has been expanded to include participation in peacekeeping operations. The SDF and the Bundeswehr are undergoing some reorganization in preparation for carrying out such missions, The pace of these changes, however, remains very slow, the great majority of German and Japanese forces remain earmarked for territorial defense, and neither nation has made any deliberate effort to increase its power projection capabilities.[73]

Civil-Military Relations

Even greater immobility may be observed in the area of civil-military relations. This is not to say that there was a complete absence of debate on this topic. On the contrary, throughout the Cold War civil-military relations remained one of the most sensitive issues on the political agenda. Nonetheless, the pressures for change were the weakest in this area of policy, and the domestic political resistance to change was the strongest.

In West Germany the chief point of contestation was over the political symbolism and how the Bundeswehr should portray its predecessors—the

---

73. The complete text of the Japanese peacekeeping law along with concomitant amendments to other laws governing the Japanese armed forces can be found in "Kokusai heiwaji katsudō nado ni tai suru Kyōryoku ni Kan suru Hōritsu," *Shinbōeironshu* 20, no. 2 (September 1992): 82–100. For more on the background of the law, see Aurelia George, "Japan's Participation in UN Peacekeeping Missions: Radical Departure or Predictable Response?" *Asian Survey* 33, no. 6 (June 1993): 560–75. On German Bundeswehr reorganization, see Otfried Nassauer, "Die NATO—Aufbruch zu neuen Ufern?" in Erich Schmidt-Eenboom and Jo Angerer, eds., *Siegermacht NATO* (Berg am See: Verlagsgesellschaft Berg, 1993), pp. 75–84; and Thomas-Durrell Young, *The New European Security Calculus: Implications for the U.S. Army* (U.S. Army War College, Strategic Studies Institute, Carlisle Barracks, March 1, 1991).

Reichswehr and the Wehrmacht—in the construction of an institutional persona that its members could use as a role model. Conservative politicians and officers periodically sought to strengthen unit cohesion through the cultivation of a sense of military tradition. In a number of respects, these traditions—especially their emphasis on discipline, obedience, and a martial ethos oriented toward killing—clashed with the principles of *innere Führung.*[74]

During the 1980s the Kohl government, concerned that German society needed a healthy sense of patriotism in order to counter the neutralist tendencies of the peace movement, raised similar issues concerning the place of the armed forces in Germany identity on the national level through a series of symbolic gestures. The most controversial of these was Kohl's 1986 visit with President Ronald Reagan to the Bittburg military cemetery, where former members of Hitler's Waffen ss, among other, ss are buried. The Kohl administration continued to attach great importance to this kind of political symbolism even after the Cold War ended, as reflected by the reinterment of the Prussian Soldier King, Friedrich II, in 1993 and the participation of German troops in the July 14, 1994, parade of the Eurocorps down the Champs d'Elysees.[75]

Innere Führung, although challenged, proved too deeply rooted to be discarded, and efforts to re-create a martial ethos within the Bundeswehr were unsuccessful. Although compromises were worked out on such peripheral issues as the names of ships or barracks, the doctrine of democratizing internal military life was retained. Likewise, even after the end of the Cold War made the military rationale for the maintenance of a mass army less credible, support for the retention of military conscription crossed party lines and was legitimated as an important means of integrating the armed forces into society.[76]

In Japan the debate centered on retaining airtight control over the activ-

---

74. See Abenheim, *Reforging the Iron Cross*; Ulrich Simon, *Die Integration der Bundeswehr in die Gesellschaft* (Heidelberg/Hamburg: R.v.Decker's Verlag G. Schenck, 1980); and Martin Esser, *Das Traditionsverständnis des Offizierkorps* (Heidelberg/Hamburg: R.v.Decker's Verlag G. Schenck, 1982).

75. For an extensive documentary overview of the Bittburg visit and the controversy surrounding it, see Ilya Lefkov, ed., *Bitburg and Beyond: Encounters in American, German, and Jewish History* (New York: Shapolsky Books, 1987).

76. See Hans-Adolf Jacobsen and Hans-Jürgen Rautenberg, eds., *Bundeswehr und Europäische Sicherheitsordnung* (Bonn: Bouvier, 1991), pp. 50–51, 55–59; and Jürgen Kuhlmann and Ekkehard Lippert, "Wehrpflicht Ade? Argumente für und wider die Wehrpflicht in Friedenszeiten," in Geld Kladrack and Paul Klein, eds., *Die Zukunft der Streitkräfte Angesichts Weltweiter Abrüstungsbemühungen* (Baden-Baden: Nomos Verlagsgesellschaft, 1992).

ities of military men and the ways in which the government portrayed the martial aspects of Japan's past.[77] The continued modernization of the Japanese military and its assumption of somewhat broader military roles inevitably led to modification of the many legislative safeguards that had been placed on the armed forces. So, for example, in 1986 the one-per-cent-of-GNP limit on defense spending was abrogated. Every time a safe-guard has been dropped, however, it has been replaced by new constraints. In the case of the one-percent barrier, a five-year rolling budget was intro-duced that made sure expansion took place at a controlled pace. Other measures were implemented as well, increasing the ability of politicians and nonmilitary bureaucrats to intervene in the military budget process.[78]

As in Germany, conservative leaders in Japan believed that the nation lacked a proper sense of patriotism. As a result, throughout the Cold War there were repeated efforts to rekindle a sense of national consciousness. And as in Germany, these concerns motivated conservative leaders to make a number of symbolic gestures designed to reconcile postwar Japan-ese society with the armed forces; the most famous such overture was Nakasone's 1986 visit to the Yasukuni shrine dedicated to the Japanese war dead. Unlike the situation in Germany, however, these efforts have had more far-reaching, concrete policy implications revolving primarily around the issue of how to treat the war in Japanese textbooks.[79] In the late 1980s and early 1990s the Japanese government succeeded in revising Japanese textbooks, including making a discussion of Japan's right to self-defense part of the curriculum and adding Admiral Tōgō Heihachirō, a hero of the Russo-Japanese war, to the list of historical role models for Japanese children.[80]

As in Germany, however, these symbolic gestures were highly contro-versial and have never been fully institutionalized. Nakasone's trip to the Yasukuni shrine attracted widespread criticism, as did other measures that appeared to link the military with religious or nationalist themes. More-

77. Hirose Katsuya, *Kanryo to Gunjin: Bunmintosei no Genkai* (Tokyo: Iwanami Shoten, 1989); *Nikkei*, February 16, 1992, p. 2, and October 16, 1993, p. 2.
78. Keddell, *The Politics of Defense in Japan*, pp. 126–56.
79. Because of the institutional structure of the German state, where education is a responsibility of state governments, this issue rarely reaches national politics. For an exception, see Dieter Lutz, *Der 'Friedens'-Streit der Kultusminister: Ein 'Schul' Beispiel* (Baden-Baden: Nomos Verlagsgesellschaft, 1984). For an overview of the Japanese debate, see Teruhisa Hori, *Educational Thought and Ideology in Modern Japan: State Authority and Intellectual Freedom* (Tokyo: University of Tokyo Press, 1988), pp. 106–212.
80. See *Asahi*, July 1, 1992, p. 1; and *Japan Times*, July 1, 1992, p. 3.

over, at the same time that Japanese textbooks began to deal more openly with military issues, the Japanese government began to allow more discussion of Japanese wartime atrocities in school texts. Parallel to these efforts was a diplomatic campaign, spearheaded by the new Japanese emperor, to apologize to other Asian nations for Japan's past misconduct in the region.[81]

In short, the core features of the German and Japanese approaches to maintaining control over the armed forces—tight bureaucratic controls in the Japanese case and integration of the armed forces into society in the German case—remained intact into the 1990s. While in both countries conservative governments sought to cast the armed forces in a more positive light, their efforts to do so met with limited success and were offset by countervailing pressures to acknowledge the terrible crimes to which Bundeswehr's and SDF's predecessors had been party. More than fifty years after the end of World War II the past continues to cast a large, inescapable shadow over the official discourse on the relationship between the armed forces and society.

As the foregoing analysis of German and Japanese security policy has demonstrated, cultural norms and values have evolved in tandem with shifts in behavior, precisely as our model predicts. Over the past fifty years, external events such as the end of the East-West conflict, the Gulf war, or shifts in the balance of power have periodically triggered domestic political debates over national security. At issue in these debates has been not only the question of how beset to realize German and Japanese interests but also the highly emotional areas of national identity and the definition of national interests. Different political actors in the German and Japanese contexts have held strong and widely divergent views on these subjects, leading to intense controversies over how to interpret external developments and how to respond to them. The extreme sensitivity of military security issues in the German and Japanese contexts has placed significant constraints on policy making in the area of security. German and Japanese political leaders are naturally reluctant to deal with such a highly sensitive issue, especially since the domestic political gains from taking a strong stance on defense are perceived by most politicians as minimal.[82]

Moreover, the overall direction of the shifts both in German and Japan-

---

81. For an overview of recent developments, see *Sekai* (February 1994), special issue on war guilt, Arai Shinichi, Sensō Sekinin to wa Nani Ka"; and Tanaka Akira, "Nihon wa Sensō Sekinin ni dō taishite kita ka."

ese behavior and in attitudes indicates a consolidation of, rather than a departure from, the antimilitarism approaches to national security that originally came together in the 1950s. Despite profound changes in their external security environments, German and Japanese policy makers have acted in a manner consistent with the core principles of the political-military cultures established by their nations in the 1950s and 1960s. In turn, German and Japanese behavior has had an increasingly significant impact on the security environments in those countries. Germany's commitment to political and economic integration has permitted the formation of a European security community, while Japan's eschewal of military power has greatly reduced tensions in the potentially volatile Asia-Pacific region.

To be sure, there have been incremental shifts all along in German and Japanese defense and national security, and such shifts are likely to continue as the two countries adjust to changes in the international system. A dramatic shift from the core principles of their political-military culture is, however, likely only if there is a major shock to the system that persuades the countries' leaders that their approach to defense and national security has been a failure. In the Japanese case, such an event would require a collapse of the U.S.-Japan alliance, combined with the emergence of a major new security threat. In the German case, even if the alliance with the United States came apart, there would remain the option of trying to find a purely European solution to the problem of nuclear deterrence. Alternatively, a failure of extended deterrence resulting in an attack on a German or Japanese population center might constitute a similar shock. Even under such extreme circumstances, however, German and Japanese behavior would not likely change overnight. Instead, there would be intense domestic political debate between different political actors about how to interpret these events and how to respond to them. The outcome of such debate would be, at least in part, strongly shaped by domestic political forces, and the kind of policies that would then be adopted are not predictable by considering external factors alone.

---

82. This is particularly true in Japan. The author has had numerous oportunities over the past five years to discuss defense issues with Japanese policy makers and it has been their *unanimous* view that a strong, prodefense position brings little electoral benefit. As a prominent liberal democratic Diet member put it to the author, "Bōei wa Hyō ni Tsunagaranai" (interview with Nagao Eiichi, Tokyo, spring 1988), a point of view that was repeated to the author many times by politicians from both the Left and the Right.

10 · Collective Identity in a Democratic Community: The Case of NATO

Thomas Risse-Kappen

The Puzzle

Why was it that the United States, the undisputed superpower of the early post-1945 period, found itself entangled in the North Atlantic Treaty Organization (NATO) with Western Europe only four years after the end of World War II? Why was it that a pattern of cooperation evolved in NATO that survived not only the ups and downs of the Cold War and various severe interallied conflicts—from the 1956 Suez crisis to the conflict over Euromissiles in the 1980s—but also the end of the Cold War? Why is it that NATO has emerged as the strongest among the post–Cold War security institutions—as compared to the Organization for Security and Cooperation in Europe (OSCE), the West European Union (WEU), not even to mention the EU's Common Foreign and Security Policy (CFSP)?

This essay summarizes, builds upon, and expands arguments developed in Thomas Risse-Kappen, *Cooperation Among Democracies: The European Influence on U.S. Foreign Policy* (Princeton: Princeton University Press, 1995). Participation in the Social Science Research Council–sponsored project under the directorship of Peter Katzenstein has greatly inspired my thinking on the subject of norms, identity, and social constructivism. For comments on the draft of this essay, I am very grateful to the project participants, in particular Peter Katzenstein. I am also indebted to Mark Laffey, David Latham, Fred H. Lawson, Stephen Walt, Steve Weber, and several anonymous reviewers for their criticism and suggestions.

Traditional (realist) alliance theory[1] at least has a simple answer to the first two questions: *the Soviet threat*. But what constituted the Soviet threat? Was it Soviet power, ideology, behavior, or all three combined? I argue in this essay that the notion of the "Soviet threat" needs to be unpacked and problematized if we want to understand what it contributed to the emergence and the endurance of NATO. I also claim that realism might provide first-cut answers to the questions above but that it is indeterminate with regard to explaining particular Western European and U.S. choices at critical junctures of the Cold War, not even to mention its aftermath. Moreover, sophisticated power-based arguments that try to account for these choices do so at the expense of parsimony. Why should they be privileged as providing the baseline story, while more elegant alternative explanations are used to add some local coloration?[2]

I provide an account for the origins and the endurance of NATO different from the conventional wisdom. NATO and the transatlantic relationship can be better understood on the basis of *republican liberalism* linking domestic polities systematically to the foreign policy of states.[3] Liberal democracies are likely to form "pacific federations" (Immanuel Kant) or "pluralistic security communities" (Karl W. Deutsch). Liberalism in the Kantian sense, however, needs to be distinguished from the conventional use of the term, as in *neoliberal institutionalism*, denoting the "cooperation under anarchy" perspective of rationalist regime analysis.[4] I present a social constructivist interpretation of *republican liberalism*, emphasizing collec-

---

1. See, for example, Hans J. Morgenthau, *Politics Among Nations: The Struggle for Power and Peace*, brief ed. (1948; reprint, New York: McGraw Hill, 1993); Kenneth N. Waltz, *Theory of International Politics* (Reading, Mass.: Addison-Wesley, 1979); George Liska, *Nations in Alliance: The Limits of Interdependence* (Baltimore: Johns Hopkins University Press, 1962); Arnold Wolfers, *Discord and Collaboration* (Baltimore: Johns Hopkins University Press, 1962). See also Ole R. Holsti et al., *Unity and Disintegration in International Alliances* (New York: Wiley, 1973).

2. On this point, see Ron Jepperson, Alexander Wendt, and Peter J. Katzenstein, "Norms, Identity, and Culture in National Security," essay 2 in this volume.

3. See, for example, Michael Doyle, "Liberalism and World Politics," *American Political Science Review* 80, no. 4 (1986): 1151–69; Robert Keohane, "International Liberalism Reconsidered," in John Dunn, ed., *The Economic Limits to Modern Politics*, pp. 165–94 (Cambridge: Cambridge University Press, 1990); Bruce Russett, *Grasping the Democratic Peace: Principles for a Post–Cold War World* (Princeton: Princeton University Press, 1993).

4. On this use of the term, see, for example, Joseph M. Grieco, "Anarchy and the Limits of Cooperation: A Realist Critique of the Newest Liberal Institutionalism," *International Organization* 42, no. 3 (Summer 1988): 485–507; Robert O. Keohane, *International Institutions and State Power: Essays in International Relations Theory* (Boulder: Westview, 1989). See also the discussion of neoliberalism in Peter J. Katzenstein, "Introduction: Alternative Perspectives on National Security," essay 1 in this volume.

tive identities and norms of appropriate behavior. To illustrate my argument, I discuss the origins of NATO, the transatlantic interactions during two major Cold War "out-of-area" crises (the 1956 Suez crisis and the 1962 Cuban missile crisis), and the persistence of NATO after the end of the Cold War.

Theorizing About Alliances
Realism and NATO: The Indeterminacy of the Conventional Wisdom

Traditional alliance theory is firmly grounded in realist thinking. Realism, however, is indeterminate with regard to explaining the origins of, the interaction patterns in, and the endurance of NATO.

Realism and the Origins of NATO

Structural realism contains a straightforward alliance theory.[5] States balance rather than bandwagon; alliances form because weak states band together against great powers in order to survive in an anarchic international system. Alliance patterns change because the international distribution of power changes. This is particularly true under multipolarity; great powers do not need allies under bipolarity. The latter structure consists of only two great powers, which are self-sufficient in terms of their ability to survive. As a result, alliances become a matter of convenience rather than necessity.

It is hard to reconcile Waltzian realism with the history of NATO. The U.S. emerged from World War II as the undisputed superpower in the international system, enjoying a monopoly (and later superiority) with regard to the most advanced weapons systems, i.e., nuclear forces. Its gross domestic product (GDP) outweighed that of all Western European states combined, not even to mention the Soviet Union. If material capabilities are all that counts in world politics, one would have expected Western Europe to align with the Soviet Union rather than with the U.S.[6]

5. For the following, see Waltz, *Theory of International Politics*, ch. 6; and Glenn H. Snyder, "Alliance Theory: A Neorealist First Cut," *Journal of International Affairs* 44, no. 1 (Spring 1990): 103–23.
6. See Stephen M. Walt, *The Origins of Alliances* (Ithaca: Cornell University Press, 1987), pp. 274–76. For thorough critiques of the Waltzian notion of bipolarity, see, for example, Richard Ned Lebow, "The Long Peace, the End of the Cold War, and the Failure of Realism," *International Organization* 48, no. 2 (Spring 1994): 249–77; R. Harrison Wagner, "What Was Bipolarity?" *International Organization* 47, no. 1 (Winter 1993): 77–106.

But the Waltzian argument rests on some peculiar assumptions about bipolarity. While great powers may not need allies to ensure their survival, client states might become an asset in the competition between the two hegemonic rivals. After all, bipolarity means that the two great powers in the system have to cope primarily with each other. As "defensive positionalists," they are expected to be concerned about relative gains and losses vis-à-vis each other and to compete fiercely.[7] The more important relative gains are, however, the more significant the acquisition of client states should become. While the loss or defection of one small ally might not be important, superpowers might fear that even small losses might set in motion a chain reaction.

Thus, if we change our understanding of bipolarity only slightly, American Cold War policies of acquiring allies around the globe, including the Western Europeans, can be explained. In other words, structural realism can be made consistent with actual U.S. behavior during the Cold War, but the theory could also explain the opposite behavior.

What about Stephen Walt's more sophisticated realism emphasizing the "balance of threat" rather than the "balance of power"?[8] Does it reduce the indeterminacy of structural realism by adding more variables? Walt argues that states align against what they perceive as threats rather than against economic and military capabilities as such. States feel threatened when they face powers that combine superior capabilities with geostrategic proximity, offensive military power, and offensive ideology. One could then argue that the proximity of the Soviet landmass to Western Europe, Moscow's offensive military doctrine backed by superior conventional forces, and the aggressive communist ideology constituted the Soviet threat leading to the formation of NATO.

There is no question that Western decision makers perceived a significant Soviet threat during the late 1940s and that this threat perception was causally consequential for the formation of NATO. The issue is not the threat perception, but what constituted it: Soviet power, ideology, behavior, or a combination of the three? As to Soviet power, the geographic proximity of the Soviet landmass—Walt's first indicator—could explain the Western European threat perception and the British and French

---

7. See Waltz, *Theory of International Politics*, pp. 106, 170–73. On "relative gains" in particular, see Grieco, "Anarchy and the Limits of Cooperation." For an argument that relative gains are particularly important under bipolarity, see Duncan Snidal, "International Cooperation Among Relative Gain Maximizers," *International Studies Quarterly* 35, no. 4 (December 1991): 387–402.
8. Walt, *The Origins of Alliances*.

attempts to lure reluctant decision makers in Washington into a permanent alliance with Europe.[9] But it is still unclear why the U.S. valued Western Europe so much that it decided to join NATO. The argument that the U.S. wanted to prevent Soviet control over the Eurasian rimland[10] makes sense only if we also assume that decision makers in Washington saw themselves as defensive positionalists in a fierce hegemonic rivalry rather than more relaxed Waltzian realists (see above). In this case, sophisticated realism is as inconclusive as structural realism.

Moreover, the Soviet Union was not considered an offensive military threat to Western Europe during the late 1940s. Military estimates did increasingly point to Soviet military superiority in Europe, but that did not lead to the perception of an imminent attack. As John Lewis Gaddis put it, "Estimates of Moscow's intentions, whether from the Pentagon, the State Department, or the intelligence community, consistently discounted the possibility that the Russians might risk a direct military confrontation within the foreseeable future."[11]

Rather, the U.S. threat perception at the time focused on potential Soviet ability to psychologically blackmail war-weakened Western Europe and to destabilize these countries politically and economically. This American view of a significant Soviet threat was concerned about actual Soviet behavior in *Eastern Europe* and the Soviet offensive political ideology—the third of Walt's indicators. If this is indeed what constituted the Soviet threat in Western eyes in the late 1940s, it can be better explained by liberal theories than by even sophisticated realism (see

---

9. On the origins of NATO, see, for example, Richard Best, *"Cooperation with Like-Minded Peoples": British Influence on American Security Policy, 1945–1949* (Westport, Conn.: Greenwood, 1986); Don Cook, *Forging the Alliance: NATO, 1945–1950* (New York: Arbor House/William Morrow, 1989); Sir Nicholas Henderson, *The Birth of NATO* (London: Weidenfeld and Nicolson, 1982); Timothy P. Ireland, *Creating the Entangling Alliance: The Origins of the North Atlantic Treaty Organization* (Westport, Conn.: Greenwood, 1981).

10. On this point, see Wagner, "What Was Bipolarity?" and Robert Jervis and Jack Snyder, eds., *Dominoes and Bandwagons: Strategic Beliefs and Great Power Competition in the Eurasian Rimland* (New York: Oxford University Press, 1991).

11. John Lewis Gaddis, *The Long Peace* (Oxford: Oxford University Press, 1987), p. 41. See also Matthew Evangelista, "Stalin's Postwar Army Reappraised," *International Security* 7, no. 3 (Winter 1982/83): 110–68; James L. Gormly, *From Potsdam to the Cold War* (Wilmington, Del.: Scholarly Resources, 1990), pp. 92–93; Melvyn P. Leffler, "National Security and U.S. Foreign Policy," in Melvyn P. Leffler and David S. Painter, eds., *Origins of the Cold War*, pp. 15–52, 25–27 (London: Routledge, 1994); Norbert Wiggershaus, "Nordatlantische Bedrohungsperzeptionen im 'Kalten Krieg,' 1948–1956," in Klaus A. Meier et al., eds., *Das Nordatlantische Bündnis, 1949–1956*, pp. 17–54 (Munich: Oldenbourg, 1993). Perceptions of a Soviet military threat increased only *after* the political confrontation was already in full swing.

below). At least, the two accounts become indistinguishable at this point.

Realism and Cooperation Patterns in NATO

Realism's indeterminacy with regard to the origins of NATO also applies to interaction patterns within the Western Alliance. To begin with, structural realism of the Waltzian variety has a clear expectation regarding cooperation among allies. If great powers do not need allies under bipolarity, they also do not need to listen to them. As Waltz put it, the contributions of smaller states to alliances "are useful even in a bipolar world, but they are not indispensable. Because they are not, the policies and strategies of alliance leaders are ultimately made according to their own calculations and interests."[12]

If this argument holds true, one would not expect much European influence on U.S. decisions during the Cold War—particularly not in cases, such as the Cuban missile crisis, when the U.S. perceived its supreme national interests at stake. I show later in this essay that this expectation proves to be wrong. Close cooperation among the allies was the rule rather than the exception throughout the history of NATO—with regard to European security, the U.S.-Soviet relationship, and "out-of-area" cases. The power asymmetry within NATO did not translate into American dominance. Rather, the European allies managed to influence U.S. foreign policy significantly even in cases when the latter considered its supreme national interests to be at stake.[13]

More sophisticated realists, however, should not be too surprised by these findings. If we assume that decision makers in Washington needed allies to fight the Cold War, we would expect some degree of cooperation within the Western Alliance, including European influence on U.S. policies. Allies who need each other to balance against a perceived threat are expected to cooperate with each other. Unfortunately, this assumption is

---

12. Waltz, *Theory of International Politics*, pp. 169, 170. Glenn Snyder applies this thought to the transatlantic alliance: "It is abundantly clear that the European allies will not do the United States' bidding when it is not in their own interest, but it is also clear that they have little positive influence over U.S. policy—when the United States does not wish to be influenced. . . . The word that most accurately describes their behavior is not domination or even bargaining, but unilateralism" (Snyder, "Alliance Theory," p. 121).
13. Details in Risse-Kappen, *Cooperation Among Democracies*. See also Fred Chernoff, *After Bipolarity* (Ann Arbor: University of Michigan Press, 1994); Helga Haftendorn, *Kernwaffen und die Glaubwürdigkeit der Allianz* (Baden-Baden: Nomos, 1994); Elizabeth Sherwood, *Allies in Crisis: Meeting Global Challenges to Western Security* (New Haven: Yale University Press, 1990).

demonstrably wrong. Cooperation among allies is by no means assured. Allies are as likely to fight each other as they are to fight non-allies—except for democratic alliances.[14] Thus we need additional assumptions about the conditions under which nations in alliances are likely to cooperate. According to realist bargaining theory, for example, we would expect a higher degree of interallied cooperation,

- the higher the perceived level of external threat
- the more allies fear that their partners might abandon them or defect, particularly in crisis situations
- the more issue-specific power resources are used in interallied bargaining situations.[15]

At this point, sophisticated realism loses much of its parsimony. Evaluating these propositions against alternative claims requires detailed process-tracing of interallied bargaining. We cannot simply assume a realist bargaining process when we find outcomes consistent with one specific version of realist theory.

Realism and the Endurance of NATO After the Cold War

The indeterminacy of realism also applies when we start using the theory to predict the survivability of NATO after the Cold War. Structural realists in the Waltzian tradition should expect NATO to wither away with the end of the Cold War. If great powers do not need allies under bipolarity for their survival, this should be all the more true when the hegemonic rivalry ceases to dominate world politics. In Waltz's own words, "NATO is a disappearing thing. It is a question of how long it is going to remain as a significant institution even though its name may linger on."[16]

In the absence of indicators of what "lingering on" means, it is hard to evaluate the proposition. I argue later in this essay that NATO is alive and well so far, at least as compared to other security institutions in Europe.

---

14. For evidence, see Bruce Bueno de Mesquita, *The War Trap* (New Haven: Yale University Press, 1981); Stuart A. Bremer, "Dangerous Dyads: Conditions Affecting the Likelihood of Interstate War, 1816–1965," *Journal of Conflict Resolution* 36, no. 2 (1992): 309–41.

15. On these propositions, see, for example, Michael Handel, *Weak States in the International System* (London: Frank Cass, 1981); Holsti, *Unity and Disintegration in International Alliances*; Glenn Snyder, "The Security Dilemma in Alliance Politics," *World Politics* 36, no. 4 (July 1984): 461–96; Jan F. Triska, ed., *Dominant Powers and Subordinate States* (Durham: Duke University Press, 1986).

16. At a U.S. Senate hearing in November 1990. Quoted from Gunther Hellmann and Reinhard Wolf, "Neorealism, Neoliberal Institutionalism, and the Future of NATO," *Security Studies* 3, no. 1 (Autumn 1993): 3–43, 17. See also John J. Mearsheimer, "Back to the Future: Instability in Europe After the Cold War," *International Security* 15, no. 1 (1990): 5–56.

364 • *Thomas Risse-Kappen*

Sophisticated realism and "balance-of-threat" arguments are indeterminate with regard to the future of NATO. On the one hand, one could argue that the Western Alliance should gradually disintegrate as a result of the Soviet withdrawal from Eastern Europe and the drastically decreased military threat. On the other hand, the Russian landmass might still constitute a residual risk to Western Europe, thus necessitating a hedge against a potential reemergence of the threat.[17] In any case, the Western offer for a "partnership for peace" to Russia is difficult to account for even by sophisticated realism.

In sum, a closer look at realism as the dominant alliance theory reveals its indeterminacy with regard to the origins of, the interaction patterns in, and the endurance of NATO. In retrospect, almost every single choice of states can be accommodated somehow by realist thinking. As a Waltzian realist, the U.S. could have concluded that the direct confrontation with the USSR was all that mattered, while the fate of the Western Europeans would not alter the global balance of power. As a more sophisticated realist, the U.S. would have decided—as it actually did—that the fate of the Eurasian rim was geostrategically too significant to leave the Western Europeans alone. If decision makers in Washington listened to their allies during the Cuban missile crisis, we can invoke realist arguments about reputation and the need to preserve the alliance during crises. Had the U.S. *not* listened to the Western Europeans during the crisis, one could have argued that superpowers do not need to worry about their allies when they perceive that their immediate survival is at stake. If NATO survives the end of the Cold War, it is "lingering on" as a hedge; if it disappears, the threat has withered away. As others have noted before, realism is not especially helpful in explaining particular foreign policy choices.[18] I now look at a liberal account emphasizing a community among democracies, collective identity, and alliance norms.

---

17. See Charles Glaser, "Why NATO Is Still Best: Future Security Arrangements for Europe," *International Security* 18, no. 1 (Summer 1993): 5–50.

18. As Kenneth Waltz himself put it, "With the aid of a rationality assumption one still cannot, from national interest alone, predict what the policy of a country might be" (Waltz, "Reflections on *Theory of International Politics*: A Response to My Critics," in Robert O. Keohane, ed., *Neorealism and Its Critics*, pp. 322–45 [New York: Columbia University Press, 1986], p. 331). On the indeterminate nature of realism, see also Robert O. Keohane, "Realism, Neorealism, and the Study of World Politics," ibid., pp. 1–26; Stephen Haggard, "Structuralism and Its Critics: Recent Progress in International Relations Theory," in Emanuel Adler and Beverly Crawford, eds., *Progress in Postwar International Relations*, pp. 403–37 (New York: Columbia University Press, 1991).

Democratic Allies in a Pluralistic Security Community: A Liberal Constructivist Approach

The U.S. had quite some latitude as to how it defined its interests in Europe. Thus we need to "look more closely at *this* particular hegemon" in order to "determine why *this* particular . . . agenda was pursued."[19] Domestic politics and structures have to be considered, and the realm of *liberal theories* of international relations is to be entered.

To avoid confusion, particularly with what is sometimes called *neoliberal institutionalism*, I reserve the term *liberal theories of international relations* for approaches agreeing that[20]

1. the fundamental agents in international politics are not states but individuals acting in a social context—whether governments, domestic society, or international institutions;

2. the interests and preferences of national governments have to be analyzed as a result of domestic structures and coalition-building processes responding to social demands as well as to external factors such as the (material and social) structure of the international system;

3. ideas—values, norms, and knowledge—are causally consequential in international relations, particularly with regard to state interests, preferences, and choices;

4. international institutions form the social structure of international politics presenting constraints and opportunities to actors.

Immanuel Kant's argument[21] that democratic institutions characterized by the rule of law, the respect for human rights, the nonviolent and compromise-oriented resolution of domestic conflicts, and participatory opportunities for the citizens are a necessary condition for peace has been

19. John G. Ruggie, "Multilateralism: The Anatomy of an Institution," *International Organization* 46, no. 3 (Summer 1992): 561–98, 592.

20. For efforts at systematizing a liberal theory of international relations, see Ernst-Otto Czempiel, *Friedensstrategien* (Paderborn: Schöningh, 1986), pp. 110–67; Doyle, "Liberalism and World Politics"; Keohane, "International Liberalism Reconsidered"; Andrew Moravcsik, *Liberalism and International Relations Theory*, 2d ed., Working Paper Series (Cambridge: Center for International Affairs, Harvard University, 1993); Russett, *Grasping the Democratic Peace*. My point of departure is, thus, what Jepperson, Wendt, and Katzenstein call "neoliberalism" in "Norms, Identity, and Culture in National Security," essay 2 in this volume. But drawing on insights from social constructivism, I argue that a liberal theory of international relations properly understood should be located in the upper-right—"sociological"—corner of figure 1 in the Jepperson, Wendt, and Katzenstein essay.

21. See Immanuel Kant, "Zum ewigen Frieden: Ein philosophischer Entwurf" (1795), in Wilhelm Weischedel, ed., *Immanuel Kant: Werke in sechs Bänden* (Frankfurt am Main: Insel-Verlag, 1964), 6:193–251.

empirically substantiated. Most scholars agree that liberal democracies rarely fight each other, even though they are not peaceful toward autocratic regimes.[22] The reasons for these two findings are less clear, since explanations focusing solely on democratic domestic structures miss the point that liberal states are *not* inherently peaceful. Rather, we need theoretical accounts that link the domestic level to interactions on the international level.[23]

Two domestic-level explanations prevail in the literature.[24] The first emphasizes *institutional constraints*. Democracies are characterized by an elaborate set of checks and balances—between the executive and the legislature, between the political system and interest groups, public opinion, and so on. It is then argued that the complexity of the decision-making process makes it unlikely that leaders will readily use military force unless they are confident of gathering enough domestic support for a low-cost war. This explanation is theoretically unconvincing. Why is it that the complexity of democratic institutions seems to matter less when liberal states are faced with authoritarian adversaries?

The second explanation focuses on the *norms* governing democratic decision-making processes and establishing the nonviolent and compromise-oriented resolution of political conflicts, the equality of the citizens, majority rule, tolerance for dissent, and the rights of minorities. These norms are firmly embedded in the political culture of liberal states and shape the identity of political actors through processes of socialization, communication, and enactment. This norm- and identity-based account appears to offer a better understanding of why it is that democratic governments refrain from violence when dealing with fellow democracies. But its exclusive focus on the domestic level still does not show why such restraints disappear when liberal governments deal with autocratic regimes.

The norm- and identity-based explanation nevertheless can be easily amended and linked to the level of international interactions. Collectively

---

22. For the state of the art, see Russett, *Grasping the Democratic Peace*. Two recent criticisms of the "democratic peace" finding seem to be empirically flawed. See Christopher Layne, "Kant or Cant: The Myth of the Democratic Peace," *International Security* 19, no. 2 (Fall 1994): 5–49; David E. Spiro, "The Insignificance of the Liberal Peace," *International Security* 19, no. 2 (Fall 1994): 50–86. For the rebuttals, see John M. Owen, "How Liberalism Produces Democratic Peace," *International Security* 19, no. 2 (Fall 1994): 87–125; Bruce M. Russett, "The Democratic Peace: And Yet It Moves," *International Security* 19, no. 4 (Spring 1995): 164–75.

23. See Owen, "How Liberalism Promotes Peace"; Thomas Risse-Kappen, "Democratic Peace—Warlike Democracies? A Social Constructivist Interpretation of the Liberal Argument," *European Journal of International Relations* 1, no. 4 (1995): 489–515.

24. See the discussion in Russett, *Grasping the Democratic Peace*, ch. 2.

held identities not only define who "we" are, but they also delineate the boundaries against "them," the "other."[25] Identities then prescribe norms of appropriate behavior toward those perceived as part of "us" as well as toward the "other." There is no reason that this argument should not equally apply to the domestic and the international realm. A sociological interpretation of a liberal theory of international relations then claims that actors' domestic identities are crucial for their perceptions of one another in the international realm. As Michael Doyle put it,

> Domestically just republics, which rest on consent, then presume foreign republics also to be consensual, just, and therefore deserving of accommodation. . . . At the same time, liberal states assume that non-liberal states, which do not rest on free consent, are not just. Because non-liberal governments are in a state of aggression with their own people, their foreign relations become for liberal governments deeply suspect. In short, fellow liberals benefit from a presumption of amity; nonliberals suffer from a presumption of enmity.[26]

Threat perceptions do not emerge from a quasi-objective international power structure, but actors infer external behavior from the values and norms governing the domestic political processes that shape the identities of their partners in the international system. Thus, France and Britain did not perceive the superior American power at the end of World War II as threatening, because they considered the U.S. as part of "us"; Soviet power, however, became threatening precisely because Moscow's domestic order identified the Soviet Union as "the other." The collective identity of actors in democratic systems defines both the "in-group" of friends and the "out-group" of potential foes. Liberal theory posits that the realist world of anarchy reigns in relations between democratic and authoritarian systems, while "democratic peace" prevails among liberal systems.

But liberal theory does not suggest that democracies live in perpetual harmony with each other or do not face cooperation problems requiring institutional arrangements. Kant's "pacific federation" (*foedus pacificum*) does not fall from heaven, but has to be "formally instituted" (*gestiftet*).[27] Since the security dilemma[28] is almost absent among democracies, they

---

25. See Alexander Wendt, "Collective Identity Formation and the International State," *American Political Science Review* 88, no. 2 (Summer 1994): 384–96.
26. Doyle, "Liberalism and World Politics," p. 1161.
27. Kant, "Zum ewigen Frieden," p. 203.
28. See John Herz, *Political Realism and Political Idealism* (Chicago: University of Chicago Press, 1951); Robert Jervis, "Cooperation Under the Security Dilemma," *World Politics* 30, no. 2 (1978): 167–214.

368 · *Thomas Risse-Kappen*

face fewer obstacles to creating cooperative security institutions. Actors of democratic states "know" through the process of social identification described above that they are unlikely to fight each other in the future. They share liberal values pertaining to political life and are likely to form what Deutsch called a "pluralistic security community," leading to mutual responsiveness in terms of "mutual sympathy and loyalties; of 'we-feeling,' trust, and consideration; of at least partial identification in terms of self-images and interests; of the ability to predict each other's behavior and ability to act in accordance with that prediction."[29]

While Deutsch's notion of pluralistic security communities is not confined to democracies, it is unlikely that a similar sense of mutual responsiveness could emerge among autocratic leaders. There is nothing in their values that would prescribe mutual sympathy, trust, and consideration. Rather, cooperation among nondemocracies is likely to emerge out of narrowly defined self-interests. It should remain fragile, and the "cooperation under anarchy" perspective to international relations should apply.[30]

If democracies are likely to overcome obstacles against international cooperation and to enter institutional arrangements for specific purposes, what about the rules and decision-making procedures of these institutions? One would expect the regulative norms[31] of these institutions to reflect the constitutive norms that shape the collective identity of the security community. Democracies are then likely to form *democratic international institutions* whose rules and procedures are aimed toward consensual and compromise-oriented decision-making respecting the equality of the participants. The norms governing the domestic decision-making processes of liberal systems are expected to regulate their interactions in international institutions. Democracies externalize their internal norms when cooperating with each other. Power asymmetries will be mediated by

---

29. Karl W. Deutsch et al., *Political Community and the North Atlantic Area* (Princeton: Princeton University Press, 1957), p. 129.
30. See, for example, Kenneth A. Oye, ed., *Cooperation Under Anarchy* (Princeton: Princeton University Press, 1986). The "democratic peace" argument does not suggest that authoritarian states are constantly in a state of war among themselves. Rather, liberal theory posits that the causes of peace among autocracies are different from the causes for the "democratic peace" and that cooperation among authoritarian regimes is likely to remain fragile.
31. Norms are "collective expectations of proper behavior for a given identity." In the following, I mainly use the term in the sense of *regulative norms* that prescribe or proscribe behavior for already constituted identities. The *constitutive norms* of these identities are the values and rules of democratic decision making in the domestic realm. For these distinctions, see Jepperson, Wendt, and Katzenstein, "Norms, Identity, and Culture in National Security."

norms of democratic decision-making among equals emphasizing persuasion, compromise, and the non-use of force or coercive power. Norms of regular consultation, of joint consensus-building, and of nonhierarchy legitimize and enable a habit of mutual influence on each other's preferences and behaviors. These norms serve as key obligations translating the domestic decision-making rules of democracies to the international arena. This is not to suggest that consultation norms exist only in alliances among democracies. But consultation means "*codetermination*" when democracies are involved.

But how are these regulative norms expected to affect interaction processes among democratic allies? First, decision makers either anticipate allied demands or directly consult their partners *before* preferences are formed and conclusions are reached. Actors then make a discernible effort to define their preferences in a way that is compatible with the allied views and to accommodate allied demands.

Second, norms serve as collective understandings of appropriate behavior, which can be invoked by the participants in a discourse to justify their arguments. Consultation norms affect the reasoning process by which decision makers identify their preferences and choices. Actors are expected to invoke the norms to back up their respective views and to give weight to their arguments.

Third, the cooperation rules and procedures are also expected to influence the *bargaining processes* among the allies. This is fairly obvious with regard to consultation. In addition, democratic decision-making procedures deemphasize the use of material power resources in intra-allied bargaining processes, thereby delegitimating to play out one's superior military or economic power in intra-alliance bargaining. Both the pluralistic security community and specific consultation norms work against the use of coercive power in bargaining processes among democracies.

But norms can be violated. Norms compliance in human interactions is to be expected only in a probabilistic sense. Instances in which actors violate specific rules and obligations are of particular interest to the analysis. If norms regulate the interaction but are breached, one would expect peculiar behavior by both the violator and the victim, such as excuses, justifications, or compensatory action.[32]

---

32. See Friedrich Kratochwil, *Rules, Norms, and Decisions: On the Conditions of Practical and Legal Reasoning in International Relations and Domestic Affairs* (Cambridge: Cambridge University Press, 1989), p. 63.

Finally, the allied community of values does not exclude democracies' driving hard bargains when dealing with each other in conflictual situations. While using material power resources to strengthen one's bargaining position is considered illegitimate among democracies, references to domestic pressures and constraints are likely to occur frequently. After all, liberal systems have in common that their leaders are constrained by the complexities of democratic political institutions. Since these procedures form the core of the value community, it should be appropriate to play "two-level games" using domestic pressures—small domestic "win-sets," in Robert Putnam's terms—to increase one's bargaining leverage.[33]

The argument presented above assumes that the values and norms embedded in the political culture of liberal democracies constitute the collective identity of a security community among democracies and that the regulative norms of the community institutions reflect these constitutive norms. This claim is subject to two objections:[34]

1. Why is it that *domestic orders*, norms, and political cultures shape the identities of actors in the international realm? Why not economic orders, such as capitalism? Why not geographic concepts, such as "the West," the "North Atlantic area," and the like? Why not gender and race, such as "white males"?

2. Democratic identities appear to be constant and acontextual rather than historically contingent. Is there never any change as to what constitutes an identity as "liberal democrat"?

As to the first point, it is, of course, trivial that actors hold multiple identities. Which of these or which combination dominates their interests, perceptions, and behavior in a given area of social interaction needs to be examined through empirical analysis and cannot be decided beforehand. I submit, however, that values and norms pertaining to questions of governance are likely to shape identities in the realm of the political—be it domestic or international. Moreover, such notions as "the West" do not contradict the argument here but seem to represent a specific enculturation of a broader liberal worldview. The same holds true for identities as

---

33. See Robert Putnam, "Diplomacy and Domestic Politics: The Logic of Two-Level Games," *International Organization* 42 (1988): 427–60; Peter B. Evans, Harold K. Jacobson, and Robert S. Putnam, eds., *Double-Edged Diplomacy* (Berkeley: University of California Press, 1993).
34. I thank Mark Laffey, Steve Weber, and an anonymous reviewer for alerting me to the following points.

"capitalists," particularly if juxtaposed against "communist order." The notion of the "free world," which Western policy makers used frequently during the Cold War to refer to their collective identity and to demarcate the boundaries against "Communism," encompassed liberal values pertaining to both the political and the economic orders.

As to the second point, and unlike several versions of neoliberalism, a sociological interpretation of the liberal argument posits historical contingency and contextuality. The zone of the "democratic peace" in the Northern Hemisphere did not fall from heaven but was created through processes of social interaction and learning.[35] The emergence of NATO is part and parcel of that story. Moreover, the norms of the democratic peace can in principle be unlearned, since collective identities might change over time. But to argue that the social structure of international relations is somehow more malleable and subject to change than material structures represents a misunderstanding of social constructivism.[36]

The argument then can be summarized as follows: Democracies rarely fight each other: they perceive each other as peaceful. They perceive each other as peaceful because of the democratic norms governing their domestic decision-making processes. For the same reason, they form pluralistic security communities of shared values. Because they perceive each other as peaceful and express a sense of community, they are likely to overcome obstacles against international cooperation and to form international institutions such as alliances. The norms regulating interactions in such institutions are expected to reflect the shared democratic values and to resemble the domestic decision-making norms.

In the following sections, I illustrate the argument with regard to the formation of NATO, two cases of inter-allied conflict during Cold War crises, and the future of the transatlantic relationship in the post–Cold War environment.

---

35. This even shows up in quantitative studies. Instances of militarized disputes among democracies have declined over time. Moreover, most disputed cases of alleged war among democracies occurred during the nineteenth and early twentieth centuries. For data, see Russett, *Grasping the Democratic Peace*, ch. 4.

36. John Mearsheimer's discussion of social constructivism—which he mislabels "critical theory," thereby lumping together a variety of different approaches—suffers from the misunderstanding that ideational factors in world politics are somehow more subject to change than material ones. Collective identities cannot be changed like clothes. See John J. Mearsheimer, "The False Promise of International Institutions," *International Security* 19, no. 3 (Winter 1994/95): 5–49.

A Liberal Interpretation of the Transatlantic Security Community
The Origins of NATO

The North Atlantic Treaty Organization represents an institutionalization of the security community to respond to a specific threat. While the perceived Soviet threat strengthened the sense of common purpose among the allies, it did not create the community in the first place.[37] NATO was preceded by the wartime alliance of the U.S., Great Britain, and France, which also collaborated closely to create various postwar regimes in the economic area. Particularly the British worked hard to ensure that the U.S. did not withdraw from Europe, as it had after World War I, but remained permanently involved in European affairs.[38]

While the European threat perceptions at the time might be explained on sophisticated realist grounds using Stephen Walt's "balance-of-threat" argument, U.S. behavior as the undisputed hegemon of the immediate post–World War II era is more difficult to understand. The U.S. faced several choices, each of which was represented in the administration as well as in the American public. President Roosevelt, for example, tried to preserve the wartime alliance with the Soviet Union until his death and to realize a collective security order guaranteed by the "four policemen" (the U.S., the USSR, Great Britain, and China), a concept that he had first proposed in 1941. His successor, President Truman, continued on this path during his first months in office. After Truman had changed his mind, Secretary of Commerce Henry Wallace still advocated a modus vivendi with the Soviet Union and the need to respect a Soviet sphere of influence in Europe until he was removed from office in September 1946. In the U.S. public, Walter Lippmann became the leading advocate of that argument when responding to George F. Kennan's containment strategy.

Early supporters of a tougher policy toward Moscow included the U.S. ambassador to Moscow, Averell Harriman, Kennan, and particularly Sec-

---

37. As Alfred Grosser put it, 1945 was "no year zero"; see Grosser, *The Western Alliance: European-American Relations Since 1945* (New York: Vintage Books, 1982), pp. 3–33. See also Robert Latham, "Liberalism's Order/Liberalism's Other: A Genealogy of Threat," *Alternatives* 20, no. 1 (1995): 111–46, on this point.

38. See, for example, John Baylis, "Britain and the Formation of NATO" (International Politics Research Paper no. 7, Department of International Politics, University College of Wales, Aberystwyth, 1989); Best, *"Cooperation with Like-Minded Peoples"*; Henry B. Ryan, *The Vision of Anglo-America* (Cambridge: Cambridge University Press, 1987).

retary of the Navy James Forrestal, while Secretary of State George Marshall steered a middle course until about 1948. How is it to be explained that this latter argument carried the day and that particularly President Truman became a firm advocate of a policy of containment?[39]

An obvious answer pertains, of course, to Soviet behavior. Western leaders, including Roosevelt, would have accepted a Soviet sphere of influence in Europe and were prepared to accommodate its security concerns— see Churchill's famous trip to Moscow in October 1944 and the Soviet-British "percentages agreement" on Southeast Europe.[40] But when the Red Army moved into Eastern Europe in 1944, Moscow immediately started to suppress potential political opposition in Romania, Bulgaria, Hungary, and, above all, Poland. Stalin broke what Roosevelt considered a Soviet commitment to free elections negotiated at Yalta, provoking the president to complain, "We can't do business with Stalin. He has broken every one of the promises he made at Yalta."[41]

The Truman administration, which had supported friendly relations with the Soviet Union until December 1945, began to change its position in early 1946, in conjunction with the Soviet reluctance to carry out the Moscow agreements to include non-Communists in the governments of Romania and Bulgaria.[42] These early disputes focused on domestic order issues in Soviet-controlled Eastern Europe. Had Stalin "Finlandized" rather than "Sovietized" Eastern Europe, the Cold War could have been avoided. In the perception of U.S. decision makers, the Soviet threat emerged as a threat to the domestic order of Western Europe, whose economies were devastated by the war. As the CIA concluded in mid-1947, "the greatest danger to the security of the United States is the possible economic collapse in Western Europe and the consequent accession to power of Communist elements."[43] U.S. administrations from Roosevelt to Truman considered Western Europe vital to American security interests, both for historical reasons (after all, two world wars had been fought over West-

39. On the origins of the containment strategy, see, for example, John L. Gaddis, *Strategies of Containment* (Oxford: Oxford University Press, 1982); Gaddis, *The Long Peace*, pp. 20–47; Deborah Larson, *Origins of Containment: A Psychological Explanation* (Princeton: Princeton University Press, 1985); David Mayers, *George Kennan and the Dilemmas of U.S. Foreign Policy* (Oxford: Oxford University Press, 1988).

40. Overview in David Dimbleby and David Reynolds, *An Ocean Apart: The Relationship Between Britain and America in the Twentieth Century* (New York: Vintage Books, 1989), pp. 170–72.

41. Quoted from Gaddis, *The Long Peace*, p. 30.

42. See Gormly, *From Potsdam to the Cold War*, pp. 94–111.

43. Quoted from Leffler, "National Security and U.S. Foreign Policy," p. 29.

ern Europe) and because it was viewed as a cornerstone of the liberal—political and economic—world order that both Roosevelt and Truman envisaged.[44] But it was not Soviet power as such that constituted a threat to these interests; rather it was the Soviet domestic order, combined with Soviet behavior in Eastern Europe, indicating a willingness to expand Communism beyond the USSR. In other words, Soviet power became threatening as a tool to expand the Soviet domestic order. Moreover, the Soviet Union also refused to join the Bretton Woods institutions of the World Bank and the International Monetary Fund, thus ending hopes that it might participate in the postwar international economic order.

This is not to suggest that the Soviet Union was solely responsible for the origins of the Cold War. Rather, differing views of domestic and international order clashed after World War II. Moscow refused to join the American liberal project based upon an open international order and free trade, free-market economies, and liberal systems of governance.[45] Roosevelt and Truman tried to accommodate the Soviet view at first but then gradually abandoned that idea in favor of tougher policies. Stalin's behavior in Eastern Europe and elsewhere—irrespective of whether it was motivated by genuine security concerns or aggressive intentions—reinforced the emerging perceptions of threat, both in the public and in the administration. Over against those promoting a modus vivendi between the U.S. and the Soviet Union, Stalin helped another worldview to carry the day in Washington, one that interpreted the post–World War II situation in terms of a long-lasting strategic rivalry between the U.S. and the USSR—the Cold War.

The emerging conflict was increasingly framed in Manichaean terms. As Anders Stephanson put it,

> [The Cold War] was launched in fiercely ideological terms as an invasion or delegitimation of the Other's social order, a demonology combined of course with a mythology of the everlasting virtues of one's own domain. This is not surprising, considering the universalism of the respective ideologies.[46]

---

44. For conflicting interpretations of U.S. strategic interests after World War II, see Gaddis, *The Long Peace*; Melvyn P. Leffler, *The Preponderance of Power* (Stanford: Stanford University Press, 1992); Leffler, "National Security and U.S. Foreign Policy," pp. 23–26; Thomas J. McCormick, *America's Half-Century: United States Foreign Policy in the Cold War* (Baltimore: Johns Hopkins University Press, 1989). For an excellent overview on U.S. historiography on the origins of the Cold War, see Anders Stephanson, "The United States," in David Reynolds, ed., *The Origins of the Cold War in Europe: International Perspectives* (New Haven: Yale University Press, 1994), pp. 23–52.
45. See Latham, "Liberalism's Order/Liberalism's Other," on this point.
46. Stephanson, "The United States," p. 50.

The liberal interpretation of Stalin's behavior transformed the Soviet Union from a wartime ally to an opponent, the "other":

> There isn't any difference in totalitarian states. . . . Nazi, Communist or Fascist, or Franco, or anything else—they are all alike.
> The stronger the voice of a people in the formulation of national policies, the less the danger of aggression. When all governments derive their just powers from the consent of the governed, there will be enduring peace.[47]

The various declarations of the Cold War—Kennan's "long telegram," Churchill's 1946 "iron curtain" speech in Fulton, Missouri, and the 1947 Truman doctrine—all made the same connection between a *liberal* interpretation of the Soviet threat stemming from its "totalitarian" domestic character, on the one hand, and a *realist* balance of power ("containment") strategy to counter it. Kennan's "long telegram" and his later "X" article connected two liberal interpretations of the Soviet threat to promote his preferred course of action.[48] He portrayed the Soviet Union as combining an ancient autocratic tradition that was deeply suspicious of its neighbors with a Communist ideology. Of course, cooperation was not an option with an opponent whose aggressiveness resulted from a historically derived sense of insecurity together with ideological aspirations that were ultimately caused by the fear of authoritarian rulers that they would be overthrown by their own people.

To what extent were these interpretations of the Soviet threat merely justifying rhetoric to gather public support for U.S. foreign policy rather than genuine concerns of decision makers? First, as argued above, there was nothing inevitable about the emergence of the Cold War, as far as U.S. decision makers were concerned. Soviet behavior, U.S. responses, the clash of worldviews, and mutual threat perceptions reinforced each other to create the East-West conflict. Second, the historical record appears to indicate that Harry Truman genuinely changed his mind about the extent to which one could cooperate with the Soviet Union during his first year in office.[49] Third, an exaggerated rhetoric constructing the Soviet Union as the

47. Quotes from Truman's speeches in March 1947, contained in Gaddis, *The Long Peace*, p. 36.
48. See Kennan's "long telegram," in U.S. Department of State, *Foreign Relations of the United States, 1946* (Washington, D.C.: U.S. Government Printing Office), 6:696–709; 'X,' "The Sources of Soviet Conduct," *Foreign Affairs* 25, no. 4 (July 1947).
49. See, for example, Robert Donovan, *Tumultuous Years: The Presidency of Harry S. Truman* (New York: Norton, 1982); Gaddis, *Strategies of Containment*, pp. 14–20; Gormley, *From Potsdam to the Cold War*.

"empire of the evil" (Reagan) created the Cold War consensus in the U.S., since public opinion and Congress at the time were reluctant to accept new commitments overseas shortly after World War II had been won. The Truman doctrine, for example, deliberately oversold the issue of granting financial aid to Greece and Turkey as a fight between "freedom" and "totalitarianism" to get the package through Congress. But this point only confirms the power of the liberal argument in creating winning domestic coalitions in the U.S.

Even after the perception of a Soviet threat had won out in Washington, the U.S. still faced choices. Joining NATO was only one of them. It could have fought the Soviet Union on its own in a bipolar confrontation. Another option was to negotiate bilateral security arrangements with selected Western European states, as the Soviet Union did with Eastern Europe between 1945 and 1948, and as British Foreign Secretary Ernest Bevin suggested in 1948.[50] Instead, the U.S. chose to entangle itself in a multilateral alliance based on the indivisibility of security, diffuse reciprocity, and democratic decision-making procedures.[51]

Since it is impossible to present a detailed history of the North Atlantic Treaty in a few pages, some general remarks must suffice.[52] First, NATO came about against the background of the emerging sense of threat in both Western Europe and the U.S. Soviet behavior in Eastern Europe and in its German occupation zone might have been motivated by Moscow's own threat perceptions and by an attempt to prevent a Western anti-Soviet bloc. But Stalin's behavior once again proved counterproductive and served to fuel Western threat perception. The Prague Communist "coup," for example, occurred precisely when negotiations for the Brussels Treaty creating the West European Union were under way and led to their speedy conclusion. The events in Czechoslovakia, as well as Soviet pressure against Norway, convinced U.S. Secretary of State Marshall that a formal alliance

50. On these alternatives, see Steve Weber, "Shaping the Postwar Balance of Power: Multilateralism in NATO," *International Organization* 46, no. 3 (Summer 1992): 633–80, 635–38. See ibid. for the following.
51. The first two notions are based on Ruggie's definition of multilateralism. See Ruggie, "Multilateralism."
52. See, for example, Cook, *Forging the Alliance*; Henderson, *The Birth of NATO*; Ireland, *Creating the Entangling Alliance*; Lawrence S. Kaplan, *The United States and NATO: The Formative Years* (Lexington: University of Kentucky Press, 1984); Ennio Di Nolfo, ed., *The Atlantic Pact: Forty Years Later* (Berlin: De Gruyter, 1991); Meier et al., *Das Nordatlantische Bündnis*; Norbert Wiggershaus and Roland G. Foerster, eds., *Die westliche Sicherheitsgemeinschaft, 1948–1950* (Boppard: Harald Boldt Verlag, 1988).

between the U.S. and Western Europe was necessary. The Soviet blockade of Berlin's Western sectors in 1948 not only "created" Berlin as the symbol of freedom and democracy—i.e., the values for which the Cold War was fought—but also proved crucial to move the U.S. closer to a firm commitment to European security.

Second, major initiatives toward the formation of a North Atlantic Alliance originated in Europe, mainly in the British Foreign Office.[53] A close transgovernmental coalition of like-minded U.S., British, Canadian, and—later on—French senior officials worked hard to transform the growing sense of threat into a firm U.S. commitment toward European security. The negotiations leading to the North Atlantic Treaty resembled a "three-level" game involving U.S. domestic politics, transgovernmental consensus-building, and intergovernmental bargains across the Atlantic. As to the last, probably the most important deal concerned Germany: the French would support U.S. policies toward the creation of a West German state in exchange for an American security commitment to Europe in terms of "dual containment" (protection against the Soviet Union *and* Germany).[54]

Third, a multilateral institution had advantages over alternative options, since it enhanced the legitimacy of American leadership by giving the Western Europeans a say in the decision-making process. In this context, it was self-evident and not controversial on either side of the Atlantic that an alliance of democratic states had to be based on democratic principles, norms, and decision-making rules. The two major bargains about the North Atlantic Treaty concerned, first, the nature of the assistance clause (article 5 of the treaty) and, second, the extent to which the consultation commitment (article 4) would include threats outside the NATO area. Neither the commitment to democratic values (preamble) nor the democratic decision-making procedures as outlined in articles 2, 3, and 8 were controversial in the treaty negotiations. Rather, the controversy between the U.S. Congress, on the one hand, and the administration together with the Western European governments, on the other, focused on the indivisibility of the mutual security assistance.[55]

---

53. See Best, *"Cooperation with Like-Minded Peoples."*
54. On the French position, see Bruna Bagnato, "France and the Origins of the Atlantic Pact," in Di Nolfo, *The Atlantic Pact*, pp. 79–110; Norbert Wiggershaus, "The Other 'German Question': The Foundation of the Atlantic Pact and the Problem of Security against Germany," in ibid., pp. 111–26; Pierre Guillen, "Frankreich und die Frage der Verteidigung Westeuropas," in Wiggershaus and Foerster, *Die westliche Sicherheitsgemeinschaft*, pp. 103–23.
55. For details on the treaty negotiations, see Cook, *Forging the Alliance*; Henderson, *The Birth of NATO*; Ireland, *Creating the Entangling Alliance*; Sherwood, *Allies in Crisis*, pp. 5–29.

In sum, a liberal interpretation of NATO's origins holds that the Cold War came about when fundamental ideas—worldviews—about the domestic and the international order for the post–World War II era clashed. The Western democracies perceived a threat to their fundamental values resulting from the "Sovietization" of Eastern Europe. While the perceived Soviet threat certainly strengthened the sense of community among the Western democracies, it did not create the collective identity in the first place. In light of the liberal collective identity and its views of what constituted a "just" domestic and international order, Stalin's behavior and his refusal to join the liberal order confirmed that the Soviet Union could not be trusted. NATO then institutionalized the transatlantic security community to cope with the threat. The multilateral nature of the organization based on democratic principles and decision rules reflected the common values and the collective identity.

Regulatory norms of multilateralism and joint decision making were not just rhetoric covering up American hegemony, but shaped the interallied relationship. These norms were causally consequential for transatlantic security cooperation during the Cold War, since they allowed for disproportionate European influence on U.S. foreign policies. During the Korean war, for example, norms of consultation had an overall restraining effect on American decisions with regard to the localization of the war in Korea instead of its extension into China, the non-use of nuclear weapons, and the conclusion of the armistice negotiations.[56]

Western Europeans also had quite an impact on the early stages of nuclear arms control, especially during the test ban negotiations when the British in particular pushed and pulled the U.S. toward an agreement. As to NATO decisions pertaining to European security, joint decision making quickly became the norm. This has been shown to be true in most crucial cases, such as decisions on nuclear strategy and deployments.[57] The evidence also suggests that the transatlantic relationship cannot be conceptualized as merely interstate relations; rather, the interaction patterns are significantly influenced by transnational and transgovernmental coalition-building processes.[58]

56. For details, see Risse-Kappen, *Cooperation Among Democracies*, ch. 3. For the following, see ibid., ch. 5.
57. See, for example, Haftendorn, *Kernwaffen und die Glaubwürdigkeit der Allianz*; Thomas Risse-Kappen, *The Zero Option: INF, West Germany, and Arms Control* (Boulder: Westview, 1988). See also Chernoff, *After Bipolarity*.
58. Transgovernmental relations are defined as interactions among subunits of national governments in the absence of central decisions. See Robert O. Keohane and Joseph S. Nye, Jr., "Transgovernmental Relations and International Organizations," *World Politics* 27 (1974): 39–62.

I will briefly discuss here two cases of interallied dispute over policies during the Cold War. The first, the 1956 Suez crisis, probably constituted the most severe transatlantic crisis of the 1950s, leading to a temporary breakdown of the community. I argue, however, that reference to a conflict of interests alone does not explain the interallied confrontation, in particular not the United States' coercion of its allies. The transatlantic dispute can be better understood in the framework of norm-guided behavior, as a dispute over obligations and appropriate behavior in a security community. The second case, the 1962 Cuban missile crisis, was the most serious U.S.-Soviet confrontation during the Cold War. I argue that U.S. decisions during the crisis cannot be explained without reference to the normative framework of the transatlantic security community.

The 1956 Suez Crisis: The Violation of Community Norms

A temporary breakdown of the allied community resulted from the 1956 Suez crisis when the U.S. coerced Britain, France, and Israel through economic pressure to give up their attempts to regain control of the Suez Canal. I suggest that the "realist" outcome of the crisis—the strong defeating the weak—needs to be explained by a "liberal" process. The American coercion of its allies resulted from a mutual sense of betrayal of the community leading to the violation of consultation norms and the temporary breakdown of the community itself.

The conflict of interests between the U.S. and its two allies was obvious to both sides from the beginning of the crisis.[59] The British and French governments knew that the U.S. profoundly disagreed with them on whether or not force should be used to restore control over the Suez Canal. The attitudes of the U.S. as compared with those of its allies were rooted in diverging assessments of the situation in the Middle East, of the larger political context, and of the particular actions by Egypt's Nasser. The U.S. made a major effort to restrain its allies from using military force by working for a negotiated settlement and the establishment of an international authority to take control of the Suez Canal. Both sides frequently exchanged their diverging viewpoints through the normal channels of

---

59. I essentially agree with Richard Neustadt's earlier analysis of the crisis. See his *Alliance Politics* (New York: Columbia University Press, 1970). For a similar argument, see Sherwood, *Allies in Crisis*, pp. 58–94. The major studies on the Suez crisis are David Carlton, *Britain and the Suez Crisis* (Oxford: Blackwell, 1988); Steven Z. Freiberger, *Dawn over Suez* (Chicago: Iven R. Dee, 1992); Keith Kyle, *Suez* (New York: St. Martin's, 1991); Diane B. Kunz, *The Economic Diplomacy of the Suez Crisis* (Chapel Hill: University of North Carolina Press, 1991); Wm. Roger Louis and Roger Owen, eds., *Suez 1956* (Oxford: Clarendon Press, 1989).

interallied communication, which remained open throughout most of the crisis. The U.S. and its allies also knew that the British were economically dependent on American assistance for the pound sterling and for ensuring oil supplies to NATO Europe, should the crisis escalate into war.[60]

Why, then, did the British and French who knew about their dependence and the American disagreement with them, nevertheless go ahead with their military plans and deceive Washington? How is their miscalculation of the U.S. reaction to be explained?

The British and French governments reluctantly agreed to U.S. attempts for a negotiated solution, first through an international conference in London in August 1956 and later through the proposal of a Suez Canal Users' Association (SCUA) in September. But the allies were not seriously interested in the success of these efforts, since their ultimate goal was not only to secure access to the Suez Canal but also to get rid of Nasser. They endorsed the American efforts to buy time and to create a favorable climate of opinion in the U.S. and the UN.

At the same time, the governments in London and Paris perceived American behavior during the crisis as at best ambiguous, if not deceiving. John Foster Dulles earned himself a reputation of "saying one thing and doing another," as Selwyn Lloyd, the British foreign minister, put it.[61] There are indeed indications that Dulles favored stronger action if Nasser rejected reasonable proposals by the London conference. In September, for example, Dulles discussed a proposal with the British prime minister to set up an Anglo-American working group that would consider means of weakening Nasser's regime.[62]

The British sense of being betrayed by the Americans increased dramatically as a result of Dulles's handling of his own SCUA proposal. Prime Minister Anthony Eden viewed it as a means to corner Nasser further and to use his expected rejection as a pretext for military action. But in an attempt to dampen the British spin on the proposal and to make it more acceptable to the Egyptians, Dulles declared that "the United States did not intend itself to try to shoot its way through" the Suez Canal. As a

---

60. See Diane B. Kunz, "The Importance of Having Money: The Economic Diplomacy of the Suez Crisis," in Louis and Owen, *Suez 1956*, pp. 215–32, 218–19; Kunz, *The Economic Diplomacy of the Suez Crisis.*
61. Selwyn Lloyd, *Suez 1956: A Personal Account* (London: Jonathan Cape, 1978), p. 38.
62. See "Memorandum of Conversation at British Foreign Office," September 21, 1956, in U.S. Department of State, *Foreign Relations of the United States, 1955–1957* [hereafter *FRUS 1955–1957*] (Washington, D.C.: U.S. Government Printing Office, 1990), 16:548–50.

result, Eden concluded on October 8 that "we have been misled so often by Dulles' ideas that we cannot afford to risk another misunderstanding. . . . Time is not on our side in this matter."[63] The British felt abandoned by the American government, which in their eyes had violated the community of purpose. London then chose to deliberately deceive Washington about the military plans in October 1956 without calculating the possible consequences. First, British officials thought, in a somewhat self-deluding manner, that the U.S. did not want to hear about the military preparations. Second, the British government was convinced in some strange way that the U.S. would ultimately back it and that allied action would somehow force Washington to support what persuasion did not accomplish. Eden and his foreign minister reckoned that the choice was clear for Washington if it had to take sides between Egypt and its European allies. What they perceived as Dulles's duplicity not only created a sense of betrayal leading to the deception in the first place, it also helped to reassure them that the Americans would ultimately support their action. In short, British decision makers firmly believed in the viability of the North Atlantic partnership. They convinced themselves that the U.S. was bound by the community and would ultimately value it. They relied on reassurances such as the one uttered by Dulles ten days before the invasion of the Suez Canal: "I do not comment on your observations on Anglo-American relations except to say that those relations, from our standpoint, rest on such a firm foundation that misunderstandings of this nature, if there are such, cannot disturb them."[64]

But Eisenhower and Dulles, despite all ambiguous statements, never wavered in pursuing two goals: (a) to prevent the use of force and (b) to reach a negotiated settlement guaranteeing safe passage through the Suez Canal. The administration mediated between its allies and the Egyptians while at the same time trying to restrain the British and French from resorting to military action. But this does not mean that Washington had to use its overwhelming power to force its allies to give up their adventure in Egypt. While the U.S. opposition to the allied action was to be expected, the use of coercive power was not. The allies could have agreed

---

63. "Eden to Selwyn Lloyd," October 8, quoted in Wm. Roger Louis, "Dulles, Suez, and the British," in Richard Immermann, ed., *John Foster Dulles and the Diplomacy of the Cold War* (Princeton: Princeton University Press, 1990), pp. 133–58, 151. For the Dulles quotes, cf. ibid., pp. 149, 150; Robert Bowie, "Eisenhower, Dulles, and the Suez Crisis," in Louis and Owen, *Suez 1956*, pp. 189–214, 204–5.
64. "Dulles to Selwyn Lloyd," October 19, *FRUS 1955–1957*, 16:760.

to disagree, since no supreme American interests were at stake.[65] The U.S. could have confined its opposition to condemnatory action in the UN General Assembly. In other words, U.S. decision makers made choices as to how to react to the allied military action.

The American decision to play hardball with the allies was triggered by a series of unilateral allied moves that violated norms of consultation and jeopardized the community of purpose in the eyes of American leaders. First, the British government decided at the end of August to get the North Atlantic Council involved in the crisis, against the explicit advice of the U.S. government. The allies apparently calculated that other Western Europeans would support their military preparations, while the administration thought that such a move would further complicate discussions at the London conference.[66]

Second, the British government told the U.S. in late September of its plans to refer the matter to the UN Security Council in order to preempt a likely Soviet move. John Foster Dulles advised against it, since he thought that such action would hinder his attempts to get the SCUA off the ground. On September 23, the British and French referred the Suez issue to the Security Council anyway.

Third, immediately before the invasion, American decision makers complained that they were left in the dark about the British and French plans and that the interallied lines of communications had gradually broken down. The State Department asked the U.S. embassies in London and Paris to find out what the two governments were up to. It received reassuring messages, since the American embassies either were deliberately misled by their sources or just second-guessed the allied governments. Intelligence information gradually came in reporting Israeli plans to invade Egypt, with possible French and British involvement.[67] When the Israeli invasion started on October 29, the U.S. administration had suffi-

---

65. U.S. anticolonialism, for example, does not explain American behavior. During the Falklands/Malvinas war in 1982, for example, the Reagan administration tacitly backed the British effort to regain the islands even though it remained officially neutral in light of its alliance obligations to both Argentina (OAS) and Britain.

66. See "Memorandum for Secretary of State," August 28, *FRUS 1955–1957*, 16:309; "Secretary of State to U.S. Embassy UK," August 30, ibid., pp. 339–40; "Dept. of State to certain diplomatic missions," August 31, ibid., pp. 344–45.

67. See "Dept. of State to U.S. Embassy UK," October 26, *FRUS 1955–1957*, 16:790; "U.S. Embassy Israel to Dept. of State," October 26, ibid., p. 785; "Dept. of State to U.S. Embassy France," October 29, ibid., pp. 815–16. For the following, see "Memorandum of Conversation at Dept. of State," October 28, ibid., pp. 803–4; "U.S. Embassy UK to Dept. of State," October 29, ibid., pp. 817–20.

cient information to suspect that France was involved in the action. But until the facts could no longer be denied, neither Eisenhower nor Dulles wanted to believe that the British government had deceived them. The sense of community led to wishful thinking by American decision makers. The U.S. then decided to bring the matter to the UN Security Council but was told by the allies that they would never support a UN move against Israel. Even then, Eisenhower did not believe what he saw. He sent an urgent message to Prime Minister Eden, expressing his confusion and demanding

> that the UK and the US quickly and clearly lay out their present views and intentions before each other, and that, come what may, we find some way of concerting our ideas and plans so that we may not, in any real crisis, be powerless to act in concert because of our misunderstanding of each other.[68]

The extent of the Anglo-French-Israeli collusion became clear only a few hours later, when the British and French issued a joint ultimatum demanding that Israel and Egypt withdraw from the Suez Canal to allow for an Anglo-French occupation of the Canal zone. The plot was immediately apparent, since the Israeli forces had not yet reached the line to which they were supposed to retreat. Eisenhower now realized that he had been misled all along and expressed his dismay about the "unworthy and unreliable ally." Later that day, he declared that he was "inclined to think that those who began this operation should be left to work out their own oil problem—to boil in their own oil, so to speak."

The secretary of state summoned the French ambassador, telling him that "this was the blackest day which has occurred in many years in the relations between England and France and the United States. He asked how the former relationship of trust and confidence could possibly be restored in view of these developments."[69]

Eisenhower and Dulles were not so much upset by the Anglo-French-Israeli use of force itself as by the fact that core allies had deliberately deceived them. The allies had not broken some minor consultation agree-

---

68. "Eisenhower to Eden," October 30, *FRUS 1955–1957*, 16:848–50. See also "Memorandum of Conversation at the White House," October 29, ibid., pp. 833–39; editorial note, ibid., pp. 840–42; Bowie, "Eisenhower, Dulles, and the Suez Crisis," pp. 208–9.
69. "Memorandum of Conversation at the Dept. of State," October 30, *FRUS 1955–1957*, 16:867–68. For the Eisenhower quotes, see "Memorandum of Conference with the President," October 30, ibid., p. 873; "Message from Eisenhower to Eden," October 30, ibid., p. 866; "Memorandum of Conversation with the President," October 30, ibid., pp. 851–55.

ments; they had violated fundamental collective understandings that constituted the transatlantic community—"trust and confidence." Once the
degree of allied deception became obvious, decision makers in Washington concluded that they were themselves no longer bound by alliance
norms. They decided to retaliate in kind and coerced their allies through
financial pressure. Now the U.S. abandoned the community, leaving its
allies no choice but to back down. As the British ambassador in Washington put it, "We have now passed the point when we are talking to friends.
. . . [W]e are on a hard bargaining basis and we are dealing with an Administration of business executives."[70]

While the U.S. administration was coercing its allies to withdraw from
the Suez Canal, it indicated at the same time that a major effort should be
made to restore the community. As soon as November 7, the president
called the whole affair a "family spat" in a telephone conversation with
Prime Minister Eden. He later tried to find excuses for the British behavior: "Returning to the Suez crisis, the President said he now believes that
the British had not been in on the Israeli-French planning until the very
last stages when they *had no choice* but to come into the operation."[71]

If the British had "no choice," they could not really be blamed for
deceiving the U.S. The two governments now engaged in almost ritualistic reassurances that their "special relationship" would be restored quickly.
President Eisenhower and Anthony Eden's successor Harold Macmillan
worked hard to reestablish the community. The Bermuda summit in
March 1957 documented the restoration of the "special relationship." In
the long term, the crisis resulted in a major change in U.S. policies toward
nuclear cooperation with the British. In 1958, Congress amended the
Atomic Energy Act to allow for the sharing of nuclear information with
Britain, which London had requested throughout the decade. The violation of alliance norms during the Suez crisis reinforced rather than reduced
the transatlantic ties.

As for NATO in general, the crisis led to a reform of its consultation procedures. The "Report of the Committee of Three on Non-Military Cooperation in *NATO*" restated the need for timely consultation among the
allies on foreign policy matters in general, not just those pertaining to

70. "Lord Caccia [UK ambassador in Washington] to Foreign Office," November 28, 1956, quoted
from Louis, "Dulles, Suez, and the British," pp. 155–56.
71. "Memorandum of Conversation between the President and Dulles," (my emphasis!), November
12, *FRUS 1955–1957*, 16:1112–14. For the preceding quote, see "Memorandum of Telephone
Conversation between the President and Sir Eden," November 7, ibid., p. 1040.

European security. The North Atlantic Council adopted the report in December 1956.[72]

But the French-American relationship never recovered. While French leaders had already been more sanguine about the interallied conflict than the British, the crisis set in motion a trend of gradually weakening the transatlantic ties between Paris and Washington. This deinstitutionalization culminated in President de Gaulle's 1966 decision to withdraw from the military integration of NATO. The French learned different lessons from the crisis than did the British, as far as the collective identity of the transatlantic community was concerned. The case shows that actors' interpretations of specific events may lead to changes in how they perceive their identity, which then results in changing their practices.

In sum, the confrontation between the U.S. and its allies developed because each side felt betrayed by the other in fundamental ways. The conflict of interests alone does not explain the confrontation. Such conflicts occurred before and afterward without leading to a breakdown of the transatlantic community, but they were usually resolved through cooperation and compromise—note, for example, the almost continuous interallied disputes over nuclear strategy and deployment options, which involved the survival interests of both sides. During the Suez crisis, however, U.S. decision makers perceived the allied deception as a violation of basic rules, norms, and procedures constituting the transatlantic community. No longer bound by the norms of appropriate behavior, the U.S. used its superior power and prevailed. Both sides knew that they had violated the rules of the "alliance game" and engaged in self-serving rhetoric to cover it up. More important, the U.S. and the British worked hard to restore the transatlantic community, suggesting that they did not regard the sort of confrontations experienced during the Suez crisis as appropriate behavior among democratic allies.

I conclude, therefore, that the Suez crisis confirms liberal expectations about discourses and practices when fundamental norms governing the relationship are violated. Norm violation challenging the sense of community among the allies provides the key to understanding the interactions leading to the confrontation, the clash, and the restoration of the community.

The 1962 Cuban Missile Crisis: Collective Identity and Norms

While the Suez crisis is a case of norm violation, the Cuban missile crisis shows the collective identity of the security community in action. It rep-

---

72. See Sherwood, *Allies in Crisis*, pp. 88–94.

resents the most serious U.S.-Soviet confrontation of the Cold War. While we know today that neither side was prepared to risk nuclear war over the Soviet missiles in Cuba, President John F. Kennedy and General Secretary Nikita Krushchev were each afraid that the other would escalate the conflict in ways that might get out of control.[73] Decision makers in Washington were convinced that the supreme national interests of the United States were at stake. Why care about allies when national survival is endangered? Indeed, the conventional wisdom about the Cuban missile crisis holds that the allies were not sufficiently consulted, even though U.S. decisions directly affected their security. Even senior officials in the administration, such as Roger Hilsman, then director of intelligence in the State Department, thought that the U.S. had chosen not to consult the allies in order to preserve its freedom of action: "If you had the French Government and the British Government with all their hangups and De Gaulle's hangups we would never have done it, it's as simple as that."[74]

I argue that—except for the first week of the crisis—there was far more interallied consultation than most scholars assume and that key allies, particularly the British and Turkish governments, knew about details of decision making in Washington. Moreover, the fate of the Western Alliance was the most important foreign policy concern for U.S. decision makers, except for the direct confrontation with Moscow and Cuba. Strategic arguments about reputation and the credibility of commitments explain these concerns only to a limited extent. First, as argued above, realism is indeterminate with regard to allied consultation when the alliance leader's survival is perceived to be at stake. Second, decision makers did not worry at all about their reputation in the Organization of American States (OAS), for example, the other U.S.-led alliance, which was even more directly

73. For details, see Richard N. Lebow and Janice G. Stein, *We All Lost the Cold War* (Princeton: Princeton University Press, 1994), pp. 19–145. See also Michael Beschloss, *The Crisis Years* (New York: Edward Burlingame Books, 1991), pp. 431–575; James Blight, *The Shattered Crystal Ball* (Savage, Md.: Rowman and Littlefield, 1990); James Blight and David Welch, *On the Brink* (New York: Hill and Wang, 1989); McGeorge Bundy, *Danger and Survival* (New York: Random House, 1988), ch. 9; Laurence Chang and Peter Kornbluh, eds., *The Cuban Missile Crisis, 1962* (New York: New Press, 1992); Raymond Garthoff, *Reflections on the Cuban Missile Crisis*, rev. ed. (Washington, D.C.: Brookings Institution, 1989).
74. "Interview with David Nunnerly," in National Security Archive, *The Cuban Missile Crisis, 1962* [hereafter *NSA:CMC*], microfiche collection (Washington, D.C.: Chadwyck-Healey, 1990), Doc. 03251. On the alleged lack of consultation, see Richard Rosecrance, *Defense of the Realm* (New York: Columbia University Press, 1986), p. 13; Sherwood, *Allies in Crisis*, p. 122; I. F. Stone, "What Price Prestige?" in Robert A. Divine, ed., *The Cuban Missile Crisis*, pp. 155–65 (Chicago: Quadrangle Books, 1971).

involved in the Cuban missile crisis. Rather, if we assume a security community of democracies, strategic concerns about reputation and credibility immediately make sense. At least, realism does not offer a better understanding of these concerns than liberal theory.

But the Cuban missile crisis also poses a puzzle for liberal propositions about the allied community of values and norms, since the U.S. violated these rules during the first week of the crisis. Whether or not to consult the allies was discussed during the very first meeting of the Executive Committee (ExComm) on October 16. Secretary of State Dean Rusk argued strongly in favor of consultation and maintained that unilateral U.S. action would put the allies at risk, particularly if the U.S. decided in favor of a quick air strike. The decision not to consult, however, did not free decision makers from concerns about the Europeans. Membership in the community of democracies formed part of the American identity, as a result of which decision makers continued to define U.S. preferences in terms of joint interests rather than unilaterally. There was unanimous consensus that U.S. inaction with regard to the Soviet missile deployment in Cuba would be disastrous for U.S. credibility vis-à-vis its allies.[75] The reputation of the U.S. government was perceived to be at stake, in both domestic and alliance politics. Decision makers in the ExComm did not distinguish between the two. As a result, the decision *not* to consult key allies during the first week strengthened the position of the "doves" in the ExComm, who argued that an air strike and military action against the Soviet installations in Cuba without prior consultation would wreck NATO.

During the second week of the crisis, the Europeans not only were regularly informed about the U.S. deliberations but had ample opportunities to influence American thinking through a variety of bilateral and multilateral channels. Among the key allies, only the British chose to take advantage of these opportunities, while France and West Germany strongly supported the U.S. courses of action. President Kennedy had almost daily telephone conversations with Prime Minister Macmillan—which even many of his staff members did not realize.

The British were the most "dovish" of the major allies. They made sure, for example, that U.S. forces in Europe were exempted from the general alert status of U.S. troops. When Macmillan was briefed about the crisis,

---

75. As Robert McNamara put it later, "For all kinds of reasons, especially to preserve unity in the alliance, we had to indicate to the Soviets that we weren't going to accept the presence of offensive missiles in Cuba" (quoted from Blight and Welch, *On the Brink*, p. 188). See also "ExComm Transcripts," October 16, 1962, *NSA:CMC*, Doc. 00622.

he assured the president that Britain would support the U.S., but he mentioned that Europeans had lived under the threat of Soviet nuclear weapons for quite some time. Since the British had internally concluded that the naval blockade of Cuba violated international law, Macmillan demanded that the U.S. made a good legal case in favor of the quarantine. He then wondered about possible Soviet reactions against the blockade, including attempts at trading American bases in Europe or even West Berlin for the withdrawal of the missiles from Cuba.[76] Kennedy perceived Macmillan's message as the "best argument for taking no action."

The British prime minister was as concerned as President Kennedy that the crisis might get out of control, and he favored a *cooperative solution*. On October 24, he told David Ormsby-Gore, the British ambassador to the U.S.: "If I am right in assuming that the President's mind is moving in the direction of negotiations before the crisis worsens, I think that the most fruitful course for you to pursue at the present might be to try to elicit from him on what lines he may be contemplating a conference."[77]

He suggested that the U.S. should raise the blockade if the Soviets refrained from putting more missiles into Cuba. When Macmillan phoned Kennedy later, he urged the president not to rush and asked whether "a deal" could be done. When the president asked for Macmillan's advice on a possible invasion of Cuba, the prime minister strongly recommended against it.[78]

Whether the British proposals for de-escalation made a crucial difference in the U.S. decision-making process is unclear. It is safe to argue, however, that the close contact between Kennedy, Macmillan, and Ormsby-Gore during the second week of the crisis strengthened and reinforced the president's view. Given Kennedy's convictions about the importance of the Western Alliance, which he expressed time and again during the crisis, it was significant that a key ally whom he trusted fully endorsed his search for a "deal."

Two alliance issues strongly influenced the president's thinking during the crisis. The first was the fate of Berlin. The American commitment to Berlin was one more reason to preclude inaction against the Soviet missiles

---

76. See Harold Macmillan, *At the End of the Day, 1961–1963* (London: Macmillan, 1973), pp. 184–90. For the following quote see "507th NSC Meeting," October 22, *NSA:CMC*, Doc. 00840.

77. "Foreign Office to Embassy Washington," October 24, in Public Records Office, London, *Diplomatic Correspondence Files* [hereafter *PRO:FO*] 371/162378.

78. See Macmillan, *At the End of the Day*, pp. 198–203, 202–4. See also Lebow and Stein, *We All Lost the Cold War*, p. 121.

in Cuba. As the president put it during the second ExComm meeting, if the Soviets put missiles in Cuba without an American response, Moscow would build more bases and then squeeze the West in Berlin.[79] Concerns about Berlin also served as another restraining factor on U.S. decisions. The city's exposure inside the Soviet bloc made it an easy target of retaliatory action against American moves in Cuba. Kennedy worried about Berlin almost constantly. Fear of Soviet action against the essentially defenseless city was one reason for his decision in favor of the blockade and against more forceful military action.[80]

Kennedy's personal and emotional commitment to Berlin was again apparent during the crucial ExComm meeting on October 27, when he was faced with the choice between an air strike and a "missile swap":

> What we're going to be faced with is—because we wouldn't take the missiles out of Turkey, then maybe we'll have to invade or make a massive strike on Cuba which may lose Berlin.

> . . . We all know how quickly everybody's courage goes when the blood starts to flow, and that's what's going to happen in NATO . . . We start these things and they grab Berlin, and everybody's going to say, "Well that was a pretty good proposition."[81]

The Berlin issue symbolized the role of the North Atlantic Alliance in the minds of U.S. decision makers throughout the crisis—precluding both inaction and a rush to escalation. Concerns about the city and the fate of Europe in general were causally consequential not by determining specific choices but by constraining the range of options available to decision makers. President Kennedy and other ExComm members treated Berlin almost as if it were another American city, for which American soldiers were supposed to die in defense of their country. It did not seem to make a difference whether the fate of Berlin or that of New York was at stake. Berlin symbolized the allied community and the values for which the Cold War was fought. It was the city's very vulnerability to Soviet pressures that made it such a significant symbol for the U.S. commitment to the defense of Europe.

While Berlin was an important concern of U.S. decision makers during

---

79. "White House Tapes and Minutes of the Cuban Missile Crisis," *International Security* 10, no. 1 (Summer 1985): 164–203, 185.

80. See, for example, the telephone conversation Macmillan-Kennedy, October 26, in Macmillan, *At the End of the Day*, pp. 209–11.

81. "October 27, 1962: Transcripts of the Meetings of the ExComm," *International Security* 12, no. 3 (Winter 1987/88): 30–92, 55, 58.

the crisis, it was peripheral to the *solution* to the crisis. The Jupiter medium-range ballistic missiles (MRBMs) deployed under NATO arrangements in Turkey and Italy became part and parcel of the crisis settlement. The Jupiter missiles had been deployed following a 1957 NATO decision, on U.S. request. In the meantime, the administration considered them dangerously vulnerable and militarily obsolete. Kennedy would have preferred their withdrawal long before, but the administration failed to persuade Turkey to give them up. By the time of the Cuban missile crisis, the Jupiter missiles had become a *political symbol* of alliance cohesion, of the U.S. commitment to NATO and to Turkey in particular, which had just returned to democratic rule.

Not surprisingly, the Jupiter MRBMs became immediately linked to the Soviet missile deployment in Cuba. Throughout the crisis, the administration was divided over a "missile swap." The split cut across divisions between departments and even led to differences of opinion within specific agencies such as the State Department and the Pentagon. The topic of the Turkish Jupiter bases also came up in various interallied discussions. A "missile swap" was discussed in the British government, but London remained opposed to an explicit "missile trade" throughout the crisis, despite its support for a "deal." At the same time, the Turkish government began to raise concerns, particularly when the Soviet ambassador in Ankara began to argue that Moscow regarded the Jupiter missiles as its "Cuba." While Dean Rusk publicly denied any connection between the Cuban missile crisis and any situation elsewhere in the world, he hinted that, in the long run, disarmament negotiations could deal with the location of weapons.[82]

The administration also considered speeding up plans for the Multilateral Force (MLF), a sea-based nuclear force of American, British, and French systems under a joint NATO command, which had originally been proposed by the Eisenhower administration. The U.S. then set its diplomatic machinery in motion to anticipate how the allies would react to withdrawal of the Jupiter missiles in such a context.[83] The U.S. ambassador to NATO, John Finletter, responded along the lines already discussed in Washington. He argued that Turkey regarded the Jupiter missiles as a

82. For details, see "Ambassador Hare, Ankara, to State Dept.," October 23, *NSA:CMC*, Doc. 01080; "Hare to State Dept.," October 24, ibid., Doc. 01260; "Rusk, Circular Cable," October 24, ibid., Doc. 01140; "Rusk to US Embassies, West Europe," October 25, ibid., Doc. 01294; "Rusk to US Embassy, Ankara," October 25, ibid., Doc. 01298.
83. "Dean Rusk to US Embassies to NATO and to Turkey," October 24, *NSA:CMC*, Doc. 01138.

symbol of the alliance commitment to its defense and that no arrangement should be made without the approval of the Turkish government. Finletter strongly advised against any open deal, but then proposed a "small southern command multilateral seaborne force on a 'pilot basis'" using Polaris submarines and manned by mixed U.S., Turkish, and Italian crews. Such an arrangement could allow the U.S. to offer the withdrawal of the Jupiters to the Soviets.[84] While the U.S. ambassador to Turkey cabled a gloomy assessment from Ankara, he also concurred that a strictly secret deal with the Soviets was possible, together with some military compensation for Turkey.[85] These cables were discussed in the ExComm meetings on October 27 and influenced the president's decisions.

Various U.S. ambassadors to NATO allies apparently talked to their host governments about a secret "missile swap" despite an explicit directive by Rusk not to talk about it. The networks provided by the transatlantic institutions made it impossible to exclude allied officials from the deliberations. British officials discussed a "missile swap"; so did NATO's permanent representatives in Paris. Most important, the Turkish foreign ministry indicated to the American and the British ambassadors that it was not completely opposed to a removal of the Jupiters, to be discussed after a suitable lapse of time and in a general NATO context.[86] The president involved the British ambassador in his deliberations and also asked the British to approach their embassy in Ankara for a view on the matter.[87]

When the crisis reached its climax on October 27, discussions that included the State Department, the Pentagon, U.S. diplomats in Europe, NATO representatives in Paris, and various allied governments—at least the British and the Turks—had been held, and a solution had emerged. The solution entailed a strictly secret deal between Washington and Moscow that included the removal of the Jupiter missiles from Turkey in exchange for military compensation, after the Soviets had withdrawn their missiles from Cuba.

On October 27, the ExComm devoted most of its meeting time to discussing the options of an air strike against Cuba versus a "missile swap."

84. "Finletter to State Dept.," October 25, *NSA:CMC*, Doc. 01328.
85. "Hare to State Dept." (Section 1), October 26, *NSA:CMC*, Doc. 01470; "Hare to State Dept." (Sections 2 and 3), October 26, NSA, *Nuclear History Documents*.
86. See "Embassy Ankara to Foreign Office," October 28, *PRO:FO* 371/162382; "Embassy Ankara to Foreign Office," October 28, ibid. 371/162381. On discussions at NATO's headquarters see "Finletter to State Dept.," October 28, *NSA:CMC*, Doc. 01602.
87. According to "Embassy Washington to Foreign Office," October 27, *PRO:FO* 371/162382.

The sense of allied community among ExComm members served as a frame of reference in which the various courses of action were discussed. Both sides in the debate referred to the need to preserve NATO. Supporters of an air strike argued that a missile trade would lead to the denuclearization of NATO and indicate that the U.S. was prepared to tamper with the indivisibility of allied security for selfish reasons. As McGeorge Bundy put it, "In their [the Turkish] own terms it would already be clear that we were trying to sell our allies for our interests. That would be the view in all of NATO. It's irrational, and it's crazy, but it's a terribly powerful fact."[88]

The president was primarily concerned that the Soviet public demand might provoke a public counterresponse by the Turkish government, which would jeopardize a secret solution to the crisis. He argued that the U.S. faced a dilemma. On the one hand, the U.S. commitment to its allies was at stake. On the other hand, many alliance members around the world might regard a missile trade as a reasonable deal and would not understand if the U.S. rejected it.[89]

In the end, the proposal of a secret deal with the Soviets together with some military compensation for the allies carried the day with the president. It was agreed that the Jupiter missiles could not be removed without Turkish approval and that therefore the U.S. would have to persuade the government in Ankara. A small group of Kennedy's advisers assembled after the ExComm meeting and discussed an oral message to be transmitted to Anatoly Dobrynin, the Soviet ambassador, by Attorney General Robert Kennedy. Dean Rusk proposed that Kennedy should simply tell Dobrynin that the U.S. was determined to get the Jupiter missiles out of Turkey as soon as the crisis was over. The group also agreed to keep absolute secrecy about this in order to preserve allied unity.[90]

Shortly after the meeting of Kennedy's advisers, the president's brother met with Ambassador Dobrynin and told him in rather dramatic terms that the crisis was quickly escalating and that the U.S. might soon bomb the missile bases in Cuba, which could lead to war in Europe. He then told Dobrynin with surprising openness that the U.S. was prepared to remove the Jupiter missiles from Turkey but could do so only if the deal was kept secret, since alliance unity was at stake.[91] Khrushchev accepted the president's proposal, thereby solving the crisis.

---

88. "October 27, 1962: Transcripts," p. 39.
89. Bromley Smith, "Summary Record of ExComm Meeting," October 27, *NSA:CMC*, Doc. 01541. For the following see "October 27, 1962: Transcripts."
90. See Bundy, *Danger and Survival*, pp. 432–34;.
91. See Dobrynin's cable to Moscow, October 27, in Lebow and Stein, *We All Lost the Cold War*, pp. 524–26.

In sum, U.S. membership in an alliance of democratic states shaped the process by which decision makers struggled over the definition of American interests and preferences during the Cuban missile crisis. One could argue, though, that the U.S. decisions were perfectly rational given the risks and opportunities at hand and that reference to the transatlantic relationship is, therefore, unnecessary to explain American behavior. The blockade, the noninvasion pledge, and the secret "missile swap" were indeed perfectly rational decisions. But a rational-choice account proves to be indeterminate *unless* alliance considerations are factored in. The opposite arguments in favor of escalating the crisis through an air strike or even an invasion were as rational as those in support of the blockade or the "missile deal." Supporters of an air strike correctly argued that the risks of escalation were minimal given the overwhelming superiority of the U.S., both locally in the region and on the global nuclear level. Only if Soviet retaliation against *Europe* was considered a problem could one make a rational argument against the air strike and other escalatory steps. *Berlin* was the American Achilles heel during the crisis, not New York City.

That U.S. decision makers did not distinguish between domestic and European concerns, that they worried as much about the fate of Berlin as about New York City, and that they regarded obsolete Jupiter missiles in Turkey as major obstacles to the solution of the crisis—these puzzles make sense if one assumes a security community of democratic nations, on behalf of which the Kennedy administration acted. Membership in the Western Alliance affected the identity of American actors in the sense that the "we" in whose name the president decided incorporated the European allies. Those who invoked potential allied concerns in the internal discourses added weight to their arguments by referring to the collectively shared value of the community. The alliance community as part of the American identity explains the lack of distinction between domestic and alliance politics as well as the sense of commitment that U.S. decision makers felt with regard to their allies. Reputational concerns and the credibility of the U.S. commitment to NATO were at stake during the Cuban missile crisis. But I submit that these worries can be better understood within the framework of a security community based on collectively shared values than on the basis of traditional alliance theory.

The End of the Cold War and the Future of NATO

Since 1985, the European security environment has changed dramatically. The Cold War is over, the U.S.-Soviet rivalry gave way to a new partnership among former opponents, Germany is united, the Warsaw Pact and even the Soviet Union have ceased to exist. Fundamental parameters in the international environment of the transatlantic relationship have been profoundly altered. The world of the 1990s is very different from the world of the 1950s and 1960s. Can we extrapolate anything from the study of European-American relations during the height of the Cold War for the future of the transatlantic ties?

Contrary to Waltzian assumptions, NATO remains alive and well so far, adjusting to the new international environment:

- In response to the end of the Cold War, NATO has started changing its force structure. Instead of heavily armored and mechanized divisions, member states are setting up intervention forces with increased mobility in accordance with the NATO decision to build an allied rapid reaction corps for "out-of-area" purposes.[92]
- As to relations with the former Cold War opponents, the North Atlantic Cooperation Council was instituted in 1991, linking the sixteen allies with Eastern Europe and the successor states of the Soviet Union. Two years later, these countries joined a "partnership for peace," creating institutionalized ties between NATO's integrated military command structure and the East European and Russian militaries. Current debates center around how central Eastern European countries such as Poland, Hungary, and the Czech Republic could join the alliance without antagonizing Russia and jeopardizing its legitimate security concerns.[93]
- The alliance has started playing a subsidiary role in UN-sponsored international peacekeeping and peace-enforcement missions, such as in the former Yugoslavia.[94] It is remarkable in this context that the profound conflict of interest among the Western powers with regard to the war in Bosnia-Herzegovina has not at all affected NATO. Rather, the U.S., Britain, France, and Germany worked hard to ensure that their disagreements over Bosnia would not adversely influence the transatlantic alliance.

---

92. If the alliance was disintegrating, one would expect the members to concentrate on the defense of their national territories rather than building light and mobile forces. See Hellmann and Wolf, "Neorealism, Neoliberal Institutionalism, and the Future of NATO," p. 22.

93. For details, see "North Atlantic Cooperation Council Statement," *NATO Press Service*, December 20, 1991; Stephen Flanagan, "NATO and Central and Eastern Europe," *Washington Quarterly* 15, no. 2 (Spring 1992): 141–51; " 'Partnerschaft für den Frieden' mit Osteuropa. Aber keine konkreten Zusagen für Mitgliedschaft," *Süddeutsche Zeitung*, January 11, 1994; "NATO Chiefs Hail New Era, But War Still Casts Clouds," *International Herald Tribune* [hereafter *IHT*], January 12, 1994; "Clinton Hints NATO Would Defend East from Attack," *IHT*, January 13, 1994.

94. See, for example, "Report by Ad-hoc Group of the North Atlantic Cooperation Council on Cooperation for Peacekeeping," *NATO Press Service*, June 11, 1993; Hellmann and Wolf, "Neorealism, Neoliberal Institutionalism, and the Future of NATO," p. 25.

I have argued here that the Western Alliance represents an institution-alization of the transatlantic security community based on common values and a collective identity of liberal democracies.[95] The Soviet domestic structure and the values promoted by communism were regarded as alien to the community, resulting in a threat perception of the Soviet Union as the potential enemy. The democratization of the Soviet system initiated by Mikhail Gorbachev and continued by Boris Yeltsin then started ending the Cold War in Western eyes by altering the "Otherness" of the Soviet sys-tem. The Gorbachev revolution consisted primarily of embracing Western liberal values.[96] While "glasnost" introduced publicity into the Soviet political process, "perestroika" democratized it. In response, Western threat perception gradually decreased, even though at different rates and to different degrees. The Germans were the first to declare the Cold War over. They reacted not only to the democratization of the Soviet system but in particular to Gorbachev's foreign policy change toward "common security." Americans came last; Gorbachev needed to give up Eastern Europe and the Berlin Wall had to tumble down in order to convince them.

It should be noted, however, that this explanation has its limits. Liberal theory as such does not suggest that democracies should behave coopera-tively toward democratizing states, as the West did toward the Soviet Union under Gorbachev. The arguments put forward in the Kantian tra-dition pertain to *stable* democracies. Since they relate to the social *struc-ture* of international relations, they cannot explain the specifics as well as the differences among the Western responses to the Gorbachev revolution, i.e., *agency*.[97] But unlike realism, a liberal argument about the transatlantic security community correctly predicts that these threat perceptions would wither away at some point when former opponents democratize and thus begin entering the community of liberal states.

---

95. See also Steve Weber, "Does NATO Have a Future?," in Beverly Crawford, ed., *The Future of European Security* (Berkeley: University of California at Berkeley, Center for German and European Studies, 1992), pp. 360–95. Emanuel Adler, "Europe's New Security Order," in ibid., pp. 287–326, shares the assessment but comes to different conclusions regarding the desirability of NATO.

96. On this point, see Daniel Deudney and G. John Ikenberry, "The International Sources of Soviet Change," *International Security* 16 (Winter 1991/92): 74–118; Henry Nau, "Rethinking Econom-ics, Politics, and Security in Europe," in Richard N. Perle, ed., *Reshaping Western Security*, pp. 11–46 (Washington, D.C.: American Enterprise Institute Press, 1991).

97. See Thomas Risse-Kappen, "Ideas Do Not Float Freely: Transnational Coalitions, Domestic Structures, and the End of the Cold War," *International Organization* 48, no. 2 (Spring 1994): 185–214.

The end of the Cold War, then, not only does not terminate the Western community of values, it extends that community into Eastern Europe and, potentially, into even the successor states of the Soviet Union, creating a "pacific federation" of liberal democracies from Vladivostok to Berlin, San Francisco, and Tokyo.[98] But liberal theory does not necessarily expect NATO to last into the next century. It only assumes that the security partnership among liberal democracies will persist in one institutionalized form or another.[99] If the democratization process in Russia gives way to authoritarian nationalism, however, liberal theorists do expect NATO to remain the dominant Western security institution and to regain its character as a defensive alliance. In this case, NATO would be expected quickly to extend its security guarantee to the new democracies in central Eastern Europe. But *institutionalist* arguments suggest that a transformed NATO will remain the overarching security community of the "pacific federation." It is easier to adjust an already existing organization, which encompasses an elaborate set of rules and decision-making procedures, to new conditions than it is to create new institutions of security cooperation among the liberal democracies in the Northern Hemisphere. The OSCE—not to mention the West European Union—would have to be strengthened much further until they reach a comparable degree of institutionalization.

NATO also provides a unique institutional framework for Europeans to affect American policies. Liberal democracies successfully influence each other in the framework of international institutions by using norms and joint decision-making procedures as well as transnational politics. Playing by the rules of these institutions, they do not just constrain their own freedom of action; they also gain access to the decision-making processes of their partners. Reducing the institutional ties might create the illusion of independence, but it actually decreases one's impact.

---

98. On liberal and institutionalist visions of the future of European security, see Adler, "Europe's New Security Order"; Ernst-Otto Czempiel, *Weltpolitik im Umbruch* (Munich: Beck, 1991); James M. Goldgeier and Michael McFaul, "A Tale of Two Worlds: Core and Periphery in the Post–Cold War Era," *International Organization* 46, no. 3 (Spring 1992): 467–91; Charles Kupchan and Clifford Kupchan, "Concerts, Collective Security, and the Future of Europe," *International Security* 16, no. 1 (Summer 1991): 114–61; Dieter Senghaas, *Friedensprojekt Europa* (Frankfurt am Main: Suhrkamp, 1991); Stephen Van Evera, "Primed for Peace: Europe After the Cold War," *International Security* 15 (Winter 1990/91): 7–57.
99. I thank Andrew Moravcsik for clarifying this point to me.

Conclusions: How Unique Is NATO?

I have argued in this essay that traditional alliance theories based on realist thinking provide insufficient explanations of the origins, the interaction patterns, and the persistence of NATO. The North Atlantic Alliance represents an institutionalized pluralistic security community of liberal democracies. Democracies not only do not fight each other, they are likely to develop a collective identity facilitating the emergence of cooperative institutions for specific purposes. These institutions are characterized by democratic norms and decision making rules that liberal states tend to externalize when dealing with each other. The enactment of these norms and rules strengthens the sense of community and the collective identity of the actors. Domestic features of liberal democracies enable the community in the first place. But the institutionalization of the community exerts independent effects on the interactions. In the final analysis, then, democratic domestic structures, international institutions, and the collective identity of state actors do the explanatory work together.

But do the findings pertaining to the North Atlantic Alliance hold up with regard to other alliances and cooperative institutions among democracies? Comparisons can be made along two dimensions: the degree of institutionalization of the community and the extent to which collective identities have developed among its members. The only international institution that appears to score higher than NATO on both dimensions is the *European Union* (EU).[100] While it is less integrated than NATO with regard to security and foreign policy making, the EU features unique supranational institutions such as the European Commission and the European Court of Justice. The EU member states also coordinate their economic and monetary policies to an unprecedented degree.[101] As far as collective identity is concerned, there is a well-documented sense of common Europeanness among the elites of the continental member states that partially extends into mass public opinion. Interaction patterns within the EU closely resemble the transnational and

---

100. Cooperation patterns among the Nordic states come to mind, too. Note that Scandinavian cooperation was the main example in Deutsch's original study on "pluralistic security communities." See Deutsch et al., *Political Community and the North Atlantic Area.*

101. See, for example, Anne-Marie Burley and Walter Mattli, "Europe Before the Court: A Political Theory of Legal Integration," *International Organization* 47, no. 1 (Winter 1993): 41–76; Stanley Hoffmann and Robert Keohane, eds., *The New European Community* (Boulder: Westview, 1991); Alberta Sbragia, ed., *Euro-Politics* (Washington, D.C.: Brookings Institution, 1992).

transgovernmental coalitions that have been found typical for decision making in NATO.[102]

Compared with NATO and the EU, the *U.S.-Japanese security relationship* appears to represent an interesting anomaly, in the sense that it is highly institutionalized, but the collective identity component seems to be weaker.[103] Japanese security was more dependent on the U.S. during the Cold War than were Western Europe and even Germany. Strongly institutionalized transnational and transgovernmental ties developed among the military and the defense establishments of the two countries. Apart from the elite level of the governing party, however, the security relationship remained deeply contested in Japanese domestic politics during the Cold War. As a result, the U.S.-Japanese security cooperation certainly qualifies as a democratic alliance establishing norms of consultation and compromise-oriented decision making similar to those of NATO. But given the lack of collective identity, it is less clear whether this alliance constitutes a "pluralistic security community" in Deutsch's sense. The U.S.-Japanese example, then, shows that there is some variation with regard to both institutionalization and identity components in alliances among democracies.

In contrast, identity politics appears to be particularly strong in the *U.S.-Israeli security relationship*, as Michael Barnett argues in this volume. Again, the variation, compared with NATO and the U.S.-Japanese alliance, seems to pertain to the identity component, while the American alliance with Israel is as highly institutionalized as the other security relationships discussed so far. As Barnett points out, recent strains in the relationship can be better explained by challenges to the collective sense of democratic community resulting from Israeli policies than by changes in the international environment in which the two states operate.

---

102. For details, see Richard Münch, *Das Projekt Europa: Zwischen Nationalstaat, regionaler Autonomie und Weltgesellschaft* (Frankfurt am Main: Suhrkamp, 1993); Anthony Smith, "National Identity and the Idea of European Unity," *International Affairs* 68, no. 1 (1992): 55–76; Ole Waever et al., "The Struggle for 'Europe': French and German Concepts of State, Nation, and European Union" (unpublished manuscript, 1993). On transnational and transgovernmental relations within the EU see, for example, David Cameron, "Transnational Relations and the Development of the European Economic and Monetary Union," in Thomas Risse-Kappen, ed., *Bringing Transnational Relations Back In: State Actors, Domestic Structures, and International Institutions*, pp. 37–78 (Cambridge: Cambridge University Press, 1995).

103. See Reinhard Drifte, *Japan's Foreign Policy* (London: Routledge, 1990); Peter Katzenstein and Yutuka Tsujinaka, " 'Bullying,' 'Buying,' and 'Binding': U.S.-Japanese Transnational Relations and Domestic Structures," in Risse-Kappen, *Bringing Transnational Relations Back In*, pp. 79–111; Peter Katzenstein and Nobuo Okawara, *Japan's National Security: Structures, Norms, and Policy Responses in a Changing World* (Ithaca: Cornell University Press, 1993). See also Thomas Berger's contribution to this volume.

So far, I have looked only at security communities among democracies. What about *alliances involving nondemocracies*? If the liberal argument presented here holds true, we should find quite different interaction patterns in such relationships, since the basic ingredients for the "democratic peace" are missing. A thorough analysis is beyond the scope of this essay. But various findings appear to suggest that, indeed, interaction patterns in nondemocratic alliances are different and conform more closely to realist expectations, particularly realist bargaining theory. As to the Middle East, for example, Stephen Walt has argued that common ideology played only a limited role in the formation of alliances among Arab states. While Michael Barnett disagrees, pointing to the significance of pan-Arabism, he also concurs that this collective identity has been weaker than the sense of community among democratic allies such as the U.S. and Israel.[104] A study comparing U.S. relations with Latin America and interaction patterns within the former Warsaw Pact concludes that these relations can well be analyzed within the framework of public choice and realist bargaining theories.[105]

In sum, these comparisons suggest that NATO is not unique but exemplifies interaction patterns and collective identities that are quite common for security communities among democracies. At the same time, these features appear to distinguish democratic alliances from other security relationships. In this sense, alliances among democracies are indeed special, since they can build upon a strong sense of community pertaining to the domestic structures of liberal states. Nevertheless, the degree of institutionalization as well as the extent to which "pluralistic security communities" have emerged varies among democracies.

---

104. See Walt, *The Origins of Alliances*; Michael Barnett, "Institutions, Roles, and Disorder: The Case of the Arab States System," *International Studies Quarterly* 37, no. 3 (September 1993): 271–96; see also Barnett's contribution to this volume.
105. See Triska, *Dominant Powers and Subordinate States*.

11 · Identity and Alliances in the Middle East

Michael N. Barnett

International relations scholarship is nearly unanimous in the view that alliances are driven by expediency rather than principle, that their primary motivation is to enhance state security in the face of some immediate or future external threat, and that ideational and domestic interests are of secondary importance. In this view, states seek alliances primarily to enhance their capabilities through combination with others, which helps to deter a potential aggressor and avoid an unwanted war, to prepare for a successful war in the event that deterrence fails, or more generally to increase one's influence in a high-threat environment or maintain a balance of power in the system. Resting on a foundation of systemic theorizing, alliances can be a product of either balancing or bandwagoning behavior, but in any form they are the result of expedience and an external threat.[1]

For their critical reading and helpful suggestions, I would like to thank the members of the project, the participants in the workshops at Stanford and Minnesota, Emanuel Adler, Peter Katzenstein, David Laitin, Martin Sampson, Stephen Walt, and the anonymous reviewers at Columbia University Press.
1. For various realist and neorealist statements, see Thucydides, *The Peloponnesian War* (New York: Penguin Books, 1954); George Liska, *Nations in Alliance: The Limits of Interdependence* (Baltimore: Johns Hopkins University Press, 1962); William Langer, *European Alliances and Alignments, 1871–1890*, 2d ed. (New York: Vintage, 1964); Stephen M. Walt, *The Origins of Alliances* (Ithaca: Cornell University Press, 1987); Edward Gulick, *Europe's Classical Balance of Power* (New York:

As security scholars identify the dynamics of alliance formation, they generally focus on two features of the state's strategic calculus: (1) the identification of the threat and (2) the determination of whether and with whom to ally in response to that threat. Both steps, according to realists, are parsimoniously and predictably propelled by power politics and systemic pressures; material factors and threats to the state's security generate the definition of the threat, and the decision to construct an external alignment (as opposed to a strategy of internal mobilization) and with whom is dependent on a rational calculation of costs and benefits that derive primarily from material factors and the state's relative military power vis-á-vis potential and immediate threats.[2] In general, the neorealist approach to alliance formation is quite insistent that material factors dominate the definition of, and the adopted response to, that threat.

This essay, in contrast, asserts that state identity offers theoretical leverage over the issue of the construction of the threat and the choice of the alliance partner. It is the politics of identity rather than the logic of anarchy that often provides a better understanding of which states are viewed as a potential or immediate threat to the state's security. Moreover, whereas realists calculate the costs and benefits of additional units of security, defined in terms of the state's relative military power, and emphasize the state's attempt to maneuver between the dual fears of entrapment and abandonment, the variable of identity also signals which states are considered more or less desirable partners. By proposing a direct link between identity and strategic behavior, and investigating that behavior in a central research domain of neorealism, I offer an alternative understanding of security dynamics.

To explore the relationship between identity and alliance formation I examine various episodes of inter-Arab and U.S.-Israeli relations. Inter-Arab relations are frequently characterized as the paragon of realist politics; Arab leaders routinely paid lip service to the ideals of pan-Arabism while engaging in power-seeking behavior. To demonstrate how identity provides theoretical leverage over these central issues surrounding alliance formation, I examine two periods in inter-Arab relations. During the early

Norton, 1955), pp. 58–62; Glenn Snyder, "Alliance Theory: A Neorealist First Cut," in Robert Rothstein, ed., The Evolution of Theory in International Relations, pp. 83–104 (Columbia: University of South Carolina Press, 1992); Kenneth N. Waltz, Theory of International Politics (Reading, Mass.: Addison-Wesley, 1979), chs. 6, 8; and Randall Schweller, "Bandwagoning for Profit: Bringing the Revisionist State Back In," International Security 19, no. 1 (Summer 1994): 72–107.
2. See, respectively, Walt, *The Origins of Alliances*, and Snyder, "Alliance Theory."

years of the Arab states system, Arab nationalism guided Arab states to identify both with whom they should "naturally" associate and the threat to Arab states; this common identity and threat, in turn, created the desire for certain normative and institutional arrangements to govern inter-Arab security politics that were reflective of their self-understanding of being Arab states. The 1955 Iraqi-Turkey Treaty, better known as the Baghdad Pact, ignited these very issues and suggests the impact of identity rather than anarchy. I then examine the Gulf Cooperation Council (GCC) and some features of the post–Gulf war security patterns, which also elevate how identity shapes the construction of the threat and signals who is considered a preferred partner.

These two episodes in inter-Arab politics also suggest ways in which changing identities are associated with changing regional security and alliance patterns. Frequently discussed as the "end of pan-Arabism," "the new realism," "the return to geography," and "the fragmentation of the Arab world," the subtext is the decline of Arab national identities and the emergence of statist identities.[3] These changes, in turn, are linked to discursive and behavioral changes in inter-Arab politics. Specifically, if Arab nationalism reminded Arab leaders that as heads of Arab states they shared interests, goals, and security threats and should actively attempt to strengthen that community and to develop close strategic ties (or at least be viewed as doing so), its observed decline and the rise of statist identities has diminished the enthusiasm for all of the above. Consequently, Arab states are exhibiting new behavioral expectations and patterns of interactions that have imprinted their security politics in general and alliance arrangements in particular.

Most analyses of the U.S.-Israeli alliance contend that it is driven by either systemic or U.S. domestic politics. My position, however, is that

---

3. See, respectively, Fouad Ajami, *The Arab Predicament: Arab Political Thought and Practice Since 1967* (New York: Cambridge University Press, 1981); Bernard Lewis, "Rethinking the Middle East," *Foreign Affairs* 71, no. 4 (1992): 99–119; and Martin Kramer, "Arab Nationalism: Mistaken Identity," *Daedalus* 122 (Summer 1993): 171–206; Ghassam Salame, "Inter-Arab Politics: The Return to Geography," in William Quandt, ed., *The Middle East: Ten Years After Camp David*, pp. 319–56 (Washington, D.C.: Brookings Institution, 1988); and George Corm, *Fragmentation of the Middle East: The Last Thirty Years* (London: Hutchinson Books, 1983). For realist-inspired explanations of inter-Arab dynamics, see P. J. Vatikiotis, *Conflict in the Middle East* (London: George Allen and Unwin, 1971), and *Arab and Regional Politics in the Middle East* (New York: St. Martin's, 1984); Walt, *The Origins of Alliances*; Shibley Telhami, *The Path to Camp David* (New York: Columbia University Press, 1990); Roger Owen, *State, Power, and Politics in the Making of the Modern Middle East* (New York: Routledge, 1992), pp. 90–92; and Alan Taylor, *The Arab Balance of Power* (Syracuse: Syracuse University Press, 1982).

Israel's collective identity, and the U.S.'s understanding that Israel shares with it certain values, are critical for understanding U.S.-Israel relations. To demonstrate the importance of identity, I examine the "crisis" in U.S.-Israeli relations that began in the late 1980s; while many look to systemic forces and the end of the Cold War, I argue that another source of the crisis resided in Israeli debates and practices that challenged its Western, liberal-democratic, character, and accordingly, the foundation of U.S.-Israeli relations. All three cases, then, are intended to demonstrate how identity, as a relational construct that emerges out of the international and domestic discourse and interactions, helps us better to understand the dynamics of alliance formation.

Identity and Alliance Formation

A mainstay of realist approaches to alliance politics is that states respond to threats from the external environment. Of central importance here is Stephen Walt's *The Origins of Alliances*. Walt modifies Kenneth Waltz's account of alliance formation by recognizing that states balance not against power but rather against threats. Because anarchy and the distribution of power alone are unable to signal which states will be identified as threats, Walt posits that the threat derives from a combination of geostrategic and military factors and "aggressive intentions."[4] To determine who constitutes a threat to the state's physical security and relative power requires a marriage of capabilities and intentions.

Walt's "balance-of-threat" approach represents an important contribution to neorealist thought, and his analytically driven narrative of Middle Eastern politics is quite compelling. Yet to what extent do Walt's theory and narrative of Middle Eastern politics offer a verdict for neorealism and materialism? I want to suggest that his theoretical framework and observations identify not the logic of anarchy but rather the politics of identity; specifically, Walt assembles strong support for ideational rather than materialist forces as driving inter-Arab politics in general and alliance formation in particular.

To begin, consider the variable of "aggressive intentions." Walt elevates this critical variable because of his recognition that the distribution of power alone cannot predict which states will be identified as a threat. Yet

---

4. Walt, *The Origins of Alliances*, pp. 22–26.

how is intent determined? In his theoretical discussion Walt offers various examples of how intent represents an important component of the construction of the threat, yet the concept of intent is left underspecified and undertheorized. By rejecting the proposition that intent is conceptually linked to anarchy or the balance of power and by failing to offer a conceptual tie in its place, Walt leaves the issue unresolved: How is intent determined? What constitutes a threat?

Although Walt's theoretical discussion does not offer any guidance concerning how intent is determined, looming large in his historical narrative is "ideology." Specifically, pan-Arabism represents both a force to be reckoned with and a potential threat to other Arab regimes by challenging their legitimacy, sovereignty, and internal stability. Briefly, pan-Arabism charged that because the West segmented and divided the Arab nation into separate Arab states, Arab states derived their identity, interests, and legitimacy from the entire Arab nation that enveloped their separate borders. A central feature of this drama was that while the Arab states system was nominally organized around sovereignty, pan-Arabism held that Arab states had an obligation to protect Arabs wherever they resided and to work toward political unification, that is, to bring the state and the nation into correspondence. pan-Arabism, in short, represented a potential threat to Arab governments, as it challenged the very territorial basis of their existence.

An Arab leader that wielded the pan-Arab "card," therefore, represented a dual challenge to other Arab governments. First, he challenged them to be viewed as working toward both a deepening of the Arab political community and their eventual political unification. By reminding them both that (his own and) their authority and legitimacy derived not from these fictitious territories created by the West but from the Arab nation, and that their duty was, in effect, to deny their own sovereignty and strengthen the bonds of Arab unity, Arab nationalism represented a threat to the Arab states' sovereignty and, hence, to the Arab leaders' external and internal security. This view helps to explain why in the 1940s a militarily powerful Egypt feared a substantially weaker Iraq that was a thousand miles from its border, that offered little military challenge, and that, in fact, offered itself up for political unification. The proposed Syrian-Iraqi federation in the late 1940s and the realized Syrian-Egyptian unification in 1958 threatened the entire region; yet the challenge derived not from the combined aggregate military power of the two states but from their making good on Arabism's pledge and challenging other Arab leaders to do the same.

Second, Arab leaders could lose tremendous legitimacy, and hence suffer a drop in their domestic and regional standing, if they were viewed as not acting to safeguard the interests, as failing to live up to the goals and aspirations, of the Arab nation. The fortunes of Arab leaders were dependent on whether they were viewed as conforming to the norms of the Arab nation; indeed, they could be the target of severe regional and domestic sanctions if they were perceived as violating its norms. The norms associated with Arabism, in other words, instructed Arab leaders how they were to behave, and one Arab leader could potentially undermine another by charging him with behavior that was inconsistent with the norms of the group. That Arab nationalism had this effect dramatizes the point that it was cultural capital, not military capabilities, that was the currency of power in Arab politics and that was deployed to shield oneself from, and to injure, one's rivals. In the game of inter-Arab politics, if you will, sticks and stones had comparatively little effect, but words could really hurt; portraying another Arab leader as acting in ways that were inconsistent with Arabism could potentially unleash domestic challenges and subject him to regional sanctions. In general, pan-Arabism represented a potential threat to the Arab state's domestic and international basis of existence, and an Arab leader who wielded the pan-Arab card could be dangerous indeed.[5]

Because Arab nationalism represented a potential threat to the sovereignty and security of Arab states, interstate interactions had a different dynamic than predicted by realist formulations. Simply put, rivalry had a strong normative element that was independent of material power. In fact, Walt recognizes as much. After surveying a series of alliances and balancing episodes in Arab politics, he concludes:

A different form of balancing has occurred in inter-Arab relations. In the Arab world, the most important source of power has been the ability to manipulate one's own image and the image of one's rivals in the minds of other Arab elites. Regimes have gained power and legitimacy if they have been seen as loyal to accepted Arab goals, and they have lost these assets if they have appeared to stray outside the Arab consensus. As a result, an effective means of countering one's rivals has been to attract as many allies as

---

5. This relates to domestic sources of alliance formation. Specifically, there is wide-ranging evidence, particularly in the non-Western context, that states often construct external alliances to counter domestic threats. See Michael Barnett and Jack Levy, "Domestic Sources of Alliances and Alignments: The Case of Egypt," *International Organization* 45, no. 3 (Summer 1991): 369–96; and Stephen David, "Explaining Third World Alignment," *World Politics* 43, no. 2 (January 1991): 233–56.

possible in order to portray oneself as leading (or at least conforming to) the norms of Arab solidarity. In effect, the Arab states have balanced one another not by adding up armies but by adding up votes. Thus militarily insignificant alliances between various Arab states often have had profound political effects.[6]

This conclusion, by singling out Arabism and ideology as driving inter-Arab interactions and by failing to forward the distribution of power as causally consequential, seems somewhat at odds with a neorealist view as it points to identity and not anarchy.

If Walt concludes that Arabism and ideology drove inter-Arab dynamics, why does he not revise his balance-of-threat model to incorporate more fully ideational factors? If he is suggesting that images, not anarchy, drives inter-Arab politics, then why not direct attention to ideational—not material—forces as primary, independent, and causal? As it stands, Walt's various historical observations are inconsistent with his materialist presuppositions, suggesting the limitations of neorealism for understanding inter-Arab politics. In my view, there are two reasons for the failure to give ideational forces their proper due. The first is a commitment to a materialism that forces Walt to reduce ideational factors to the level of ideology and to see them as parasitic on the material. Rather than considering how Arabism might in fact shape the identity, if not the interests, of Arab leaders, Walt reduces its status to that of an instrument used by Arab leaders to further their domestic and regional standing—simply put, as a legitimator of foreign policy. Although in his analytical discussion Walt recognizes that "aggressive intentions" drive the construction of the threat and are autonomous with respect to the distribution of power, he fails to consider what other theoretical field might generate the identification of hostile intent. The need to try to minimize the potential causal force of identity is also evident in his discussion of U.S.-Israeli relations; for instance, he dismisses the possibility of "ideological solidarity" between the U.S. and Israel because the "U.S. is [not] a welfare-state theocracy such as Israel."[7] In general, Walt seems incapable of fully acknowledging just how inconsistent his empirical observations are from his theoretical presuppositions because of his loyalty to materialism.

Perhaps another reason why Walt retreats to anarchy is because of the observation that Arab states, who supposedly shared an identity, have

---

6. Walt, *The Origins of Alliances*, p. 149.
7. Ibid., p. 200.

showed quite a flair for conflict and not for cooperation. In other words, because a shared identity is more closely associated with conflict than with cooperation, then it must be a realist world.[8] Yet the observation that the existence of a shared identity is associated with conflict is worth greater reflection. To begin[why assume that a shared identity necessarily generates a pacific structure and cooperation? After all, a community of Saddam Husseins is unlikely to father a secure environment, while a community of Mahatma Gandhis will encourage all to leave their homes unlocked.] Perhaps a more reasonable stance is to consider the possibility that conflict can take place among those actors that have a shared identity.[10] Conflict, after all, is part of any social relationship; George Simmel told us this a century ago in his highly insightful, but generally underappreciated, essay "Conflict."[11] In other words, the mere existence of conflict does not in and of itself entail a realist world or derive from anarchy; conflict has many sources, and the challenge is to consider reasons other than anarchy for why actors that have a shared identity might also exhibit conflict and hostility.

Because interstate interactions and alliance formation are better connected conceptually to identity than to anarchy, reducing identity to ideology and assuming that the ideational is parasitic on the material relegates to a residual category what is, in fact, central.[12] Specifically, while anarchy and

---

8. See John J. Mearsheimer, "The False Promise of International Institutions," *International Security* 19, no. 3 (Winter 1994/95): 37–40, for a similar view.

9. This is consistent with Wendt's observation that "anarchy is what states make of it"; Alexander Wendt, "Anarchy Is What States Make of It: The Social Construction of Power Politics," *International Organization* 46, no. 2 (Spring 1992): 391–425.

10. Walt observes that certain ideologies are likely to generate suspicion and fear while others are not; *The Origins of Alliances*, pp. 36, 267. Specifically, he argues that a Pan-Arabism that is associated with unification and can only have one "leader" is likely to generate fear, suspicion and rivalry, while democracies and monarchies are not likely to generate the same dynamics. Walt, in other words, appears to be suggesting that identity, and not anarchy, drives interstate dynamics in important ways.

11. George Simmel, *Conflict and the Web of Group-Affiliations* (New York: Free Press, 1964).

12. Walt's implicit recognition but ultimate rejection of the causal impact of ideational factors, and his subsequent retreat to materialism, are aptly captured by Jeffrey Alexander's observation of what occurs when individualists are confronted by the limitations of their theories for understanding interactions and group behavior: "When unresolved tensions develop in general theories, theorists will resort to ad hoc ways to resolve them. To cope with these tensions they will introduce, in what is usually an ad hoc and unthought-out way, theoretical categories which are residual to, or outside of, the logically developed systemic strands of their argument. . . . While residual categories are the result of theoretical tensions, for the sake of interpretation it is often more useful to move backwards, from one's discovery of the residual categories back to the basic tensions which they have been developed to obscure" (Jeffrey Alexander, *Twenty Lectures* [New York: Columbia University Press, 1987], pp. 124–25).

material factors provide little leverage and are not analytically linked to "aggressive intentions," identity offers a better conceptual handle in two ways. First, assorted literatures conclude that there is an important relationship between identity and the construction of the threat. To begin, identity emerges as a consequence of taking into consideration a relevant "other." While not all states with a shared identity will define threats in the same way, will treat all those outside the group as a threat, or will agree on the means to confront the threat, there is an important connection between identity and threat.[13] In other words, Arabism might affect the identity and interests of, and the socially acceptable policies available to, Arab leaders in ways that fundamentally shape their desired and available security policies. In fact, we readily accept the proposition that there is a relationship between identity and threat when it comes to ethnic, tribal, and religious groups, and there is no reason to dismiss a similar connection in the context of a different corporate actor called the state.[14] For instance, in the current climate, that is absent a clearly identifiable external danger, those that compose the self-selected Western community are elevating domestic characteristics—most notably, markets and democracy—as markers to distinguish between those who represent threats and those who do not. Walt, for instance, recognizes that an Arab identity and Arab nationalism caused Arab states to identify Israel as a threat and enemy.[15] To be sure, this hostility did not overcome collective action problems and free riding, yet it did prescribe what was acceptable and legitimate and suggests an important relationship between identity and the definition of the threat. In general, identity might be better able to "predict whether two states will be friends or foes, will be revisionist or status quo powers, and so on," and a shared identity is likely to generate a shared definition of the threat.[16]

Second, a possible source of conflict among actors that share an identity is their constitutive norms. Those states that share a basic identity and

13. See William Connolly, *Identity/Difference* (Ithaca: Cornell University Press, 1992), for a general treatment. That the definition and cohesion of the group are shaped by an outside threat or entity is, of course, a central proposition in much sociological thinking and many works on nationalism. See, for instance, Simmel, *Conflict and the Web of Group-Affiliations.*

14. For other treatments of the relationship between state identity and threat, see Gerrit Gong, *The Standard of "Civilization" in International Society* (New York: Oxford University Press, 1984); Iver Neumann and Jennifer Welsh, "The Other in European Self-Definition: An Addendum to the Literature on International Society," *Review of International Society* 17 (1991): 327–48; and David Campbell, *Writing Security* (Minneapolis: University of Minnesota Press, 1992).

15. Walt, *The Origins of Alliances*, p. 204.

16. Wendt, "Anarchy Is What States Make of It," p. 398.

organize themselves into a self-constituted group are likely to construct norms that instruct them on how they are to enact their identity. This suggests two possible sources of conflict. First, actors with a shared identity might very well debate and contest their associated norms. After all, while Pat Buchanan and I both identify ourselves as Americans, we have very different understandings of the norms that are associated with that identity, and those understandings are not easily reducible to our material circumstances or interests. What exists for actors in the domestic arena also applies to states in the international system. My argument is that inter-Arab politics largely concerns the debate over the norms that should govern Arab politics that are directly related to issues of identity. In general, that actors who have a shared identity will disagree over what constitutes acceptable behavior for the members of the group represents a potential source of conflict.

The proposition that actors with a shared identity might debate the norms that are to regulate their relations and are tied to conceptions of self generates a second, earlier observation: that actors will vie to present themselves as acting in a manner that is consistent with the group's norms and to portray others as acting in a manner that is inconsistent with those norms and thus potentially threatening to the group. In other words, rivalry is not over military power but rather it is over images and the presentation of self; threats, therefore, derive from a rival's attempt to portray itself as acting in a manner that violates the group's norms. Arab leaders, for instance, have attempted to present themselves as acting to further the interests of the Arab nation and to present others as potentially undermining those interests. Similarly, Arab leaders forged alliances and divisions around different positions concerning the norms that should govern inter-Arab politics; this is to be expected, given that norms, rather than militaries, potentially posed the threat to the regime's domestic and regional standing.

Consequently, portraying a member of the group as violating the group's norms potentially threatens that member's standing, if not its very status in the group. Said otherwise, there is generally some positive relationship between the state's expressed identity, its membership in the group, and its behavior; the behavior cannot be totally inconsistent with the self-proclaimed identity without challenging the state's relationship to the group. Therefore, disregarding these norms that define the group can undermine the state's identity and relationship to that group. For instance, the literature on the "democratic peace" notes the presence of constitutive norms that signify that "civilized" states do not go to war; therefore, going to war with a member of the community challenges the state's membership in the community of democratic states. The case of the Baghdad Pact illustrates the development of and debate over the norms that are intended to define and give meaning to the Arab nation and shows how Iraq's alliance with Turkey represented a challenge to the meaning and future of Arab nationalism and unleashed a debate over the norms to govern Arab politics.

In general, by exploring, first, that actors with a shared identity are likely to have a shared construction of the threat and, second, that actors with a shared identity might clash over the norms that are to govern their behaviors that are a reflection of that shared identity, I contend that identity is linked to the construction of the threat and represents a potential source of alliance formation.

In contrast to the neorealist view that the choice of the alliance partner is largely dependent on a rational calculation of costs and benefits that derive primarily from material factors, I want to consider how identity potentially shapes the choice of the alliance partner, and provides the foundation of the alliance. First, whereas neorealists presume that strategic calculations exhaust the state's consideration of a potential alliance partner, there is evidence that it frequently employs identity criteria to evaluate a prospective partner's "worthiness." Identity, in short, makes some partners more attractive than others. For instance, it is noteworthy that democratic states generally align with one another and do not ally against each other during times of war.[17] In Arab politics, the West, not to mention Israel, is not usually ranked high on the list of desirable strategic partners. The importance of identity for determining who is considered a worthwhile strategic partner is explored in the case of the Baghdad Pact and the GCC. In general, given the absence of an immediate threat (which is frequently the case), identity will factor into the state's choice of ally.

Second, identity not only provides some leverage over the choice of an alliance partner, but it also suggests that the maintenance of that alliance can be dependent on the parties' mutual identification. Consequently, a shared identity might not help to cement the basis of the alliance, but a change in identity can undermine the alliance's foundation. Because an important basis for the strategic association is not simply shared interests

---

17. Jack Levy, "Domestic Politics and War," *Journal of Interdisciplinary History* 18, no. 3 (1988): 653–73. Also see Thomas Risse-Kappen's contribution to this volume, essay 10.

in relationship to an identified threat but rather a shared identity that promotes an affinity and mutual identification, the language of community rather than the contractual language of alliance arguably better captures this type of strategic association.[18] To participate and to be counted as a member of a community requires that the state proclaim oneself as a member of the community, and express and uphold those values and norms that constitute it. To do so, the state must have a stable identity that has the "capacity *to keep a particular narrative going.*"[19] Therefore, being part of an association of like-minded states involves having a dominant historical narrative, an identity, that is consistent with that of the community. "In order to have a sense of who we are," Charles Taylor observes, "we have to have a notion of how we have become, and of where we are going."[20] The community becomes an important source of that identity and that narrative, and those within the community frequently express similar historical roots, a common heritage, and a shared future.

Communities and societies can be understood as engaging in a continuous debate over their collective identity.[21] As Edward Said observes, "We need to regard society as the locale in which a continuous contest between adherents of different ideas about what constitutes the national identity is taking place."[22] In this respect, states can have an "identity conflict," which is likely to emerge under two conditions.[23] First, it may result whenever there are competing definitions of the collective identity that call for contradictory behaviors. Although referring explicitly to the notion of role conflict, (with minimal translation errors), identity conflict might be seen to exist

> when there are contradictory expectations that attach to some position in a social relationship. Such expectations may call for incompatible perfor-

---

18. This is related to the concept of security communities. See Karl W. Deutsch, *Political Community and the North Atlantic Area* (Princeton: Princeton University Press, 1957); Emanuel Adler and Michael Barnett, "Pluralistic Security Communities: Past, Present, and Future" (Working Paper Series on Regional Security, no. 1, Global Studies Research Program, University of Wisconsin–Madison, 1994).

19. Anthony Giddens, *Modernity and Self-Identity* (Stanford: Stanford University Press, 1991), p. 54, emphasis in original.

20. Quoted from Giddens, ibid.

21. Connolly, *Identity/Difference*, p. 204; and Samuel Kim and Lowell Dittmer, "Whither China's Quest for National Identity?" in L. Dittmer and S. Kim, eds., *China's Quest for National Identity* (Ithaca: Cornell University Press, 1993), p. 241.

22. Edward Said, "The Phony Islamic Threat," *New York Times Magazine*, November 21, 1993, p. 62.

23. Lowell Dittmer and Samuel Kim, "In Search of a Theory of National Identity," in Dittmer and Kim, *China's Quest for National Identity*, pp. 6–7.

mances; they may require that one hold two norms or values which logically call for opposing behaviors; or they may demand that one [identity] necessitates the expenditure of time and energy such that it is difficult or impossible to carry out the obligations of another [identity].[24]

Identity conflict can also exist whenever definitions of the "collective self are no longer acceptable under new historical conditions."[25] In other words, a crisis might emerge whenever the state's collective identity (or the very debate over that identity) is at odds with the demands and defining characteristics of the broader community (which represents an additional source of the state's identity).

Maintaining a stable identity that is consistent with this larger community may be particularly challenging for some states at some moments because of changed international and domestic factors. At the international level, a change in systemic patterns, caused by transnational, economic, or military politics, can trigger wide-scale domestic change and debates concerning the collective identity and the state's relationship to the wider community. This has been particularly noticeable in recent years, as many states have debated the national identity and its relationship to other international communities, most notably the "West." At the domestic level, changes in territorial boundaries, the political economy, and demography can also enliven the debate over the collective identity. In any event, identity concerns not only the state's external "self" but also its internal one.

Relatedly, constitutive norms can pertain not only to the external behavior of states but also to their domestic behavior and arrangements. That is, being a member in the community is shaped not only by the state's external identity and associated behavior but also by its domestic characteristics and practices. Indeed, states apparently attempt to predict a state's external behavior based on its internal arrangements; this is most obvious in the expectation that democratic states will settle their differences short of war. Therefore, the failure to order the domestic polity in a particular way can potentially undermine the state's status in the group.[26] In general, my con-

24. Sheldon Stryker, *Symbolic Interactionism: A Social Structural Perspective* (Reading, Mass.: Benjamin/Cummings, 1980), p. 73.
25. Dittmer and Kim, "In Search of a Theory of National Identity," p. 7.
26. Relatedly, identity shapes the boundaries of the community. Whereas structuralists argue that the boundaries of any security association are determined along systemic lines, namely those that ally against the identified external threat, the language of identity suggests that boundaries are shaped by identity considerations. This raises the possibility that some states are probational members of the community—that is, they are not full-fledged members. Because of the state's domestic configurations, its foreign policy behavior, or the way the community constructs the state, the

cern is how identity conflict undermines both the state's ability to keep a particular narrative going, and, accordingly, the state's membership in the community. This issue is explored in the case of U.S.-Israel relations.

In sum, I am employing the concept of state identity to gain theoretical leverage over strategic behavior in general and alliance formation in particular. Identity, first, provides a better conceptual link to the construction of the threat than do anarchy and other materialist derivations and, second, potentially informs as to who is deemed an attractive ally. The following cases are intended to illustrate these two central points concerning alliance formation.

Identity and Alliances in Arab Politics

From the inception of the Arab states system through the late 1960s, Arab nationalism had a powerful hold over the Arab states. Two points deserve immediate attention. First, there is a relationship between the Arab identity and the definition of the threat. Although before the 1900s the Arab world lived in separate and relatively isolated political communities, soon after that time, the combination of imported ideas of nationalism from the West, changes in social structure because of an expanding world economy, the Ottoman Empire's "Turkification" program of 1908, and primarily the mandate system and Zionism following World War I caused Arab leaders and masses alike to consider their relationship to one another and to develop an Arab political identity and loyalty.[27] The fear generated by these intrusions did not subside after the independence of the Arab states, for the Jewish presence had become the State of Israel, and the West made known its intentions to maintain influence over this important geostrate-

---

membership of some states is less "natural," less taken for granted. Accordingly, probational members will have their behavior more fully scrutinized and monitored. The probational status of some states suggests that they might be "liminal" states. Liminal actors can be thought of as " 'betwixt and between' existing orders. Liminars, whether their rites of passage are ritual or revolutionary, are between identities. In politics, they are between allegiances. This state is marked by ambiguity, ambivalence, and contradiction, yet it is from this disorder that new orders arise. In reflecting on the differences that mark out the liminal, people give meaning to their nationalities" (Anne Norton, *Reflections on Political Identity* [Baltimore: Johns Hopkins University Press, 1988], p. 53.)

27. For good overviews of Arab nationalism, see A. A. Duri, *The Historical Formation of the Arab Nation* (New York: Croom Helm, 1987); Bassam Tibi, *Arab Nationalism,* 2d ed. (New York: St. Martin's, 1990); Rashid Khalidi, "Arab Nationalism: Historical Problems in the Literature," *American Historical Review* 96 (December 1991): 1363–73; Rashid Khalidi et al., eds., *The Origins of Arab Nationalism* (New York: Columbia University Press, 1991); and Martin Kramer, "Arab Nationalism."

gic ground. A common Arab identity, in short, was linked to a common definition of the threat.

Second, Arab nationalism can be understood as the belief that Arab states have shared identities and interests; the Arab nation envelops and allocates a common Arab identity to the segmented Arab states system. Since the independence of the Arab states in the 1940s, the relationship between Arab nationalism and the sovereign Arab states has been a defining feature of the debates over how Arab states should organize their relations. In short, how were Arab states to enact their identity? What norms were associated with Arab nationalism? Briefly, if Arab states assumed that they had a common Arab identity, they exhibited a range of expectations concerning how that Arab identity should affect inter-Arab strategic cooperation; Arab states forged allegiances depending on the positions they held on these key issues. At one end was the expectation that Arab states should work toward unification. If the West had divided the Arab nation into separate states to keep it weak and vulnerable to Western interests, then the surest and quickest way to restrengthen the Arab nation was to create a single Arab state. In this version, Arab nationalism meant territorial unification. As reflected by the League of Arab States, however, the Arab states were generally suspicious of any efforts to restrict their sovereignty or to undermine their territorial basis of power. Although this was particularly true of Lebanon (which feared Syria's territorial claims), Saudi Arabia, and Egypt, even Jordan, Syria, and Iraq, which more actively flirted with the idea of unification (no doubt in part because these three states were the most artificial and, accordingly, their populations the most susceptible to the rally of unification), demonstrated tremendous wariness regarding unification.

Although most Arab leaders had little taste for a pan-Arabism that demanded unification, the existence of Arabism encouraged Arab states to organize themselves somewhere between sovereignty and unification; because their security was interdependent, Arab states should act in concert and consultation with other Arab states. The clearest expression of this was the attempt to develop close strategic ties and military integration, and the articulated norm that Arab states should settle their disputes short of war. These principles were embodied in the Treaty of Joint Defence and Economic Cooperation Among the States of the Arab League (better known as the Collective Arab Security Pact), signed April 13, 1950, which pledged them to settle their conflicts through nonviolent means (article 1), to engage in collective defense (article 2), and to integrate their military and foreign policies (article 5).[28] Such noble gestures notwithstanding, the lofty rhetoric and far-reaching treaty had very little practical effect.

Although there was little real movement toward unification or military integration, the history of the period exhibits numerous instances and episodes in which Arab leaders responded to the expectations that they develop (or at least be viewed as supporting the development of) close strategic ties among Arab states and, at the bare minimum, that Arab states not adopt any policies that potentially might harm the security of the Arab nation.[29] The fact of being an *Arab* state, therefore, generated certain expectations, and defying those expectations could have major consequences for an Arab leader's domestic and regional standing. In general, Arab leaders had been involved in a continuous debate over the norms to govern inter-Arab relations.

Beginning in the early 1950s, two events intensified the discussion over the norms associated with Arabism. The first was the Egyptian revolution in 1952, which brought about a change not only in regime but in foreign policy orientation. King Faruq's commitment to Arabism did not extend much beyond a desire to rid the British from Egypt and to assert Egypt's role as leader of the Arab world if only to discourage radical Arab demands. At first Nasser and the Free Officers appeared to be loyal to Faruq's policies, as they concentrated their energies on evicting Britain from Egypt. Yet Nasser expressed a greater commitment to Arab unity, a desire born largely of his experiences in the Palestine War of 1948 and his belief that Arab unity was the best method for resuscitating Arab power. It was, then, Nasser's understanding that Egypt's fate and security could not be separated from those of the other Arab states (and that he could gain considerable personal power from this message).[30] As a sign of events to come, on July 4, 1953, Nasser launched the "Voice of the Arabs" to broadcast his message of Arab unity to the Arab world. The second development was that the U.S. and Britain, both perceived threats to the Arab nation, were signaling their determination to become more deeply

---

28. See Patrick Seale, *The Struggle for Syria* (Berkeley: University of California Press, 1986), pp. 90–91, for a discussion of the events leading to the treaty. See Taylor, *The Arab Balance of Power*, pp. 125–27, for the text.

29. See Bruce Maddy-Weitzman, *The Crystallization of the Arab State System* (Syracuse: Syracuse University Press, 1993), and Seale, *The Struggle for Syria*, for excellent treatments of the politics of the pre-1955 period.

30. Gamal Abd' Nasser, *The Philosophy of the Revolution* (New York: Buffalo, Smith, Keyze, Marshall, 1959); Seale, *The Struggle for Syria*, pp. 193–94; and Taylor, *The Arab Balance of Power*, p. 30.

416 • *Michael N. Barnett*

involved in the region. Both nations were hoping, though for somewhat different reasons, to establish alliances with Arab states.[31] The principal signal that the Cold War had come to the Middle East was the Turkish-Pakistani alliance of April 1954, which created a strategic link to Britain and the U.S. This treaty precipitated a major debate in the region concerning the proper, and ideally collective Arab, response to this renewed surge from the West. Throughout the debate, Arab leaders exhibited approach-avoidance behavior toward each other and the West: while most were highly conservative and suspicious of any actions that might lead to an erosion of their sovereignty or encourage Arabist sentiments, they also desired closer cooperation because, first, it would increase their power vis-á-vis the West and their standing among their populations and, second, the failure to be associated with the group's norms could lead to a decline in popular support.

Similarly, while most Arab states were quite fearful of the West, they also accepted the reality that Britain and the increasingly engaged U.S. were great powers that could provide both arms and badly needed resources for regime maintenance.[32] Iraq seemed the most favorably disposed toward an association with the West. Not only was it fearful of potential encroachment by the Soviets to the north, but Iraq believed that only the West could provide the resources it so desperately required.[33] Nasser, though generally pro-West, more than willing to talk to Dulles, and highly attracted to the capital and arms of the West, was extremely sensitive to any agreement that hinted at Egypt's and the Arab world's subordination to the West. Therefore, the debate between Iraq and Egypt was not about making a deal with the West per se but rather it was about the belief that Arab states should coordinate their security and foreign policies before any deal and that such a deal should not leave the Arab world vulnerable to the West.

---

31. Eisenhower and Dulles intended to build a fire wall of alliances to contain the Soviet Union. A critical section of this wall would be the "Northern Tier" in the Middle East; with its geostrategic proximity to the Soviet Union and its incredible oil reserves, the Arab states were viewed as a major prize in the Cold War contest. Britain was engaged in its own strategic search, attempting to establish alliances where it once had mandate rights; the Middle East was Britain's remaining souvenir of the empire, and it was determined to retain a presence for both symbolic and geostrategic reasons. See Seale, *The Struggle for Syria*, pp. 186–92.

32. Many Arab-Islamic states were not wary of the Soviet Union because it was an unknown quantity and communist. Still, the Soviet Union was an immediate beneficiary of these intrusions by the West; incensed by Iraq's defection, concerned with Israeli military operations, and unable to locate a Western arms supplier, Egypt and Syria concluded arms deals with the Soviets in 1955.

33. Seale, *The Struggle for Syria*, p. 200.

After months of dialogue and debate, something of a solution was reached at the Arab Foreign Ministers Conference held in Cairo in December 1954. There the Arab governments crafted two resolutions: (1) "that no alliance should be concluded outside the fold of the Collective Arab Security Pact" and (2) "that cooperation with the West was possible, provided that a just solution was found for Arab problems and provided the Arabs were allowed to build up their strength with gifts of arms."[34] In other words, a strategic relationship with the West was possible after consultation with and consensus among the other Arab states.[35] Arab leaders had seemingly navigated between Arab nationalism and realpolitik, between the two ideas that they must coordinate their policies because they were Arab states and that as sovereign entities they could construct any alliance they desired.

Hence, the January 13, 1955, announcement of a strategic alliance between Iraq and Turkey sent shockwaves through the Arab world.[36] It is important to recognize that Turkey was not just any non-Arab state; rather, it was the successor to the Ottoman Empire that had ruled the region for more than three centuries. Many Arab leaders could remember Ottoman rule; therefore, Iraq's alliance with Turkey not only handed the West a possible port of entry into the Arab world but also represented an alliance with an old antagonist. More disturbing, however, was that it represented a direct challenge to a stripped-down version of Arabism that bound Arab states to coordinate their foreign policies before reaching any formal agreement with the West: if this watered-down Arabism had no force, then it had little meaning. Egyptian minister Sallah Salim captured the mood: "The Arab World is now standing at a crossroads: it will either be an independent and cohesive unit with its own structures and national character or else each country will pursue its own course. The latter would mean the beginning of the downfall of Arab nationhood."[37]

Therefore, the challenge offered by the Baghdad Pact was not a shift in

---

34. Ibid., p. 211.
35. Ibid., p. 205.
36. Iraq's decision to sign the treaty apparently derived from the belief that Arab unity offered little protection and security from the Soviet Union, that other Arab countries would follow its lead, and that it needed cooperation with Turkey on the Kurdish issue to maintain Iraq's internal cohesion. See Albert Hourani, *History of the Arab Peoples* (Cambridge: Harvard University Press, 1991), p. 363; and Seale, *The Struggle for Syria*, pp. 199–201.
37. Quoted from Seale, *The Struggle for Syria*, p. 217.

military power[38] but rather a move toward Arabism and the belief that Arab states should coordinate their policies because they had common identities and interests.[39] More to the point, the ensuing debate and conflict (1) concerned the norms that should govern Arab states and (2) was waged through presentational politics in general and Nasser's attempt to portray Iraq as having violated the norms of Arabism in particular. For instance, newspaper headlines throughout the Arab world strongly condemned the treaty. In Egypt, a major Arab daily wrote in its headlines: "Iraqi Government Demolishes All Efforts to Strengthen the Arab League and Bolster the Arab Collective Security Pact."[40] The "Voice of the Arabs" beamed:

> While the Arab States are preparing to hold a meeting of their Foreign Ministers to consider and agree on the unification of their foreign policy, the consolidation of the Collective Security Pact, and the strengthening of the Arab League, the Arab World is taken unaware by a communique issued by two countries. . . . How can it be justified that Iraq took part in this communique and indeed did so on her own when the meeting is about to be held?[41]

Responding to whether Iraq as an independent state had the right to enter into any treaty it wants, Egyptian minister Sallah Salim said: "Although Iraq is an independent sovereign state, she nevertheless has obligations and responsibilities toward the League of Arab States and the Arab Collective Security Pact. Is there any state, in the Atlantic Pact, for example, free to make any decisions it chooses even if it be contrary to that pact?"[42]

In response to the treaty, Arab governments met in Cairo from January 22 though February 6. Egypt, Lebanon, Saudi Arabia, Syria, and Jordan— states with different governmental structures, military capacities, and location in the distribution of power—uniformly condemned the Iraqi action

---

38. Walt, *The Origins of Alliances*, pp. 58–60. Although Walt initially characterizes the events surrounding the Baghdad Pact as related to the balance of power, his narrative recognizes the importance of ideational forces in causing the alliances.

39. "The [Arab] League's policy, assiduously promoted by Egypt, of noncooperation with the West until Arab national objectives had been realized has frequently found Iraq and Egypt in opposite camps. The controversy over the Baghdad Pact is, of course, an outstanding illustration" (Robert McDonald, *The League of Arab States* [Princeton: Princeton University Press. 1965], p. 77). Also see Elie Podeh, *The Quest for Hegemony in the Arab World: The Struggle over the Baghdad Pact* (New York: Brill, 1995).

40. Foreign Broadcast Information Service Daily Report, *FBIS*, January 14, 1955, pp. A1–2.

41. Ibid., pp. A4.

42. Ibid., January 17, 1955, pp. A7.

as undermining Arabism and the Collective Arab Defense Treaty. Nasser unveiled his own response the evening of January 25: the "establishment of a unified Arab army under one command along the same lines as the proposed European army."[43] The overall result of the conference must have been somewhat disappointing to Egypt, the most vocal opponent of the pact, and somewhat heartening to Iraq. Although it passed several resolutions condemning Iraq's actions, pledged not to join the treaty, and decided to send a delegation to Iraq to try and persuade Nuri al-Said of the error of his ways, the conference adjourned without reaching any real conclusion or issuing a final statement. The delegation was apparently unsuccessful, for Iraq and Turkey signed the treaty on February 24.[44]

Four days later, on February 28, Israel attacked a military installation in Gaza. The combination of Israel's attack on Egypt and Iraq's defection from the Arab fold had a tremendous impact on Nasser and the Arab world. Nasser now found himself riding a tide of popular support across the region. In response to both the treaty and Arab governments' rather tepid opposition, protests against the treaty erupted in Jordan, Syria, and Saudi Arabia. King Hussein of Jordan had been attempting to lean on British power as a way of propping up his regime and keeping at bay both regional and domestic rivals. The Baghdad Pact completely undermined his policy, as domestic forces both caused him to desist from any consideration of signing it[45] and forced him to dismiss John Glubb as head of Jordan's Arab Legion, a symbol of British presence, in March 1956.[46] King Saud of Saudi Arabia calculated that Iraq was attempting to gather the resources and prestige to launch another challenge for Fertile Crescent unification, which would represent both an external threat and a source of internal instability.[47] Syria was the real battleground for the pact, and the debate over whether to join was both a sign and a cause of its increasingly Arab nationalist and neutralist leanings;[48] that it abstained from joining was counted as a loss for Iraq and a victory for Nasser.

---

43. Ibid., January 26, 1955, pp. A1.
44. Although Nuri al-Said was highly defensive of the pact and felt highly susceptible to Nasser's charges; Waldemar Gallman, *Iraq Under General Nuri: My Recollections of Nuri al-Said, 1954–1958* (Baltimore: Johns Hopkins University Press, 1964), p. 72.
45. Peter Mansfield, *The Ottoman Empire and Its Successors* (New York: St. Martin's, 1973), p. 119.
46. Hourani, *History of the Arab Peoples*, p. 363; J. C. Hurewitz, *Middle East Politics: The Military Dimension* (Boulder: Westview, 1982), pp. 318–19.
47. Nadav Safran, *Saudi Arabia: The Ceaseless Quest for Security* (Ithaca: Cornell University Press, 1988), pp. 78–79.
48. Seale, *The Struggle for Syria*, ch. 17.

These domestic pressures, unleashed by Iraq's affront to Arabism, caused the other Arab states to become allies. Egypt offered to replace the now moribund Collective Arab Security Pact with its "own security community by a series of treaties with Syria and Saudi Arabia (1955), and eventually, with Jordan and Yemen (in 1956)."[49] In other words, Egypt forged a series of alliances with some Arab states that concurred with Nasser's brand of Arabism (Syria) and others that did not (Jordan, Lebanon, and Saudi Arabia), and the latter states chose to ally themselves with Nasser's vision of regional life rather than risk a decline in regional standing or a domestic backlash. It was Nasser's normative vision and ability to portray Iraq in a particular manner, not his military, that caused this alliance with Egypt and against Iraq.

The Baghdad Pact would have its most direct and immediate effect on its very Iraqi signatories: in July 1958 the Free Officers' revolution, led by General Qasim and Colonel Aref, overthrew the Iraqi government (Nuri al-Said was killed while trying to escape the city). Although many factors contributed to the revolution, the Baghdad Pact, the Suez War of 1956, and Iraq's subsequent isolation in the Arab world, contributed to the military's and masses' increasing dissatisfaction with the government's policies.[50]

> The pact not only perpetuated the undesired connection with the English and guaranteed them the privilege they had hitherto enjoyed, but also entailed a severing of Arab ranks and an open taking of sides in the "cold war." It alienated, in other words, neutralist, nationalist, and pan-Arab opinion.[51]

Indicative of how the Baghdad Pact and Arabism affected the Free Officers was a directive signed by the party on the eve of the July 14 coup, in which a central point was that the future Iraqi government would henceforth "pursue an independent Arab national policy . . . convert the 'Arab Union' into an authentic union between Iraq and Jordan . . . and unite on a federal basis with the U.A.R."[52] After coming to power, the Free Officers immediately suspended Iraq's participation in future pact security meetings and then, in March 1959, withdrew completely from the treaty.

---

49. McDonald, *The League of Arab States*, pp. 233–34; also Hurewitz, *Middle East Politics*, p. 463.
50. Marion Farouk-Sluglett and Peter Sluglett, *Iraq Since 1958* (London: Taurus, 1990), pp. 43–44, 47.
51. Hanna Batatu, *The Old Social Classes and the Revolutionary Movements of Iraq* (Princeton: Princeton University Press, 1978), p. 679.
52. Ibid., p. 804.

Although not all segments of Iraqi society supported this more radical brand of Arab nationalism,[53] they were unified in their rejection of the Baghdad Pact and its symbolic defection from the Arab fold.

The controversy surrounding the pact highlights a number of key issues concerning the relationship between identity and strategic behavior that run counter to neorealist arguments. First, the Arab nation's definition of the threat was directly linked to the Arab identity: Arab nationalism partially emerged in response to intrusions from the Ottoman Empire and the West. In short, the definition of *intent*, of who is considered friend and foe, is better determined by the politics of identity than by the logic of anarchy. Second, the Baghdad Pact represented a challenge not to the balance of power per se but to Arab nationalism and its emerging and contested norms. The pact unleashed a debate among Arab states concerning what behavior was and was not proper for *Arab* states, that is, how Arab states were to enact their identity. At the core of it was a concern about how Arab states should organize their relations as Arab states, and a conviction that because they had a shared identity and interdependent security they should coordinate their policies. Iraq's alliance with Turkey and the West not only symbolized an alliance with actors who were considered to be hostile to the Arab nation, but the means by which it forged that agreement violated even the most minimal understanding of the norms that were to guide the behavior of Arab states. Simply put, the conflict was about the norms that were to govern their shared identity.

Third, in the ensuing debate Arab states dueled with symbols and images, but not militaries, attempting to portray themselves as expressing and furthering the aspirations of the Arab nation and their rival as potentially injuring those very interests. In short, rivalry was driven by presentational, not military, politics. Arab leaders could either profit or suffer, depending on how they were situated by regional and domestic actors in relation to the group's norms; if Nasser's ascending fortunes represent one side of the coin, Iraq's Nuri al-Said's fate demonstrates the other.

Fourth, the power of these norms is exemplified by the individual and collective response of the Arab states to the pact. Not only was the response shaped by Arabism and not anarchy, but most Arab leaders quickly acknowledged that Iraq's actions posed a threat to any collective spirit; and if they were not visibly exercised over Iraqi actions, then their

53. Ibid., p. 817; Majid Khadduri, *Independent Iraq*, 2d ed. (New York: Oxford University Press, 1960), pp. 307–9.

populations were quick to remind them of their "true" preferences and where their loyalties should reside.[54] Indeed, the transnational identity of Arabism placed very similar demands on Arab leaders and caused them both to reject the pact and to embrace an alliance among themselves.

Finally, the Baghdad Pact deposited two currents of Arab nationalism in inter-Arab politics. The first was the search for Arab unity as advanced by Nasser and other state and societal actors throughout the Arab world. The other, however, did not necessarily encourage Arab unification and close inter-Arab consultation; it encouraged neutralism and anticontainment.[55] That is, the debate over the Baghdad Pact contributed to the development of strong prohibitionary norms that signaled to Arab leaders that certain actions could not be undertaken for fear of estrangement and retribution from the Arab community. The legacies of the Baghdad Pact were both the growing expectation among societal forces that Arab leaders should be seen working toward the cause of Arab nationalism and unification and the constraints that it imposed on their future security policies.

The GCC and Post–Gulf War Security Arrangements

The Gulf Cooperation Council and the post–Gulf war security arrangements illustrate the continuing salience of identity for shaping alliance formation; yet these episodes, in combination with the Baghdad Pact, also suggest how a change in state identities—specifically the declining significance of an Arab national identity and the emergence of statist identities—can shape security and alliance politics.[56]

Few paid much heed when Oman, Bahrain, the United Arab Emirates, Qatar, Saudi Arabia, and Kuwait signed the GCC charter in Abu Dhabi on May 25, 1981. After years of failed Arab experiments in regional associa-

---

54. Writing at the time of the post–June 1967 soul-searching in the Arab world, Mohammed Haykal wrote in the Egyptian paper *Al-Ahram* that he hoped that masses would act at present as they had during the Baghdad Pact: "Our past experience is still within our memory. In a situation less dangerous than the one we are facing now, the Arab national force destroyed the Baghdad Pact in Baghdad itself without a single shot from outside Iraq and before the winds of social revolution had begun to blow" (cited from *BBC World Broadcasts*, ME/2548/A/3, August 21, 1967).

55. Boutros-Ghali reflected: "The controversy between Iraq and the other Arab states over the formation of the Baghdad Pact . . . is interesting from a historical viewpoint inasmuch as it was the starting point of a nonalignment policy adopted by the Arab states. . . . The revolution of July 14, 1958, in Baghdad sanctioned the victory of the nonaligned states" ("Arab Diplomacy: Failures and Successes," in George Atiyeh, ed., *Arab and American Cultures*, p. 232 [Washington, D.C.: AEI Press, 1969]).

56. See Michael Barnett, "Sovereignty, Nationalism, and Regional Order in the Arab States System," *International Organization* 49, no. 3 (Summer 1995): 479–510, for an explanation for the shift in these state identities.

tions and federation, yet another attempt on the periphery of Arab nationalism did not warrant excessive hype. What motivated the Gulf Arab states to form an exclusive club? Shared economic concerns certainly played a role. The GCC states, after all, were all oil-exporting states (with the exception of Oman) and had experienced rapid economic development and industrialization since the 1970s. Alongside these economic factors, however, was a shared identity. Geographic contiguity had left a legacy of cultural, strategic, political, and economic interaction, which, in turn, produced a regional identity (*khaliji*). For instance, in June 1980, before the Iran-Iraq war, the amir of Bahrain called for tightening Gulf relations among the Arab states because it is an *Arab* Gulf and those in the region are *khaliji*.[57] Furthermore, in contrast to most other Arab states (with the exception of Jordan) that had nonmonarchical forms of governance, the GCC states were all monarchies. On this basis alone, Iraq, Iran, and the Yemens were relatively poor candidates for the GCC.[58] These states, moreover, were Sunni Muslim and embraced some type of Islamic polity. Consistent with the view that this was an association of like-minded states, the final statement of the GCC's inaugural meeting proclaimed that their common destiny, shared interests and values, and common economic and political systems produced a natural solidarity.[59] The GCC states, in short, were "natural" allies, sharing key biographical features and historical characteristics, and by creating the GCC they aspired to construct a "psychologically satisfying political community."[60]

The GCC states also differentiated themselves from the other Arab states.[61] Although the Gulf states identified themselves as Arab—after all, they immediately joined the League of Arab States (Saudi Arabia was a

57. *FBIS-Near and Middle East*, June 18, 1980, pp. C1–5.
58. Joseph Twinam, "Reflections on Gulf Cooperation, with Focus on Bahrain, Qatar, and Oman," in John Sandwick, ed., *The Gulf Cooperation Council*, p. 30 (Boulder: Westview, 1987); author interview with Abdalla Bishara.
59. See Abu Dhabi Domestic Service, May 26, 1981. Cited from *FBIS-NES*, May 27, 1981, pp. A1–2; and Gulf News Agency, May 26, 1981. Cited in *FBIS-NES*, June 4, 1981, pp. A10–11.
60. Twinam, "Reflections on Gulf Cooperation," p. 23. Twinam later notes: "The main goals were both a more secure environment for the GCC states and meeting the aspirations of their citizens for a closer Gulf identity" (p. 29). Also see Emile Nakhleh, *Gulf Cooperation Council: Policies, Problems, and Prospects* (New York: Praeger, 1986), p. 57; and author interview with Abdalla Bishara.
61. See Michael Morony, "The Arabisation of the Gulf," in B. R. Pridham, ed., *The Arab Gulf and the Arab World*, pp. 3–28 (New York: Croom Helm, 1988); and Robert Landen, "The Changing Pattern of Political Relations Between the Arab Gulf and the Arab Provinces of the Ottoman Empire," in Pridham, *The Arab Gulf and the Arab World*, pp. 41–64, for brief overviews of the relationship between the Gulf and other Arab regions. Abdalla Bishara, the first secretary-general of the GCC, added that the Gulf states had been the "butt of Arab jokes," considered something of a backwater of the Arab world; author interview.

founding member) upon independence and supported core Arab issues such as Palestine—the GCC states also were rather wary of and aloof from the rest of the Arab world. For instance, while the Gulf leaders waved at the GCC's role in furthering Arab aspirations, such rhetoric was always quickly followed by aggressive claims that the Gulf Arab states were a separate entity bounded by common culture and interests and, accordingly, were different from the other Arab states.[62] Indeed, the GCC states tended to perceive other Arab states as something of a threat: their traditional fear that close cooperation might trigger memories of and hopes for unification heightened beginning in the 1970s when the Gulf Arab states became the Gulf Arab *oil* states—leading them to become highly suspicious of the economic motivations underlying any new expressions of fraternal devotion from other Arab states. Therefore, the GCC states hoped to use their new association to isolate the Gulf from the other Arab states.[63] In general, the GCC states expressed the belief that their shared identity made them natural allies, desired to cooperate to further their shared interests, and drew a symbolic boundary between themselves and other Arab states and, therefore, opposed including the other states in their association. Indeed, the GCC, alongside the other subregional organizations that emerged in the 1980s (the Arab Maghrebi Union and the Arab Cooperation Council) suggested a weakening Arab national identity and emerging statism.[64]

The shared identity shaped not only the choice of with whom they felt most comfortable but also, relatedly, their common construction of the threat. At the time of the GCC's inception there was little thought that it would become a full-fledged security organization; the opinion was that any discussion of this sort was highly premature and unrealistic.[65] However, the GCC states soon began to explore the possibility of security cooperation because of external and internal security threats. Most prominent, though arguably not most alarming, was the Iran-Iraq war, which threatened to involve the GCC states both directly and indirectly—namely, through the possibility of a direct Iranian assault, the closing of the ship-

62. Ralph Braibanti, "The Gulf Cooperation Council: A Comparative Note," in John Sadwick, *The Gulf Cooperation Council*, p. 206 (Boulder: Westview, 1988).
63. Ghassam Saleme, "Inter-Arab Politics," pp. 239, 249–50.
64. Salame, "Inter-Arab Politics," p. 239; and Tibi, *Arab Nationalism*, p. 24.
65. Author interview with Abdalla Bishara. Separated from the rest of the Arab world because of the British protectorate over much of the Gulf region, the rapid independence of many of the Trucial states after 1960 caused many to contemplate security cooperation and some form of association to replace the British presence; see Riad El-Rayyas, "Arab Nationalism and the Gulf," in Pridham, *The Arab World and the Gulf*, pp. 87–90. Still, little happened on this front until these security threats.

ping lanes, and the attempt by Iran to destabilize them from within. The Iran-Iraq war, in short, catalyzed the GCC states to take defensive measures. Yet what strategies would they adopt? States have numerous options available to them for increasing their security: they can extract from their societies, or construct alliances, or some combination of the two—but neorealism says very little about the direction or the form of that policy search.[66]

To begin, the GCC states decided to construct some type of external alignment since an internal mobilization strategy was highly unattractive, given a sparse manpower base, geostrategic vulnerability, and limited resources. Although there was a wealth of opportunities, for helping hands were being extended from near and far, the Gulf states jettisoned any Arab or superpower involvement, preferring to maintain an exclusive club of like-minded Gulf Arab states.

Why did the Gulf states spurn the offers from other Arab states? A pan-Arab response, the very arrangement vocalized and nominally pursued before 1967, might be attractive for both ideational and strategic considerations. Although the Collective Arab Security Pact still existed and the Arab League still operated, neither these nor any type of collective Arab effort was ever seriously entertained. There were quasi-strategic reasons for shunning an alliance with all other Arab states: Egypt was estranged from the Arab world because of the Camp David Accords; any agreement with Iraq would seem highly offensive to Iran and therefore would threaten to widen the war; and Syria was considered a "rogue" state, a reputation only enhanced by its support of Iran, and its radical rhetoric was particularly offensive to the more conservative Gulf monarchies. That said, an underlying fear was that an Arab alliance might stimulate greater demands for inter-Arab cooperation and perhaps greater sharing of the oil wealth. Such demands were legitimated by the understanding that oil was an "Arab" resource and that they were part of the same Arab nation; therefore, a strategic arrangement might only encourage the view that the Gulf oil states had an obligation to redistribute the wealth among other members of the "family."

If the Gulf states did not favor a pan-Arab response, then what of an alliance with one of the superpowers? After all, such an alliance would provide an immediate increase in external security, and both the Soviets and the Americans were actively courting the Gulf states. Yet the GCC states

---

66. Michael Barnett, *Confronting the Costs of War: Military Power, State, and Society in Egypt and Israel* (Princeton: Princeton University Press, 1992).

rebuffed such overtures.[67] In fact, a point of consensus among the GCC states was to keep the superpowers at bay, to establish regional independence, and to resist foreign intervention.[68] Two prominent factors guided this objection to superpower presence. First, the GCC feared that superpower involvement would increase regional instability and expand the severity and boundaries of the war. Although the superpowers were arming the region, to solicit a greater role for one superpower would automatically invite suspicions and intrusions by the other, quickly turning what was ostensibly a regional conflict into an international conflict. Such an escalation would only further imperil the GCC states.

Second, any increase in external security might decrease internal security. Nearly all Arab-Islamic societies (and this was true of the GCC states) were highly sensitive to an explicit alliance with the U.S. and feared that too visible a presence might trigger domestic instability. Consequently, a U.S. alliance might increase external security while unleashing domestic insecurity. In general, the GCC states were wary of any visible relationship with the West or the Soviet Union, because of the fear that their interventions might invite both regional and domestic instability.

That a superpower or a pan-Arab alliance might have negative domestic repercussions—that is, igniting Arab nationalist sentiments in either case—not only highlights the role of identity but also demonstrates that the GCC states were arguably more alarmed by domestic, rather than interstate, threats. "Gulf security in the context of the GCC," observes Emile Nakhleh, "is directly equated with the continued stable existence of the present regimes and forms of government in the Gulf States."[69] The real impetus for security cooperation, in fact, came not from the Iran-Iraq war per se but from internal instability, namely militant Shi'a activity.[70] The

---

67. While Oman had a low-level, but highly controversial, strategic agreement with the U.S., the other Gulf states condemned its actions and actively discouraged any greater U.S. (or Soviet) presence in the region. In 1985 Kuwait both received a shipment of weapons from the Soviet Union and allowed the U.S. to reflag its oil tankers following the "tanker wars."

68. *FBIS-NES*, September 20, 1984, 5, 184, p. C1.

69. Nakhleh, *Gulf Cooperation Council*, p. 44.

70. See Joseph Kechichian, "The GCC and the West," *Journal of American-Arab Affairs* 29 (Summer 1989): 28; Nakleh, *Gulf Cooperation Council*, p. 39; and Ursula Braun, "The Gulf Cooperation Council's Security Role," in Pridham, *The Arab World and the Gulf*, p. 255. The Omani information minister provided the following distinction between security and defense policy: "There is a very big difference between the security strategy and the defense strategy. The security strategy deals with the firmness of the internal front of the GCC states, while the defense strategy deals with resisting external threats to these states" (*WAKH*, November 6, 1985, cited from *FBIS-NES*, 216, November 7, 1985, C3).

attempted coup in Bahrain in mid-1981, and the string of bombings in Kuwait in December 1983 (rumored to have been fomented by Iran) alarmed the Gulf Arab states and prodded them to cooperate against this security threat and to safeguard their "political security."[71] As Sultan Qabas of Oman commented:

> I firmly believe that the main threat facing the Gulf is the attempt to destabilize it from within—by exporting terrorism across the national borders. We should watch out for destabilization attempts, particularly because domestic instability can blow the door open to foreign intervention. I believe that this the main hazard.[72]

The GCC saw these internal developments as a threat shared by the Gulf Arab states; therefore, they had no intention of involving other Arab states in their security precautions. As noted by Bahraini interior minister Amir Nayif: "Gulf coordination [to combat terrorism] with other states . . . has not yet materialized."[73] Nor would it.[74]

In sum, identity played a role in shaping: the boundaries of the association; the definition of the threat; and who qualified as a desirable alliance partner. First, the common identity of the Gulf Arab states shaped who was a candidate for membership; not only did they identify themselves as sharing key ideational features based on a common history, culture, and government, but other Arab states were viewed as "different" and even as potential threats. Second, their shared identity lent naturally to a shared definition of the threat. This became particularly clear vis-á-vis internal threats; as Sunni monarchies they viewed the threat to their regimes as deriving largely from Shi'ite elements. Third, as the GCC states confronted

---

71. *KUNA*, April 4, 1984, cited in *FBIS-NES*, 5, 67, April 5, 1984, C1.

72. *MENA*, April 4, 1985, cited in *FBIS-NES*, 85, 66, April 5, 1985, C2–3.

73. "Al-Hawadith," March 6, 1987, pp. 30–31. Cited in *FBIS-NES*, March 10, 1987, p. 3.

74. That the GCC was able to construct some modest cooperation against their shared internal threats emboldened them to undertake military cooperation. The first GCC meeting commissioned a discussion group to consider their security needs, which became the first paper on the concept of collective defense in 1982 (author interview with Abdalla Bishara). Soon thereafter the GCC developed a series of elaborate and sustained measures designed to increase military coordination and cooperation: a rapid deployment force, the outline for a unified army, an early warning network, a series of joint maneuvers through the "Peninsula Shield" exercises, attempted coordination of military procurement to standardize equipment and training, an integrated training academy. As Bahraini minister of foreign affairs Shaykh Muhammad Khalifa observed: "We feel we have started a never-ending effort, because every coordination action has unknown results" (*WAKH*, April 24, 1984, cited in *FBIS-NES*, 5, 81, April 25, 1984, C1). See Braun, "The Gulf Cooperation Council's Security Role," for an overview of GCC security cooperation.

internal and external threats, they desired to construct some type of external alignment because of their domestic limitations. To be sure, there were strategic rationales for avoiding an alliance with either the superpower or other Arab states, yet also prominent were ideational and normative concerns. Specifically, the underlying fear was that, first, an Arab alliance might stir pan-Arab sentiments if not unleash redistributive claims on the oil wealth by their Arab brethren, and, second, an alliance with the West would violate Arabist norms. In short, while strategic factors were certainly part of the story behind the GCC and the response to these perceived internal and external security threats, identity was a critical factor in shaping the definition of the threat and the alliance response.

Post–Gulf War Security Arrangements

During the Gulf war the GCC acted as the primary conduit for expressing the revulsion by the region's Arab states to the Iraqi invasion of Kuwait, and its "Saudi-controlled skeleton military command structures were . . . mobilized immediately afterwards to integrate Gulf military forces into the Coalition."[75] Moreover, that the Gulf states participated in the Gulf coalition under the GCC flag while the Syrian and Arab states were integrated as individual states in the coalition symbolizes the division between the Gulf Arabs and the rest of the Arab world.[76]

Notwithstanding the modest expressions of security cooperation among the Arab states in general and the GCC states in particular, Iraq's invasion of Kuwait—simply put, the sight of one Arab state swallowing another whole—caused Arab leaders to proclaim the end of Arab nationalism, the need for a "new realism," and the view that state interests were not interchangeable with, and took primacy over some conception of, the Arab national interest.[77] I want to discuss briefly four ways in which the weakening hold of Arab national identities and the emerging statist identities imprinted post–Gulf war inter-Arab dynamics and alliance behavior.

To begin, the emerging statism and the decline of Arabism nearly erased

---

75. George Joffe, "Middle Eastern Views of the Gulf Conflict and Its Aftermath," *Review of International Studies* 19 (1993): 191.

76. See F. Gregory Gause III, *The Oil Monarchies* (New York: Council on Foreign Relations, 1993), ch. 5, for a good discussion of the Gulf states' post–Gulf war security policies.

77. See Lewis, "Rethinking the Middle East"; Kramer, "Arab Nationalism"; Ibrahim Karawan, "Arab Dilemmas in the 1990s: Breaking Taboos and Searching for Signposts," *Middle East Journal* 48 (Summer 1994): 433–54; and Muhammad Faour, *The Arab World After Desert Storm* (Washington, D.C.: United States Institute of Peace Press, 1994); and author interview with Abdalla Bishara.

the assumption that as Arab states they had shared security threats and should consider pan-Arab security arrangements. As acknowledged by then Egyptian foreign minister Boutros Boutros-Ghali, "The painful realities resulting from Iraq's invasion of Kuwait and its usurpation of the territory of a fraternal Arab state include the collapse of the traditional concept of pan-Arab security."[78] The secretary-general of the Arab League nearly pronounced the last rites of the Collective Arab Security Pact: "It must be clear that the concept of security is the biggest responsibility of each individual state. Each state determines the needs and boundaries of its security on its own, because this concerns its people and its future. We should basically assume that there should be no interference in any country's security. We must acknowledge and proceed from this basic principle."[79] Relatedly, at an Arab League meeting, Arab states agreed for the first time that each could identify its own security threats.[80] These testimonials suggest that the emergence of statist identities and the corresponding decline of Arab national identities enabled Arab leaders to assert that they no longer shared a definition of the threat or should attempt to coordinate their security.

Second, as Arab states recognized that pan-Arab security arrangements were a thing of the past, they also proclaimed that regional order should be premised on sovereignty. Immediately following the Gulf war, the Arab states displayed some security camaraderie through the Damascus Declaration. Announced in March 1991, the Gulf states, Syria, and Egypt pledged further strategic and military cooperation, with an understanding that the last two would be well compensated for their military commitments and troops.[81] The declaration, however, soon became a dead letter, testifying to the very differences between two regions of the Arab world.[82] Indeed, the real importance—and the only surviving principle—of the declaration was not its promise of further military cooperation but its insistence on sovereignty as the basis of inter-Arab politics. Coming on the heels of Iraq's denial of Kuwaiti sovereignty and claim that Gulf oil belonged to the Arabs, the GCC states held sovereignty and

---

78. Interview and date not given. Cited in *FBIS-NES*-91–059, March 27, 1991, pp. 9–10.

79. *FBIS-NES*-92–232, December 2, 1992, pp. 1–2. See also the "Memorandum of Understanding" signed between the Arab League and the GCC; *FBIS-NES*-92–034, February 20, 1992, p. 3.

80. Oded Granot, "Outcome of Arab League Conference Analyzed," *Ma'ariv*, in *FBIS-NES*, March 31, 1994, p. 3.

81. For the text of the Damascus Declaration, see *FBIS-NES*-91–152, August 7, 1991, pp. 1–2.

82. As noted by Ihsan Bakr in Egypt's *Al-Ahram*, "We have to acknowledge the apprehensions of the people in the Gulf, or at least some of them, who fear an *Arab* presence in the Gulf, because the past is not very encouraging" (June 7, 1992, p. 9, cited in *FBIS-NES*-92–114, June 12, 1992, 9–10).

security as indistinguishable. Secretary-General Bishara's interpretation of the declaration was that it recognized the legitimacy of the Arab states' borders, the right of each state to arrange its own security, and the exclusive claim to its resources—that is, its sovereignty and exclusivity.[83] Although Arabism once challenged and undermined the sovereignty of the separate Arab states, its decline meant that Arab states were more willing to recognize the norms of sovereignty as the basis of regional order.[84]

Third, the rise of statism and the decline of Arabism ushered in a debate over the desired regional order: an all-Arab regional order versus a "Middle Eastern" order.[85] That is, to what extent should regional arrangements be exclusive to Arab states or include non-Arab states? In this respect, perhaps the surest barometer of the emergence of statism and sovereignty was the transformation of the Arab-Israeli conflict from an ideological struggle into an interstate conflict. The decline of the Arab political community, the hardening of the Arab states, and a diminished responsiveness to "core" Arab concerns means that Israel is more fully recognized as a legitimate member of the region.[86] That Israel negotiates bilaterally with the Palestinians and the various Arab states represents a fundamental change in the organization of the Arab-Israeli conflict and reflects the emergence of state-national interests that are linked to a regional order premised on sovereignty.[87]

Fourth, the emerging statism also shaped the permissible alliance arrangements: whereas once the Gulf states shunned the West and outside powers for fear of offending Arabist sympathies, the emerging statism meant that each state was responsible for its own security and was now permitted to construct its security arrangements as it saw fit, though still

---

83. *FBIS-NES*-92–241, December 15, 1992, pp. 10–11.

84. Barnett, "Nationalism, Sovereignty, and Regional Order in Arab Politics."

85. Kramer, "Arab Nationalism," p. 198; Karawan, "Arab Dilemmas in the 1990s"; and "Arafat Suggests Formation of Mideast 'Regional Order'," *FBIS-NES*, February 4, 1994.

86. Paul Noble, Rex Brynen, and Baghat Korany, "Conclusion: The Changing Regional Security Environment," in B. Korany, P. Noble, and R. Brynen, eds., *The Many Faces of National Security in the Arab World*, p. 281 (New York: St. Martin's, 1993).

87. As one editorial lamented, "The paradox of the negotiations between the Arabs and Israel are [*sic*] more acceptable—and maybe successful—than the Arabs' negotiations with one another. And the enmity with Israel has begun to drop to low levels, compared with inter-Arab hostilities. The negotiations with it over the demarcation of its border are much easier than negotiations among Gulf states, on the grounds that Israel is more acceptable" (Abd-al-Bari Atwan, *al-Quds al-Arabi*, December 23, 1994; cited in *FBIS-NES*, December 30, 1994, p. 3).

within limits.[88] The U.S., for instance, now found itself openly wined and dined by the GCC states. The same GCC secretary-general who before the Gulf war was quite unbending in his objection to a superpower presence was now advertising that he had "no reservations" concerning a more visible foreign presence: "Every state has an inalienable and legitimate right to defend its sovereignty and territory using the methods and means available to it, including inviting foreign forces to that end."[89] Kuwaiti defense minister Shaykh al-Sabah, who previously chastised Oman for its security agreement with the U.S., likened the defense agreement with the U.S. to the Damascus Declaration, thereby equating defense agreements with Arab and Western states.[90] Many Arab states, in effect, were now claiming that the U.S. was preferable to their Arab brothers as a security partner. The emerging statism, in short, erased a prewar security taboo: an explicit alliance with the U.S. In general, although Arabism had been in decline for several years, the Gulf war was the midwife to pronounced statist identities and interests and the decline of any politically meaningful Arab identity in inter-Arab politics. These developments imprinted the region's security patterns.

In sum, while these post–Gulf war security patterns can be partly attributed to the severity of the external threat, namely, the shock of the Iraqi invasion of Kuwait, that alone is unable to explain why Arab leaders were now able to entertain those very policies that were once prohibited by the transnational norms associated with Arabism. To fully understand these shifts requires incorporating the relationship between changing identities and norms. This can be illustrated by contrasting the post–Gulf war security arrangements and patterns with the Baghdad Pact. Whereas the Baghdad Pact was defined by a contest over images and a conflict over the constitutive norms that should flow from an Arab identity, the post–Gulf war security arrangements are not only absent these very dynamics but, in fact, Arab leaders go out of their way to argue the irrelevance of the Arab national identity for shaping the state's current security policies (thereby providing indirect testimony to the past potency of that identity and its

---

88. While the U.S. has concluded several strategic agreements with the Gulf states, these agreements are always quite careful to limit U.S. visibility for fear of offending local sensitivities. Consequently, the U.S. has forgone military bases in favor of stockpiling and over-the-horizon agreements.

89. "Sawt al-Kuwayt al-Duwali," July 21, 1992, p. 9; cited in *FBIS-NES*-92–142, July 23, 1992, p. 2.

90. "Defense Minister on Army, Security Accords." *FBIS-NES*-007, January 10, 1992, p. 10. The London-based *al-Quds al-Arabi* editorialized that the Gulf Summit Declaration of December 1991 was evidence that the Gulf states had abandoned their Arab brothers for isolation and demonstrated real hostility toward the Arabs; *FBIS-NES*-27–003, January 6, 1992, p. 5.

associated norms). Identity politics has defined inter-Arab dynamics and developments over the years, and no understanding of Arab politics is complete without it.

U.S.-Israeli Relations

There are two generalized views concerning what matters for understanding U.S.-Israeli relations, each of which has serious defects for explaining the U.S.'s continuous strategic support of the State of Israel since 1948. The first situates U.S.-Israeli relations within the same systemic forces and strategic logics that envelop other interstate relations. Regardless of the long-standing pledges by U.S. policy makers of their support for Israel's security and sovereignty, the level of support followed the phases of the Cold War.[91] Specifically, it was not until after 1967 that the U.S. began to fully integrate Israel into its containment strategy, and, true to systemic form, it was only then that Israel received tremendous military and economic assistance from the U.S.; conversely, the end of the Cold War caused many to ponder Israel's coming strategic irrelevance.[92]

Yet systemic theorists have a difficult time explaining why the U.S. was so quick to extend security guarantees in the late 1940s despite the absence of a strategic rationale and to continue such guarantees when they were perceived as undermining the security goals of the U.S.—as was frequently the case during the Cold War when the U.S. attempted to cultivate strategic alliances with the Arab states and since the end of the Cold War when the continued level of support and commitment betrays any compelling strategic imperative. When all is said and done, U.S. support for Israel has

---

91. Michael Handel, "Israel's Contribution to U.S. Interests in the Middle East," in Harry Allen and Ivan Volgyes, eds., *Israel, the Middle East, and U.S. Interests*, pp. 80–85 (New York: Praeger, 1983); and A. F. K. Organski, *The $36 Billion Bargain* (New York: Columbia University Press, 1990).

92. Michael Barnett, "From Cold Wars to Resource Wars: The Coming Decline in U.S.-Israeli Relations?" *Jerusalem Journal of International Relations* 13, no. 3 (September 1991): 99–117. A possible objection to the U.S.-Israeli case is that its uniqueness renders it a poor place for theory testing and plausibility probes. Many of the so-called unique features of Israel and U.S.-Israeli relations first suggest complexity and not uniqueness and second require explanation and not dismissal. Moreover, even if U.S.-Israel relations does exhibit some atypical qualities—what social relationship does not?—this does not justify its exclusion as a case. The idea of using exceptional and atypical cases for theory development has become a more widely accepted methodological practice in recent years. See Michael Barnett, "The Methodological Status of the Israeli Case," in Michael Barnett, ed., *Israel in Comparative Politics: Challenging Conventional Wisdom* (Albany: State University of New York Press, 1996), for a detailed discussion of the methodological status of the Israeli case.

continued against the backdrop of changing security circumstances, distributions in the balance of power, and the place of Israel in U.S. strategic doctrine.

The second view, that of the primacy of domestic politics, attempts to explain a relationship that seemingly defies systemic reasoning. Various mechanisms, most notably electoral politics and interest-group pressures, cause American leaders to adopt consistently a pro-Israel policy even when strategic logic suggests a more "balanced" approach if not a pro-Arab policy.[93] The implication, accordingly, is that these subsystemic pressures "distort" the formulation of U.S. foreign policy as it steers away from "objective" national interests and takes a pro-Israel position.[94] Although this domestic politics view helps to explain the level of U.S. strategic assistance, it does not provide an adequate explanation of its very existence. To begin, the level of aid and strategic support is not correlated with the rumored role of domestic politics.[95] Moreover, the effectiveness of domestic groups is dependent on their ability to provide a sustained justification for U.S. support that is consistent with the beliefs and values of most Americans.[96] Consequently, not only is there little evidence that domestic politics explains the consistent existence and high levels of support for Israel, but the very effectiveness of these interest groups is dependent on an existing cultural and ideational field that resonates with the arguments raised by these groups.

In short, those who put forward the domestic politics position offer convincing critiques of the systemic view, and those who champion a systemic view offer several persuasive arguments against the domestic politics position. Their mutual criticisms are fairly convincing. The result, however, is that the issue of U.S.-Israeli relations defies the expectations of either systemic or domestic politics; there has been a continuity in strategic association that survives changes in systemic politics and exists even in the absence of electoral or domestic pressures. How else might we explain this continuity?

I offer a third view: identity politics matters. Although domestic and

---

93. Mohammed Ayoob, "The Security Problematique of the Third World," *World Politics* 43, no. 2 (1991): 257–83.

94. Cheryl Rubenberg, *Israel and the American National Interest* (Urbana: University of Illinois Press, 1986).

95. Organski, *The $36 Billion Bargain*, p. xv.

96. Camille Mansour, *Beyond Alliance: Israel and U.S. Foreign Policy* (New York: Columbia University Press, 1994); Abraham Ben-Zvi, *The United States and Israel: The Limits of the Special Relationship* (New York: Columbia University Press, 1990), pp. 16–17; and James Lee Ray, *The Future of American-Israeli Relations* (Lexington: University of Kentucky Press, 1985), p. 25.

systemic pressures affected the level of U.S. support for Israel, it is the existence of a shared identity and transnational values that is the foundation of this relationship. The oft-heard mantras—"the only democracy in the Middle East," and "shares values and principles"—signify something substantial and causal and gives meaning and substance to the term *special relationship*.[97]

Suggesting that shared identities and values are the foundation of U.S.-Israeli relations does not imply that it is impermeable to corrosive forces. A shared identity is based on two factors: the U.S. must view Israel as having a common identity; and Israel's collective identity and associated practices must be consistent with those of the U.S.[98] Here resides the potential hurdle. Israel's identity is not firmly ensconced in the story lines that dominate and define the Western community and embrace the U.S.; indeed, it frequently challenges the dominant narratives that define that community. U.S.-Israeli relations is dependent upon Israel's having a particular identity, though for a variety of reasons Israel has difficulty keeping that identity going. I argue that Israel's identity crisis provoked a crisis in U.S.-Israeli relations in the late 1980s and discuss how this crisis potentially undermined the U.S.-Israeli alliance and how the Israeli polity responded to this crisis.

Israeli Collective Identity

Three strands constitute Israel's collective identity: religion, nationalism, and the Holocaust.[99] Although each has varied in prominence and meaning, all three provide an attenuated link between Israel and the U.S. First,

---

97. See Mansour, *Beyond Alliance*, for an excellent review of the shortcomings of the literatures that treat U.S.-Israeli relations as driven by either systemic or domestic politics and an interesting discussion of how cultural factors and shared values represent its real foundation. Ben-Zvi, *The United States and Israel*, begins with the assumption that the special relationship is dependent on shared beliefs and then proceeds to examine the conditions under which the "national interest" can overcome normative power. See Peter Grose, *Israel in the Mind of America* (New York: Alfred A. Knopf, 1983), and Seth Tillman, *The United States in the Middle East* (Bloomington: Indiana University Press, 1982), for other statements that acknowledge shared identity and values as the basis of U.S.-Israeli relations.

98. Morton Halperin, "Guaranteeing Democracy," *Foreign Policy* 91 (Summer 1993): 105–22; and Samuel Huntington, "The Clash of Civilizations," *Foreign Affairs* 72 (Summer 1993): 22–49, provide a fairly simplistic but effective representation of how U.S. policy makers see both themselves and those who are part of the community. Although the relationship is equally dependent on Israel's reading of the U.S., I focus on the debate over Israel's identity both for illustrative purposes and because it was here that the real challenges existed.

99. Amos Elon, "The Politics of Memory," *New York Review of Books*, October 7, 1993, p. 4.

Israel has a Jewish identity—it is a Jewish state.[100] Although its Jewish identity represents an important connection with a West that claims a Judeo-Christian heritage, it also acts as a distancing agent. Specifically, although the specific meaning of, and practices that are associated with, being a Jewish state have been hotly contested in Israeli politics, the role of religion in guiding everyday life means that Israel contrasts decidedly with other Western states that are secular in character.[101] Israel's civil laws, customs, national holidays, education curricula, right of return, and a host of other cultural and political practices are all explicitly guided by Jewish law and custom. In this important respect, Israel's domestic makeup and organizing principles contrast with those of the West. Indeed, people in the West who declare that Islam represents a threat to the West's "way of life" because the former does not separate the state and religion are implicitly suggesting that Israel has more in common with its Arab-Islamic neighbors than it does with the West.

Zionism, a response to the Jewish community's exclusion from and persecution in European Christian society, maintains an ambivalent relationship to the West.[102] Although its main ideological sources—Judaism, socialism, secular nationalism, and liberalism—provide something of a link, it is a weak connection because of Zionism's underlying premise that Jews are unsafe in the Western community.[103] In short, Zionism and the very need for a Jewish State exists because of the Western community and its long and virulent history of anti-Semitism.

The Holocaust is the third strand of Israel's identity.[104] To be sure, the Holocaust represents an important reason for the West's commitment to the Jewish state. Yet one important lesson of the Holocaust is that Jews cannot trust their safety and security to non-Jews, even in so-called progressive and civilized countries. The lessons of the Holocaust not only instruct Israel to be wary of a Western (Christian) community but also challenge the dominant narrative of the Western community that views itself as liberal, democratic, and tolerant. As a living memorial of the Holo-

---

100. S. N. Eisenstadt, *Change and Continuity in Israeli Society* (New York: Humanities Press, 1974).
101. The debate over Israel's Jewish identity is perhaps best illustrated in the continuing controversy over "Who is a Jew?"
102. Shlomo Avineri, *The Making of Modern Zionism* (New York: Basic Books, 1981).
103. Baruch Kimmerling, "Between the Primordial and the Civil Definitions of the Collective Identity," in E. Cohen, M. Lissak, and U. Almagor, eds., *Comparative Social Dynamics*, p. 262 (Boulder: Westview, 1985).
104. Elon, "The Politics of Memory"; Tom Segev, *The Seventh Million* (New York: Hill and Wang, 1993).

caust, Israel represents a constant reminder to the West that its history does not resemble the self-image of enlightenment and tolerance.[105] All three strands, then, provide a tenuous link to the West and the U.S., represent the West as something of a threat (which, ironically, Israel shares with the Arab states), challenge the West's self-understanding of being progressive and civilized, and, finally, provide a justification for a defiant and aggressive self-help posture and foreign policy.[106]

If these three strands of Israel's collective identity represent a less-than-firm link to the West and the U.S., a fourth serves both to embed it in the West and to differentiate it from the surrounding Arab states: its status as a liberal democracy. Since Israel's inception in 1948, Israeli leaders and supporters have identified its democratic character as a major justification for its support. Although Israel's status as a democracy generally goes unchallenged—for it does have a relatively free press, a competitive party system, free and fair elections, and so on—there are two potential problems. The first is the Arab minority in the Israeli state, a minority that is viewed by Israeli authorities as having dual loyalties, and therefore as being unable to accept the full benefits, obligations, and markings of Israel citizenship, i.e., military service. The second, more visible and frequently cited concern is Israel's record in and hold over the territories captured in the 1967 war. Israel's democratic character within the "Green Line" contrasts decidedly with that in the occupied territories. Notwithstanding the various justifications used to exculpate Israel's presence and policies in the territories, those who reside there live in tremendous insecurity, without the same civil rights and protections available to Israeli citizens. These issues become more salient when considering the possibility of Israeli sovereignty over these territories.[107]

This brief discussion of Israel's collective identity suggests that, while

---

105. Although the Holocaust has been internalized within the American historical consciousness, it has been in a particular American way. For instance, the Holocaust Museum in Washington, D.C., is a testimony to both the need to resist future Holocausts and ambiguous role of the U.S. in protecting and overcoming the Holocaust. See David Schoenbaum, *The United States and the State of Israel* (New York: Oxford University Press, 1993), p. 321. The contradictions were ever-present at the commemorative ceremony with Elie Wiesel, a Holocaust survivor, imploring President Clinton, the leader of the West, to do something to stop the modern-day Holocaust in Bosnia.

106. See Segev, *The Seventh Million*, for illustrations of how the legacy of the Holocaust translates into particular foreign policy actions.

107. While those states that are "core" members of the West might not be able to live up to its supposed standards, their status is taken for granted (and in this respect these questions are hardly ever addressed), and transgression is viewed as an occasional, and excusable, lapse—not cause for questioning its very identity and membership within the community.

there are strong links to the West and Israelis identify themselves as part of the West, its collective identity is always negotiated and highly vulnerable to counternarratives. This provides the background for the examination of U.S.-Israeli relations since the mid-1980s: to investigate how Israel's identity "crisis" helps to account for the progressive strains in the relationship. In response to this crisis, Israeli leaders and partisans began to accentuate and promote Israel's "Western" and democratic character and identity in order to reproduce the U.S.-Israeli alliance and to distinguish Israel from its neighboring Arab states.

An Alliance Under Duress

U.S.-Israeli relations can be divided into three periods. The pre-1967 period reveals two, almost contradictory, behavioral patterns. On the one hand, there was the unquestioned and unequivocal support of the U.S. for the State of Israel. Whence came this impulse? Shared values and sentiments are nearly always recognized as primary factors in explaining this rush to protect and guarantee Israel's sovereignty. Americans saw something in themselves when they saw Israel:

> Even as [Americans] go their own way, in pursuit of their own national interests, Americans and Israelis are bonded together like no two other sovereign peoples. As the Judaic heritage flowed through the minds of America's early settlers and helped to shape the new American republic, so Israel restored the vision and the values of the American dream.[108]

Richard Murphy, a former assistant secretary of state for Near and Middle Eastern affairs, observes that the strategic alliance was used for the moral commitment;[109] that is, the strategic is parasitic on the ideational. There are innumerable testimonials to the belief that the U.S.-Israeli relationship is undergirded by shared values rather than shared threats.

These stated commitments, however, cannot erase a legacy of U.S. policies that often represented more of a threat than a support to Israeli security. Truman quickly followed his recognition of the Israeli state with an arms embargo, Eisenhower and Dulles asked Israel whether it might be willing to withdraw from the Negev in return for an alliance between the U.S. and Egypt, and the U.S. refused to sell Israel any weapons until the

---

108. Grose, *Israel in the Mind of America*, p. 316.
109. Interview with author.

mid-1960s. In general, the strategic and ideational imperatives of the U.S. produced a nearly schizophrenic attitude toward Israel.

For a variety of reasons, revolving largely around a changing U.S. containment and strategic posture, U.S.-Israeli relations grew by leaps and bounds after 1967. The upturn was particularly noticeable under Reagan, when the conservative tide and the "second cold war" furthered Israel's standing in the eyes of the U.S. government (and this was particularly true when compared to the Carter years).[110] The peaks came in 1984 with the Memorandum of Understanding, which pledged to deepen military and strategic cooperation with Israel, and in 1987 when Israel attained quasi-NATO status (which led some in the U.S. to contemplate the "NATOization of Israel"). Many Israelis interpreted these developments as evidence of Israel's important, nearly indispensable, place in U.S. security strategy, creating tremendous optimism in Israel.[111] Writing in the Israeli paper *HaMishmar*, Wolf Blitzer exclaimed that with the memorandum, "We are on the threshold of a new era in relations between Washington and Jerusalem."[112]

This era, however, was not the one that Blitzer and others imagined. No sooner had the festivities subsided than U.S.-Israeli relations entered a third period, one of difficulties, leading to a genuine concern that the special relationship was not that special. Although some deemed it a clash of personalities, President Bush and Secretary of State Baker against Shamir, many others argued that the crisis was a natural by-product of the end of the Cold War and the loss of Israel's strategic role. I want to propose, however, that three events—the end of the Cold War, the debate over Greater Israel, and the *intifada*—challenged the foundations of U.S.-Israeli relations by challenging Israel's identity.

The most frequently evoked reason for the crisis was the end of the Cold War. The traditional interpretation is that absent the Cold War Israel became strategically irrelevant; therefore, the crisis was provoked by a change in the international distribution of power. Yet this systemic reading of the Cold War is open to a constructivist twist. The very categories

---

110. That Reagan would frequently quote biblical scripture and openly discuss Israel's place in biblical prophecy only served to strengthen the link between the U.S. and the Jewish state.

111. "The idea was harmful, especially once it took root in the popular mind, for it created an erroneous perception of what Israel can allow itself to do in its relations with the United States, and thus provided indirect support for annexationist and other extreme policies" (Yehoshafat Harkabi, *Israel's Fateful Hour* [New York: Harper and Row, 1988], p. 129).

112. May 28, 1984, pp. 7, 12, cited in *FBIS-NES*, 5, 107, June 1, 1984, 15–6.

East and *West* became indistinguishable from the Cold War itself, and this international structure distributed identities and roles to states depending on their place within that structure. That the international system through the structure of the Cold War distributed identities to states is apparent in the myriad debates over the national identity—for instance, in Turkey and the U.S.—that have erupted since the demise of the Cold War. The same can be said of Israel. For two decades Israel had been an integral part of the Western containment network, proudly guarding U.S. military and foreign policy interests and profiting greatly in both status and resources. Yet Israel's place within the containment network was sold on the basis of its identity and its potential strategic utility; it was not just any ally but a "stable and reliable" ally because of its democratic features and Western values. In this respect, Israel's role in the Western community, its very identity as a Western state, derived in part from—or at the very least reinforced by—the Cold War. The decline of the Cold War, then, potentially usurped not just Israel's identification with the Western community but a source of Israel's Western identity as well.[113]

A greater challenge to Israel's collective identity emerged in the debate over "Greater Israel." Although this debate preceded Israel's control over the territories as a consequence of the June 1967 war, it has intensified considerably since then.[114] There are two alternative visions of Israel's collective identity with respect to the territories. The first argues for a "State of Israel," an Israel that resides within negotiated pre-1967 borders as the best hope for maintaining Israel's security, and its civic, democratic, and Jewish character. The Labour Party and leftist movements expressed tremendous concern that Israel is endangering its commitment to democracy and its Jewish character by maintaining its hold over the territories. Therefore, those in this camp demand a change in Israeli policies not only on security and humanitarian grounds but also because of a belief that a continuation would threaten Israel's collective identity as a Western, Democratic, Jewish state.

Those who championed a "Greater Israel" hoped to extend Israel's sovereignty to the territories, what they prefer to call by the biblical names Judea and Samaria to symbolize the Jewish people's historical and religious

---

113. This is consistent with the proposition that identity is partly informed by an outside threat; consequently, the demise of that threat can potentially undermine the actor's identity. See Simmel, *Conflict and the Web of Group-Affiliations.*
114. Kimmerling, "Between the Primordial and the Civil Definitions of the Collective Identity."

bond to this land. Beginning with Zev Jabotinsky, the founder of Revisionist Zionism, and carried forward by Menachem Begin and Yitzhak Shamir, the champions of Eretz Israel evidenced a willingness to forgo (or at least risk) Israel's democratic character to maintain Jewish control over the territories. Specifically, to extend sovereignty over these territories and its nearly one million Palestinians would automatically change Israel's demographic character and, in time, threaten to turn the Jews of the Jewish state into a minority.[115] In general, this debate over Israel's boundaries and sovereignty had immediate and direct implications for Israel's democratic future; in this important respect, it had immediate and direct implications for Israel's status as a "Western" state.

The third event is the *intifada*. The Israeli response to the Palestinian uprising not only undermined the portrait of a "benign" occupation but also led many to question Israel's "Western" character. The images of routine beatings, detention, Defense Minister Rabin's "iron fist" policy, and other violations of human rights caused many to mumble that Israel resembled a "Third World" and not a "Western" state.

The images and reports transmitted to the U.S. affected the American government's (and community's) view of Israel.[116] U.S. officials were deeply troubled by Israel's response to the *intifada*. Assistant Secretary of State for Middle East Affairs Richard Murphy argued that the *intifada* would not go away and that the U.S. was opposed to many of the policies adopted by Israel to contain it.[117] Noting that some began to ques-

---

115. Those who championed Greater Israel had three immediate methods for resolving the possibility that Arabs might outnumber Jews in a future Israel. One was to deny that this demographic revolution would ever occur either because of alternative projected birthrates, anticipated immigration, or desired Palestinian emigration. The second, articulated by the political party Moledet, was to "transfer" Palestinians to Arab states through either forced means or incentive packages. A final option, visibly and starkly articulated by Meier Kahane's Kach Party, was to deny citizenship to the Palestinians in an expanded Israel. Kahane argued that Israel could not be both Jewish and democratic, and since Israel would always be a Jewish state the Arabs would never be citizens. Although Kach was a minority party that was eventually ruled unconstitutional by the Israeli Supreme Court in 1984, Kahane and his followers touched a raw nerve in Israeli politics as they challenged Israel's democratic character and image.

116. The Jewish American leadership was quite sensitive to Israel's deteriorating status as a consequence of the decline of the Cold War and its occupation policies and altered their presentation of Israel accordingly to highlight its democratic character. For instance, testimony by the American Israel Public Affairs Committee (AIPAC) to the House Foreign Affairs Committee on Israel's aid package between 1982 and 1993 reveals a pronounced emphasis on Israel's democratic character and Western identity. In general, the vanishing strategic rationale caused supporters of Israel to focus on the base reason for U.S.-Israeli relations: their shared identity and values.

117. *FBIS-NES*-88–174, September 8, 1988, pp. 50–51.

tion whether Israel was still part of the West, Murphy later reflected that the intifada created a shockingly different context for U.S.-Israeli relations, captured vividly by the CBS film of Israeli soldiers breaking the bones of those accused of throwing stones. Such pictures reverberated throughout the administration and caused many to wonder about its friend.[118]

Although U.S. policy had always maintained that Israeli settlements on the occupied territories were both illegal and an obstacle to peace, there were greater urgency and determination by American officials to differentiate U.S. support for Israel from support for Israeli policies in the territories. In other words, support for Israeli sovereignty did not extend to support for Israeli sovereignty over a Greater Israel that had a large Palestinian population absent civil rights. For instance, the House Foreign Affairs Committee, a mainstay of U.S. support for Israel, recognized Israel's commitment to democracy, noted the "striking contrast between Israel and the Arab states in this regard,"[119] but was troubled that the shared values that joined U.S. and Israel might be eroding:

> America's links with Israel are broad and deep, based on shared values, common interests, and a commitment to democracy, rule of law and freedom. Nevertheless, the subcommittee is troubled by the continuing cycle of violence between Israelis and Palestinians . . . and evidence of on-going human rights violations in the West Bank and Gaza.[120]

The House, in other words, was troubled that a traditional marker used to separate Israel and the Arab states in the American mind was deteriorating because Israeli behavior more closely resembled that expected from the Arab states. No doubt Israel's presence and policies in the territories were eroding the foundations of the special relationship.

The most visible sign of the changing times was the emerging debate over U.S. assistance to Israel. In response to Israel's post–Gulf war request for a $10 billion loan guarantee, the U.S. made the assistance conditional on Israel's assurance that these funds would not be used for settlement expansion. Shamir vehemently objected to the condition, arguing that it intruded on Israel's domestic affairs and hindered the humanitarian mission of absorbing the Russian and Ethiopian Jews. Tensions rose through

118. Interview with author.
119. Committee on Foreign Affairs, *Foreign Assistance Legislation for Fiscal Year 1994: Part 2*, Subcommittee on Foreign Affairs (Washington, D.C.: U.S. Government Printing Office, 1993), p. 60.
120. Ibid., p. 21.

fall 1991 and early 1992, with Bush and Baker holding firm and Shamir believing that they were bluffing and that Congress would come to Israel's rescue. Shamir miscalculated. Not only did Bush refrain from bending but Shamir wrongly predicted that a confrontation with the U.S. would not damage his popularity.[121]

Because the U.S. was Israel's primary military benefactor, a crisis, particularly one that was potentially avoidable, might conceivably risk Israeli security. The Labour and Likud parties present two different understandings of whether Israel's confrontational tactics risked U.S. support and methods for managing the relationship. Labour politicians have a history of expressing greater deference and are generally more reserved and measured in their criticisms and confrontational rhetoric; Likud, on the other hand, often declared that confrontation would not beget confrontation. Yehoshafat Harkabi contrasts these two styles and hypothesizes how Likud's policies might undermine Israeli security in the following way:

> A widely-held but erroneous belief is that Ben-Gurion's view of world opinion is contained in his remark: "It doesn't matter what the 'goyim' say, it matters what the Jews do." . . . [Yet] he believed that a positive international attitude toward Israel was a precondition for Israeli security. . . . The capacity to achieve goals depends not only on the strength of the local forces that have to be overcome, but also on the support of these goals in the world community.[122]

Harkabi provided a causal chain to illustrate why certain policies and practices must be changed: such practices will create moral gaps between Israel and the West; these gaps, in turn, will erode U.S. support for Israel; and, finally, they will encourage adventurism among the Arab states. Provoking the U.S. and aggravating the "hand that feeds you" was not only bad manners but also needlessly endangering Israel's security.

These issues culminated in the 1992 Israeli elections, in which Israel's identity crisis was played out, pitting the "two Yitzhaks"—Shamir and Rabin—against each other, with their two alternative visions of Israel's relationship to the territories and collective identity. Since 1967 Israel's debate over the territories has been the primary vehicle for discussing the nation's collective identity. The end of the Cold War, the post–Gulf war

---

121. While approximately 20 percent of those polled said that a deterioration in relations would increase their support for Shamir, more than 40 percent said that it would undermine it; *Davar*, March 30, 1992, p. 2, cited in *FBIS-NES*-92–062, March 31, 1992, p. 19.
122. Harkabi, *Israel's Fateful Hour*, p. 205.

peace process, and the confrontation with the U.S. over the loan guarantees combined to focus the Israeli election on its future relationship to the territories and the question of whether it was willing to endure the costs of Shamir's policies. The subtext, then, was Israel's collective identity: Yitzhak Rabin advocated a State of Israel theme, while Yitzhak Shamir championed Greater Israel. By openly campaigning that Israel could not afford the economic, strategic, and psychological costs of maintaining a permanent presence over the territories, Rabin was implicitly arguing that at stake were Israel's collective identity, relationship to the West, and relationship to the U.S. Rabin's victory was interpreted by many as a victory for those championing a State of Israel message.

The debate over Israel's collective identity—or at the very least the recognition that Israeli policies in the territories would shape that identity—carried over from the elections to the peace process. Israel's decision to recognize the PLO and sign the Declaration of Principles was profoundly shaped by the visions of its collective identity. In an interview the night of the historic handshake between himself and Yasir Arafat, Prime Minister Rabin explained why Israel had to cede territory to Palestinians:

> I believe . . . annexation will bring . . . racism to Israel, [and] that racism and Judaism are in contradiction by their very essence. Israel that will preach racism will not be a Jewish state by my understanding. . . . Otherwise [Israel will have to give the Palestinians] full civilian rights as we give to every individual who is an Israeli citizen. . . . Every one of them, once inside, can be a full Israeli citizen . . . [and will constitute] 35 percent of the voters to the Knesset. . . . They'll dictate if Israel will be a Jewish state with a destiny to serve the Jewish people all over the world, or we will become another small Jewish country . . . because 35 percent of the voters will be non-Jewish. . . . I don't expect [the Palestinians] to be Zionists. And if Israel will lose the Zionists from its very existence, Israel will be an entirely different country. . . . Therefore, whoever speaks now about the whole land of Israel speaks either of a racist Jewish state which will not be a Jewish or a binational state. I prefer Israel to be a Jewish state not all over the land of Israel.[123]

Acknowledging a direct link between a continuation of certain practices and Israel's collective identity, Rabin was responding to the twenty-five-

---

123. Interview with Yitzhak Rabin on the *MacNeil-Lehrer Newshour*, Monday, September 13, 1993. Also see Ben Lynfield, "Rabin Tries to Make Less of 'Greater Israel,' " *Christian Science Monitor*, January 25, 1994, p. 22.

year-old identity crisis caused by Israel's capture of the territories in the 1967 War and saying that the only way to resolve that crisis in favor of a Western, Democratic, and Jewish Israel was to relinquish Israel's control over the territories.[124]

Another way to reinforce Israel's identity as part of the West was to discover a common threat. Earlier I argued that a common threat can reinforce or shape a common identity; it is through the recognition of a shared threat that actors acknowledge that they share not only interests but also values and beliefs. Although U.S.-Israeli relations already had a strong ideational component before Israel's post-1967 strategic role in U.S. containment policy, this role reinforced both Israel's identity as part of the West and the U.S.-Israeli alliance. Therefore, the end of the Cold War stripped Israel of not only its strategic role but also a reinforcing beam of its identity. Although still very much in the making, and by no means approximating the status of the Cold War, many Israeli and Western leaders argue that Islam represents a common threat.[125] It is unknown whether Israeli leaders cynically or sincerely thrust Islam forward as the new threat: while undoubtedly many Israelis feel threatened by radical Islam, Israeli leaders are probably aware of the potential strategic payoff from a threat also identified by the West.[126] In either case, if the U.S. recognized the threat to the West posed by Islamic fundamentalism, then U.S.-Israeli relations might be righted and their shared identities reinforced.

This discussion highlights two key features of the relationship between identity, practices, and membership in the community. First, being part of the community entails not only having a particular identity but also abid-

---

124. More recent events, including Israel's decision to label Kach and Kahana Hay as terrorist organizations after the terrorist attack in Hebron in February 1994, was also read through the image of the Western "self" in general and the belief that Israel's democratic and liberal identity were being challenged from within. See, for instance, "Rabin Addresses Knesset on Hebron Massacre," *FBIS-NES*, March 1, 1994, pp. 31–33; and Clyde Haberman, "Israel Votes Ban on Jewish Groups Linked to Kahane," *New York Times*, March 14, 1994, p. 1.

125. This "Islam vs. the West" debate has become a particularly troubling and vocal one in the U.S. over the past few years, beginning soon after the Iranian revolution but gathering momentum and contributors since the end of the Cold War. For a sampling of the literature, see Ghassan Salame, "Islam and the West," *Foreign Policy* 90 (Spring 1993): 22–37; Huntington, "The Clash of Civilizations"; and Said, "The Phony Islamic Threat."

126. Ariel Sharon claimed that the U.S. and Israel are threatened by Arab-Muslim fundamentalism and that the U.S. should begin discussions with Israel on how best to confront this mutual threat. IDF Radio, 28 March 1992, cited in *FBIS-NES*-92–061, March 30, 1992, pp. 27–28. Yitzhak Rabin also argued that Islam represents a shared threat, implying that Israel has not only a new strategic role but also a shared identity. Daniel Williams, "U.S. Offers to Sell Israel Upgraded Fighter Jets," *Washington Post*, November 16, 1993, p. 31.

ing by the community's norms. The constitutive norms, in other words, demanded not that the "average stream" of behavior converge around certain practices and expectations, but rather that it abstain from those practices that were antithetical to the very qualities that define membership in the community. If Israel's membership is dependent on its liberal character and values, then these domestic debates over its future relationship to, and practices in, the territories potentially threatened its collective identity as a "Western" state and, accordingly, the U.S.-Israeli alliance. Therefore, both foreign policy actions and the constitutive norms that define state-society relations are important markers of identity.

Second, the desire to adhere to the norms of the Western community for both instrumental and ideational reasons served to reproduce and (potentially) encourage the development of new identities. If one reason for the interest of Israeli leaders in altering their policies in the territories was to ensure an uninterrupted flow of U.S. assistance, these policy changes, in turn, promoted certain identities and denigrated others. Yet instrumental logic alone does not fully capture the nature of the debate over the territories or the reason for the recent changes, for equally important was the desire by various Israeli constituencies to promote a particular political identity, to adhere to a particular vision of Zionism, and to be part of the liberal, Western community.

In sum, most interpretations of U.S.-Israeli relations view it as a product of either domestic or systemic politics, but thus far most analyses of the crisis in U.S.-Israeli relations refer to the collapse of the Cold War and Israel's strategic relevance. My focus on identity highlights how shared values and common identities are the foundation of U.S.-Israeli relations and how the crisis was nothing less than an "identity" crisis, which challenged Israel's Western, liberal character and, therefore, U.S.-Israeli relations. Because ideational factors represented the source of the crisis, the Israeli polity moved (consciously or not) to redirect its collective identity and to stabilize U.S.-Israeli relations. By conceptualizing the U.S.-Israeli alliance as forged by shared identity and not simply a shared security interest, we are better able to understand how this partnership preceded and outlasted any systemic threat that might have given rise to its existence.

Rather than following the lead of neorealism and reducing nonmaterial forces to the level of ideology and parasites on the material, this essay demonstrates how state identity offers important insights into the dynamics of security cooperation and alliance formation. Although Walt and other neorealists treat Arabism as little more than an ideology that is used to legitimate state interests deriving from anarchy, Arabism shaped the identity, interests, and policies available to Arab leaders in ways that left its mark on inter-Arab security dynamics and alliance politics. To begin, identity provides theoretical leverage over the construction of the threat. While neorealists concede that the construction of the threat cannot be derived from structural factors alone, they have yet to offer an alternative proposition for explaining this elementary feature of alliance formation. If history and a collective memory are obvious factors in producing a definition of the "other" and the threat, many approaches to security politics tend to view them as secondary considerations and as background material rather than as a central feature of what is doing the explaining and what is to be explained.

Similarly, identity provides a handle on who is considered to be a desirable alliance partner. Whether a state is a "natural" security partner cannot be derived from material forces alone, for the degree of naturalness is highly dependent on familiarity and identity. For instance, U.S. officials often claimed that Israel is a preferable strategic partner to the Arab states (despite the latter's advantaged geostrategic condition) because of its democratic character and liberal values. The GCC's membership was based on ideational factors, a shared history, and a similar political profile, which meant placing symbolic boundaries between Gulf and non-Gulf Arab states. In short, identity potentially signals whom to balance against and whom to bandwagon with.

Far from suggesting the primacy of identity and the irrelevance of material forces, I recognize that both are important explanatory variables, though with different causal weight at different historical moments. Sometimes identity politics will figure centrally; at other times a strategic logic might provide an exhaustive explanation. There is no theoretical or empirical justification, however, for assuming the primacy of one over the other. My sense is that neorealism's insistence on material factors is premised not only on its theoretical presuppositions but also on the mistaken assumption that a shared identity lends naturally and only to cooperation. That is, neorealism observes that because even states that have a shared identity have, at times, conflicting interests if not outright hostility, then it must be a realist world. Yet there are many sources of conflict, and there is no a priori reason to dismiss the possibility of identity. The case of the Baghdad Pact vividly illustrates, first, how inter-Arab politics and alliances were driven by presentational politics and not by military power and, second, an intense debate over which behavioral expectations were and were not consistent with being an Arab state. Arab states positioned themselves, fought, and forged alliances depending on their view of the demands and expectations that Arabism made on Arab states. In general, even actors that have a shared identity and identification of the threat can struggle over the norms that concern how they are to enact their identity.

These cases also demonstrate that identity is not a static construct but rather is socially constructed, and that this social construction process can be used to good effect for understanding alliance dynamics and changes in security patterns. To understand the social construction of state identity, however, requires examining not only interstate interactions but also state-society relations. The discussion of the changing alliance patterns in inter-Arab politics is connected to a weakening of the Arab national identity and the emergence of statist identities, which are a consequence of regional interactions and state formation processes.[127] These ideational shifts are associated with changing patterns of inter-Arab politics, including the definition of the threat and who is considered an acceptable ally. The case of U.S.-Israeli relations suggests how the state's membership in the community and the basis of the association is dependent on mutual identification, that is, shared identities. Yet because identities are socially constructed they are susceptible to change, and such a change can create a "crisis," if not undermine the very basis of the relationship. To understand the source of this crisis, however, requires incorporating changes in the international system structure as well as debates over the national identity.

In sum, the language of identity offers an alternative approach for understanding security politics and security cooperation. All three cases demonstrate how identity, as a relational construct that emerges out of the international and domestic discourse and interactions, imprints security politics and helps us to understand the dynamics of alliance formation.

---

127. Barnett, "Sovereignty, Nationalism, and Regional Order in Arab Politics."

Part · 3
Implications and Conclusions

12 • Norms, Identity, and Their Limits: A Theoretical Reprise

Paul Kowert and Jeffrey Legro

> It is neither the borders nor the men who make a nation; it is the laws, the habits, the customs, the government, the constitution, the manner of being that comes from all of this. The nation is in the relations of the state to its members: when its relations change or cease to exist, the nation vanishes.
>
> —Jean-Jacques Rousseau
> Correspondance générale

Unlike Rousseau, many contemporary students of international politics treat the material facts of a nation's existence—its physical capabilities, technological achievements, geographical location, and so on—as the final arbiters of political outcomes. Not only are the laws, habits, and customs that Rousseau emphasizes considered epiphenomena, but they are notoriously elusive subjects for social scientific inquiry. Volumes such as this one therefore necessarily devote considerable effort to justifying their own approach and subject matter. The authors of the preceding essays seek to show in great detail, and in a wide variety of settings, that custom is often more important than capability and that social prescription often super-

The authors wish to thank the participants of the Social Science Research Council/MacArthur Workshops at Cornell University (February 5–7, 1993), the University of Minnesota (January 14–16, 1994), and Stanford University (October 7–9, 1994), as well as members of the Mershon Center Research Training Group (RTG) on the Role of Cognition in Collective Political Decision Making at Ohio State University for discussions that enriched this essay. We are also indebted to Ethan Cherin, Martha Finnemore, Peter Katzenstein, Nicholas Onuf, Diana Richards, Stephen Walt, Katja Weber, the other participants in this book project, and two anonymous reviewers for their helpful comments and advice. Kowert gratefully acknowledges support from the International Relations Department at Florida International University and from a National Science Foundation grant (DIR-9113599) to the Mershon Center RTG at the Ohio State University. Legro is grateful for support from the Department of Political Science at the University of Minnesota.

sedes material self-interest. This essay critically reviews these efforts and considers the payoff for international relations theory of a focus on norms.

Norms, including the laws, habits, and customs to which Rousseau refers, are social prescriptions. While such prescriptions take many forms, this volume focuses first on norms that regulate the behavior of important actors in international politics.[1] Norms are thus tied to actors. "New Thinking" in the Soviet Union was a norm, as was "hard realpolitik" in Mao's China. Both prescribe behavior for national policy-making elites (and, on another level, for nations). The changing collective beliefs about the use of nuclear or chemical weapons, the legitimacy of military intervention, and even the spread of democracy are all examples of widespread

---

1. Jepperson, Wendt, and Katzenstein define norms, in the second essay of this volume, as "collective expectations about proper behavior for a given identity." This is consistent with our definition, but naturally one might distinguish among many different types of norms. Some regulate morality, others prescribe accepted (but not ethically required) practice, and still others regulate the character of actors themselves. The latter type of norm, which we term *identity*, is discussed below.

Norms may also differ in their effects, in the extent to which they are known and accepted as just, in the explicitness of their content or provisions, in the uniformity of their application, in the degree to which sanctions accompany violations, in the degree to which they are internalized, and in the modes of their transmission. See Judith Blake and Kingsley Davis, "Norms, Values, and Sanctions," in Robert E. L. Faris, ed., *Handbook of Modern Sociology* (Chicago: Rand McNally, 1964); Robert E. Edgerton, *Rules, Exceptions, and Social Order* (Berkeley: University of California Press, 1985); and Janice E. Thomson, "Norms in International Relations: A Conceptual Analysis," *International Journal of Group Tensions* 23 (1993): 67–83. The common analytical divide between constitutive and regulative norms, for example, is a distinction based on effect: constitutive norms create or grant properties while regulative norms specify the proper enactment of these properties. On this distinction, see David Dessler, "What's at Stake in the Agent-Structure Debate?" *International Organization* 43, no. 3 (Summer 1989): 454–58; and Friedrich Kratochwil, *Rules, Norms, and Decisions: On the Conditions of Practical and Legal Reasoning in International Relations and Domestic Affairs* (Cambridge: Cambridge University Press, 1989). Others make a related distinction between descriptive and prescriptive norms. Because we focus in this article only on norms with prescriptive or regulative effects, we leave aside many of these distinctions. Thus even our treatment of identity focuses explicitly on the regulative (rather than merely constitutive) effects of norms. We concentrate, in other words, not on how collective understandings describe or constitute actors but on how they regulate the "proper" identity of actors.

Another related distinction also deserves brief mention. Essays 1 and 2—and several of the empirical essays (notably those by Berger, Johnston, and Kier)—devote attention to "culture" as well as to norms or identity. Because we focus on social prescription, we avoid the more general term *culture*, which may include a wide variety of social knowledge apart from (prescriptive) norms. We do not attempt, therefore, to capture every aspect of the arguments offered in the empirical essays. What is distinctive about this volume, in our view, is its emphasis on social prescriptions of both identity and behavior (see Katzenstein's essay 1 and its discussion of culture). For a recent account of culture as collective knowledge that does *not* (necessarily) involve prescription, see Judith Goldstein and Robert O. Keohane, *Ideas and Foreign Policy: Beliefs, Institutions, and Political Change* (Ithaca: Cornell University Press, 1993). For a multifaceted account of the impact of culture on international politics, see Jongsuk Chay, *Culture and International Relations* (New York: Praeger, 1990).

and evolving political norms. These too prescribe and regulate the practice of agents in international politics.

We wish, however, to maintain one important distinction among the different types of norms discussed in this essay. In much the same way that Wendt has distinguished between structure and agent in international relations theory, we will distinguish between *norms* as the regulative cultural content of international politics and *identities*—regulative accounts of actors themselves.[2] Another example may help to clarify this distinction. Charles Kindleberger has argued that the rise of free trade in mid-nineteenth-century Europe came not from changing material interests but rather from the spread of a laissez-faire ideology.[3] This ideology itself consists of a web of normative claims (about the efficacy of new trade practices, for example). But it also incorporates an account of the identity of actors who may legitimately participate in and govern trade (the legitimate practices of sovereign nations, for example, continued to differ from those of colonies). Identities, therefore, are prescriptive representations of political actors themselves and of their relationships to each other. We thus divide social prescription into these two categories: prescriptive accounts of actors themselves (identities) and behavioral prescriptions for the proper enactment of these identities (behavioral norms).[4] When maintaining this distinction is unimportant, however, we will occasionally use the latter term (norms) in the more general sense described above to indicate social prescriptions *including* regulative accounts of actor identity.

This essay raises two questions about social prescriptions in world politics. First, what are the consequences of behavioral norms and identities? What, in other words, is the payoff of the "sociological turn" in international relations theory away from individualism and materialism toward a focus on collective interpretation? The central claim of this

---

2. Alexander Wendt, "The Agent-Structure Problem in International Relations Theory," *International Organization* 41, no. 3 (Summer 1987): 335–70; see also Dessler, "What's at Stake in the Agent-Structure Debate."

3. Charles Kindleberger, "The Rise of Free Trade in Western Europe, 1820–1875," *Journal of Economic History* 35 (1975): 20–55.

4. This distinction corresponds closely to Jepperson, Wendt, and Katzenstein's distinction in essay 2 between portfolios of identities and regulations for the behavior of "already-constituted identities." It also parallels, very roughly, the distinction between the two axes of international relations theory that they discuss (see their figure 2.1). Theories that emphasize the cultural, regulative content of the environment in which actors move (the x-axis) are theories of norms. Theories that focus on the way the environment shapes cultural representations of actors themselves (that is, theories high on the y-axis) are theories of identity.

volume is that international relations theory cannot afford to ignore norms. This essay assesses that claim by considering the impact of norms on the interests, beliefs, and behavior of actors in international politics. Demonstrating that impact does not invalidate other theories of international relations. Rather, it points to analytical blind spots and gaps in existing accounts. In so doing, it not only casts light into the shadows of existing theory but raises new questions (and offers new explanations) as well.

If norms are important, a second question naturally emerges: Where do the norms themselves come from? While the preceding essays devote considerable effort to answering the first question, they rarely address the second one. But they nevertheless offer some insights into potential answers. The second section of this essay therefore identifies three possible avenues to norm building. For the most part, these "sources" of norms remain ill-defined, incompletely theorized, and understudied. But if one accepts the central contention of this volume—that norms matter to the conduct of international politics—then the origins of norms is a natural subject for further study.

The third section of this essay considers several other difficulties with ongoing efforts to investigate the role of norms in international politics. While the practitioners of international politics (national leaders, for example) may believe they know norms when (and if) they see them, identification and categorization remain difficult problems for social scientists. Moreover, the fluidity of social norms and the complex interplay between physical reality and interpretation complicate such scholarship enormously. And the fact that at least some political actors are aware of norms and actively seek to manipulate them further confounds the efforts of scholars. This essay concludes, therefore, with an overview of the promise and perils of a focus on norms in international politics.

How Norms Matter

Norms have attracted attention in disciplines across the social sciences, including psychology, sociology, anthropology, economics, and political science. Such wide interest undoubtedly stems in large part from a desire to explain otherwise perplexing behavior. Why do actors adhere to social rules even in situations where these rules may run counter to their own material interests?[5] What, more generally, is the fabric that holds pluralistic societies together? And when will these societies, facing each other across national boundaries, adhere to a set of (admittedly looser) rules for international conduct? These are critical concerns for students of international relations.

The international arena is often characterized as having a minimalist order because it is "anarchic"—that is, it lacks a sovereign to enforce rules, leaving only appeals to armed force to resolve clashes of interest between states.[6] Scholars of post–World War II international relations, especially in security affairs, consequently tend to downplay the role of norms. Realists focus primarily on material capabilities and argue that norms, where they exist, merely ratify underlying power relationships. And while (neo)liberal theorists more often accord an independent role to norms, they nevertheless concentrate on explicit contractual arrangements (such as those embodied in regimes) intended to resolve collective action problems. This volume, however, argues that norms play a much broader role in world politics, shaping both cooperation *and* conflict in ways that are invisible to theories that focus either on material structural forces or on individual choice.

The argument here is not that approaches such as realism or liberalism are "wrong." Rather, it is that the micro- and macrofoundations of these perspectives are not equipped to account for the full range of political norms and their consequences. Indeed, the central assumptions of such theories direct attention away from the cultural variables on which this volume focuses. Thus, a useful starting point for this section on the consequences of norms is with these very gaps in existing approaches. Such gaps are important because they point directly to the most important effects of norms—and because they highlight the relevance of norms for mainstream international relations theory. This section considers first,

5. See Jon Elster, *The Cement of Society: A Study of Social Order* (Cambridge: Cambridge University Press, 1989); and Jack P. Gibbs, *Norms, Deviance, and Social Control: Conceptual Matters* (New York: Elsevier, 1981). Scholars may have different interests in studying order—some hope to undermine it, others to strengthen it. For an interpretivist assessment of "order" as a social construct, see Nicholas Onuf, *World of Our Making: Rules and Rule in Social Theory and International Relations* (Columbia: University of South Carolina Press, 1989), pp. 127–59.
6. Hedley Bull defines order as "an arrangement of social life such that it promotes certain goals or values" (*The Anarchical Society: A Study of Order in World Politics* [New York: Columbia University Press, 1977], p. 4).

therefore, the "economic" approach that provides the dominant micro-foundation of both neorealist and neoliberal theory. It then turns to the formal structuralism that serves as a macrofoundation to both bodies of theory.[7]

Neoclassical microeconomics, in both its orthodox and its institutional versions, offers an important account of the microfoundations of social order. In the orthodox approach, social behavior and outcomes are a product of the rational choices of individuals who maximize their satisfaction (utility) by efficiently matching available means to their desired ends. The main factor that conditions actor choice is change in "prices" based on market forces (supply and demand) that tend to stabilize in equilibrium.[8]

In international relations theory, several approaches adopt this economic individualism. Strategic and game theoretic perspectives on conflict and cooperation employ a generic version of the economic approach to understand the dynamics of strategic choice and the circumstances (costs) that shape actor decisions.[9] More generally, realist (and particularly neore-alist) international relations theory rests on orthodox microeconomic foundations. Neorealists thus view states as generic entities, like firms, that respond rationally to costs in an international "market" defined by a distribution of capabilities among states. Robert Gilpin, to take a prominent example, explicitly adopts microeconomic language and analogies.[10]

While it may offer considerable advantages, the orthodox economic approach and its application to international relations tend to marginalize the importance of both behavioral norms and actor identity. In this spare version of economic individualism, norms play no independent role apart from the strategic choices of actors, since explanation focuses on agents that respond rationally to the "objective" environment (i.e., shifting prices

---

7. These schools—neoclassical individualism and formal structuralism—represent different extremes of the schema developed in essay 2 (figure 2.1). The former ignores the way that structures (either material or normative) constitute actors, whereas the latter ignores the cultural content of the environment.

8. Gary Becker, *The Economic Approach to Human Behavior* (Chicago: University of Chicago Press, 1976); Jack Hirschleifer, "The Expanding Domain of Economics," *American Economic Review* (1985), pp. 53–68.

9. Duncan Snidal, "The Game Theory of International Politics," in Kenneth Oye, ed., *Cooperation Under Anarchy* (Princeton: Princeton University Press, 1986); Arthur Stein, *Why Nations Cooperate* (Ithaca: Cornell University Press, 1990).

10. Robert Gilpin, *War and Change in the International System* (Princeton: Princeton University Press, 1981). See also Robert O. Keohane, *Neorealism and Its Critics* (New York: Columbia University Press, 1986); and Kenneth Waltz, *Theory of International Politics* (Reading, Mass.: Addison-Wesley, 1979).

in the markets for security and welfare).[11] And actors themselves are posited as unitary, calculating, self-interested agents.[12] When conceptions of actor identity and roles cleave to these minimalist assumptions, then orthodox economics can only provide an extremely sparse account of behavioral variations in actors facing similar constraints. The neoclassical model possesses no theory of differences in goals.

Another, less orthodox variant of neoclassical theory directs greater attention toward the institutional framework of individual choice. This school accepts the rational egoism of orthodox theory but accords institutionalized rules a special role in resolving problems of aggregation and coordination. These rules facilitate repeated interaction and, as Michio Morishima has argued, may contribute to long-run economic success.[13]

---

11. Many of the arguments in this volume distinguish themselves from rationalism, but that does not imply that they espouse "irrationalism." Rather, the point is that "rationalist" arguments are based on narrow self-interest that is influenced primarily by material-economic forces. A sociological approach rejects the basis of realist rationality—that states are driven primarily by the international power distribution—as too limited. Instead it argues that a range of social phenomena help to constitute and constrain agents. Once an agent knows what it is and what it wants, it will move instrumentally (even in the sociological model) to achieve its goals within the material and normative constraints it faces. The virtue of the sociological approach is that it fills in some of the more interesting lacunae of rationalism (e.g., the character and goals of actors).

12. Albert Hirschman, "Three Ways of Complicating Some Categories of Economic Discourse," *Economics and Philosophy* 1 (1985): 7–21; Robert Jervis, "Realism, Game Theory, and Cooperation," *World Politics* 40 (1989): 317–49; and Amartya Sen, "Rational Fools," *Public Affairs and Philosophy* 6 (1977): 317–44.

13. For discussions of how rules facilitate repeated interaction, see Robert Axelrod, *The Evolution of Cooperation* (New York: Basic Books, 1984); Andrew Schotter, "The Evolution of Rules," in Richard N. Langlois, ed., *Economics as a Process: Essays in the New Institutional Economics*, pp. 117–33 (Cambridge: Cambridge University Press, 1986); Robert Sugden, *The Economics of Rights, Co-operation, and Welfare* (Oxford: Blackwell, 1986); and R. Sugden, "Spontaneous Order," *Journal of Economic Perspectives* 3 (1989): 85–97.

Morishima argues that the adoption of Confucian ethics during the Meiji period produced an economically functional civic code that contributed to Japan's long-run commercial success. Similarly, Ramsey McMullen attributes the decline of the Roman Empire to a failure by the Roman state to encourage social norms capable of reining in corruption. And Greif extends this argument to the commercial success of Western traders during the Middle Ages. See Avner Greif, "Reputation and Coalitions in Medieval Trade: Evidence on the Maghribi Traders," *Journal of Economic History* 49 (1989): 857–82; Avner Greif, "Institutions and International Trade: Lessons from the Commerical Revolution," *American Economic Review* 82 (1992): 128–33; Avner Grief, "Cultural Beliefs and the Organization of Society: A Historical and Theoretical Reflection on Collectivist and Individualistic Societies," *Journal of Political Economy* 102 (1994): 912–50; Ramsey McMullen, *Corruption and the Decline of Rome* (New Haven: Yale University Press, 1988); and Michio Morishima, *Why Has Japan "Succeeded"? Western Technology and the Japanese Ethos* (Cambridge: Cambridge University Press, 1982). For a discussion of these points and for an extended account of the economic role of social norms, see also Jean-Philippe Platteau, "Behind the Market Stage Where Real Societies Exist—Part I:

When individual preferences do not aggregate to a consistent "collective" interest, as discussed by Kenneth Arrow, these institutions may provide a framework of order that permits collective decision making.[14] Similarly, institutions may coordinate expectations and actions in situations where there are multiple equilibria. A focus on institutions thus permits the theorist to examine mechanisms for dealing with the costs of uncertainty, information acquisition, and transactions rather than assuming a perfect and frictionless market.[15]

The study of regimes is the most prominent example of the institutionalist microeconomic approach in international relations theory. Neoliberal institutionalists explicitly acknowledge the collective rules (norms) that constrain and enable individual choice, but they continue to treat actor identities and interests themselves as preexisting and fixed.[16] And to the extent that they *are* considered, norms (embodied in institutions) derive exclusively from rational egoistic choice.[17] Their origins are thus limited to the preexisting preferences of agents, and their consequences tend to reflect this constraint. Identity thus remains

The Role of Public and Private Order Institutions," *The Journal of Development Studies* 30 (1994): 533–77; and J.-P. Platteau, "Behind the Market Stage Where Real Societies Exist—Part II: The Role of Moral Norms," *The Journal of Development Studies* 30 (1994): 753–817.

14. Kenneth Arrow, *Social Choice and Individual Values* (New Haven: Yale University Press, 1951); Kenneth Schepsle, "Institutional Arrangements and Equilibrium in Multidimensional Voting Models," *American Journal of Political Science* 23 (1979): 27–59; and Kenneth Schepsle and Barry Weingast, "The Institutional Foundations of Committee Power," *American Political Science Review* 81 (1987): 85–104.

15. Douglass North, *Structure and Change in Economic History* (New York: Norton, 1981); D. North, *Institutions, Institutional Change, and Economic Performance* (Cambridge: Cambridge University Press, 1990); and Oliver E. Williamson, *Markets and Hierarchies: Analysis and Antitrust Implications* (New York: Free Press, 1975).

16. See, for example, Robert O. Keohane, *International Institutions and State Power* (Boulder: Westview, 1989); and Stephen D. Krasner, ed., *International Regimes* (Ithaca: Cornell University Press, 1983).
This is not true in the most "sociological" versions of regime theory. For example, Oran Young defines institutions as "recognized practices consisting of easily identifiable roles, coupled with collections of rules or conventions governing relations among the occupants of these roles" (O. Young, "International Regimes: Toward a New Theory of Institutions," *World Politics* 39 [1986]: 107). Young thus explicitly addresses the identities that define agent roles, but it is unusual for neoliberal institutionalists to devote much attention to the constitution of actors themselves (as opposed to the rules that govern actor behavior).

17. Axelrod, *The Evolution of Cooperation*; Keohane, *International Institutions and State Power*; Oye, *Cooperation Under Anarchy*; Philip Pettit, "Virtus Normativa: Rational Choice Perspectives," *Ethics* 100 (1990): 725–55; Edna Ullmann-Margalit, *The Emergence of Norms* (New York: Oxford University Press, 1977).

marginalized, even in more expansive neoliberal institutionalist arguments.[18]

In contrast to the bottom-up view of economic individualism, structural approaches adopt a top-down logic. Structure can be conceptualized as having two aspects: material and social. The material aspect of structure refers to the relative position of subgroups within a society and the distribution of material capabilities among them. Social structure refers to the cultural context of actor behavior—the dominant beliefs and understandings that characterize a society.[19] Most theories of international relations, as already suggested above, have placed far greater emphasis on the material aspects than on the social attributes of structure. And this tendency is evident in structural theories at both the international and the domestic levels of analysis.

At the level of the international system, neorealism's materially grounded view of structure has played an influential intellectual role, particularly in security studies.[20] For neorealists, the structure of the interna-

---

18. To be sure, some rational choice theorists have gone beyond their customary focus on strategy in an effort to model individual preferences and beliefs. Aaron Wildavsky argued, in his 1986 presidential address at the 82d annual meeting of the American Political Science Association, that international relations theorists (and neoliberal institutionalists in particular) should devote greater attention to preference formation. See A. Wildavsky, "Choosing Preferences by Constructing Institutions: A Cultural Theory of Preference Formation," *American Political Science Review* 81 (1987): 3–21. See also Vinod Aggarwal, "A General Theory of Preference Formation" (manuscript); also published, in a different version, as "Obiettivi, Preferenzie, e Giochi: Verso una Teoria della Contrattazione Internazionale," in Paolo Guerrieri and Pier Carlo Padoan, eds., *Politiche Economiche Nazionale e Regimi Internazionali* (Milan: Franco Angeli, 1990); Vinod Aggarwal and Pierre Allan, "Modeling Game Change: The Berlin Deadline, Berlin Wall, and Cuban Missile Crises" (paper prepared for delivery at the 1990 annual meeting of the American Political Science Association, San Francisco, August 29–September 2, 1990); and Michael D. Cohen and Robert Axelrod, "Coping with Complexity: The Adaptive Value of Changing Utility," *American Economic Review* 74 (1984): 30–42. But there is no obvious *rational* explanation for these beliefs (or for the character of actors themselves). Offering such an account, in fact, would take rational choice theorists well into the domain of "substantive" rationality (Weber's *Wertrationalität*)—a move that they have, so far, wisely resisted.

19. Material structures, of course, are interpreted by actors and thus "shade into" social structures. Moreover, social structures themselves may range from the formal and legalistic to the informal and "customary." Even within virtually identical formal structures, behavior may vary widely depending on informal beliefs and practice. While formal laws prohibit jaywalking in many places, for example, the practice of jaywalking varies according to cultural practice—it is widespread in some areas and rare in others.

20. Other systemic theories, based on different material notions of structure, also accord only a minor role to norms and social structures. Wallerstein's modern world system approach, for example, explains international relations as a product of the material nature of the global capitalist system that leads to a hierarchy of power (i.e., core, semiperiphery, periphery) with accompanying institutions

tional system is sketched primarily along a single dimension: the distribution of power, defined in terms of material capabilities. Realism assumes that states generally perceive this balance in an accurate fashion and respond accordingly to secure their own relative advantage wherever possible.[21] And if they fail to do so, they are likely to fall victim to a process of "natural selection" at the international level. Thus the system as a whole rewards realist adaptation. In this approach, customs and beliefs far removed from the distribution of power are relatively unimportant. Norms, where they matter at all, matter only at the discretion of (or in service to) the power structure.[22] Neoliberal institutionalism, on the other hand, more readily allows for the possibility that norms, conventions, and principles may over time become uncoupled from "material" structure, thus exerting a limited independent influence. Even this approach, however, usually focuses on formal treaties and institutions rather than on less formal social expectations. And it grants norms an independent influence only when the (materially) functional imperatives of the international system are relatively modest. Many neoliberal theorists have thus been particularly reluctant to focus on informal structure and norms in the area of security studies.[23]

At the level of the nation-state, analysts have also relied on material or formal notions of structure and functional approaches to the problem of order. For example, Peter Gourevitch, Peter Katzenstein, and Stephen

---

(e.g., strong and weak states). Hegemonic stability theory likewise bases systemic structure on relative power. See Robert Gilpin, *U.S. Power and the Multinational Corporation* (New York: Basic Books, 1975); R. Gilpin, *War and Change in the International System*; and R. Gilpin, *The Political Economy of International Relations* (Princeton: Princeton University Press, 1987). And other cyclic theories trace structure to the long-term fluctuations of the international economy; see Joshua Goldstein, *Long Cycles: Prosperity and War in the Modern Age* (New Haven: Yale University Press, 1988).

21. Another variant of this argument is the "security dilemma," which posits an international structure of insecurity independent of actors' understandings (and relying, instead, on such putatively "objective" factors as the offense-defense balance). But this balance and the dilemma itself are affected by collective beliefs that vary independently of power, as in the cases of the U.S.-British condominium before World War I and the U.S.-European alliance after World War II against the Soviet Union. See Stephen R. Rock, *Why Peace Breaks Out* (Chapel Hill: University of North Carolina Press, 1989); and Stephen M. Walt, *The Origins of Alliances* (Ithaca: Cornell University Press, 1987).

22. For example, see Waltz on socialization and emulation and Posen's account of the sources of nationalism: Kenneth N. Waltz, "The Emerging Structure of International Politics," *International Security* 18 (1994): 44–79; Barry Posen, "Nationalism, the Mass Army, and Military Power," *International Security* 18 (1993): 80–124.

23. See Robert Jervis, "Security Regimes," in Krasner, *International Regimes*, pp. 173–94; R. Jervis, "From Balance to Concert: A Study of International Security Cooperation," *World Politics* 38 (1985): 58–79; and Charles Lipson, "International Cooperation in Economic and Security Affairs," *World Politics* 37 (1984): 1–23.

Krasner have all traced foreign economic or security policies to variations—derived from differences in material capabilities—in state political structures.[24] Others, such as Barry Posen and Jack Snyder, point to similarity in organizational structures (e.g., the pursuit of maximum autonomy and size) to account for similarities in military doctrine.[25] But, as with structural theories at the international level, these domestic structural theories make scant room for cultural norms to exert an independent effect.[26] Conceptions of both the actors and the environment are, in these models, functionally derived from materially "objective" structures.

Both the economic individualist and the structural functionalist approaches are silent, therefore, on what this volume identifies as critical. The authors of the preceding essays find considerable variation in the preferences and character of actors in international politics so that, even when actors face similar constraints, they may respond in different ways. And bringing social, normative structures into sharper focus greatly facilitates an account of behavior in those situations that neorealists and neoliberals find perplexing. The authors of this volume thus explicitly problematize the assumptions—economic rationalism and formal, material structuralism— of the dominant approaches to international relations thought and are consequently able to shed new light on a variety of ways in which norms matter. Their arguments can be grouped into three categories, focusing on: (1) the effects of norms on interests, (2) the ways norms shape instrumental awareness of links between interests and behavior, and (3) the effects of norms on other normative structures (including actor identities). These three effects are shown schematically in figure 12.1 (see also the related discussion and diagram in Jepperson, Wendt, and Katzenstein's essay 2).

---

24. Peter Gourevitch, *Politics in Hard Times: Comparative Responses to International Economic Crises* (Ithaca: Cornell University Press, 1986); Peter J. Katzenstein, ed., *Between Power and Plenty: Foreign Economic Policies of Advanced Industrial States* (Madison: University of Wisconsin Press, 1978); and Stephen D. Krasner, *Defending the National Interest* (Princeton: Princeton University Press, 1978). See also Matthew Evangelista, *Innovation and the Arms Race: How the United States and the Soviet Union Develop New Military Technologies* (Ithaca: Cornell University Press, 1988).

25. Barry Posen, *The Sources of Military Doctrine* (Ithaca: Cornell University Press, 1984); Jack Snyder, *The Ideology of the Offensive* (Ithaca: Cornell University Press, 1984).

26. An exception is Katzenstein's two-volume study of the "corporatist compromise" in the small European states. These states' common ideology of democratic corporatism, resulting from their peculiar vulnerabilities, nevertheless allows for considerable variation, ranging from Swiss, Belgian, and Dutch liberal corporatism to Austrian and Scandinavian brands of social corporatism. Peter J. Katzenstein, *Corporatism and Change: Austria, Switzerland, and the Politics of Industry* (Ithaca: Cornell University Press, 1984); and Katzenstein, *Small States in World Markets: Industrial Policy in Europe* (Ithaca: Cornell University Press, 1985).

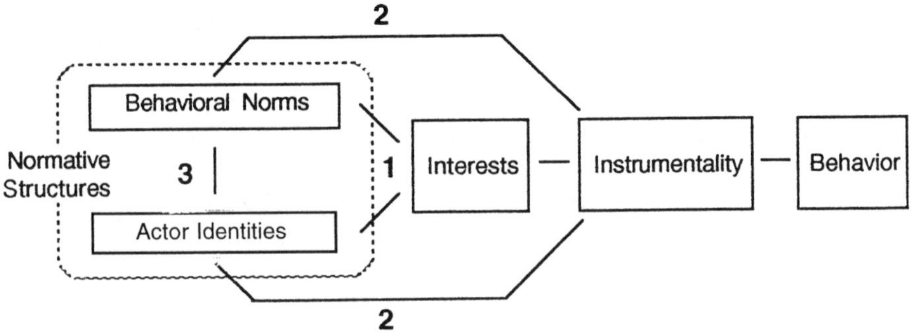

FIGURE 12.1 Consequences of Political Norms

Of course, not every author in this volume emphasizes all three of these effects: the essays trace a variety of different paths through figure 12.1. The remainder of this section considers these paths in more detail, focusing on the three effects of norms listed above.

Interests

Theories of norms address gaps in economic rationalist accounts most directly by examining (rather than merely assuming) the construction of actor interests. In fact, norms may even shape an actor's interests or preferences in ways that contradict the strategic imperative of the international environment (as specified, for example, in realist balance of power theories) or the functional need to cooperate. In Finnemore's analysis of military intervention, for example, states may intervene to accomplish humanitarian objectives even when no obvious economic or strategic rationale is present. As she points out, a realist could identify few interests that explain the commitments Western nations have made in Somalia or Cambodia. But theories that allow for a fuller range of national goals—including humanitarian goals—are more readily able to account for evolving patterns of intervention. Similarly, Eyre and Suchman find evidence that developing countries—which may face very different strategic problems or threats—will tend to buy very similar types of weapons. These choices, they argue, have little to do with the external threats these states face. Instead, global norms of modernity shape the interests of national elites, directing their attention toward symbols of status and power such as advanced (but often inappropriate) weaponry.

Domestic-level norms may also shape state interests in ways that contradict the material international structure. Kier argues that the interwar preferences of both civilian and military leaders for military doctrine (either offensive or defensive) were defined more by internal culture than by the external balance of power. While the military aspired to professionalism, French civilians focused on how military policy affected their own domestic power rather than on external threats. And Risse-Kappen shows that norms associated with the spread of democracy, in a later period of European history, once again shaped preferences—this time promoting a new European alliance structure (NATO). Again, this argument contrasts sharply with the realist expectation that states should ally against the strongest power regardless of ideological or political considerations. Finally, Johnston describes a remarkably constant parabellum strategic culture in China that, he argues, has produced a consistent set of Chinese interests despite changes in China's strategic position with respect to other powers. In fact, Johnston finds that this strategic culture determined the character of China's involvement in external politics, thus reversing the primacy that realism usually accords to the international system.

Instrumentality

Norms affect not only actor interests but also the ways actors connect their preferences to policy choices. More precisely, norms shape the instruments or means that states find available and appropriate. In other words, norms shape actors' awareness and acceptance of the methods and technologies on which they might rely to accomplish their objectives. Some means, of course, may be ignored simply because they are outside the knowledge set of the actors involved, however functional or technologically viable they might otherwise be. Jacob Viner argues, for example, that wealth-seeking states failed for some time to understand that free trade actually served their goals better than mercantilist autarky.[27] And, in security studies, others have pointed to a "cult of the offensive" before World War I that biased choices of military doctrine at a time when defense (as ample evidence from the Boer and Russo-Japanese wars indicated) was functionally more appropriate.[28]

Even when actors are aware of a wide array of means to accomplish their policy objectives, they may nevertheless reject some means as inappropriate because of normative constraints. Finnemore's discussion of military

---

27. Jacob Viner, "Power Versus Plenty as Objectives of Foreign Policy in the Seventeenth and Eighteenth Centuries," *World Politics* 1 (1948): 1–29.
28. Stephen Van Evera, "The Cult of the Offensive and the Origins of the First World War," *International Security* 9 (1984): 58–107; and Snyder, *The Ideology of the Offensive.*

intervention suggests, for example, that while states now have broader humanitarian goals that extend to more parts of the world, they simultaneously confront increasing normative constraints on the enactment of these goals. Unilateral intervention, even to accomplish humanitarian objectives, is seen as less and less appropriate. Ignoring this norm would have both international and domestic consequences that most leaders are unwilling to risk. And not only do such prohibitions shape actors' adoption of means, but their self-understanding (identity) also determines which means are acceptable. Price and Tannenwald thus argue that the widespread tendency to distinguish nuclear and chemical weapons from "conventional" weapons, and to prohibit their use, stems in important ways from norms of "civilization" (including prescriptions for a "civilized state," a particular identity). A civilized state, so the argument goes, cannot adopt these means—even in warfare. A rationalist and functionalist framework, they contend, cannot explain such restrictions when nothing about "unconventional" technologies distinguishes them from any other means of warfare. Burying the enemy alive in trenches and caves, or killing by immolation with a flamethrower, is hard to distinguish functionally (or even morally) from death by gas. Indeed, the World War II firebombing campaigns in Japan were every bit as brutal and even more lethal than the atomic bombs used later. Nor can realism account for the reluctance of states to use unconventional weapons, despite the military advantage they might have produced, in those cases where one combatant had no ability to respond in kind (as in Korea, Vietnam, or the Persian Gulf war). The taboo against chemical, biological, and nuclear weapons thus emerges as a subjective and socially determined phenomenon.

Domestic norms have also helped to define the means that actors consider acceptable and effective. Kier's analysis of interwar France indicates that the norms of military organizational culture, in combination with France's broader political-military culture, had a definitive impact on whether offense or defense was chosen as the guiding principle of military doctrine. Thus norms shape not only civilian and military preferences (as noted above) but also the means for accomplishing these goals. While an offensive military doctrine was objectively possible (and Kier argues that the French military was well aware of German developments in offensive doctrine), the prevailing organizational wisdom among French officers was that short-term conscription afforded no means to attain the operational goals of an offensive strategy. French officers believed themselves constrained, therefore, to a defensive strategy. Similarly, in both Germany and Japan, Berger finds that internal cultural norms dictated an antimilitarist defense policy.[29] These countries still desired security, but the perceived lessons of World War II highlighting the costs of unilateral defense prohibited the development of military tools that were affordable and that, from a realist viewpoint, would enhance security in an anarchic, uncertain world where even allies cannot be trusted completely. Once again, these cultural norms do not simply parallel systemic constraints as neorealism or neoliberalism might suggest; instead, they reflect internal social values and ideas.

Normative Structure

Not only do norms affect actor interests and awareness of instrumentality, but they also affect other normative structures. A good deal of this volume, in fact, is preoccupied with this kind of normative effect (which is circumscribed by the dotted line in figure 12.1). Behavioral norms, for example, may encourage certain national identities. Diffuse, underlying norms at one level may shape specific norms at another level.[30] These effects are complex and frequently appear to be circular, but interactions among norms have profound consequences for the other effects of norms (on interests and instrumentality) already examined.

In their discussion of interactions between norms, several authors in this volume focus on the ways in which identity shapes prevailing rules for behavior. Barnett shows, for example, that pan-Arabism strongly influenced Arab national identities and inter-Arab politics, promoting a specific pattern of strategic ties that required consultation, placed limits on the use of force to resolve intracommunity conflicts, and excluded Western participation. And while the Persian Gulf war signaled an apparent end to whatever pan-Arabism remained in the region, the reemergence of statist identities paved the way for new patterns of sovereign behavior and new alliances with the West. In another case of alliance politics, Risse-Kap-

---

29. Kier and Berger (and Johnston) generally use the term *culture* rather than discussing specific social norms or prescriptions (see the first essay for further discussion of culture and its relationship to norms and identity). But in each of these essays, there is obvious concern for the effects of norms. The military's culture prescribes how the military *ought* to be constituted as a professional organization and how its members *ought* to behave. Kier also shows that these norms were subject to vehement dispute. The culture of the French Left, for example, included very different prescriptions for the role and identity (presumably bourgeois) of the military. Thus, while culture does not always involve prescription, the arguments in these essays do clearly involve cultural norms.

30. See, for example, Robert Axelrod's discussion of "metanorms" in "An Evolutionary Approach to Norms," *American Political Science Review* 80 (1986): 1095–111.

pen argues that democratic identity promoted reciprocity and consultation within the NATO alliance. Even the trying circumstances of the Suez crisis, during which these norms were violated, served only to redouble the efforts of NATO partners to build better institutions for cooperation.[31]

Not only does identity shape rules for behavior within the political environment, but behavioral norms can also interact powerfully with conceptions of identity. Sociologists and anthropologists have noted that some identities are challenged so severely by certain behavioral prescriptions that individuals would rather risk death than permit the two to remain in conflict. For example, Clifford Geertz describes a Balinese elite who marched into Dutch machine-gun fire rather than accept a way of life (and its attendant norms) that included foreign domination.[32] Samurai of ancient Japan committed *seppuku* in the face of lost honor. And in times of starvation, elderly Eskimos committed suicide rather than burden their families.[33] In each of these cases, individuals chose to negate their own identity rather than permit it to conflict with prevailing behavioral norms.[34] And in each case the outcome is, to say the least, puzzling when viewed from the perspective of economic rationalism.

In international relations, sovereignty is the quintessential norm that demarcates global political space into nation-states, thereby conferring legitimacy on some actor conceptions (nationhood, for example) and not on others (such as supranational movements). Indeed, much of this volume focuses on the way prescriptive accounts of the political environment shape conceptions of identity. German and Japanese antimilitarism, as

---

31. Risse-Kappen notes, of course, that these efforts to strengthen the ties binding NATO members were not accepted unanimously. The French-American relationship, in particular, deteriorated from this point onward. But, by the time of the Bermuda summit in March 1957, the British and the Americans had already begun to restore their "special relationship."
For an interesting related discussion of possible conflicts between norms of democracy and deterrence within NATO, see Josef Joffe, "Democracy and Deterrence: What Have They Done to Each Other?" in Linda Miller and Michael J. Smith, eds., *Ideas and Ideals: Essays on Politics in Honor of Stanley Hoffmann*, pp. 108–26 (Boulder: Westview, 1993).
32. Clifford Geertz, *Negara: The Theatre State in Nineteenth-Century Bali* (Princeton: Princeton University Press, 1980).
33. Edgerton, *Rules, Exceptions, and Social Order*, p. 28.
34. In each of these cases, it is not merely identity (as a Balinese, a Japanese, or an Eskimo) that is in conflict with a particular external threat. Rather, identity is in conflict with culturally accepted practice for meeting those threats. One cannot simultaneously remain a good Balinese and allow foreign domination. It is not the *fact* of Dutch rule that is at issue: it is the *acceptance* of this rule that is incompatible with the Balinese elite's identity. The conflict, in each of these cases, is directly between behavioral rules and actor identity. The suggestion of change in the former implies the negation of the latter.

Berger indicates, owes much to the common experience of these two countries as they emerged from World War II (and to the prescriptive consequences that this experience entailed). Of course, their experiences were not identical. Nor were the roles that they adopted: Japan became a merchant state, while Germany sought closer ties to the West through formal alliances and institution-building. But in both cases the collective lessons of wartime defeat became embedded in political-military cultures that have since prevented the development of strong military resources to match the international position of these states.

The preceding discussion has noted that norms at several different *levels* may affect interests and instrumentality. This observation introduces a distinction—which is rarely treated explicitly in the empirical essays of this volume—between "levels of norms." And this distinction suggests, in turn, that norms may interact across these levels. Consider, for example, the vision of systemic structure adopted by hegemonic stability theory or Kenneth Waltz's discussion of systemic polarity, both of which propose a direct link between the distribution of power in the international arena and peace.[35] Despite the materialist orientation of such theories, the structures that they feature involve considerable normative content. A nation-state system, whatever its polarity, requires a conception of the world as meaningfully divided according to state boundaries. And theories that focus on power require some collective knowledge about what national capabilities are meaningful and about how they are distributed. Differences in the content of these underlying structures may thus cause the hegemony of one nation to differ considerably from that of another, as John Ruggie has argued in a comparative analysis of Dutch, British, and American hegemony.[36] And, as several authors in this volume argue, these underlying normative structures greatly influence specific behavioral norms and identities.

Herman suggests, for example, that Soviet perceptions of international structure were multifaceted (and certainly not the product of material structures alone). The *mezhdunarodniki* were informed more by the underlying norms of detente (such as the Basic Principles Agreement) than by those of competitive bipolarity. These structures pushed the New Thinkers toward a reconceptualization of Soviet identity (as a less "revolu-

---

35. See Gilpin, *War and Change in the International System*; Waltz, *Theory of International Politics*.
36. John G. Ruggie, "International Regimes, Transactions, and Change: Embedded Liberalism in the Postwar Economic Order," in Krasner, *International Regimes*, pp. 195–231.

tionary," more "normal" state). And their more liberal interpretation of international structure, in turn, also encouraged the transfer and consideration of new prescriptions for foreign and domestic security policies—of new behavioral norms, in other words. Interestingly, while detente may have encouraged greater pluralism in Soviet domestic politics for a time, Herman also argues that underlying normative structures (of "normalcy") eventually promoted isomorphism and convergence around New Thinking. Several other authors make similar arguments. Eyre and Suchman trace the acquisition of symbolically modern weapons by developing countries to underlying structures of national sovereignty. And Price and Tannenwald's account of weapons taboos relies strongly on preexisting structures of national sovereignty, "civilization," and technology. Before a weapon can be considered unconventional, the distinction between conventional and unconventional weapons in the context of national self-help must be meaningful—it must be institutionalized within existing global structures. And given this context, weapons taboos are not only possible but *functional* since they serve to demarcate civilized and uncivilized nations (another institutionalized distinction). Thus diffuse normative structures and institutions (e.g., "It is meaningful to speak of 'conventional weapons' and 'civilized states'") permit specific identities and behavioral norms (e.g., "We are a civilized nation" or "This weapon is not conventional"), resulting finally in specific means knowledge and behavioral prohibitions (e.g., "We will not use nuclear or chemical weapons").

To summarize, then, norms matter in a wide variety of ways. Diffuse normative structures such as sovereignty or even "civilization" shape the particular identities of actors on the international stage, as well as the rules for enacting these identities. The character of actors also influences the way they interpret the rules that apply to them. And, conversely, these rules limit the types of identities that are viable. This interlocking web of norms, in turn, shapes the particular interests of political agents. And it shapes their beliefs about the available (and best) instruments for achieving their goals. Neorealist and neoliberal theories of international politics offer no comparable model for specifying the interests of actors, nor can they account for persistent differences in interpretation of seemingly objective political structures. For all of these reasons, the sociological turn in international relations theory described here holds considerable promise. Of course, the sociological approach is not without its challenges. But before a consideration of some of these difficulties, a prior question merits discussion: What processes generate social norms?

pretty weak overall

The Sources of Norms

The irony of the criticism of neorealist and neoliberal theory voiced here is that, while the authors of this volume often take existing international relations theory to task for treating the construction of political actors and their preferences as exogenous, the essays that make up the body of this book tend to treat their own core concepts as exogenously given. To be sure, they acknowledge, often explicitly and at some length, that actor identity and behavioral norms are socially constructed. But this is generally a starting point, from which the essays proceed to focus on the impact of these social constructions (which is, after all, their primary concern). Arab, European, Chinese, Japanese, and Soviet political identities are all shown to have a great impact on strategic behavior in international politics . . . an impact that rationalist theory tends to ignore. And in some cases, the historical development of these identities is described, occasionally in detail. But about the *process* of identity construction, the authors have relatively little to say. And without any theory of how such identities are constructed and evolve, this research struggles to contribute more to an understanding of political behavior than the work that it criticizes.

The next task for scholars such as these is to take their own criticisms seriously and to develop more explicitly theoretical propositions about the construction of sociopolitical facts—the process of building collective norms and political identities.[37] At least some of the authors in this volume might resist this task on the grounds that such generalizations are impossible. Indeed, while the essays are both "descriptive and explanatory," as Jepperson, Wendt, and Katzenstein observe in essay 2, they often seem to view the generative processes of norm building and evolution as unique to the cases they examine. And yet there is considerable material in these essays from which to construct plausible hypotheses about norm creation that might be applied to other cases.

---

37. We substitute the term *norm building* for *norm creation* because norms are rarely (if ever) created de novo. Instead, they rely on preexisting cultural knowledge and institutions. Nevertheless, the importance of particular behavioral regulations and identities does rise and fall over time. In some cases, this process may occur so rapidly that a new norm appears to be "created," as in the case of prohibitions against the use of nuclear weapons. Undeniably, this norm drew on prohibitions against the use of other "unconventional" weapons. But since not all highly destructive weapons are taboo, it is not unreasonable to ask how this particular norm, pertaining to this weapon, came into being. Although we avoid the term for the sake of clarity, we therefore do not believe it is meaningless to ask how norms are "created."

This section takes up the task of identifying candidates for generalizable theory—*not* about the ways that social constructions cause (or enable, or give meaning to) certain political outcomes but about the sources of norms themselves. Where do collective political norms come from? How are the identities of states, military organizations, alliances, and other international actors constructed? In this section, we seek to distill, from the essays in this volume and from the broader social science literature, some tentative answers to these questions. In fact, the previous section has already pointed to one source of norms: other norms (possibly at other levels). But it is difficult to generalize about this source of norms because of their historical specificity and because of the potential for circular reasoning ("norms cause norms"). Therefore, we will not revisit the interaction between norms discussed above but focuses instead on three other processes that generate, maintain, and change political norms: (1) ecological, (2) social, and (3) internal.

Ecological processes derive from the pattern of relations between actors and their environment. Social processes stem from the relations between actors themselves. And, as the term implies, internal processes spring from the internal characteristics of actors. Internal processes, therefore, are reductive, while both ecological and social processes are irreducible to individual actors (and thus, in some sense, systemic).

Ecological Processes

Ecological processes result from the patterned interaction of actors and their environment. In some cases, actors confront a rapidly (or dramatically) changing environment.[38] In other cases, continuities are more obvious; and in still other cases, the characteristics of the environment are unclear. The third category of cases, which we will consider first, point to the role of ambiguity in social knowledge. Ambiguity is not a function of particular actors or of the environment itself in the abstract. A political situation appears ambiguous only *to* actors, depending on their relationship to it. Arguments about the role of ambiguity in the creation of social norms have an old pedigree. In 1939, Muzafer Sherif described a series of experiments that suggested that collective, normative agreement was much easier in ambiguous settings (e.g., those in which a clear frame of reference is lacking) than in more clear-cut situa-

---

38. See Harry Eckstein, "A Culturalist Theory of Political Change," *American Political Science Review* 82 (1988): 789–804.

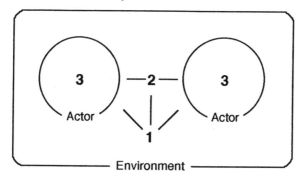

FIGURE 12.2 Three Sources of Political Norms

tions.[39] His argument finds some confirmation in this volume. Herman proposes, for example, that in the Soviet Union the vision articulated by Gorbachev "was sufficiently vague to permit political forces with relatively moderate agendas to claim allegiance to a common ideal even as they strived to head off any radical change."[40] At the outset, at least, politicians with different agendas could all claim to be New Thinkers. And while he is not so explicit, Barnett provides numerous clues that pan-Arab identity, to the extent that it existed, relied on a similar ambiguity to smooth over many important differences among Arab nations. When events such as the Baghdad Pact and, later, the Persian Gulf war brought these differences into sharper relief, the weak norms (and identities) of Arabism suffered greatly.

But the effects of ambiguity are . . . ambiguous. The authors of this volume take pains to point out that almost every aspect of international politics requires considerable social interpretation, no matter how incontrovertible materialists may take it to be. What counts, therefore, as an unambiguous international situation? By what metric can social scientists determine that one norm is more ambiguous than another? Put another way, how can differences in the degree of normative ambiguity be mea-

---

39. Sherif projected a dot of light on a wall in an otherwise darkened room. The autokinetic effect makes the dot appear to move, and Sherif investigated the extent to which a confederate could influence judgments about this movement. But even in this scenario, there is nothing inherently ambiguous about the situation that Sherif created. It was ambiguous only given the autokinetic effect and the visual acuity of the human subjects that Sherif used in his experiment. See Muzafer Sherif, *The Psychology of Social Norms* (New York: Harper, 1939).
40. See Herman, essay 8 in this volume, p. 287. Herman also notes that while virtually all New Thinkers he interviewed invoked the idea of a "normal country" to describe their hopes for their nation's future, "not all of them meant precisely the same thing" (Herman, essay 8 in this volume, p. 294). Here again ambiguity serves a useful role.

sured? And should one assume that ambiguous norms are *always* easier to establish than highly specified ones? After all, prohibitionary norms regarding the use of nuclear weapons flourished only after nuclear weapons were clearly distinguished from other weapons. In this case, clarity rather than ambiguity hastened the institutionalization of the nuclear taboo. The ways in which ambiguity relates to norm and identity construction thus remain in need of elaboration.

A second ecological process argument addresses the problem of norm and identity maintenance rather than their emergence. This argument stresses the passage of time and continuity in the environment, positing simply that iteration strengthens norms, quite apart from any other efforts to reinforce or undermine them. In other words, the longer a norm goes unchallenged, the more it tends to "solidify." Finnemore places great emphasis, for example, on the growth and solidification of humanitarian norms (including, but not limited to, norms of humanitarian intervention such as multilateralism) over "the past fifty or one hundred years."[41] And Price and Tannenwald link iteration to both norms and identities; compliance with weapons taboos over time, they contend, both strengthens non-use norms and "reinforces the identity of states."[42]

While the iteration hypothesis seems plausible and is appealing in its simplicity, it seems equally possible that the opposite might sometimes occur: norms or identities, although unchallenged, might simply "fade away" over time, pass out of style, or for a variety of reasons become irrelevant. What, for example, of the prohibition in the Hague Regulations of 1907 against the attack or bombardment of undefended towns, villages, dwellings, or buildings? Rather than being challenged directly, this norm has simply lost force with the passage of time and the development of modern mass armies requiring a "nation at arms."[43] Since time is not

41. Finnemore also notes that the passage of time permits greater institutionalization in formal international organizations such as the United Nations; see Finnemore, essay 5, p. 160.
42. Berger's finding that support for new political-military cultures in Germany and Japan increased slowly over time also fits well with the iteration hypothesis. See Price and Tannenwald, essay 4, and Berger, essay 9.
43. Nor is it sufficient to explain away the decline of the "aerial bombardment of undefended areas" prohibition simply by pointing out that its frequent violation undermined the norm. Chemical weapons, after all, were widely used in World War I; yet the taboo against chemical weapons is now strong, while aerial bombardment has become permissible.
Some might even argue that this norm, while often violated, remains in effect. To be sure, attacking undefended *noncombatants* would appear to violate current norms of warfare. But it seems difficult to argue that attacking undefended *cities* or *buildings* is a similar violation in light of the role that so many civilian technologies (telecommunications, power generation, etc.) can play in modern war-

equally kind to all norms, some further refinement of this hypothesis seems in order.

A third ecological process argument expressed in this volume addresses *changes* in norms. This proposition—that dramatic shocks in the environment (to the international system, for example) loosen commitments to existing identities and behavioral norms—is an institutionalist's version of Mancur Olson's argument in *The Rise and Decline of Nations*.[44] But whereas Olson focused on the ways in which systemic shocks eliminate redistributive agreements and redefine material incentives within a society, this volume opens the question of how such agreements and incentives themselves are constructed. One way of putting the argument is to say that an obvious shock to the international (or domestic) political system provides political capital for the proponents of change within a political system. The shock "proves" that politics must be conducted differently . . . or thought about differently. In this volume, the shock hypothesis finds its strongest exposition in Berger's discussion of German and Japanese identities after World War II. Berger argues that a national identity or a political-military culture will change rapidly only when it is "challenged by a major external shock" and "placed under great strain." Otherwise, cultural change is likely to be slow and incremental. World War II, he contends, provided just such a massive shock to the political-military cultures of militarism in Germany and Japan. Similarly, Barnett suggests that the shock of the Persian Gulf war helped to crystallize the dependence of Gulf Arab states on the West, reinforced emergent statism, and thereby allowed what had previously been taboo—a security alliance with the United States.

One difficulty with this type of argument lies in defining what counts as a shock. In Berger's case, the impact of World War II seems so decisive that one would expect it to qualify as a systemic shock whatever the definition. This allows Berger to avoid definitional issues. But how shocking

---

fare. The aerial bombardment of Iraq during the Persian Gulf war—and particularly the American emphasis on precision-guided munitions targeted at specific buildings—illustrates this distinction.
44. Mancur Olson, *The Rise and Decline of Nations: Economic Growth, Stagflation, and Social Rigidities* (New Haven: Yale University Press, 1982). See also Stephen Krasner, "State Power and the Structure of Foreign Trade," *World Politics* 28 (1976): 317–47. On the twin shocks of World War I and the Depression, see Jeff Frieden, "Sectoral Conflict and U.S. Foreign Economic Policy, 1914–1940," in G. John Ikenberry, David Lake, and Michael Mastanduno, eds., *The State and American Foreign Economic Policy*, pp. 59–90 (Ithaca: Cornell University Press, 1988). And on the oil shocks of the 1970s, see G. John Ikenberry, "Market Solutions for State Problems: The International and Domestic Politics of American Oil Decontrol," in Ikenberry, Lake, and Mastanduno, *The State and American Foreign Economic Policy*, pp. 151–77.

must shocks be? What is it about the Persian Gulf war that qualifies it as a major systemic shock? Moreover, the "rally 'round the flag" effect must be reconciled with this general argument. Some shocks, at least initially, reinforce rather than challenge existing collective beliefs. The Japanese attack on Pearl Harbor, for example, strongly reinforced American identity. On the other hand, it served to undermine norms of isolationism that until that time had been quite strong. Not only does greater attention to the circumstances under which shocks will reinforce rather than challenge existing norms seem desirable, but also the relationship of shocks at one level to norms at another deserves further exploration. Barnett alludes to this phenomenon in his discussion of the *intifada*, which not only provided a shock to domestic norms of democracy within Israel but, as a result, also called into question the alliance relationship of Israel to the United States.

Social Processes

Social process arguments of norm building take the form of generalizations about the way human beings, organizations, states, or other political agents interact.[45] At least two such arguments appear in the foregoing essays. The first of these is also perhaps the most straightforward: norms are spread through a simple process of social diffusion.[46] Although they do not elaborate, several authors allude to this process. Risse-Kappen, for example, finds that "transgovernmental networks" greatly facilitated the development of a common identity (and norms of reciprocity and consultation) within NATO. Finnemore suggests that international organizations encouraged a similar process involving the spread of humanitarian norms, while Herman argues that New Thinking in the Soviet Union was "essentially homegrown . . . [and] nurtured in an oppressive system."[47]

In the most explicit discussion of diffusion, Eyre and Suchman suggest that affinities such as common heritage or language may serve to increase

45. For an account of norm creation as a problem of strategic interaction, see Arthur Stein, "Normative Equilibrium and International Politics" (paper presented at the conference "Norms and Emulation in International and Domestic Behavior," Palm Springs, Calif., January 13–16, 1994).
46. This notion has been developed in some detail by sociologists and by political scientists who focus on "epistemic communities." See Mary Fennell and Richard Warnecke, *The Diffusion of Medical Innovations: An Applied Network Analysis* (New York: Plenum Press, 1988); Claude Fischer and Glenn Carroll, "Telephone and Automobile Diffusion in the United States, 1902–1937," *American Journal of Sociology* 93 (1988): 1153–78; Peter Hall, *The Political Power of Economic Ideas: Keynesianism Across Nations* (Princeton: Princeton University Press, 1989); and "Knowledge, Power, and International Policy Coordination," *International Organization* 46 (special issue, 1992):
47. Herman, essay 8 in this volume, p. 310.

the chances for norm or identity diffusion. Unfortunately, they do not take up this argument in any detail in the empirical section of their essay.

As appealing and straightforward as the social diffusion hypothesis is, it leaves many questions unanswered. Are new collective understandings expected simply to seep across "transgovernmental networks" like ever-widening inkblots? If not, then what operational criteria will allow us to identify the most prominent paths for diffusion? And *which* ideas will be communicated across these linkages? Why humanitarian norms instead of self-help ones, particularly given the rise of highly nationalist identities in some areas of the globe? Even if these questions are addressed, a more fundamental problem remains. Jepperson, Wendt, and Katzenstein, following Durkheim, call attention to the difference between *shared* understandings and *collective* understandings—the latter presumably being the concern of this volume.[48] But diffusion seems to explain the sharing rather than the "collectivizing" of norms. The process by which shared knowledge becomes a collective norm remains underspecified. While these difficulties deserve further attention, the empirical essays nevertheless make a strong case that social diffusion is responsible for the emergence of many of the norms considered in this volume.

A second social process account of norm building draws on "interaction role theory" and suggests that norms—and particularly identity—emerge from a process of in-group/out-group differentiation and social role definition.[49] It may encourage New Thinking in the Soviet Union, for example, to be able to oppose it to the "old thinking" of Brezhnev and Gromyko. Identifying the out-group helps to reify its supposed values (old thinking), which may then be opposed to in-group values. Another statement of the role relation argument can be found in Barnett's discussion of security communities in the Middle East. Barnett argues that

---

48. For a belief (or norm) to be shared does not necessarily mean that it is institutionalized or, in some other way, a property of a collective. On this point, see also Ronald L. Jepperson and Ann Swidler, "What Properties of Culture Should We Measure?" *Poetics* 22 (1993/94). Saying that a certain percentage of Americans have patriotic beliefs is different, for example, from saying that Americans as such are patriotic. Only the latter is a statement of a collective norm. But despite this discussion, it often seems difficult to distinguish between the two in practice. Is New Thinking the shared representation of a new foreign policy agenda among Soviet elites or is it a property of some collective, ultimately institutionalized in *perestroika*? Perhaps it is both. But, if so, it is not clear what evidence of its presence would help us to distinguish between its shared existence and its collective existence.

49. Stephen Walker, ed., *Role Theory and Foreign Policy Analysis* (Durham: Duke University Press, 1987); and S. Walker, "Symbolic Interactionism and International Politics: Role Theory's Contribution to International Organization," in Martha Cottam and Chih-yu Shih, eds., *Contending Dramas: A Cognitive Approach to International Organization*, pp. 19–38 (New York: Praeger, 1992).

identity is profoundly social—a product of continuous debate within the community, of evolving historical narratives, and of competing social portrayals (some of which posed great challenges to leaders in the Middle East). Barnett thus goes beyond simple in-group/out-group distinctions to argue that social interaction may produce a variety of relational (and interrelated) identities as actors take up various roles with respect to each other. Israel's role as an American ally in the Middle East, for example, also promotes (arguably) a democratic Israeli identity. And the Iraq-Turkey Treaty of 1955 "sent shockwaves through the Arab World" because it placed Iraq in a new role vis-à-vis the West and thereby challenged its Arab identity—an identity that was itself founded on role relations and the perceived threat from the West (a homogeneous out-group) to Arab states.

Barnett's discussion of role relations points the way to a more complex account of roles in international politics. Despite the advantages of parsimony, a degree of complexity may be partly unavoidable, since nations (not to mention other political actors) can relate to each other in so many different ways. Kal Holsti offers a typology of no fewer than seventeen specific national role conceptions defined, at least in part, through social interaction.[50] These national roles include: regional leader, independent, faithful ally, liberator, and defender of the faith. And, more recently, Richard Herrmann has proposed twenty-seven categories of national role images based on differential social comparisons of capability, culture, and threat. Herrmann does go on to argue, however, that only a small subset of these (notably: enemy, ally, degenerate, colonial, and imperial) is likely to be common.[51] Finally, Martin Sampson and Stephen Walker tie these role conceptions to cultural norms in a study that speaks directly to

50. Kal J. Holsti, "National Role Conceptions in the Study of Foreign Policy," *International Studies Quarterly* 14 (1970): 233–309.

51. See Richard K. Herrmann, *Perceptions and Behavior in Soviet Foreign Policy* (Pittsburgh: University of Pittsburgh Press, 1985); R. K. Herrmann, "The Power of Perceptions in Foreign-Policy Decision Making: Do Views of the Soviet Union Determine the Policy Choices of American Leaders?" *American Journal of Political Science* 30 (1986): 841–75; and Richard K. Herrmann and Michael P. Fischerkeller, "A Cognitive Strategic Approach to International Relations: Theory and Practice in the Persian Gulf" (manuscript, 1994).

Herrmann argues that states, in the course of their interaction, make judgments about their relative capabilities (superior, comparable, or inferior), cultures (superior, comparable, or inferior), and interactions (threat, opportunity, or mutual interest). Different combinations of these judgments yield twenty-seven categories. A smaller number are likely to dominate, however, because some combinations make little sense. It seems unlikely, for example, that an "enemy" should simultaneously be

Berger's discussion of militarism in Germany and Japan. Sampson and Walker offer a different comparison—between France and Japan—but reach much the same conclusion: that differences in national role conceptions (identity) explain decisions about militarization in these two societies.[52]

Typologies of national roles take an important step toward analytical generalization. But role relation arguments do not always offer clear predictions, perhaps because they emphasize a highly contingent process of role creation. It remains unclear which social roles will become linked together and whether or not such linkages must be functional. Nor is it obvious how role relation theory should account for different levels of analysis. It may well make sense, after all, to speak both of a single Japanese identity (which relies greatly on Japanese distinctiveness—a relational concept) and of many Japanese identities, some more nationalist than others (indeed, Berger makes such an argument for both Japan and Germany). Much the same could be said for the Israeli identities that Barnett examines. While two-level games have received considerable attention among international relations theorists, two-level roles have not.

Internal Processes

Unlike other paths to the generation of norms, internal processes operate *within* political actors. For this reason, scholars interested in the phenomena of collectives often ignore internal processes, usually with the dismissive rationale that psychological or rational choice arguments cannot account for the generation of truly *social* norms or knowledge structures. Judith Goldstein and Robert Keohane, in their recent book *Ideas and Foreign Policy*, thus take pains to distinguish their work from psychological

---

viewed as posing a "high" threat and yet having "low" capabilities. One of the components of such a role image will, over time, be revised. Some will object to Herrmann's and other similar approaches to identity on the grounds that they overlook "intrinsic" components of identity, focusing instead only on relational aspects of identity definition. Whether identity is more an intrinsic property of actors or a function of their social interaction and environment is impossible to say. At the extreme, however, the contention that identity is fully and solely intrinsic *precludes* any investigation of its sources—they would consequently be held unknowable, as in rationalist theory, discussed above. This contention would have the effect, therefore, of foreclosing the very kind of inquiry that this volume (and this essay, in particular) undertakes.

52. Martin W. Sampson and Stephen W. Walker, "Cultural Norms and National Roles: A Comparison of Japan and France," in Walker, *Role Theory and Foreign Policy Analysis*, pp. 105–22.

approaches.[53] And in his paper on the evolution of Soviet New Thinking, Herman takes both rational choice and psychological theories to task for their failure to integrate social and political processes into their accounts of learning.[54] But despite this implied criticism, Herman's subject matter lends itself easily to an internal process interpretation. In fact, Douglas Blum has offered an account of the evolving New Thinking in the Soviet Union that parallels Herman's in many respects but explicitly emphasizes cognitive rather than social processes.[55]

While internal processes do not themselves operate at the level of the collective, their effects may nevertheless be felt at other levels. In fact, Johnston's reliance on cognitive mapping to construct an image of the parabellum strategic culture in Maoist China is a tacit adoption of this internal process premise.[56] Limitations of space do not permit a full discussion here of the ways individual-level processes may result in collective political norms. But three examples should suffice to give some indication of the variety of internal process arguments.

The first of these examples emphasizes a psychological process and is closely related to one of the social process arguments discussed above. Role-relation hypotheses about the construction of norms emphasize a process of social interaction encouraging role definition. But the definition of social roles might also, as considerable research suggests, stem from cognitive or motivational processes within individuals. In fact, the reluctance of the authors of this volume to place emphasis on people's *need* for identity in social relations—a need so strong that they will invent in-group and out-group identities and differences even when there is no rational basis for doing so—makes sense only in the light of this volume's general preoccupation with social rather than individual processes.[57] Marilyn

---

53. Goldstein and Keohane, *Ideas and Foreign Policy.*
54. Eyre and Suchman, Finnemore, and Risse-Kappen also distance their arguments from rational choice approaches.
55. Douglas W. Blum, "The Soviet Foreign Policy Belief System: Beliefs, Politics, and Foreign Policy Outcomes," *International Studies Quarterly* 37 (1993): 373–94.
56. See Johnston, essay 7 in this volume; also see Katzenstein's discussion in essay 13 of efforts by both rational choice and cognitive theorists to provide a microfoundation for the analysis of collective norms.
57. On in-group and out-group identities, see Richard Cottam, *Foreign Policy Motivation: A General Theory and a Case Study* (Pittsburgh: University of Pittsburgh Press, 1977); Paul A. Kowert, "The Cognitive Origins of International Norms: Identity Norms and the 1956 Suez Crisis" (paper presented at the 35th annual meeting of the International Studies Association, Washington, D.C., March 28–April 1, 1994); Penelope Oakes and John C. Turner, "Distinctiveness and the Salience of Social Category Memberships: Is There an Automatic Perceptual Bias Towards Novelty?" *European Journal of Social Psychology* 16 (1986): 325–44; Henri Tajfel, ed., *Differentiation Between Social Groups: Studies in the Social Psychology of Intergroup Relations* (London: Academic Press, 1978); H.

Brewer's theory of "optimal distinctiveness," however, traces identity formation to the individual's need to perceive distinctions between self and other, and to justify one's own behavior.[58] Taking another approach, John Turner argues that social identities emerge instead from cognitive miserliness. According to Turner, "the first question determining group-belongingness is not 'Do I like these other individuals?' but 'Who am I?' "[59] Turner's self-categorization theory emphasizes the mental heuristics that cause people, for reasons of cognitive efficiency, to focus selectively on information that confirms simplifying group stereotypes. In the case of either cognitive or motivational arguments, the result is the same: stable in-group and out-group identities—precisely the sort of identity on which this book places so much emphasis.[60]

Another internal process argument focuses on the use and interpretation of language. It would, of course, be inappropriate to identify the "linguistic" path to norm construction *solely* with an internal process since neither the grammar nor the content of a language is reducible to individual speakers. But, by the same token, speech act processes begin their opera-

Tajfel, *Human Groups and Social Categories: Studies in Social Psychology* (Cambridge: Cambridge University Press, 1981); and H. Tajfel et al., "Social Categorization and Intergroup Behavior," *European Journal of Social Psychology* 1 (1971): 149–78.

58. Marilyn Brewer, "The Social Self: On Being the Same and Different at the Same Time," *Personality and Social Psychology Bulletin* 17 (1991): 475–82; and M. Brewer, "The Role of Distinctiveness in Social Identity and Group Behavior," in Michael Hogg and Dominic Abrams, eds., *Group Motivation: Social Psychological Perspectives* (London: Harvester Wheatsheaf, 1993).

59. John C. Turner, "Towards a Cognitive Redefinition of the Social Group," in Henri Tajfel, ed., *Social Identity and Intergroup Relations*, p. 16 (Cambridge: Cambridge University Press, 1982). For a comparative analysis of several other cognitive theories of group identification, see Richard R. Lau, "Individual and Contextual Influences on Group Identification," *Social Psychology Quarterly* 52 (1989): 220–31.

60. This discussion of internal psychological processes has, for reasons of brevity, focused only on the microfoundation of identity. But cognitive and motivational psychologists have also undertaken numerous research projects investigating the construction of behavioral norms. See, among others, Jerry Burger, "Desire for Control and Conformity to a Perceived Norm," *Journal of Personality and Social Psychology* 53 (1987): 355–60; Martha Cottam, "Problem Representation After the Cold War" (paper presented at the 35th annual meeting of the International Studies Association, Washington, D.C., March 28–April 1, 1994); Daniel Kahneman and Dale Miller, "Norm Theory: Comparing Reality to Its Alternatives," *Psychological Review* 93 (1986): 136–53; Brian Ripley and Dwain Mefford, "The Cognitive Foundations of Regime Theory" (paper prepared for delivery at the 1987 annual meeting of the American Political Science Association, Chicago, 1987); Donald Sylvan and Stuart Thorson, "Ontologies, Problem Representation, and the Cuban Missile Crisis," *Journal of Conflict Resolution* 36 (1992): 709–32; and Stephen Walker, "The Motivational Foundations of Political Belief Systems: A Re-Analysis of the Operational Code Construct," *International Studies Quarterly* 27 (1983): 179–202. Jonathan Mercer has also employed Turner's self-categorization theory to argue that both the identities and the behavioral repertoires of nation-states are likely to be constructed in ways that mirror common realist assumptions; see J. Mercer, "Anarchy and Identity," *International Organization* 49 (1995): 229–52.

tion at the level of the individual.[61] Livia Polanyi et al. argue, for example, that "we need comprehensive textual analyses if we wish to identify and explore cultural expectations of normal and abnormal conduct, good or bad self and other identifications, possible or impossible or necessary historical development within particular security cultures."[62] Their objective, rephrased in the terms of this book, is a linguistic account of norms and identity.[63] To this end, they propose a "linguistic discourse model" that identifies regularized processes and multiple levels of speech: speech events (gestures, facial expressions, and so on), words, phrases, clauses, sentences, multi-sentences, and finally texts. Textual instruction devices—including analogies, metaphors, and varied forms of negation or emphasis—all serve as definitional wayposts in the construction of a discourse. In a similar vein, both Friedrich Kratochwil and Nicholas Onuf argue that social meanings and institutions are constructed out of the practical linguistic rules that operate within individuals but that have profound normative, constructive effects.[64] In a sense, these linguistic theorists go one step further than cognitive psychologists: they argue that people must not only make sense out of their world, but must then communicate those mental representations to others . . . and that the process of communication *is* a process of making sense. This process inevitably, they would argue, produces norms (in fact, the process *is* the production of norms). And while the "semantic dimensions of the language" permit some normative constructions, they render other constructions unintelligible.[65]

---

61. Our claim here is more modest than it may seem. We do not contend that language can be reduced entirely to the behavior of individuals or that individuals are even "primary." It may largely rely, instead, on collective representations that exist completely apart from the thoughts or actions of any particular person. But the act of speech itself does begin with the human (biological and psychological) capacity for speech. In the following discussion, we briefly consider several regularities in the processes of speech that may serve to generate norms.

62. Livia Polanyi et al., "Retelling Cold War Stories: Uncovering Cultural Meanings with Linguistic Discourse Analysis" (working paper, "Security Discourse in the Cold War Era," Center for Studies of Social Change, New School for Social Research, New York, 1993), p. 8.

63. For related work, see Hayward Alker, "Fairy Tales, Tragedies, and World Histories: Towards Interpretive Story Grammars as Possibilist World Models," *Behaviormetrika* 21 (1987): 1–28; H. Alker et al., "Text Modeling for International Politics: A Tourist's Guide to RELATUS," in Valerie M. Hudson, ed., *Artificial Intelligence and International Politics* (Boulder: Westview, 1991), pp. 97–126; and Sergio Alvarado, *Understanding Editorial Text: A Computer Model of Argument Comprehension* (Boston: Kluwer Academic Publishers, 1990).

64. Kratochwil, *Rules, Norms, and Decisions*; and Onuf, *World of Our Making*.

65. On the semantic dimensions of language, see Kratochwil, *Rules, Norms, and Decisions*. Also see Onuf, *World of Our Making*, pp. 66–95.

Although psychological and linguistic theories are often set in opposition to rational choice theories—at least in the field of international relations—rigid distinctions of this type are illusory. The cognitive efficiency invoked by Turner's self-categorization theory might easily be restated in rational choice terms. And Hayward Alker and his colleagues working in the fields of discourse analysis, artificial intelligence, and computer modeling have already examined in some detail the links between storytelling, motivation, and economic activity in iterated Prisoner's Dilemma games.[66] In these theories, strategic agency plays an important role. But the internal process version of agency emphasizes not the normative constructions that interact through the behavior of actors who subscribe to them, but rather the (exogenously given) goals of agents themselves. A more straightforward restatement of the argument in rational choice terms is that the efforts of utility maximizers to attain efficient outcomes encourage norm construction as a device that reduces transaction costs.[67] There is, of course, a large body of neoliberal research (on declining hegemony and regimes) that has focused almost exclusively on this pathway to norm creation.[68] For neoliberals, norms are strictly functional at their inception, serving the (innate or given) interests of strategic actors.[69] They reduce transaction costs and facilitate agreement among political

Neither Kratochwil nor Onuf would classify his own work under the rubric of "individual-level processes." To do so would be akin to suggesting that a language can be *private* (a claim that Onuf specifically rejects; see Onuf, *World of Our Making*, pp. 47–49, esp. n. 12, and pp. 78–81). But our claim here is not that language or the social rules it engenders are reducible to individual behavior. Rather, they stem from a process of communication that, like processes of thinking, feeling, and (rationally) choosing, begins its operation at an individual level. For a related effort to bridge the gap between psychology and discourse, focusing on the concept of voice—which once again grows out of individual speech acts but which also acquires collective, cultural content—see the discussion of identity politics in Edward Sampson, "Identity Politics: Challenges to Psychology's Understanding," *American Psychologist* 48 (1993): 1219–30.

66. Hayward Alker, Roger Hurwitz, and Karen Rothkin, "Fairy Tales Can Come True: Narrative Constructions of Prisoner's Dilemma Game Play" (paper presented at the annual meeting of the American Economic Association, Anaheim, Calif., January 5, 1993).

67. See Platteau, "Behind the Market Stage Where Real Societies Exist—Part I"; Platteau, "Behind the Market Stage Where Real Societies Exist—Part II"; Sugden, *The Economics of Rights, Co-operation, and Welfare*; and Ullmann-Margalit, *The Emergence of Norms*.

68. Robert O. Keohane, *After Hegemony: Cooperation and Discord in the World Political Economy* (Princeton: Princeton University Press, 1984); and Krasner, *International Regimes*.

69. Price and Tannenwald (essay 4 in this volume) give an example of the role of agency in creating a norm that turned out not to be very functional from the point of view of the agent. They observe that the efforts of the chemical industry to play up developments in chemical warfare in order to secure tariff protection facilitated the creation of a chemical weapons taboo—something that the industry evidently had not expected and that ultimately ran counter to its business interests.

agents.[70] And they help to encourage behavior congenial to the interests (and identity) of the hegemon that (neoliberals assume) created them.

Whatever the flaws of internal process accounts of norm building, it seems inappropriate to dismiss them merely because they are not (by definition) "social" theories of collective knowledge. As a wide variety of cognitive, linguistic, and economic research shows, norms may also arise from the aggregate effects of processes that operate within individuals. Moreover, such reductive arguments may have another practical advantage: they are often better specified and may lead more easily to generalizable predictions than do the sociological theories emphasized in this volume. Remedying the "weakness" of the latter theories is, of course, precisely the justification for books such as this one.

To be sure, internal process theories are not immune to criticism. A particularly important gap in the individualist approach is the problem of aggregating individual choices. The aggregation problem is common to psychological, linguistic, and rational choice approaches. But it has received particular attention from rational choice theorists, who point out that social order can be difficult to understand from the point of view of atomistic choice when strategic situations do not encourage stability or equilibrium. As noted above, Arrow has demonstrated that certain individual preference orderings yield no consistent social preference ordering.[71] And Jon Elster argues that many strategic interactions produce either no equilibrium, multiple equilibria, or unstable equilibria.[72] Both Arrow and Elster suggest that norms themselves may play a role in resolving these aggregation problems. Elster argues that norms afford predictability, and for Arrow they take the form of "consensus on social objectives" that align individual interests. In either case, the implication is that norms precede and constrain the strategic interaction of individuals. For this reason, Alexander Field argues that an economic approach cannot explain institutions.[73] If they are to be productive, efforts to account for norms on the basis of internal processes must squarely address the aggregation problem.

---

70. Deborah Avant, "The New Institutional Economics and the Origin of Norms of Warfare" (paper presented at the 35th annual meeting of the International Studies Association, Washington, D.C., March 28–April 1, 1994); Keohane, *After Hegemony*; North, *Institutions, Institutional Change, and Economic Performance*; and Katja Weber, "Hierarchy Amidst Anarchy: Transaction Costs and International Cooperation" (Ph.D. diss., University of California, Los Angeles, 1992).

71. Arrow, *Social Choice and Individual Values*.

72. Elster, *The Cement of Society*.

73. Alexander Field, "Microeconomics, Norms, and Rationality," *Economic Development and Cultural Change* 32 (1984): 683–711.

The authors of the preceding essays provide ample reason to suspect that further investigation of the social construction of norms and identity would be fruitful. They offer an intriguing variety of proto-theories (schematically summarized in figure 12.2) about the genesis of norms and identities. While some of these theories have been tested in other disciplines (sociology and psychology, for example), they deserve similar attention from students of international politics.

Challenges in the Study of Norms

In addition to the issue of generalizing about norm construction, the sociological turn in international relations theory faces several other theoretical and methodological challenges. This section examines five of them. The first, confronted in some way by the authors of each empirical paper in this volume, is to decide on criteria for identifying and measuring norms. It is not always apparent how, from a social scientific perspective, one can be certain that a norm is present. A second problem—in some sense the reverse of the first—is that norms often seem to be all too present. In other words, the field may suffer from an embarrassment of norms. A third problem is that norms figure in efforts to account for both continuity and change, with occasionally confusing results. A fourth problem is the difficulty of specifying the relationship between the normative and the material worlds. And finally, the fifth problem is the potentially confounding effect of agency on normative analysis. The criticisms offered in this section do not reflect a desire to undermine or reject the sociological approach to international relations. In fact, as we have argued, many of these problems are shared by (and may be more intractable within) the mainstream rationalist research program.[74] The following discussion is simply an attempt to stake out challenges that lie ahead. Addressing these challenges will improve research efforts that make up the "sociological turn."

Knowing Norms

This volume generally treats norms as collective beliefs regulating the behavior and identity of actors. But that definition leaves important questions unanswered. To what degree must norms be shared before they can be called collective? And on what does their regulative authority depend?

---

74. For a recent, general critique of the rationalist research program, see Donald P. Green and Ian Shapiro, *Pathologies of Rational Choice Theory* (New Haven: Yale University Press, 1994).

To argue that certain norms are influential is to suggest that their effect may vary with their strength. Thus Price and Tannenwald indicate that, as the taboo against using unconventional weapons has become more robust, the use of these weapons has declined. But by what criteria can one assess norm robustness (independent of the very outcomes one seeks to explain)? Some have linked a norm's strength to its institutionalization.[75] But this simply pushes the problem back to one of measuring institutionalization—no easy task itself.[76] And the chore is complicated by the widely accepted notion that some behavioral violations of norms do not necessarily invalidate the norms. At a certain point violations clearly do begin to undermine norms. But how do we assess that point?

Rational choice scholars have faced similar problems in identifying and measuring actor preferences or interests. Relying on what actors say can be misleading because of the strategic role of deception in public statements. Judging interests according to behavior, on the other hand, invites circularity. The unhappy compromise is to rely on "revealed preferences"—desires exhibited in past behavior. But such a move assumes that preferences do not change (or at least that they have not *yet* changed). And as game theorists themselves emphasize, action is not a sure guide to preferences since it also reflects actors' assessments of strategic circumstances and constraints.[77]

In general, students of norms have taken two different approaches to identifying their subject matter. The first is to focus their attention on what actors do—that is, whether actor behavior complies with norms or not (and, if not, how other actors respond). But if some degree of deviation from norms does not necessarily imply their repudiation, then this "revealed norm" method is unreliable.[78] A case of incest, for example, does

75. Keohane, *International Institutions and State Power*, pp. 4–5; Kratochwil, *Rules, Norms, and Decisions*, p. 62.
76. This problem has also plagued the neoliberal institutionalist research program. It has been difficult to assess regime strength without referring to criteria that are conceptually related to regime effects. Discussions of different criteria for assessing institutionalization include: Keohane, *International Institutions and State Power*, pp. 4–5; Joseph Nye, "Nuclear Learning and U.S.-Soviet Security Regimes," *International Organization* 41 (1987): 375; and Roger Smith, "Institutionalization as a Measure of Regime Stability: Insights for International Regime Analysis from the Study of Domestic Politics," *Millennium: Journal of International Studies* 18 (1989): 234–36. For a related discussion in comparative politics, see Samuel Huntington, *Political Order in Changing Societies* (New Haven: Yale University Press, 1968).
77. Snidal, "The Game Theory of International Politics."
78. See Blake and Davis, "Norms, Values, and Sanctions"; Edgerton, *Rules, Exceptions, and Social Order*; and Friedrich Kratochwil and John G. Ruggie, "International Organization: A State of the Art on an Art of the State," *International Organization* 40, no. 4 (Autumn 1986): 753–76.

not by itself invalidate prohibitions against incest. Likewise, in Risse-Kappen's study, the violation of an alliance consultation norm during the Suez crisis did not lead to a collapse of the Atlantic security community or to the illegitimacy of its norms. Nor have the many violations of the chemical weapons taboo led (so far) to its irrelevance. And, at any rate, this approach permits only the post hoc recognition of norms.

A second approach is to focus on what actors say—that is, how they justify or defend their actions. Because an interpretive approach sees norms as communication devices, perhaps their presence and efficacy are indeed better judged by the pleas for understanding, rationales, and normative justifications than by behavior itself. The problem here, as for the rational choice theorist, is to distinguish manipulation and deception from more "genuine" forms of communication. How should one interpret proclamations of support for nuclear nonproliferation when a nation simultaneously works to build nuclear weapons . . . or worse, claims that nuclear or chemical weapons are too horrible to use, even when preparations for attack are under way? At the very least, then, it seems necessary to study *both* rhetoric *and* behavior over time—an approach adopted by most of the essays in this volume.

Efforts to identify and measure norms also suffer from a bias toward "the norm that worked." Most studies of norms, including those in this volume, focus only on a single, specific norm—or, at most, on a small set of norms. Typically, the norms under consideration are effective norms or ones that seem to have obvious consequences.[79] Yet, in order to understand how norms work, studies must allow for more variation: the success or failure, existence or obsolescence of norms. A companion study to Price and Tannenwald's examining weapons taboos that did *not* take hold would be instructive.[80] But normative research has tended to overlook the emerging norms that never quite made it, the portfolio of identities that were never realized, and the international structures that might have been. These counterfactuals, analyzed in conjunction with comparable cases of success, should lead to a more substantial research program.[81] Addressing

---

79. See, for example, James Mayall, *Nationalism and International Society* (Cambridge: Cambridge University Press, 1990); James Lee Ray, "The Abolition of Slavery and the End of International War," *International Organization* 43 (1989): 405–39; Janice E. Thomson, *Mercenaries, Pirates, and Sovereigns* (Princeton: Princeton University Press, 1994).

80. In the case of prohibitions during World War II, see Jeffrey W. Legro, *Cooperation Under Fire: Anglo-German Restraint During World War II* (Ithaca: Cornell University Press, 1995).

81. A related bias in the study of norms is the "good norms" problem. Analysts tend to focus on those issues that are normatively desirable—e.g., the spread of democracy, the rise of human rights,

these identification and measurement problems is a formidable task for work in this area—but not one that is necessarily intractable. And the particular virtue of the empirical essays in this volume, unlike research that overlooks behavioral norms and that fails to problematize actor identity, is that these essays have at least begun to confront these important variables.

An Embarrassment of Norms

An equally troubling issue for those working in the sociological tradition is not the difficulty of identifying norms but their ubiquity. Several of the empirical essays in this volume make it clear that norms are multifaceted and that many different identities can exist side by side in a collectivity.[82] In one sense, this is an advantage of sociological analysis rather than a problem, since it allows a richer account of political behavior. Moreover, while rationalists must assume that preferences are ordered transitively in order to aggregate interests in a collectivity, the sociological approach faces no similar constraint with respect to norms or identities. But because multiple norms can influence actors—with competing or even contradictory prescriptions for behavior and for identity—it is difficult to predict which norms will be most influential. Without clear conceptual definition and convincing measures of norm salience, the consequences of norms are likely to be indeterminate. One can almost always identify, post hoc, a norm to explain a given behavior.[83]

Examples of this problem are manifold. Finnemore recognizes that increasingly dense organization in global politics has facilitated the rise of humanitarian norms, but she argues that these norms run counter to other important institutional structures such as sovereignty and self-help. It is clear neither in the abstract nor in the concrete terms of the case that

---

the integration of world society, and prohibitions against the use of force. Yet undesirable norms are equally possible. Examples include norms of military autonomy and the use of force, economic domination, the acceptability of intrastate violence (e.g., civil war), and the disintegrative tendencies that exist in international politics (e.g., nationalism, religious exclusivity). These issues too deserve attention from the emerging sociological approach. By focusing on security affairs, this volume takes a step toward exploring a fuller range of normative consequences. But "bad" or threatening norms remain understudied.

82. Diana Richards, "Interests and Identities in International Relations Theory" (paper presented at the annual meeting of the Midwest Political Science Association, Chicago, April 6–8, 1995). The analogous problem for rationalist (economic individualist) international relations theory is the prospect of an "embarrassment of interests" in which any behavior can be explained by reference to some interest (often inferred ex post facto from the behavior).

83. For a lucid discussion of these problems, see Stephen Welch, *The Concept of Political Culture* (New York: St. Martin's Press, 1993).

Finnemore discusses whether humanitarian or "isolationist" norms will ultimately prevail. But whatever the outcome, one could easily point to norms as a cause![84] Or, to take another example, Barnett discusses a variety of competing regional, Arab, and statist identities. Each of these identities has different implications for behavior. But, once again, which will prevail?

Perhaps a resolution to this problem will come from a reintegration of different levels of analysis (or more specifically, "levels of norms") within the sociological approach.[85] A neorealist would almost certainly argue that there is a hierarchy of global political structures such that norms must conform to certain structures even though they may violate others.[86] When basic national interests are challenged, for example, a self-help system will punish the states that do not respond appropriately. Structures such as these are functionally dominant in a neorealist analysis. And, even if we do not accept neorealist functionalism, the need for a "replacement" framework relating collective beliefs at different levels to one another is clear.[87] Otherwise, it is difficult to avoid the criticism that "anything goes"—that any behavior can be explained with reference to some norm. In reaction to this position, several of the authors in this volume, including Eyre and Suchman, Finnemore, and Price and Tannenwald, focus on normative structures that they take to be decisive at the international level. Others (Berger, Kier, and Johnston) accord more

---

84. Finnemore might reasonably object that she never claims to make a deterministic argument about whether, when, or which norms will prevail. On the contrary, she specifically disavows such an intention because of the multiplicity of relevant norms and because of exogenous influences on state interests and behavior. Our point, therefore, is the *same* as Finnemore's—that multiple and conflicting international norms limit the prospects for predictive generalization.

85. A constructivist might offer a much different solution to this problem. The meaning and force of rules, from a constructivist perspective, rely on the possibility of their violation. Affirming a norm thus *requires* its potential negation—otherwise the norm ceases to have meaning. In a more general sense, all norms must therefore explain their violation as well as their affirmation. David Campbell argues, in this vein, that the modern discourse of international security and foreign policy depends on (and therefore must define and create) insecurity and foreignness; see David Campbell, *Writing Security: United States Foreign Policy and the Politics of Identity* (Minneapolis: University of Minnesota Press, 1992). From this perspective, the causal questions that concern the authors of this volume simply become irrelevant when understood in a larger interpretive context.

86. Eyre and Suchman note, citing Anthony Giddens, that the current world system can actually be decomposed into several systems: an information system, a nation-state system, a capitalist economy, and so on. They warn that we should not exaggerate the extent to which these systems are integrated. See Eyre and Suchman, essay 3 in this volume; and A. Giddens, *The Nation-State and Violence* (Berkeley: University of California Press, 1987).

87. Swidler labels a less functionalist alternative to the traditional realist framework "sociological realism." See Ann Swidler, "The Ideal Society," *American Behavioral Scientist* 34 (1991): 563–80.

impact to domestic structures. The great variety of norms that these authors identify, however, makes a cross-level, integrative analysis a challenging task.

Continuity and Change

Another complication for research on political norms is the difficulty of accounting for both stasis *and* change. One of the central contributions of the sociological turn in international relations theory is its move away from static conceptions of fixed identities and interests. This volume problematizes both state and other collective identities. But while social interaction among actors may produce new collective identities, existing normative structures also shape the properties and behavior of agents. Consequently, the sociological approach pursues an explanation both for patterns of stability *and* for cases of change.

At the heart of the problem is the inertial force of cultural constructs such as norms: this inertia tells us why certain patterns persist, but not why they change. Of course, a culture may *consistently* demonstrate patterns of change, as Harry Eckstein contends in the case of modern societies, but then the problem becomes one of accounting for observed continuities (themselves a deviation from more fluid patterns).[88] The problem, in other words, is accounting for both stasis and change in the same culture. To do so, normative theorists must usually appeal to ad hoc arguments about forces external to a given culture. Thus Berger focuses on the shock of World War II to explain the rise of new cultures in Japan and Germany. And while Arab and regional identities may explain continuity in the Gulf Cooperation Council, they cannot *also* explain its demise and the emergence of alliances with the West. So Barnett, like Berger, invokes an external shock: the Persian Gulf war.

While cultures may certainly have multiple themes (or subcultures) that are in tension, explanations for the hierarchy of these different cultural elements (including multiple identities) are poorly developed at present. Several approaches to this difficulty have been proposed. Ann Swidler sees culture, for example, as a "tool kit" from which actors choose different types of actions. But, as already noted, if the available tools allow for both any action *and* its opposite, then their explanatory role is suspect. Indeed, Swidler accords exogenous "structural constraints" and "historical circumstances" substantial influence in dictating which "strategy of action" is

---

88. Eckstein, "A Culturalist Theory of Political Change."

selected.[89] Similarly, in this volume Kier grants considerable leeway to historical circumstance in shaping both the organizational culture of the French military and the fears of civilian elites. And yet a greater appreciation for the hierarchical integration of cultural themes suggests at least a degree of cultural and normative stability. Finnemore, although clearly concerned with change and evolution in humanitarian norms over a 150-year period, thus maintains that normative change may be guided by principles of logical consistency. Expanding definitions of "humanity" led naturally (although perhaps not unavoidably) to the expansion of associated human rights. Likewise, Eckstein finds evidence of a more uniform process at work in culture. He proposes that changes in culture occur in response to environmental changes and argues that these changes will ordinarily work to maintain existing patterns.[90] He allows that rapid contextual changes and even the instrumental efforts of agents (such as revolutions) may lead to cultural discontinuities. But these sources of change cannot themselves be explained within the logic of culture itself.

Constructivists appear to offer another approach to the problem of change and continuity, relying on a conceptualization that views structures and agents as linked in a dialectical synthesis. The interaction among agents and between agents and structures both produces and reproduces these entities.[91] The key issue, of course, is whether "reproduction" or "different" production (i.e., change) will occur. And to answer this question, constructivists once again appeal to exogenous historical conditions. While historical contingency is undoubtedly central to understanding specific events, it does not easily lend itself to theoretical generalization.[92] In

---

89. Ann Swidler, "Culture in Action: Symbols and Strategies," *American Sociological Review* 51 (1986): 280.

90. Eckstein, "A Culturalist Theory of Political Change."

91. John G. Ruggie, "Continuity and Transformation in the World Polity: Toward a Neorealist Synthesis," *World Politics* 35, no. 2 (January 1983): 261–85; J. Ruggie, "Territoriality and Beyond: Problematizing Modernity in International Relations," *International Organization* 47 (1993): 845–65; Alexander Wendt, "Anarchy Is What States Make of It: The Social Construction of Power Politics," *International Organization* 46, no. 2 (Spring 1992), pp. 391–425; and Alexander Wendt, "Collective Identity Formation and the International State," *American Political Science Review* 88, no. 2 (June 1994): 384–96.

92. As a possible first step toward such generalization, some theorists emphasize the way that small historical events can have enormous and persistent implications. Thus, an appreciation of historical contingency does not require that *anything* could happen. See, for example, the discussion of path dependence and punctuated equilibrium in Brian Arthur, "Competing Technologies, Increasing Returns, and Lock-in by Historical Events," *Economic Journal* 99 (1989): 116–31. Also see Stephen Krasner, "Sovereignty: An Institutional Perspective," in James Caporaso, ed., *The Elusive State: International and Comparative Perspectives* (Newbury Park, Calif.: Sage, 1989).

fact, this line of reasoning suggests that social scientific inquiry can offer nothing more than a historically descriptive and highly contingent account. Although this proposition is inconsistent with the overall tenor of this volume, it occasionally finds exposition in the empirical essays (in Price and Tannenwald's observation, for example, that the chemical weapons taboo owes much to a series of fortuitous events). But while some historians and interpretive theorists might find common ground in this approach, it seems too pessimistic and too restrictive.

The bulk of the studies in this volume suggest yet another approach to change and continuity. While a single culture may be inadequate to explain both change and stasis, an appreciation for levels of culture—that is, different facets of culture nested within one another—may help. The preceding essays suggest multiple levels of nested norms, ranging from organizational culture (Kier) to strategic culture (Johnston) to political-military culture (Berger, Kier, and perhaps Herman) to international technological and political norms (Barnett, Eyre and Suchman, Finnemore, Price and Tannenwald, Risse-Kappen). This solution is remarkably similar to the rationalist attempts to deal with anomalies by demonstrating that actors are maximizing their welfare in different nested games.[93] Of course, the danger for realists of both traditional and sociological stripe is an endless appeal to nests within nests of interests or norms. But in general the authors in this volume adopt the position that norms and identity are constructed through regularized processes, often with relatively stable effects. Even their discussions of historical contingency do not imply that all conceivable outcomes were equally likely.

Material and Normative Worlds

While the sociological perspective rejects the realist preoccupation with uniquely material forces, students of norms cannot afford to ignore the material world. Norms do not float "freely," unencumbered by any physical reality. They are attached to real physical environments and are promoted by real human agents (though norms, of course, are not themselves material). But the relationship of normative to material structures is rarely examined or explicitly theorized, despite the likelihood that the influence of norms may be related to the characteristics of the material structures in

---

93. George Tsebelis, *Nested Games: Rational Choice in Comparative Politics* (Berkeley: University of California Press, 1990).

which they are embedded or the qualities of the actors that adopt or promote them. Norms backed by the United States are likely to become more
widespread and effectual than otherwise similar norms originating in Lux-
embourg. While the differing capabilities of these two nations are
undoubtedly a matter of interpretation, it is difficult to ignore the overwhelming material contrasts.

Scientific, technological, political, economic, religious, and even
artistic structures all involve both formal and informal, physical and
interpretive components. While Kier argues in this volume that the
French choice of strategic doctrine in the interwar period did not derive
functionally from perceptions about the state of military technology
(favoring either a defensive or offensive stance), the history of warfare
offers many examples of how technology was decisive in other ways.
When Americans rushed to develop nuclear weapons, their expectations
were eventually rewarded by a Japanese surrender.[94] Very often, as in the
latter case, actors are keenly aware of such technological change, even
though they may be unsure of its impact. And perhaps the material
aspects of cultural and religious similarities between Israel and the
United States help to explain the close relationship between these two
nations. Or, to take another example, the economic and technological
performance of the United States undoubtedly contributed strongly to
the persuasiveness of Western values reflected in Soviet New Thinking
(*and* helps to explain why the West itself seemed to derive so little from
Soviet norms during the interactions that Herman describes). In each of
these instances, it is hard to overlook the possible connection between
material developments and normative changes. To suggest a role for
material influences on norms does not imply that norms stem directly
from physical capabilities as realism more or less expects. But neither do
collective understandings exist in a material vacuum. And a more synthetic conceptualization of the interaction between the material and the
interpretive worlds remains necessary.[95]

---

94. A determined constructivist might argue that, even in the case of nuclear weapons, technology
was not initially decisive. Indeed, postwar U.S. presidents have often worried that nuclear weapons
will not be sufficient to deter the threat of the day. We should also point out that Kier's argument
applies equally to nuclear weapons—the technology does not clearly favor a particular military doctrine apart from the various (different) ways it is socially interpreted.
95. To take one example of such a synthesis, Keegan offers an intriguing historical account of the
interaction between cultures of warfare and technology; see John Keegan, *A History of Warfare* (New
York: Knopf, 1993).

Agency and Norms

One of the most important effects of norms, as we noted earlier in this essay, is their influence on the interests of political actors. But we also found the reverse to be true: agents sometimes set out to manipulate or change norms. Actors may be well aware of the potential advantages accruing to those who control certain norms. Hans Morgenthau thus warned long ago that rationalizations and justifications should not be allowed to conceal the true nature of foreign policy.[96] Identifying the "true nature" of foreign policy is no easy task. But some agents are clearly able to use norms in an instrumental fashion to further their own interests rather than simply being held captive to various normative mandates.[97]

In World War II, countries sometimes abided by restrictions on the use of force (e.g., strategic bombing, submarine warfare) not out of ethical restraint but instead to retain domestic or international support. At the same time, some states tried to arrange situations that would cast another party as a "violator" and thus justify otherwise prohibited measures in retaliation.[98] In such cases, both support and violation of prohibitionary norms were functions of strategic calculations that had little to do with the norms themselves. In this volume, Eyre and Suchman, Johnston, and Herman all point to other ways that leaders use norms instrumentally to enhance their own positions. The development of New Thinking in the Soviet Union, for example, was not merely an academic exercise and cannot be divorced from the strategic behavior of the *mezhdunarodniki* who promoted these new understandings in an attempt to change the course of Soviet foreign policy and, perhaps, to improve their own positions. In this case, promoting a certain redefinition of the situation (as a "failed" Brezhnev-Gromyko foreign policy) served the political interests of the liberal reformers.[99]

---

96. But he also cautioned against assuming that moral limitations play no role in international politics; see Hans Morgenthau, *Politics Among Nations* (New York: Knopf, 1973), pp. 230–31.

97. A nice statement of this point is Foucault's claim that "the successes of history belong to those who are capable of seizing these rules, to replace those who had used them, to disguise themselves so as to pervert them, invert their meaning, and redirect them against those who had initially imposed them." See Michel Foucault, "Nietzsche, Genealogy, History," in Paul Rabinow, ed., *The Foucault Reader*, pp. 85–86 (New York: Pantheon, 1984); also see Richard Price, "A Genealogy of the Chemical Weapons Taboo," *International Organization* 49 (1995): 73–103.

98. Legro, *Cooperation Under Fire.*

99. Herman would also argue that the Soviet reformers took political risks for which they occasionally paid a price (personal communication with the authors). We do not mean to suggest, therefore, that the norms they promoted can easily be construed as completely self-serving. Especially during the early years of the Reagan administration, the reformers left themselves open to harsh criticism from Soviet conservatives.

Even an actor's own identity can be manipulated for instrumental reasons. Kier provides an excellent example of this process, noting the extent to which military organizations construct their identity for strategic purposes: battlefield effectiveness requires a self-conception incorporating professionalism, obedience, and esprit de corps. In this case, effectiveness relies on strategic behavior designed to encourage particular (military) identities. Or, to take another example, Barnett argues that Israel manipulated its own identity for strategic advantage. Israeli leaders emphasized Israel's Western and democratic character so that Americans would see "something in themselves when they saw Israel." American "identification" with Israel was critical, Israeli leaders realized, to the continued flow of financial support from the United States.

These examples illustrate a distinction, which is not always acknowledged in the empirical papers of this volume, between *internal* and *external* norms.[100] Internal norms are representations of the environment or constructions of identity as it appears to an actor. External norms, on the other hand, are representations of situations or actors to others.[101] Some might object to this distinction on the grounds that, because norms are a collective phenomenon, all norms must be external. At the level of the individual, this is true. An internal norm for an individual is not a norm at all but merely an idea. But many of the actors discussed in this volume are not individuals but collectives (foreign policy elites, militaries, and nations, for example). For such actors, identity is different from the presentation of identity—though both involve regulative content. And the fact that actors manipulate self-presentation (that is, external norms) strategically does not mean that such norms are irrelevant. On the contrary, these manipulations would be pointless if norms did not matter.[102] The instrumental manipulation of norms poses a more fundamental problem, however, than distinguishing internal from external norms. If

---

100. See, however, Finnemore's distinction between identity and identification.

101. On such "external" representations, see Erving Goffman, *The Presentation of Self in Everyday Life* (Garden City, N.Y.: Doubleday, 1959); and A. Paul Hare and Herbert Blumberg, *Dramaturgical Analysis of Social Interaction* (New York: Praeger, 1988).

102. In fact, these manipulations may come to matter even to the manipulators; see Kevin McKillop, Michael Berzonsky, and Barry Schlenker, "The Impact of Self-Presentations on Self-Beliefs: Effects of Social Identity and Self-Presentational Context," *Journal of Personality* 60 (1992): 789–808; and Barry Schlenker and J. T. Trudeau, "The Impact of Self-Presentations on Private Self-Beliefs: Effects of Prior Self-Beliefs and Misattribution," *Journal of Personality and Social Psychology* 58 (1990): 22–32. For similar dynamics in "myths" and strategic culture, see Jack Snyder, *Myths of Empire* (Ithaca: Cornell University Press, 1991); and Charles A. Kupchan, *The Vulnerability of Empire* (Ithaca: Cornell University Press, 1994).

actors self-consciously manipulate external norms, then the social scientific study of norms, their origins, and consequences is greatly complicated. Not only do the variables in such an analysis interact, but some variables (agents) are directly *aware* of other variables. In such cases, many social scientific models must be applied with greater caution than usual. Linear regression models, for example, might be inappropriate for certain analyses. Such instrumental awareness may violate assumptions about the independence of error components in the linear model, and it is very likely to introduce additional problems of multicollinearity and serial correlation. Quasi-experimental research designs also suffer when their subjects "know too much." Researchers should be cautious when their subjects are not only aware of the "experiment" but also actively trying to change its parameters. For these reasons, the instrumental manipulation of norms poses special difficulties for social scientific analysis. This issue, in turn, foreshadows a more philosophical problem—the double hermeneutic (the interpretation by scholars of the interpretations of actors) in social science.[103]

Since scholarly inquiry is itself interpretation (thus the product of agency), can it presume to investigate interpretive phenomena such as norms without, by the nature of the scientific enterprise, altering their meanings? This is not the place for an extended discussion of the philosophy of social science, but a few concrete examples drawn from the empirical essays may help to clarify the point. It seems almost undeniable that the norms of New Thinking in the Soviet Union, parabellum strategic culture in Maoist China, or reciprocity among NATO allies mean the same thing to the authors of this volume as they did (or do) to the relevant political actors themselves. Can the effects of sociopolitical norms then be stated precisely, or are these effects (like the norms themselves) so much a matter of interpretation that any attempt to measure them distorts them? The analogy in physics is the Heisenberg uncertainty principle. But while physicists no longer find efforts to locate electrons within the electron shell of an atom meaningful (because this cannot be known except by measurement procedures that themselves define the possible locations), this volume undertakes a closely analogous task in the domain of international politics. The practical objection, therefore, is that there should be a Heisenberg uncertainty principle of interpretive analysis. And if the nor-

---

103. Anthony Giddens, *The Constitution of Society: Outline of the Theory of Structuration* (Cambridge: Cambridge University Press, 1984); and A. Giddens, *New Rules of Sociological Method: A Positive Critique of Interpretative Sociologies* (Stanford: Stanford University Press, 1993).

mative interpretations of actors are themselves unknowable except by an equally interpretive procedure carried out by social scientists, then it is no longer clear who or what is being studied.

This is a problem that confronts all social science.[104] Those working in the sociological tradition are neither more nor less prone to it (although they may be more likely to recognize it). The criterion for judging international relations scholarship is not therefore the extent to which it replaces interpretation with "objectivity." Rather, it is the extent to which it provides better historical accounts and raises new questions.[105] And while the other essays of this volume are mostly concerned with assessing the plausibility of norm-based portraits of political behavior, this paper argues that they succeed in doing much more. Not only are they able to tell stories about international politics that realists, neoliberals, and neorealist structuralists (among others) have difficulty telling, but they also point the way toward numerous intriguing relationships between underlying cultural structures, norms, identities, interests, and behavior—relationships that students of international politics have scarcely begun to investigate.

So messy

As this essay has suggested, there are (if anything) too many rather than too few plausible generalizations that describe the causes and effects of norms. The practical task is therefore to sort out unrelated, rival, and contradictory hypotheses rather than to reject the whole enterprise on the grounds that social norms can operate in a wide variety of ways. One method of doing this is to search for regularized pathways between norms, identities, interests, and behavior. One need not subscribe to functionalism in order to search for such patterned behavior. Indeed, there is considerable danger that a naïvely teleological view of norm function will obscure both "deeper" causes and counterfactual hypotheses. Many of the authors in this volume consequently resist functionalist arguments. But whether or not social norms are functional, this volume finds evidence that they are in some cases quite stable and that when they change they do

---

104. Thomas S. Kuhn, *The Structure of Scientific Revolutions* (Chicago: University of Chicago Press, 1962). See also Hayward Alker, "The Return of Practical Reason" (unpublished review article, 1993); and Martin Hollis, *The Cunning of Reason* (Cambridge: Cambridge University Press, 1987).
105. What counts as a "better" historical argument is too philosophical a question to examine here in any detail. Simply put, however, "good" arguments are a matter of interpretation within the culture of social scientists. This certainly does not mean that all claims to historical "truth" are equally valid; social science offers many criteria for evaluating the performance of theories. These criteria are the social norms that make the professional study of international relations possible.

so in predictable ways (in response to shocks or ambiguities, for example). General accounts of the causes and consequences of norms, such as those offered in this essay, thus provide a basis for rejecting the pessimistic claim that every interpretation of political reality is unique in all respects and that theory is impossible.

In fact, this volume is ambitious in its approach to international relations theory. It rejects the extreme historical constructivist position that generalizations about how actors will interpret their environment (political or otherwise) are impossible. Moreover, it rejects the materialist position that the physical reality of this environment governs cultural interpretations of it. And it rejects the tendency of rationalist theory to assume fixed goals and identities of actors. To attempt theory simultaneously on all of these fronts—that is, theory within the upper-right quadrant of Jepperson, Wendt, and Katzenstein's figure 2.1—would go beyond ambition if the authors also rejected the insights of scholarship in the other quadrants. But while this volume identifies shortcomings in the micro- and macrofoundations of mainstream approaches, it does not reject realism, liberalism, or their structural variants out of hand. In a broad analytical sense, there is a complementary relationship between the sociological perspective and these more traditional approaches. Accounts (and theories) of norms and identity fill gaps where other perspectives fall short. Of course, this complementarity can be overstated. A realist would not argue that threatened states will buy weapons for their symbolic (rather than military) value or that they will avoid other weapons—chemical or nuclear— that might serve their interests. Nor would a realist expect a nation to select a military doctrine that satisfies certain domestic and organizational interests but that leaves the nation woefully unprepared for the next war. Eyre and Suchman, Price and Tannenwald, and Kier—to take three examples—do not merely supplement realism; to a point, at least, they challenge it.[106]

The payoff of the sociological turn in international relations theory, therefore, is not merely incremental (i.e., more detailed historical accounts than are otherwise possible). It redirects scholars' attention toward consequential variables and processes that might otherwise go unnoticed. Norms and identity are both facets of culture and, as such, have been invis-

---

106. Nor would a realist argue that states will enter into alliance relationships for reasons of cultural affinity or normative symbolism. Barnett and Risse-Kappen both contrast their approaches, therefore, to realist theories of alliance formation such as that proposed by Walt. See Walt, *The Origins of Alliances*.

ible to scholars who choose to investigate more tangible, less value-laden phenomena. This essay highlights the analytical and explanatory significance of social norms. The final essay of the volume argues that this work is also timely and particularly relevant for problems of the post–Cold War order.

13 • Conclusion: National Security in a Changing World

Peter J. Katzenstein

> *The approach of "rational behavior," as it is typically interpreted,*
> *leads to a remarkably mute theory. . . . The purely economic man*
> *is indeed close to being a social moron. Economic theory has been*
> *much preoccupied with this rational fool decked in the glory of his*
> *one all-purpose preference ordering. To make room for the different*
> *concepts related to his behavior we need a more elaborate structure.*
> —Amartya Sen
> *"Rational Fools"*

In the late phases of the Cold War American discussions about a newly emerging international order concentrated on changes in America's global position. Paul Kennedy's historical analysis of the rise and fall of great powers argued that, for reasons of material resources, like all other great powers America was destined to lose its position of international preeminence.[1] At best, the United States could affect the process of secular decline. Francis Fukuyama's essay and subsequent book "The End of History"[2] analyzed a broader range of factors and concluded, to the contrary, that America had prevailed in the great ideological conflicts of the twentieth century. Focusing on material resources and ideology, these two analyses reached dramatically different conclusions.

For their careful readings and critical comments of previous drafts, I would like to thank the members of the project; the participants at the Social Science Research Council/MacArthur Workshops at the University of Minnesota and Stanford University in 1994; and Emanuel Adler, Tom Christensen, Lynn Eden, Gunther Hellmann, Ron Jepperson, Mary F. Katzenstein, Robert Keohane, Jonathan Kirshner, Audie Klotz, Atul Kohli, Henry Nau, Jack Snyder, Janice Thomson, Stephen Walt, Alexander Wendt, and two anonymous readers for Columbia University Press.
1. Paul Kennedy, *The Rise and the Fall of the Great Powers: Economic Change and Military Conflict from 1500 to 2000* (New York: Random House, 1987).
2. Francis Fukuyama, "The End of History," *National Interest*, no. 16 (Summer 1989): 3–18; Francis Fukuyama, *The End of History and the Last Man* (New York: Free Press, 1992).

In a similar vein, the disintegration of the Soviet Union is yielding a proliferation of different interpretations. Some insist on the primacy of strong states, the continuity of the balance of power, and the inescapability of war.[3] Others see a pandemonium of ethnic wars and wars of rage caused by the excessive weakness, not strength, of contemporary states.[4] Still others argue that states will continue to be central actors, together with large corporations, regional security communities, and world civilizations.[5] Our interpretations shape the views we hold of the international position of the United States and change in the world at large.

Adherents and critics of the two leading paradigms of international relations, realism and liberalism, did not succeed in explaining adequately, let alone predicting, the peaceful end of the Cold War and the breakup of the Soviet Union. It is, therefore, a good time to reconsider the conventional analytical assumptions that informed national security studies during the Cold War. Are there alternative ways of conceptualizing international relations and security affairs that are both systematic and comprehensive?

Our understanding of the international security environment inevitably privileges some factors at the expense of others. This book is no exception. It emphasizes culture and identity as important determinants of national security policy. Without a particular political problem or a well-specified research question, it makes little sense to privilege cultural context over material forces or problematic, constructed state identities over unproblematic, given ones. By the same logic, it makes little sense to make the opposite mistake, focusing exclusively on material resources or assuming that state identities can be taken for granted.

This essay argues that in American scholarship realism and liberalism

3. Kenneth N. Waltz, "The New World Order," *Millennium: Journal of International Studies* 22, no. 2 (1993): 187–95; Kenneth N. Waltz, "The Emerging Structure of International Politics," *International Security* 18, no. 2 Fall 1993): 44–79; John J. Mearsheimer, "Back to the Future: Instability in Europe After the Cold War," *International Security* 15, no. 1 (Summer 1990): 5–56.

4. Daniel P. Moynihan, *Pandaemonium: Ethnicity in International Politics* (New York: Oxford University Press, 1993); Ken Jowitt, *New World Disorder: The Leninist Extinction* (Berkeley: University of California Press, 1992).

5. U.S. Congress, Office of Technology Assessment, *Multinationals and the National Interest: Playing by Different Rules*, OTA-ITE-569 (Washington, D.C.: U.S. Government Printing Office, September 1993); Emanuel Adler and Michael Barnett, "Pluralistic Security Communities: Past, Present, and Future,' Working Paper Series on Regional Security, Global Studies Research Program, University of Wisconsin, Madison, 1994; Samuel P. Huntington, "The Clash of Civilizations?" *Foreign Affairs* 72, no. 3 (Summer 1993): 22–49.

have converged greatly in recent decades. Next, it summarizes the book's approach, hypotheses, and findings and then considers briefly two issues, sovereignty and regionalism. Third, it argues that the concept and the approach to national security should be broadened. Finally, it presents the current confusions about the purposes motivating American foreign policy as being rooted not in the transitory phenomena of daily politics but in the confusion about American identity.

Realism and Liberalism

Traditional disagreements between realism and liberalism are deep. The skepticism of realists is rooted in their analysis of bloody and often evil conflicts in world politics. By contrast, the optimism of liberals derives from the existence of embryonic communities of humankind.[6] Since World War II international relations scholars have drawn a sharp distinction between a realist stance that took note of the shattering political experiences of the 1930s and 1940s and an idealist or legalist stance that did not. Hans Morgenthau, John Herz, and Henry Kissinger, among others, brought from Europe to the United States the doctrine of realpolitik, which Kenneth Waltz, Robert Gilpin, and other scholars reformulated as social science theory.[7]

Despite important substantive differences, the gap between realist and liberal perspectives has narrowed. In the 1950s and 1960s realists focused on the Cold War. Economic theories and strong assumptions about the rationality of decision makers informed their analysis of nuclear deterrence. As systematic explanatory factors, culture and identity did not exist. Liberals focused on the astonishing transformation that the process of European integration had brought to a part of the world that in the twen-

---

6. Michael Lorriaux, "The Realists and Saint Augustine: Skepticism, Psychology, and Moral Action in International Relations Thought," *International Studies Quarterly* 36, no. 4 (December 1992): 401–20.

7. Hans J. Morgenthau, *Politics Among Nations: The Struggle for Power and Peace* (New York: Knopf, 1985); John H. Herz, *International Politics in the Atomic Age* (New York: Columbia University Press, 1959); Henry Kissinger, *A World Restored: Metternich, Castlereagh, and the Problems of Peace, 1812–22* (Boston: Houghton Mifflin, 1957); Henry Kissinger, *Diplomacy* (New York: Simon and Schuster, 1994); Kenneth N. Waltz, *Theory of International Politics* (Reading, Mass.: Addison-Wesley, 1979); Robert Gilpin, *War and Change in World Politics* (New York: Cambridge University Press, 1981); Frank W. Wayman and Paul F. Diehl, "Realism Reconsidered: The Realpolitik Framework and Its Basic Propositions," in Frank W. Wayman and Paul F. Diehl, eds., *Reconstructing Realpolitik*, pp. 3–26 (Ann Arbor: University of Michigan Press, 1994).

tieth century had spawned two global wars.[8] Many liberals were deeply skeptical of the relevance of models of rationality to questions of nuclear strategy.[9] Many realists remained unpersuaded that in the process of integration states would cede sovereignty on vital issues of "high politics."[10]

With the growing importance of economic issues in world politics, the gap between realism and liberalism narrowed during the 1970s. At the beginning of that decade interdependence theory had a decidedly liberal cast. It highlighted new sets of transnational relations not captured by traditional state-centric models of international politics.[11] But the oil shock of 1973, the move to flexible exchange rates, and subsequent creeping trade protectionism helped to clarify the political dynamics of two kinds of interdependence, sensitivity and vulnerability, that affect societies and states differently. By the end of the 1970s interdependence theory had been reformulated as a set of descriptive models that approximated, more or less closely, two ideal types: traditional state-centric international politics as analyzed by realism, on the one hand, and a novel form of complex interdependence amenable to liberal analysis, on the other.[12]

The elaboration of regime theory in the 1980s has been the latest step in the substantial convergence of realist and liberal theories of international politics. "Modified structural realists" and "neoliberal institutionalists" have done a large amount of theoretically informed, empirical research. This has broadened the middle ground between "hard" neorealist scholars, who deny the political effects of regimes altogether, and "soft" Grotian scholars, who see in regimes more than mere mechanisms that facilitate the coordination of conflicting policies. This middle ground bridges a chasm that for decades had separated the fields of international relations and international law.

Furthermore, economic models of politics and choice theoretic perspectives have deeply affected the centrist versions of realist and liberal the-

8. Ernst B. Haas, *Beyond the Nation-State: Functionalism and International Organization* (Stanford: Stanford University Press, 1964); Karl W. Deutsch et al., *Political Community and the North Atlantic Area* (Princeton: Princeton University Press, 1957).

9. Philip Green, *Deadly Logic: The Theory of Nuclear Deterrence* (New York: Schocken, 1968); Karl W. Deutsch, *The Analysis of International Relations* (Englewood Cliffs, N.J.: Prentice Hall, 1968), pp. 124–30.

10. Stanley Hoffmann, "Obstinate or Obsolete? The Fate of the Nation-State in Western Europe," *Daedalus* 95, no. 3 (Summer 1966): 862–915.

11. Robert O. Keohane and Joseph S. Nye, eds. *Transnational Relations and World Politics* (Cambridge, Mass.: Harvard University Press, 1972).

12. Robert O. Keohane and Joseph S. Nye, *Power and Interdependence: World Politics in Transition* (Boston: Little, Brown, 1977).

ories, thus reinforcing a convergence in perspective. Realists and liberals alike contributed to the discussion of hegemonic stability that an economist, Charles Kindleberger, had started.[13] Microeconomics was very important to the specification of neorealism. And institutional economics has become central to neoliberalism. Preferences are assumed to be fixed. Explicitly accepting the rationality premise, Judith Goldstein and Robert Keohane, for example, write that "actions taken by human beings depend on the substantive quality of available ideas, since such ideas help to clarify principles and conceptions of causal relationships, and to coordinate individual behavior. Once institutionalized, furthermore, ideas continue to guide action in the absence of costly innovation."[14] Bypassing the social effects (identity and culture) that this book underlines, their analysis views ideas as mechanisms by which actors with given identities seek to achieve their preexisting goals.

This is not to argue that the process of convergence has eliminated all important differences between realism and liberalism. These two perspectives continue to disagree strongly, most notably on the effect that institutions can have in moderating or transforming international conflicts, and on the dynamics of redistributive conflicts.[15] But the stark difference that separated realism and liberalism in the 1950s and 1960s has become more muted. The end of the Cold War and the relatively peaceful disintegration of the Soviet Union have not disrupted this substantial convergence between current formulations of realist and liberal perspectives. Neorealism carries on in focusing largely on the balance of material forces in the international state system; neoliberalism continues to study the potentially moderating effects of international institutions on conflicts between states.[16] In a clarifying exchange over the relative merits of neorealism and neoliberalism, Keohane invokes the collective identity of all scholars of

---

13. Charles P. Kindleberger, *The World in Depression, 1929–1939*, rev. ed. (Berkeley: University of California Press, 1986).

14. Judith Goldstein and Robert O. Keohane, "Ideas and Foreign Policy: An Analytical Framework," in Judith Goldstein and Robert O. Keohane, eds., *Ideas and Foreign Policy: Beliefs, Institutions, and Political Change*, p. 5 (Ithaca: Cornell University Press, 1993).

15. Robert O. Keohane, ed., *Neorealism and Its Critics* (New York: Columbia University Press, 1986); David A. Baldwin, ed., *Neorealism and Neoliberalism: The Contemporary Debate* (New York: Columbia University Press, 1993); John J. Mearsheimer, "The False Promise of International Institutions," *International Security* 19, no. 3 (Winter 1994/95): 5–49, and a set of replies of liberal scholars to be published in the same journal (vol. 20, Summer issue), in 1995.

16. Waltz, "The New World Order"; Waltz, "The Emerging Structure"; Robert O. Keohane, Joseph S. Nye, and Stanley Hoffmann, eds., *After the Cold War: International Institutions and State Strategies in Europe, 1989–1991* (Cambridge, Mass.: Harvard University Press, 1993).

international affairs interested in better theory. Students of realism and liberalism should break down artificial barriers between academic doctrines.[17] For Keohane the possibility exists that "perhaps in the next few years, analysts who are willing to synthesize elements of realism, liberalism, and arguments about domestic politics will be able to better explain variations" in different aspects of world politics.[18]

Cataclysmic international change has affected the political sensibilities and intellectual intuitions of some realists and liberals. Henry Nau and Joseph Nye, for example, have articulated nuanced realist and liberal positions that seek to integrate culture and identity into their analyses.[19] Nau is a realist with moderately conservative views. In light of the specific conditions of the inflation-ridden years of the early 1980s and in the interest of stable economic growth as an essential prerequisite for a peaceful international order, Nau favors a unilateral American approach to international problems. Nye is a liberal with moderate views. Seeking to strengthen the role of international institutions that embody many of America's values and interests, he favors multilateral diplomacy.

In making their theoretical moves, Nau and Nye follow some traditional realists and liberals who paid attention to culture and identity. Carl Schmitt, for example, was an uncompromising realist who insisted that identity, the distinction between friend and foe, was a central, defining element of the state.[20] Indeed, Christoph Frei argues that Schmitt may well have borrowed the distinction between friend and foe from Hans Morgenthau's dissertation.[21] Morgenthau's discussion of power acknowledges that international politics operates within a framework of rules and through the instrumentality of institutions. "The kinds of interests deter-

17. Robert O. Keohane, "Institutional Theory and the Realist Challenge After the Cold War," in Baldwin, *Neorealism and Neoliberalism*, p. 293. The analytical assumptions of a sociological formulation of liberalism that Keohane invokes only in passing are more compatible with the perspective of this volume than with the perspective of neoliberalism and its total neglect of issues of identity (ibid., pp. 271, 289), for they focus, in the words of Joseph Nye on "the transformative effect of transnational contacts and coalitions on national attitudes," or identity; Joseph S. Nye, Jr., "Neorealism and Neoliberalism," *World Politics* 40, no. 2 (January 1988): 246.

18. Keohane, "Institutional Theory and the Realist Challenge After the Cold War," p. 296.

19. Henry R. Nau, *The Myth of America's Decline: Leading the World Economy into the 1990s* (New York: Oxford University Press, 1990); Joseph S. Nye, *Bound to Lead: The Changing Nature of American Power* (New York: Basic Books, 1990); Robert L. Paarlberg, *Leadership Abroad Begins at Home: U.S. Foreign Economic Policy after the Cold War* (Washington, D.C.: Brookings Institution, 1995).

20. Carl Schmitt, *Der Begriff des Politischen* (Munich: Duncker and Humblot, 1932).

21. Christoph Frei, *Hans J. Morgenthau: Eine intellektuelle Biographie* (Bern: Paul Haupt, 1993), pp. 168–72. I am indebted to Gunther Hellmann for drawing my attention to this point and to Frei's work.

mining political action in a particular period of history depend upon the political and cultural context within which foreign policy is formulated."[22] And ever since Kant, different strands of liberal thought have attached much greater importance to norms and identities than does neoliberal institutionalism.

For Nau and Nye, American foreign policy is determined fully neither by the distribution of material capabilities in the international system nor by the rules of international organizations. What also matters for Nau, for example, is the influence of the ideas that shape the purposes and policies of governments, specifically those of the United States. A cocoon of consensus-building shapes social values. As these purposes have converged among many of the major states since 1945, American interests have been well served. Similarly, Nye stresses the importance of institutions and culture for a transformation of power. He argues that the importance of "hard" power is declining while the importance of "soft" power is rising.[23] Hard power relies on tangible resources and military or economic threats or inducements to affect the behavior of others directly. Soft power relies on intangible resources that include culture, ideology, and institutions that shape the preferences and thus coopt behavior.[24]

Nau struggles with the problem of how to specify the influence of national ideas on the international convergence of purpose, especially in light of some of the glaring social pathologies that have marked American society during the last four decades. Nye has difficulty articulating clearly the relational implications of his concept of "soft power" and demonstrating empirically how it, and America's stipulated cultural, ideological, and institutional preeminence, is affecting different features of international politics. But both Nau and Nye point the way for future reformulations of realist and liberal perspectives by seeking to incorporate into their analysis social factors that are central to this book. Put differently, they are utterly persuasive by pointing to the need for both realism and liberalism to embed their analyses in a broader sociological perspective.

The effect of culture and identity varies across time and space. "Idealism" is not a political doctrine, as was thought in the 1950s, but a type of

---

22. Morgenthau, *Politics Among Nations*, p. 11.
23. Nye does not offer any suggestions for how we might explain this important change. The concluding pages in essay 2 try to develop one possible line of argument.
24. Nye, *Bound to Lead*, pp. 31–32, 188.

social science theory.[25] Indeed, Ronen Palan and Brook Blair have argued that neorealism has been inoculated with an exceptionally heavy dose of German idealism.[26] *Culture* and *identity* are summary labels for phenomena that have an objective existence. The crumbling of the structures that had defined and been reinforced by the Cold War highlights their relevance for an analysis of national security.

Summary and Extensions

The empirical studies in this book deal with subjects central to the field of national security studies: arms proliferation, intervention, deterrence and weapons of mass destruction, military doctrine and strategic culture in part 1 and several of these topics as well as civil-military relations, arms control, and alliances in part 2. This section briefly summarizes the approach, hypotheses, and findings of the empirical essays. Avoiding an artificial distinction between international and domestic politics, it then briefly considers sovereignty and regionalism in world politics.

Summary

All the empirical essays in this volume are problem-focused. In most instances the questions they pose are similar to those at the center of the mainstream literature on national security. Why have weapons proliferated throughout the developing world (essay 3)? What determines the choice between offensive and defensive military doctrines (essay 6)? How did "New Thinking" in the Soviet Union help bring about the end of the Cold War (essay 8)? Why do Japan and Germany refuse to seize the opportunities for enhancing their political and military profiles in the post–Cold War world (essay 9)? What will happen to NATO (essay 10)? And what is the relation between threat and the process of alliance formation in the Middle East (essay 11)?

But in several instances the motivating questions differ from those normally asked by students of national security. How have nuclear and chemical weapons become delegitimated as "weapons of mass destruction" and

25. Christian Reus-Smit, "Realist and Resistance Utopias: Community, Security, and Political Action in the New Europe," *Millennium: Journal of International Studies* 21, no. 1 (1992): 1–28; Robert W. McElroy, *Morality and American Foreign Policy: The Role of Ethics in International Affairs* (Princeton: Princeton University Press, 1992).
26. Ronen P. Palan and Brook M. Blair, "On the Idealist Origins of the Realist Theory of International Relations," *Review of International Studies* 19 (1993): 385–99.

how can we explain this change (essay 4)? How and why, rather than if and when, do humanitarian interventions occur (essay 5)? What is the relation between the self-help behavior of states and realist conceptions of the state in the international system (essay 7)? It is one of the advantages of the sociological perspective that on questions of national security it can both address existing questions in the field and, going beyond that, raise new ones.

Some of the essays articulate conventional, structural, rationalist, or functional explanations for the questions that interest them. And they point to the limitations of these explanations in accounting for the empirical evidence at hand. For example, Dana Eyre and Mark Suchman (essay 3) argue that conventional realist analysis views weapons proliferation as a consequence of states preparing for war as the ultimate means for defending their security. But if that were true, states should possess militaries in some rough proportion to both the magnitude and the quality of the threats they face. States confronting large internal security threats, for example, should have militaries and weapons that are very different in their configurations than states that face only minimal threats. But the size and functional specialization of many Third World militaries differ from what a conventional explanation would lead us to expect. Specifically, many Third World states spend too much of their money on "big ticket" items that are not useful in dealing with the actual internal security threats that they face.

Furthermore, Elizabeth Kier (essay 6) shows how prevailing explanations of the choice between offensive and defensive military doctrines are rooted in structural and functional styles of analysis. For functional reasons having to do with their size, autonomy, and prestige, military organizations, the conventional literature argues, prefer offensive doctrines. Furthermore, existing explanations argue that civilian intervention in the development of doctrine occurs in response to the objective incentives that the international balance of power provides. With few qualifications, Kier's analysis undercuts both of these claims.

Thomas Berger (essay 9) also shows realist explanations of Japanese and German security policy to be either indeterminate or empirically wrong, as neither state has sought to translate its growing capabilities in the last two decades into commensurate military power. Furthermore, liberal explanations that focus on Japan and Germany as trading states operating in international markets have trouble explaining why some important elements of Japanese and German antimilitarism arose even before complex interdependence created a benign international environment. And Thomas Risse-Kappen (essay 10) argues that structural realism, balance of power, hegemonic stability, and rationalist-institutional explanations are indeterminate or wrong in either explaining the origin of NATO or accounting for how over time NATO solved the collective action problem of harmonizing divergent national policies.

Other essays point to what they regard as some debilitating weaknesses that make conventional explanations ill-suited for helping to explain particular aspects of national security. Richard Price and Nina Tannenwald, for example, argue in essay 4 that rationalist, interest-based explanations of the "taboo" status of chemical and nuclear weapons are either indeterminate or wrong, for such explanations assume that some objective characteristics of weapons delegitimate them as weapons of war. Furthermore, conventional accounts have difficulty explaining why chemical and nuclear weapons were not used when it might have been advantageous and the deterrent effects of reliance on these weapons were not evident—for example, in the Pacific islands fighting during World War II. Martha Finnemore (essay 5) suggests that humanitarian interventions pose important logical problems for realist theory. Such interventions bring into conflict two of the theory's core assumptions, self-help and sovereignty. In cases of intervention, the target state ceases to be an autonomous actor. Furthermore, the shift to multilateral interventions as the main legitimate form of intervention in the last decades and the occurrence of interventions in situations in which the interests of the intervening states are often not at stake, either directly or indirectly, pose important anomalies to conventional accounts.

Alastair Johnston (essay 7) seeks to establish the superiority of an analytical perspective that stresses the effects of strategic culture over those of the international system emphasized by conventional models of structural realism. Robert Herman (essay 8) finds conventional structural and rationalist explanations limited because they posit a deterministic relation between structure and behavior and thus fail to engage political processes that he sees as central to any understanding of the transformations in Soviet politics and foreign policy in the 1980s. In a similar vein, Michael Barnett (essay 11) criticizes existing theories of balance of power and balance of threat for failing to engage a broad range of social processes that are essential for explaining how collective identities and the construction of threats shape processes of alliance formation in the Middle East.

The empirical essays make claims that both compete with and complement conventional explanations. In some instances they offer alternative explanations, for example, in the case of arms proliferation and military doctrine. In other instances, they make problematic what conventional theories take for granted—concepts such as deterrence, humanitarian intervention, or threats leading to alliance formations—thus complementing existing accounts. Finally, such complementarities also exist where the essays establish that the stipulated effects of general structural theories are indeterminate and thus unhelpful—for example, in answering questions about NATO and the security policies of China, the Soviet Union, Germany, and Japan. The analysis of social effects on national security thus can offer a useful alternative to conventional theories; it can cause us to ask new questions about aspects of national security previously taken for granted; and it can offer a more fine-grained analysis of issues that conventional theories cannot deal with easily.

In their descriptions and explanations, the empirical essays trace two kinds of social effects on national security policies: processes that affect the identity of actors, and thus the interests these actors hold, and processes that shape the interests of actors directly without redefining identities. For example, internationally recognized standards of what it means to be a modern state, Eyre and Suchman (essay 3) and Finnemore (essay 4) argue, have noticeable effects on what kinds of weapons governments buy, whom they consider to be "human," and how they organize military interventions. Price and Tannenwald (essay 4) describe historical, political, and moral developments that have created a taboo around weapons of mass destruction, developments that are not reducible either to objective characteristics of the weapons themselves or to the structural power relations between states. And in their analyses of the effects of the organizational culture of the French military and of Chinese strategic culture, Elizabeth Kier (essay 6) and Alastair Johnston (essay 7) show how cultural effects help shape the interests that guide actors in the military doctrines they adopt and the security policies they adhere to. These cultural effects vary, depending on whether they operate in the polity at large or in particular military organizations (the French case) or whether they are reinforced by specific aspects of political ideology (the Chinese case).

Robert Herman (essay 8) and Thomas Berger (essay 9) trace the effects that Soviet, German, and Japanese contested definitions of identity have had on previously unchallenged views of state interest. But Herman's analysis of "New Thinking" stresses for the most part cognitive elements, not unlike those discussed in the global models of statehood in essays 3 and 4, while Berger's analysis underlines prescriptive elements. Finally, Thomas Risse-Kappen (essay 10) and Michael Barnett (essay 11) analyze how collective identities of liberal democracies and pan-Arabism define the threats that states face in the international system and thus shape the interests that motivate their alliance policies. The difference in these two cases is that over time the collective identity of the democratic member states of NATO strengthened, and with it the North Atlantic security community, while the pan-Arabic movement weakened greatly after 1967, in the face of the growing identities of separate Arab states.

The essays avoid tautological reasoning. Instead of relying on policies as indicators of "revealed cultural preference," the authors analyze various kinds of texts and interview materials to infer the presence or absence of specific social effects. The analysis in these essays, as in the conventional explanations that they engage, is primarily interested in drawing causal inferences between stipulated effects and observed behavior. For example, although Eyre and Suchman are as interested as are the other authors in the effects that modern notions of statehood have on policy, their analysis simply assumes that a model of a modern military exists as part of an ensemble of models that helps define the modern world polity in which contemporary states operate. Essay 3 argues that if such a model exists, then it should have a range of observable effects, and the essay goes on to investigate those effects. Alternatively, Kier establishes the effects of the organizational culture of the military on military doctrine. But she is not interested in analyzing the sources of organizational culture and the degree to which and how it can change. Finally, to different degrees all of the remaining essays are interested in processes of cataclysmic or gradual change that alter some of the social processes that shape national security policies.[27]

In their methods of analysis these essays do not differ from the qualitative case study and historical narrative that are typical of the literature on national security. Eyre and Suchman's statistical analysis and the genealog-

---

27. For a number of reasons this volume resists the temptation of developing typologies—for example, of norms and identities. Since actor identities are often relational, they involve the coding of processes of political construction rather than simply the coding of the political properties of actors. The typologizing of processes is not an easy task and requires considerably more data than are at hand to date in this field of study. Typologies are useful for organizing a substantial body of empirical material. Outside of a rationalist framework, however, national security studies has paid little systematic attention to either norms or identities. The line of work that this book represents is at an early stage. Furthermore, typologies are ahistorical and acontextual. To be fruitful, most scholars argue, the analysis of norms, identities, and cultures must be contextual and historical.

510 • Peter J. Katzenstein

ical reconstruction of historical processes of change in the analysis of the chemical weapons taboo in essay 4 illustrate, furthermore, that the analysis of social effects and processes can rely equally well on hard quantitative or soft interpretive methods. What distinguishes this book's approach is not distinctive methods but the analytical specification of effects that conventional theories typically slight.

In some instances these effects do not merely help define interests in ways that we tend to overlook but also make intelligible what from a structural or rationalist perspective may look like "dysfunctional" behavior. Essay 3 suggests, for example, that modern militaries in Third World countries have been a source of profound political instability for many of the political regimes that equip these militaries with modern weapons. Relatedly, the effects of the chemical weapons taboo were so strong, Price and Tannenwald argue, that the United States refrained from using these weapons when, in the absence of clear Japanese deterrent effects, it would have been advantageous to rely on them during the late stages of World War II in the Pacific. Kier (essay 6) illustrates that the reason for France's lack of adequate preparation for war in 1939 had cultural roots. Herman (essay 8) argues that the Soviet Union sacrificed an empire in the interest of meeting the "Western" standards of behavior that New Thinking and transnational contacts had spread among members of the political elite.[28] Similarly, Berger's analysis underscores what from the vantage point of conventional theories looks like a profound "irrationality" of Japanese and German policy during the Persian Gulf war. For these two states resisted vigorously, and at considerable economic and political cost to themselves, the strong pressure that the United States brought to bear on them to join a broad international coalition against Iraq.

Since the approach of this book seeks to explain the interests that actors hold, rather than taking them as given, the notion of "dysfunctional" or "irrational" behavior makes little sense, for such a notion implies what this book's approach seeks to investigate, the existence of an objectively "best"

---

28. To be sure, realist and rationalist explanations help us to understand why the Soviet military permitted the reformers to seize power in the first place. For without reform, the military believed, Soviet defeat in the high-technology arms race of the Cold War would be unavoidable. But these explanations are not useful, Herman argues, in helping us to understand policies of voluntary retrenchment—imposing a unilateral moratorium on nuclear testing, deliberately undercutting the leadership of several Eastern European allied governments intent on cracking down on democracy movements, offering only token resistance to German unification on Western terms, and acquiescing in the UN Security Council to a U.S.-led Persian Gulf intervention—that the reformers eventually adopted.

standard for behavior. But just about any behavior can be construed to be "functional" or "rational" from some perspective. The trick is not to define one best standard against which all performance is measured, but to make intelligible the political logic inherent in different kinds of substantive rationalities.

Although all the essays argue that social effects have causal significance, the tightness or looseness of the link between social effects and observed behavior varies. In some instances the link is loose, as in the global models of statehood that inform the analysis of arms proliferation and military intervention in essays 3 and 4. Essay 10 refers to instances in which the United States actually did not comply with specific rules of the norm of consultation while at the same time acquiescing in the diffuse norm of taking Allied interests into account. And essay 7 reports the existence of a large gap between China's idealized, Confucian-Mencian strategic culture and security policy and the absence of such gap in the case of its parabellum, operational strategic culture. Depending on the content of a country's strategic culture and the nature of a chosen policy, Johnston's analysis suggests, the tightness of the link between social effects and observed behavior varies.

Most of the essays investigate how social effects define the interests that actors hold. Hence standards of appropriate behavior among allies, as described in essay 10, appeal to collective understandings. They are not arguments deployed for selfish reasons, as a rationalist interpretation would suggest. Instead they are the articulation of preferences that have been formed in light of historical experience. Instances in which allies make appeals to such standards in order to elicit compliance by others while covering their own noncompliance would rapidly undermine any existing collective understanding. Analogously, Kier (essay 6) argues that we need to make a sharp distinction between the causal effects of organizational culture on the one hand and the invocation of specific myths, created for particular political purposes, on the other. The defensive lesson of Verdun and World War I, for example, took on legendary proportions, but only after the organizational culture of the French military had already shaped a defensive military doctrine. Causal primacy hence lies with this factor, not with historical myths. Finally, the invocation of standards of appropriate behavior is often closely linked to issues of political power— for example, in the case of the invocation by Arab states of the taboo against chemical weapons as an attempt to redress a discriminatory nuclear nonproliferation regime as discussed in essay 4.

The social effects that are analyzed here typically are institutionalized.

The taboo against chemical weapons, essay 4 argues, was institutionalized even before the invention of modern chemical weapons, a plausible explanation for the success of those who ostracized these weapons as instruments of war in the twentieth century. The antinuclear taboo, by way of contrast, was institutionalized only in the 1960s and 1970s, two decades after Hiroshima and Nagasaki. In the diverse data on the social effects that the essays report, only pan-Arabism appears to be conspicuously uninstitutionalized.

There is, however, considerable variation in the specificity or diffuseness of the social effects that the essays analyze. The global models of statehood that shape arms proliferation and intervention policies, Eyre and Suchman as well as Finnemore argue, are diffuse. The taboo against weapons of mass destruction and the effects of organizational culture of the military, on the other hand, are specific (essays 4 and 6). And as in several other of the essays, Risse-Kappen's discussion in essay 10 points to the coexistence of both, specific consultation norms with the diffuse obligation of taking allied interests into account in foreign policy making. Breaking specific norms can under some circumstances reinforce a diffuse sense of obligation toward allies who have not been consulted but whose interests must be taken into account.

This argument provides a ready link to the moral basis of American hegemony that Lea Brilmayer has analyzed lucidly.[29] One of the advantages of the sociological-institutional perspective lies in its ability to lend itself to reconnecting empirical analysis to philosophical discussions about the purposes of political action and the nature of political community. Scholarly analysis of national security and international politics has sidestepped these issues during the last three decades. It should not.

Extensions

Paul Kowert and Jeffrey Legro (essay 12) reflect on both the effects and the origins of norms. They argue that norms are an interlocking web, spanning different levels of analysis and shaping the interests of actors, the beliefs that actors hold about the best means available for achieving their objectives, and larger normative structures. But Kowert and Legro note also that, in the effort to convince us that the social constructions of norms and identity matter, the empirical essays, like the conventional theories

29. Lea Brilmayer, *American Hegemony: Political Morality in a One-Superpower World* (New Haven: Yale University Press, 1994).

that they criticize, tend to take their own core concepts as exogenously given.[30] With a few notable exceptions, such as the genealogy of the chemical weapons taboo in essay 4, the empirical essays have little to say about the manner by which collective identities and norms are constructed through different generative processes: ecological, social, and internal. Extension into the domain of social psychology offers a possible microfoundation for sociological approaches. Although it signifies the continued importance of psychology to our understanding of national security, such a move insists that besides individual cognition and motivation we must be attentive as well to collective and social origins.[31] Relatedly, the research program on national role perceptions should be of great interest to those who are rediscovering the importance of social facts in international politics and national security.[32]

Other approaches for the construction of a microfoundation of an institutional perspective are possible. They include theories of practical knowledge and action based on advances in ethnomethodology, the analysis of cognitive aspects of routine social behavior, the taken-for-grantedness element in cognition, and the analysis of a habitus that seeks to explain why strategically oriented actors so often do not seek to alter social structures that are not in their interest.[33] Furthermore, research into the microfoundations of norms and identities cannot avoid paying close attention to language.[34] In contrast, conventional realist and liberal theories

---

30. Sociological-institutional scholarship thus would do well to emulate Alexander George. Criticizing structural theories for their black-boxing of important processes that translate structural effects, he has shown us how to make "process theory" a respectable cousin of "substantive theory"; see Alexander L. George, *Bridging the Gap: Theory and Practice in Foreign Policy* (Washington, D.C.: United States Institute of Peace Press, 1993), pp. xxi–xxii. Glenn H. Snyder, "Process Variables in Neorealist Theory," *Security Studies* 5, no. 3 (Spring 1996), in press, has tried to enrich neorealist theory by developing more systematically the concepts of "process" and "relationship."

31. On the basis of social psychological research, Jonathan Mercer offers an interesting realist critique of Wendt's constructivist account of anarchy. See his article "Anarchy and Identity," *International Organization* 49, no. 2 (1995): 229–52. Alastair Johnston's essay in this volume is a useful reminder that, contra Mercer, realism and constructivism are not necessarily antithetical, for realism can itself be viewed as a powerful social construction. See also Stephen Haggard, "Structuralism and Its Critics: Recent Progress in International Relations Theory," in Emanuel Adler and Beverly Crawford, eds., *Progress in Postwar International Relations*, p. 430 (New York: Columbia University Press, 1991).

32. Stephen G. Walker, ed., *Role Theory and Foreign Policy Analysis* (Durham: Duke University Press, 1987).

33. Paul J. DiMaggio and Walter W. Powell, introduction to Walter W. Powell and Paul DiMaggio, eds., *The New Institutionalism in Organizational Analysis*, pp. 15–27 (Chicago: University of Chicago Press, 1991).

34. Albert Yee, "The Causal Effects of Ideas Themselves and Policy Preferences: Behavioral, Institutional and Discursive Formulations" (unpublished paper, Brown University, 1993); Sanjoy Banerjee,

seek the microfoundation for structural theories in economics and the rational actor assumption. Essay 12 illustrates that much work has been done in other social science fields that is very relevant for the approach of this book and that should be incorporated more systematically into future work.

This book's focus on the social effects that operate on national security spans both international and domestic politics.[35] Conventional theories, by contrast, typically operate exclusively at the level of the international system while conceding to "reductionist" theories of domestic politics the task of accounting for elements of national variation. This distinction has always been in tension with real-world politics, which the organization of this volume seeks to sidestep. Instead, the empirical essays analyze in one framework international and national effects that shape national security. In part 1 the essays by Eyre and Suchman, Price and Tannenwald, and Finnemore focus primarily on international models of statehood that inform national security policy on issues such as weapons procurement, non-use of nuclear and chemical weapons, and military intervention. At a different level of analysis but from the same norms-based perspective, the essays by Kier and Johnston focus instead at the national level on the effects of the organizational and strategic culture of the military. In part 2 Herman and Berger explain national security policy in terms of Soviet, Japanese, and German collective identities. From a similar identity-based vantage point, but at a different level of analysis, Risse-Kappen and Barnett examine the waxing and waning of international security communities in the North Atlantic area and of alliances in the Middle East as well as U.S.-Israeli relations. The book's analytical categories thus permit us to sidestep the traditional "level-of-analysis problem."[36] I will illustrate this advantage briefly with reference to our understanding of sovereignty and regionalism as important factors that are shaping world politics.

"International Interaction as a Psychocultural Process: Examples from the Partition of India" (paper prepared for delivery at the 1994 annual meeting of the American Political Science Association, New York, September 1–4, 1994).

35. It thus follows those scholars who are self-conscious in avoiding any sharp distinction between international and domestic levels of analysis; Peter Evans, Harold Jacobson, and Robert Putnam, eds., *Double-Edged Diplomacy: Interactive Games in International Affairs* (Berkeley: University of California Press, 1993).

36. In a different way, though, a sociological perspective may also emphasize differences between levels of analysis. This volume offers some evidence for the preliminary hypothesis that the constitutive effects of norms are stronger at the international level, while their regulative effects are stronger at the domestic level.

Sovereignty

A sociological perspective affects how we think about the institution of sovereignty, in the view of conventional theories the supposed foundation of international anarchy and state autonomy. Writing from a realist perspective, Stephen Krasner acknowledges that the system of 1648 did not create states acting as "billiard balls." The principle of unquestioned state sovereignty never triumphed. Instead the practice of intervention, before and after 1648, has left state sovereignty deeply problematic, and with it the sharp distinction between international and domestic levels of analysis.[37] Economic, social, and environmental issues that increasingly permeate state boundaries reinforce that trend. Sovereignty is an institution that shapes state identity. It is not a natural fact of international life. Instead it is politically contested and has variable political effects.[38]

A broader historical and cultural perspective, extending beyond the modern Western state system, illustrates that sovereignty is a problematic, fundamental institution distinctive of the modern Western system rather than a universal institution typical of all international systems. The international relations of other historical eras and civilizations have been based on other fundamental institutions.[39]

Reus-Smit, for example, argues that in Western history different state systems have created different fundamental institutions governing the relations between states.[40] Ancient Greece, for example, relied for centuries on a successful system of third-party arbitration not codified by international law. By contrast, the modern Western system relies on law and multilateral diplomacy. The cause for such variation in institutional practice lies in changing state identities. These identities reflect not international sovereignty but domestic values concerning the moral purpose of the state. Such values are not invariant but historically and culturally specific. They originate in dominant states and then diffuse internationally, affecting the behavior of weak and strong states alike.

---

37. Stephen D. Krasner, "Westphalia and All That," in Goldstein and Keohane, *Ideas and Foreign Policy*, pp. 235–64.

38. John Boli, "Issues of Sovereignty in the World Polity: An Institutionalist Research Agenda" (unpublished paper, n.d.); Thomas J. Biersteker and Cynthia Weber, eds., *State Sovereignty As Social Construct* (Cambridge: Cambridge University Press, in press); Palan and Blair, "On the Idealist Origins."

39. Adda B. Bozeman, *Politics and Culture in International History* (Princeton: Princeton University Press, 1960); Neta Crawford, "A Security Regime Among Democracies: Cooperation Among Iroquois Nations," *International Organization* 48, no. 3 (Summer 1944): 345–86.

40. Christian Reus-Smit, "The Moral Purpose of the State: The Social Identity, Legitimate Action, and the Construction of International Institutions" (Ph.D. diss., Cornell University, 1995).

In the Chinese context, sovereignty is defined not only by equality between states but also by the capacity of the Chinese state to encompass others.[41] With a combination of hierarchy and anarchy as its distinctive trait, the Chinese system, like the Ottoman Empire, was made up of suzerain states. In this instance issues of political or military domination and resistance do not fall into discrete spheres of international and domestic politics. They occupy a sphere that links both. Tributary trade, not third-party arbitration or international law and multilateralism, was the distinctive fundamental institution of the Sino-centric world. And it was the strength of domestic coalitions fighting over different, and changing, definitions of Chinese state identity that shaped the policy interests of the Ming dynasty.

What was true of ancient China is also true of contemporary world politics. Sovereignty is not the basic defining characteristic of an international anarchy. Instead there are numerous examples of various types of sovereignty, which suggests that sovereignty is not an unquestioned foundational institution of international politics that can be assumed or analyzed at the level of the international system. Contemporary conflicts in the Russian Federation, for example, offer a telling example. Between July 1990 and January 1991, fourteen of the sixteen autonomous republics in Russia declared their sovereignty and renamed themselves. A few months later four of the five autonomous oblasts did the same and were recognized by the Russian Supreme Soviet on July 2, 1991.[42] Before the dissolution of the Soviet Union only the North Caucasus republic of Chechnya forced the issue of independence, which in December 1994 exploded into war. The Russian Federation Treaty signed in March 1992 creates three types of units with various types of sovereignty inside Russia: sovereign republics, other administrative units of varying size and autonomy, and the cities of Moscow and St. Petersburg.

Institutionalized definitions of nationhood do not have to treat nations

41. Arthur Waldron, "Chinese Strategy from the Fourteenth to the Seventeenth Centuries," in Williamson Murray, MacGregor Knox, and Alvin Bernstein, eds., *The Making of Strategy: Rulers, States, and War*, pp. 85–114 (Cambridge: Cambridge University Press, 1994); Morris Rossabi, ed., *China Among Equals: The Middle Kingdom and Its Neighbors, 10th–14th Centuries* (Berkeley: University of California Press, 1983); Alastair Iain Johnston, *Cultural Realism: Strategic Culture and Grand Strategy in Chinese History* (Princeton: Princeton University Press, 1995). Adam Segal, "War, Walls, or Trade: Changing Conceptions of Chinese State Identity and Ming Foreign Relations" (unpublished paper, Government Department, Cornell University, Ithaca, New York, 1994).
42. John W. Slocum, "Will Russia Disintegrate? Separatism, Regionalism, and the Future of the Russian Federation" (unpublished paper, Peace Studies Program, Cornell University, 1993), p. 5.

simply as internally homogeneous and externally sharply delimited social groups. Nations are not fixed or real. Nationality struggles in Russia and the Commonwealth of Independent States (CIS) can be viewed instead not as "struggles of nations, but the struggles of institutionally constituted national elites—that is, elites institutionally defined as national—and aspiring counter-elites."[43] A map of Russia thus resembles a quilt made up of republics proclaiming the precedence of their laws over those of the Russian Constitution. John Slocum concludes that "the concept of sovereignty, so much at stake in the struggle over Russian federalism, is becoming increasingly irrelevant in the world at large. A fragmented Russia, which hangs together on some level and not on others, seems perfectly in tune with the times."[44]

In contrast to Russia, contemporary Europe offers a very different example of far-reaching attempts to pool state sovereignty of various sorts across different parts of Europe and different issues areas. Neorealism either denies that international institutions in Europe have any important effects[45] or interprets such effects as resulting primarily from the interests of "middle-rank" countries like France and Italy, which seek to gain some voice over the growing power of Germany.[46] Neoliberal institutionalism interprets European international politics by pointing to a particularly dense set of institutions that facilitate problems of coordination. In this view institutions are important because they reduce uncertainty and create efficiencies that may contribute to the redefinition of interests and thus

---

43. Rogers Brubaker, "Nationhood and the National Question in the Soviet Union and Post-Soviet Eurasia: An Institutionalist Account," *Theory and Society* 23 (1994): 48; David Laitin, "Identity in Formation: The Russian-Speaking Nationality in the Post-Soviet Diaspora" (paper prepared for delivery at the 1994 annual meeting of the American Political Science Association, New York, September 1994); Ted Hopf, "Identity and Russian Foreign Policy" (unpublished paper, University of Michigan, August 1994); Jessica Eve Stern, "Moscow Meltdown: Can Russia Survive?" *International Security* 18, no. 4 (Spring 1994): 40–65.

44. Slocum, "Will Russia Disintegrate?" p. 18.

45. Mearsheimer, "Back to the Future."

46. Joseph M. Grieco, "State Interests and International Rule Trajectories: A Neorealist Interpretation of the Maastricht Treaty and European Economic and Monetary Union," *Security Studies* 5, no. 3 (Spring 1996), forthcoming. Joseph M. Grieco, "The Maastricht Treaty, Economic and Monetary Union, and the Neo-realist Research Programme," *Review of International Studies* 21, no. 1 (January 1995): 21–40. Neorealism fails to convince in this instance, since it sidesteps altogether the central question of why Germany has an interest in a policy that neorealist theory suggests favors its European competitors. An important part of the answer, as Grieco recognizes elsewhere, lies in German domestic politics and thus falls outside the domain of neorealist theory altogether. See Joseph M. Grieco, "Understanding the Problem of International Cooperation: The Limits of Neoliberal Institutionalism and the Future of Realist Theory," in Baldwin, *Neorealism and Neoliberalism*, p. 338.

modify behavior. Neoliberals interpret the partial pooling of sovereignty in Europe as a series of nested games that link states in ongoing interactions that limit the range of their bargaining tactics. Political elites make strategic use of international institutions to escape from both the democratic controls and the political fragmentation of domestic societies.[47] Furthermore, the structures and processes of European integration offer new opportunities for domestic actors to strike transnational bargains that change domestic coalitions, institutions, and policies.

But institutions do not merely create efficiencies. They also express identities, for example by affecting the character of statehood. John Ruggie, for one, sees in the EU "the first truly postmodern international political form."[48] International politics in the EU is neither national nor intergovernmental nor supranational. It no longer takes place from twelve distinct starting places with twelve separate, single, and fixed viewpoints. The processes "whereby each of the twelve defines its own identity—and the identities are logically prior to preferences—increasingly endogenize the existence of the other eleven. Within this framework, European leaders may be thought of as entrepreneurs of alternative political identities."[49] Because territorial conflict has become a less central component of state identity in Western Europe, the EU has tamed and transformed its member states in significant ways. European identity links both international and national levels of politics and shapes the preferences and interests that actors hold.

This sociological perspective makes it possible for us to capture variations in state identity that are glossed over by conventional theories. In

47. Wayne Sandholtz, "Choosing Union: Monetary Politics and Maastricht," *International Organization* 47, no. 1 (Winter 1993): 1–39.
48. John Gerard Ruggie, "Territoriality and Beyond: Problematizing Modernity in International Relations," *International Organization* 47, no. 1 (Winter 1993): 140. Ruggie's formulation is giving short shrift to Canada, arguably the first postmodern state par excellence. Quebec's search for "sovereignty association" bears some resemblance to the EU. According to Quebec comedian Yvon Deschamps, ideally an independent Quebec would exist within a united Canada. See Clyde H. Farnsworth, "Quebec Separatists Split on Timing and Terms of Referendum," *New York Times*, April 18, 1995, p. A9. The United States is not free of its own sovereignty problems. In 1990, 287 reservations for American Indians, and almost as many tribes, were recognized as distinct nations. These reservations sometimes resemble Third World enclave economies, often lacking extradition agreements with surrounding county governments. See Peter T. Suzuki, "The Indian Reservation in the Comparative PA Course" (paper prepared for delivery at the Eighteenth National Conference on Teaching Public Administration, Seattle, March 24–25, 1995).
49. Ruggie, "Territoriality and Beyond," p. 172; Ann-Marie Burley and Walter Mattli, "Europe Before the Court: A Political Theory of Legal Integration," *International Organization* 47, no. 1 (Winter 1993): 41–76.

their response to the crisis of fall 1993 in the European Exchange Rate Mechanism (ERM), France and Britain took different positions, arguably reflecting attempts to maintain different political identities in Europe. David Cameron thus argues that the politics of European monetary cooperation is explained best in terms of the effects that identity has on the definition of interests.[50] France and Germany cooperated in a series of currency crises to maintain their privileged European partnership. In contrast to Britain, France refused to drop out of the ERM, largely because of considerations of identity.[51] State identities thus can have powerful effects on conceptions of state interest.

Institutional perspectives that neglect questions of identity also have great difficulties in accounting for German policy on questions of European monetary integration. While neoliberal institutionalism offers powerful explanations for why Germany has come to like the ERM as a way of shaping European politics, it tells us little about why Germany's political leadership appears to be so committed to the goal of full monetary integration in the EMU, a policy that would greatly reduce the power of German monetary policy in Europe. The effect of Europe on German identity offers us a clue. In his essay Thomas Berger points to the fundamental consequences that the changing purpose of the state has had for the character of German identity. Put succinctly, he describes the transformation of German state identity from territorial aggrandizement to individual entitlement, from warfare to welfare. Furthermore, as Thomas Risse-Kappen shows in his essay, the North Atlantic security community has had lasting effects on the identity of all member states, including Germany. In short, German identity now encompasses more international aspects than ever before in modern times. In fact, the German government accepted national unification in 1990 only under the condition that it be legitimated internationally by all European states. Europe thus has become a very important component of German national identity.

Like Germany, many European states are finding their "home" in a broadening European community. Identity politics is thus central to an understanding of the politics of regional integration. But as Michael Bar-

---

50. David Cameron, "British Exit, German Voice, French Loyalty: Defection, Domination, and Cooperation in the 1992–93 ERM Crisis" (paper prepared for delivery at the 1993 annual meeting of the American Political Science Association, Washington, D.C., September 1993).

51. This line of reasoning could be extended to a comparison of Germany and France. Despite some remarkable similarities in their international placement after World War II, West Germany and France have often behaved very differently. These differences are arguably related to different state identities.

nett's analysis of Mideast politics illustrates, collective regional identities can be built "down" as well as "up." A sociological perspective can help us analyze conflict and war as well as peaceful cooperation.

Regionalism

An analytical focus on social effects of culture and identity permits us to examine international politics not only along dimensions of power, types of alliances, or geography. We may gain much from thinking of world regions as social constructs. Sometimes regions emerge spontaneously. At other times political actors deliberately fashion them.[52] The North Atlantic region, for example, subsequently institutionalized in NATO, was a political creation of the mid-1940s, designed to bring the United States politically closer to Britain and the European continent, in defiance of the logic of cartographers. With the reestablishment of democracy in the mid-1970s, political elites emphasized Spain's European identity rather than its traditional Iberian–Latin American identity.[53] Greece succeeded in joining Europe largely because it could play on its recognized identity as the home of European culture and civilization.[54] In a similar vein, since 1989 the Central European democracies have been competing in their attempts to show that they are returning to "Europe," with the Czech Republic apparently winning first prize. And Russian politicians are creating a new region of "the near abroad" to legitimate possible future interventions in the affairs of members of the CIS. Such political constructs often, but not always, reflect particularly dense social transactions that tie different societies to one another.[55] And they often, but not always, can enhance economic and social density.

On this point the contrast with neorealism is stark. This theory insists that states live in an international environment marked by an inescapable security dilemma. With the end of the Cold War and bipolarity, for example, neorealists argue that international politics is returning to multipolarity. "Assuming Russia recovers, and China holds itself together, we can expect as in the old days to have a world of five or so great powers, probably by the first decade of the next millennium . . . if unity is not achieved,

52. Adler and Barnett, "Pluralistic Security Communities."
53. Michael Marks, "The Formation of European Policy in Post-Franco Spain: Ideas, Interests, and the International Transmission of Knowledge" (Ph.D. diss., Cornell University, 1993).
54. Michael Herzfeld, *Ours Once More: Folklore, Ideology, and the Making of Modern Greece* (Austin: University of Texas Press, 1982).
55. Deutsch et al., *Political Community and the North Atlantic Area*.

Germany may get tired of playing European games, some years hence and go off on its own."[56] States play games and have distinct identities that permit them to go their own ways when the game is over. But the language of multipolarity and games is analytically quite limiting, as Charles Kegley and Gregory Raymond have argued.[57] It imposes an artificially uniform analytical perspective upon a political reality that differs substantially in different regions of the world.[58]

A sparse conception of international structure can capture elements of international politics better in some regions than in others. Considering the basic values that motivate the contemporary Chinese state, realism offers important, though limited, political insights into some aspects of the Asian balance of power.[59] In contrast to Western Europe and the North Atlantic area, during the last several decades no security community has emerged in Asia. The Cold War never imposed as clear a split on Asia as it did on Europe, hence the end of the Cold War had a less dramatic effect on the Asian balance of power. The logic of military balancing that no longer is central to West European politics still remains an important aspect of Asian international politics.[60]

Indeed, since the end of the Cold War in Europe, Asian governments have moved very quickly to set up new multilateral international institutions or to deepen existing ones. This offers strong support for the insights of neoliberal institutional theory. Institutions do serve the purpose, among others, of reducing uncertainty and thus facilitating policy coordination. But this is not the only effect that institutions have, even in Asia. The network structures that are increasingly integrating Asian political economies under the umbrella of Japanese *keiretsu* systems and through Chinese ethnic and familial ties are informal and, by European standards, politically

---

56. Waltz, "The New World Order," p. 194.

57. Charles W. Kegley, Jr., and Gregory Raymond, *A Multipolar Peace? Great-Power Politics in the Twenty-first Century* (New York: St. Martin's, 1994), p. 121.

58. Peter J. Katzenstein, "Regions in Competition: Comparative Advantages of America, Europe, and Asia," in Helga Haftendorn and Christian Tuschhoff, eds., *America and Europe in an Era of Change*, pp. 105–26 (Boulder: Westview, 1993); Peter J. Katzenstein, "Introduction: Asian Regionalism in Comparative Perspective," in Peter J. Katzenstein and Takashi Shiraishi, eds., *Network Power: Japan and Asia* (Ithaca: Cornell University Press, 1997).

59. Realist theories are likely to be wrong in their analyses if they overlook either the significance of comprehensive definitions of national security going beyond narrow military concerns or the legacy of the Sino-centric world system for the national security policies of Asian states in the 1990s.

60. Applied to Asia, however, realism still faces the problem of yielding analyses that are indeterminate. See Peter J. Katzenstein, *Cultural Norms and National Security: Police and Military in Postwar Japan* (Ithaca: Cornell University Press, 1996).

underinstitutionalized.[61] But they are, in the words of Joel Kotkin, instances of a new form of tribalism in the global economy. They illustrate how race, religion, and identity are central in shaping important trends in the global economy.[62]

Regional politics in Europe offers another illustration of the role of the profound effects that collective identity has on interests and policies. The phenomenal success of the national institution of the welfare state since 1945 has had a lasting effect on the basic values that define the substantive purposes of policy both at home and abroad. This transformation is most evident in Germany in the center of Europe and the locus classicus of a virulent ethnically or racially based form of nationalism. Although current citizenship requirements still reflect the view of a national community bound together by ancestral lineage, the political realities of the 1990s are different. Contemporary German nationalism has become a nationalism not of collective assertion but of individual entitlement. With unification the expectation of the Kohl government, widely shared by the older generation of the social democratic leadership, assumed a repetition of the experience of joint sacrifice and pulling together, 1950s style.

What happened instead was the display of a "possessive individualism" that took the chancellor's election promises literally: national unification without individual sacrifice. This nationalism of entitlement has not shown itself as clearly in any other European state in recent years. But there exists no substantial evidence undermining the expectation that the German form of welfare state nationalism distinguishes Western Europe at large.[63] The effect that the institution of the welfare state has had on collective identities in Germany and throughout Europe, and hence on the content of policy interests, I would argue is of much greater political importance for an understanding of the national security policies of Western European states than are the stipulated, though unmeasured, efficien-

---

61. Katzenstein, "Introduction: Asian Realism."
62. Joel Kotkin, *Tribes: How Race, Religion, and Identity Determine Success in the New Global Economy* (New York: Random House, 1993).
63. The reappearance of a virulent and xenophobic nationalism in the politics of many European states, including Germany, reflects an erosion (in the case of Italy, an implosion) of the political center-right. Underlying trends of increasing social diversity have been apparent for two decades, paralleling, although in less dramatic form, developments toward the creation of a multicultural regime in the United States. The broadening of the spectrum of collective identities in Europe has accelerated with the end of the Cold War. In the 1990s Christian democracy is losing its grip over the right-wing political spectrum. This development mirrors the erosion of social democratic support among groups favoring environmental movements in the 1980s.

cies that international institutions create as conceived by rationalist theories.

Different world regions thus embody different substantive domestic purposes that shape state sovereignty. And regions are parts of a global system that, in turn, is affecting them differently. Global processes like transnational capital flows, the increasing salience of human rights, or the risks of environmentally unsustainable developments thus have different political effects on states situated in different regions of the world. Today there exists no general threat to the state system as the basic organizing principle of international politics. Everywhere states retain minimal sovereignty. But an increasing number of agenda-setting and legitimacy-creating polities are organized on a global scale.[64] This is one step in the direction that Hedley Bull has called the "neo-Medievalism" of contemporary international politics:[65] a move, more or less halting in different regional settings, toward multiple, nested centers of collective authority and identity. One advantage of a sociological perspective is that it can capture analytically the variability of the effects that varying substantive values informing state sovereignty and different regional contexts have on the national security policies of states. Little is gained, and much is lost, when our theories foreclose a systematic investigation, at multiple levels of analysis, of the possibility that culture and identity can interact in shaping the interests of specific states seeking to protect their national security.

Going Beyond Traditional National Security Studies

This book's exclusive focus on traditional military issues meets traditional definitions of national security. The subject matter of the case studies is central to the substantive concerns of conventional approaches to questions of national security. The analytical issues are thus joined on grounds that provide a hard test for the sociological approach that this book puts forward.

We do not, however, endorse in this volume the insistence on restricting security studies only to states and military issues. Traditional strategic studies continues to be an important part of the field of security studies.

---

64. John Meyer, "Rationalized Environments," in W. Richard Scott and John W. Meyer, eds., *Institutional Environments and Organizations* (Beverly Hills: Sage, 1994), pp. 28–54.
65. Hedley Bull, *The Anarchical Society: A Study of Order in World Politics* (New York: Columbia University Press, 1977), pp. 254–55.

And the state continues to be an important actor on questions of security. But changes in world politics have broadened the security agenda that confronts states. And nonstate actors are of great relevance to traditional issues of military security. Furthermore, theoretical debates about how strategic and security studies relate to the social sciences suggest that commonly made analytical distinctions—for example, between international and domestic politics, security issues and economic issues, facts and values—often hinder rather than help our description and explanation of real world events.[66] These analytical distinctions often pose conceptual barriers that reflect a binary view of the world. In distinguishing between "inside" and "outside," "us" and "them," that view often takes collective identity as an unexamined defining characteristic of international politics.[67] In light of recent political and theoretical developments, it serves no purpose to restrict scholarship to only one part of the field of national security studies.[68]

Developments in world politics speak for broadening the field of security studies in two directions, encompassing nonmilitary issues and nonstate actors. First, a focus on economic issues could analyze, for example, policies that relate to questions of military conversion and are thus clearly relevant to traditional national security studies. But it could also concentrate on broader issues of food security, as in Africa, or human rights, as in Haiti, because such issues can have direct effects on the military intervention of states. Furthermore, for governments of rich states the economic development of their poor neighbors is also becoming a security issue. Fear of mass migration, for example, and the social and political instabilities that it can engender, characterizes the political relations of the United States and Mexico, France and Northern Africa, and Germany and its Eastern neighbors.

Furthermore, collapsing political structures have put ethnic and

---

66. Such compartmentalization had great intellectual benefits in the 1970s and 1980s. It supported, for example, the creation of a "conventional" scholarly field of national security that followed the canons of social science rather than simply tracking policy developments, as had often been the case in the 1950s and 1960s.

67. R. B. J. Walker, *Inside/Outside: International Relations As Political Theory* (Cambridge: Cambridge University Press, 1993).

68. When conventional analytical perspectives in the field of national security engage issues that provide hard tests for their preferred mode of analysis—broader security issues and nonstate actors—theoretical debate and empirical research on national security issues are likely to be enriched greatly. See, for example, Daniel Deudney, "The Case Against Linking Environmental Degradation and National Security," *Millennium: Journal of International Studies* 19, no. 3 (Winter 1990): 461–76.

national conflict even higher on the agenda of national security studies than they have been since 1945. The analysis of the effects of ethnic and national identities on security, as compared with competing class, gender, race, or religious identities, raises vexing political and theoretical problems. An empirically grounded analysis should steer clear of both the essentialism of rationalist perspectives (which, typically, take actor identities to be unproblematic) and the fluidity of postmodern perspectives (which often see identity as being shaped by specific combinations of contingency and agency). Security studies should not be narrowly restricted to states and questions of military security only. But neither should it be broadened so much that it comes to encompass all issues relating directly or indirectly to the violence between individuals and collectivities. Broader security studies can add to the traditional analysis of national security if the issues and actors that it studies have some demonstrable links to states and questions of military importance.

Theoretical developments in the social sciences, in international relations, and in the specific field of national security studies provide a second main reason why the intellectual agenda of security studies should be broad, not narrow. The dominant theoretical issues no longer relate, as they did in the 1970s and early 1980s, to debates between realist, pluralist, and structural-global analytical perspectives—that is, academic versions of conservatism, liberalism, and Marxism. Rather, the central theoretical debates now engage rationalist and constitutive explanatory approaches to theory.

This book targets realism's and rationalism's neglect of important effects and processes that shape the nature of political interests and the character of political actors. But the approach of this volume shares with realism and rationalism an insistence on linking analytical arguments to evidence. Other approaches, such as critical theory, postmodernism, and feminist theory, are divided on many issues. They offer much more profound and unsettling challenges to the field of national security studies and international relations theory than do disagreements between different types of explanatory theory. Critical theory investigates the knowledge interests that tie security studies to the institutions and individuals that control the levers of power. Feminist theory proposes to rethink all of the basic categories of analysis—man, state, and war—central to the field of military strategy and important in the field of security studies. And postmodernist theory seeks to deconstruct, among others, core concepts of security studies, such as state sovereignty, and thus to subvert the entire field of security studies and decenter its theoretical discourse. These approaches are themselves divided between critical theory that works toward some foundationalism of shared knowledge and postmodernism that does not, with different strands of feminist theory to be found in either camp. Typically, they all question the research strategy of realist, rationalist, and constructivist explanatory theory.

The theoretical debates that are occurring in the social sciences and in international relations, as well as in the fields of security and strategic studies, are likely to broaden the range of analytical approaches. One reason is generational change. When asked what constituted progress in the field of economics, a young Paul Samuelson is reported to have replied, "Obituaries." Younger scholars, whose political experiences were not formed by the Cold War, are likely to experiment with a broader range of theories to understand a new political reality. A second reason is the geographic diffusion of centers of learning and intellectual innovation in a more pluralist world. European peace researchers, for example, cannot suppress a polite yawn when American students of security studies rehearse vigorously arguments in the 1990s that Europeans debated in the 1960s and 1970s. And Asian scholars and policy makers are plainly bewildered by American debates about whether the definition of security should be restricted only to military issues or should encompass economic and other issues as well. From the Asian perspective it makes neither political nor intellectual sense to adhere to a narrow scope of security studies. In light of these reactions, Paul Samuelson might also have answered, "Intellectual currents outside of U.S. national security studies."[69]

National security studies are exposed to the differing insights of sociological or constructivist and economic or rationalist perspectives. This book tries to follow Max Weber onto the middle ground that he sought to preserve in the original "battle of the methods."[70] In the late nineteenth century, that battle pitted Gustav Schmoller and the German historical

69. See, for example, a number of outstanding essays on international relations theory published in the excellent inaugural issue of *Zeitschrift für Internationale Beziehungen* 1, no. 1 (1994).
70. Richard Swedberg, " 'The Battle of the Methods': Toward a Paradigm Shift?" in Amitai Etzioni and Paul R. Lawrence, eds., *Socio-Economics: Toward a New Synthesis*, pp. 13–33 (Armonk, N. Y.: M. E. Sharpe, 1991). During the last decade the relationship between economics and sociology has once again become a lively source of debate. See, for example, James N. Baron and Michael T. Hannan, "The Impact of Economics on Contemporary Sociology," *Journal of Economic Literature* 32 (September 1994): 1111–46; Harald Müller, "Internationale Beziehungen als kommunikatives Handeln: Zur Kritik der utilitaristischen Handlungstheorien," *Zeitschrift für Internationale Beziehungen* 1, no. 1 (1994): 15–44; *Rationality and Society* 4, no. 4 (October 1992); *Journal of Institutional and Theoretical Economics (JITE)* 150, no. 1 (March 1994); James Johnson, "Habermas on Strategic and Communicative Action," *Political Theory* 19, no. 2 (May 1991): 181–201; Jon

school of economics against Carl Menger and the challenge of the British, neoclassical tradition. Neoclassical theory stressed choice, individual units, rationalism, a market logic, prediction, and explanation. The historical school emphasized constraints, collectivities, irrationalities, a logic of society, description, and explanation. Contemporary theoretical debates in the field of security studies, as throughout the social sciences, are restating core aspects of the old debate in modern form.

Disciplinary debates within each of the two camps and their various subdivisions tend to be isomorphic. They focus on the causal priority and sequence of the major analytical variables as they relate to the formulation of actor interests and choices. In the economic-rationalist perspective this debate affects how we think about the causal relationships among preferences, institutional rules, organizational structures, and choice. In the sociological-constitutive perspective it affects how we think about the causal relationships among identities, norms, interests, and practice. The discussions within different paradigms illustrate a substantial amount of parallelism in perspectives, albeit expressed in different analytical languages. Students of security seeking to relate their substantive interests to either camp thus focus on the intersection between power and policy on the one hand and preferences, institutional rules, organizational structures, norms, identity, and interests on the other.

But discussions within paradigms are theoretically less illuminating than the emerging debates across paradigms. Such debates sometimes bring radically different perspectives closer together. Some rationalists, for example, are in the early stages of seeking an active engagement with students of culture. For cultural processes may offer a solution to the vexing problem of multiple equilibria and the 'common knowledge' assumption.[71] Alternatively, cross-paradigm debates can also divide more clearly from one another analytical perspectives that once were thought of as sharing much

Elster, *The Cement of Society: A Study of Social Order* (Cambridge: Cambridge University Press, 1989); Mark Granovetter, "Economic Action and Social Structure: The Problem of Embeddedness," *American Journal of Sociology* 91, no. 3 (November 1985): 481–510; and Anthony Oberschall and Eric M. Leifer, "Efficiency and Social Institutions: Uses and Misuses of Economic Reasoning in Sociology," *Annual Review of Sociology* 12 (1986): 233–53.

71. John A. Ferejohn, "Rationality and Interpretation: Parliamentary Elections in Early Stuart England," in Kristen Renwick Monroe, ed., *The Economic Approach to Politics* (New York: Harper Collins, 1991), pp. 279–305; Robert H. Bates and Barry R. Weingast, "A New Comparative Politics: Integrating Rational Choice and Interpretivist Perspectives" (unpublished paper, Harvard and Stanford Universities, October 1994); James Johnson, "Symbol and Strategy: Cultural Bases of Political Possibility" (unpublished paper, University of Rochester, 1992).

in common. For example, all variants of institutional analysis oppose a decontextualized and atomistic account of choice behavior. And all model the way institutional arrangements mediate, shape, and channel collective and individual choices. But the new rational choice institutionalism in economics and political science focuses on the institutional context of and constraint on interested action. It remains indebted to the Weberian distinction between a world of brute or material facts and a world of perceived or interpreted facts. This perspective contrasts, however, with the world of institutional facts that are at the center of the new post-Weberian institutionalism in sociology.[72] This version of institutionalism focuses not on institutional constraints on interests and actors but on the institutional constitution of both interests and actors. Put differently, sociological institutionalism makes problematic what economic institutionalism takes for granted, actor identities and the interests they entail.

Cross-paradigm debates are as complicated now as they were at the end of the nineteenth century, for the temptation is great to merely retranslate the core constructs of another perspective or discipline into one's own, rather than trying to understand which parts of reality another perspective might in fact illuminate more forcefully than a familiar mode of thought. This appears to be true of all social science. As much as it might wish, the field of national security studies is unlikely to escape from a broadening of analytical perspectives and competing empirical claims. The only question is whether the new "battle of methods" will split the field further into different camps, both committed to empirical research, that speak past each other or will lead to joint intellectual advance. Eventually the choices we make as scholars and teachers will be reflected in which journals and book series publish our research findings, in how we train our graduate students, and in how we teach our undergraduate students. Acknowledging the intellectually profitable and personally uncomfortable frictions that occur in cross-paradigm discussions, this book aims at broadening the middle ground for an analysis of national security.

America in a Changing World

Shocks produce traumas. For the survivors of the California earthquake the traumas are emotional. For foreign policy specialists who watched the

---

72. Friedrich Kratochwil, "Regimes, Interpretation, and the 'Science' of Politics: A Reappraisal," *Millennium: Journal of International Studies* 17, no. 2 (Summer 1988): 263–84. Friedrich V. Kratochwil, *Rules, Norms, and Decisions* (New York: Cambridge University Press, 1988), pp. 22–28.

Cold War end unexpectedly and the Soviet Union disintegrate peacefully, the traumas are cognitive. Disagreement about the future course of American foreign policy runs deep. Conventional theories do not consider important factors that contributed to the cataclysmic changes of 1989–1990. Their conceptual lenses overlook the cultural-institutional context and identity as important causes that are creating widespread confusion about the purposes to which American power should be applied now that the Soviet Union has disappeared. In contrast, Ernest May identifies the central importance of culture and identity when he argues that "American foreign policy issues have historically involved one question not asked in the same way elsewhere: Who are we?"[73]

Although none of the empirical essays deal with American foreign policy directly, their arguments contain a number of implications that point to the contradictory impulses of American security policy on the international system. Eyre and Suchman suggest that the United States affects the militarization of international politics directly, as one of the largest weapons exporters in the world. Furthermore, by defining the model of what constitutes a modern military, the United States reinforces global militarization also, though indirectly. By implication, the United States also shapes the concepts and language by which modern militaries frame security issues, with obvious effects on the international security environment. Johnston's analysis of the causal effects of China's strategic culture of hard realism reminds us of the political significance of such collective norms. At the same time, American foreign policy has also created political developments that push in very different directions. Risse-Kappen and Herman show in their essays that the creation of a North Atlantic security community, embodying the principle of multilateralism and the exchange of ideas during the period of detente, as well as President Bush's policy of reassurance in 1989–1991 created the political space that allowed New Thinkers to operate and that helped push Gorbachev to adopt radical reform policies.

Over time some of these factors get magnified for reasons not directly related to American foreign policy. For example, the powerful effect of the presence of the United States in Germany and Japan after World War II eventually made these two states abstain from the militarization of international politics—based on the reassurance that the protection of the U.S. military has provided to date. Herman's paper illustrates that important

---

73. Ernest R. May, " 'Who are We'?" *Foreign Affairs* 73, no. 2 (March–April 1994): 135.

elements of New Thinking in the Soviet Union, such as the concept of "defensive defense," acquired political significance because of contacts between Soviet and German research institutes.

Today American foreign policy is unsteady because the norms and doctrine that inform it remain politically undefined. Price and Tannenwald show how the norms of non-use of chemical and nuclear weapons evolved not in a linear fashion but in response to political contingencies, historical conjunctures, and accident. Finnemore's analysis of intervention norms documents important secular changes in shared identities and in liberal egalitarian notions of humanity. They are now embodied in international legal precepts that have eliminated the legitimacy of unilateral interventions for national gain. Realpolitik efforts to ignore claims for humanitarian intervention in strategically unimportant states will prove politically impossible to sustain in at least some cases, such as Rwanda.

If humanitarian interventions cannot be avoided and if they must be multilateral, U.S. policy makers should strengthen multilateral institutions so that they can act more efficiently and effectively when they must carry out what have become normatively necessary tasks. But at the end of the Cold War, we do not find a broadly accepted model or set of social norms that shapes U.S. policy. Instead American politics shows a deep division between a Congress committed to unilateralism and an executive favoring multilateralism. Similarly, the U.S. military, Kier's analysis of French military doctrine implies, should now reevaluate its military doctrine to adjust to new contexts. It remains to be seen whether peace enforcement in the Third World and low-intensity conflicts will replace, for example, the army's traditional focus on Europe and mechanized warfare.

Domestic debate about American foreign policy resembles a masquerade ball. Conservatives who favored an assertive foreign policy, including intervention, in the interest of defending the free world before 1989, have turned isolationist. None of the growing number of trouble spots in the Third World threatens vital American interests and thus merits engagement. Liberals who had advocated caution in foreign affairs before 1989 now insist that if international pandemonium is left unchecked, this will have deleterious consequences for the American body politic. Hence, they favor multilateral engagement in defense of basic human rights. In terms of public debate, American foreign policy reacts to the push and pull of the same forces as it did before 1989. The masques are the same. But the faces and voices that they conceal differ.

With the end of the Cold War and the breakup of the Soviet Union, the relative power of the United States has increased sharply. Yet we do not live in a world in which international security issues gravitate around only one superpower. For the United States is reluctant to commit its military might. Unilateral military action is unlikely, since few, if any, of the many conflicts in the world threaten vital American interests. And multilateral action is also unlikely, since the American political elite and public do not trust international peacekeeping and peace-enforcing efforts that the United States government cannot fully control. Yet American influence does not exist simply because of America's military might, for that might is often not usable in the many conflicts that affect the national security of states around the world. American influence exists also by virtue of the fact that the United States is recognized in most capitals around the world as the only military superpower.

On economic issues the distinction between the territorial economy of the United States and American global economic presence makes it difficult to come to an overall assessment of America's position. The territorial economy of the United States is holding its own in competition with Europe, but the accelerating pace of economic change in Asia is undermining, in relative terms, the strength of American producers in that part of the world. The American territorial economy creates a large number of jobs while real wages, uniquely among the leading capitalist states, stagnate or decline. In the international division of labor, American multinational corporations remain highly competitive, as has been true for the last several decades.

Finally, on questions of mass culture the assessment of America is equally indeterminate. The United States is unrivaled in exporting its popular culture to all corners of the globe, from fast-food chains to movies and rock music. Japan and Germany have made limited inroads, for example, in the world of fashion and international cuisine, but their cultural appeal is very limited compared with the pervasive American presence in the global culture market. Furthermore, that presence has intensified over time. In the process of becoming, in Walt Whitman's apt phrase, a "world nation, " however, the United States is largely giving over to marketing considerations any specificity of what it means to be American.[74] For *ET* and *Jurassic Park* to be successful culture products, they must abstract from the American context

---

74. David Rieff, "A Global Culture?" *World Policy Journal* 10, no. 4 (Winter 1993/94): 74; Carl Bernstein, "The Leisure Empire," *Time*, December 24, 1990, pp. 56–59; Paarlberg, *Leadership Abroad Begins at Home*, pp. 48–56.

in which they were produced. These are global stories that do not package American values. Distinctive to the strong global appeal of America's popular culture is the fact that it transcends the specificity to time and space. As is true for military and economic issues, in the realm of mass culture America appears to be both present and absent on the global scene.

The United States thus finds itself enmeshed in global contexts that are partly of its own making. As Samuel Huntington argued in a seminal essay published in 1973, the nature of the American empire was powered by the spread of transnational organizations. Since 1945 they were developed largely out of American national organizations, both governmental and nongovernmental. Access to foreign societies became as important as accords with foreign governments. America expanded into the international system not only by controlling foreign people and resources but also by deploying American people and resources. American expansion was typified not by the acquisition of foreign territory and the power to control but by the penetration of foreign society and the freedom to operate. This expansion was quintessentially American: segmental, pluralistic, and operational. By and large, and despite some significant exceptions, American expansion was not colonial. The mechanisms of expansion were variegated and involved a mixture of competition, coercion, and emulation.[75]

In the end, this American empire proved vastly superior to the territorially based one of the Soviet Union. But with the end of the Cold War, Huntington argues, the United States is locked, once again, in a conflict of global proportions. In Huntington's view the Cold War has given way to a clash of civilization that makes issues of cultural authenticity central to international politics.[76] Indeed, Huntington's economic and cultural arguments are close cousins. The pervasiveness of America's informal empire and the increasing intensity of international cultural conflicts are probably causally related.

Civilizational clashes are in this view the defining characteristic of a new type of international relations. Civilizations are not replacing states. Instead, Huntington argues, they are becoming the relevant cultural contexts in which states must act.[77] State interests will no longer be

---

75. Samuel P. Huntington, "Transnational Organizations in World Politics," *World Politics* 25, no. 3 (April 1973): 338, 342–45.
76. Huntington, "The Clash of Civilizations?"
77. Don Puchala, "International Encounters of Another Kind" (paper prepared for presentation at the annual meeting of the International Studies Association, Washington, D.C., March 30–April 2, 1994.

defined as much by ideological interests as by civilizational ones. Although they are real, the defining characteristics of civilizations (history, language, culture, tradition, religion) cannot be grasped easily. Similarly, although the boundaries between civilizations are not hard and fast, they are basic.[78] Civilizations are becoming more important as the religious and political fundamentalism of non-Western states is challenging the interests and values of the West. Iran, Turkey, Egypt, and Algeria are examples.

This argument is appealing to some because, like Doctor Doolittle's push-me-pull-you, it has two heads and thus can take on all comers—those who assume identities to be essential and those who assume them to be constructed. Under the wide umbrella of civilization, identities can be thought of as constantly contested and constructed in a fluid political life. Political leaders can deliberately choose to refashion the identity of a Turkey, a Mexico, an Australia, or a Russia.[79] But this is not the central thrust of Huntington's argument. His analysis views the basic factors defining civilizations as objective and not amenable to political change. Indeed, at times in the analysis civilizations, not states, bandwagon and balance, and act on the international stage.[80] Ethnic and religious slaughter in Yugoslavia results from five hundred years of history, not from the political gambits of a Milosevic or a Tudjman during the last five years. This view of civilizational identity as immutable permits Huntington to articulate the most controversial part of his analysis. An apparent, old civilizational multipolarity conceals an underlying, new bipolarity, which pits the "West against the rest."[81]

Huntington's conclusion is open to serious question on many grounds.[82] Four points concern me here. His analysis does not specify the full range of outcomes that occurs when the states or empires that are carriers of civilizations clash. In history that range encompasses more than "clashes." Don Puchala's preliminary inventory of some historical episodes lists a much broader array of outcomes that includes absorption, hybridization, hege-

78. Ian S. Lustick, *Unsettled States, Disputed Lands: Britain and Ireland, France and Algeria, Israel and the West Bank–Gaza* (Ithaca: Cornell University Press, 1993).
79. Huntington, "The Clash of Civilizations?," pp. 24, 42–44, 48.
80. Ibid., pp. 26–27, 30, 35, 39–41, 48.
81. Ibid., pp. 26, 39–41, 48.
82. Some of these issues are aired in a number of short articles published in *Foreign Affairs* 72, no. 5 (November–December 1993), and discussed by James Kurth in "The *Real* Clash," *National Interest*, no. 37 (Fall 1994): 3–15. They were discussed frankly at a special panel of the 1993 annual meeting of the American Political Science Association.

mony, rejection and resurgence, obliteration and genocide, isolation and suspicion, and cross-fertilization.[83]

Second, Huntington is erroneously one-sided in the conclusion he draws from his analysis. Karl Deutsch's comparison of world regions and civilizations strikes a better balance. Deutsch argues that the distinctiveness of the West is strongest with respect to social and political institutions. And, equally important, almost all Western traits can also be found in one or more world regions and civilizations. "The peoples and culture of the West are like those of other regions, only more so. This is why the West and the rest of the world could learn from each other in the past and can continue to do so in the future."[84]

Third, identities are neither totally fluid nor primordial. They are historically contingent and must be understood contextually. The resurgence of Islam illustrates the point. "Islam" operates as a construct that includes Iran in the Middle East and gives that country a leading role in the politics of that region. By contrast, "pan-Arabism" as the reigning ideology of the 1960s sought to exclude non-Arab Iran from the Middle East. A politically focused anti-imperialism of the 1960s has given way to a diffuse anti-Westernism in the 1990s. Definitions of collective identity are thus subject to change over time. Unsurprisingly, contemporary Islamic civilization is not a homogeneous actor on the world stage. Saudi Arabia and Iran express clashing visions of traditionalism and radicalism and are deeply divided over the social and cultural purposes of Islamic civilization. Static and totalizing wholes such as "Islam" and "Christianity," or "totalitarian Communism" and "democratic Capitalism," do not offer fruitful ways for analysis and harbor the risk of seriously misleading public policy.[85]

Finally, the United States itself reveals a great flaw in Huntington's attempt to reimpose intellectual order on an inchoate world, based on the equation of American with Western identity. Huntington acknowledges this possibility in the form of a rhetorical question: Is it possible that "de-Westernization of the United States" may lead to its "de-Americaniza-

83. Puchala, "International Encounters of Another Kind."
84. Karl W. Deutsch, "On Nationalism, World Regions, and the Nature of the West," in Per Torsvik, ed., *Mobilization, Center-Periphery Structures and Nation-Building: A Volume in Commemoration of Stein Rokkan*, p. 86 (Bergen: Universitetsforlaget, 1981).
85. Susanne Hoeber Rudolph, "Religion, the State, and Transnational Civil Society," in Susanne Hoeber Rudolph, ed., *Transnational Religion, the State, and Global Civil Society*, pp. 21–23 (forthcoming).

tion"?[86] The question is more than rhetorical. It is real. To be sure, the American celebration of cultural diversity, remarkably uniform as it is in its tenor, is not pushing the United States toward disintegration. But cultural diversity is real nonetheless. "Oklahoma city has five mosques, four Hindu temples, one Sikh *gurudwara*, and three Southeast Asian Buddhist temples. . . . There are said to be 70 mosques in the Chicago metropolitan area. . . . It is surprising to find that Muslims outnumber Episcopalians in the U.S. and are likely to outnumber Jews in the near future."[87] These demographic facts eliminate the dubious anchor of an uncontested, stable American or Western identity that clashes with the "rest." In a world where "our" Japanese can beat "their" Japanese,[88] will "our" Muslims fight "theirs"?

The United States may begin to follow in Canada's footsteps and become the second postmodern nation. Canada's central government has made multiculturalism its official policy, and Canadian identity on questions of security is defined in terms of international peacekeeping rather than the defense of national sovereignty. But in contrast to Canada through its politics, economics, and culture, the United States has a profound influence on the "rest." It offers a microcosm of the political and cultural pluralism that marks the world. The social statistics of the United States belie the presumption of cultural homogeneity. Traditional pillars of American identity are growing weaker: standardized school curricula, a common language, mass conscription, and a skilled industrial working class. Other institutions gain strength: the media and pop culture, high-tech warfare, and a bifurcated service economy. Thus the United States is increasingly institutionalizing its own "multicultural regime" as a form of postmodern politics.[89]

The incoherence of American policy and politics expresses this increasing diversity and, with the end of the Cold War, the weakening of a sense of collective identity. The hollowing out of the American economy by American multinational corporations and the segmentation of American culture by media conglomerates are part of the same social process. They

---

86. Samuel P. Huntington, "If Not Civilizations, What? Paradigms of the Post–Cold War World," *Foreign Affairs* 72, no. 5 (November–December 1993): 189–90.

87. Rudolph, "Religion, the State, and Transnational Civil Society," p. 4.

88. Walter Feinberg, *Japan and the Pursuit of a New American Identity: Work and Education in a Multicultural Age* (New York: Routledge, 1993).

89. James Kurth, "The Post-Modern State: Is America a Nation?" *Current* 348 (December 1992): 26–33; Kurth, "The *Real* Clash."

reflect the logic of an informal American empire that is reorganizing the world along transnational lines while helping to disorganize the American nation-state. We can observe a similar process in Europe. But it takes a different form and works more obliquely.[90] Civilizations will provide the relevant context for state action. With its identity demonstrably changing in important ways, however, the "West" is unlikely to confront the "rest." America's growing cultural heterogeneity makes implausible the fixing of a particular "us" that can be opposed to an alien "them." America's collective identity can no longer be reinforced by the invocation of an overpowering foreign enemy—unless, of course, one was to reinvent that enemy for political reasons in a new cultural gestalt.

An eroding sense of collective identity in the United States reinforces rather than weakens the transnational diffusion of American values. For as John Ruggie argues compellingly, the multilateral vision of world order that has been at the core of the American expansion in the twentieth century mirrors America's collective identity. To become American is a matter of individual choice, not birth. America sees itself as it sees the world it would like to create: a willful community created by individual choices that are based on a universal organizing principle.[91]

With the end of the Cold War, national security specialists are eager to find a new compass for the United States. The difficulty in constructing a coherent grand strategy does not lie primarily in the complexity of the material and normative constraints and incentives that confront the United States in the international arena. It lies rather in the contested collective U.S. identity and lack of purpose that make a clear definition of American interest so difficult. It is easy to forget that on the eve of the war with Iraq the American public was more deeply divided about whether or not to fight than it had been before any of the other major U.S. military campaigns in the twentieth century. America's position in the world is thus shaped by the two factors that this book has privileged in its analysis throughout: real and perceived cultural conflicts and the contestations of collective identities at home and abroad.

90. Michael Geyer, "Historical Fictions of Autonomy and the Europeanization of National History," *Central European History* 22, nos. 3–4 (1989): 316–42.

91. John Gerard Ruggie, "Third Try at World Order? America and Multilateralism After the Cold War," *Political Science Quarterly* 109, no. 4 (Fall 1994): 564–65; Alexander L. George, "Domestic Constraints on Regime Change in U.S. Foreign Policy: The Need for Policy Legitimacy," in Ole R. Holsti, Randolph M. Siverson, and Alexander L. George, eds., *Change in the International System*, pp. 233–62 (Boulder: Westview, 1980).

But the difficulty in devising a new American strategy runs deeper. In an attempt to meet its intellectual critics on their chosen ground, this book has been self-conscious in focusing on the state's military security. Yet the concept of national security is evidently in a process of broadening. Outside of the United States and the halls of government nonmilitary and nonstatist definitions of national security are becoming more widely shared. In Europe and Asia political and economic definitions of security are debated more seriously than in the United States. And in many states, especially in the Third World, the main worry is not, and should not be, about how to make the state more secure from other states. Rather the focus is, and should be, on how to make citizens more secure from the capriciousness of states.

Furthermore, the search for a new coherent strategy is impaired by the fact that the United States does not live with a few scores of other states in an anarchic international system. Nor does it belong to international institutions whose effects on policy coordination extend only to the reduction of uncertainties and the increase in transparency. Instead the United States is part of a variegated set of complex social structures and processes that constitute a global system. Although they are relevant for governments and states, these processes typically are not organized solely around states. They may or may not take institutional form and thus affect the interest calculations of governments. But they touch often on norms and identities that matter in domestic and international politics.

Today's problem is no longer that of E. H. Carr, one of avoiding the sterility of realism and the naïveté of idealism.[92] Our choice is more complex. We can remain intellectually riveted on a realist world of states balancing power in a multipolar system. We can focus analytically with liberal institutionalists on the efficiency effects that institutions may have on the prospects for policy coordination between states. Or, acknowledging the partial validity of these views, we can broaden our analytical perspective, as this book suggests, to include as well culture and identity as important causal factors that help define the interests and constitute the actors that shape national security policies and global insecurities.

---

92. E. H. Carr, *The Twenty Years' Crisis, 1919–1939: An Introduction to the Study of International Relations*, 2d ed. (London: Macmillan, 1956), pp. 11–12.

Index